# FOR REFERENCE

### Do Not Take From This Room

D0073618

# HANDBOOK OF
# AMERICAN
# FILM GENRES

# HANDBOOK OF AMERICAN FILM GENRES

Edited by WES D. GEHRING

**GREENWOOD PRESS**

New York • Westport, Connecticut • London

WITHDRAW ITHACA COLLEGE LIBRARY

**Library of Congress Cataloging-in-Publication Data**

Handbook of American film genres / edited by Wes D. Gehring.
   p. cm.
  Bibliography: p.
  Includes indexes.
  ISBN 0-313-24715-3 (lib. bdg. : alk. paper)
  1. Motion pictures—United States—Handbooks, manuals, etc.
2. Film genres.  I. Gehring, Wes D.
PN1993.5.U6H335  1988
791.43'75'0973—dc19                    87-31784

British Library Cataloguing in Publication Data is available.

Copyright © 1988 by Wes D. Gehring

All rights reserved. No portion of this book may be
reproduced, by any process or technique, without the
express written consent of the publisher.

Library of Congress Catalog Card Number: 87-31784
ISBN: 0-313-24715-3

First published in 1988

Greenwood Press, Inc.
88 Post Road West, Westport, Connecticut 06881

Printed in the United States of America

The paper used in this book complies with the
Permanent Paper Standard issued by the National
Information Standards Organization (Z39.48-1984).

10 9 8 7 6 5 4 3 2 1

To Eileen, Sarah, and Emily; my family; and my grandmother, Phyllis Morf Leonhart McIntyre.

# Contents

# Preface

This book was inspired by two limitations frequently found in texts on American film genres. First, there was a need for a text which would examine an expanded number of genres. The best two genre books on the market, Thomas Schatz's *Hollywood Genres* and Barry K. Grant's *Film Genre: Theory and Criticism,* were limited to six genres, respectively.[1] These numbers were consistent with Stuart M. Kaminsky's pioneer work, *American Film Genres,* which examines approximately eight genres, depending on how one counts Kaminsky's fascination with variations of the crime movie, to which he devotes several chapters.[2] Only slightly larger numbers are addressed in both a more recent Grant anthology, *Film Genre Reader* (eleven genres, with some of the pieces recycled from his other collection), and Steven C. Earley's rather pedestrian *An Introduction to American Movies* (twelve genres).[3] Thus, the book in hand examines eighteen genres, with much of the increase coming from both a more ambitious look at "comedy genres" and the inclusion of such "nontraditional" genres as the problem film, the art film, and the biography picture. Other genres included are swashbuckling adventure film, western, gangster film, film noir, World War II combat film (in the category Action/Adventure); horror, science fiction, and fantasy (in The Fantastic); and the musical and the melodrama (in Songs and Soaps).

The reasoning behind the order of the chapters in each division is as follows: In the action/adventure section the adventure chapter goes first because it broadly addresses the division, even to the point of mentioning several of the other member genres. The western and gangster chapters follow because of their pivotal positions as archetypal American genres. Film noir is next because it is in part an outgrowth of the gangster film, or more broadly, the crime movie. The World War II combat chapter is last since it is the most specific of the divisions.

The comedy section saves the most familiar type (the clown genre) for last, and begins with the most often confused—screwball comedy. The three chapters sandwiched in between (populist, parody, and black humor) seem the most natural bridge. For instance, populism follows screwball because the former is sometimes mistaken for the latter, especially in the films of director Frank Capra.

Similar and/or other significant factors can be applied to the chapter order of the other divisions, too. For example, in the fantastic category, the genre order (horror, science fiction, fantasy) follows the historical emergence of each as a film genre of study. The same applies, though to a lesser extent, to the divisions of songs and soaps and the nontraditional genres.

The need to examine an expanded number of genres seemed most pressing in comedy. There is the tendency for genre authors either to limit their comedy focus to the screwball variety or to simply call comedy the broadest of all genres and proceed to lump every conceivable type into one very overworked chapter. As comedy theorist Jim Leach has observed with humorous insight, "a genre which encompasses the visions of Jerry Lewis *and* Ernst Lubitsch is already in trouble."[4] He goes on to request a more ambitious examination of the comedy genre*s*, noting what many film comedy enthusiasts have long felt— "if a genre is defined too loosely (as in the case of 'comedy') it ceases to be of any value as a critical tool."[5]

This book attempts to address that limitation by devoting five chapters to five different comedy genres: screwball, populist, parody, black, and clown. This is not meant to imply that these are the limit of all possible comedy genres. But the five would seem to represent the most obvious types visible to the student of film humor. Hopefully, they should provide a more thorough framework from which to study and enjoy the varied richness of comedy. Moreover, though chapters were written as autonomous units, they are frequently cross-referenced to better facilitate one's understanding of the comedy issues at hand.

Second, there was a need for a more thorough guideline-oriented genre study. To better facilitate reader insight, this volume's formulaic subjects have been showcased in an ambitious, fittingly formulaic manner. That is, each genre chapter is systematically broken into the following sections: a historical/analytical overview, a bibliographical overview of the genre's key literature, a checklist of these texts, and a filmography of the genre's pivotal movies. Such an arrangement assists the reader in comparing different genres and gives him or her a solid, working foundation for further study. Despite that old gag about an anthology editor being someone who spends his time *raiding* good books, the reader of an essay collection such as this is undoubtedly best served when each contribution is an original piece (though having a common framework), written specifically for a shared goal.

Despite this common framework, certain minor variations occur in the chapter structures. For instance, there is some information contrast between filmographies from chapter to chapter. Thus, the horror filmography includes credits for things like special effects or makeup, categories not so central in other film lists. Moreover, the filmographies themselves are limited to the most central movies in each genre. This was done to give the reader with limited time a more selective choice. Because of this, however, movies cited in the text do not always appear in the filmography.

Along similar lines, not every source noted in each chapter's bibliographical overview appears in the checklist. For example, references can be brought in for certain points but are not relevant to the focus of the chapter. Or a weak source might be cited in the overview but not listed in what are essentially *recommended* readings (the checklist). However, a reference in the overview was necessary in order to show its checklist omission was simply not a mistake.

This has been a most ambitious project, but it does not purport to be the end-all to the subject at hand. Like all material aiming for insightfulness, its goal is to further challenge the inquisitive mind. Thus, additional genres not included but worthy of possible further consideration would include disaster films, sports movies, and erotic films.

The publication of most books merits many thank-yous, and this is especially true of a work such as this. I am most grateful to Marilyn Brownstein, Greenwood Press's humanities editor and the catalyst for this book. Her ideas and support made the volume possible and her sensitive leadership has had an effect on all my Greenwood books.

To credit an essay collection as dependent on its contributors is an understatement. The insights of these people fill the pages and quite literally decide the fate of the book and its organizer, hopefully qualifying me for that comic definition of an editor as someone who uses scissors and taste. Thus, they have provided a most happy fate for the reader. All contributors are proven scholars who have fine-tuned their ideas in the classroom, the ultimate liberal arts laboratory (see the About the Contributors section). Moreover, in an age frequently driven by the philosophy of "What's in it for me?," these teacher/scholars set pencil to paper out of an obligation to that most sacred of human enterprises—the exchange of ideas. Significant thank-yous are just not possible.

With regard to my own genre chapter contributions, these were built upon a lifelong fascination with comedy which started with the humor of my father and both grandfathers. Laughter is very special in my family. Through the years and the books, so many people have helped me that I would need a second volume to list them all. However, I would be remiss if I did not credit the staffs of six archives—the Library of Congress (especially the divisions of Motion Pictures, Copyright, and Manuscripts), the Billy Rose Theatre Collection of the New York Public Library at Lincoln Center, the Research Annex of the New York Public Library (521 West 43rd Street), the Museum of Modern Art's Department of Film (New York), the Academy of Motion Picture Arts and Sciences Library (Beverly Hills), and the American Film Institute (Beverly Hills).

Closer to home, additional thank-yous are in order for the strong support of my department chairman, John Kurtz, and my teaching colleague, Darrel Wible; Janet Warrner, my typist and general troubleshooter; and Vera McCoskey, interlibrary loan librarian at Ball State University's Bracken Library.

Further acknowledgments are in order for the support and suggestions of family, friends (in particular, Conrad Lane and Joe Pacino), colleagues (especially the professional conferences where early versions of several comedy chapters were presented), and students (particularly, members of my annual American Film comedy seminars). I wish also to credit humor scholar Larry Mintz, who besides supporting my comedy writing through the years, indirectly influenced this book by his recent editing of *Humor in America: A Research Guide to Genres and Topics.*[6] His request of an overview chapter on American film comedy better helped me prepare for the writing of this volume's comedy chapters. And because of the earlier inception of his book, and my involvement therein, I was privy to an ongoing, mini workshop on editing.

Finally, my family merits a truckload of praise for their patience, understanding, and advice through all the mini-crises that constitute editing and writing a book.

## NOTES

1. Thomas Schatz, *Hollywood Genres* (New York: Random House, 1981); Barry K. Grant, ed., *Film Genre: Theory and Criticism* (Metuchen, N.J.: Scarecrow Press, Inc., 1977).

2. Stuart M. Kaminsky, *American Film Genres* (Dayton, Ohio: Pflaum, 1974).

3. Barry K. Grant, ed., *Film Genre Reader* (Austin: University of Texas, 1986); Stephen C. Earley, *An Introduction to American Movies* (New York: Mentor Books, 1979).

4. Jim Leach, "The Screwball Comedy," in *Film Genre: Theory and Criticism*, ed. Grant, p. 75.

5. Ibid, pp. 75–76.

6. Lawrence E. Mintz, *Humor in America: A Research Guide to Genres and Topics* (Westport, Conn.: Greenwood Press, 1988).

# HANDBOOK OF
# AMERICAN
# FILM GENRES

# 1

# Introduction

WES D. GEHRING

"All this has happened before. And it will all happen again."

So begins one of my daughter's fairy tales, and it is a fitting description of the genre film. *Genre* is a French word for a literary type. In film study it represents the division of movies into groups which have similar subjects and/or themes. Sometimes this is an easy task, when your genre is of a given time and place, such as the western. From film frame one it is generally obvious you are in the American West of the second half of the nineteenth century, especially when you are bombarded with more western icons (ten-gallon hats, six-guns, etc.) than you would be in a Zane Grey museum.

Some genres are not so immediately obvious. For instance, screwball comedy is not limited to one period and place, although it is often set in the present in the milieu of the idle rich. This genre is more defined by the eccentric courtship of the screwball couple. Sister genres would include the musical and the melodrama—again, types *not* dependent on a given time and place and readily recognizable icons.

Historically, genre lineage can be traced back to the seemingly always intellectually present *Poetics* of Aristotle, wherein the literature of the day was broken down into types. Thus, for much of the recorded history of man, varying formulaic genre guidelines have been present and growing, though not without detractors. This is best exemplified by the nineteenth-century Romantic movement, which felt the genre structure limited the artist, as did most rules. The still popular notion that ''the artist'' must create something entirely new each time stems from this.

The significance of genre stories, however, long predates the *Poetics*, and might just be addressed by repeating a question which frequently surfaces in genre study: Why does an audience member keep returning to a favored story type (genre) which a formalistic structure often makes predictable? Such repetition would seem a bit irrational, rather like the joke with which Woody Allen closes *Annie Hall* (1977): A guy tells his psychiatrist that his brother believes himself to be a chicken. When the doctor asks, "Why don't you turn him in?" he receives the reply, "I would, but I need the eggs."

The genre fan seems "egged on" by man's need for the repetitive reaffirmation of certain ritualistic experiences, such as good triumphing over evil, the promise of finding the perfect love, the comic underdog winning—things which do not occur so frequently, if at all, in real life. Even in the case of a genre like black comedy, where the absurdity and ugliness of both man and the modern world are directly addressed in dark, or sick, humor, genre helps one cope through laughter. Multifaceted viewer catharses are a genre given. Thus, the need for the ritualistic experience is as old as man and the first oral tales shared around primitive campfires. Despite today's sophisticated high-tech wrappings, genre entertainment would seem to fulfill the most ancient of needs.

There are seven key reasons to pursue genre study. The first and most compelling is at the heart of all liberal arts education—to provide both a systematic overview of mankind's masterworks while providing personal insight for the individual. To what genre(s) do you most frequently return? Why? What primal messages, or assurances, are provided by your genre(s)?

Second, as with any schematic approach to the arts, genre study helps one organize the ever burgeoning number of films—categorizing them into smaller, more manageable groups. An added plus for the genre approach is that it is probably the classification system most familiar to viewers. While they may have never formally articulated this before, most people have some definite expectations concerning at least the most mainstream of genres, such as the western and the gangster film (genres often considered the most inherently American). After all, through the years much of the Hollywood product—the "canned" goods, if you will—has been produced and marketed along genre lines. Using a popular model as a production guideline is an old and efficient way of doing things. It is for that reason that genre theorist Barry K. Grant's description of genre movies as the "Model T's" of popular entertainment has about it the perfect tongue-in-cheek appropriateness.[1] Bear in mind, however, that thorough genre study also takes one beyond formulaic fundamentals and reveals all the creatively complex options still available. These might be specific variations on a ritualistic experience or the broad impact some auteurs have had on a given genre model, such as directors John Ford on the western and Howard Hawks on screwball comedy. In fact, genre study has often been the chief beneficiary of any number of auteur works because the focus director was invariably identified with a specific genre.

Third, genre study also acts as a natural corollary to what celebrated nineteenth-century literary critic Matthew Arnold called the "touchstone" method—producing a guide to what the reader/viewer can expect from a given work, or in this case, genre.[2] Since few people have the viewing opportunities of the film critic, genre analysis steers one to the pivotal examples of whatever genre(s) one might prefer.

Fourth, because even watershed films rarely encapsulate everything there is to know about a given movie type, genre study also allows one both to better appreciate the significant elements of the individual film and to examine other viable directions it could have taken, subjects which might not readily be apparent without a broader understanding of the parent genre itself.

Fifth, genre study keeps one alive to the cultural changes forever taking place in the world at large. That is, genre analysis frequently operates on a contradiction. It is very much formulaic *but* at the same time must be flexible enough to incorporate the ongoing changes affecting all genres. Such changes would include the undercurrent of paranoia over communist witch-hunting which surfaced in 1950s science fiction films or the Vietnam antiestablishment 1960s and the emergence of the antihero in most traditional genres (especially the western), not to mention the evolution of black comedy as a mainstream genre itself.

At the risk of sounding blasphemous, even pioneer genre writings by pivotal film critics like Robert Warshow (on the western and the gangster film) and James Agee (on comedy) are not without some restrictiveness. Warshow has problems with *My Darling Clementine* (1946), *Kiss of Death* (1947), *High Noon* (1952), and *Shane* (1953); Agee has reservations about comedy outside the silent era.[3] Genre criticism exists as a guide for the inquiring mind (highlighting recurring patterns of cultural significance in the arts), not as a dictator of said patterns. As influential genre author John G. Cawelti has observed, "When genre critics forget that their supertexts are critical artifacts and start treating them as prescriptions for artistic creation, the concept of genre becomes stultifying and limiting."[4]

Sixth, to the ongoing credit of Warshow and Agee, however, as well as André Bazin and those who have followed, genre criticism has given credibility to the study of popular culture. Most specifically for the book in hand, this has meant the elevation in importance of the Hollywood studio film. Whereas its genre product was once often considered merely interchangeable links of entertainment sausage squeezed out of a fun factory, today's film historian is capable of such hosannas as comparing the Hollywood studio era to the days of Elizabethan repertory theater companies, most famous for a playwright named Shakespeare.[5] This is called high praise. To put it even more succinctly, one has only to recycle the title of film scholar Gerald Weales's excellent book on a portion of the studio period—*Canned Goods as Caviar*.[6]

Yes, things have changed greatly since 1939, often considered the watershed year of studio creativity, when a young but already celebrated Hollywood director named William Wellman kidded an academic-oriented film audience with the observation: "Cinema appreciation . . . must be rather like going to school to learn the aesthetic differences between a Pontiac and an Oldsmobile."[7] Of course, the nature of popular culture has also changed greatly in the intervening years, which leads one to the next and possibly most startling point for genre study.

Seventh, genre criticism is now starting to act as a bridge between the mainstream popular film and the art film, the latter probably still most closely associated with Swedish filmmaker Ingmar Bergman, whose 1950s films so helped create a demand for these more personalized works—such as *The Seventh Seal* (1956) and *Wild Strawberries* (1957). Traditionally, the art film has been considered a nongenre movie because recurring characters and themes were not as readily apparent. However, a marriage has now taken place between the popular film and art cinema. This has accompanied the 1950s decline of the studio system with the emergence of numerous, influential art house European auteurs, especially those associated with the French New Wave (see this volume's parody chapter); a new wave, most specifically François Truffaut and Jean-Luc Godard, whose films still managed to pay homage to traditional Hollywood genres; the rise of a 1960s young, antiestablishment audience—complemented by the real arrival of film studies on college campuses; and the materialization since the 1960s of American directors pursuing art house themes (from Arthur Penn to Woody Allen). William C. Siska, author of the art film chapter in this volume, pinpoints *Annie Hall* (1977) as the "crossover film" from which this union can be dated. Indeed, one might say Allen tested the popular film-art cinema market even earlier with *Love and Death* (1975), his critically and commercially successful parody of the art film, as well as high art in general (see the parody chapter). Consequently, the application of genre study has come full circle, from credibility for the mainstream popular film to a recognition of its increasing ties with art cinema. In addition, revisionist film theorists are even starting to redefine some popular film products along art film lines, such as Dudley Andrew's provocative claiming of the Frank Capra Middle America film *Meet John Doe* (1941) in his book *Film in the Aura of Art*.[8]

These have been the seven key reasons to pursue genre study. No doubt, additional factors could be cited. But one then begins to court the overkill factor that once inspired the definition of a film censor as "someone who even sees three meanings in a double-entendre." Suffice it to say that genre criticism has become an important tool in the ongoing study of film. And regardless of what the future holds, genre analysis in some form (such as the recent fascination with the more complex "compound genre"; see the parody chapter) will continue to exist because "All this has happened before. And it will all happen again."

## NOTES

1. Barry K. Grant, ed., *Film Genre Reader* (Austin: University of Texas Press, 1986), p. x.

2. Matthew Arnold, "Preface to the 1853 Edition of Poems," in *Critical Theory Since Plato,* ed. Hazard Adams (Chicago: Harcourt Brace Jovanovich, 1971), p. 580.

3. Robert Warshow, "The Gang as Tragic Hero" (1948) and "Movie Chronicle: The Westerner" (1954), in *The Immediate Experience* (Garden City, N.Y.: Doubleday, 1962), pp. 127–33 and 135–54; James Agee, "Comedy's Greatest Era" (1949), in *Agee on Film*, vol. 1 (New York: Grosset and Dunlap, 1969) p. 2–19.

4. John G. Cawelti, "The Question of Popular Genres," *Journal of Popular Film and Television*, Summer 1985, pp. 55–56.

5. Gerald Mast, *A Short History of the Movies*, 2d ed. (Indianapolis: Bobbs-Merrill, 1976), pp. 265–66.

6. Gerald Weales, *Canned Goods as Caviar: American Film Comedy of the 1930s* (Chicago: University of Chicago Press, 1985).

7. Ibid., p. 1.

8. Dudley Andrew, chapter 5, "Productive Discord in the System: Hollywood *Meets John Doe*," in *Film in the Aura of Art* (Princeton, N.J.: Princeton University Press, 1984), pp. 78–97. See this volume's chapter 8 on populist comedy for further discussion.

# ACTION/ADVENTURE GENRES

# 2

# The Adventure Film

THOMAS SOBCHACK

"Ultimately, our familiarity with any genre seems to depend less on recognizing a specific setting than on recognizing certain dramatic conflicts that we associate with specific patterns of action and character relationships."[1]

The adventure genre is a major genre category like romance, crime, or mystery, identifying a broad sweep of conflicts and actions. There are no "adventure" films as such, but the term loosely connects a number of more specific genres, all dealing with "adventures," but particularized by certain plot formulas, settings, character networks, icons, and conventions of action which together mark out the range of this category. Most observers include the swashbuckler or sword-fighting picture, the war film or military combat film, the safari or jungle film, and the disaster film under the adventure rubric. Although these groups of films may appear a disparate lot, their patterns of action and character relationships display characteristics which clearly link them together and distinguish them from other genres.

In one sense, all non-comic genre films are based on the structure of the romance of medieval literature: a protagonist either has or develops great and special skills and overcomes insurmountable obstacles in extraordinary situations to successfully achieve some desired goal, usually the restitution of order to the world invoked by the narrative. The protagonists confront the human, natural, or supernatural powers that have improperly assumed control over the world and eventually defeat them. This pattern, though found in other genres like the western, the sports film, or the horror film, is most clearly visible in those films conventionally understood as adventure films—the swashbuckler, the war film, safari/jungle epic, and the survival film. In these films mankind is depicted as living in a world fraught with perils of all kinds, but through the

exemplary effort, cooperation, and bravery of individuals and groups, the social order, without which man would perish, is maintained against all threats
to its stability. And yet it is the very hallmark of the adventure films that they
give free play to activities which are outside the normal framework of the
everyday world, taking place as they do in situations and settings in which
social restraints upon the characters are minimal.

Hence the key factor which identifies the adventure film is that its characters
and their conflicts are located in the romantic past or in an inhospitable place
in the present or in the midst of a large-scale war or in some sort of isolation
from ordinary life. Adventure films need that sort of distance from the everyday
world in order to maximize the dangers and thus to increase the magnitude of
the efforts of the characters. If they succeed or fail, it must be on a stage larger
than life, a place where heroes can perform splendid deeds, where nobility can
be tested by adversity.

The exotic settings and flamboyant actions of the characters in adventure
films also provide wonderful opportunities for filmic presentation. Spectacle—
the depiction of wide vistas of the geography of faraway places, frames full of
colorful costumes, masses of people, animals, and objects—playing out events
of epic proportions, in and of itself, is a central feature of the adventure genre.
Simply seeing this plenitude is one of the pleasures inherent in all film, and
nowhere is this pleasure more amply produced than in adventure films. Whether
it is the sight of pirate ships booming over the waves, their sails filled with a
driving wind, a safari trekking over the steaming veldt, or two armies clashing
on a plain, the adventure film provides inherent spectacle.

D. W. Griffith knew the appeal of such spectacle. His use of the long shot
of battles and his focus on the movement of rescues and chases in *Birth of a
Nation* and *Intolerance* impressed audiences. Although one could claim both
of these films as the archetype of the adventure film in feature-length form, it
was not until the 1920s that adventure films became a recognizable genre. Douglas
Fairbanks in such films as *The Mark of Zorro* (1920), *The Three Musketeers*
(1921), and *The Thief of Bagdad* (1924) almost single-handedly invented and
popularized the swashbuckler, while Rudolph Valentino added voluptuous romance to the formula of the dashing hero in his films. Anti-German war films
abounded during World War I, but made a resurgence later in the 1920s. *The
Big Parade* (1925), *What Price Glory?* (1926), and *Wings* (1927) were very
popular. Visual spectacle made all forms of the adventure film a natural for
silent movies.

And yet the addition of sound added a dimension which amplified all of the
spectacle previously only available to the eye by adding spoken dialogue, sound
effects, and music to fill out and expand the power of the image. Though films
featuring Tarzan, lord of the jungle, had been made in the silent period, the
trumpeting of elephants, the jibbering of monkeys, and the echoing cry of Tarzan himself increased the exotic effect. The authentic sound of cannons, ma-

chine guns, and airplane motors made war films sound as death defying as they looked. And swashbucklers gained immensely from the sound of sword on sword, the crashing of waves, and the strains of melodramatic music during moments of intense conflict. An essential part of the adventure formula is a stirring speech, a call to action by the hero as he rallies his comrades around him. Synchronized dialogue made this possible.

During the 1930s the framework of the adventure film was formalized within the context of sound; the basic patterns remained the same throughout the studio years of the 1940s and the 1950s, changing little until the 1960s. This is the ''classic'' period of Hollywood production in which all genres evolved somewhat in response to changes in society, yet maintained an overall consistency. As the studio system dissolved, however, audience acceptance of the tried-and-true formulas waned. From the 1960s to the present, the adventure film dramatically changed its tone. Except for the disaster films of the early 1970s which treated their premises with sincerity, most modern adventure films suggest irony or parody of their basic tenets. For example, *The Three Musketeers,* based on the Dumas novel, had been made essentially as conventional sword and swagger adventure in 1933, 1948, and 1951 (even Edwin S. Porter had produced an hour-long version in 1912). Richard Lester's 1974 *Three Musketeers*, however, was clearly an attempt to show the famous swordsmen as vain, obtuse, stupid, brawling hooligans, paid mercenaries of a vapid king, engaged in petty duels while the social order crumbled around them, and not as the noble heroes of romantic fiction. In short, Lester's treatment of the genre was antiheroic.

This is not to say that the adventure film in its classic form is no longer a viable entity. In 1974, the same year as Lester's film, Richard Chamberlain appeared in *The Count of Monte Cristo,* a made-for-television film which had little trace of irony. He also appeared in a theatrical remake of *King Solomon's Mines* in 1985 which was also treated conventionally. And the glorious achievements of American servicemen were noted without parody in the Rambo films made by Sylvester Stallone. The story of Indiana Jones in *Raiders of the Lost Ark* (1981), though given a peculiar nostalgic note by being set in the past, appeared at least on one level to be doing the expected: thrilling the audience with countless hairbreadth escapes and dynamic chases.[2] There is no way to predict audience response where genre films are concerned. Sometimes the standard, classic formula, treated with respect, may prove successful. At other times parody and irony capture viewers' imaginations. Perhaps it is safe to say that the potential for irreverence is always present in the world of genre films. Mack Sennett's comedians parodied all the romantic heroes and genres of the silent era, even as the serious films found their audiences. In fact, the same person could thrill to the exploits of Douglas Fairbanks one week, and laugh hysterically at Will Rogers humorously imitating Fairbanks the next.

Let us look first at the standard form of the adventure film, to examine its patterns of action and character networks in order to discover how the genre works in the first place, and then see what elements in the standard formula lend themselves to irony and parody.

As noted earlier, the adventure genre is really a grouping of several more well-defined genres—the swashbuckler, the war film, the safari film, and the survival film. Despite their surface differences in topography, costumes, time periods, and iconography, two major plot structures are clearly discernible. One focuses on the lone hero—the swashbuckler, the explorer who searches for the golden idol, the great hunter who leads the expedition, the lord of the jungle—and the other focuses on a hero interacting with a microcosmic group— the sergeant of a patrol, the leader of a squadron, the person who leads a group of castaways out of danger and back to civilization.

The lone hero pattern is most obvious in the swashbuckler. There a decent, law-abiding member of a society (as in nearly all adventure films, a male fig- ure, although there is at least one pirate film in which the protagonist is a female) is cast into the role of outlaw because the society in which he lives has been corrupted from within: a tryannical ruler has come to power and bent law and order to his own selfish ends in *Captain Blood* (1935) and *The Adventures of Robin Hood* (1938), or some social injustice has put the hero in an adversary position to the prevailing social order as in *Scaramouche* (1952) and the three sound versions of *The Prisoner of Zenda* (1937, 1952, 1979). Once outlawed, the hero makes every effort to restore order to society. Sometimes this means literally placing the absent or kidnapped ruler on the throne by overthrowing the false regent; sometimes it is enough that the hero, through his actions, reminds the society that it is time to reexamine its institutions and cast out the people who have been corrupting them.

For the most part, there is no attempt at changing those institutions. The prevailing social structure is never questioned. In this respect, the swashbuckler is extremely conservative. If kings rule, that is just fine as long as they are decent kings. In *Captain Blood,* Errol Flynn rebels against constituted authority only when it is clear that James II of England is a tyrant. Later, when he learns that a new king, William of Orange, has accepted the throne, Flynn gives up privateering and patriotically enlists to serve under the new, presumably benign rule. In *The Scarlet Pimpernel* (1934) the revolutionaries of France are depicted as villains, whereas the aristocrats are shown to be the representatives of a proper, well-organized, humane, law-abiding society who need to be rescued from the brutish rabble. Political stability and the status quo of traditional social structures are prominent values of this genre.

Nevertheless, before the end of the swashbuckler, the hero—invariably of noble blood and descended from an aristocratic family—must become a part of the masses. After recognizing the injustice of his society, the hero separates himself from his peers and allies himself with the poor and the downtrodden, the tortured and the imprisoned. The hero dramatically moves from aristocracy to democracy and thus represents a paradox of the genre. Never fully assimilating himself into the common herd, always flamboyant and marked by his superior intelligence, grace, and fighting skills, he still expresses the notion that all men can treat each other equally, that distinctions between men based on rank, privilege, and birth are outmoded and unjust in themselves. Robin Hood leaves Locksley Hall and joins his merry men in the forest and stresses egalitarianism. Scaramouche joins a troupe of traveling players and becomes an actor, a member of a profession that absorbs all talented individuals no matter what their backgrounds might be. Captain Blood becomes a common prisoner aboard a slave ship where he is thrown in with men from all walks of life.

Frequently the hero's democratic guise creates one of the stumbling blocks to successful union with the heroine, who usually is aristocratic. The romantic subplot of most swashbucklers is surprisingly like the main plot of a romantic comedy—the male and female meet, hate and distrust each other after an initial attraction, bicker and argue throughout the film, and finally resolve their differences at the end in a marriage or the promise of one—except that the hero must rescue the heroine from physical danger at least once during the course of the film. Repelled by the brusqueness of the hero's approach at first, the swashbuckler heroine comes to realize that moral value and social value are represented by action and intent and not by the superficial trappings of title, wealth, costume, or manners. When the heroine has come to understand this proposition, the hero can throw off his democratic disguise and reenter the aristocracy. The two will wed and create a better society, one which retains all the best of the old rules but will ensure that those rules be administered fairly and justly.

In addition to the connection with romantic comedy, the swashbuckler shares certain elements with the musical comedy where the hero is also defined as much by his physical expressiveness as by his good deeds. Many of the directors who made swashbucklers also were known for their musicals, and it is easy to see similarities in function and structure between sword fights and dance numbers. George Sidney, for example, directed musicals like *Anchors Aweigh* (1945), *Showboat* (1951), and *Kiss Me, Kate* (1953), and in the same period swashbucklers like *The Three Musketeers* (1948), *Scaramouche* (1952), and *Young Bess* (1953). Gene Kelly plays a song-and-dance man and a swashbuckling hero in *Singin' in the Rain* (1952) where the connection between the two styles is made comically clear when the film-within-the-film Kelly is making changes its title from "The Dueling Cavalier" to "The Dancing Cavalier." Dancing and swordplay are linked not merely by choreography but by their emphasis on style. The dancers and the sword fighters who are most graceful deserve to win because physical proficiency is identified with moral value. Although a fine fencer in real life, Basil Rathbone always looks clumsier in his duels with Errol Flynn simply because he is the villain.

Unlike the hero in other adventure films, the swashbuckling hero, like a precursor of James Bond, will often distance himself from his actions and situation to comment upon them ironically. Hence the swashbuckler, even in its most serious forms, is very close to self-parody. Because the hero is frequently in disguise, he is a performer aware that he is giving a performance, capable of giving asides to the audience. In the 1948 *The Three Musketeers,* when Gene Kelly, in the middle of a deadly serious duel, turns a particularly acrobatic somersault and lands neatly, ready to parry an opponent's thrust, it's done not only for the viewer's amusement but for the character's as well. Personal style and a literate self-consciousness are as fundamental a part of this genre as swords, sailing ships, plumed hats, and caskets of jewels.

Though he may have helpers or a crew to work with, the hero of biblical epics, tales of spies or test pilots, explorer stories, safari films, jungle pictures, and the swashbuckler, is essentially a loner, one distinguished from the crowd by superior skills and intelligence, a cut above the ordinary man, a hero in the more traditional sense of the term. Not so the hero of the second large category of adventure films—the survival films. In these the hero is a part of a small group, relatively inconspicuous at first, who works with that group to ensure its survival against great odds and then returns to virtual anonymity after the danger is past and the group's safety is secured. The heroes of war films and disaster films are just regular guys who find themselves in jeopardy within a group thrown together by chance—they all find themselves booked on a partic-ular plane or ship or they are assigned to a particular platoon or boot camp. Even when the group is formed by individuals making a choice—they volunteer for a special mission against the enemy or join a famous squadron or outfit— the implication is clear that no one in the group is superior to any other, that is, until the action develops and the challenges and dangers test the mettle of the group's members. Then the primary hero will emerge to do his extraordi-nary feats, but always within the context of the group.

Survival films, located primarily in a contemporary context, have a grimmer tone than those adventure films featuring the lone hero. Because settings, cos-tumes, and situations, as well as heroes, tend to be less exotic and more im-mediately familiar to the audience, survival films provide fewer opportunities for viewers to romanticize the activities of the characters. After all, everyone knows that "war is hell!" and being held hostage by a group of terrorists is no picnic. We know from daily newscasts that these are everyday occurrences. Nevertheless, the underlying structures of the survival film are similar to those of the romance. They both emphasize the heroic triumph over obstacles which threaten social order and the reaffirmation of predominant social values such as fair play and respect for merit and cooperation.

These values are highlighted in the war and disaster film, seen as the essen-tial ingredients which ensure the survival of the group, even more than the physical and mental skills of the protagonist. In fact, the hero's most important function is to instill, and inspire the group to practice, these values, which are important for the perpetuation of society at large. But rather than dealing with society in its largest numbers (the swashbuckler is often about the fate of the country as a whole), the survival films must first identify and isolate a microcosm of the society. Isolation allows the society to test itself and its components in a circumscribed and easily identified arena, and it allows all the myriad obstacles facing society to be represented by one large and dramatic obstacle. A group is isolated in the desert when a plane crashes in *The Flight of the Phoenix* (1966). An overturned ocean liner contains the microcosm of *The Poseidon Adventure* (1972). Prisons, either civilian or military, provide the isolation in such films as *Stalag 17* (1953), *The Great Escape* (1963), and *Escape from Alcatraz* (1978). An escape and a mode of transportation are combined in *The Runaway Train* (1986) to isolate the group. Almost all war movies contain a natural separation into smaller groups—the squad, the platoon, the company—allowing for the creation of a democratic microcosm containing a wide spectrum of character types and ethnic groups, specifically organized to fulfill clearly defined objectives. Whether it's a special group like the criminals in *The Dirty Dozen* (1967) or an average group as in *The Boys in Company C* (1978), the isolation presents the opportunity for a close examination of the interaction of individuals to each other and the group enterprise.

At the beginning of the survival film, the various characters are shown in everyday situations without life-threatening stress. Then the characters are separated from the society as a whole and confronted with the problem of survival. Most of the time in a survival film is spent depicting the process whereby the group, cut off from the securities and certainties of the ordinary support networks of civilized life, forms itself into a functioning, effective unit. People learn that they can't do it alone, that certain members of the group are good at certain tasks, that everyone has moments of doubt, but each in his own way can help. It is interesting to note that even though stereotypes abound—the self-sacrificing mother, the good-hearted prostitute, the loyal nurse, the frail creature reduced to hysterics—women often play a decisive role in the success or failure of the group in survival films. Certainly much more so than in those adventure films based more closely on the romance featuring the lone hero.

In fact, it is necessary to lean heavily on the idea of character types to certify the notion that the mini-society of the isolated group is, indeed, representative of the variety and difference that make up any social entity. Any such group is essentially made up of *individuals,* all primarily interested in their own happiness, success, pleasure, and survival. Indeed, in the course of normal life, these individuals usually see themselves in competition with the others in the society for these values. It is only when disaster strikes that the value of cooperation and concern for the good of the whole comes into play. Thus the group in a survival film is usually made up of very distinct characters, almost caricatures. We will recognize a range of personal qualities (courage, cowardice, humor, intelligence, selfishness, self-sacrifice and so forth); a range of ethnic, religious, and economic types (the Jew, Catholic, black, Native American, Hispanic, rich snob, redneck populist, and so forth); and a range of skills, either professionally acquired or amateurishly cultivated (the engineer, the computer nerd, the radio ''ham,'' the Olympic swimmer, the pastor, the used-car salesman). Such a breadth of social strata allows the viewer to observe a range of behavior, to see played out the many possible ways in which the average social being might respond if placed in similar life-threatening situations. Through identification with the ordinary characters, the viewer can play out potential ways of meeting crises. Clearly all of the skills and qualities which aid in the group's survival are considered positive; those which serve only individual interests are seen as negative. The black marketeer in a wartime prison camp, the coward whose fear makes him desert his post, thereby threatening the safety of others, the bully who uses the isolation of the disaster as a pretext for enlarging his own ego at the expense of the group, all usually experience rejection from the group, if not actual death, for their failure to think of the group's mutual safety first.

One of the basic lessons of the survival film is that crisis creates its own democracy; all sorts of persons from all walks of life, socially acceptable under normal circumstances or not—criminals and prostitutes often redeem themselves in these films, witness *The Dirty Dozen*—have crucial roles to play if they expend themselves to benefit the group and to reaffirm the value of social order. No matter what they've done in the past, they become worthy of praise if they join in the common cause. In all survival films, some members of the microcosm will end up sacrificing themselves for the good of the group. The "villains" are those too concerned with personal welfare, or those too intellectual to act swiftly, or too cynical, or too neurotic, who by their actions obstruct the group's aim of reuniting with the larger society. The hero of the survival film comes to the fore because his skills of perseverance, practicality, and leadership are needed by the group, but once the group reenters the larger society, he is willing to disappear into the crowd. Marked by none of the personal style, quick wit, and self-reflexivity of the swashbuckling hero, the survival film hero is always thoughtful and earnest. John Wayne was the perfect actor for such roles. In fact, personal style and idiosyncratic behavior are seen as undesirable qualities in a survival film hero because of their individualistic, antisocial implications. This is the hero who says afterwards, "Aw, shucks, anybody could have done it. I just did my duty." Unlike the swashbuckler, the survival film is less interested in the aloof loner than it is in the ways in which a variety of individuals hinder or contribute to the creation of social order.

In either case, however, whether focusing on an individual hero or a microcosmic group's survival, the adventure film always plays out the mythic ideal of social unity. All the abnormal, exotic, excessive activity of individuals is a necessary component to be sure. During the course of an adventure film, the audience can vicariously live out their fantasies of personal prowess and vigorous action in heightened, emotionally intense, extraordinary situations, and can be moved by images of titanic struggle against the opposing forces which seek disruption—political upheaval, war, disaster—yet the ending, the closure of the adventure, always returns the viewer to the position of social conformity. All the values in the traditional adventure film uphold and reinforce the status quo, the idea of stability and regularity in the workings of the social order. As Aristotle said, man is a social animal and must never lose sight of that fact. The adventure film will always strive to remind us of that precept.

## BIBLIOGRAPHICAL OVERVIEW

Perhaps because the adventure film is an amorphous category, really a catch-all for several more specific genres, it is not surprising that there are very few books and articles devoted to adventure films. What is surprising, however, is that except for the war film, there are very few published works worth reading on any of the more specific genres. A major critical book has yet to be written about the safari or jungle film, the swashbuckler, or the disaster film. If the spy film is included as an adventure genre, there is no single book about it either. To be sure, there are popular treatments given over to some of these areas: a book on Tarzan films, for example, and biographies of Errol Flynn and Douglas Fairbanks which contain some useful information about the swash-bucklers these actors appeared in. But there has been an amazing neglect of scholarly interest in what has to be, after all, one of the most consistent and popular areas of Hollywood production.

Though not limited to a discussion of films exclusively, one book stands out above all the others as an introduction to that "complex of situations and conflicts" which constitutes the matrix, the field, of the adventure film. John G. Cawelti's *Adventure, Mystery, and Romance* (1976) covers all forms of presentation—films, literature, and drama—which revolve about the elements listed in his title, paying particular attention to the way these elements are materialized in popular and not high culture forms. Cawelti probes the psychological underpinnings of these stories, how audiences both desire structure and are structured by narratives which revolve around adventure, mystery, and romance modes of expression. He finds the desires of readers and viewers located in the experience of the works which induce and cater to these attributes.

Cawelti first makes the observation that the popular mind associates such narratives with violence and sex. Government panels and citizens' groups are always being formed to investigate the effect such depictions have on viewers, usually fearing a negative influence on the impressionable minds of the young. Too much viewing of scenes of violence and sex presumably leads some audience members to imitative behavior. Cawelti argues against this position by changing the terms. He says that what the audience finds vicariously in adventure narratives is not violence and sex but danger and sex. In a world which is for most people quite ordinary, he posits the need for moments of confrontation with "the ultimate excitements of love and death," but in a structured context—the fictional work—which also intensifies the experience of order and stability.[3] Thus stories of adventure, mystery, and romance provide a dual satisfaction unavailable in everyday life. The audience can eat its cake and have it, too.

Unquestionably, Cawelti's view derives from Aristotle's *Poetics,* just as the detractors derive their fears from Plato's view of fiction as presented in *The Republic.* But Cawelti quotes a variety of modern commentators as well. For example, he cites Harry Berger, Jr., who sees the desire for stability and the desire for excitement as the two drives which produce culture. "Man has a need for order, peace, and security, for protection against the terror and confusion of life, for a familiar and predictable world." But Berger sees an equally strong drive which is the opposite: "man positively needs anxiety and uncertainty, thrives on confusion and risk, wants trouble, tension, jeopardy, novelty, mystery, would be lost without enemies," and so forth.[4]

Building upon the definition that genre fictions are "moral fantasies," Cawelti sets up a typology.[5] Though only some of these apply to the adventure film, they demonstrate the thoroughness of Cawelti's views. First of all, the moral fantasy will embody the values defined by the culture's norms. If in time those norms change, that will be reflected in the genre's notion of who or what is good. But there are basic human goods which seem to have existed in Western culture from the time of the Greeks to the present. Cawelti says we all desire Victory, Love, and Knowledge; each type of genre displays a plot pattern which recognizes these desires. Stories of adventure are about heroic action—the search for justice. Stories of romance are about the meeting of a girl and a boy and the birth of love—the search for true love. Stories of mystery are about unraveling the mystery—the search for truth. Stories of horror and science fiction are about the encounter with a monster or an alien—the search for survival. In all these genres humans undergo suffering and unhappiness, but eventually they are rewarded for their troubles.

For Cawelti, "the central fantasy of the adventure story is that of the hero— individual or group—overcoming obstacles and dangers and accomplishing some important and moral mission."[6] This type of story goes back to the earliest epics. What this story represents, in all action genres in which the protagonist is successful, is basically the victory over death. There are, however, other subsidiary values: "the triumph over injustice and the threat of lawlessness in the western; the saving of the nation in the spy story; the overcoming of fear and the defeat of the enemy in the combat story";[7] the return to civilization in the safari/jungle story (with or without prize); and the restoration of proper authority in the swashbuckler.

For Cawelti, then, the genres which deal with adventure, mystery, and romance synthesize these two desires, the quest for order and the flight from ennui. As fictions, as stories following extremely codified forms, genres are ordered and conventional, their conflicts neatly resolved by the end of the story. Yet at the same time, they are filled with images of excitement, danger, uncertainty, violence, and sex. Thus the audience, held in the comfort and security of the fictional form, can experience the anxiety and suspense, the thrills and chills of the situations depicted. Like the thrill of riding a roller coaster at the amusement park, the feeling of excitement is high, while the real danger is low, and it only lasts a specified amount of time. Cawelti invokes Jean Piaget on play and likens the experience of these narratives to the function of play.[8] The tensions and frustrations of everyday life are temporarily transcended. And, of course, like Piaget, Cawelti sees this as a good both for the individual and the society.

Cawelti does not sidestep the Marxist critique of such experiences, however. He recognizes that the satisfaction of desires as represented in the adventure, mystery, and romance genres is a fantasy, the therapeutic value temporary. Yet the history of culture suggests that civilized human beings, social human beings, have a bona fide need for stories of this kind in order to keep alive a vision of the ideal in the face of the practical forces impinging upon them. It's well enough to say that people should change the conditions of their existence and make the world a better place through their actions, but most people living in the social community simply don't. The burden of everyday life is too great. But most people have the desire for moral action, and perhaps rather than diffuse such desires, these kinds of generic stories serve to remind the participants of the potential for higher goals.

There are two general patterns for these adventure tales, says Cawelti. There are those with ''superheroes'' whose actions and exploits are exaggerated and perhaps defy credulity. These are popular with youthful audiences. The other broad pattern displays an ''ordinary hero,'' one who uses only the normal human attributes to solve the conflicts of the narrative. These stories appeal to adult audiences. James Bond is a ''superhero'' who nevertheless fits the tastes of the latter audience.

Cawelti then breaks down this basic pattern of adventure stories by setting and time. For example, the swashbuckler is set anywhere from the late Middle Ages to the nineteenth century in Europe. The combat story is almost exclusively tied to a specific historical war. The safari/jungle film has to be in some exotic location (even Antarctica) during the time of exploration when Western culture and native culture are still in conflict. The disaster film is nearly always in the postindustrial period and very frequently contemporaneous with the making of the film.

Cawelti does not deal at any great length with individual adventure films in his book. Yet his work is recommended reading for anyone who is interested in the psychological dimensions of generic fictions whether they occur in film, literature, or drama. Erudite, scholarly, and yet extremely lively, *Adventure, Mystery, and Romance* is a seminal inquiry into genres and the genre experience.

A quick look at a reference bibliography on film books will find one entitled *Adventure in the Movies* by Ian Cameron. The title itself should, of course, make it clear that the book is not about the adventure genre per se, but about the quality of adventure found in a variety of movies. Cameron covers war films, safari films, horror films, science fiction films, westerns—indeed any film which has adventure in it. For him, adventure is a kind of heightened excitement produced by the perils of the protagonist in a wide array of films. Though the text is competently written, most of the pages are taken up with still photos from favorite films. Cameron presents himself as a member of the movie audience reminiscing about the wonderful and fabulous films of the past, but there is little analysis of generic form and function in this book.

The same may be said about most books on the war film, too. Perhaps because war films are so closely identified with actual historical wars, the primary approach of these books seems to be historical and sociological, not filmic. Nevertheless, the books make important observations about the fantasy of war films and their function as propaganda. That is, they discuss the films made during World War II as aspects of the war effort—how accurate did they depict what was really happening at the front, how effective were they in keeping up morale, and so forth—rather than focusing on the archetypal situations inherent in generic patterns or showing how the films worked as repetitions and variations of earlier films. In the better books, some of this material does show up, making them well worth reading for the person interested in the war film as a genre film.

Tom Perlmutter's book, called simply *War Movies,* appears in a series from Castle Books which by and large are picture books. But Perlmutter goes much further and gets into some very accurate observations about the nature of this kind of film. The book is selective but covers films made from World War I up to Vietnam. Thus one gets a good sense of the historical development of the genre.

Lawrence Suid, on the other hand, examines very closely the ties between Hollywood and the War Department in World War II and after in his monumental study *Guts and Glory.* What he demonstrates in great detail, with references to copious amounts of correspondence, is that the government had a great hand in dictating the story values of films made about the military from the 1930s on. In some cases the use of military equipment and personnel by Hollywood producers was contingent upon the narrative reflecting the image the government wanted promoted. Military advisers assigned to guarantee the authenticity of battle sequences, costumes, organizations of ranks, and so forth frequently asked for and got major changes in the script of the film. This is a most fascinating and revealing look at an aspect of filmmaking not generally known.

Two other books whose texts contain much rewarding information about the scope and function of the war film were published in 1974 with the same title. Ivan Butler and Norman Kagan each authored *The War Film* from different publishers. Both select a wide variety of films about the various wars from the past to the present and show the changes and development of these films within the context of film history and the history of the nation in the twentieth century.

One of the problems engendered by any discussion of genre, that of definition, arises in most war film books. Perhaps it would be better to speak of the "combat" film rather than the war film as the subgenre of the adventure film (see chapter 6). Films in which men come together to engage in battle have very recognizable patterns of conflict and action which engender subsequent films; that is, they do live up to genre expectations. There are other films that use wartime as a background and a setting for their narratives, but they do not focus on the military in action.

Stanley J. Solomon, for example, in his book *Beyond Formula: American Film Genres,* refers to a number of films as "war" films, which do not fit the popular definition. He mentions Griffith's film *America,* as well as *Birth of a Nation* and *Intolerance,* but few would agree that these are typical adventure genre combat films. Nevertheless they fit into Solomon's thesis: they are films which go "beyond formula." It is always a difficult decision, drawing the line between films that are in a genre and those that become nongenre films when they stretch the limits of the generic formulas and conventions. Solomon does at least distinguish between combat and noncombat films. For example, he gives a close reading to *Casablanca* as a film in which war is a theme. On the other hand, he says war films are only definable in "terms of a certain kind of atmosphere."[9] The problems inherent in definition are apparent to Solomon, as the following remark suggests: "Thus the spy film is a category of war films when the spying is carried on by different nations, but becomes a category of crime films if carried on, for instance, between rival companies or gangs."[10] Ultimately, each writer has to set up a working definition of the subject at hand.

Information on the silent swashbuckler can be found in Lewis Jacobs's *The Rise of the American Film,* but Jacobs groups films on the basis of content and not a more modern definition of genre. He mentions Thomas Ince's 1914 version of *Typhoon* as one of the first "adventure" films, covers all of Douglas Fairbanks's films, and notes such silent films as *The Prisoner of Zenda, The Sea Hawk,* and *Beau Brummel,* the latter starring John Barrymore.

Although there is no definitive work on the jungle/safari film, Richard Maynard's *Africa on Film: Myth and Reality* mentions the 1932 Tarzan film, *King Solomon's Mines, Trader Horn,* and other films set in Africa. His treatment is from a sociological perspective. Gabe Essoe's Citadel Press book *Tarzan of the Movies* also contains some fascinating lore about that well-known figure.

Finally, *Film Genre: Theory and Criticism,* an anthology edited by Barry K. Grant, contains several interesting essays on the disaster film, the biblical epic, and the sports film (which is often defined as a subgenre of the adventure genre).

This survey of written material on the adventure genre certainly suggests that there is a great deal of work to be done. Though the war film has been covered from a number of perspectives, the other genres have been given very little attention. The area is wide open for trailblazers who wish to open up the dark continent of the adventure film to the scrutiny of criticism.

## NOTES

1. Thomas Schatz, *Hollywood Genres* (New York: Random House, 1981), p. 21.
2. See Frank Tomasulo's article, "Mr. Jones Goes to Washington," *Quarterly Review of Film Studies,* Fall 1982, pp. 331–40, for an analysis of the hidden ideological messages contained in this film.
3. John G. Cawelti, *Adventure, Mystery, and Romance* (Chicago: University of Chicago Press, 1976), p. 16.
4. Ibid.
5. Ibid., p. 37.
6. Ibid., p. 36.
7. Ibid., p. 40.
8. Ibid., p. 18.
9. Stanley J. Solomon, *Beyond Formula: American Film Genres* (New York: Harcourt, 1976), p. 244.
10. Ibid., p. 245.

## BIBLIOGRAPHICAL CHECKLIST

### Books

Barbour, Alan G. *Days of Thrills and Adventure*. New York: Macmillan, 1976.
Butler, Ivan. *The War Film*. Cranbury, N.J.: A. S. Barnes, 1974.
Cameron, Ian. *Adventure in the Movies*. New York: Crescent Books, 1974.
Carey, John. *Spectacular: The Story of Epic Films*. Secaucus, N.J.: Castle Books, 1974.
Cawelti, John G. *Adventure, Mystery, and Romance*. Chicago: University of Chicago Press, 1976.
Connell, Brian. *Knight Errant: A Biography of Douglas Fairbanks, Jr*. London: Hodder and Stoughton, 1955.
Cook, Alistair. *Douglas Fairbanks: The Making of a Screen Character*. New York: Museum of Modern Art, 1940.
Essoe, Gabe. *Tarzan of the Movies*. Secaucus, N.J.: Citadel Press, 1968.
Flynn, Errol. *My Wicked, Wicked Ways*. New York: Putnam, 1959.
Hirsch, Foster. *The Hollywood Epic*. New York: A. S. Barnes, 1978.
Kagan, Norman. *The War Film*. New York: Pyramid, 1974.
McConnell, Frank D. *The Spoken Seen: Film and the Romantic Imagination*. Baltimore: Johns Hopkins University Press, 1975.
Maynard, Richard. *Africa on Film: Myth and Reality*. Rochelle Park, N.J.: Hayden Press, 1974.
Parish, James R., and Don E. Stanke. *The Swashbucklers*. New Rochelle, N.Y.: Arlington House, 1975.
Perlmutter, Tom. *War Movies*. Secaucus, N.J.: Castle Books, 1974.
Richards, Jeffrey. *Visions of Yesterday*. London: Routledge and Kegan Paul, 1973. Imperialism in film.
Shinder, Colin. *Hollywood Goes to War*. London: Routledge and Kegan Paul, 1974. A British view of the period 1939–1952.
Smith, Julian. *Looking Away: Hollywood and Viet Nam*. New York: Scribners, 1975.

Solomon, Stanley J. *Beyond Formula: American Film Genres*. New York: Harcourt Brace Jovanovich Inc., 1976.

Suid, Lawrence. *Guts and Glory*. Reading, Mass.: Addison Wesley, 1978.

Thomas, Tony. *The Great Adventure Films*. Secaucus, N.J.: Citadel, 1976.

Walsh, Raoul. *Each Man in His Time*. New York: Farrar, Straus, and Giroux, 1974.

Zinman, David H. *Saturday Afternoon at the Bijou*. New Rochelle, N.Y.: Arlington House, 1973.

### Shorter Works

Durgnat, Raymond. "Epic, Epic, Epic, Epic, Epic." In *Film Genre: Theory and Criticism*, ed. Barry K. Grant. Metuchen, N.J.: Scarecrow Press, 1977, pp. 108–17.

McInery, Peter. "Apocalypse Then: Hollywood Looks Back at Vietnam," *Film Quarterly*, Winter 1979–1980, pp. 21–32.

Sayre, Nora. "Winning the Weepstakes: The Problems of American Sports Movies." In *Film Genre: Theory and Criticism*, ed. Barry K. Grant. Metuchen, N.J.: Scarecrow Press, 1977, pp. 182–94.

Suid, Lawrence. "Hollywood and Vietnam," *Film Comment*, September–October 1979, pp. 20–25.

Yacowar, Maurice. "The Bug in the Rug: Notes on the Disaster Genre." In *Film Genre: Theory and Criticism*, ed. Barry K. Grant. Metuchen, N.J.: Scarecrow Press, 1977, pp. 90–107.

## SELECTED FILMOGRAPHY

1924  *The Thief of Bagdad* (138 minutes).
United Artists. Director: Raoul Walsh. Screenplay: Lotta Woods. Cast: Douglas Fairbanks (The Thief of Bagdad), Anna May Wong (The Mongol Slave).

1927  *Wings* (130 minutes).
Paramount. Director: William A. Wellman. Screenplay: Hope Loring, Harry D. Lighton; from John M. Saunders's story. Cast: Clara Bow (Clara Preston), Charles Rogers (John Powell), Richard Arlen (David Armstrong), Gary Cooper (Cadet White).

1932  *Tarzan the Ape Man* (100 minutes).
MGM. Director: W. S. Van Dyke. Screenplay: Cyril Hume adapted the *Tarzan* series of novels by Edgar Rice Burroughs, film dialogue by Ivor Novella. Cast: Johnny Weissmuller (Tarzan), Maureen O'Sullivan (Jane Parker).

1935  *Captain Blood* (98 minutes).
Warners. Director: Michael Curtiz. Screenplay: Casey Robinson adapted the Rafael Sabatini novel. Cast: Errol Flynn (Peter Blood), Olivia de Havilland (Arabella Bishop), Basil Rathbone (Levasseur).

1938  *The Adventures of Robin Hood* (102 minutes).
Warners. Director: Michael Curtiz. Screenplay: Norman Reilly Raine, Seton I. Miller. Cast: Errol Flynn (Robin Hood), Olivia de Havilland (Maid Marian), Basil Rathbone (Sir Guy of Gisbourne).

1939    *Only Angels Have Wings* (120 minutes).
Columbia. Director: Howard Hawks. Screenplay: Jules Furthman, from a story by Hawks. Cast: Cary Grant (Geoff Carter), Jean Arthur (Bonnie Lee), Thomas Mitchell (Kid Dabb).

1943    *Air Force* (124 minutes).
Warners. Director: Howard Hawks. Screenplay: Dudley Nichols. Cast: John Garfield (Aerial Gunner), Gig Young (Co-Pilot), Harry Carey (Crew Chief).

1949    *Sands of Iwo Jima* (109 minutes).
Republic. Director: Alan Dwan. Screenplay: Harry Brown, James Edward Grant, from a Harry Brown story. Cast: John Wayne (Sgt. Stryker), John Agar (Pfc. Conway), Forrest Tucker (Cpl. Thomas).

1950    *King Solomon's Mines* (102 minutes).
MGM. Director: Compton Bennett/Andrew Marton. Screenplay: Helen Deutsch, based on the H. Rider Haggard novel. Cast: Deborah Kerr (Elizabeth Curtis), Stewart Granger (Alan Quartermain), Richard Carlson (John Goode).

1951    *The African Queen* (103 minutes).
United Artists. Director: John Huston. Screenplay: James Agee and John Huston adapted the C. S. Forester novel. Cast: Humphrey Bogart (Charlie Allnut), Katharine Hepburn (Rose).

1952    *Scaramouche* (115 minutes).
MGM. Director: George Sidney. Screenplay: Ronald Miller, George Froeschel, based on a Rafael Sabatini novel. Cast: Stewart Granger (André Moreau), Eleanor Parker (Lenore), Janet Leigh (Aline de Gavrillac), Mel Ferrer (Marquis de Maynes).

1970    *Airport* (137 minutes).
Universal. Director: George Seaton. Screenplay: Seaton, from the novel by Arthur Hailey. All-star cast includes Burt Lancaster (Mel Bakersfield), Dean Martin (Vernon Demerest), Jean Seberg (Tanya Livingston), George Kennedy (Patroni).

1972    *The Poseidon Adventure* (117 minutes).
20th Century-Fox. Director: Ronald Neame. Screenplay: Stirling Silliphant, Wendell Mayes, based on the Paul Gallico novel. All-star cast includes Gene Hackman (Rev. Frank Scott), Red Buttons (James Martin), Shelley Winters (Belle Rosen).

1977    *Star Wars* (121 minutes).
20th Century-Fox. Director: George Lucas. Screenplay: Lucas. Cast: Mark Hamill (Luke Skywalker), Harrison Ford (Han Solo), Carrie Fisher (Princess Leia Organa), Alec Guinness (Ben Kenobi). (Although full of the trappings of science fiction, this film is basically Arthurian romance.)

1981    *Raiders of the Lost Ark* (115 minutes).
Paramount. Director: Steven Spielberg. Screenplay: Lawrence Kasdan, from a George Lucas and Philip Kaufman story. Cast: Harrison Ford (Indy), Karen Allen (Marion), Denholm Elliott (Brody).

# 3

# The Western

THOMAS SCHATZ

"This is the West, sir. When the legend becomes fact, print the legend."
　　　　　　　—Newspaper editor in *The Man Who Shot Liberty Valence*

"The Western is the only genre whose origins are almost identical with those of the cinema itself. . . ."
　　　　　　　—André Bazin, in "The Western: or the American Film
　　　　　　　　　　　　　　　　　　　　　　Par Excellence" (1953)[1]

The western is the richest and most complex of all American genres, cinematic or otherwise, and the most enduring of all the stories that our society continually tells itself. As an American foundation myth it has been endlessly updated, transformed, and reworked through an array of discursive forms, from wood carvings and folk ballads to pulp novels and cigarette ads. Its lineage can be traced back through centuries of American lore to Indian captivity tales and colonial folk music, to the writings of James Fenimore Cooper and other less renowned fiction writers, and particularly to the popular accounts of the "taming" of the American West in the latter half of the nineteenth century. But the western story has been told most frequently, most powerfully, and most accessibly on film. Not until the emergence of the cinema in the early twentieth century as a genuine mass medium, in fact, did the western gain the widespread circulation and thus the "cultural currency" to be considered as something of a national legend.

This is a complex and perhaps a contradictory cultural issue, for to consider the circulation of western stories via the cinema is also to consider the formal and commercial imperatives of the burgeoning mass medium. From as early as 1903 with the huge success of Edwin S. Porter's *The Great Train Robbery*, western stories were perceived as marketable commodities, and they were repeated and varied until certain basic structural features—many of them specific to the film medium—were clearly understood by both filmmakers and audiences alike. These economic imperatives demanded the repetition of the western story and the steady refinement of its narrative and thematic conventions, but it was the very existence of the movie industry and the social climate it represented that ensured the western's "larger" cultural and ideological status.

The rise of Hollywood signaled the arrival of America's urban-industrial age, a period when traditional values and established notions of family and community, of the social and political order, and of individual freedom and initiative were radically transformed. Hollywood movies were among the first and were certainly the most widespread and accessible manifestations of an emergent "mass culture" which brought with it new forms of cultural expression. The western genre was among the more prevalent of those forms, and in a very real sense it was "about" the very same conflicts that the new industrial age (and thus the movies themselves) had come to represent—conflicts between rural and urban lifestyles, between agrarian traditions and the conditions of modern city life, between the nineteenth and twentieth centuries, between the old world and the new. The half-century "life span" of the genre, then, might be seen as the period necessary for our society to collectively work through those conflicts, to resolve the ideological contradictions that infused the western genre with its basic dramatic structure and its thematic nexus. And thus the so-called death of the western in the late 1960s and early 1970s as a mass media staple may indicate an ideological as well as a historical distance from the virtual world that the genre repeatedly displayed.

In essence, of course, the western is both historically and geographically specific; it traces the settling of the American West (defined generally as the land west of the Mississippi) from the end of the Civil War until the early twentieth century. In this sense the western is tied more directly to social and historical "reality" than virtually any other film genre, with the possible exceptions of the gangster films and bio-pics of the 1930s and the combat films made during and after World War II. But as Robert Warshow so aptly pointed out in his study of the gangster film, every genre gradually generates its own distinct reality. "It is only in the ultimate sense that the type appeals to the audience's experience of reality," Warshow argued. "Much more immediately, it appeals to the previous experience of the type itself; it creates its own field of reference." [2]

This was particularly true of the western, since the historical reality it portrayed already had been "processed" for popular consumption not only by writers and painters but by self-styled purveyors of their own mythology, especially such outright hucksters of the symbol as Bill Cody and Wyatt Earp. But given the cinema's commercial, ideological, and formal-narrative imperatives, it was inevitable that historical reality yield to a romanticized and formulaic treatment. Jon Tuska, who has done extensive research into the filming of the West, suggests that movie westerns might be categorized as formula, as historical romance, and as historical reconstruction.[3] Predictably enough, Tuska finds that formulary westerns and historical romances far outnumber authentic reconstructions.

The narrative structure of the formulary and romantic western is essentially the same. As Tuska puts it: "There is conflict within the community. The hero eventually decides to take part in the conflict and his involvement precipitates the death-struggle between himself and one or more villains."[4] The conflict invariably is resolved in the most fundamental of all western plot conventions, the climactic gunfight. In the formulary western the outcome of the struggle is altogether predictable: the hero prevails, simply because the formula demands it. Here the historical romance differs. "What happens in the romantic historical reconstruction," observes Tuska, "happens for an ideological reason."[5] A historical romance does not simply play out the familiar formula, as a B-grade western might do, thus repressing the sociopolitical and cultural stakes involved in American history (which did, after all, involve the near extermination of an entire race and the appropriation of their land in the name of progress and Manifest Destiny). Instead it steadily discloses its own "internal"—i.e., textually specific—value system, its own particular skew on the issues and conflicts inherent within the western "story."

This necessarily varies from one western to another, even if the films in question depict the same historical figures and events—the Earps and Clantons fighting for control of Tombstone, say, or Custer and Crazy Horse at the Battle of the Little Big Horn. We have little trouble with the idea that different film versions of these events tell the story differently, because each telling creates its own narrative context and, beyond that, each is specific to the political and ideological stakes of its era. It is no surprise, for instance, that Custer's legendary Last Stand against the Sioux and Cheyenne in 1876 would be depicted as a glorious and heroic military venture in *They Died With Their Boots On,* since it was produced by a Hollywood studio in 1942 when nationalism, xenophobia, and a call to arms were the order of the day. Nor was it surprising when some thirty years later in *Little Big Man,* the same event was portrayed as a self-destructive imperialist venture of absurd proportions, since it was directed by the iconoclastic Arthur Penn at the height of the American antiwar movement, when antiestablishment sentiments were running rampant among the "youth culture" for which the film was targeted.

All three types—the historical reconstruction, the historical romance, and the formulary western—have been prevalent throughout the genre's development, and in fact all three are at work in any one western film. The conventions of feature filmmaking, and especially the demand that conflict be resolved by an individual, goal-oriented protagonist, require that even the most accurate depiction of historical events be romanticized to some degree. And at the same time, even the most banal and predictable formulation requires a minimum of historical authenticity simply to be recognized as a western.

Given the quest for standardization of both the filmmaking process and the film product in the commercial cinema, formulary westerns have dominated Hollywood's output from the very earliest years. In fact, André Bazin's assertion about the cinema and the western sharing certain origins applies to economic and institutional as well as formal-aesthetic qualities. The prototype for studio-based feature film production was refined by Thomas Ince between 1912 and 1915, and most of the products that he rolled off the studio assembly line were mass-produced formula westerns featuring the likes of William S. Hart. And in the late 1920s and early 1930s, when the logistical problems of sound production severely limited location shooting and complex camera work, thus curtailing the production of A-class feature westerns, still formulary B-westerns remained a cinematic staple. In fact, a number of outfits like Republic Pictures were created in the 1930s primarily to crank out B-grade westerns for a seemingly insatiable market.

Basic to the western story in whatever formulation is an elemental conflict between civilization and savagery. This is the thematic nucleus and the defining characteristic of the genre, and it informs virtually every aspect of its narrative composition, from character and setting to plot structure and thematics. This basic conflict is expressed in a variety of oppositions: East versus West, America versus Europe, garden versus desert, social order versus anarchy, individual versus community, town versus wilderness, cowboy versus Indian, schoolmarm versus dancehall girl, and on and on. The narrative trajectory of any western animates the governing civilization-savagery opposition, generating a conflict—or more likely a whole series of conflicts—that are steadily intensified until a consummate, climactic confrontation becomes inevitable.

The opening to virtually any western immediately cues us to just how the basic oppositions will be animated in this particular "telling" of the generic tale. Consider the opening of John Ford's classic, *Stagecoach* (1939). The film opens with a shot of Monument Valley, an arid landscape that provides—quite frequently, for Ford—a powerful evocation of the West's "natural" hostility toward progress and civilization. As the credits wind down we notice two riders approaching, and as they near the camera Ford dissolves from this vast panorama to the exterior of a cavalry camp. The horizon is suddenly cluttered with tents, flagstaffs, and soldiers. The two riders gallop into camp and dismount, and another dissolve takes us into the telegraph office where a group of uniformed men are huddled around a telegraph. Just before the lines go dead, the machine emits a single coded word: "Geronimo."

This is a striking example of both narrative and generic economy: it establishes the setting and the general historical context of the story, and at the same time it fleshes out the classical conventions of the genre at large. Hollywood's depiction of the American West presents a vast wilderness dotted with occasional oases—frontier towns, cavalry outposts, isolated campsites—which are linked with one another and with the civilized East by the railroad, the stagecoach, the telegraph, and other "tentacles" of social progress reaching westward. Each oasis is a veritable society in microcosm, plagued by conflicts both internal and external. In *Stagecoach,* for instance, which depicts the journey of eight people via stage through hostile Indian country from one frontier community (Tonto) to another (Lordsburg), we are always aware of an array of conflicts. The internal stability of one community is threatened most dramatically by the murderous Plummer brothers, who are terrorizing the town of Lordsburg; and there are other less immediate threats to social order as well: an embezzling banker, a timid whiskey salesman, a self-righteous women's group (the Law and Order League) which runs a suspected prostitute and an alcoholic physician out of town. At the same time, Geronimo and his band of renegade "Injuns" provide an external threat, as does the inhospitable landscape itself.

Significantly, all of these issues and conflicts are established before Ford's hero, John Wayne as the Ringo Kid, is even introduced. Typically, the hero embodies these oppositions: he is a naive, moral man of the earth who, just before the story opens, has escaped from prison (where he has been unjustly incarcerated) to kill the Plummers and thus avenge the death of his father and brother. Ringo is a classic westerner, embodying the talents and capabilities of the savage (he is capable of violence, good with a gun), but he feels a necessary allegiance to the force of civilization. His pursuit of the Plummers, in fact, has both a personal and a communal motivation: his obsessive desire for vengeance will also rid Lordsburg of a disruptive antisocial force.

The ambivalence of the western hero is evident in other sympathetic characters as well, particularly Doc Boone (Thomas Mitchell), the philosophical inebriate, and Dallas (Claire Trevor), the whore with the proverbial heart of gold. Both are being run out of Tonto by the Law and Order League as the story opens, and both are befriended by Ringo once he joins the stage en route to Lordsburg. Like Ringo, both are social outcasts who have violated society's precepts in order to survive. And like Ringo, when various crises arise, these two are the most dependable passengers on the stage. Those crises are resolved favorably, but here again is glimpsed a certain fundamental and not altogether obvious sense of ambiguity.

All drama involves conflict, and in Hollywood genre movies—or at least in their classical formulation—conflict is resolved in a way that celebrates both heroic action and the status quo. In *Stagecoach,* the cavalry rescues the stage from the rampaging Indians just in time for Ringo to face down the Plummer brothers in a gunfight on main street. Ringo prevails, predictably enough, but Ford and Screenwriter Dudley Nichols add an interesting and significant twist in the film's epilogue. Ringo and Dallas, who have fallen in love during the journey, are allowed by Doc Boone and the sheriff to flee to Ringo's ranch "just across the border." As the two ride off together, Doc Boone, ever the cultural commentator, muses to the sheriff: "Well they're saved from the blessings of civilization." This presents at once a cynical and an optimistic vision: the repressive and inadequate social system has been salvaged, but only by an agent—the violent hero—who has no place within that society. Yet at the same time, the flight of the uncivilized outlaw-hero and the reformed prostitute to start their own family, itself a society in microcosm, keeps the promise of some utopia in the wilderness open as at least a viable possibility.

Although the image of the western hero as an ambivalent figure who embodies the savage and civilized was always essential to the genre, many (perhaps most) classical westerns did not play out this ambivalence in terms of plot resolution. Narrative conflict often was resolved with the suggestion that the westerner might repress his violent, antisocial tendencies and settle down within the community. The promise of marriage and family for Ringo and Dallas at the end of *Stagecoach* is indicative of this tendency, although their shared status as social outcasts and their final flight to Mexico qualify any one-dimensional reading of the film's outcome. A more simplistic and perhaps more typical example of the genre's penchant for prosocial resolution appears in *The Westerner,* a 1940 film starring Gary Cooper as Cole Hardin, who mediates a violent confrontation between anarchic cattlemen and defenseless, idealized homesteaders.

Hardin strikes up a close friendship with representatives of both groups. On one side is Judge Roy Bean (Walter Brennan), the self-appointed "law west of the Pecos" who nearly lynches Hardin early on when he mistakes him for a horse-thief, but then the two bond together in their mutual regard for rugged individualism and a pragmatic survival-of-the-fittest mentality. On the other is Jane Ellen (Doris Davenport), the daughter of a homesteader who emerges as their spokesperson and brings out the more civilized impulses in Cole Hardin. The woman-domesticator eventually wins over the hero, who turns against Roy Bean and kills him in a climactic gunfight. And in a brief epilogue, the two are pictured gazing out of the window of their own homestead at the "promised land," with the westerner apparently content to hang up his saddle and guns and to take up farming and child-rearing.

This closing image runs counter to the contradictory makeup of the western hero, of course, and thus strains both narrative logic and the hero's distinctive status. Here Cole Hardin has acquiesced to society's emasculating and depersonalizing demands and severely compromised the very nature of his appeal. Much more satisfying are those westerns which have the hero ride off into the sunset at film's end after the requisite showdown, thereby reinforcing the genre's prosocial stance without compromising the hero's essential individuality and antisocial tendencies. This allows the western in its classical formulation to "play it both ways," to celebrate a certain idealized sense of the community and of social order while also emphasizing the self-reliant, rugged figure whose capacity for violence and obstinate individualism put him at odds not only with the forces that threaten the community but with the very same community that he feels compelled to protect since it is incapable of protecting itself.

The hero's ambivalent status was foregrounded through a distinctive narrative device that appeared in many westerns, especially during the late 1940s and afterward, while the genre was outgrowing its more simplistic classical formulation. This device was the incorporation into the familiar constellation of characters of another mediating figure: the initiate hero. In a whole series of successful westerns—notably *Red River* (1948), *Shane* (1952), *The Searchers* (1956), *Rio Bravo* (1958), *The Magnificent Seven* (1960), *Ride the High Country* (1962), *El Dorado* (1967), *Little Big Man* (1970), *The Cowboys* (1972), and *The Shootist* (1976)—the narrative is filtered through the perceptions of a young man, often only a child, who is at first mystified by the heroic westerner but gradually comes to understand the contradictory lifestyles and value systems of those living inside and outside the community. Invariably the initiate opts to remain in the realm of Woman, Hearth, and Home—i.e., in the domain of domestication—while the traditional westerner, having served his heroic function, leaves the community.

Curiously enough, as the western genre evolved and the formula was further refined and embellished through repetition, the western hero maintained his ambivalent status while the frontier community and its denizens were depicted in increasingly negative terms. In fact, one of the most fascinating and complex aspects of the western's steady evolution as a cinematic form is how stable—if not downright static or reactionary—the western hero has been while the community has taken on a more "progressive" and orderly and at the same time a more malevolent status. In the postwar westerns, in fact, the hero takes on guise of a mythic figure caught in real time: the westerner is depicted in ever more heroic and idealized terms, while the community is seen more realistically—assuming that the "reality" of contemporary urban life is alienating, bureaucratic, institutionalized, ruthlessly capitalistic, and ultimately dehumanizing.

If we see the western as a historical narrative which served ideologically to enable the audience (i.e., the public) to negotiate a transition from its rural-agrarian past and into its urban-industrial (and postindustrial) age, then the diverging depictions of the hero and the community seem altogether logical. American audiences after World War II necessarily became more familiar with both the hero and the genre and also grew less optimistic about the utopian promise of urbanization, industrialization, and high technology. Images of the western community changed accordingly, which of course affected the hero's motivation and sense of mission. Hence the "psychological" westerns of the late 1940s and 1950s which displayed the hero's largely ineffectual efforts to handle his growing incompatibility with civilization as well as the cumulative weight of society's unreasonable expectations.

Perhaps the most celebrated example of this generic strain is *High Noon*, whose release in 1950 marked an onslaught of adult westerns with psychologically complex heroes and confounding social issues. The story takes place on the day that the local sheriff (Gary Cooper) is due to retire and wed his Quaker fiancée (Grace Kelly). All this is disrupted when he learns that an outlaw gang is headed for town to kill him. The tension mounts as the sheriff waits, since his fiancée urges him not to face the outlaws and the townspeople either evade or ignore his pleas for assistance. The sheriff and his fiancée face the outlaws, despite her religious convictions against violence, and after disposing of the outlaws in a climactic gunfight Cooper throws his badge into the dirt and leaves the community to fend for itself.

Several years later another successful "adult western," *Rio Bravo* (1959), provided a belated response to what director Howard Hawks considered the knee-jerk liberalism of Fred Zinneman's *High Noon*. This film presents an even more helpless and claustrophobic community, but this time the local lawman (John Wayne) and his deputies (Walter Brennan, Dean Martin, and Ricky Nelson) refuse any offers of assistance from the obviously inept townspeople. Wayne repeatedly insists that "this is no job for amateurs," and he and the others take on a veritable army of gunfighters hired by a local rancher to break his brother out of jail. The lawmen prevail and thus both the heroes and the community emerge with their integrity intact. But still the hero's incompatibility with the community is altogether obvious; he is motivated more by his professional pride and personal code than by any genuine commitment to the quality of life in the community.

In this sense the "professional western" was something of an answer to the psychological westerns of a few years earlier. The psychological western posed an implicit question: how could the morally upright, self-reliant western hero continue to defend a repressive, cowardly, and thankless community without breaking down? The professional western offered one of two responses, both of which were informed with the values of entrepreneurial capitalism as well as rugged individualism: either the westerner becomes a paid lawman and develops an antagonistic rapport with the bureaucrats who hire him, or else he becomes an outlaw. And as the community's collective notion of law and order progressively squeezes out those rugged individualists who made that order possible, the latter course becomes increasingly attractive to the classical westerner. At some point, the "honor among thieves" and self-styled autonomy of the outlaw is preferable to the emasculating demands of social institutions and the domesticating impulse of Woman.

Thus many westerns from the late 1950s onward involve a collective led by an aging but still charismatic hero whose demand for material or monetary compensation for their violent activities, whether those activities be prosocial or antisocial, undercuts the classical hero's unspoken moral code. The more significant professional westerns of the 1960s and 1970s—*The Magnificent Seven* (1960), *The Professionals* (1966), *El Dorado* (1967), *The Wild Bunch* (1969), *Butch Cassidy and the Sundance Kid* (1969), *The Cowboys* (1972), *The Great Northfield Minnesota Raid* (1972), *The Missouri Breaks* (1976), and *The Long Riders* (1980)—center on characters who, by traditional generic standards and values, are both heroic and villainous, both civilized and savage, both good and evil. And society itself in these films, which invariably overwhelms and either displaces or destroys the collective, is seen not as a community of helpless citizens and homesteaders but as a vast, insensitive bureaucratic machine.

Gone, then, is the utopian vision of the classical western. The heroic loner whose moral vision and sense of justice set him apart from—and ultimately above—the community he defended, gradually has evolved into a cynical, self-serving, and self-conscious Everyman. There have been occasional films in which the westerner goes out with something more than a whimper, however. In *The Wild Bunch,* directed by Sam Peckinpah in 1969, for example, the outlaw collective reestablishes its heroic credentials even in the face of extinction. Like the professional groups in *The Magnificent Seven, Butch Cassidy and the Sundance Kid,* and other professional westerns, the Bunch has been forced by legal and military forces to flee into Mexico. There they take up with a corrupt bandit army which, just before the outbreak of World War I, is collaborating with the Germans. In a climactic bloodbath that is both suicidal and redemptive, the Bunch decides to confront the entire bandit army. Peckinpah transforms the apocalyptic finale into a superrealist dream, a ballet of blood and death that is shot and cut with multiple cameras running at different speeds.

The result is one of the most powerful and disconcerting sequences in any western—clearly Peckinpah's effort to choreograph the genre's dance of death. But while *The Wild Bunch* may have signaled the genre's death throes, it scarcely marked its termination. In fact, in the late 1960s and the 1970s there was something of an upsurge in western production which seems to have been brought on by a number of forces. One was the convergence of the antiwar movement and the film industry's pursuit of America's youth as a "target market." Vietnam itself proved to be too sensitive a setting for films that examined the United States' militaristic and colonialist/imperialist impulses, while the western genre provided an apt metaphor for what was happening in Southeast Asia, particularly the cavalry-versus-Injun variation that dealt with Manifest Destiny and the calculated destruction of the Native American race. Hence a spate of "Vietnam westerns" like *Little Big Man* (1970) and *Ulzana's Raid* (1972), which were overtly critical of the jingoism and the racial-cultural chauvinism that seemed to inform both the "taming of the West" and the U.S. involvement in Vietnam.

Another aspect of this upsurge in western production was the influx of foreign films during the 1960s after the Hollywood studio system collapsed and exhibitors who were in need of product began relying more on foreign distributors. By this time filmmakers from other countries—Akira Kurosawa from Japan, for example, or Sergio Leone from Italy—had appropriated the western and revitalized it for artistic or ideological reasons quite their own. Japanese samurai films like Kurosawa's *The Seven Samurai* and Leone's "spaghetti westerns" like *A Fistful of Dollars* and *The Good, the Bad and the Ugly* did excellent business internationally and breathed new life into the genre. The Leone films also revitalized the career of Clint Eastwood, who has succeeded John Wayne as the quintessential western hero.

After establishing his screen persona in a TV western, *Rawhide,* in the early 1960s, Eastwood left the country to do features in Europe where his westerns with Leone reestablished his market value in the States. Significantly, Eastwood has become the top box-office attraction worldwide alternating between western characters (in *Hang 'Em High, High Plains Drifter, The Outlaw Josey Wales,* et al.) and urban crime-fighters (in *Dirty Harry, Magnum Force, The Enforcer,* et al.). Eastwood has almost single-handedly kept the western genre alive in the 1980s, and he seems to be a key transitional figure—as a producer and director as well as a star persona—from the western genre to its logical generic successor, the urban crime film. The fact that Eastwood can move so effectively between the two narrative formulas says less about his flexibility as a performer than the essential similarities between the narrative and thematic qualities of each form. Both feature ascetic, self-reliant loners who have the skills and capabilities (and perhaps even the inclinations) of the threatening forces, but whose sense of absolute social justice allies them with the social system.

While the urban crime genre seems to be the narrative successor to the western, other films were taking a more self-conscious or "modernist" tack, working to subvert and expose the genre's conventions. Two 1970s filmmakers were especially effective in demystifying the western: Robert Altman with *McCabe and Mrs. Miller* (1971) and *Buffalo Bill and the Indians* (1976), and Arthur Penn with *Little Big Man* and *The Missouri Breaks.* The opening sequence of *Little Big Man,* in which an anthropologist prepares to tape-record the meandering recollections of Jack Crabbe, effectively "frames" the story and establishes a basic opposition between history and popular mythology. The use of flashback structure throughout the rest of the narrative, the establishment of Crabbe as an unreliable narrator, the anthropologist's insistence that he uncover "history" rather than simply relate "tall tales"—all of these render the reconstruction of the past a necessarily subjective process, particularly as done by Crabbe (and Penn).

Penn knows what he is about, of course. His first feature film was *The Left-Handed Gun* (1958), an altogether unsympathetic portrayal of Billy the Kid (Paul Newman) as not only psychologically complex but genuinely psychotic and painfully antiheroic. After making *Little Big Man,* Penn gave an interview in which he acknowledged the inherent ideological power of the western form but shied away from seeing the genre as a full-blown myth. "I think our myths started way back," said Penn, but qualified the western's status as myth: "I don't even know that you could call it mythology. I think it's just tales, yarns. . . . I think the yarns are coming down to us and, of course, they're full, loaded material."[6] Penn suggested that one way to "unload" the genre of its ideological baggage is "to go by a more opaque way than saying this is a direct representation of what went on."[7] This clearly is what he did with *Little Big Man* through the various framing and distancing devices, and consequently the film is "about" not only the story of Custer and the Little Big Horn but the very process whereby history is transformed into myth.

What is so fascinating about Robert Altman's *McCabe and Mrs. Miller* is that it achieves the same kind of opacity and generic self-consciousness without resorting to any kind of framing or distancing devices. In fact, McCabe manages somehow both to honor and to subvert the western genre's conventions, accommodating the structural demands of the form while repeatedly calling into question its implicit values and worldview. The film stars Warren Beatty as McCabe, a legendary figure in the Pacific Northwest who transforms the small mining community of Presbyterian Church into a thriving economic community and eventually is killed in a gunfight while protecting the town from three hired killers. This sounds conventional enough, but consider the details. McCabe rides into the dismal community during an evening rainstorm and within weeks, as the weather deteriorates, he has established a modest brothel, thus bringing women to the virtually all-male mining community.

But McCabe is only a small-time entrepreneur. Not until the arrival of Mrs. Miller (Julie Christie), a professional madame with her own stable of whores, do McCabe's business and the town's economic climate really begin to flourish. Local mining interests covet McCabe's enterprise, however, and decide to buy him out, but McCabe bungles the transaction and becomes the target of the corporation's hit men. In a remarkable showdown conducted during a snowstorm while the townspeople battle a fire in a half-built and never-attended church, McCabe manages to kill the three hit men but is himself mortally wounded. As he is slowly covered by drifting snow, Mrs. Miller finds solace in a pipeful of opium.

In the end, McCabe joins those countless other western heroes who demonstrate time and again what "a man's gotta do." Whether or not his efforts are interpreted as being futile depends on the disposition, the generic literacy, and the sense of irony in the interpreter, though, which underscores not only the subtlety of Altman's direction but the inherent ambivalence of the genre itself. Even a self-conscious and "subversive" rendition of the western genre like *McCabe and Mrs. Miller* still bears traces of the classical paradigm and might indeed be read as a straight retelling of the western tale. But that is not to say that the genre was still fueled by the same ideological imperatives in the 1970s that it was during its classical stage. Altman, like Penn and perhaps even Kurosawa and Leone, might well have been motivated more by the formal-aesthetic traditions which any telling of the western invokes than by the social and political implications of the western tale. In other words, the western genre—like the code of the western hero himself in the latter stages of the genre's development—had become something of an end in itself, disconnected from its social and historical moorings. The genre's style, in effect, had outlived its substance: it had in fact become its substance.

How else can we explain the death of the genre as a staple in mainstream entertainment forms? The western lives on in other media, of course. Pulp fiction still exploits the form, reprinting Zane Grey and translating Louis L'Amour so long as a subculture of aficionados keeps that market alive and the paperback sales hold up. And advertising will recirculate western images (the Marlboro

Man, the Ford Mustang) so long as the "residue" of the genre lingers in the cultural ether and still carries meaning for the general public. But the story itself has run its course, and only the leverage of a Clint Eastwood or some other producer-director whose career is on the upswing—Michael Cimino with *Heaven's Gate* (1980), for instance, or Lawrence Kasdan with *Silverado* (1986)—will get yet another western movie made. But these exercises in nostalgia can do little to revitalize the genre. The general public, and especially the American youth whose disposable income determines the general ebb and flow of media trends in the 1980s, no longer seems to need the western story to negotiate its rural agrarian traditions and come to terms with its historical roots. The culture has moved on: the western was vital to that transition, but now it is only baggage that we carry with us via film retrospectives and late-night television.

## BIBLIOGRAPHICAL OVERVIEW

At the outset I cited André Bazin's observation that the origins of the western are closely akin to those of the cinema itself. That notion has a curious parallel in cinema studies—namely, that the origins of western genre study are directly related (and in some ways even "identical," to use Bazin's term) to the birth and development of cinema studies. In fact, whether film scholars directly invoke the issue of genre or it simply remains a "structuring absence" in their work, the genre issue has been a dominant concern in cinema studies over the past two decades.

This is scarcely surprising, given the prevalence of genres and story formulas in commercial filmmaking. Because of the cost and complexity of feature filmmaking—which of course involves distribution and exhibition as well as the production of movies—the film industry has always sought to standardize and thus to economize the filmmaking process. Hence there has been a heavy reliance on convention, particularly via genre production, since any genre represents a whole system of narrative conventions whose currency already has been established in the marketplace.

Genre study itself has a tradition dating back centuries, at least as far back as Aristotle's *Poetics,* but curiously enough the earliest scholarly work in film acknowledged those traditions only by indirection. The birth of "serious" film criticism and university film studies coincided with the rise of "auteurism" during the 1960s.[8] At first glance, auteur criticism might be seen as an opposition to genre study—an effort, in effect, to develop a critical theory based more on a Romantic conception of the individual artist (director-as-author/auteur) and the creative process rather than the convention-bound nature of the products themselves. But there was a strong antielitist and popular-cultural bias in auteurism, since critics argued not only that commercially successful directors like Howard Hawks and Alfred Hitchcock were worthy of note, but also that they should not be dismissed simply because they worked in such seemingly low-brow forms as the western and the thriller. What's more, auteurists argued that someone like John Ford was a more significant film artist for his westerns than for those films that were more esteemed in the bastions of high culture, particularly his literary adaptations (*The Grapes of Wrath, How Green Was My Valley*, et al.) or his documentaries (*The Battle of Midway, December 7th*).

By the late 1960s, theories of authorship and genre reached a kind of symbiosis. The more work that was done with auteur directors, especially those who worked in Hollywood, the more evident it became that virtually all of the American cinema's auteur directors were in fact "genre auteurs."[9] That is, they refined their technical skills and distinctive styles working with only one or two familiar narrative-cinematic formulas. This brings us back to the western genre specifically, since so many of the early auteur studies focused on directors who had worked with the western genre. The two most important studies of this type were Peter Wollen's "The Auteur Theory," which appeared in his book *Signs and Meaning in the Cinema*,[10] and Jim Kitses's "Authorship and Genre," which was the introduction to *Horizons West*, an analysis of the work of three western directors.[11] Both of these were published in 1969, and both really did more to advance genre study than they did to promote auteurism.

Wollen's piece provided an elaborate comparison of the films of John Ford and Howard Hawks, paying special attention to their westerns. Wollen argued most persuasively that the two directors animated the western genre in quite different ways, and that to apprehend this difference one might apply a "structural approach" which has "evident affinities with methods which have been developed for the study of folklore and mythology."[12] Wollen was struck by the ways that both Ford and Hawks repeatedly fleshed out certain oppositions or "antinomies" in their films, particularly in the depiction of their heroes. He went on to note that "the protagonists of fairy-tales and myths, as Lévi-Strauss has pointed out, can be dissolved into bundles of differential elements, pairs of opposites," and that "we can proceed with the same kind of operation in the study of films."[13]

Jim Kitses followed much the same line of reasoning in *Horizons West*, arguing that "central to the [western] form we have a philosophical dialectic, an ambiguous cluster of meanings and attitudes that provide the traditional thematic structure of the genre." The structure itself was based on a "series of antinomies," with two fundamental oppositions governing all the others: wilderness versus civilization and individual versus community."[14] Kitses refers to Henry Nash Smith's seminal study of the myth of the American West, *The Virgin Land*, and like Peter Wollen he is intrigued by the notion of western filmmaking as a form of contemporary mythmaking. But Wollen's conception of mythology came from anthropology via Claude Lévi-Strauss, whose *Structural Anthropology* and other subsequent works were transforming that field and a number of others as well—Lévi-Strauss, of course, being the founding father of contemporary structuralism. Kitses relied instead on Northrop Frye, the literary critic and historian whose *Anatomy of Criticism* was equally influential in his own field but which developed a considerably different—and more "literary," as one might guess—conception of myth.

Following Frye, Kitses considered myth a formal vehicle for sacred or pantheistic narrative content. "In strict classical terms of definition," wrote Kitses, "myth has to do with the activity of the gods and as such the western has no myth."[15] It is interesting that Kitses's analysis of the structure of the western brought him close to what might be termed a "structuralist" interpretation of the genre, but his allegiance to Frye prevented him from making that final—and vital—connection. Kitses was not alone in his debt to Northrop Frye nor in his tendency to define myth in terms of narrative content rather than structure or function. John Cawelti in his provocative treatise on the western, *The Six-Gun Mystique* (published in 1970), opted for the term "formula" rather than "genre" specifically to avoid the issue of myth. "For Frye myths are universal patterns of action," stated Cawelti, and he argued that as such they cannot exist within a formula whose imagery and ideology are specific to a given historical context.[16]

Cawelti took a different tack, though, when discussing the western as a form of "social and cultural ritual,"[17] and he later defined ritual as "a means of affirming certain basic cultural values, resolving tensions and establishing a sense of continuity between present and past."[18] This definition brought Cawelti much closer to the structuralist conception of myth (and of genre) which was just emerging in American film studies, engendered more than anything else by the belated arrival of semiotics and structuralism from France. By 1970, Lévi-Strauss's work in structural anthropology had spread to other fields, with Roland Barthes applying structuralist concepts to an array of popular culture forms, and Christian Metz developing a theory and methodology of "cine-structuralism." Like Lévi-Strauss, these structuralist critics were heavily influenced by Swiss linguist Ferdinand de Saussure, who a half century earlier had proposed a theory of "semiology" (or "semiotics"), a science which might study "the life of signs within a society."[19] Culture itself was seen from this perspective as a vast array of signifying systems, including not only the movie industry at large but its various genres as well.

Actually, film genres were a special kind of signifying system not only because of their "currency" as conventionalized and value-laden signifying systems but also because of the particular way in which they structured social reality and continually reexamined certain basic cultural conflicts. In this sense genre theory was moving beyond the literary notion of genres as stories with a certain content, seeing them instead as narratives with specific kinds of structuring principles and thus with a certain cultural function. Robin Wood aptly indicated this shift in perspective in an essay entitled "Ideology, Genre, Auteur."[20] Wood suggested that to really understand the western or any other genre, we need to look beyond its distinctive "motifs" and "archetypes" and ask why the genre was created and why it persists. According to Wood, "What we need to ask, if genre theory is ever to be productive, is less What? than Why? We are so used to the genres that the peculiarity of the phenomenon is too little noted.''[21]

Wood answered this "Why genre?" question in ideological terms, concentrating on the formal composition and rhetorical strategy of the genre in question. Wood perceived America, like any active, dynamic cultural system, to be rife with internal conflicts and contradictions: between entrepreneurial capitalism and egalitarianism, for example, or between self-fulfillment and the common good. Wood argued that "the development of genres is rooted in the sort of ideological tensions" that characterize American society at large. "All the genres can be profitably examined in terms of ideological oppositions," with the genres themselves serving as "different strategies for dealing with ideological tensions.''[22] Genre theorist Thomas Sobchack developed a similar line of reasoning, arguing that genre films resolve the "tensions of cultural and social paradoxes.''[23] Popular narrative formulas like the western celebrate both heroic individual action and also the collective ideals and values of the community. Thus he argued that the central conflicts are "between the individual and the group, between self-realization and communal conformity.''[24]

By now theories of film genre and particularly of the western were corresponding quite closely with Lévi-Strauss's conception of myth. In identifying and analyzing any myth, Lévi-Strauss looked not for some "pantheistic" or otherwise metaphysical content but rather certain structural and functional features. He defined myth as "a whole system of references which operates by means of a pair of cultural contrasts: between the general and the particular on the one hand and nature and culture on the other.''[25] And in a seminal essay entitled "The Structural Study of Myth," Lévi-Strauss suggested that in mythology these "bundles of oppositions" are organized in a distinctive fashion. "If there is meaning to be found in mythology," he argued, "this cannot reside in the isolated elements which enter into the composition of a myth, but only in the way the elements are combined.''[26] The nature and function of the combinations themselves become evident through repeated usage—through the varied "tellings" of the mythic tale. In a key passage describing the variations of a myth, Lévi-Strauss might just as easily have been describing the individual films that comprise a genre:

A myth exhibits a "slated" structure which seeps to the surface, if one may say so, through the repetition process. However, the slates are not absolutely identical to each other. And since the purpose of myth is to provide a logical model capable of overcoming a contradiction (an impossible achievement if, as it happens, the contradiction is real), a theoretically infinite number of slates will be generated, each one slightly different from the others.[27]

Thus mythmaking itself emerges as a basic human activity which structures human experience—whether social or personal, whether physical or metaphysical—in a distinctive and consistent fashion. A society's mythology represents its populace speaking to its collective self, cultivating a whole network of stories and images designed to animate and resolve the conflicts of everyday life. Consider the basic similarities between cultural mythmaking and genre filmmaking: how the society at large participates in isolating and refining certain stories, the fact that those stories are essentially problem-solving strategies whose problems cannot be fully resolved (hence the infinite variations), the tendency for heroic redeemer-figures to mediate the opposing values inherent within the problem, and the ongoing effort to resolve the problem in a way that reinforces the existing social and conceptual order. Genre films, much like the folk tales of primitive cultures, serve to defuse the threats to the social order and thereby to provide some logical coherence to that order.

The key figure in extending Lévi-Strauss's work from a primitive to a contemporary cultural context was Roland Barthes, who in *Mythologies* contended that the mythmaking impulse in primitive societies survives in the form of ideology. "The very principle of myth," wrote Barthes, is that "it transforms history into nature."[28] Today this process serves to naturalize those familiar belief systems like Christianity, democracy, capitalism, monogamy, heterosexual romantic love, and so on. The power of myth and ideology is evidenced by the fact that these belief systems do indeed seem natural, they seem to be common-sensical or self-explanatory, even though they are in no way biologically motivated and may be peculiar only to certain nation-tribes.

As might be expected, these ideas have been applied most frequently and most effectively to the western genre, although one of the most important contributions of a structuralist approach is that it enabled film theorists and critics to address the fundamental notion of "genre-ness"—that is, the structural and functional qualities that virtually all cinematic formulas have in common. There is a danger here of being too reductive, of perceiving all film genres in terms that are so simplistic that we lose sight of the distinctive qualities and appeal of the individual genres. But Barthes argued that even this penchant for reductivism is a form of narrative condensation and is basic to mythmaking. In an essay entitled "Myth Today," which concludes *Mythologies,* Barthes wrote: "In passing from history to nature, myth acts economically: it abolishes the complexity of human acts, it gives them the simplicity of essences, it does away with all dialectics, with any going back beyond what is immediately visible, it organizes a world which is without contradiction because it is without depth."[29]

This seems to be an apt description of any genre in its least sophisticated and most conventional formulation. As Robin Wood suggested, "It is probable that a genre is ideologically 'pure' . . . only in its simplest, most archetypal, most aesthetically deprived form," which he equated with Hopalong Cassidy westerns.[30] Only in such simplified versions did the genre's "logical model" overcome the cultural contradictions—the thematic "antinomies"—that the western repeatedly addresses but clearly cannot ever really resolve. In more ambitious and sophisticated westerns, however, particularly those later in the genre's development, we find narratives that do in fact acknowledge the complexity of human acts, that grapple directly with contradictory values, that display formal and thematic depth. By the 1960s and 1970s, in fact, the genre began to exhibit—and on a fairly consistent basis—qualities often associated with high narrative artistry, qualities like irony, ambiguity, formal self-consciousness, and so on.

Recourse to auteurism begins to explain this. Many commercial filmmakers, producers and screenwriters as well as directors, certainly were savvy enough to recognize and exploit the inherent complexities of the genres in which they so often worked. But it is also significant that these complexities surface more frequently later in the genre's development. What this suggests is that as both artists and audience became more familiar with the genre's system of conventions, the more they wanted to see those conventions being embellished, reworked, manipulated, and perhaps even subverted or openly questioned. Leo Braudy suggested that "change in genre occurs when the audience says, 'That's too infantile a form of what we believe. Show us something more complicated.' "[31]

This raises the related issues of viewer "literacy" and generic "evolution." One of the more provocative and influential analyses of the western's evolution was developed by Christian Metz in *Language and Cinema* in his chapter "Textuality and Generality." Metz argued that as early as 1946, with John Ford's *My Darling Clementine,* the "classic" western had assumed "an accent of parody which was an integral part of the genre, and yet it remained a Western." He stated that the "superwesterns" of the 1950s (what we referred to above as the psychological and adult westerns) actually "passed from parody to contestation," openly challenging the traditional values associated with the hero and the form itself: still these films "remained fully westerns." Then in many recent westerns, suggested Metz, "contestation gives way to 'deconstruction': the entire film is an explication of the [generic] code and its relation to history. One has passed from parody to critique, but the work is still a Western." Metz's contention was that with every stage of its evolutionary process, the western sustained its essence, its generic identity—which, like Kitses, Wollen, et al., Metz defined in terms of the basic oppositions and cultural conflicts that it repeatedly addresses. He concluded his discussion with the observation: "Such is the infinite text one calls a genre."[32]

Significantly, Metz's view of generic evolution focused on "internal" dynamics, that is, on the genre itself as a more or less closed narrative and conceptual system. But the public's desire to see the western form embellished has to do not only with its previous experiences with the genre itself but also with its experience of social reality "outside" the cinema and its genres, and indeed a number of critics developed theories of generic evolution that keyed on cultural, political, or even economic and industrial trends that were external to the genre. Philip French in his study *Westerns,* for example, argued (quite persuasively) that after World War II, when the genre passed out of its classical stage, a productive way to consider its development is in relation to the national political climate, and more specifically to the succession of U.S. presidents. Thus he described the Eisenhower western, the Kennedy western, the Johnson western, and so on.[33] Sociologist Will Wright followed a similar argument in *Sixguns and Society,* contending that "the narrative structure [of the western] varies in accordance with the changing social actions and institutions."[34] For Wright, the economic as well as the political climate was an important factor, although he allowed that the "oppositions" which identify the western are "fundamental in the consciousness of the society" and thus do not change.[35]

The most effective studies of the western's evolution have followed a structuralist approach, analyzing this process in terms of a complex interplay of internal and external forces. Clearly Warshow was correct when he suggested that any genre creates "its own field of reference," but for the form to have any vitality at all it must maintain contact with the world that it represents and with the values and attitudes of the public. As both "post-structuralist" and those in the burgeoning cultural studies camps have argued, the meaning of the western or of any other genre does not reside "in" the films but rather in the consciousness—both individual and collective—of those who consume and interpret them. We may dismiss this or that western as mere "entertainment," but for it to hold the viewer's interest it must somehow appeal to what is meaningful in his or her own lived experience.

Thus the apparent death of the western a decade or so ago marks the culmination of both an internal and an external development. On the one hand, its passing manifests the kind of internal dynamic that Metz talked about whereby the genre seemed quite literally to "deconstruct" itself out of existence once it began to question its own narrative and ideological conventions. But on the other hand, it would seem that the form lost its cultural currency because the issues and conflicts that it repeatedly addressed, at least in the historical and geographical context of the western, no longer carried the same relevance for the moviegoing public. This is not to say that certain of the antinomies which informed the western are no longer "at issue" in our society, but rather that they have been appropriated by other narrative forms—the space epic, for example, or the urban crime film.

Since the western has lost its favor with the general public, it seems to have lost much of its appeal for critics and scholars as well. But just as western films served a purpose for the public, providing a context for working through certain basic cultural contradictions, so too has the genre served its purpose for film scholars. Studies of the western brought a new sophistication to auteur analysis and, even more importantly, they motivated an important shift into structuralism and anthropology that marked a vital advance in cinema studies. There have in more recent years been a few interesting books on the western— William T. Pilkington and Don Graham's anthology *Western Movies,* for example, and Jon Tuska's *The American West in Film: Critical Approaches to the Western*.[36] But like *Heaven's Gate, Silverado,* and the other occasional western movies of recent years, these studies have been exercises in nostalgia, more retrospective than forward-looking. Perhaps the genre still has some life in it, both as a popular formula and as the object of productive film scholarship. Chances are it has run its course as a mainstream media form, but that it will continue to motivate productive criticism and scholarship. We are only beginning to really understand how genres work in and on our society, and as long as we seek that understanding we will study the western, which worked harder and longer than any other genre in media history.

## NOTES

1. André Bazin, "The Western: or the American Film Par Excellence," *What Is Cinema,* vol. 2 (Berkeley: University of California Press, 1971), p. 140.

2. Robert Warshow, "The Gangster as Tragic Hero," in *The Immediate Experience* (Garden City, N. Y.: Doubleday, 1962), p. 147.

3. Jon Tuska, *The American West in Film* (Westport, Conn.: Greenwood Press, 1985), pp. 3–39.

4. Ibid., p. 18.

5. Ibid., p. 19.

6. From an interview with Arthur Penn, reprinted in George H. Lewis, ed., *Side-Saddle on the Golden Calf* (Pacific Palisades, Calif.: Goodyear Publishing, 1972), p. 123.

7. Ibid.

8. What has come to be known as the "auteur theory" began in France as "la politique des auteurs" and was developed by a group of critics writing for the Parisian film journal *Cahiers du Cinéma.* For a fairly comprehensive survey of its development in America, see the sections devoted to film authorship in Gerald Mast and Marshall Cohen, eds., *Film Theory and Criticism* (New York: Oxford University Press, 1974), and in Bill Nichols, ed., *Movies and Methods* (Berkeley: University of California Press, 1976). See also Andrew Sarris, *The American Cinema* (New York: E. P. Dutton, 1968).

9. For a more detailed treatment of this notion, see Thomas Schatz, "The Genre Film and the Genre Director," in *Hollywood Genres* (New York: Random House, 1981), pp. 6–13.

10. Peter Wollen, *Signs and Meaning in the Cinema* (Bloomington: University of Indiana Press, 1969), pp. 74–115.

11. Jim Kitses, *Horizons West* (Bloomington: Indiana University Press, 1969), pp. 7–28.

12. Wollen, *Signs and Meaning,* p. 93.

13. Ibid., p. 94.

14. Kitses, *Horizons West,* p. 11.

15. Ibid., p. 13.

16. John G. Cawelti, *The Six-Gun Mystique* (Bowling Green, Ohio: Bowling Green State University Press, 1970), p. 30.

17. Ibid., p. 32.

18. Ibid., p. 73.

19. Ferdinand de Saussure, excerpt from *A Course in General Linguistics,* first pub-

lished in Paris in 1916 and reprinted in *The Structuralists: From Marx to Levi-Strauss,* ed. Richard and Fernande DeGeorge (Garden City, N. Y.: Doubleday, 1972), pp. 58–79. The reference in the text appears on page 62 of DeGeorge.

20. Robin Wood, "Ideology, Genre, Auteur," *Film Comment,* January–February 1977, pp. 46–51.

21. Ibid., p. 47.

22. Ibid.

23. Thomas Sobchack, "Genre Film: A Classical Experience," *Literature/Film Quarterly,* Summer 1975, p. 201.

24. Ibid.

25. Claude Lévi-Strauss, *The Savage Mind* (Chicago: University of Chicago Press, 1965), p. 135.

26. Claude Lévi-Strauss, "The Structural Study of Myth," in DeGeorge and DeGeorge, eds., *The Structuralists,* p. 105.

27. Ibid, p. 109.

28. Roland Barthes, *Mythologies* (New York: Hill and Wang, 1957), p. 129.

29. Ibid., p. 143.

30. Wood, "Ideology, Genre, Auteur," p. 47.

31. Leo Braudy, *The World in a Frame* (Garden City, N. Y.: Anchor Press/Doubleday, 1976), p. 179.

32. Christian Metz, *Language and Cinema* (New York: Praeger, 1975), pp. 148–61.

33. Philip French, "Politics, etc., and the Western," *Westerns* (New York: Viking Press, 1973), pp. 12–48.

34. Will Wright, *Sixguns and Society: A Structural Study of the Western* (Berkeley: University of California Press, 1975), p. 27.

35. Ibid.

36. William T. Pilkington and Don Graham, *Western Movies* (Tempe: University of New Mexico Press, 1979), and Jon Tuska, *The American West in Film.*

## BIBLIOGRAPHICAL CHECKLIST

### Books

Barthes, Roland. *Mythologies.* New York: Hill and Wang, 1975.

Bogdanovich, Peter. *John Ford.* Berkeley: University of California Press, 1968.

Braudy, Leo. *The World in a Frame.* Garden City, N.Y.: Anchor/Doubleday, 1977.

Cawelti, John. *Adventure, Mystery, and Romance.* Chicago: University of Chicago Press, 1976.

———. *The Six-Gun Mystique.* Bowling Green, Ohio: Bowling Green State University Press, 1971.

DeGeorge, Richard, and Fernande DeGeorge, eds. *The Structuralists: From Marx to Lévi-Strauss.* Garden City, N.Y.: Doubleday, 1972.

Fenin, George, and William K. Everson. *The Western: From Silents to Cinerama.* New York: Orion Press, 1962.

French, Philip. *Westerns.* New York: Viking Press, 1973.

Frye, Northrop. *Anatomy of Criticism.* Princeton, N.J.: Princeton University Press, 1957.

Kaminsky, Stuart. *American Film Genres.* Chicago: Pflaum, 1974.

Kitses, Jim. *Horizons West: Anthony Mann, Budd Boetticher, Sam Peckinpah: Studies of Authorship within the Western*. Bloomington: Indiana University Press, 1969.

Lévi-Strauss, Claude. *The Raw and the Cooked: Introduction to a Science of Mythology*. Evanston, Ill.: Harper and Row, 1964.

————. *The Savage Mind*. Chicago: Chicago University Press, 1962.

Lewis, George H. *Side-Saddle on the Golden Calf*. Pacific Palisades, Calif.: Goodyear Publishing, 1972.

McBride, Joseph, and Michael Wilmington. *John Ford*. London: Secker and Warburg, 1974.

Mast, Gerald, and Marshall Cohen, eds. *Film Theory and Criticism*. New York: Oxford University Press, 1974.

Metz, Christian. *Language and Cinema*. New York: Praeger, 1975.

Nichols, Bill, ed. *Movies and Methods*. Berkeley: University of California Press, 1976.

Sarris, Andrew. *The American Cinema*. New York: E. P. Dutton, 1968.

Schatz, Thomas. *Hollywood Genres*. New York: Random House, 1981.

Smith, Henry Nash. *The Virgin Land*. Cambridge: Harvard University Press, 1950.

Tuska, Jon. *The Filming of the West*. Garden City, N.Y.: Doubleday, 1976.

————. *The American West in Film: Critical Approaches to the Western*. Westport, Conn.: Greenwood Press, 1985.

Warshow, Robert. *The Immediate Experience*. Garden City, N.Y.: Doubleday, 1962.

Wollen, Peter. *Signs and Meaning in the Cinema*. Bloomington: Indiana University Press, 1969.

Wright, Will. *Sixguns and Society*. Berkeley: University of California Press, 1975.

### Shorter Works

Bazin, André. "The Western, or the American Film Par Excellence," in *What Is Cinema?*, vol. 2. Berkeley: University of California Press, 1971, pp. 140–48.

Browne, Nick. "The Spectator and the Text: The Rhetoric of Stagecoach," *Film Quarterly*, Winter 1975–1976, pp. 26–38.

Engle, Gary. "*McCabe and Mrs. Miller:* Robert Altman's Anti-Western," *Journal of Popular Film*, Fall 1972, pp. 268–87.

Lévi-Strauss, Claude. "The Structural Study of Myth," *Journal of American Folklore*, October–December 1955, pp. 428–44. Citations in this essay from the reprinted version in DeGeorge and DeGeorge, *The Structuralists*, pp. 169–94.

Sobchack, Thomas. "Genre Films: A Classical Experience," *Film/Literature Quarterly*, Summer 1975, pp. 196–204.

Wood, Robin. "Ideology, Genre, Auteur," *Film Comment*, January–February 1977, pp. 46–51.

## SELECTED FILMOGRAPHY

(The following films are those on which Thomas Schatz focused—The editor.)

1939    *Stagecoach* (97 minutes).

Wanger/United Artists. Producer/Director: John Ford. Screenplay: Dudley Nichols, from the story *Stage to Lordsburg* by Ernest Haycox. Cast: John Wayne (The Ringo Kid), Claire Trevor (Dallas), Thomas Mitchell (Dr. Joseph Boone), Andy Devine (Buck), John Carradine (Hatfield), Donald Meek (Samuel Peacock), Louise Platt (Lucy Mallory), George Bancroft (Sheriff Curly Wilcox), Berton Churchill (Banker Henry Gatewood).

1940    *The Westerner* (97 minutes).
United Artists. Samuel Goldwyn production. Director: William Wyler. Screenplay: Jo Swerling and Niven Busch, from the story by Stuart N. Lake. Cast: Gary Cooper (Cole Hardin), Walter Brennan (Judge Roy Bean), Doris Davenport (Jane Ellen Mathews), Fred Stone (Caliphet Mathews).

1952    *High Noon* (84 minutes).
United Artists. Stanley Kramer production. Director: Fred Zinneman. Screenplay: Carl Foreman, from the story "Tin Star" by John W. Cunningham. Cast: Gary Cooper (Will Kane), Thomas Mitchell (Jonas Henderson), Lloyd Bridges (Harvey Pell), Katy Jurado (Helen Ramirez), Grace Kelly (Amy Kane).

1959    *Rio Bravo* (140 minutes).
Warner Brothers/Armada. Producer/Director: Howard Hawks. Screenplay: Jules Furthman, Leigh Brackett, from a short story by B. H. McCampbell. Cast: John Wayne (John T. Chance), Dean Martin (Dude), Walter Brennan (Stumpy), Angie Dickinson (Feathers), Ricky Nelson (Colorado).

1969    *The Wild Bunch* (145 minutes).
Warner Brothers–Seven Arts. Producer: Phil Feldman. Director: Sam Peckinpah. Screenplay: Walon Green and Peckinpah, from a story by Green and Roy N. Sickner. Cast: William Holden (Pike), Ernest Borgnine (Dutch), Robert Ryan (Thornton), Edmond O'Brien (Sykes), Warren Oates (Lyle Gorch), Jaime Sanchez (Angel), Ben Johnson (Tector Gorch).

1970    *Little Big Man* (150 minutes).
National General/Cinema Center. Producer: Stuart Millar. Director: Arthur Penn. Screenplay: Calder Willingham, based on Thomas Berger's novel. Cast: Dustin Hoffman (Jack Crabbe/Little Big Man), Faye Dunaway (Mrs. Pendrake), Martin Balsam (Allardyce T. Merriwhether), Richard Mulligan (Gen. Custer), Chief Dan George (Old Lodge Skins).

1971    *McCabe and Mrs. Miller* (121 minutes).
20th Century-Fox. Producer: David Foster and Mitchell Brower. Director: Robert Altman. Screenplay: Altman and Brian McKay, based on the novel *McCabe* by Edmund Naughton. Cast: Warren Beatty (John Q. McCabe), Julie Christie (Mrs. Miller), René Auberjonois (Patrick Sheehan), Hugh Millais (Dog Butler), Shelley Duvall (Ida Coyl).

# 4

# The Gangster Film

JOHN RAEBURN

Although the gangster movie appeared in embryonic form before World War I (with D. W. Griffith's *Musketeers of Pig Alley* [1912], for example), not until the late 1920s did it become a distinct genre. Prohibition and the notoriety of crime barons like Al Capone were the genre's most obvious precipitants. Prohibition provided a new, lucrative, and well-publicized field of activity for racketeers, one which required a high degree of coordination and organization, transforming the "crook" into the "gangster." The men whose organizations supplied alcohol to otherwise law-abiding citizens, moreover, were regarded by many Americans as suppliers of legitimate needs, even as heroic subverters of state tyranny. Such men were newsworthy, and like other media the film industry moved to capitalize on their activities.

The city's new significance also paved the way for the gangster film, as did a reevaluation of the American success tradition. Cities had grown astonishingly in size and importance during the latter half of the nineteenth century, but not until after the Great War did the nation begin to perceive itself as an urban rather than rural society. The city's preeminence exposed a set of cultural cleavages—between WASPs and ethnics, middle class and working class, rural beliefs and urban practices—that the gangster saga could dramatize with unusual force. Perhaps because the 1920s were a period of unparalleled economic expansion and prosperity (not, however, for farmers or much of the working class), a number of writers explored the implications of the American success ethic and exposed its liabilities for the individual and for the culture itself. Among these writers were Theodore Dreiser, Sinclair Lewis, Van Wyck Brooks, Matthew Josephson, and preeminently F. Scott Fitzgerald, whose 1925 novel, *The Great Gatsby,* featured a gangster as its eponymous hero. As Fitzgerald realized, the gangster hero lent himself admirably to an examination of the American myth of success in the modern city.

By the late 1920s urban criminals were staples of the Broadway stage in melodramas like *The Gang War, The Racket,* and *Four Walls,* and they began to appear in movies as well, most notably in *Underworld* (1927), a silent directed by Josef Von Sternberg. Cultural conditions were ripe for the emergence of the gangster film genre, but it waited upon the development of sound technology to bring it into being. As the western is a genre of silences (the stillness of open spaces, the terseness of cowboy speech), the gangster film is one of sounds, even of cacophony. The city the gangster hero must traverse and dominate is a dense, crowded, noisy place, and the throbbing motor and squealing tires of his automobile and the staccato of his guns confirm his sovereignty in it; moreover, his aggressive use of criminal argot (and often his accented English) as well as his reiteration of his guiding principles (e.g., ''Do it first, do it yourself, and keep on doin' it.'') are essential linguistic indicators establishing his character and social bearing.[1]

The first all-talking film, *Lights of New York* (1928), in fact, did feature tough-talking gangsters, but *Little Caesar* (1930) was the first genuine gangster film in focusing explicitly and unswervingly on the character of the gangster and on his relation to larger cultural values and beliefs. Because by definition the gangster is beyond the boundaries of conventional society, he perforce presents a critique of that society. The movie audience's privileged position, however, allows it to see the gangster as he himself cannot, at once in opposition to normative social order and as a caricature of some of its most cherished beliefs. The social critic Daniel Bell calls (actual) crime a ''Coney Island mirror'' of American culture, illuminating in an exaggerated way its morals and manners; the criminal's duel with the law, he says, is a morality play in which the illicit desires of ordinary citizens are given expression before ''final judgment and the force of law'' are invoked to rebuke those desires.[2] Robert Warshow took a more sophisticated view in a seminal essay written in 1948. He called the movie gangster a tragic hero because he illuminated the terrible dilemma implicit in the American success ethic: failure is a kind of death, but success—establishing one's individual preeminence—leaves one alone, hated, and vulnerable. ''The effect of the gangster film,'' wrote Warshow, ''is to embody this dilemma in the person of the gangster and resolve it by his death. The dilemma is resolved because it is *his* death, not ours.''[3]

*Little Caesar*'s commercial and artistic success spawned a host of gangster films, at least twenty-five in 1931 and forty. in 1932, before the cycle lost momentum. Notable among these were *Public Enemy* (1931) and *Scarface* (1932), which along with *Little Caesar* represent the best of what Thomas Schatz calls the ''classical'' period of the genre, when the films transparently conveyed to their audiences their social messages.[4] Most film historians have considered *Scarface* the finest of these three films, perhaps because it came last and can be fitted into an evolutionary scheme, perhaps because its producer Howard Hughes in later years withdraw it from circulation, thereby giving it the status of a suppressed classic, most likely because its director Howard Hawks was enshrined as a pantheon director in the heyday of auteur criticism in the 1960s.

But whatever the excellences of *Scarface* and *Public Enemy*—and they are many—*Little Caesar* is the most powerful and compelling of these early gangster films, not only establishing the conventions of the genre but doing so within an economical, tightly organized, and consistently sure-handed form.

The film's director, Mervyn LeRoy, had a successful, long, and undistinguished career as a director and producer of mostly mediocre films. But his work in the early 1930s at Warner Brothers was anything but mediocre.[5] The visual style of *Little Caesar* was unadorned, straightforward, perfectly attuned to its subject matter; seen today, the film has an almost primitive quality in the spareness of its mise-en-scène, the filmic equivalent of the stripped language and compressed structure of Hemingway's short stories written in the 1920s. Edward G. Robinson's bravura performance as Rico Bandello, a snarling bantam rooster of a man, endows the character with both pathos and demonic hubris, providing him a stature a less gifted actor would have missed.

Rico is single-minded in his ambition to rise in the city to which he has come from somewhere in the West (thus reversing the direction Americans traditionally took in search of success, the city by the 1920s having replaced the open spaces as the arena in which to achieve). He joins a gang and by dint of his determination, self-discipline (he doesn't drink or trifle with women), and superior business acumen overthrows each of his superiors until only the WASP gangland czar, "The Big Boy," is left above him. Each of Rico's moves up the ladder of success is indicated by an ascending scale of status indicators: grander apartments/offices, flashier clothes, gaudier jewelry, longer cigars. The city in which Rico makes his mark is an abstract place; he calls it only "The Big Town" and the audience sees little of actual city streets. The limited iconographic range of the film no doubt reflected a desire to minimize costs, but it has the effect of allegorizing the story.

Rico's ascent thus parallels those of the ambitious and capable heroes of the American Dream, men of lowly origins who rise to the top of their professions. Two scenes near the middle of the film, however, define the limits and the limitations of Rico's new estate. In one Rico is summoned to a conference with The Big Boy, in whose tastefully furnished apartment Rico is gauche and out of place. He doesn't know how to deal with the butler, he's confused by the offer of "a cocktail or a splash of brandy," he mistakes the value of a painting for the cost of its frame. What is clear to the audience, if not to Rico, is that he can never achieve the genteel, cultured preeminence of The Big Boy. American society is open to new talent up to a point, but the wrong class or ethnic origins, lacking "advantages," condemn one to a supporting role. In another scene, Rico's colleagues honor him with a banquet, an imitation of similar ceremonial occasions sponsored by businessmen or politicians. The testimonials are windy and banal, Rico's response equally bland, the whole affair having a distinct air of cant and hypocrisy. Behind the dais on which Rico is enthroned is a banner inscribed "Friendship Loyalty," a motif symbolized on the evening's program by a pair of turtle doves. Friendship and loyalty, though, are precisely what Rico does not and cannot have; his preeminence at the banquet is based on his abjuration of these values in favor of self-interest and aggression. Individual achievement of the kind Rico aspires to leaves one alone, cut off from genuine friendship and community.

Rico first arrived in The Big Town with a sidekick, Joe Massara, his accomplice in his hinterland petty crimes. For Rico "money isn't everything"; it's power he wants, to tell people what to do and "have your own way or nothing." Joe does not have a similar imagination of personal mastery; he wants to be a dancer and to make a lot of money, and he is willing to sell himself to the highest bidder. When Joe gets his first dancing job, the nightclub manager says "$100 ought to buy you"; in this sense, Rico is incorruptible. Even though Rico coerces Joe's help on a heist at the nightclub at which Joe performs, Joe throughout the film tries to extricate himself from the relationship with Rico, just as Rico tries to maintain it. Rico's affection for Joe makes him human, less a driven monomaniacal monster of ambition and destruction. Even Rico needs intimacy and companionship, and these needs, the film suggests, are antithetical to the will to power. Some film historians have seen this relationship as a covertly homosexual one, which it may well be, but more interesting is the way it exposes a tension in American culture between a belief in individualism and a belief in community. Normative American society lives unreflectively with that contradiction; the gangster film exposes it and assesses its costs.

Rico unregenerately dies on an anonymous city street, the victim of this contradiction. He is unable to kill Joe at point-blank range when he (rightly) suspects Joe is going to betray him. Then, on the lam in a flophouse, his pride in his immaculate individualism provokes him into a final, hopeless confrontation with the police, who have publicly impugned his brains, nerve, and courage. His famous dying words, "Mother of Mercy, is this the end of Rico?" not only ambiguously mingle his acceptance of death and his disbelief that he cannot triumph over it, but also in their use of the third person suggest a stature which transcends the merely personal.

Like *Little Caesar, Scarface* also alluded to Al Capone in its title, but any actual resemblances to the character of the Chicago gang chieftain were merely fortuitous. Hawks and Ben Hecht, who wrote the screenplay, claimed to want to recapitulate the saga of the Borgias in modern terms, although little of this idea remains in the finished film. A more likely inspiration seems to have been *The Great Gatsby*. Fitzgerald's gangster hero is both pathetic and noble, driven by his ambition to acquire a spurious refinement but redeemed by the purity of his vision of transcendence. Hecht's screenplay wittily alludes to Fitzgerald's novel by naming the woman Tony pursues Poppy (Gatsby's beloved was named Daisy) and by having him similarly woo her with a display of his shirts to demonstrate his wealth and power. Like Gatsby with Daisy, Tony sees Poppy as the ultimate monument to his success; he says to her, "I've got everything but what I want." And again like Gatsby, Tony develops cultural pretensions:

he attends a performance of *Rain* and promises himself "to see more shows like this—you know, serious."

*Scarface* derives in part from *The Great Gatsby,* but it is also a critique of it. Gatsby's business dealings are left vague, and while there is a rumor that he once killed a man, it is unsubstantiated. His single-minded pursuit of Daisy has an impersonal purity about it, making it a kind of grail quest. Tony Camonte is a vicious, amoral, violent, and rapacious killer, driven by his lust for power to destroy everyone who stands in his way. "The World is Yours," says the Cook's sign Tony gazes at eagerly several times in the movie, and it is clear he takes it literally. Poppy is for him no equivalent of the grail, either; one of the audience's first views of her is of her derriere as she bends over from the waist. Moreover, he seems to harbor incestuous feelings for his flapper sister. As Thomas Schatz writes, Tony's "primitive brutality, simple-minded naivete, and sexual confusion make him a figure with little charisma and virtually no redeeming qualities."[6] Hawks and Hecht thought of themselves as hard-bitten realists, insiders who knew the real man; their film would be a more accurate rendition of the gangster hero than Fitzgerald's novel and a salutary corrective to the soft romanticism indulged in by the novelist. Even the brooding chiaroscuro of Hawks's visuals contrasted with the omnipresent pastels in Fitzgerald's prose.

But Tony Camonte, like Rico, will have his tragic apotheosis, the consequence of his determined pursuit of success and power being compromised by his feelings of family solidarity. Protecting his sister's virtue, Tony murders his righthand man and the police close in on the hideout where he and his sister have taken refuge. After she is killed he tries to flee, is captured and cravenly begs the police not to shoot, but then thinks better of it and is cut down in a hail of machine-gun fire as he tries to make a break. The film's final scene, a close-up of the Cook's sign filling the screen, reminds the audience of the distance between Tony's ambition and his fate.

In *Scarface* as in *Little Caesar* the forces of social order, as represented by the police, execute but do not determine the gangster hero's downfall; in *Public Enemy,* it is left to a rival gang to destroy Tom Powers, the title figure. The fundamental cause of his death, however, is the same as Rico's and Tony's: his self-reliant individualism is weakened by his attachment to another person—to the idea of community, in other words—impelling him to a suicidal attack on the friend's assassins.

The friend is again male, as in *Little Caesar,* a sidekick whom Tom Powers dotes on more than he does any of the women he attracts. The gangster film has a strong misogynist strain, nowhere more so than in *Public Enemy.* In one of the American cinema's most famous scenes, James Cagney, who played Tom Powers with unforgettable brio, grinds a grapefruit into the face of the woman he is living with when her nagging annoys him. Their relationship had begun on a different plane, however, in a nightclub when Tom whispers something suggestive to her, making her giggle coyly. But eroticism has been leached

out by the domesticity they have established. Male relationships are not subject
to such vicissitudes and seem to be less threatening to the gangster hero's sturdy
independence (but as we have seen, ultimately are not). The gangster film's
misogyny aligned it with similarly formulated cultural documents of the postwar period, such as Hemingway's stories and those of hard-boiled writers like
Dashiell Hammett, all of them expressing a conflicted attitude about the liberated "new women" who were supplanting their Victorian mothers. The gangster film touched a sensitive cultural nerve: *Variety* reported that 75 percent of
the New York audience for *Public Enemy* was male, a significantly higher
proportion than the usual film audience.[7]

*Public Enemy*'s misogyny exposed a constellation of dualisms implicit in all
the classic gangster films, linking fear of women to the theme of individual
achievement. The movie contrasts the jaunty, ebullient Tom Powers with his
drab, conventional older brother, Mike. A streetcar conductor, Mike lives at
home with his immigrant mother and a woman who is either his sister or his
wife (it is impossible to tell which, so insipid is his sexuality). He patriotically
enlists in the AEF in 1917, is wounded, and returns home to the same dreary
job which he hopes to escape by Benjamin Franklin–like study and industry.
Tom thinks the army is for suckers, lives in an apartment, dresses well, drives
a flashy roadster, and has plenty of ill-gotten money to throw around. He is
also attractive to glamorous women like Gwen, played by Jean Harlow, whose
taste runs to men who are "not polite and considerate," although such women
never supplant his male comrades. The brothers thus diagram the cultural tensions between a middle-class ethos of home and family and a vision of individual achievement. One may be an indistinguishable part of the crowd or can be
"somebody"; be a marginal white-collar worker or a plutocrat; privilege duty
or follow one's self-interest; live a life of sexual restraint or express a vital
sexuality; have genteel aspirations or give rein to one's impulses. Too near an
attachment to women and the domesticity they represent threatens the gangster
hero's spontaneous self-fulfillment.

In dramatizing these tensions the gangster film raised subversive questions
about cultural priorities, questions only nominally resolved by the violent deaths
of their heroes in the last reel. Their heterodoxy roused the fears of censors—
although violence, not anarchic individualism, was a more convenient locus for
attack—and after 1933 the fearful Hollywood studios responded to pressure
from cultural guardians by transforming the gangster hero into the crusading
G-man or district attorney, putting all the gangster's energy and drive on the
side of the law, or by making him a penitent misfit doomed by his irrelevance
in a society remaking itself under the New Deal.[8] None of the films employing
these formulas had the energy, cultural interest, or aesthetic distinction of the
classic films.

The genre's first renaissance began with *The Roaring Twenties* (1939), the
first of three remarkable gangster films directed by Raoul Walsh which together
constitute a kind of trilogy; it was followed by *High Sierra* (1941) and *White*

*Heat* (1949). They are linked by an elegiac tone, the gangster hero becoming a poignant reminder of a morally ambiguous but ultimately heroic past, and by a correlative historical perspective in which the meaning of the American experience is reassessed. This self-conscious historicism brought something new to the gangster film, further enriching its cultural significance and establishing a new convention for the genre.

*The Roaring Twenties,* as its title suggests, is the most overtly historical. Resembling Dos Passos's *U.S.A.* trilogy in its blending of documentary and fiction, it neatly condenses the interbellum period into a 1920s of frenzied economic irresponsibility followed by a 1930s in which the economic debacle wrought by the 1920s is cathartic, leading to a more mature, responsible society. That, at least, is the film's overt theme. But Eddie Bartlett, the exemplar of the 1920s played with his usual energy by James Cagney, is a far more charismatic figure than Lloyd Hart, an erstwhile corporation lawyer become crime-busting district attorney who represents the 1930s. Near the end of the movie, Eddie says in the 1930s people are trying to build things up, not "tear things apart like we used to." Perhaps so, but the film has in fact celebrated Eddie's heroic efforts in the 1920s to create a business empire and to acquire a genteel woman who will top off his business success, à la Gatsby. That the empire crumbles in the 1929 crash and the woman marries the dull district attorney only increase Eddie's poignance. His dreams of success were exactly those of generations of American achievers, and if bootlegging is the only avenue for achievement open to him and the woman is bound by her class prejudice to choose the insipid Lloyd over him, then the fault lies not so much in Eddie as in the meretriciousness of a culture which could only provide such impoverished materials to a man of Eddie's extraordinary abilities.

Implicit in the classic gangster films was an indictment of American culture for providing no more appropriate arena than crime in which the gangster hero could work his indomitable will, but it was a recessive theme in those movies, which instead emphasized the drivenness and loneliness of their heroes. *The Roaring Twenties* provided a richer cultural and historical context than the classic films, but it, too, concluded with the hero dying alone on an anonymous street in the city he once had dominated. Mortally wounded by his onetime confederates, he staggers up and dies on the steps of a church, a resonant symbol of the social institutions which have been unable to provide him with opportunities commensurate with his abilities. His epitaph—it could be that of every film gangster—is pronounced by a woman of his own class, a flapper who has unrequitedly loved him. When a cop asks her who he is and what his business was, she says, "He was once a big shot."

If *The Roaring Twenties* saw the 1930s as a time of social regeneration, at least nominally, *High Sierra* made them the last gasp of an era in which personal authenticity was still a possibility for Americans. Roy Earle, the film's Dillinger-like hero just out of prison, is identified with the victims of the Depression when on a nostalgic visit to his Indiana boyhood home he is nervously asked by the farmer presently occupying it if he is from the bank, and again when he establishes a friendship with the utterly decent patriarch of a family of dispossessed Ohio farmers migrating to California in their jalopy. These representatives of a passing rural way of life are contrasted with those of the new urban order, the smug, supercilious rich idling in the resort Tropico Springs and the vapid, frivolous lower–middle class living in Los Angeles bungalows. Although the film never says why Roy left the farm, it was clearly for the same reason so many farm boys did: only the cities provided opportunities in modern America for a man of his energy, ambition, and competence. But with his code of honor (even among thieves), his basic chivalry, and his invincible independence, Roy is an anachronism in this new world.

Like a pastoral hero, he finds himself between two worlds, here defined chronologically as well as spatially. The old America is passing almost unmourned; the new one is repellent to him. A man of the past, Roy values above all else independence and freedom, but the only real possibility for freedom in modern America left to him is in death. He is shot down alone in a mountain fastness, the emblem of that lost America, high above a rabble of gawking spectators and a modern media circus reporting his death throes to a credulous audience in the nation's cities. The classic gangster films undertook an exploration of the paradoxes of American individualism; *High Sierra* was a dirge for its demise.

But it was not dead yet. Cody Jarrett in *White Heat,* the most extraordinary of Walsh's fine trilogy, is yet another American individualist, as his first name's allusion to nineteenth-century western heroics suggests. The movie begins like a western: Cody daringly holds up a mail train at California's eastern boundary by leaping off an overpass onto the train's tender and commandeering the engine. Its finale is as modern as its opening is antique. Cody dies atop an enormous refinery tank in Long Beach, the last bit of land before the Pacific, after a payroll robbery goes awry, destroyed in a mushroom cloud that can only remind viewers of a nuclear explosion. Thus the movie evokes a century of American history, East to West, the machine in the garden to the industrial cityscape, the sidearm to the A-bomb.

Eddie Bartlett and Roy Earle were essentially men of personal decency as well as unusual ambition and skill; violence was always forced on them, never sought. Cody Jarrett shares their drive and acumen, but he is a pathological monster. He murders the trainmen in cold blood, orders the execution of an injured member of his gang, shoots a rival in the back, kills a betrayer by locking him in a car trunk and then casually shooting him. All of these killings he relishes. But the film nonetheless compels viewers to admire Cody, to want him to succeed, and simultaneously to abhor his egregiousness, with perhaps more of the former than the latter. Some of this complexity of response stems from point of view—movies almost inevitably invite identification with their protagonists—some of it from the power of James Cagney's performance as Cody, but a good deal of it is cultural, too. The film shapes the antagonism between Cody and his enemies in such a way as to evoke maximum sympathy for his attempts to overcome them.

Cody's enemies are everywhere. Within his gang, a rival and Cody's duplicitous wife conspire to destroy him. But his major antagonist is the federal government, abetted by an extraordinary panoply of modern technology. The government, moreover, insinuates into Cody's confidence one of its agents by exploiting its knowledge of his psychological maladies. This secret agent becomes Cody's trusted confidant; as in the classic films, too intimate an attachment to another is lethal. The agent's betrayal of Cody's trust makes rancid the entire government operation. The federal government, then, is portrayed in *White Heat* unsympathetically, deploying the impersonal power of technology in clandestine snooping operations and callously exploiting personal intimacy. (It is probably not coincidental that the film was made at the outset of the McCarthy era.) Cody's modus operandi, on the other hand, is old-fashioned: he has no organization to speak of, only his own imperial will, his code premised on individual achievement, making it to "the top of the world," not on organizational allegiance.

For all his pathological violence, then, Cody is a representative of an older individualistic America, one being extinguished by the impersonal forces of technology, urbanization, and bureaucratization. As a historical anomaly he is doomed. The film's conclusion is a brilliant distillation of this theme. Trapped in the urban, entirely man-made environment of a chemical factory at the western edge of the continent, Cody is shot twice at long-range by the very bureaucrat he has befriended, but dies only when he destroys himself by detonating the towering tank on which he has made his last stand. He is intransigent to the last: "they haven't got Cody Jarrett," he shouts, pounding his chest, "in here, they haven't got him." Like Rico, he imagines himself in the third person, an epitome rather than a mere individual.

If the classic films emphasized the gangster's lonely isolation in a microcosm of American society, and the Walsh trilogy balanced between indicting overreaching gangsters and a deteriorating society, *Bonnie and Clyde* (1967) and *The Godfather I and II* (1972, 1975), the best films of the genre's second renaissance, portrayed a normative culture so lethally inimical to human needs that the only way to survive and find meaning in it was to create an alternative criminal society to nourish one's need for intimacy, fulfillment, and individual dignity. Intimacy doomed the early gangster heroes; in these most recent films, the criminal family is the only haven in a heartless world. All three films were made during the Vietnam era, when skepticism about American values reached an apogee, and reflected this widespread malaise. Like the Walsh films, moreover, all three adopted a historical perspective in their reassessment of American culture.

*Bonnie and Clyde* is set in the 1930s and loosely based on the exploits of two authentic desperadoes. Failed banks, evicted farmers, Okies on the road suggest a cultural breakdown. But the film does not adduce this social disorganization to explain Bonnie and Clyde's criminality; rather, the Depression provides a context in which their search for personal authenticity and intimacy—themes of the 1960s, not the 1930s—may be detached from the particular social confusions of the Vietnam period and at the same time evoke it by suggesting a culture in which the individual's fate is problematic. Passivity is the lot of the Depression's victims; Bonnie and Clyde assert their wills and by opposition to normative society create an identity which would otherwise be denied them. Ambition for personal success is a weaker motive with them than with earlier gangster heroes; they talk about having fancy clothes and being served in fine hotels, but the quality of their relationship is clearly more important to them than money. Just so, they are rural gangsters and it never seems to occur to them to head for a large city.

Like their filmic predecessors, they are doomed because of their aggression against social order, although as the movie makes clear such fantasies of violent aggression are endemic in normative society. Bonnie comes to understand their fate, as Clyde never fully does. He overcomes his sexual impotence as their intimacy ripens but holds on to his dreams of fame and omnipotence to the end. Bonnie, on the other hand, writes a ballad celebrating their intimacy which concludes with the line, "But it's death for Bonnie and Clyde." Her recognition of fate and mortality and her unwillingness either to retreat before it or to dissemble about it give her a tragic stature, linking her with earlier gangster heroes who less articulately also asserted their indomitable pride in the face of retributive death.

*Bonnie and Clyde* provoked a firestorm of criticism. Its director, Arthur Penn, daringly mixed scenes of clownishness with graphic violence so that the film's tone, complex but never uncertain, played with generic expectations; the comedy made a number of reviewers misperceive the film as a lighthearted and unambiguous paean to youthful criminality. The real Bonnie and Clyde were not like this, these critics said, thus foolishly confusing the realm of art with that of facticity. The same confusion appeared in some of the reviews of *The Godfather,* which was condemned on the grounds that the Mafia was unlike its simulacrum portrayed in the movie. But *The Godfather* and its sequel, *The Godfather: Part II,* were not filmed as documentaries; like all gangster films, they used crime as a metaphorical vehicle to explore questions of wider cultural value. They are the richest, most complex and ambitious gangster films ever made, and are among the signal achievements of the entire American cinema.

Taken together, the two *Godfather* films constitute at once a history of twentieth-century American culture, a family saga chronicling a rise in power and influence with a corresponding moral decline, and a network of penetrating portraits in individual psychology. Earlier gangster films alluded to crime as a ladder of social mobility for immigrants and as an arena in which intraethic and interethnic conflicts were fought out, but never depicted these with such specificity, density, or historical acuity. Likewise, earlier films implicitly demonstrated how criminal activity replicated that of legitimate business; the *God-*

*father* films charted the development of a criminal business empire as it passed through free market and oligopolistic phases into a virtual monopoly, and explored correspondingly its imperialist expansionism as domestic markets became saturated or politically tenuous. They also explicitly paralleled the hegemonic global ambitions in the larger American culture following World War II with organized crime's similar desire for control, and *The Godfather: Part II* especially dramatized the moral consequences of exercising such power.

In *The Godfather* family solidarity among the Corleones nurtures its members and protects them against a normative society consistently portrayed as unjust, repressive, and corrupt. After the death of Don Vito, the family's founding father—a death which comes while he is playing with his grandson, a brilliant anticlimactic reversal of the gangster film's conventions—the family's coherence begins to erode as the new don, his son Michael, instigates a bloody purge which includes his brother-in-law. In *The Godfather: Part II* the family's disintegration accelerates under the pressure of Don Michael's icy and megalomaniacal ambitions for power, until at the end he is left virtually alone in his Nevada fortress, his brothers and sister dead or alienated, his wife gone, his children unknown by him. This loss of everything that once had meaning is the equivalent of the earlier gangster hero's death, with this difference. Rico's death, and that of his avatars, had an ironic nobility engendered by the distance between his dreams of grandeur and the squalor of his end. In his failure, he is tragically human and evokes our pity. Don Michael Corleone is no less alone in life than Rico was in death, but his success makes him repellent and contemptible and brings us at last face to face with the moral consequences of that remorseless American will to power which has always been the irreducible subject of the gangster film.

It is tempting to see the *Godfather* films as the ultimate gangster saga, an achievement beyond which subsequent movies cannot go. No gangster film since, to be sure, has approached the *Godfather* films' thematic ambition and complexity or their aesthetic sophistication, although a handful have shown comparable aspirations. But the genre's durability has been in its adaptation to changing cultural conditions, and it seems virtually certain that new cultural imperatives will sooner or later bring forth a reformulated gangster film commensurate with a new era.

## BIBLIOGRAPHICAL OVERVIEW

"The Gangster as Tragic Hero," written by Robert Warshow in 1948, remains the seminal work for understanding the genre. Prior to Warshow's essay, the gangster film had been largely a despised genre, provoking condemnations from defenders of civic virtue for its gratuitous violence, its pandering to its audience's appetite for sensationalism, its encouragement of antisocial behavior. The *Christian Century,* a magazine of progressive uplift, for example, rhetorically asked in 1931, "What use is it to support schools and churches and boys' clubs only to have them offset by vicious movies?'' (October 21, 1931, p. 1015). For such critics, the idea that gangster films were works of art was unimaginable; they were a mere commodity and, like impure food, capable of poisoning the nation's health. During the 1930s a few writers like Jay Leyda and Lewis Jacobs resisted this dubious moralism but they also focused on questions of instrumentality more than of art. Leyda thought the gangster film ''show[ed] a certain section of America to itself'' and prepared the way ''for the clearer social statements of the reformist films that followed.'' For Jacobs, the ''new realism'' of the gangster movies in the early 1930s reflected the social disenchantment of audiences in the early Depression years.

Warshow was likewise interested in the audience's relation to the gangster film, but he assumed an audience more alert and attuned to the metaphorical resonances of movies than had earlier commentators. For him the movies were not only a mass medium but an art form as well, capable of eliciting from their audience richly calibrated responses. He saw gangster movies as an antidote to the spurious and self-congratulatory optimism of modern American culture as well as a form which imagined the psychic costs of the success ethic which otherwise so dominated the mentality of Americans. The gangster hero ''is what we want to be and what we are afraid we may become.'' His aggressive, totally self-interested pursuit of power only magnifies the dreams Americans were taught to follow; his end, dying alone in a gutter, measures the cost of those dreams. For its audiences, then, the gangster film qualified the cultural belief that success was sufficient unto itself, while at the same time making that success sufficiently attractive so as to induce a vicarious response. For Warshow the gangster movie was complex and paradoxical, not simplistic; moral, not moralistic; tragic, not melodramatic. It was, in short, an art form of the most immediate cultural significance.

Every subsequent study of the gangster film, of which there are now a good number, is indebted to Warshow's brief essay. Many of these later studies conflate the ''crime'' film (including films involving capers, private eyes, the police, juvenile delinquents, and so forth) with the ''gangster'' film, a not illegitimate pairing although one which in its capaciousness sometimes encourages plot summary and flaccid generalization, as well as militating against close analysis of individual works and a specification of their significance in the genre's history.

Richard Whitehall's ''Crime Inc.'' (1964) is just such a breezy listing of dozens of films, of little value except as a compendium of titles. Harry Hossent's *Gangster Movies: Gangsters, Hoodlums and Tough Guys of the Screen* (1974) is a coffee-table book of the same ilk, and virtually worthless. John Gabree's *Gangsters: From ''Little Caesar'' to ''The Godfather''* (1973), which combines a breathless history of the genre with a modified auteurist approach, is only slightly more substantial. The perils of writing briefly about scores of films are evident in Gabree's entirely misleading summary of *White Heat* as a ''throwback to an earlier time, a remake of the attempts to revitalize the gangster film in the late thirties.'' His critical acuity is weak as well, as when he describes *The Godfather*'s ''pale colors'' being ''like a series of pretty watercolors''; whatever else one might say about the look of Gordon Willis's photography in Francis Ford Coppola's film, its rich chiaroscuro did not even slightly resemble a watercolor. These studies masquerade as critical/historical works; John Baxter's *The Gangster Film* (1970) is more honest. It is unabashedly a compendium, in alphabetical order, with some 200 entries of actors, directors, and other figures associated with the crime film, each of them with a limp critical tagline and a filmography. The book also indexes over 900 films which Baxter considers within the genre.

The best of these *omnium gatherums* is Carlos Clarens's *Crime Movies* (1980), although it does not entirely overcome the limitations inherent in trying to discuss so many films (as his title suggests, Clarens cuts a wide swath, alluding to several hundred movies). Its pace is always brisk, sometimes breakneck, relying on pedestrian plot summaries for a number of lesser films. But the book does provide a thoughtful conspectus of the genre's major films as they relate to lesser movies made in the same period.

The focus of Stephen Louis Karpf's *The Gangster Film: Emergence, Variation, and Decay of a Genre, 1930–1940* (1973) is narrower, but it too mostly relies on plot synopses and the isolation of general themes to carry its thesis, which is that the genre progressively decayed during the 1930s. Karpf's thesis is misleading, as when, for example, he argues that *The Roaring Twenties* is little more than a knockoff of *Public Enemy,* and his analyses of individual films are banal. Andrew Bergman's *We're in the Money: Depression America and Its Films* (1971) more intelligently examines several of the decade's gangster films in their cultural context, although his discussions tend to treat films as mere plots rather than as complex aesthetic creations.

Cultural history rather than genre history is the organizing principle of Eugene Rosow's *Born to Lose: The Gangster Film in America* (1978), and this broader purview allows Rosow to explore usefully how developments in America culture and in the film industry affected the gangster film. Rosow's political commitments sometimes lead him into reductiveness, as when he argues that ''gangster films were poised between two alternatives that confronted America's crumbling economic system: socialism and fascism,'' and his attention to the genre after the 1930s is too cursory, but his book is a valuable, even essential one. Its profuse illustrations richly complement the text, unusual in a book about the movies.

Colin McArthur's *Underworld USA* (1972) is a pioneering study of the dynamics of genre, although more about thrillers than true gangster films. It has been superseded by Thomas Schatz's fine *Hollywood Genres* (1981), which devotes a suggestive chapter to gangster movies. Schatz's discussion of the nature of genres and their cultural functions is unusually intelligent, the most trenchant formulation of genre theory to date.

Individual films have not been well-served in much of the writing about the gangster genre. Too often their basic plot lines are adduced to support a windy generalization with no attention to the formal elements which distinguish a movie from a synopsis. John G. Cawelti's long essay, "The Artistic Power of *Bonnie and Clyde*," collected in his *Focus on Bonnie and Clyde* (1973), is a notable exception to this tendency and one of the very best studies of any film of whatever kind. In it he methodically and imaginatively analyzes the film's visual texture and strategy, its structure and rhythm, its use of sound and silence, and demonstrates how the film's formal constituents amplify and sometimes modify the basic story of the screenplay. Cawelti's essay, which triumphantly brings together artistic and cultural perspectives, ought to be a model for movie critics and historians.

Jack Shadoian's *Dreams and Dead Ends: The American Gangster/Crime Film* (1977) examines in detail some eighteen movies, from *Little Caesar* through the *Godfather* films, divided into a half-dozen groups corresponding to chronology and thematic similarity. In general, Shadoian's book is strongest when it examines specific films, weakest when it tries to relate them to larger cultural developments. These historical generalizations tend to be somewhat superficial. Like Cawelti, although with not quite as much detail or rigor, Shadoian intelligently explores the relationship between filmic form and meaning. His analyses of *Little Caesar, Public Enemy, High Sierra,* and *White Heat* are especially rewarding. His discussion of the *Godfather* films is less successful, perhaps because he is so intent on using them to support his thesis that they represent a "modernist emphasis," that is, "an articulate and consciously conceived nonillusionistic cinema," and thus he oversimplifies them.

What is clearly needed now are additional close analyses such as Cawelti and Shadoian provide, analyses which may then be employed in a more sophisticated history of the genre as a whole and a more complex understanding of its relation to larger patterns in American culture. Far from being exhausted, the study of these films has hardly begun.

## NOTES

1. Jay Leyda cites Gilbert Seldes's argument that " 'in the gangster picture the talkies found themselves' " and subsequent movies of all kinds " 'were more terse in speech and vigorous in action because of the invigoration which this type of picture brought to the screen.' " "Post-War American Films: The Gangster Film," *Film Notes,* Series 4, Program 8 (New York: Museum of Modern Art, n.d.), n.p.

2. Daniel Bell, "Crime as an American Way of Life: A Queer Ladder of Social Mobility," in his *The End of Ideology* (Glencoe, Ill.: Free Press, 1960), pp. 116–17.

3. Robert Warshow, "The Gangster as Tragic Hero," in his *The Immediate Experience* (New York: Atheneum, 1970), p. 133.

4. Thomas Schatz, *Hollywood Genres* (New York: Random House, 1981), pp. 81–82.

5. His early directorial skill may also be seen in *Two Seconds* (1931) and especially *I Am a Fugitive from a Chain Gang* (1932).

6. Schatz, *Hollywood Genres*, p. 91.

7. *Variety,* 29 April 1931, p. 9.

8. For a discussion of these films, see Carlos Clarens, *Crime Movies* (New York: Norton, 1980), pp. 116ff.


## BIBLIOGRAPHICAL CHECKLIST

### Books

Baxter, John. *The Gangster Film.* New York: A. S. Barnes, 1970.

Bergman, Andrew. *We're in the Money: Depression America and Its Films.* New York: New York University Press, 1971.

Cawelti, John G. *Focus on Bonnie and Clyde.* Englewood Cliffs, N.J.: Prentice-Hall, 1973.

Clarens, Carlos. *Crime Movies: From Griffith to "The Godfather" and Beyond.* New York: W. W. Norton, 1980.

Gabree, John. *Gangsters: From "Little Caesar" to "The Godfather."* New York: Pyramid, 1973.

Jacobs, Lewis. *The Rise of the American Film.* 1939; repr. New York: Teachers College Press, 1968, pp. 509–15.

Karpf, Stephen Louis. *The Gangster Film: Emergence, Variation, and Decay of a Genre, 1930–1940.* New York: Arno, 1973.

Leyda, Jay. *The Gangster Film.* New York: Museum of Modern Art Film Library Programs, Series 4, Program 8, n.d.

McArthur, Colin. *Underworld USA.* New York: Viking Press, 1972.

Parish, James R., and Michael R. Pitts. *The Great Gangster Pictures.* Metuchen, N.J.: Scarecrow Press, 1976.

Rosow, Eugene. *Born to Lose: The Gangster Film in America.* New York: Oxford University Press, 1978.

Shadoian, Jack. *Dreams and Dead Ends: The American Gangster/Crime Film.* Cambridge, Mass.: MIT Press, 1977.


### Shorter Works

Alley, Kenneth D. *"High Sierra*—Swan Song for an Era," *Journal of Popular Film* 5, nos. 3 and 4, 1976, pp. 248–62.

Bell, Daniel. "Crime as an American Way of Life." In his *An End to Ideology.* Glencoe, Ill.: Free Press, 1960, pp. 115–36.

Clark, Thomas. *"White Heat:* The Old and the New," *Wide Angle,* Spring 1976, pp. 60–65.

Hennelly, Mark M., Jr. "American Nightmare: The Underworld in Film," *Journal of Popular Film* 6, no. 3, 1978, pp. 240–61.

Kaminsky, Stuart M. "Little Caesar and Its Role in the Gangster Film Genre," *Journal of Popular Film,* Summer 1972, pp. 209–27.

Mate, Ken, and Pat McGilligan. "Burnett," *Film Comment,* January–February 1983, pp. 58–68.

Mitchell, Edward. "Apes and Essences: Some Sources of Significance in the American Gangster Film," *Wide Angle,* Spring 1976, pp. 18–23.

Schatz, Thomas. "The Gangster Film." In his *Hollywood Genres: Formulas, Filmmak-ing, and the Studio System.* New York: Random House, 1981, pp. 81–110.

Simon, William. "An Analysis of the Structure of *The Godfather: Part I,*" *Studies in the Literary Imagination,* Spring 1983, pp. 75–89.

Warshow, Robert. "The Gangster as Tragic Hero." In his *The Immediate Experience.* 1962; repr. New York: Atheneum, 1971, pp. 127–33.

Whitehall, Richard. "Crime Inc.," *Films and Filming,* January–February–March 1964, pp. 7–12, 17–22, 39–44.

## SELECTED FILMOGRAPHY

1930    *Little Caesar* (77 minutes).
First National. Producer: Hal B. Wallis. Director: Mervyn LeRoy. Screenplay: Francis Edwards Faragoh; adaptation by Robert W. Lee; from a novel by W. R. Burnett. Cast: Edward G. Robinson (Rico Bandello), Douglas Fairbanks, Jr. (Joe Massara), Glenda Farrell (Olga Strassof), Sidney Blackmer (The Big Boy), Thomas Jackson (Flaherty).

1931    *The Public Enemy* (83 minutes).
Warner Brothers. Producer: Darryl Zanuck. Director: William Wellman. Story: Kubec Glasman and John Bright; adaptation by Harry Thew. Cast: James Cag-ney (Tom Powers), Edward Woods (Matt Doyle), Donald Cook (Mike Powers), Joan Blondell (Mamie), Jean Harlow (Gwen), Mae Clark (Kitty).

1932    *Scarface: The Shame of a Nation* (99 minutes).
Distributing Co.: United Artists. Producing Co.: Howard Hughes Productions. Director: Howard Hawks. Screenplay: Seton I. Miller, John Lee Mahin, W. R. Burnett, and Ben Hecht; from a novel by Armitage Trail [Maurice Coon]. Cast: Paul Muni (Tony Camonte), Ann Dvorak (Cesca Camonte), Karen Morley (Poppy), Osgood Perkins (Johnny Lovo), Boris Karloff (Gaffney), George Raft (Rinaldo).

1939    *The Roaring Twenties* (106 minutes).
Warner Brothers. Producer: Hal Wallis. Director: Raoul Walsh. Screenplay: Jerry Wald, Richard Macauley, and Robert Rossen; from a story by Mark Hellinger. Cast: James Cagney (Eddie Bartlett), Priscilla Lane (Jean Sherman), Humphrey Bogart (George), Gladys George (Panama Smith), Jeffrey Lynn (Lloyd Hart).

1941    *High Sierra* (100 minutes).
Warner Brothers. Executive Producer: Hal B. Wallis. Associate Producer: Mark Hellinger. Director: Raoul Walsh. Screenplay: John Huston and W. R. Burnett, from Burnett's novel. Cast: Humphrey Bogart (Roy Earle), Ida Lupino (Marie Garson), Joan Leslie (Velma), Henry Travers (Pa), Arthur Kennedy (Red), Alan Curtis (Babe), Barton MacLane (Jake Kranmer), Henry Hull (Doc), Willie Best (Algernon).

1949    *White Heat* (114 minutes).
Warner Brothers. Producer: Louis F. Edelman. Director: Raoul Walsh. Screen-play: Ivan Goff and Ben Roberts; from a story by Virginia Kellogg. Cast: James Cagney (Cody Jarrett), Margaret Wycherly (Ma Jarrett), Virginia Mayo (Verna Jarrett), Steve Cochran (Big Ed), Edmund O'Brien (Hank Fallon), John Archer (Phillip Evans).

1967   *Bonnie and Clyde* (111 minutes).
Distributing Co.: Warner Brothers–Seven Arts. Producing Co.: Tatira–Hiller Productions. Producer: Warren Beatty. Director: Arthur Penn. Screenplay: David Newman and Robert Benton. Cast: Warren Beatty (Clyde Barrow), Faye Dunaway (Bonnie Parker), Michael J. Pollard (C. W. Moss), Gene Hackman (Buck Barrow), Estelle Parsons (Blanche Barrow), Dub Taylor (Malcolm Moss), Denver Pyle (Capt. Frank Hamer), Evans Evans (Velma Davis), Gene Wilder (Eugene Grizzard).

1972   *The Godfather* (175 minutes).
Paramount. Producer: Albert S. Ruddy. Director: Francis Ford Coppola. Screenplay: Mario Puzo and Francis Ford Coppola; from a novel by Puzo. Cast: Marlon Brando (Vito Corleone), Al Pacino (Michael Corleone), James Caan (Sonny Corleone), Richard Castellano (Clemenza), Robert Duvall (Tom Hagen), Sterling Hayden (McCluskey), John Marley (Jack Woltz), Richard Conte (Barzini), Diane Keaton (Kay Adams).

1975   *The Godfather: Part II* (200 minutes).
Paramount. Producer/Director: Francis Ford Coppola. Screenplay: Francis Ford Coppola and Mario Puzo; from a novel by Puzo. Cast: Al Pacino (Michael Corleone), Robert Duvall (Tom Hagen), Diane Keaton (Kay), Robert De Niro (Vito Corleone), John Cazale (Fredo Corleone), Talia Shire (Connie Corleone), Lee Strasberg (Hyman Roth), Michael V. Cazzo (Frankie Pentangeli).

# 5

# Film Noir

JACK NACHBAR

"Someday fate, or some mysterious force, can put the finger on you
or me for no reason at all."

—Tom Neal in *Detour* (1945).

"First you dream, then you die."

—Cornell Woolrich

Film noir (black film) is the title bestowed by the French on a group of American films produced between the early 1940s and the late 1950s, with their peak of production from about 1945 through 1950. In general, as their name suggests, films noir were dark in both storyline and physical texture. The world of film noir is the city, primarily at night, indifferent to suffering, with the possibility of violence or death around every corner. Within this world characters lie, deceive, and kill one another in a desperate struggle to avoid their own fated destructions. It is a world where a giggling Tommy Udo (Richard Widmark) happily pushes a wheelchair-bound old woman down flights of stairs to her death in *Kiss of Death* (1947). It is a world where the hired killer Raven (Alan Ladd), when asked in *This Gun for Hire* (1942) how it feels to kill someone, smiles and says, ''It feels fine.'' It is a world in *Kiss Me Deadly* (1955) in which a search for a killer and a ''great whatsit'' leads to a blonde woman killer and a nuclear device. It is a world in which the movie titles themselves—*So Dark the Night* (1946), *Born to Kill* (1947), *The Guilty* (1948), *Criss Cross* (1949), *Night and the City* (1950)—suggest despair, compulsions, and betrayals.

James Damico has attempted to summarize what he believes is the common storyline of film noir:

Either because he is fated to do so by chance, or because he has been hired for a job specifically associated with her, a man whose experience of life has left him sanguine and often bitter meets a non-innocent woman of similar outlook to whom he is sexually and fatally attracted. Through this attraction, either because the woman induces him to it or because it is the natural result of their relationship, the man comes to cheat, attempt to murder, or actually murder a second man to whom the woman is unhappily or unwillingly attached (generally he is her husband or lover), an act which often leads to the woman's betrayal of the protagonist, but which in any event brings about the sometimes metaphoric, but usually literal destruction of the woman, the man to whom she is attached, and frequently the protagonist himself.[1]

Because film noir incorporates films from a number of different genres, however, Damico admits that his model must allow for wide variance. Thus, while *The Scarlet Street* (1945), *The Postman Always Rings Twice* (1946), and *The Pitfall* (1948) fit the pattern perfectly, other films do not. In a prison film, for example, *Brute Force* (1947), we learn that all five of the main convict characters owe their prison terms to earlier relations with different women. And the highly violent attempted breakout which leads to all of their deaths also was motivated by their earlier relationships. In *White Heat* (1949), a gangster picture, Cody Jarrett (James Cagney) is driven to crime and then insanity not by a sexual partner, but by his mother.

Noir protagonists are on a collision course with fate. Driven by greed or lust or their own psychotic impulses, they create a pattern of existence for themselves, from which there is no escape, which must lead to their actual or near destruction. The initial choice may seem trivial. Al Roberts (Tom Neal) decides to hitchhike west in *Detour,* and through no real fault of his own beyond his own lack of faith in himself, becomes involved in two killings and ends the film picked up for murders he did not commit. Foster Hirsch divides noir protagonists into three classes.[2] The first class is investigators such as private detective Philip Marlowe (Dick Powell) in *Murder My Sweet* (1944). The second group is victims such as middle-aged frump Christopher Cross (Edward G. Robinson in *The Scarlet Street* (1945). The third class is psychopaths such as the murderess with amnesia Louise Graham (Joan Crawford) in *Possessed* (1947). All three types, once "they have been singled out by a dark and capricious fate . . . are hurled into an abyss, their lives fatally disrupted, their personalities inevitably stained and transformed."[3]

If film noir males are destroyed or nearly destroyed by fate, the noir woman is fate's emissary, a siren leading the man to ruination. Called a "bitch goddess" by Stephen Farber because he believes she acts primarily out of greed for wealth,[4] the noir woman lures men with "stormy, dangerous, and above all exciting sexuality"[5] with which she first seduces them, then later betrays them. Three of the most famous noir women serve as ideal examples. Phyllis Dietrichson (Barbara Stanwyck) in *Double Indemnity* (1944) first seduces the weak-willed Walter Neff (Fred MacMurray), then convinces him to murder her husband for the insurance money, and finally shoots him. Kathie Moffett (Jane Greer) in what many critics believe is the definitive film noir, *Out of the Past*

(1947), seduces detective Jeff Bailey (Robert Mitchum) and then convinces him to double-cross his gangster client so, unknown to Bailey, she can escape with $40,000. Three years later, Kathie turns up again, betrays Bailey again, and finally kills him. Kitty Collins (Ava Gardner) in *The Killers* (1946) so casts Swede (Burt Lancaster) under her spell that he first goes to prison to save her from being arrested and two years later becomes involved in a robbery for her sake only to be double-crossed by her, leaving him with no money and the blame for Kitty's double-crossing of the entire gang of thieves. Swede is so broken by Kitty that six years later he waits in passive acceptance as he is tracked down by hired killers and murdered.

In the midst of their evil machinations, noir women are made up and lit to look mysterious and sensual. Never in films before or since has the sexually aggressive female been so evil or so glamorously attractive. There are, naturally, also good women in films noir, mostly girl-next-door types, docile and domestic, but they pale in the aura of the sexual power and charisma of the dark ladies.

The environment within which the noir characters struggle to survive is the city, its high buildings creating a sense of claustrophobic entrapment, its hidden alleyways at night threatening sudden violence, and the interiors of its labyrinthine office buildings suggesting the confusion and the panic of finding no way out. In most film noir, this nightmare landscape is filmed at odd angles with diagonal lines continually cutting the screen thus increasing the grotesque, menacing quality of the city.

In addition, there are strong contrasts of black and white lighting, putting the characters in menacing shadows, and suggesting their dubious natures by showing faces half lit, half in darkness. All of these environmental and stylistic elements create a metaphor for the inner lives of the characters, suggesting their confusion and their instability.

## MAJOR INFLUENCES ON FILM NOIR

It can be argued, of course, that all of the history of art is present in any work of art. Most film scholars agree, however, that certain specific European and American artistic developments contributed directly to the development of film noir plots, characters, style, and the pessimistic noir worldview.

### The Influence of German Filmmakers

During the 1920s, working mostly at the state supported Universal Film A. G. (U.F.A.) studios in Berlin, a number of German filmmakers developed a style influenced by the stage expressionism developed principally in Germany by Max Reinhardt. The aim of the expressionists was to distort physical reality to suggest a subjective, psychological state. To do this, props and acting styles were intentionally distorted, and lighting on films tended to be a striking chiaroscuro, dramatic contrasts of areas of light and dark. Many films, such as

*The Cabinet of Doctor Caligari* (1919), *The Last Laugh* (1925), and *Variety* (1927), employed these techniques to express traditional Germanic angst, a wrenching of the soul in the face of fate. During the 1930s a number of German and Austrian directors emigrated to America, among them Fritz Lang, Otto Preminger, Billy Wilder, Robert Siodmak, and Edgar G. Ulmer, all of whom used expressionistic techniques to express an angst-saturated worldview in their American films. These same men are best known for their films noir. In addition, German expressionism on screen heavily influenced many of the primary directors of film noir, including Orson Welles, Anthony Mann, Jules Dassin, and Robert Aldrich.

### Italian Neorealism

As the violence of war left Rome, Italian filmmakers, their studios bombed-out rubble, took to the streets to make their pictures, creating films with a documentary look, featuring location shooting and footage of the everyday lives of common people. Such films as Roberto Rossellini's *Rome, Open City* (1945), Vittorio De Sica's *Bicycle Thieves* (1948), and Lucino Visconti's *La Terra Trema* (1948) became internationally acclaimed as masterpieces. Dubbed neorealism, this style of filmmaking became influential all over the world, including Hollywood, where it influenced film noir directors such as Henry Hathaway, Anthony Mann, and Jules Dassin. Beginning with *The House on 92nd Street* in 1945, many films noir adopted the neorealist look, and the urban landscapes of noir became real locations, making the threat of the city more immediately menacing. The advertising for *Kiss of Death* (1947) and *The Naked City* (1948) even bragged of their actual location scenes. In some noirs such as *Cry of the City* (1948) and *D.O.A.* (1949) location shooting is combined with stylized expressionist lighting and compositions to produce a world both real and nightmarish.

### American Gangster and Horror Films of the 1930s and 1940s

Early 1930s gangster pictures such as *Little Caesar* (1931) and *Scarface* (1932) contributed to noir one of its dominant themes: the American dream of success through crime. More importantly, they also suggested the noir theme of a fated doom. In *Scarface,* for example, director Howard Hawks always places the letter X on screen near a person about to be killed, thereby suggesting that each of their deaths is inevitable. Gangster films thus provide a valuable border between Greek tragedy, which is the core source of film noir, and the noir films themselves. Oedipus is doomed by his ego; Tony (Paul Muni) in *Scarface* is fated to die for his incestuous love of his sister; Bert (John Dall) and Annie Laurie (Peggy Cummins) in *Gun Crazy* (1950) are pointed toward their own violent deaths by their obsession with guns. One of the first films in the film noir cycle, *High Sierra* (1941), was a classic gangster picture and provided a direct link between the two types of films.

Horror movies provided directors of American sound films their first opportunities to use expressionistic techniques to create environments full of menace and dread. It is probably no coincidence that RKO, in a series of classic low-budget horror movies produced in the early 1940s by Val Lewton including *Cat People* (1942) and *The Body Snatchers* (1945), was also the studio most active in the production of films noir.[6] Robert Wise, who worked on several of the Lewton horror films, went on to directing noir films including *Born to Kill* (1947) and *The Captive City* (1952).

## Pulp Writers of the 1920s and 1930s

In general, the pulps were fiction magazines printed on cheap pulpwood paper, costing between ten cents and a quarter. Pulps began about the turn of the century but were most popular between 1920 and 1945. By 1920 they had evolved from short story anthologies to specialized magazines organized around such genres as westerns, war stories, and science fantasy.[7] Two pulp genres that indirectly influenced film noir were the weird menace pulps and avenger hero pulps.

Weird menace pulps such as *Weird Tales* and *Dime Mystery Detective* created hallucinatory worlds full of menacing fiends and, often, suggested erotic sadism. They described worlds beyond all control of normal human order where the only means of survival was power and violence. Such 1930s avenger pulps as *The Shadow, The Spider,* and *The Avenger* described an America so caught in the embrace of evildoers that normal law enforcers were helpless. Justice in avenger pulps was satisfied by vigilantes in masks creeping through the night to violently stamp out crime without the complication of the law-and-order process. Both weird menace pulps and avenger pulps contributed to film noir stylized worlds dominated by evil and characterized by acts of violence as the normal means of resolving conflicts.

More directly influential than the weird menace or avenger pulps was the hard-boiled detective story, primarily as it developed in the pulp *Black Mask* in the 1920s. The *Black Mask* writers, most notably Dashiell Hammett and Raymond Chandler, brought their detectives, to paraphrase Raymond Chandler in his famous essay, "The Simple Art of Murder," out of the drawing rooms of the classical detective story and into the "mean streets" where they belong because that is where violent death most commonly happens.[8] The city of the hard-boiled detective *is* the film noir city, a place of cheap hotels, seedy bars, and dimly lit rooms, a place where life is cheap and nearly everyone, especially women, lies, cheats, and steals. This city is usually described by the detective himself in a cynical idiom emphasizing surface details, a tone also adopted by film noir. It is hardly surprising that some of Hammett's and Chandler's books became classic films noir, such as *The Maltese Falcon* and *The Big Sleep* (1946) respectively. It is also hardly surprising that James M. Cain, a hard-boiled stylist whose best-selling novels emphasized middle-class murder, also provided stories for such famous films as *Double Indemnity, The Postman Always Rings Twice* (1946), and *Mildred Pierce* (1945).

One other pulp writer needs to be mentioned as an influence on film noir. Cornell Woolrich, in dozens of pulp stories and serials, many of which were later used in radio thrillers and films, created "the most powerful [suspense stories] ever written—stories full of fear, guilt, and loneliness, breakdown and despair, and a sense that the world is controlled by malignant forces preying on us."[9] If the hard-boiled detective writers created the noir environment, Woolrich, in stories like "Borrowed Crime" and books such as *The Black Path of Fear* (1944), creates the feel of film noir, a personal sense of a hostile world gone out of control. Among the papers found in Woolrich's apartment after his death in 1968 was a fragment saying, "I was only trying to cheat death. I was only trying to surmount for a little while the darkness that all my life I surely knew was going to come rolling in on me some day and obliterate me. I was only trying to stay alive a little brief while longer, after I was already."[10] When has the essense of film noir ever been better expressed?

## FILM NOIR IN AMERICAN CULTURE

Several filmographies of film noir identify hundreds of films noir made during the 1940s and 1950s. It is perhaps rather surprising, then, to discover that very few films noir were highly successful at the box office. Of the 298 films named in the top money-making movies list published by the *Motion Picture Herald* between 1944 and 1956, the years of peak film noir production, only nine are consensus films noir, barely 3 percent of the total.[11] Yet film noir was commercially successful enough that it was extended even into such unlikely genres as comedy (*Monsieur Verdoux* [1947] and the hilarious *Unfaithfully Yours* [1948]) and westerns (*Colorado Territory* [1948] and *The Furies* [1950]). The main reason for this disparity between high production numbers and a low percentage of major hits is the simple fact that a high percentage of films noir were low-budget B films made to play on the bottom end of double features. Consequently, the noir use of night scenes, location shooting, and low-key lighting all were ways of avoiding expensive sets and long shooting schedules. Made cheaply, B movies could be profitable with far less rental income than what A movies needed to generate. And since small, independent movie theaters often changed films several times a week, there was always playing time available, even for the cheaply made B's.[12]

Film noir's second-class status on postwar American movie screens locates noir's dark content at the heart of other mass media materials also on the edges of the mainstream. Radio detective shows, for example, like *The Adventures of Sam Spade*, provided yet another outlet for the hard-boiled heroes of the pulps. Suspense shows on the radio such as *Suspense* and *Inner Sanctum* usu-

**Some Major Influences on Film Noir**

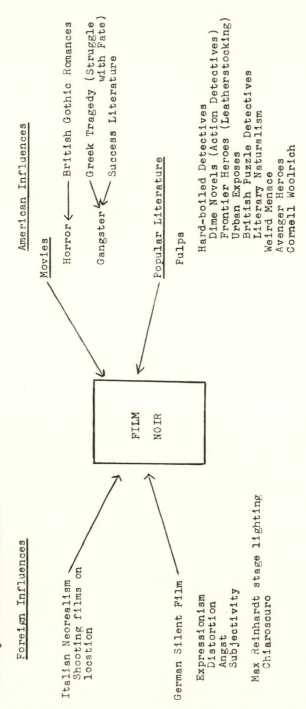

Foreign Influences

Italian Neorealism
Shooting films on
location

German Silent Film

Expressionism
Distortion
Angst
Subjectivity

Max Reinhardt stage lighting
Chiaroscuro

American Influences

Movies

Horror ← British Gothic Romances

Gangster ← Greek Tragedy (Struggle
with Fate)
Success Literature

Popular Literature

Pulps

Hard-boiled Detectives
Dime Novels (Action Detectives)
Frontier Heroes (Leatherstocking)
Urban Exposes
British Puzzle Detectives
Literary Naturalism
Weird Menace
Avenger Heroes
Cornell Woolrich

FILM

NOIR

ally featured characters terrified by forces outside themselves. Occasionally, the suspense shows adapted the short stories of Cornell Woolrich. B movie serials, intended mostly for kids, served up fast action, constant danger, and a life-and-death situation at the end of every fifteen-minute episode. Off-brand comics, before they were driven out of business in 1954 by the Comics Code, served up for their preadolescent and early adolescent fans large dollops of crime comics picturing plenty of close-up shootings, and at the E.C. comics factory, artists churned out grisly horror stories showing torture, dismemberments, and every imaginable variation of how to die horribly. Finally, the late 1940s and early 1950s was the age of the lurid paperback. Drugstores all over America included racks of twenty-five–cent paperbacks featuring covers with partially clad women with unusually large breasts, often holding a gun, looking erotic and deadly at the same time.[13] The king of the lurid paperbacks was, of course, Mickey Spillane, whose impulsively violent hero, Mike Hammer, in a series of hard-boiled detective stories beginning with *I the Jury* in 1947, found pleasure in first seeing women naked and then killing them.

All of these entertainments, usually condemned by the "proper" elements of society, suggest a mood or feeling that existed on the bottom half of the double feature of life. In 1951, for example, while respectable audiences were seeing the colorful optimism in *An American in Paris,* kids were seeing the latest chapter of *Batman* on Saturday afternoon or paging through *The Vault of Horror* at the barbershop. Their older brothers, in the meantime, were at the drugstore thumbing their way through the girlie magazines or scanning Spillane's *One Lonely Night* looking for the dirty stuff. And that night the entire family might walk to the neighborhood Bijou and see a film noir like *The Racket, Roadblock,* or *The Killer That Stalked New York.*

What did it all mean, this walk into a dark alley away from the power of positive thinking? A reasonable list of reasons is offered by Colin McArthur:

It seems reasonable to suggest that [the continuance of angst in thrillers] into the postwar period was stimulated by the uncertainty of the cold war, that its misogyny was connected with the heightened desirability and concomitant suspicion of women back home experienced by men at war, and that its obvious cruelty was related to the mood of a society to whom the horrors of Auschwitz and Hiroshima had just been revealed.[14]

While there is no reason to quarrel with McArthur's list of reasons, the list does not explain why film noir and the other dark entertainments of the period prospered in an era where the best-sellers and the box-office bonanzas were, for the most part, much more optimistic. One major clue to solving this mystery is provided by Barbara Deming in her marvelous book, *Running Away from Myself: A Dream Portrait of America Drawn from Films of the Forties.* Deming examines a number of popular A films over a broad range of genres including musicals, romantic fantasies, war movies, suspense thrillers, and domestic melodramas. She finds that in all of these films, beneath surfaces of generally upbeat conclusions, when the films are looked at together, they reveal an endless circle of frustration and uncertainty.

The figures I have presented seem together to form a hopeless circle. The hero who sees nothing to fight for; the hero who despairs of making a life for himself; the hero who achieves success but finds it empty; and the malcontent who breaks with life to find himself nowhere—each mourns a vision of happiness that eludes him.[15]

If Deming is correct, apparently the worldview of the optimistic A films in reality is not so different from that of the more cynical, low-budget films noir. Both deal with anxious men, running desperately after happiness, but living in great fear that happiness has passed them by forever.

Another clue to the relationship between the high and low ends of the popular entertainments of the noir era is supplied by Sylvia Harvey in her article "Woman's Place: The Absent Family of Film Noir." Harvey notes that, quite simply, family life is a rarity in film noir and that the misogyny so commonly perceived in film noir is directed in the films against women whose sexual power or ambitions or greed leads them to deviate from their conventional family roles as wives and mothers.[16] We can see Harvey's point in two of the few films noir to feature women protagonists. In *Mildred Pierce,* Mildred (Joan Crawford) leaves her husband to manage her own restaurant. This eventually leads her to believe she is a murderess. When she is finally cleared, she reconciles with her husband. In *The Reckless Moment* (1949), Lucia Harper (Joan Bennett), with her husband away on business, desperately struggles to replace him as head of their well-to-do family, including covering up an accidental killing by her headstrong daughter. This eventually leads to the deaths of two more men, one trying to blackmail her, the other trying to help her. Mildred's adventure into the business world makes her a bad wife and mother and she nearly hangs for it. Lucia's attempt to fill her husband's role leads her deeper and deeper into deceit and treachery. To overstep the boundaries of one's family destiny is to sin and suffer.

Film noir is the flip side of the postwar baby boom and the American middle-class flight to the suburbs. But because it deals with anxieties, repressions and brutality does not mean that its perspectives contradict the values of quiet conformity, corporate security, and family ideals we associate with the era. If many of the good-time hits of that generation—*Meet Me in St. Louis* (1944), *Blue Skies* (1946), *Cheaper by the Dozen* (1950), and *Seven Brides for Seven Brothers* (1954)—suggest some doubts about reaching those ideals, the films noir point to the dangers and horrible consequences of not reaching them. Noir showed its audiences that the world is malevolent and to be too ambitious for money or sex or power leads to violence and death. The only logical alternative was to seek a life of total safety.

The film most critics choose as representing the end of the classic period of film noir is Orson Welles's *Touch of Evil* in 1958. By that time Hollywood no

WITHDRAWN
ITHACA COLLEGE LIBRARY

longer had much need for film noir. Wide-screen films in color were standard in American movie theaters by 1958, thus eliminating noir's menacing texture that had worked best on more claustrophobic small screens in films shot in black and white. The B movie had also expired in the competition with television by 1958. The low-budget exploitation pictures that succeeded the B's were aimed primarily at an adolescent audience not interested in highly stylized musings on the absurdity of human existence. Films noir still appear occasionally, however. Some of them, such as *Chinatown* (1974) and *Taxi Driver* (1976), are brilliant new variations on the plots of the noir era. Others, such as *Body Heat* (1981), are essentially remakes of earlier noir classics. *Body Heat* retells the story of *Double Indemnity,* merely changing the locale and the immediate circumstances. Since film noir was discovered by British and American critics in the 1970s, young filmmakers are showing an interest in the form. Joel and Ethan Coen's 1983 *Blood Simple,* shot on a classic noir low budget, is loaded with stylistic flourishes and drips with angst. "In Texas, you're on your own," says the film's murderous main character, and by film's end he is on his own, cold dead. Conditions in Hollywood and in the rest of America will probably never again be right for a classic noir era, but films noir will in all likelihood continue to trickle onto our movie screens, telling us not to be too cocksure of ourselves, telling us to be careful out there.

## BIBLIOGRAPHICAL OVERVIEW

Film noir was primarily an American movie phenomenon, but it was first discovered and described by the French. Soon after the end of World War II, French *cinéastes* began viewing the American films of the 1940s which the war had made unavailable earlier. They were surprised at the darkness of the themes and style many of these films contained in comparison with the films of the 1930s which had provided them with their previous expectations about Hollywood films. In 1946 critic Nino Frank introduced the term *film noir* for these darker films, a term he had derived from a series of hard-boiled books being published in France under the title *Série Noire.*[17] A series of articles about film noir in French publications evolved in 1955 into the first book-length study of the topic, Raymond Borde and Étienne Chaumeton's *Panorama du Film Noir Américain.*

It was another fifteen years before British and American writers following the French lead began to study film noir as a subject. The first article in English about film noir was a chapter from Charles Higham and Joel Greenberg's monograph, *Hollywood in the Forties,* published in 1968. In that chapter, entitled "Black Cinema," the authors use the term *film noir* to describe films that contain "a world of darkness and violence . . . and above all shadow upon shadow upon shadow."[18] Little space, however, is given to a general description of film noir. Instead, Higham and Greenberg use "black cinema" as a descriptive term to unite a discussion of the works of notable noir directors such as Robert Siodmak, Fritz Lang, and Billy Wilder. The first full-length study of film noir, Amir Karimi's *Toward a Definition of the American Film Noir* (1970) was published two years after Higham and Greenberg's pioneering effort. Karimi's book, an Arno Press reprint of his doctoral dissertation, provides considerably more background than *Hollywood in the Forties,* but it is limited as a resource by its restricting its study to films released before 1950 and by its emphasis on the relationship between the film noir and the detective story.

While Higham and Greenberg, and Karimi put cracks in the dike holding back writing on film noir, the floodgates which would release a rush of written analysis in the 1970s and 1980s, were opened by two articles which appeared in the early 1970s, Raymond Durgnat's "Paint It Black: The Family Tree of the Film Noir" (1970), and Paul Schrader's "Notes on Film Noir" (1972). Both articles provided the kind of background and descriptive observations which proved to be invaluable starting places for later writers, dozens of whom would refer to Durgnat and Schrader before presenting ideas of their own.

Durgnat's essay attempted to order the multigenred variety of pictures that form the film noir canon by placing them in eleven categories: (1) crime as social criticism, (2) gangsters, (3) on the run (fugitives trying to escape), (4) private eyes and adventurers, (5) middle-class murder, (6) portraits and doubles, (7) sexual pathology, (8) psychopaths, (9) hostages of fortune, (10) blacks and reds, (11) Guignol, horror, fantasy.[19] Although such a description and listing was invaluable for showing many of the themes and variations within film noir, Durgnat's categories were overly inclusive, incorporating such dubious items as *King Kong* (1933) and *2001: A Space Odyssey* (1968). Schrader's essay, on the other hand, is much narrower in its inclusions than Durgnat's and thus has been more influential. According to Schrader, film noir is mainly distinguished by style and tone. His essay describes these characteristics and discusses four "catalytic elements that are the sources for film noir's dark tonality: (1) World War II and postwar disillusionment; (2) postwar realism; (3) German expressionist lighting brought to Hollywood by German expatriate directors; and (4) the "hard-boiled" school of crime and detective stories.

A number of books and dozens of articles centering on film noir themes, directors, and individual films have appeared since Durgnat's and Schrader's influential articles. Books strictly on film noir have, for the most part, been elaborate filmographies each containing several hundred films or attempts to define the aesthetic and cultural conditions that led to and are reflected in the film noir canon.

The first of the filmographies, *Film Noir: An Encyclopedic Reference to the American Style* (1979), edited by Alain Silver and Elizabeth Ward, is also the most ambitious and most generally useful. Besides production and cast credits, and a plot synopsis, each entry also includes interpretive commentary that is sometimes quite insightful. There are also useful appendices and an index. Unfortunately, since a number of writers contributed to the book, the quality of the commentaries is inconsistent. Worse, there are a number of factual errors and mistakes in the plot summaries.

The second book-length filmography, *A Reference Guide to the American Film Noir, 1940–1958* (1981) by Robert Ottoson, is more accurate and consistent than Silver and Ward's book. It also includes the most complete bibliography yet published. Two minor omissions limit this otherwise admirable resource. First, the cast credits do not include the names of the characters played. Second, the filmography stops at 1958, thus excluding the occasional film noir of the 1960s and 1970s such as *Point Blank* (1967), *Night Moves* (1975), and *Taxi Driver* (1976), which are all included in Silver and Ward. The most recent filmography, *Dark City: The Film Noir* (1984) by Spencer Selby, is the least useful of the three books. Although partial credits for almost 500 films are included with useful appendices and an index, extended commentary appears for only twenty-five movies. Annotation for the others is only a single sentence.

Of the two book-length general studies of film noir, Jon Tuska's *Dark Cinema: American Film Noir in Cultural Perspective* (1984) is at one and the same time the more detailed and the more exasperating. In the first half of *Dark Cinema*, Tuska describes some of the major influences on film noir; Greek and Roman tragedy, hard-boiled writing, German expressionist films, and certain American movies of the 1920s and 1930s. Although this material is presented competently, its relevance to film noir gets hopelessly obscured. Tuska seems to have an encyclopedic knowledge of his materials, and he tends to pedantically drone on for page after page, needlessly quoting scholarship, endlessly piling on irrelevant details, until dozens of pages have accumulated before film noir is even briefly mentioned. The second half of the book, devoted to film noir itself, also occasionally bogs down in unnecessary details but manages to usefully discuss the subject. A chapter is given to defining film noir, and a chapter each is devoted to noir women, noir men, and noir directors.

The other general study of film noir is Foster Hirsch's *The Dark Side of the Screen: Film Noir* (1981). Hirsch covers nearly the same territory as Tuska, but unlike Tuska, Hirsch comes to the point and writes with clarity and enthusiasm. In addition, *The Dark Side of the Screen,* unlike Tuska's book, is stuffed full of dozens of photos, each a clear illustration of what is being discussed in the text. These photos, so often merely fillers in other books about movies, prove essential in presenting ideas about a type of film perhaps best known for its visual characteristics.

The single other widely distributed book-length study of film noir points a possible way to future research of these films. *Women in Film Noir* (1978), edited by E. Ann Kaplan, presents an anthology of eight articles unified by their concern about the implications of the powerful, sexual, but finally evil women characters that dominate so many films noir. Most of the articles focus on individual films, *Gilda* (1946), *The Blue Gardenia* (1953), *Mildred Pierce* (1945), *Double Indemnity* (1944), and *Klute* (1971). Two more general essays discuss the absence of family and the visual portrayal of women in film noir. Overall, the anthology is provocative reading, but it also suggests that quality, lengthy research on film noir may be on specific elements of the films rather than the general subject.

Most of the individual articles published on film noir examine specific films within the noir canon. Some articles, however, have made important contributions to our understanding of the general topic. Among these are two essays by Janey Place. In "Some Visual Motifs of Film Noir" (1974), written with Lowell S. Peterson, Place, using a number of frame enlargements, describes how "the 'dark mirror' of film noir creates a visually unstable environment in which no character has a firm moral base from which he can confidently operate."[20] Techniques for the noir "dark mirror," such as low-key lighting, are described and illustrated with a simple clarity that is understandable even to readers with little or no knowledge of filmmaking techniques. In another article featuring numerous photo illustrations, "Women in Film Noir" (1978), Place argues convincingly that the noir spider woman, dramatized as evil because of her sexual aggressiveness, is nevertheless one of the few types of women on screen who are strong-willed and powerful.[21]

Two other articles also provide rays of light into the dark world of film noir. In "No Way Out: Existential Motifs in the Film Noir" (1976), Robert G. Porfirio shows that noir may owe as much to French notions of living in an absurd world as to Germanic angst. As Porfirio points out, within both film noir and existentialism is an "emphasis on man's contingency in a world where there are no transcendental values or moral absolutes, a world devoid of any meaning but the one man himself creates."[22] In "Conspiracy City" (1980), Richard Dorfman argues that during the 1970s film noir evolved into "conspiracy cinema." According to Dorfman, in conspiracy cinema, films such as "The Parallax View (1974) and *Three Days of the Condor* (1975), "the individual must ferret out a conspiracy, the nature of which both he and the audience are not aware of, while in film noir the hero perceives the danger from the beginning and must act, often alone, to defuse it."[23] In all of the books and articles published about film noir, there seems to be an emerging consensus about many of the stylistic and thematic consistencies common within the noir canon of films. One question remains as yet unresolved, however, and this question is a fundamental one: is film noir a genre or is it something else? A majority believe it is something else, although what that "else" is remains somewhat at issue. Raymond Durgnat, for example, says expressly that "film noir is not a genre . . . and [it] takes us into the realm of classification by motif and tone."[24] Paul Schrader in "Notes on Film Noir" agrees with Durgnat that film noir is not a genre and that tone is one of its distinguishing characteristics, but Schrader also adds style and mood as noir essentials. Janey Place, however, in "Women in Film Noir" describes film noir as a "movement," a type of film that occurs in specific historical periods such as Italian neorealism or Soviet socialist realism. For Place, classifying film noir in such a manner enables us to analyze the body of films as products of a certain cultural mindset during a certain era.[25]

Those arguing that film noir is indeed a genre are James Damico and Foster Hirsch. Damico, in "Film Noir: A Modest Proposal" (1978), argues that film noir can best be studied as a cultural manifestation only after the common elements of films noir are pinpointed and understood. These common elements are conventions, and it is sets of common plot and thematic conventions that are normally referred to as genres. Damico cites critics René Wellek and Austin Warren in *Theory of Literature,* and Northrop Frye in *Anatomy of Criticism,* for his ideas about genre. He illustrates his thesis by attempting to articulate the conventional plot of film noir, which was quoted earlier in this essay.

In *The Dark Side of the Screen,* Hirsch attempts to establish film noir as a genre by demonstrating that noir has all of the categories of movie conventions we normally associate with film genres. Genres have "conventions of narrative structure, characterization, theme, and visual design," and, says Hirsch, film noir has all of these ingredients, even down to conventional acting styles by noir performers.[26] Hirsch's central task in *The Dark Side of the Screen* becomes one of describing the genre's conventions, demonstrating their origins in other genres in various mass media, and explaining the cultural implications of the public acceptance of noir's genre conventions mainly during the years immediately after World War II.

One final voice in the debate over whether or not film noir is a genre is that of Jon Tuska in *Dark Cinema.* Tuska does not seem especially interested in debating the genre-nongenre question; he says film noir is mainly a "perspective on life" based on a "confrontation with nihilism."[27] This premise leads him to conclude that most movies classified as films noir really are not noir. Tuska argues that "a truly *black* film" should be distinguished from *film gris* (gray film) and melodrama. *Films gris* and melodramas have typical noir plots and/or noir stylistics, but contain a happy resolution. A true film noir must leave a "continuing, persistent *malaise* in its wake . . . a film noir cannot have a conventional happy ending and still be considered a film noir."[28]

Whether film noir is a genre, a subgenre, a mood, a movement, or merely a handy way of discussing the most stylized movies in the history of American film is still a question almost as murky as the movies themselves. What is clear, however, is the fact that after more than a decade of lagging behind the French in the study of the black-shaded films of the 1940s and 1950s, British and American film analysts are catching up fast. Film noir has been one of the most written about film subjects of the 1970s and 1980s. The end of substantial written work on this elusive but fascinating subject is nowhere in sight.

## NOTES

1. James Damico, "Film Noir: A Modest Proposal," *Film Reader,* no. 3 (1978), p. 54.

2. Foster Hirsch, *The Dark Side of the Screen: Film Noir* (San Diego: A. S. Barnes, 1981), p. 167.

3. Ibid., p. 178.

4. Stephen Farber, "Violence and the Bitch Goddess," *Film Comment,* November 1974, p. 9.

5. Janey Place, "Women in Film Noir," in *Women in Film Noir,* ed. E. Ann Kaplan (London: BFI, 1978), p. 36.

6. Spencer Selby, *Dark City: The Film Noir* (Jefferson, N.C.: McFarland, 1984), p. 211.

7. A good general history of the pulps is Ron Goulart, *An Informal History of the Pulp Magazine* (New York: Ace Books, 1972).

8. Raymond Chandler, *The Simple Art of Murder* (New York: Ballantine Books, 1972).

9. Francis M. Nevins, Jr., Introduction to *The Black Path of Fear* by Cornell Woolrich (New York: Ballantine Books, 1982), p. vii.

10. Quoted in Nevins, p. xiv.

11. Compiled from Cobbett Steinberg, *Reel Facts* (New York: Vintage Books, 1982), pp. 18–22. The nine films are *The House on 92nd Street* (1945), *Mildred Pierce* (1945), *Gilda* (1946), *Notorious* (1946), *Spellbound* (1946), *Nora Prentiss* (1947), *Possessed* (1947), *Key Largo* (1948), and *Detective Story* (1951).

12. The connection between film noir and the needs of the Hollywood assembly line is presented in detail in Paul Kerr, "Out of What Past? Notes on the B Film Noir," *Screen Education,* Autumn–Winter 1979–1980, pp. 45–65.

13. The evocative covers of and stories in the lurid paperbacks are shown and described in Geoffrey O'Brien, *Hardboiled America: The Lurid Years of Paperbacks* (New York: Van Nostrand Reinhold, 1981).

14. Colin McArthur, *Underworld USA* (New York: Viking Press, 1972), pp. 66–67.

15. Barbara Deming, *Running Away from Myself: A Dream Portrait of America Drawn from Films of the Forties* (New York: Grossman Publishers, 1969), p. 201.

16. Sylvia Harvey, "Woman's Place: The Absent Family of Film Noir," in *Women in Film Noir,* ed. Kaplan, pp. 22–34.

17. Jon Tuska, *Dark Cinema: American Film Noir in Cultural Perspective* (Westport, Conn.: Greenwood Press, 1984), p. xxi.

18. Charles Higham and Joel Greenberg, *Hollywood in the Forties* (New York: A. S. Barnes, 1968), pp. 19, 21.

19. Raymond Durgnat, "The Family Tree of the Film Noir," *Cinema* (U.K.), nos. 6–7 (1970), pp. 49–56. A somewhat revised listing appeared in *Film Comment,* November–December 1974, pp. 6–7.

20. Janey Place and Lowell S. Peterson, "Some Visual Motifs of Film Noir," *Film Comment,* January–February 1974, p. 32.

21. Place, "Women in Film Noir," p. 54.

22. Robert G. Porfirio, "No Way Out: Existential Motifs in the Film Noir," *Sight and Sound,* Autumn 1976, p. 213.

23. Richard Dorfman, "Conspiracy City," *Journal of Popular Film and Television,* 1980, p. 435.

24. Durgnat, "The Family Tree," p. 49.

25. Place, "Women in Film Noir," pp. 36–39.

26. Hirsch, *The Dark Side of the Screen,* p. 72.

27. Tuska, *Dark Cinema*, p. xvi.
28. Ibid., pp. 151–52.

## BIBLIOGRAPHICAL CHECKLIST

### Books

Alloway, Lawrence. *Violent America: The Movies 1946–1964*. New York: Museum of Modern Art, 1971.

Borde, Raymond, and Étienne Chaumeton. *Panorama du Film Noir Américain*. Paris: Editions du Minuit, 1955.

Deming, Barbara. *Running Away from Myself: A Dream Portrait of America Drawn from the Films of the Forties*. New York: Grossman, 1969.

Eisner, Lotte H. *The Haunted Screen: Expressionism in the German Cinema and the Influence of Max Reinhardt*. Berkeley: University of California Press, 1969.

Hirsch, Foster. *The Dark Side of the Screen: Film Noir*. San Diego: A. S. Barnes, 1981.

Kaplan, E. Ann, ed. *Women in Film Noir*. London: British Film Institute, 1978.

Karimi, Amir Massoud. *Toward a Definition of the American Film Noir*. New York: Arno Press, 1970.

McArthur, Colin. *Underworld USA*. New York: Viking Press, 1972.

McCarthy, Todd, and Charles Flynn, eds. *Kings of the Bs: Working Within the Hollywood System*. New York: E. P. Dutton, 1975.

Madden, David, ed. *Tough Guy Writers of the Thirties*. Carbondale: Southern Illinois University Press, 1968.

O'Brien, Geoffrey. *Hardboiled America: The Lurid Years of Paperbacks*. New York: Van Nostrand Reinhold, 1981.

Ottoson, Robert. *A Reference Guide to the American Film Noir, 1940–1958*. Metuchen, N.J.: Scarecrow Press, 1981.

Ray, Robert B. *A Certain Tendency of the Hollywood Cinema, 1930–1980*. Princeton, N.J.: Princeton University Press, 1985.

Rosow, Eugene. *Born to Lose: The Gangster Film in America*. New York: Oxford University Press, 1978.

Selby, Spencer. *Dark City: The Film Noir*. Jefferson, N.C.: McFarland, 1984.

Shadoian, Jack. *Dreams and Dead Ends: The American Gangster/Crime Film*. Cambridge, Mass.: MIT Press, 1977.

Silver, Alain, and Elizabeth Ward, eds. *Film Noir: An Encyclopedic Reference to the American Style*. Woodstock, N.Y.: Overlook Press, 1979.

Tuska, Jon. *Dark Cinema: American Film Noir in Cultural Perspective*. Westport, Conn.: Greenwood Press, 1984.

———. *The Detective in Hollywood*. New York: Doubleday, 1978.

Wolfenstein, Martha, and Nathan Leites. *Movies: A Psychological Study*. New York: Atheneum, 1970.

Wood, Michael. *America in the Movies*. New York: Basic Books, 1975.

### Shorter Works

Appel, Alfred, Jr. "The End of the Road: Dark Cinema and *Lolita*," *Film Comment*, September–October 1974, pp. 25–31.

————. "Fritz Lang's American Nightmare," *Film Comment,* November–December 1974, pp. 12–17.

Butler, Jeremy G. "*Miami Vice* and the Legacy of Film Noir," *Journal of Popular Film and Television,* Fall 1985, pp. 127–38.

Cohen, Mitchell S. "Villains and Victims," *Film Comment,* November–December 1974, pp. 27–29.

Coursen, David. "Closing Down the Open Road: *Detour,*" *Movietone News,* 29 February 1976, pp. 16–19.

Damico, James. "Film Noir: A Modest Proposal," *Film Reader,* February 1978, pp. 48–57.

————. "The Light Is Dark Enough: Film Noir Comedies of the Forties," *Movietone News,* 4 November 1977, pp. 2–7.

Dorfman, Richard. "Conspiracy City," *Journal of Popular Film and Television* 7, no. 4, 1980, pp. 434–56.

————. "*D.O.A.* and the Notion of Noir," *Movietone News,* 29 February 1976, pp. 11–16.

Durgnat, Raymond. "Paint It Black: The Family Tree of Film Noir," *Film Comment,* November–December 1974, pp. 6–7.

Dyer, Richard. "Homosexuality and Film Noir," *Jump Cut* 16, 1977, pp. 18–21.

Everson, William K. "British Film Noir," *Films in Review,* June–July 1987, pp. 340–46.

Farber, Stephen. "Violence and the Bitch Goddess," *Film Comment,* November–December 1974, pp. 8–11.

Flinn, Tom. "*The Big Heat* and *The Big Combo:* Rogue Cops and Mink-Coated Girls," *Velvet Light Trap* 11, 1974, pp. 23–28.

————. "Out of the Past," *Velvet Light Trap,* Fall 1973, pp. 38–43.

————. "Three Faces of Film Noir," *Velvet Light Trap,* Summer 1972, pp. 11–16.

Gregory, Charles. "Living Life Sideways," *Journal of Popular Film* 5, nos. 3 and 4, 1976, pp. 289–311.

Gross, Larry. "Film *après* Noir," *Film Comment,* July–August 1976, pp. 44–49.

Harvey, John. "Out of the Light: An Analysis of Narrative in *Out of the Past,*" *Journal of American Studies,* April 1984, pp. 73–87.

Higham, Charles, and Joel Greenberg. "Black Cinema," in *Hollywood in the Forties.* New York: A. S. Barnes, 1968.

House, Rebecca R. "Night of the Soul: American Film Noir," *Studies in Popular Culture* 9, no. 1, 1986, pp. 61–83.

Kerr, Paul. "Out of What Past? Notes on the B Film Noir," *Screen Education,* Autumn–Winter 1979–1980, pp. 45–65.

Krutnik, Frank. "Desire, Transgression and James M. Cain: Fiction into Film Noir," *Screen,* May–June 1982, pp. 31–44.

Madden, David. "James M. Cain and the Movies of the Thirties and Forties," *Film Heritage,* Summer 1967, pp. 9–25.

Maltby, Richard. "Film Noir: The Politics of the Maladjusted Text," *Journal of American Studies,* April 1984, pp. 49–71.

Place, Janey A., and Lowell S. Peterson. "Some Visual Motifs of Film Noir," *Film Comment,* January–February 1974, pp. 30–32.

Place, Janey, "Women in Film Noir," in *Women in Film Noir,* ed. E. Ann Kaplan. London: British Film Institute, 1978, pp. 35–67.

Polan, Dana. "College Course File: Film Noir," *Journal of Film and Video*, Spring 1985, pp. 75–83.

Porfirio, Robert G. "No Way Out: Existential Motifs in the Film Noir," *Sight and Sound*, Autumn 1976, pp. 212–17.

———. "Whatever Happened to the Film Noir?: *The Postman Always Rings Twice* (1946–1981)," *Literature/Film Quarterly* 13, no. 2, 1985, pp. 102–11.

Schrader, Paul. "Notes on Film Noir," *Film Comment*, Spring 1972, pp. 8–13.

Silver, Alain. "*Kiss Me Deadly:* Evidence of a Style," *Film Comment*, March–April 1975, pp. 24–36.

Telotte, J. P. "A Consuming Passion: Food and Film Noir," *Georgia Review*, Summer 1985, pp. 397–410.

———. "Film Noir and the Dangers of Discourse," *Quarterly Review of Film Studies*, Spring 1984, pp. 101–12.

———. "*Kiss Me Deadly*'s Apocalyptic Discourse," *Journal of Popular Film and Television*, Summer 1985, pp. 69–79.

Whitehall, Richard. "Some Thoughts on Fifties Gangster Films," *Velvet Light Trap*, Winter 1974, pp. 17–19.

Whitney, John S. "A Filmography of Film Noir," *Journal of Popular Film* 5, nos. 3 and 4, 1976, pp. 320–71.

Wood, Nancy. "Women in Film Noir," *Cine-Tracts*, Spring 1979, pp. 74–79.

Wood, Robin. "Ideology, Genre, Auteur," *Film Comment*, January–February 1977, pp. 46–51.

## SELECTED FILMOGRAPHY

1941    *The Maltese Falcon* (100 minutes).

Warner Brothers. Producer: Hal B. Wallis. Director: John Huston. Screenplay: John Huston, from the novel by Dashiell Hammett. Cast: Humphrey Bogart (Sam Spade), Mary Astor (Brigid O'Shaughnessy), Gladys George (Iva Archer), Peter Lorre (Joel Cairo), Barton MacLane (Lt. Detective Dundy), Lee Patrick (Effie Perine), Sydney Greenstreet (Kasper Gutman), Ward Bond (Detective Tom Polhaus).

1944    *Double Indemnity* (106 minutes).

Paramount. Producer: Joseph Sistrom. Director: Billy Wilder. Screenplay: Billy Wilder and Raymond Chandler from the novel by James M. Cain. Cast: Fred MacMurray (Walter Neff), Barbara Stanwyck (Phyllis Dietrichson), Edward G. Robinson (Barton Keyes), Jean Heather (Lola Dietrichson), Tom Powers (Mr. Dietrichson), Porter Hall (Mr. Jackson), Byron Barr (Nino Zachetti).

1945    *Scarlet Street* (102 minutes).

Universal. Producer: Fritz Lang. Director: Fritz Lang. Screenplay: Dudley Nichols, from the novel and play *La Chienne* by Georges de la Fouchardiere. Cast: Edward G. Robinson (Christopher Cross), Joan Bennett (Kitty March), Dan Duryea (Johnny Prince), Margaret Lindsay (Millie), Rosalind Ivan (Adele Cross), Samuel S. Hinds (Charles Pringle), Arthur Loft (Dellarowe), Vladimir Sokoloff (Pop Lejon).

*Detour* (68 minutes).

Producers Releasing Corporation. Producer: Leon Fromkess. Director: Edgar G.

Ulmer. Screenplay: Martin Goldsmith. Cast: Tom Neal (Al Roberts), Ann Savage (Vera), Claudia Drake (Sue), Edmund MacDonald (Charles Haskell, Jr.), Tim Ryan (Diner Proprietor), Roger Clark, Pat Gleason, Esther Howard.

1946    *The Killers* (105 minutes).
Universal. Producer: Mark Hellinger. Director: Robert Siodmak. Screenplay: Anthony Veiller, from the short story by Ernest Hemingway. Cast: Burt Lancaster ("Swede"—Ole Andreson), Edmond O'Brien (Jim Riordan), Ava Gardner (Kitty Collins), Albert Dekker (Colfax), Jeff Corey (Blinky), Virginia Christine (Lilly), Vince Barnett (Charleston), Charles D. Brown (Packy).

1947    *Brute Force* (98 minutes).
Universal-International. Producer: Mark Hellinger. Director: Jules Dassin. Screenplay: Richard Brooks, from a story by Robert Patterson. Cast: Burt Lancaster (Joe Collins), Hume Cronyn (Capt. Munsey), Charles Bickford (Gallagher), Sam Levene (Louie), Howard Duff (Soldier), Art Smith (Dr. Walters), Roman Bohnen (Warden Barnes), John Hoyt (Spencer).

*Out of the Past* (94 minutes).
RKO. Producer: Warren Duff. Director: Jacques Tourneur. Screenplay: Geoffrey Homes (Daniel Mainwaring), from his novel *Build My Gallows High*. Cast: Robert Mitchum (Jeff Bailey), Jane Greer (Kathie Moffet), Kirk Douglas (Whit Sterling), Rhonda Fleming (Meda Carson), Richard Webb (Jim), Steve Brodie (Fisher), Virginia Huston (Ann), Paul Valentine (Joe Stefanos).

1949    *White Heat* (114 minutes).
Warner Brothers. Producer: Lou Edelman. Director: Raoul Walsh. Screenplay: Ivan Goff and Ben Roberts; suggested by a story by Virginia Kellogg. Cast: James Cagney (Cody Jarrett), Virginia Mayo (Verna Jarrett), Edmond O'Brien (Hank Fallon/Vic Pardo), Margaret Wycherly (Ma Jarrett), Steve Cochran (Big Ed Somers), John Archer (Phillip Evans), Wally Cassell (Cotton Valetti), Fred Clark (the Trader).

1950    *Night And The City* (95 minutes).
20th Century-Fox. Producer: Samuel G. Engel. Director: Jules Dassin. Screenplay: Jo Eisinger; from the novel by Gerald Kersh. Cast: Richard Widmark (Harry Fabian), Gene Tierney (Mary Bristol), Googie Withers (Helen Nosseross), Hugh Marlowe (Adam Dunn), Francis L. Sullivan (Phil Nosseross), Herbert Lom (Kristo), Stanislaus Zbyszko (Gregorius), Mike Mazurki (Strangler).

*D.O.A.* (83 minutes).
United Artists. Producer: Leo C. Popkin. Director: Rudolph Maté. Screenplay: Russell Rouse and Clarence Greene. Cast: Edmond O'Brien (Frank Bigelow), Pamela Britton (Paula Gibson), Luther Adler (Majak), Beverly Campbell (Miss Foster), Lynn Baggett (Mrs. Phillips), William Ching (Halliday), Neville Brand (Chester), Henry Hart (Stanley Phillips).

1953    *The Big Heat* (89 minutes).
Columbia. Producer: Robert Arthur. Director: Fritz Lang. Screenplay: Sydney Boehm; from the novel by William P. McGivern. Cast: Glenn Ford (Dave Bannion), Gloria Grahame (Debby Marsh), Jocelyn Brando (Katie Bannion), Alexander Scourby (Mike Lagana), Lee Marvin (Vince Stone), Jeanette Nolan (Bertha Duncan), Peter Whitney (Tierney), Willis Bouchey (Lt. Wilkes).

1955   *Kiss Me Deadly* (105 minutes).
United Artists. Producer: Robert Aldrich. Director: Robert Aldrich. Screenplay: A. I. Bezzerides; from the novel by Mickey Spillane. Cast: Ralph Meeker (Mike Hammer), Albert Dekker (Dr. Soberin), Paul Stewart (Carl Evello), Maxine Cooper (Velda), Gaby Rodgers (Gabrielle/Lily Carver), Wesley Addy (Pat), Juano Hernandez (Eddie Yeager), Nick Dennis (Nick).

1958   *Touch of Evil* (95 minutes).
Universal-International. Producer: Albert Zugsmith. Director: Orson Welles. Screenplay: Orson Welles; from the novel *Badge of Evil* by Whit Masterson. Cast: Charleton Heston (Ramon Miguel ''Mike'' Vargas), Janet Leigh (Susan Vargas), Orson Welles (Hank Quinlan), Joseph Calleia (Pete Menzies), Akim Tamiroff (Uncle Joe Grandi), Joanna Moore (Marcia Linnekar), Marlene Dietrich (Tanya), Ray Collins (Adair).

1974   *Chinatown* (131 minutes).
Paramount–Penthouse–The Long Road Productions. Producer: Robert Evans. Director: Roman Polanski. Screenplay: Robert Towne. Cast: Jack Nicholson (J. J. Gittes), Faye Dunaway (Evelyn Mulwray), John Huston (Noah Cross), Perry Lopez (Escobar), John Hillerman (Yelburton), Darrell Zwerling (Hollis Mulwray), Diane Ladd (Ida Sessions), Roy Jenson (Mulvihill).

1981   *Body Heat* (113 minutes).
Warner Brothers. Producer: Fred T. Gallo. Director: Lawrence Kasdan. Screenplay: Lawrence Kasdan. Cast: William Hurt (Ned Racine), Kathleen Turner (Matty Walker), Richard Crenna (Edmund Walker), Ted Danson (Peter Lowenstein), J. A. Preston (Oscar Grace), Mickey Rourke (Teddy Lewis), Kim Zimmer (Mary Ann), Jane Hallaren (Stella).

# 6

## The World War II Combat Film

KATHRYN KANE

Film genre criticism is the practice of critically examining a selection of films that have a common element—such as subject matter—to determine whether those common elements are significant and whether they actually serve to unite a number of films into a cohesive group. Such a grouping would reveal whether the common elements are merely fortuitous or symptomatic of a shared underlying structure. The advantage of examining films through such groupings is to better understand the individual parts of each film and to reveal dimensions of the films that would not otherwise be apparent or seem significant when the film is viewed separately. The end result is a more complete and accurate understanding, and even assessment, of the individual film—and of the filmmaking process.

John G. Cawelti's study of the western, *The Six-Gun Mystique,* is a landmark analysis of a film group in terms of scope, consistency, and detail. Others since have followed his lead. What Cawelti did was to posit a paradigm for a group of similar films—westerns—based on a defining structure of the group, the frontier conflict between the forces of civilization and those of savagery. He then traced this structure through the narrative elements of character, plot, and setting.

Thus, for Cawelti, everything in the western became an aspect of the underlying structure. The western setting, for example, is not a mere backdrop for the action, but a source of conflict in itself, something to be tamed or contended with, a visual embodiment of the central conflict (e.g., the fort as the advance of civilization), or an image of the dramatic and/or moral position of the characters (e.g., the savage's association with the wilderness). In Cawelti's western, a complex of characters act out the various permutations of the conflict. Certain types represent civilization (the schoolteacher, the banker, the cleric), while others represent savagery (Indians, outlaws), with the hero poised in between. And the action, no matter what specific form it takes, centers on the struggle for supremacy of civilization over savagery.

The value of Cawelti's study, and others like it, is the ability to identify many patterned similarities in the films' narratives which yield up an underlying structure, not only in the individual film but also in the group of similar films. As a result, it becomes evident that the group of films may have a meaning or possibilities of meanings of which the individual film is one expression. In a real sense, then, the whole is more than the sum of its individual parts.

*The Six-Gun Mystique,* along with essays by André Bazin, Jim Kitses, and Robert Warshow, suggests not only the kinds of similarities that may be contained in particular groups of films and therefore characteristic of them, but also that at least part of the meaning of a film is contingent on its relationship to a group.

There are a number of films which have been made over a span of decades and which, like the western, bear strong resemblance to each other, iconographically and narratively, especially in plot and character. They have generally been only superficially studied, often dismissed as "guts and glory," jingoistic propaganda pieces populated by ethnic stereotypes and have even been considered embarrassing minor works of otherwise respected auteurs. This chapter is an effort to allay some misconceptions, offer more precise terminology, and argue the existence of a remarkable group of films containing some individual gems.

The films in question are commonly, and loosely, referred to as war films. What is generally meant by that term, and what will be referred to here as the combat film, is those films that depict the activities of uniformed American military forces in combat with uniformed enemy forces during World War II. This eliminates discussion of costume dramas with major battle scenes, all other wars, spy dramas, films made during the war years which may refer in passing to those historical events but do not take them as the basic narrative structure. It remains for other studies to determine the nature or degree of relevance of films of Korean and Vietnam combat to this core genre.

For convenience, too, this discussion will be limited to analysis only of those combat films made during the period of 1942 to 1945. Although these years correspond to the actual years of World War II, the purpose is not to make any historical cause-and-effect connections between the films and the world outside them. Rather, this time may be said to be the formative period for the combat film genre, and the films made then to form the nucleus of that genre. Twenty-four films produced during this period meet the definition of uniformed American forces in combat with uniformed enemy forces. By definition, no World War II combat films could have been made prior to 1942, and in fact none were released for two years after the end of the war, making this a convenient cutoff. However, it should be noted that between 1948 and 1970, at least one World War II combat film was released every year.

As with Cawelti's study of the western, analysis of the combat film reveals an underlying structure of dualities, or oppositions, which are embodied in the narrative elements of the films. Here, too, is the mythic struggle between the forces of good and evil, civilization and savagery. But the combat film differs significantly from the western's mythology in that the protagonists generally did not choose to be where they are, are not taking part in this action to improve their lot or for any idealistic purpose. Rather, they are Everyman swept up by forces of history beyond their understanding, carried into a wasteland to "slay the dragon," hoping to survive to return home. There is no question of turning a wilderness into a garden; the wilderness has no intrinsic value, is sterile.

Why the men fight, then, why they are engaged in this war, what the ideological or political issues or causes might be, are not relevant topics of discourse in the films. For the purposes of the films, the war began when the Japanese attacked Pearl Harbor. To a lesser, and much less clear, extent, America became involved in the war in Europe only after it had to retaliate against the Japanese and in that event, became belligerents in Europe to help its Allies against their enemy. Significantly, very few films in this period portray combat in the European theater as it involved American forces. A number of films do portray the voluntary activities of individual Americans who enlist in the Royal Armed Forces, though.

If the causes of the war are not the main issue of the films, though, how the war is waged is. Not only do opposing dualities structure the films, but their conflicts also provide the dynamic tension that sustains the existence of—and interest in—the combat film for decades after the cessation of the historical events that spawned them.

The primary dualities are obvious: War and Peace, Civilization and Savagery. These essential dualities are extensively played out as the conflict between good and evil or American/Allies and Enemy (Japanese/German), including, for example, democratic vs. totalitarian, tolerant vs. oppressive, religious vs. atheist, fertile vs. sterile, etc. In the combat films of this period, these dualities are set forth. It remains for later films to explore their ramifications and possible inversions—for example, the kind-hearted Nazi officer or the resentful Japanese commandant, the oppressive American commander, and so on.

Other dualities exist and provide much of the narrative tension: honor vs. brutality, duty vs. self-interest, cooperation vs. individual heroism, sacrifice for others vs. personal pain. These dualities, acted out in action and in each individual's attitude toward how to fight this war, are presented in the films of this period much as morality plays, but in a number of films, and particularly in some made after this period, become much more complex and even more inverted, to show that the dualities are not so black and white, nor so clearly separated into good and evil columns. Ironically, such films are often called antiwar films, when they in fact represent a predictable place on the genre continuum as established in this formative period.

These dualities form the structure of the films and of the genre. They are embodied in the narrative elements of theme, setting, character, and plot.


## THEME

The combat films of this period may be said to be inarticulate about the causes of the war, and why the protagonists are where they are, doing what they are doing. In depicting the mythic contest, they must of necessity identify the forces of good and those of evil. They do this by demonstrating who the antagonists are, what values they represent, and how they fight. It is important to note that the films demonstrate by example what they are about; they do not intellectualize, yet values are tested in the films in order to validate their truth.

Americans are defined as the forces of good through their common attributes, which are contrasted with those of the enemy, in terms of dualities (e.g., democratic vs. totalitarian). They are people of controlled and reasoned forcefulness, with a democratic yet hierarchic world order, led by knowledgeable, capable, and humane leaders. Evocations of American culture—popular music, food, romantic rituals, home life, modern technology—are frequent and underscore a tranquil yet progressive society. The enemy, in contrast, is a creature of chaos, uncontrolled violence, and immorality. Americans are idealistic, speaking frequently of liberty, with films making constant references to symbols from American history; the enemy is cynical, negative, and enslaving.

An extraordinary number of the films of this period concern American defeats: *Bataan, Back to Bataan, Air Force, Wake Island, They Were Expendable, So Proudly We Hail,* and *Cry Havoc.* Many other films depict struggling American forces losing early encounters with the enemy, only to finally triumph in the end. The result is not only to clearly delineate good and evil forces, but also to justify the eventual violence of the forces of good as righteous retribution. In an oblique manner, then, the films do explain ''why we fight'' as a defensive war, in spite of the foreign location and eventual aggressiveness of Americans, who earn the right to victory through the suffering inflicted on them.

How Americans fight also earns them the right to victory. The sneak attack on Pearl Harbor is portrayed again and again *(Flying Tigers, Air Force, Wake Island, Stand By for Action, So Proudly We Hail)* or referred to, damning the Japanese as a treacherous enemy. Japanese soldiers feign injury or death and then attack unsuspecting Americans *(Bataan, Guadalcanal Diary, Destination Tokyo)*, and call to Americans from the jungle in broken English *(Marine Raiders, Objective, Burma!)*. The enemy beats women and children *(God Is My Co-Pilot, Back to Bataan)* and bombs hospitals *(Cry Havoc!, So Proudly We Hail, Sahara)*. In contrast, Americans are committed to waging war honorably; as Colonel Madden says, ''This is a dirty war and we've got to fight it the right way'' *(Back to Bataan)*. Americans are honorable in their respect for life—no unnecessary killing, bombing only military targets, caring for prisoners—and in their belief in fair play—no sniping, no sneaky ruses.

Two values in combat that some Americans must struggle to learn because of their conflict with traditional self-reliance and individuality are cooperation and duty. Lectures occur in numerous films about the need to work together and subordinate the desire for individual action to the common effort—no "one man armies." Lieutenant Brickley is told by his commander, "Listen, son. You and I are professionals. If the manager says 'sacrifice' we lay down the bunt and let someone else hit the home runs" *(They Were Expendable)*. Men, and women, often are called on to sacrifice their happiness, safety, or lives for others and do so willingly. "You and I don't count," Sandridge tells Dorinda, "yet if we do the job we have to do, we could be great people" *(A Guy Named Joe)*.

Women, as emblems of love and home, are cherished by Americans. They generally stay home as guardians of civilization and underline the contrast of war and peace as they see their men off and welcome them home again, and appear in memory or flashbacks in chastely romantic scenes or caring for children. Those women who do appear in combat zones, as nurses, pilots, or other military functionaries, retain their role as civilizing force. The enemy does not value women, love or romance, or children; he is sterile.

## SETTING

The combat films embody the duality of civilization vs. savagery/good vs. evil in a remarkable way. The natural world is chaotic, treacherous, mysterious, a wasteland. Order and harmony come from modern technology, which, as embodied in warships, becomes an extension of home. In combat, Americans attempt to reconstruct their society not only by imposing rules of behavior in the conduct of the war, but also by cushioning themselves from the outside world with a technology.

Since most of these films take place in the Pacific, the terrain is jungle. Those that take place in Europe show bleak, bombed-out landscapes, shells of buildings, rocky mountains, and muddy ground. The enemy is perfectly at home in this wilderness. Japanese soldiers hide in the jungle and caves, are not affected by bad food (they fish in the rivers and Americans starve in *Objective, Burma!*) or bad water *(Bataan),* and move around freely and comfortably while Americans struggle. They are regarded as animals, monkeys, mad dogs—jungle beasts.

Americans in these films protect themselves from the wilderness in their warships, which take on human—and specifically female—qualities. The B-17 bomber *Mary Ann* is treated reverentially by her crew, maternally brings them together and helps youngsters to mature, and plucks her crew from the infernos of Wake and Bataan. The tank *Lulubelle* enables her crew to hold off a German regiment from a desert oasis until it surrenders to get water *(Sahara).* The USS

*Warren,* a destroyer, not only brings a green young ensign to maturity and sinks an enemy cruiser, but actually serves as a nursery for infants saved from a lifeboat and a maternity ward for two women who give birth *(Stand By for Action).* The USS *Copperfin,* a submarine, withstands prolonged depthcharging to protect her crew—"This ship has taken more than she should have to"— and inspires great loyalty from them—"Copperfin, sweetheart, I love you!" *(Destination Tokyo).*

Warships not only provide a place of comfort and continuity to crewmen, allowing them to set up housekeeping, but also impose a sense of order on the war by defining the spatial relations between Americans and the enemy. But because it does become home, and the center of communal life for its crew, the warship prompts an emotional bond among crew and between crew and ship. Moreover, an attack on this ship, or damage to it, is considered desecration. Finally, much is made of the superiority of American technology—its warships—over that of the enemy, another means of demonstrating the preeminence of good over evil. *Mary Ann* is a superior airplane, as are *Warren* and *Copperfin.* The PT boats are a revolutionary new weapon *(They Were Expendable).*

In contrast, Americans not protected by a warship must deal directly with their hostile environment and suffer for it. They not only are less comfortable and less protected, but lacking a warship, are also less powerful and less mobile. They are more vulnerable to enemy treachery and strength. But they also are at the mercy of a malevolent wilderness, where they suffer from heat, insects, disease, and the constant threat of a hidden enemy. They never really know where they are, either on their way to some obscure island in the middle of a vast expanse of ocean, or moving from one faceless place to another in the wilderness. One soldier: "What town did we just take?" Second soldier: "That was San Raviolio." First soldier: "I thought we took that yesterday?" Second soldier: "Nah, that was San Something Elsio" *(The Story of G.I. Joe).* Americans rarely speak any language other than English, relying on natives to communicate with them. The enemy often speaks English to Americans.

Americans rely on their technology to enable them to triumph over their environment and ultimately over the enemy. Their faith is rewarded in the end, but when they are deprived of their technology, they can be destroyed, a process depicted graphically in *Objective, Burma!.*

## CHARACTER

The cast of character types in the combat films of this period embody the values of the films and demonstrate the attributes that define Americans as good. The protagonists in most films are the group of soldiers/airmen/sailors who will wage combat against the enemy. The group comprises representatives of various ethnic and geographic groups, ages, military ranks and attitudes toward the war. Each classification serves a function beyond representing a diverse society.

White Anglo-Saxon Protestants (WASPS) are the most represented ethnic group. By virtue of their frequency, their prominent positions and the deference others give them, they tend to be the norm for the group. They are serious, though good-humored, not comical or passionate, but middle-class, somewhat sophisticated and educated, and from small towns or agricultural states. The major exception to this general behavior is in films about fighter pilots, who are almost exclusively WASPS, and frequently infantile. Officers are usually WASPS.

The Irish are almost as prevalent as the WASPs and appear in all ranks, including many officers. They can be somewhat staid, like the WASPs, or more comic, tough, and proletarian. They are home-loving and sentimental, often prizing their women for their maternalism (Murphy's bride kisses him on the cheek and pulls his blanket up when he falls asleep on their wedding night in *The Story of G.I. Joe;* Mike plays a record of his wife's voice in *Destination Tokyo;* Irish chiefs serenade Lieutenant Ryan's sweetheart with "Dear Old Girl" in *They Were Expendable*). They are religious, respectful of authority, and occasionally slightly rebellious but come around to cooperation easily. They manifest many of the values of the group.

Jews are confined mostly to the enlisted ranks: Corporal Weinberg *(Air Force),* Corporal Feingold *(Bataan),* Private Friedman *(Walk in the Sun),* and Private Klein *(Guadalcanal Diary).* Although there are not a lot of them, they tend to be comic, popular, genial, optimistic, and somewhat vulgar. They also serve a function in being peacemakers in the group when personal conflicts arise.

Polish Americans appear, especially early in the period: Winocki *(Air Force),* Matowski *(Bataan),* Woliczek *(So Proudly We Hail),* and Warnicki *(The Story of G.I. Joe).* They are never officers, except for native Poles who join the RAF. They are tall and blond, home loving, friendly, and a little slow-witted and stubborn. At worst, they may become obsessed with revenge and make mistakes which lead to their deaths. They are then examples of how not to wage war.

Italians appear late in the period: Private Migliori *(Objective, Burma!),* Private Rivera *(Walk in the Sun),* and Private Dondaro *(The Story of G.I. Joe).* They physically resemble the Jews in being small, dark, and somewhat vulgar, but they are very tough and passionate. They also are more sexually active and loyal to their officers, and they serve as models for masculine behavior that allows affection between men.

In addition to ethnicity, where a person comes from provides certain traits. Brooklyn gave many sons to combat films as a miniature melting pot. WASP, Irish, Italian, and Jewish characters claim Brooklyn as home. They are vulgar in grammar and taste, popular and comic, proletarian, happy, and unambitious. They demonstrate a correlation between social class and military rank—with the lowest levels virtually parallel and those at the bottom satisfied to be there.

New Yorkers, as the other big-city representatives, are neither as talkative nor as comic as their neighbors. They are more self-aware, sober, and mature. They tend to be noncommissioned officers, again paralleling military and social orders.

Texans are common, too. Tall and lanky in contrast to their urban counterparts, they speak correctly but with an accent, suggesting more education. They are self-contained and prone to individual action, but cooperate easily. As somewhat more educated, from agricultural areas, apparently middle-class, they tend to be officers.

While regions correlate to social class and military rank, age correlates to experience. Kids are close to their mothers, admire their superiors, are more religious—and so represent those values. As they learn to adopt the lessons of how to wage war honorably, and face the enemy, they grow to maturity. They also lose their innocence, another duality that causes tension. The kid has to lose his innocence or die, but all the men realize their own loss and mourn it. The kid is taken in hand by an older man, the veteran of the group, and guided along; they share the traits of being religious and perceiving the maternal qualities of women. The older man also provides stability for the group and continuity with the past. The kid and the older man almost always appear together. The rest of the men are neither too young nor too old.

As indicated above, rank tends to parallel social rank, which is determined by ethnic and regional background. Rank also demonstrates something of a natural order to the world. Officers are better educated, and their frequent use of football images suggests college experience. Other men tend to use baseball images of the common man. Officers are tough, capable soldiers and never wrong in their military decisions. The competence of officers is taken for granted by everyone in these films. On those occasions when the men question their orders, they obey them anyway and the validity of the orders is ultimately borne out. Officers may be misunderstood, but they are not wrong. The higher ranking they are, the more able they presumably are, but the less part they take in the action. However, they do serve to legitimize the action. The few generals portrayed in the films—Doolittle *(Thirty Seconds Over Tokyo)*, Chenault *(God Is My Co-Pilot)*, Stilwell *(Objective, Burma!)*, MacArthur *(They Were Expendable)*, Gilpatrick *(A Guy Named Joe)*—are, with one exception, historic figures. They make the decisions and plans that others carry out and their success proves them right. They, or anonymous War Department officers, are often pictured in Washington, D.C., with the Capitol Dome or other landmark behind them as they discuss plans or cut orders, implying continuity with the hierarchy of the government and the shared infallibility of leadership.

One final convention of characters is their attitude toward the waging of war and the function that serves. The comic generates goodwill and relieves tension. The woman chasers are occasions for negative humor; they are disapproved of because they do not value women and the sanctity of the home highly enough. Comics rarely are killed, and woman chasers either convert to a romantic relationship or are killed. In the natural order of the combat films of this period, observance of values is rewarded, and those who ignore repeated warnings to change their ways are punished.

The enemy-hater is one who becomes so obsessed with killing that he loses sight of the common good and the need for controlled force. Although prompted by the desire to avenge the death of another, his passion for killing kills him (Alvarez in *Guadalcanal Diary,* Olivia in *So Proudly We Hail,* Frenchie in *Sahara*). The lone wolf, who self-centeredly acts alone for his own glory (Woody in *Flying Tigers,* Lieutenant Coe in *Eagle Squadron,* Captain Sandridge in *A Guy Named Joe*), is distrusted by others because of his refusal to cooperate in common efforts; he is killed and serves as an example to others of the need to work together and subordinate self. The malcontent resents the military and the need to take orders (Winocki in *Air Force,* Todd in *Bataan,* McCloskey in *Wake Island*). Their personal grudge is shown to be based on faulty reasoning and they generally change their ways; again they are examples of the need to subsume self for the common good.

The dualities embodied in the characters provide considerable tension in these films which is generally not deeply explored nor its many ramifications considered. The films are more concerned with defining the structural elements of the genre, and it remains for later films to stretch and invert them.

## PLOT

Perhaps the ultimate in the combat films' dualities and the narrative conflicts they cause is the plot. There are two axes here. The action can focus on victory or defeat, and on the pulling together of the characters into a strongly united group with shared values and affections, or the disintegration of the group through death in combat. The movement toward victory or defeat is depicted in scenes of combat. The movement toward integration and disintegration is depicted in scenes of general behavior in and out of battle. One aspect of each axis appears and forms the action of all the films.

In most films, the group reaches eventual victory and in the course of that action becomes integrated: *Air Force, Back to Bataan, Crash Dive, Eagle Squadron, Flying Fortress, Flying Tigers, Destination Tokyo, Guadalcanal Diary, God Is My Co-Pilot, Gung Ho!, A Guy Named Joe, Marine Raiders, Stand By for Action, Thirty Seconds Over Tokyo,* and *A Wing and a Prayer.* In some films, the group achieves victory but most are killed: *The Story of G.I. Joe, Objective, Burma!, Sahara,* and to some extent, *A Walk in the Sun.* In other films, the group is killed and is defeated: *Bataan, So Proudly We Hail, They Were Expendable,* and *Wake Island.* It can be argued that in two cases, the group pulls together psychologically in the course of a defeat: *Bataan* (everyone dies—disintegration—but they are friends in the end) and *Cry Havoc!.*

Combat itself is the cause of any disintegration, in that men get killed, whether victory or defeat is the outcome. Groups never disintegrate psychologically, only physically. On the other hand, integration, the psychological uniting of the members of the group into a cohesive whole with shared values and purpose, is the cause of victory. Over and over again, the films insist that victory can only be achieved through honorable and cooperative means. Even in the many films in which the outcome is military defeat, the films claim moral victory because, through the efforts of the integrated group, time was purchased for others to arm themselves and, inspired by the group's sacrifice, to avenge their deaths with ultimate victory.

The mythic struggle of the combat films is elaborately placed in a historic contest in many of the films. (It should be clear by now that the generic world and requirements of the films, and the selectivity of the filmmaking process, preclude the possibility of the films actually serving as pseudodocumentaries of World War II combat, although that is the impression they try to give.) Many films open with a map of the area of combat to be shown *(Bataan, Cry Havoc!, Destination Tokyo, Thirty Seconds Over Tokyo)* or the terrain *(Back to Bataan, Eagle Squadron, God Is My Co-Pilot, Objective, Burma!)*. They may be dedicated to the branch of service about to be portrayed and play an American anthem or service theme song; all of this is done during the credits. Then a prologue often sets the scene in terms of location and year ("Somewhere in the South Pacific, July 26, 1942" in *Guadalcanal Diary*, for example). The events preceding the film's action may be recounted. All of this sets the historic framework of the film's action.

An epilogue summarizes the moral and often calls for action: "So fought the heroes of Bataan, making possible the victories in the Coral Sea" *(Bataan);* "This is not the end. There are other leathernecks who will exact a just and terrible vengeance" *(Wake Island);* Ernie Pyle's comments, "I hope we can rejoice with victory . . . that all together we will try to reassemble our broken world" *(The Story of G.I. Joe)*.

The body of the film then, in general, shows the transmission and reception of orders, assembling of the group, communication to the men of the mission, preparation of weapons, general conversation and relaxation, departure from home, arrival at destination, alternating scenes of combat and life in the combat zone, aftermath.

Daily life in the combat zone is a sequence of rituals: cigarette smoking and coffee drinking, a kid learning to shave, playing records or reading mail from home, sitting or lying down in groups talking, letter writing, listening to music. These scenes often track the progress of integration of the group and can include subplots, such as a developing romance, the conversion of the malcontent, and the adoption of pets, which represent the unity of the men, someone to care about them and their vulnerability.

Again, the films of this period define and set out the elements of narrative of the combat film genre. Some of them make unusual, even extraordinary use of the new conventions, revealing their conflicts and ramifications, turning them around, allowing things to happen that strict adherence to stereotyping wouldn't allow. For example, Sergeant Warnicki, the capable, responsible Polish American respected by the men he commands, breaks down mentally under the strain of battle, a fate not likely for a strong, major character *(The Story of G.I. Joe);* though never overtly stated, the implicit criticism of leadership for the number of deaths in the group *(Objective, Burma);* the cynicism of the malcontent to the end—and he's correct but criticized *(Bataan).*

By 1948, such films as *12 O'Clock High* and *Command Decision* began to examine more closely some of the dualities contained in the genre. These two films in particular looked at the conflict between the decisions of a commanding officer according to what worked and the commonly expressed values, and the emotional toll that conflict took on him as his men died following his orders. In the 1950 film *Halls of Montezuma* an officer suffers debilitating migraine headaches going into battle. Men suspicious of their officers' competence and courage is a frequent theme in the late 1940s and 1950s, but they are proved wrong.

The 1956 film *Attack!* inverted the conventions that guaranteed the competence of the military hierarchy, and justified with ultimate victory the suffering that soldiers must go through. In this film, the commanding officer twice fails to reinforce his men, resulting in their deaths. An enraged lieutenant, his arm ripped off during an attack when an enemy tank runs over it, returns to kill his officer but instead dies at his feet. The panicked officer mocks the fallen lieutenant and is supported by his superior, who hopes to build a political career in civilian life through this officer. The officer is shot by another lieutenant who calls the general's headquarters to report the incident. The film does not show whether he reaches the general nor what the outcome will be, but the evidence of the film substantiates overall faith in traditional values and justice, despite pockets of corruption in the ranks.

The 1980 film *The Big Red One,* which traces the progress of a squad of soldiers in the famous First Division through North Africa, Sicily, D-day, Belgium and Czechoslovakia, is a remarkably faithful example of the combat genre film, updated with more swearing and remarks about sexuality. The central group is small—the sergeant, Griff, Johnson (a pig farmer), Vinci (a street kid), and Zab (a writer from the Bronx)—but tightly knit, protecting each other and refusing to get to know newcomers to the squad because they don't want to get too attached to men who are constantly in danger of being killed. ("You know how to smoke out a sniper? You send a guy out in the open and see if he gets shot," Zab explains, as the men argue about whose turn it is to take the point and tell the sergeant he should send a newcomer.) Although the film is clear that war is insane (the squad liberates an insane asylum and an inmate grabs a gun, shooting it and saying, "I am one of you, I am sane.") and sacrilegious, it is equally clear that this war is a just war, that the enemy is fighting for a perverted cause, oppressing people who hate them, and guilty of the horrors of the concentration camps. Nevertheless, waging war is dehumanizing, since the sergeant's justification, "We don't murder, we kill," is echoed by an enemy sergeant, to whom a soldier responds, "It's the same thing." The soldiers in this film are young and decent, honoring a deal with a young Sicilian boy to bury his mother, delivering a baby, caring for the people liberated from the camp. When the sergeant unknowingly kills a German four hours after the end of the war (as he had done in World War I), and in spite of his grief over the death of another young boy, he fights to save the aforementioned German. The lesson of this film: "Surviving is the only glory in war." The plot is one of group integration and victory; the icons are reassuringly familiar.

No thorough in-depth examination has been done of the combat film through the years, including the shifts of values or in conventions over time and due to the political and ideological conditions of the Korean and Vietnam wars. Evidence that the conventions are still dynamic lies not only in *The Big Red One* but also in such recent films on Vietnam as *Go Tell the Spartans* and *Apocalypse Now*.

*Go Tell the Spartans* depicts the actions of military assistance advisory group team 7, commanded by Major Barker. The setting is conventional jungle and military outposts, though the iconography is updated: olive drab fatigues with white name tags over the pocket, baseball caps, 1960s military equipment, including helicopters. The values of the group—relaxed, informal, disillusioned, defiant, pragmatic—are put in perspective by two men: native Lieutenant Hamilton who spouts patriotic slogans about the need to kill communists (ideological speeches are infrequent and uncomfortable in earlier films) and is laughed at by the others, and a Vietnamese sergeant called Cowboy who tortures and beheads prisoners and urges the killing of women and children as possible enemies (that he is extreme, but proved correct, makes him a conventional "enemy hater" type). References to venereal disease, divorce, and promiscuity demonstrate that the value of the home, and the woman as representative of the home, is no longer so compelling; the major remains a major after being discovered in a tryst with a general's wife. Soldiers drink and take drugs, are "burned out" and act irrational—the occasional behavior of a few men has here become more common and more frequent, showing a lack of moral purpose. All here are volunteers, either idealistic or career military, providing assistance to the Vietnamese—"it's their war." But there is an implicit regret that old values are no longer so operative.

The plot requires the group to capture a town in the jungle, of no intrinsic worth but strategically important. When the town is attacked, Major Barker brings in reinforcements for Lieutenant Hamilton. When the group still is surrounded and the situation becomes hopeless, they are ordered to fly all Americans out, leaving the Vietnamese soldiers behind. Corporal Corsey refuses to leave the other soldiers, and Major Barker unexpectedly jumps out of the departing helicopter and stays behind with them. Ultimately the entire group, except Corsey, is killed.

Throughout the film, soldiers speak of the futility of their sacrifice. One says their officers are making the same mistakes the French did. Barker says,

"Sometimes I get the feeling we're in a goddamned loony bin." In the town, the soldiers view an inscription, taken from the battle of Thermopylae, over the entrance to a cemetery where French soldiers are interred: "Stranger, when you find us lying here, go tell the Spartans we obeyed their orders. 300 Spartans died trying to hold this pass." The Vietnamese soldiers are portrayed as the equals of the Americans, but the Vietnamese military hierarchy is shown to be corrupt. As he decides to remain and fight, Barker says, "This war's a sucker's tour, going nowhere, round and round in circles."

In the end, Corsey, wounded, views the stripped bodies of the dead and wanders through the town past the cemetery. A wounded enemy aims his gun at him, then drops it. Corsey looks at him and says, "I'm going home, Charlie" and keeps walking. The overall lesson here is that this war does not have the high moral purpose of World War II, it is not an American war, and soldiers do not face soldiers but people who could be innocent civilians. Nevertheless, the disillusion comes from idealism betrayed by incompetence and corruption at the highest levels, a willingness to join Vietnamese peers in a fight to victory for their country tempered by confusion over the cause of the war and the abhorrent way it's carried out. How war is waged is still central to the film; Corsey is a hero and admirable because he fights loyally, bravely, and honorably, and even cynical Major Barker agrees that Corsey is correct in his behavior and values. It is a sad and angry film mourning the betrayal of what the combat genre represents at its finest.

In contrast to this film is *Apocalypse Now,* a confused film that is part combat film, part something else. This film takes as its central character the loner of the conventional combat film, and alternately portrays him as an assassin, criminal, seedy alcoholic obsessed with violence and war, and on the other hand, as a relatively sane stranger on a journey through a land peopled by crazed killers, cynical manipulators, drug takers, and assorted bizarre characters who are officers and men of the American forces in Vietnam. Ordered to assassinate a maverick American colonel who is "operating without any decent restraint, beyond the pale of any acceptable human contact," Captain Willard feels qualms of conscience, for no American officers have been included in the six men he's already killed. The boat crew that takes him upriver consists of Chef, a machinist from New Orleans "who's not wrapped too tight"; Lance, a famous surfer from Los Angeles; Mr. Clean, a seventeen-year-old black from the south Bronx; and Philips, the black chief in charge of the boat. The crew, a group that denies the ties of a conventional group—for example, refusing an offered cigarette in a conventional group ritual because "I don't smoke"—is killed by journey's end. Conventional values are upended. Arrogant Americans nonchalantly swamp native boats, American airborne cavalry viciously attack peaceful civilians and glory in the destruction, women entertainers provide erotic dances and must be flown to safety as troops swarm onstage, a priest says mass during battle. As the boat crew inspects a native sampan, Mr. Clean suddenly opens fire and kills the civilians who show no evidence of enemy activity.

When Chef tries to save one wounded woman, Willard cold-bloodedly shoots her so the mission can continue. The balance provided by *Spartans*—that innocent-looking women and children can and will kill Americans and are the enemy—is absent. The result is total perversion of conventional values, a world where "there's enough insanity and murder to go around for everyone," where the potential of war to dehumanize decent Americans has been realized to a far greater extent than before.

A purpose for the war, or rules by which it should be fought, is not coherently dealt with, nor is evidence supplied for statements such as "The war was being run by a bunch of four star clowns who were going to end up giving the whole circus away." The absence of those conventional values, their perversion in terms of the genre, is what makes the actions of the film so outrageous, the characters so unsettling. The film exerts a peculiar fascination when viewed by itself, but when viewed in the context of the combat film of World War II, it ironically becomes both less coherent and more disturbing.

The conflicts of the dualities of the World War II combat film make it rich for exploring the depiction in film of the nature of war and what it demands of those who wage it, and what they demand of themselves. Development, exploration, and inversion of the genre's conventions over the years provide a fascinating view of the artistic process of observing and stretching the limitations of a genre and, eventually, of film referencing previous films. A thorough examination of the combat film over the years is long overdue.

## BIBLIOGRAPHICAL OVERVIEW

Little scholarly attention has been given to the combat film as such, nor in fact has much attention been given to the films of the war years.

Harry Sauberli's master's degree thesis, "Hollywood and World War II: A Survey of Themes of Hollywood Films about the War, 1940–1945" (1967), and Roger Manvell's *Films and the Second World War* (1974) are useful for their organization of data about industry production during the war years, but merely provide plot synopses and film reviews rather than in-depth analysis.

Norman Kagan's *The War Film* (1974) is helpful in its selected analyses of some films and identification of shifts in themes and treatment over the years. The author also is careful to separate combat films from other kinds of war films (e.g., espionage). *The Films of World War II*, edited by Joe Morelle, Edward Z. Epstein, and John Griggs (1973), relies on plot synopses and lots of stills and quotes from reviews. *Film, Book 2: Films of Peace and War*, edited by Robert Hughes (1962), is a mixed bag like the others, but moralistic. It spends some time discussing the "antiwar" film, while failing to define that or the "war" film or to distinguish between the two.

None of these works, in fact, attempts to define the war film, often grouping Russian newsreels with comedies about the housing shortage.

Some of the best and most perceptive analyses of the World War II combat film were contained in reviews by Manny Farber and James Agee of the films when released. In his reviews for the *New Republic* during the war years, Farber categorized different kinds of films about the war: (1) the branch of service film, praising one of the armed forces; (2) half-fictional battle accounts; (3) the resistance of nations; and (4) the home front.[1] Farber himself preferred the first two types of films—the combat film. He also explored what the films were doing. These films, he said, presented a service type, with characters treated in groups and given ethnic names, having average looks and being friendly. These characters, according to Farber, were also short on ideas and emotions.[2] The films, he said, "defused death's blow" by presenting the war as righteous, the causes of the war, the solidarity of the home front, and the humanity of the men in a kind of shorthand, consisting of a wound or individual death, a sweetheart and a dog, respectively.[3]

In another column Farber refers to the crew of *Air Force* as "ten stock Americans taken from the drawer marked 'Service picture types.'"[4] And in his review of *A Guy Named Joe* he describes the hero type of these films as more average and less eccentric than the tall, shy cowboy and the short, tough man of the underworld, less exotic and more pedestrian than Cooper or Bogart, and the ideal family man.[5]

Farber and Agee both praised *The Story of G.I. Joe*, Farber saying the film had "more firmness about its feeling and concept than any Hollywood movie has about anything in years,"[6] and Agee, writing for *Nation*, said it was "an act of heroism to make this film."[7] Parker Tyler's 1946 article "The Waxworks of War" 1947 (in *Magic and Myth of the Movies*, 1970) is another early and perceptive review of the combat film.

*Visions of War: Hollywood Combat Films of World War II* (1982), by Kathryn Kane, analyzes the combat films of 1942–1945 in considerable detail in terms of theme, character, setting, and plot. The book includes a detailed analysis of six films from this period: *Bataan, Objective, Burma!, Air Force, Guadalcanal Diary, The Story of G.I. Joe*, and *They Were Expendable*.

Finally, *Guts & Glory: Great American War Films* (1978), by Lawrence H. Suid, provides interesting background on the production of a number of combat films up through the mid-1970s. Suid is chiefly interested in the working relationship between the filmmakers and the military as story consultants, providers of equipment and extras, censors, and clients. Tracing this relationship through the years helps to account to some extent for the shifts in treatment of combat in later films, as the two sides became less dependent on and trustful of each other. Suid also makes some interesting observations about thematic shifts in the films, though he does not discuss the individual films or the genre in great critical detail or depth.

## NOTES

1. Manny Farber, "Movies in Wartime," *New Republic*, 3 January 1944, p. 19.
2. Ibid.
3. Ibid.

4. Manny Farber, *"Air Force,"* *New Republic,* 22 February 1943, p. 254.
5. Manny Farber, *"A Guy Named Joe,"* *New Republic,* 17 January 1944, p. 84.
6. Manny Farber, *"The Story of G.I. Joe,"* *New Republic,* 13 August 1945, p. 199.
7. James Agee, *"The Story of G.I. Joe,"* *Nation,* 15 September 1945, p. 264.

## BIBLIOGRAPHICAL CHECKLIST

### Books

Deming, Barbara. *Running Away from Myself.* New York: Grossman, 1969.
Editors of *Look* Magazine. *Movie Lot to Beachhead.* New York: Doubleday, Doran, 1945.
Hughes, Robert, ed. *Film, Book 2: Films of Peace and War.* New York: Grove Press, 1962.
Jones, Dorothy B. *The Portrayal of China and India on the American Screen, 1896–1955.* Cambridge, Mass.: MIT Press, 1955.
Kagan, Norman. *The War Film.* New York: Pyramid Productions, 1974.
Kane, Kathryn. *Visions of War: Hollywood Combat Films of World War II.* Ann Arbor: University of Michigan Research Press, 1982.
Manvell, Roger. *Films and the Second World War.* New York: A. S. Barnes, 1974.
Miller, Don. *"B" Movies: An Informal Survey of the American Low Budget Film, 1933–1945.* New York: Curtis Books, 1973.
Morelle, Joe, Edward Z. Epstein, and John Griggs, eds. *The Films of World War II.* Secaucus, N.J.: Citadel Press, 1973.
*Movies at War.* New York: War Activities Committee, 1942.
*Movies at War.* New York: War Activities Committee, 1943.
Sennett, Ted. *Warner Bros. Presents.* New Rochelle, N.Y.: Arlington House, 1972.
Suid, Lawrence H. *Guts & Glory: Great American War Movies.* Reading, Mass.: Addison-Wesley, 1978.
Thorp, Margaret. *America at the Movies.* New York: Arno Press and the *New York Times,* 1970.

### Shorter Works

Agee, James. *"A Guy Named Joe,"* *Nation,* 8 January 1944, p. 52.
———. *"A Walk in the Sun,"* *Nation,* 5 January 1946, p. 24.
———. *"Objective, Burma,"* *Nation,* 24 February 1945, p. 230.
———. *"The Story of G.I. Joe,"* *Nation,* 15 September 1945, pp. 264–66.
———. *"They Were Expendable,"* *Nation,* 5 January 1946, p. 24.
———. *"Thirty Seconds Over Tokyo,"* *Nation,* 2 December 1944, p. 699.
Anderson, Lindsay. "The Method of John Ford." In *The Emergence of Film Art,* ed. Lewis Jacobs. New York: Hopkinson and Blake, 1969, pp. 230–45.
Brady, Thomas F. "The OWI Criticizes Hollywood's War Films," *New York Times,* 13 September 1942, sec. 8, p. 3.
Farber, Manny. *"Air Force,"* *New Republic,* 22 February 1943, pp. 254–55.
———. *"Bataan,"* *New Republic,* 21 June 1943, pp. 329–30.
———. *"A Guy Named Joe,"* *New Republic,* 17 January 1944, p. 84.
———. "Movies in Wartime," *New Republic,* 3 January 1944, pp. 16–20.

————. *"Objective, Burma!,"* *New Republic,* 5 March 1945, p. 335.

————. "Real War," *New Republic,* 7 September 1942, pp. 283–84.

————. *"So Proudly We Hail,"* *New Republic,* 27 September 1943, p. 426.

————. *"The Story of G.I. Joe,"* *New Republic,* 13 August 1945, p. 190.

Hines, Al. "Movies of World War II," *Holiday,* September 1949, pp. 19–20.

Jacobs, Lewis. "World War II and the American Film," *Cinema Journal,* Winter 1967–1968, pp. 1–21.

Jones, Dorothy B. "Hollywood Goes to War," *Nation,* 27 January 1945, pp. 93–95.

————. "Hollywood's War Films 1942–44." In *Annual Communications Bibliography: Supplement to Volume 1 of Hollywood Quarterly.* Berkeley: University of California Press, 1942.

McClure, Arthur F. "Hollywood at War: The American Motion Picture and World War II, 1939–1945," *Journal of Popular Film,* Spring 1971, pp. 122–35.

Othman, Frederick C. "War in a World of Make-Believe," *Saturday Evening Post,* October 17, 1942, pp. 28–29.

Pinthus, Kurt. "History Directs the Movies," *American Scholar,* Autumn 1941, pp. 483–97.

Sauberli, Harry Albert, Jr. "Hollywood and World War II: A Survey of Themes of Hollywood Films about the War, 1940–45." Master's thesis, University of Southern California, 1967.

Tyler, Parker. "The Waxworks of War." In *Magic and Myth of the Movies.* New York: Simon and Schuster, 1947, pp. 132–74.

## SELECTED FILMOGRAPHY

1942    *Stand By for Action* (109 minutes).
MGM. Producer: Roy Z. Leonard. Director: Roy Z. Leonard. Screenplay: George Bruce, Jean L. Balderston and Herman J. Mankiewicz. Cast: Robert Taylor (Lt. Masterman), Brian Donlevy (Lt. Cmdr. Roberts), Charles Laughton (Adm. Thomas), Walter Brennan (Chief Johnson).

*Wake Island* (87 minutes).
Paramount. Producer: Joseph Sistrom. Director: Joe Farrow. Screenplay: Frank Butler, W. R. Burnett. Cast: William Bendix (Smacksy Randall), Brian Donlevy (Maj. Caton), Robert Preston (Joe).

1943    *Air Force* (124 minutes).
Warner Brothers. Producer: Hal B. Wallis. Director: Howard Hawks. Screenplay: Dudley Nichols. Cast: John Ridgely (Capt. Quincannon), James Brown (Lt. Tex Rader), John Garfield (Winocki), Harry Carey (Sgt. White), George Tobias (Weinberg).

*Bataan* (114 minutes).
MGM. Producer: Irving Starr. Director: Tay Garnett. Screenplay: Robert D. Andrews. Cast: Robert Taylor (Sgt. Dana), Thomas Mitchell (Sgt. Feingold), Lloyd Nolan (Cpl. Todd), Robert Walker (Seaman Purckett).

*Destination Tokyo* (135 minutes).
Warner Brothers. Producer: Jerry Wald. Director: Delmer Daves. Screenplay: Delmer Daves and Albert Malz. Cast: Cary Grant (Capt. Cassidy), John Garfield (Wolf), Dane Clark (Tin Can), Alan Hale (Cookie).

*God Is My Co-Pilot* (90 minutes).
Warner Brothers. Producer: Robert Buckner. Director: Robert Florey. Screenplay: Peter Milne and Abem Finkle. Cast: Dennis Morgan (Col. Scott), Alan Hale (Father Mike), Raymond Massey (Gen. Chenault).

*Guadalcanal Diary* (93 minutes).
20th Century-Fox. Producer: Bryan Foy. Director: Lewis Seiler. Screenplay: Lamar Trotti. Cast: Lloyd Nolan (Sgt. Hook Malone), Richard Jaeckel (Chicken Anderson), William Bendix (Taxi Potts).

*A Guy Named Joe* (120 minutes).
MGM. Producer: Everett Riskin. Director: Victor Fleming. Screenplay: Dalton Trumbo. Cast: Spencer Tracy (Capt. Sandridge), Irene Dunne (Dorinda Durston), Van Johnson (Capt. Randall), James Gleason (Gen. Gilpatrick).

*Sahara* (97 minutes).
Columbia. Producer: Zoltan Korda. Director: Rudolph Mate. Screenplay: Zoltan Korda and John Howard Lawson. Cast: Humphrey Bogart (Sgt. Joe Gunn), Rex Ingram (Tambul).

*Thirty Seconds Over Tokyo* (138 minutes).
MGM. Producer: Sam Zimbalist. Director: Mervyn LeRoy. Screenplay: Dalton Trumbo. Cast: Spencer Tracy (Gen. Doolittle), Van Johnson (Capt. Lawson).

1944 *Marine Raiders* (91 minutes).
RKO. Producer: Robert Fellows. Director: Harold Schuster. Screenplay: Warren Duff. Cast: Pat O'Brien (Maj. Lockhard), Robert Ryan (Capt. Craig), Ruth Hussey (Ella Foster).

1945 *Back to Bataan* (95 minutes).
RKO. Producer: Robert Fellows. Director: Edward Dmytryk. Screenplay: Ben Barzman and Richard H. Landau. Cast: John Wayne (Col. Joe Madden), Anthony Quinn (Capt. Andres Bonifacio).

*Objective, Burma!* (142 minutes).
Warner Brothers. Producer: Jerry Wald. Director: Raoul Walsh. Screenplay: Ronald MacDougall and Lester Cole. Cast: Erroll Flynn (Capt. Nelson), James Brown (Sgt. Tracy).

*The Story of G.I. Joe* (109 minutes).
United Artists. Producer: Lester Cowan. Director: William Wellman. Screenplay: Guy Endore, Leopold Atlas, and Philip Stevenson. Cast: Robert Mitchum (Capt. Walker), Burgess Meredith (Ernie Pyle).

*They Were Expendable* (135 minutes).
MGM. Producer: John Ford. Director: John Ford. Screenplay: Frank Wead. Cast: Robert Montgomery (Lt. Brickley), John Wayne (Lt. Ryan), Donna Reed (Lt. Davyss), Ward Bond (Chief Mulcahy).

*A Walk in the Sun* (117 minutes).
20th Century-Fox. Producer: Lewis Milestone. Director: Lewis Milestone. Screenplay: Robert Rossen. Cast: Dana Andrews (Sgt. Tyne), Richard Conte (Rivera).

# COMEDY GENRES

# 7

# Screwball Comedy

WES D. GEHRING

"Chivalry is not only dead, it's decomposing."
Rudy Vallee to Claudette Colbert in *The Palm Beach Story* (1942).

In the mid-1930s a new genre arose in American cinema based upon the old "boy meets girl" formula—gone "topsy-turvy."[1] It generally presented the eccentric, female-dominated courtship of the American rich, with the male target seldom being informed that open season had arrived. The genre was called "screwball comedy."

The birth and initial success of the genre were tied to a period of transition in American humor which had gained great momentum by the late 1920s. The dominant comedy character had been the capable crackerbarrel type of a Will Rogers; it now became an antihero best exemplified by the *New Yorker* writing of Robert Benchley and James Thurber or by the film short subjects of Leo McCarey's Laurel and Hardy. The new genre dressed up the surroundings and added beautiful people, but this was more a reflection of the need to mass-market feature films than a substantive difference. The outcome was essentially the same: an eccentrically comic battle of the sexes, with the male generally losing.

There is no easy way of explaining why the transition from capable to incompetent comic hero took place. Yet if an explanation were attempted, it would probably focus on the issue of relevance. In a world that seems more irrational every day, the antihero is fated to be forever frustrated. His frustration is the result of his attempt to create order—as did his nineteenth-century comedy counterparts—but now in a world where order is impossible. The common-sense platitudes of any updated crackerbarrel philosopher are inadequate in today's crises. The antihero is "incapable of inventing homespun maxims about hundred-megaton bombs, or of feeling any native self-confidence in the

face of uncontrollable fallout."[2] He eventually deals with this frightening outside world by not dealing with it at all. Instead, he focuses "microscopically
upon the individual unit . . . that interior reality—or hysteria. . . . In consequence, modern humor deals significantly with frustrating trivia."[3]

The term *screwball* first appeared in the mid-1930s and referred to an eccentric person.[4] The word probably has ties with such late nineteenth-century colloquial expressions as having a "screw loose" (being crazy) and becoming
"screwy" (drunk).[5] Since the mid-1930s *screwball* has also been used in baseball to describe both the eccentric player and "any pitched ball that moves in
an unusual or unexpected way."[6] All of these characteristics describe performers in screwball comedy films: the crazy Carole Lombard, the often drunken
William Powell, and the unusual or unexpected movement of Katharine Hepburn.

The use of the term in baseball may have been stimulated by the world
champion St. Louis Cardinals of 1934 (the year from which screwball comedy
is usually dated), a team noted for its nutty behavior and nicknamed the Gas
House Gang. The team's success was largely the result of pitching brothers
Dizzy and Daffy Dean, with Dizzy being the principal source of Cardinal eccentricity. The zany antics of Dizzy were not, moreover, limited to the sports
page. On April 15, 1935, he made the cover of *Time* magazine, with the accompanying article placing him among a "small company of super-celebrities"
which included Shirley Temple and Eleanor Roosevelt—super-celebrities whose
antics had "become the legend of their time."[7] While there was hardly a pre-
ponderance of baseball references in screwball comedy literature, they occasionally occurred. For example, *Variety*'s review of *My Man Godfrey* (1936)
described Lombard as "so screwy . . . she needs only a rosin bag to be a
female Rube Waddell" (a Dizzy Dean–type, turn-of-the-century pitcher). And
a review of genre hit *I Met Him in Paris* (1937) characterized it as a "cleaned
up version of Noel Coward's *Design for Living*—with a keg of beer at third
base."[8]

Study of screwball comedy should begin with the realization that the genre
parodies the traditional love story. The more eccentric partner, invariably the
woman, usually manages a victory over the less assertive, easily frustrated
male. The heroine often is assisted by the fact that only she knows that a
"courtship" is going on. By the time the male becomes aware of the courtship
(such as Cary Grant's absent-minded professor, end-of-movie resignation to the
fact in the pivotal *Bringing Up Baby*, 1938), the final buzzer has sounded,
signaling an end to his comfortably rigid bachelor lifestyle. Film historians
Thomas Sobchack and Vivian C. Sobchack have appropriately defined "the
predatory female who stalks the protagonist" as a basic genre convention.[9] The
inevitability of the woman's victory is nicely summarized by Barbra Streisand
at the close of *What's Up, Doc?* (1972, a film largely derived from the Katharine
Hepburn–dominating *Bringing Up Baby*). Streisand accepts "Professor" Ryan
O'Neal's romantic surrender at film's close with the apt observation, "You
can't fight a tidal wave."

The female's domination of the screwball male also exists upon a more self-conscious level. Stanley Cavell has written of his fascination with *The Lady Eve*'s "daring declaration" of its "awareness of itself, of its existence as a film."[10] The "daring declaration" he has in mind is the Barbara Stanwyck–directed scene of the handsome but awkward and naive Henry Fonda's first entrance into the ship's dining room/nightclub. The viewer watches the reflected image of Fonda in Stanwyck's makeup mirror as she narrates to the point of providing dialogue and direction for both the antihero and the many coquettes interested in the fortune from his family's brewery ("Pike's Pale, the Ale That Won for Yale").

Cavell's observation "that the woman [Stanwyck] is some kind of stand-in for the role of director fits our understanding that the man [Fonda], the sucker, is a stand-in for the role of the audience."[11] Cavell's realization of the Stanwyck-as-director, film-within-a-film nature of this scene is insightful. But while he relates this incident to the generally self-conscious nature of the genre, he misses the opportunity to add two other observations: this is another strong screwball comedy heroine, and such woman-as-director scenes frequently occur in other films of the genre.

Excellent variations occur in both *My Favorite Wife* (1940) and *The Ex-Mrs. Bradford* (1936). The funnier, more traditional example presents Irene Dunne's in-film comic manipulation of Cary Grant in *My Favorite Wife*, when she "directs" the reenactment of his marriage proposal to his second wife (Gail Patrick). While Stanwyck's "direction" of Fonda might be labeled omnipotent narration because the antihero male is unaware of her, Dunne's assumption of the director's role follows more customary lines. Still, the female "director" has the male jumping through hoops.

The heroine as director of a film-within-a-film scene goes beyond the merely metaphorical in *The Ex-Mrs. Bradford*. In this *Thin Man*–like film (though a more vulnerable William Powell is now teamed with Jean Arthur), Arthur orchestrates a movie-closing marriage to Powell using a minister who has already been filmed going through the ceremony (with more apparent direction from Arthur). Thus, Powell and Arthur face a truly "cinematic" minister on a screen within the movie, while the viewer becomes witness to probably the best example of screwball heroine as film director.

Despite the general superiority in the genre of the female over the male, with her apparently antisocial approach to the traditionally male-dominated courtship ritual, the game still has the most conservative of goals: the heroine's madcap maneuvers are often used to capture a male and break him—or save him—from any real antisocial rigidity. This is best summed up with the term *marriage,* or the promise of marriage (sometimes remarriage), which ends the screwball comedy, reaffirming one of the most traditional institutions in Western society. But the apparent duality of the heroine helps explain the often contradictory view of screwball comedy from feminist critics. For example, Molly Haskell's chapter "The Thirties," in *From Reverence to Rape: The Treatment of Women in the Movies,* sketches the genre as a generally positive, rebellious trend; Marjorie Rosen's *Popcorn Venus: Women, Movies and the American Dream* all but ignores it.[12]

As a teacher who frequently uses the genre in class, I have found the same divided response with regard to the heroine. Students, especially feminists, have ambivalent feelings toward the heroine. They generally tend to like her madcap means but have difficulty accepting the end: all this just for a man. The negativist position among feminist critics is probably articulated most baldly by Karyn Kay: "In modern screwball comedies the narrative inevitably unwinds to a reiteration of this man-above-woman world order."[13]

Screwball comedy is not part of the traditional ("determinate time and space") genres in which action generally occurs at a specific time and place, as with the western, the war film, and the gangster picture.[14] The determinate genre generally has its hero enter a specific physically contested space, achieve a definite resolution, then exit said space. Thus, in an archetypal western like John Ford's *My Darling Clementine* (1946), Wyatt Earp (Henry Fonda) and his brothers ride into a contested space in the American West called Tombstone, a town suffering under the presence of the evil Clantons (led by Walter Brennan). After a "battle" at the OK Corral, in which the Clantons are killed and Tombstone's conflict is fully resolved, Wyatt Earp and one surviving brother move on.

In contrast, screwball comedy is a genre of indeterminate time and space, like the musical and the melodrama. It is not limited to one period and place, although it is often set in the present in the milieu of the rich. The genre actually is defined by the eccentric courtship of the screwball couple and by the often tenuous plot, which revolves around their slapstick romantic encounters. Thus, the performers become unusually significant; the recurrent appearance of a Cary Grant or a Carole Lombard might be the only immediately discernible unifying element.

Screwball comedy deals "not with threatened space, but with a 'civilized' society whose characters have no exit and must learn to adjust their own personal dispositions to accommodate that of their cultural milieu."[15] Thus, it is conservative in the sense that to co-exist in a society is to know compromise. Moreover, unlike the sometimes vigilante violence which closes determinate time and space genres, screwball comedies occasionally even add courtroom scenes at or near the film's end. Though comic, they represent another attempt at civilized compromise. At no time is the genre's courtroom comedy so outrageous that it totally undercuts the system—something the truly iconoclastic Marx Brothers' courtroom scene is designed to do in *Duck Soup* (1933).

Little has been written about the development of screwball film as a genre of comedy. The most popular explanations for the birth of the genre have come from the sociological outgrowth of 1930s Depression America, and from censorship, the suppression of sexuality in 1930s films by way of the imposition of the Motion Picture Production Code in 1934.

Most analysts suggest that 1934 should be considered as the beginning of the screwball genre because of the appearance of three films. Frank Capra's *It Happened One Night* was a prototype, although this tale of a runaway heiress (Claudette Colbert) had a stronger male lead (Clark Gable) than would become the genre norm. While *It Happened One Night* was a bigger commercial hit, Howard Hawks's *Twentieth Century* (adapted by Ben Hecht and Charles MacArthur from their play) had more of what would typically be considered screwball in years to come, including the escaped meandering of one certified crazy and an ongoing comic battle royal between John Barrymore and Carole Lombard.

Pivotal 1934 also produced director W. S. Van Dyke's adaptation of Dashiell Hammett's comedy mystery *The Thin Man*. Its central character, Nick Charles, is more capable than the usual screwball comedy male, but he does represent a transition toward the type. He is not of the Sherlock Holmes mold, a hero who can deduce six dozen things about a suspect merely from his footprints. Charles can be frustrated. He is more vulnerable, more human, and decidedly funnier than the classical detective, attributes that make him a first cousin to the screwball male. Moreover, Hammett biographer William F. Nolan has described Charles as a detective who came out of retirement "only because his wife nagged him into it."[16] Thus, he seems all the closer to the screwball male.

In 1934 the antihero, screwball-like male even appeared in the comedy gangster film *The Whole Town's Talking* (not released until early 1935), in which mild-mannered accountant Mr. Jones (Edward G. Robinson) is a dead ringer for Public Enemy Number One, "Killer" Bannion (also played by Robinson). Although the film does not display the high-society trappings that characterize most screwball comedies, it does include many of the genre's other essentials, most notably in the nature of Robinson's relationship with co-star Jean Arthur. In fact, Arthur's impersonation of a gun moll during one of the film's many mistaken-identity scenes may have served as Katharine Hepburn's model for her own gun moll scene in screwball comedy's celebrated *Bringing Up Baby*.

The script for *The Whole Town's Talking* (1935) was adapted from a story by W. R. Burnett, probably best known for his novel *Little Caesar,* from which the classic gangster film of the same name was adapted (1930). Interestingly, however, Thurber's story, "The Remarkable Case of Mr. Bruhl" (anthologized in *The Middle-Aged Man on the Flying Trapeze,* 1935) also deals with a mousey little man and a look-alike gangster. There seemed to be an antiheroic Zeitgeist in the air.

Forgotten today is the period significance of *My Man Godfrey*. Though seldom left off anyone's list of classic screwball comedies, during the 1930s it also rated near pioneer status. More than any of its predecessors, *My Man Godfrey* offered a whole household full of screwballs. Thus, for many Depression critics, *My Man Godfrey* represented a more obvious starting point for the genre. The great 1930s film critic Otis Ferguson suggested just this during the period when he credited it with having been the first film to rate the label screwball: "With *My Man Godfrey* in the middle of 1936, the discovery of the word screwball by those who had to have some words to say helped build the thesis of an absolutely new style of comedy."[17]

This 1936 coming of age also helps explain why 1937 seems to have been such a watershed year for the genre. Five screwball classics appeared: *Easy Living, Topper, The Awful Truth, Nothing Sacred,* and *True Confession.* Leo McCarey won an Academy Award for his direction of the film frequently labeled the definitive screwball comedy: *The Awful Truth.*[18] And while the heavens dropped riches on *Easy Living*'s Jean Arthur in the form of a mink coat, *Topper* examined how two "ectoplasmic screwballs" could work their way to heaven.[19]

*Topper* gave the genre a whole new excuse for eccentricity—visitation by the most free-spirited of couples (Cary Grant and Constance Bennett). As *New York Times* film critic Frank S. Nugent so nicely put it, "their car crashed and turned them into double-exposures."[20] Thus, their good deed to guarantee their safe entry into heaven was to be the loosening up of the most rigid of milquetoast males—Roland Young as Topper. The vanquishing of rigidity, the goal of all good screwball comedies, would naturally succeed—but not before Young comically gyrated himself through this film and two sequels, *Topper Takes a Trip* (1938) and *Topper Returns* (1941). Young received an Academy Award nomination for Best Supporting Actor (1937) for his *Topper* performances and quite possibly motivated Steve Martin's more recent screwball gyrations in the inspired *All of Me* (1984). In the latter case, however, Martin's body becomes partially inhabited by a spirit (Lily Tomlin), something with which not even Young had to contend. *All of Me* demonstrates yet another variation of female domination.

The successive late 1937 releases of *Nothing Sacred* and *True Confession* (both starring Carole Lombard) also inspired film critic Nugent to write a special *New York Times* salute to the actress. Never one to avoid complementing a film comedy review with additional comedy, Nugent appropriately labeled his article "A Christmas Carole."[21] Coming upon the previous year's *My Man Godfrey,* Lombard was given a screwball comedy notoriety still associated with her name.

Cary Grant also starred in two of those 1937 screwball classics—*Topper* and *The Awful Truth.* And with his next two films (*Bringing Up Baby* and *Holiday,* both 1938), Cary Grant was fast approaching an eclipse of even Lombard. As film critic Andrew Sarris would later observe, Grant was "the only actor indispensable to the genre."[22] Grant was able to mix comic frustration (frequently in the most slapstick manner) with traditional leading-man handsomeness. In fact, film critic Ferguson might have been describing Grant when he defined the screwball performer as "the funny character with or without the funny pants."[23]

The early 1940s films of writer-director Preston Sturges, particularly *The*

*Lady Eve* (1941) and *Palm Beach Story* (1942), are also of major importance to the genre. As the initial thrust of the movement faded, Sturges's work was a comic culmination of the genre's mixture of slapstick and sophistication.

Screwball comedies continue to be made today, as evidenced by Blake Edwards's *10* (1979) and *Micki and Maude* (1984), and Steven Gordon's *Arthur* (1981), all of which star today's economy-sized Cary Grant: Dudley Moore. But they appear with neither the fanfare nor the frequency of the 1930s and early 1940s films. There are no easy explanations for this slackening, but it is undoubtedly true that both screwball comedy's antiheroics and its "new image of courtship and marriage . . . with man and wife no longer expecting ecstatic bliss, but treating . . . living as a crazy adventure sufficient to itself" are now the norm in American humor.[24]

To understand the genre fully it is necessary to examine the relationship between the screwball comedy characters of the 1930s and the full blossoming of the comic antihero in American humor during the preceding decade. The emergence of the antihero marked a pivotal period in American humor. He supplanted the crackerbarrel philosopher, marking the full transition from a rural figure full of wisdom learned through experience to a frustrated urban misfit, more childlike than manly.

The comic antihero is characterized by five key elements: his abundant leisure time, his childlike naivete, his life in the city, his apolitical nature, and his frustration—all of which are in marked contrast to the traits of the crackerbarrel figure. The screwball comedy character follows the antihero pattern, except that the feature films tend to glamorize the surroundings with beautiful people in luxurious settings and soften the battle of the sexes.

Screwball comedy focuses on the leisure life, often in high-society style. A review of the fantasy screwball comedy *I Married a Witch* (1942) nicely describes the condition with the phrase "caviar comedy."[25] The titles of two other celebrated examples of the genre express the film's ambience quite nicely: Mitchell Leisen's *Easy Living* (1937, from a Preston Sturges script) and George Cukor's *Holiday* (1938, from the Philip Barry play).

If a character does flirt with a profession in a screwball comedy, it is usually in a field Middle America does not view as serious or "real" employment. Instead the genre showcases the actors in *Twentieth Century*, newspaper reporters in *It Happened One Night*, or "painter" Douglas of *Theodora Goes Wild*. In fact, Douglas's martinet film father puts pressure on him at one point, saying, "You owe at least that much to me, especially after your choice of a profession."

Probably the most celebrated example of a character in a profession seemingly nebulous to many Americans is the absent-minded professor, a type fully realized by Cary Grant in Hawks's *Bringing Up Baby*, though one might also nominate Jimmy Stewart as professor in the hilarious *Vivacious Lady* (1938) or the professor-like snake scholar Henry Fonda in *The Lady Eve*. Hawks had, however, a penchant for the genre's absent-minded professor. After *Bringing*

*Up Baby,* there were the eight professors of *Ball of Fire* (1941), headed by Professor Gary Cooper. Hawks's 1951 comedy *Monkey Business* gave us Grant once again as Professor Barnaby Fulton, who thinks he has discovered a youth serum. In 1964 Hawks cast Rock Hudson as a professional author in *Man's Favorite Sport?*

The second commonality between the antihero and the screwball comedy male is that both are childlike. One traditionally associates the childlike with comedy, but the association has a special focus here. Whereas the capable crackerbarrel figures were caretakers for a nation, the screwball comedy male is often in a situation where he quite literally is being taken care of. In *Ruggles of Red Gap* (1935), the fiftyish Egbert (Charles Ruggles) gets a haircut under the supervision of his wife; Arthur (Dudley Moore) has all his duties supervised by his servant Hobson (John Gielgud) in *Arthur* (1981, a comic relationship which also seems to borrow from P. G. Wodehouse's classic "couple"—Bertie Wooster and his all-knowing servant Jeeves).

The childlike males, in the apparent antiheroic tradition of James Thurber, often have a dog—an obvious corollary of childhood. Thurber wrote about the dog because he felt it was the one animal that had been domesticated so long it had taken on most of man's frustrations. A dual focus of frustration, male and canine, plays an important part in several screwball comedies, including *The Awful Truth, Theodora Goes Wild,* and *Bringing Up Baby.* In the Neil Simon–scripted *Seems Like Old Times* (1980), the frustrations of the husband (Charles Grodin) are mirrored repeatedly in his wife's (Goldie Hawn) pack of dogs. This more recent example is especially important because *Seems Like Old Times* is a conscious celebration of the screwball genre.

The dog sometimes represents a surrogate child for a screwball couple who "play house" when one partner, usually the male, is not adult enough for a real marriage. A custody fight over Mr. Smith at the divorce proceedings in *The Awful Truth* allows director Leo McCarey to extend his parody of divorce without the real pathos a human child would have given the scene. Since a dog is used, any sexuality between the couple is not undermined by a "family" situation. (In *Bringing Up Baby,* having a pet represent a surrogate child is addressed much more baldly; "Baby" in the title is actually a tame leopard.)

The settings for these films often accent the childlike quality in the male. In fact, what might be described as a toyshop mise-en-scène frequently surfaces in the genre: the childhood playroom of *Holiday* (1938), the toy-strewn attic of *My Favorite Wife* (1940), Robert Benchley's playroom office in *Take a Letter, Darling* (1942). *Arthur* again provides a recent showcase of screwball consistency, because Arthur's bedroom could double as the Macy toy department.

Another parallel between the worlds of the antihero and the screwball comedy male is that both focus on an urban setting. (The elegance of the urban playgrounds of the idle rich—the art deco nightclubs, restaurants, town houses, and Hollywood-style fantasy settings—helps to explain the popularity of screwball comedy with a Depression-era audience.) Unlike the capable crackerbarrel hero, who had a close rapport with his setting—rural America—the screwball comedy male does not fully identify with his milieu. For him the city is symbolic of the irrationality of modern life. He remains frustrated no matter where he is; the city gives him at once a luxurious setting for his frustration and another cause for it besides the female. Indeed, for him the urban environment may even represent victimization. In *My Favorite Wife,* urbanite Cary Grant both feels and is made to appear effeminate, especially when juxtaposed with the macho, back-to-nature Randolph Scott, who was shipwrecked on a desert island for seven years with Grant's wife (Irene Dunne). A supporting player even mistakes Scott for Johnny Weissmuller—still cinema's greatest Tarzan.

Screwball comedy takes America's fundamental Jeffersonian democracy-based fear of cities, the unnatural mixing of too many people, and turns it into fun. The genre is full of "crazies," such as the lunatic asylum escapee in *Twentieth Century* who thinks he is rich and "bankrolls" John Barrymore's play and also puts up "repent" stickers everywhere, or the "weiner king" with a real bankroll who pays Claudette Colbert's bills and gives her culinary advice in Sturges's *Palm Beach Story* (1942).

Urban crazies symbolize both a warning and an answer in the genre. The warning implies that the fast-paced, emasculating urban lifestyle—modern living itself—could eventually put all of us in mental jeopardy if something is not done. Just as medical science derives vaccines from the bacteria that cause diseases, screwball comedy recommends a small dose of the irrational. As a practical defense the male needs to assume a certain eccentricity, as the female of the genre and American humor in general have done (such as the half-baked females on Thurber's family tree in *My Life and Hard Times*). In an irrational world, it is safest and most productive to behave irrationally.

A fourth characteristic shared by the antihero and the screwball comedy protagonist is the absence of political interest. The screwball comedy character is constantly buffeted about by the day-to-day frustrations of a seemingly irrational world. He is hardly capable of planning his leisure time, let alone entering politics. *Crucial* issues that arise in the genre would include how to dunk a donut *(It Happened One Night);* who gets custody of the dog in divorce proceedings *(The Awful Truth);* whether a dog hid Cary Grant's missing dinosaur bone and, if so, where *(Bringing Up Baby);* whether one can buy a pajama top or bottom and break up the set *(Bluebeard's Eighth Wife,* 1938); how one keeps Henry Fonda from spilling things *(The Lady Eve);* why duck hunting should be discouraged in passenger trains *(The Palm Beach Story);* and more recently, the need for martinis while bathing *(Arthur).*

Recognizing screwball comedy's nonpolitical nature also sheds light on a key misunderstanding of the genre: the tendency to include the films of director Frank Capra. After *It Happened One Night,* this director's career took a fascinating but decidedly nonscrewball turn. The Capra heroes who follow, like the classic trio of Mr. Deeds, Mr. Smith, and John Doe, are from the American humor tradition of the political crackerbarrel, hardly that of screwball comedy.

It should be underlined that while Capra's 1930s and 1940s films after *It Happened One Night* invariably centered on populist politics, screwball comedy keyed on madcap romance. Indeed, as film critic Jim Leach has observed, Capra's post–*It Happened One Night* films "would much better be described as populist comedies."[26] Leach expands:

Capra's vision is not really screwball at all . . . whereas the only positive strategy in screwball comedy is to accept the all-pervasive craziness, the populist comedy argues that what society regards as crazy (Mr. Deeds' attempt to give away his fortune) is really a manifestation of the normal human values with which society has lost touch.[27]

Moreover, while Deeds must face a sanity hearing, a true screwball comedy would not progress at all if eccentric behavior (the genre norm) were subject to the courtroom. The inherent naturalness of kookiness to the genre is best articulated by the matter-of-fact fashion in which John D. Hackensacker III (Rudy Vallee) tells his *Palm Beach Story* sister (Mary Astor): "You know, Maude [Astor], someone meeting you for the first time, not knowing you were cracked, might get the wrong impression."

A fifth commonality between the worlds of the antihero and the screwball comedy male is that both focus on frustration. The antihero is always frustrated by women, a situation also generally evident in the screwball comedy. Preston Sturges articulated the tendency toward female ascendancy in the genre in the title of *The Lady Eve,* which also features a cartoon serpent in the delightful opening and closing credits. Not surprisingly, the Lady Eve (Barbara Stanwyck) wraps the sweet boob of a man-child (Henry Fonda) around her little finger during two different courtships, after appropriately starting things off by hitting him with an apple. So great is her mastery of this simple male that Stanwyck even convinces Fonda she is two different women. (References to Eve, direct and metaphorical, occur so frequently in screwball comedy that she should be declared the patron saint of the genre.)

These, then, have been the five keys linking the genre to the world of the comic antihero. This linkage is important for five reasons. First, the most logical (yet most neglected) approach to screwball comedy is to study it in the broad context of American humor. It then becomes obvious that the screwball comedy feature film, drawing from a rich antiheroic tradition that existed in 1920s America, was able to broaden the audience for this comic misfit. It is time the genre's ties with this evolution in American humor were recognized.

Second, the genre is about madcap romance, not populist politics. This cannot be reiterated too often, because the standard interpretation of the genre has focused frequently on politics, especially the Capra films that followed *It Happened One Night.* Screwball comedy, however, is about madcaps, not messages. In fact, the genre has, on occasion, even parodied Capra's work. For example, the opening of *Nothing Sacred* (1937) is a comic send-up of the populist small-town beginning of *Mr. Deeds Goes to Town* (1936). And Ralph

Bellamy's failed attempt to read his romantic poetry to Irene Dunne in *The Awful Truth*—as well as to sing it to her in *Lady in a Jam* (1942)—parodies Gary Cooper's (the ultimate populist hero) recitation to Jean Arthur in *Mr. Deeds*.

Third, despite the genre's frequent Looney Tune activities, its comedy is inherently conservative, generally with the goal of capturing a male and breaking him, or saving him, from any real antisocial rigidity. Granted, it is an unorthodox courtship, even a satire of the traditional romance, but it is still a courtship. Female individualism is directed entirely at male conquest; it is not a commodity meant to exist outside of the romantic situation of "all's fair in love and war." One feels comic tension at the close of most screwball comedies—since they often bridge ninety previous minutes of largely comic differences. But marriage, remarriage, or promise of either, is a final humorous concession to a genre that exists within the compromises of society. Thus, screwball comedy is not to be confused with the comic iconoclasm of the Marx Brothers.

Fourth, the evolution of the comic antihero paralleled the adaptation of film to another new phenomenon—the talkie. Appropriately, only picture-plus-sound could adequately showcase the marriage of slapstick to witty dialogue, which was screwball comedy's rendition of the antihero. The popular birthdate given the genre (1934) coincides with the time it took sound technology to catch up with the visual. Sound also defused the comic centralness of the silent clowns. Thus, the lesser nature (the in-film frustrations) of the antiheroic screwball comedy male was reinforced by a sound system more geared to a decentralized focus, such as the comic battle of the sexes.

And fifth, the antiheroic screwball comedy is just one of *many* genres to be found under the humor umbrella. More film comedy differentiation needs to be done. Just as it is essential that screwball comedy finds its natural ties with the comedy antihero movement, it is equally important that other comedy genres, such as the populist, be examined more thoroughly. Too often in the past, film comedy has simplistically been called the broadest of all genres; this seemed to authorize the dumping together of a truly amazing number of comedy bedfellows. It is time to move beyond this to a greater understanding of the appreciation for all film comedy genres.

## BIBLIOGRAPHICAL OVERVIEW

Despite screwball comedy's significance in both film and comedy history, its nature remains something of a controversy. Film critic Brian Henderson's "Romantic Comedy Today: Semi-Tough or Impossible" (1978) observes: " 'Screwball comedy' [is] a term one finds in critical contexts of all sorts. Beneath the common term, however, there is no agreement, neither from critic to critic nor within the work of a single critic."[28] Earlier that same year film critic Andrew Sarris had written: "Film historians have never agreed on exactly what constitutes a screwball comedy and what movies qualify for the category.''[29] Since 1978 the issue was only intensified, including Wes D. Gehring's 1983 monograph *Screwball Comedy: Defining a Film Genre*. This monograph, which is the foundation for this chapter, for Gehring's article "Screwball Comedy: An Overview," and for his 1986 book *Screwball Comedy: A Genre of Madcap Romance*, contends that the most obvious base from which to examine the genre is the structural change which American humor underwent in the 1920s and 1930s.

Currently, there are only two other book-length studies of the genre: Ted Sennett's *Lunatics and Lovers* (1971), and Stanley Cavell's *Pursuits of Happiness: The Hollywood Comedy of Remarriage* (1981). Interestingly enough, the books take diametrically opposite approaches. Sennett looks through the small end of the telescope, briefly examining 230 films, while Cavell uses telescope's large end, scrutinizing a mere seven works in seven chapters.

The main strength of Sennett's work is as a reference, especially the appendix material and the filmography. Appendix 1 is devoted to paragraph-length biographies of key screwball comedy players. Appendix 2 applies the same approach to genre directors; appendix 3 examines the writers. The appendix material is followed by a 230-entry filmography (arranged by year, 1932-1944), with each film also receiving a one-sentence synopsis.

The main text of the book is divided into ten chapters, each representing a subgrouping of the genre. The self-explanatory chapter titles are "The Cinderella Syndrome," "Wife, Husband, Friend, Secretary," "Poor Little Rich Girls (and Boys)," "Lamb Bites Wolf," "Bats in Their Belfry," "The Thin Man, Topper, and Friends," "Boss-Ladies and Other Liberated Types," and "Stage to Screen." The only exceptions to this subgenre categorizing are in the opening chapter overview, "A World of Lunatics and Lovers" (from which the book's title is taken), and a late chapter devoted to a genre director, "The Amazing Mr. Sturges."

Sennett's group of films and facts is truly amazing, but he does not take the reader beyond this. Instead of topping off this impressive and important body of information with some big-picture analysis of the genre, or its meaning in relaltionship to American comedy, film art, and the individual and/or society at large, the book ends just as things should be beginning.

Another problem is that Sennett establishes no criteria to determine just what screwball comedy is. Granted, this is no easy task. But some filter device is necessary, or else all lines of demarcation become unclear. For example, he includes material which should be in a personality comedian genre, such as Joe E. Brown's *Alibi Ike* (1935). Membership in Sennett's 230-film survey is definitely too broad.

In contrast, Harvard professor Stanley Cavell's *Pursuits of Happiness* examines a mere seven films: *The Lady Eve* (1941), *It Happened One Night* (1934), *Bringing Up Baby* (1938), *The Philadelphia Story* (1940), *His Girl Friday* (1940), *Adam's Rib* (1949), and *The Awful Truth* (1937). Cavell more than makes up for the absence of analysis in *Lunatics and Lovers*. His primary lesson is that a number of key screwball films are comedies not of a couple's initial courtship but rather the more romantically (and, one should add, comically) interesting situation found in a second courtship after a separation and/or divorce. But while Sennett's book becomes too entangled in an almost film-by-film tradition of the genre, Cavell's work frequently suffers from tunnel vision. An example is the earlier Cavell comparison likening *The Lady Eve*'s Stanwyck to an in-film director but his failure to see its frequent application to the genre at large.

Conversely, while Cavell's pivotal comparison of forest scenes in *Bringing Up Baby* to those in Shakespeare's *A Midsummer Night's Dream* is insightful, the frantic country activities of this screwball comedy are not typical of the pastoral sojourns in most films of the genre which include a rural sidetrip.[30] Generally, such an outing provides both audience and actors with a film-closing breather, full of more resignation than resolution (the real screwball of the film's focus couple is just not going to change). Even those screwball comedies which commit more time to their country excursions, commensurate lengthwise with that in *Bringing Up Baby,* rarely showcase the comic nightmare intensity of this film. For example, in *Theodora Goes Wild* (1936), there is a leisurely pace to the fishing and berry picking of Irene Dunne and Melvyn Douglas. In fact, the segment's biggest laugh depends upon it. The two are returning from an early morning fishing trip on foot and unhurried, content in each other's company. They are so blissfully oblivious that neither realizes their slow steps have positioned them (in the most casual of fishing attire) right in front of *the* church in town just as the Sunday service is letting out. As in most screwball comedies, the real zaniness in *Theodora Goes Wild* takes place in the city. In this case, that is quite literally where Theodora goes wild.

Cavell's forty-two–page introduction, sometimes brilliant, sometimes meanderingly obtuse, can also be irritating. For example, he frequently takes an apologetic stance toward film study, as if he were writing in an earlier era when the medium's position in academic circles was on shaky ground: "I AM NOT INSENSIBLE, whatever defenses I may deploy, of an avenue of outrageousness in considering Hollywood films in the light from time to time, of major works of thought."[31] Thus, his frequent flights of intellectual comparison, such as his juxtapositioning of Kant and Capra (while not without interest), sometimes seem an extension of that apologetic stance, as if mere film or film figures could be elevated by association.

Historically, a good place to begin an examination of shorter works on screwball comedy is Lewis Jacobs's brief discussion of the genre in his chapter "Contemporary Film Content" in the watershed *The Rise of the American Film: A Critical History* (1939). Sociological film historian Jacobs ties the birth of the genre to the Depression—crazy activities in a "crazy world." Thus, he has become the father figure of what is still a popular approach to the genre.

Later pivotal sociological historians are Richard Griffith and Arthur Mayer, and Andrew Bergman. Griffith and Mayer devote a segment of their chapter "The New Deal" to screwball comedy in *The Movies* (1957), which examines America film history largely through stills and commentary. But the Jacobs-like commentary is disappointingly brief for a reference which is frequently noted in other screwball essays, such as the aforementioned Sarris essay.

Bergman's "Frank Capra and the Screwball Comedy, 1931–1941," Chapter 10 from his book *We're In the Money: Depression America and Its Films* (1971), ties his sociological approach to one director. Capra *is* screwball comedy to Bergman. While I do not subscribe to Bergman's thesis (see earlier references to Capra within this chapter), it is an essay which has been influential. (The most ambitious expansion of the Capra position comes in Thomas Schatz's "The Screwball Comedy," chapter 6 of his *Hollywood Genres.*)

As noted earlier, the other popular explanation for the birth of the genre is tied to censorship and the Motion Picture Production Code. Three specific authors come to mind: Molly Haskell, Andrew Sarris, and E. Rubinstein. The most concentrated along these lines, Sarris's "The Sex Comedy Without Sex," from the March 1978 *American Film,* should also have the subtitle "With Review." While his underlying argument is that the genre was a result of censorship code implementation—thus his article's ironic title—the essay's main strength is in its examination of earlier sociological positions.

Rubinstein's "The End of Screwball Comedy: *The Lady Eve* and *The Palm Beach Story,*" from the Spring/ Summer 1982 *Post Script,* divides itself between pivotal screwball director Sturges and a general look at the genre. In the latter case, this soon zeroes in on censorship. But in contrast to Sarris's systematic examination of earlier sociological positions, Rubinstein's piece showcases the censorship thesis with a more breezy, even winsomely comic tone: "Pulling the wool over their eyes [the censors] was a sport so widely played . . . that the sport became a genre . . . screwball comedy." [32]

Haskell's aforementioned "The Thirties" chapter actually predates the Sarris and Rubinstein essays, but her censorship premise is so fleeting (though historically important to note) that it has been relegated to third. The chapter is more important as a myriad of women's issues from the decade.

The most heated discussion of the genre within a feminist framework occurred, however, in the Summer 1976 *Film Quarterly,* where Leland A. Poague's "A Short Defense of Screwball Comedy" appeared as a response to a Fall 1975 Karyn Kay review of *Part-Time Work of a Domestic Slave.* Kay had, in a lengthy aside, linked twentieth-century screwball comedy with the "Noah" plays of the medieval ages, in which Mr. and Mrs. Noah battle as to whether she will board the ark. In either case, Kay saw the male as clearly dominant. Poague's interpretation diametrically opposed this. Following Poague's article, a Kay rebuttal appeared. Among other things, she incorporated *The Taming of the Shrew* into her defense. Ironically, Haskell had already written the best of defenses two years earlier when she observed that screwball comedies "celebrate difficult and anarchic love rather than security and the suburban dream

. . . favoring movement over stasis, and speech and argument over silent compliance.''[33]

Though it could be argued that Jacobs's sociological stance on the genre has had such influence that every variation since then might be labeled *revisionist,* that title might best be applied to two 1970s essays. The first was pluralist film critic Pauline Kael's ''Raising Kane,'' from her controversial *The "Citizen Kane" Book* (1971). While the central purpose of both the essay and the book was to shift the limelight from Orson Welles to Herman J. Mankiewicz, Kael's writing also celebrates the 1930s film comedy and the neglected screenwriter. Yet, just as she can overstate her main thesis, anti-auteurist Kael would seem to overreact to screenwriter neglect by suddenly granting them the lion's share of the credit.

Jim Leach's ''The Screwball Comedy,''from the Barry K. Grant–edited anthology *Film Genre: Theory and Criticism* (1977), is less well-known than Kael's piece but more insightful. Most revisionist is his placement of Capra's post–*It Happened One Night* films in the populist rather than the screwball comedy camp. Though he was not the first to note this, he addresses it more directly than had anyone else up to that time.

Leach also discusses the genre's relationship to slapstick, sexuality, and even film noir. Several screwball directors are discussed, but Hawks, appropriately, receives the most sustained attention. Leach's closing plea speaks to, in part, the need for an awareness of the multitude of comedy genres which exist, something which the volume in hand attempts to address.

Before this bibliographical survey is closed, several general overviews merit mentioning. There are five pivotal ones (briefly examined chronologically). First, the aforementioned Ferguson piece, ''While We Were Laughing'' (1940; see note 17), provides a period reflection on the genre, accenting the special impact of *My Man Godfrey.* Second, William Thomaier's ''Early Sound Comedy'' (*Films in Review,* 1958) is a brief but informative survey of the genre from 1934 to 1941, proceeding at a methodical year-by-year pace. Third, Donald W. McCaffrey's ''Sophisticated and Almost Satirical,'' chapter 7 from his *The Golden Age of Sound Comedy: Comic Films and Comedians of the Thirties* (1973), is a genre survey which takes *Easy Living* as its model, including to a lesser extent *Nothing Sacred.* As these focus films suggest, the essay is refreshing because McCaffrey is unconventional. There is no question his key films are of the genre, but they generally do not receive this much attention. Fourth, Bernard Drew's chatty ''High Comedy in the Thirties'' (1976; in *Movie Comedy,* edited by Stuart Byron and Elisabeth Weis) briefly assesses the genre within the decade and beyond, despite the title. In fact, it is best when discussing the post-1940 direction of key screwball alumnae. Fifth, the Sobchacks (see note 9) examine any number of screwball fundamentals in the ''Genre Films'' chapter of their *An Introduction to Film* (1980). For example, they nicely update the genre's ties to the frequently all too loosely applied New Comedy of ancient Greece. Thus, they recognize the genre is more likely to vest additional wisdom in one member of the couple as opposed to an outside adviser in the pure New Comedy tradition. They also improve upon Brian Henderson's examination of the genre as a subdivision of romantic comedy.

These, then, have been recommended readings for the student of screwball comedy. Because the subject frequently celebrates the absent-minded professor, there is a self-conscious reluctance to stop writing for fear of aping this genre character. But since not to finish would be even more antiheroic, suffice it to say that familiarity with this literature will provide a fundamental background for the study of screwball comedy.

## NOTES

1. A key element of Henri Bergson's theory of comedy, as applied to character development, addresses situations of "inversions" or "topsyturvydoms," where one takes "certain characters in a certain situation" and pulls a switch: "Thus, we laugh at the prisoner at the bar lecturing the magistrate; at a child presuming to teach its parents; in a word, at everything that comes under the heading of 'topsyturvydom.' " "Topsyturvydom" seems an especially appropriate term for a genre born in the Depression, especially one in which the stereotyped sexual role models of the American courtship system are reversed. See also Henri Bergson, "Laughter," in *Comedy,* ed. Wylie Sypher (Garden City, N.Y.: Doubleday Anchor Books, 1956), p. 121.

2. Hamlin Hill, "Modern American Humor: The Janus Laugh," *College English,* December 1963, p. 174.

3. Ibid.

4. Joseph Weingarten, *American Dictionary of Slang and Colloquial Use* (New York: Joseph Weingarten, 1954), s.v. "screwball"; William Freeman, *A Concise Dictionary of English Slang* (1955; repr. London: English Universities Press, 1958), s.v. "screwball"; Harold Wentworth and Stuart Flexner, eds., *The Pocket Dictionary of American Slang* (1960; repr. New York: Pocket Books, 1967), s.v. "screwball."

5. Eric Partridge, *Dictionary of Slang and Unconventional English* (1937; repr. New York: Macmillan, 1970), s.v. "screw loose" and "screwy."

6. Wentworth and Flexner, *Pocket Dictionary of American Slang,* p. 287.

7. "Me 'n Paul" (cover story), *Time,* 15 April 1935, p. 52.

8. *My Man Godfrey* review, *Variety,* 23 September 1936, p. 16; *I Met Him in Paris* review, *Variety,* 9 June 1937, p. 15.

9. Thomas Sobchack and Vivian C. Sobchack, Chapter 4, "Genre Films," in *An Introduction to Film* (Boston: Little, Brown, 1980), p. 208.

10. Stanley Cavell, *Pursuits of Happiness: The Hollywood Comedy of Remarriage* (Cambridge, Mass.: Harvard University Press, 1981), p. 66

11. Ibid.

12. Molly Haskell, "The Thirties," in *From Reverence to Rape: The Treatment of Women in the Movies* (Baltimore: Penguin Books, 1974), pp. 126, 130–35, 137–38; and Marjorie Rosen, *Popcorn Venus: Women, Movies and the American Dream* (New York: Avon Books, 1974).

13. Karyn Kay, *Part-Time Work of a Domestic Slave* review, *Film Quarterly,* Fall 1975, p. 56

14. Thomas Schatz deals with determinate and indeterminate space throughout his

"Hollywood Film Genre As Ritual: A Theoretical and Methodological Inquiry" (Ph.D. diss., University of Iowa, 1976). This served as the foundation for his recent *Hollywood Genres: Formulas, Filmmaking, and the Studio System* (New York: Random House, 1981).

15. Schatz, "Hollywood Film Genre As Ritual," p. 145.

16. William F. Nolan, *Hammett: A Life at the Edge* (New York: Congdon & Weed, 1983), p. 129.

17. Otis Ferguson, "While We Were Laughing" (1940), in *The Film Criticism of Otis Ferguson*, ed. Robert Wilson (Philadelphia: Temple University Press, 1971), p. 24.

18. For more on McCarey see Wes D. Gehring's *Leo McCarey and the Comic Anti-Hero in American Film* (New York: Arno Press, 1980).

19. *Topper* review, *New York Times*, 21 August 1937, p. 21.

20. Frank S. Nugent, *Topper Takes a Trip* review, *New York Times*, 31 December 1938, p. 11.

21. Frank S. Nugent, "A Christmas Carole," *New York Times*, 19 December 1937, sec. 10, p. 7.

22. Andrew Sarris, "The Sex Comedy Without Sex," *American Film*, March 1978, p. 15.

23. Ferguson, "While We Were Laughing," p. 24.

24. Raymond Durgnat, Chapter 19, "Lightly and Politely," in *The Crazy Mirror: Hollywood Comedy and the American Image* (1970; repr. New York: Dell, 1972), p. 122.

25. Herb Stone, *I Married a Witch* review, *Rob Wagner's Script*, 19 December 1942, in *Selected Film Criticism*, ed. Anthony Slide (Metuchen, N.J.: Scarecrow Press, 1983), p. 85.

26. Jim Leach, "The Screwball Comedy," in *Film Genre: Theory and Criticism*, ed. Barry K. Grant (Metuchen, N.J.: Scarecrow Press, 1977), p. 82.

27. Ibid., pp. 82–83.

28. Brian Henderson, "Romantic Comedy Today: Semi-Tough or Impossible?" *Film Quarterly*, Summer 1978, p. 12.

29. Sarris, "The Sex Comedy Without Sex," p. 9.

30. Cavell, *Pursuits of Happiness*, pp. 142–45, 153–54, 156, 261.

31. Ibid., p. 8.

32. E. Rubinstein, "The End of Screwball Comedy: *The Lady Eve* and *The Palm Beach Story*." *Post Script*, Spring/Summer 1982, p. 39.

33. Haskell, "The Thirties," p. 126.

## BIBLIOGRAPHICAL CHECKLIST

### Books

Cavell, Stanley. *Pursuits of Happiness: The Hollywood Comedy of Remarriage*. Cambridge, Mass.: Harvard University Press, 1981.

Gehring, Wes D. *Screwball Comedy: A Genre of Madcap Romance*. Westport, Conn.: Greenwood Press, 1986.

———. *Screwball Comedy: Defining a Film Genre*. Muncie, Indiana: Ball State University Press Monograph Series, 1983.

Sennett, Ted. *Lunatics and Lovers*. New Rochelle, N.Y.: Arlington House, 1971.

## Shorter Works

Bergman, Andrew. Chapter 10, "Frank Capra and the Screwball Comedy, 1931–1941." In *We're In the Money: Depression America and Its Films*. 1971; repr. New York: Harper & Row, 1972.

Drew, Bernard. "High Comedy in the Thirties" (1976). In *Movie Comedy*. Ed. Stuart Byron and Elisabeth Weis. New York: Penguin Books, 1977.

Durgnat, Raymond. Chapter 19, "Lightly and Politely." In *The Crazy Mirror: Hollywood Comedy and the American Image*. 1970; repr. New York: Delta, 1972.

Ferguson, Otis. "While We Were Laughing" (1940). In *The Film Criticism of Otis Ferguson*. Ed. Robert Wilson. Philadelphia: Temple University Press, 1971.

Gehring, Wes D. "Screwball Comedy: An Overview," *Journal of Popular Film and Television*, Winter 1986, pp. 178–85.

Griffith, Richard, and Arthur Mayer. "The New Deal." In *The Movies*. New York: Simon and Schuster, 1957. (The latest update, 1981, added a third author, Eileen Bowser.)

Haskell, Molly. "The Thirties." In *From Reverence to Rape: The Treatment of Women in the Movies*. Baltimore: Penguin Books, 1974.

Henderson, Brian. "Romantic Comedy Today: Semi-Tough or Impossible?" *Film Quarterly*, Summer 1978, pp. 11–23.

Jacobs, Lewis. Chapter 25, "Contemporary Film Content." In *The Rise of the American Film: A Critical History*. 1939; repr. New York: Teachers College Press, 1971.

Kael, Pauline. "Raising Kane." In *The "Citizen Kane" Book*. Boston: Little, Brown, 1971.

Kay, Karyn. "Controversy and Correspondence: Karyn Kay Replies," *Film Quarterly*, Summer 1976, pp. 63–64.

————. "Part-Time Work of a Domestic Slave," *Film Quarterly*, Fall 1975, pp. 52–57.

Leach, Jim. "The Screwball Comedy." In *Film Genre: Theory and Criticism*. Ed. Barry K. Grant. Metuchen, N.J.: Scarecrow Press, 1977.

McCaffrey, Donald W. Chapter 7, "Sophisticated and Almost Satirical." In *The Golden Age of Sound Comedy: Comic Films and Comedians of the Thirties*. New York: A. S. Barnes, 1973.

Poague, Leland A. "Controversy and Correspondence: A Short Defense of Screwball Comedy," *Film Quarterly*, Summer 1976, pp. 62–63.

Sarris, Andrew. "The Sex Comedy Without Sex," *American Film*, March 1978, pp. 8–15.

Schatz, Thomas. Chapter 6, "The Screwball Comedy." In *Hollywood Genres: Formulas, Filmmaking, and the Studio System*. New York: Random House, 1981.

Sobchack, Thomas, and Vivian C. Sobchack. Chapter 4, "Genre Films." In *An Introduction to Film*. Boston: Little, Brown, 1980.

Thomaier, William. "Early Sound Comedy," *Films in Review*, May 1958, pp. 254–62.

## SELECTED FILMOGRAPHY

1934  *It Happened One Night* (105 minutes).
Columbia. Producer: Harry Cohen. Director: Frank Capra. Screenplay: Robert Riskin, from the Samuel Hopkins story "Night Bus." Cast: Clark Gable (Peter Warne), Claudette Colbert (Ellie Andrews), Walter Connolly (Alexander Andrews), Roscoe Karns (Oscar Shapeley), James Thomas (King Westley), Ward Bond and Eddy Chandler (bus drivers).

*Twentieth Century* (91 minutes).
Columbia. Producer/Director: Howard Hawks. Screenplay: Ben Hecht, Charles MacArthur, from their play, based on the play *Napoleon on Broadway*, by Charles Bruce Milholland. Cast: John Barrymore (Oscar Jaffe), Carole Lombard (Mildred Plotka/Lily Garland), Walter Connolly (Oliver Webb), Roscoe Karns (Owen O'Malley).

1936  *My Man Godfrey* (93 minutes).
Universal. Producer/Director: Gregory LaCava. Screenplay: Morrie Ryskind, Eric Hatch, from the Hatch novel. Cast: William Powell (Godfrey Parke), Carole Lombard (Irene Bullock), Alice Brady (Angelica Bullock), Gail Patrick (Cornelia Bullock), Jean Dixon (Molly), Eugene Pallette (Alexander Bullock), Allan Mowbray (Tommy Gray), Mischa Auer (Carlo).

1937  *Topper* (89 minutes).
Distributing Co.: MGM. Producing Co./Producer: Hal Roach. Director: Norman Z. McLeod. Screenplay: Jack Jerne, Eric Hatch, Eddie Moran, from the Thorne Smith novel *The Jovial Ghosts*. Special Effects: Roy Seawright. Cast: Constance Bennett (Marion Kerby), Cary Grant (George Kerby), Roland Young (Cosmo Topper), Billie Burke (Mrs. Topper), Alan Mowbray (Wilkins), Eugene Pallette (Casey), Arthur Lake (elevator boy).

*The Awful Truth* (89 minutes).
Columbia. Producer/Director: Leo McCarey. Screenplay: Vina Delmar, adaptation by Dwight Taylor of the Arthur Richman play. Cast: Irene Dunne (Lucy Warriner), Cary Grant (Jerry Warriner), Ralph Bellamy (Daniel Leeson), Alexander D'Arcy (Armand Duvalle), Cecil Cunningham (Aunt Patsy), Esther Dale (Mrs. Leeson), Joyce Compton (Toots Binswanger/Dixie Belle Lee).

1938  *Bringing Up Baby* (102 minutes).
RKO. Producer/Director: Howard Hawks. Screenplay: Dudley Nichols, Hager Wilde, from a Wilde story. Cast: Katharine Hepburn (Susan), Cary Grant (David Huxley), Charles Ruggles (Maj. Horace Applegate), Walter Catlett (Slocum), Barry Fitzgerald (Mr. Gogarty), May Robinson (Aunt Elizabeth), Fritz Feld (Dr. Lehmann).

1940  *My Favorite Wife* (88 minutes).
RKO. Producer: Leo McCarey. Director: Garson Kanin. Screenplay: Bela Spewack and Samuel Spewack, from a Bella and Samuel Spewack, Leo McCarey story. Cast: Irene Dunne (Ellen), Cary Grant (Nick), Randolph Scott (Burkett),

Gail Patrick (Bianca), Ma (Ann Schoemaker), Scotty Beckett (Tim), Mary Lou Harrington (Chinch), Donald MacBride (hotel clerk), Granville Bates (judge).

1941   *The Lady Eve* (97 minutes).

Paramount. Producer: Paul Jones. Director/Screenplay: Preston Sturges, from the Monckton Hoffe story "Two Bad Hats." Cast: Barbara Stanwyck (Jean), Henry Fonda (Charles Pike), Charles Coburn ("Colonel" Harrington), Eugene Pallette (Mr. Pike), William Demarest (Muggsy/Ambrose Murgatroyd), Eric Blore (Sir Alfred McGlennan/Keith), Melville Cooper (Gerald).

1942   *The Palm Beach Story* (88 minutes).

Paramount. Assoc. Producer: Paul Jones. Director/Screenplay: Preston Sturges. Cast: Claudette Colbert (Gerry Jeffers), Joel McCrea (Tom Jeffers), Mary Astor (Princess), Rudy Vallee (John D. Hackensacker III), Sig Arno (Toto).

1952   *Monkey Business* (97 minutes).

20th Century-Fox. Producer: Sol C. Siegel. Director: Howard Hawks. Screenplay: Ben Hecht, I. A. Diamond, Charles Lederer, from a Harry Segall story. Cast: Cary Grant (Prof. Barnaby Fulton), Ginger Rogers (Edwina Fulton), Charles Coburn (Oliver Oxley), Marilyn Monroe (Lois Laurel), Hugh Marlowe (Hank Entwhistle), Howard Hawks (off-screen voice in opening scene).

1972   *What's Up Doc* (94 minutes).

Distributing Co.: Warner Brothers. Producing Co.: Saticoy Production. Producer/Director: Peter Bogdanovich. Screenplay: Buck Henry, Robert Benton, David Newman, from a Bogdanovich story. Cast: Barbra Streisand (Judy Maxwell), Ryan O'Neal (Prof. Howard Bannister), Kenneth Mars (Hugh Simon), Madeline Kahn (Eunice Burns), Austin Pendleton (Frederick Larrabee), Sorrell Book (Harry).

1981   *Arthur* (96 minutes).

Distributing Co.: Warner Brothers. Producing Co.: Orion Pictures. Producer: Robert Greenhut. Director/Screenplay: Steve Gordon. Cast: Dudley Moore (Arthur Bach), Liza Minnelli (Linda Marolla), John Gielgud (Hobson), Geraldine Fitzgerald (Martha Bach), Jill Eikenberry (Susan Johnson), Stephen Elliott (Burt Johnson), Ted Ross (Bitterman), Barney Martin (Ralph Morolla).

# 8

# Populist Comedy

WES D. GEHRING

"There you are, Norton [potential fascist leader]—the people, try and lick that."
—Harry Connell (James Gleason) to D. B. Norton (Edward Arnold) at the close of Capra's *Meet John Doe* (1941).

As the screwball comedy draws upon the evolution of the comic antihero in American humor (see preceding chapter), the populist comedy has direct ties with the country's long-term crackerbarrel Yankee humor tradition. However, this is not an essay about *P*opulism, the short-lived political party of the late nineteenth century, but rather *p*opulism—the basic belief that the superior and majority will of the common man is forever threatened by a usurping, sophisticated, evil few.

Other characteristics frequently associated with populism include a celebration of rural and/or small-town life, mythic-like leaders who have risen from the people (also reflecting the movement's often patriotic nature), adherence to traditional values and customs (mirroring the phenomenon's strong sense of nostalgia), anti-intellectualism (in an elitist sense), faithfulness to honest labor, and general optimism concerning both man's potential for good and the importance of the individual.

Appropriately, historian George McKenna describes populism in his watershed book on the subject (*American Populism,* 1974) as "the perennial American 'ism' with its roots extended at least as far back as the American revolution."[1] In 1976 populist purist Lawrence Goodwyn decried the generalization of what the actual Populist party represented.[2] But the frequent application since then of a broadly generic populism to a number of settings (past and present) makes this generalization both natural and necessary.

Of course, as populist historian Harry Lazer noted, also in 1976, this does not imply that the true meaning of populism is obvious. Yet Lazer isolated a pivotal refrain when he declared: "A basic working definition of populism is the belief that the majority opinion of the people is checked by an elitist minority."[3]

Ten years later academic author Ronald Lee underlined the significance of this common man credo when he quoted similar fundamental definitions by several populist historians (including Lazer).[4] Thus, Lee also noted Peter Wiles's observation that "populism is any creed or movement based on the following major premise: *virtue resides in the simple people, who are the overwhelming majority, and in their collective traditions*" and Edward A. Shils's comment that "populism proclaims the will of the people as such is supreme over every other standard."[5]

When this power-to-the-people genre combines with American film comedy, a seemingly diverse collection of films surfaces, from the crackerbarrel Yankee 1930s movies of Will Rogers to the 1980s world of *Moscow on the Hudson* (1984). However, the archetype author of the populist film comedy is Frank Capra, whose key works fully showcase crackerbarrel Yankee American humor.[6] Thus, a further examination of populism vis-à-vis the five criteria which characterize this humor movement reveals the unique ties between populism and this mainstream tradition of American humor. The significance of this link directs the student of populism or American humor to examine both subjects jointly, instead of making a choice between the two, as in the past.[7] It should be kept in mind, however, that Richard Griffith's popular "fantasy of good will" approach to Capra, where the people bail out the savior-like hero, is not a populist comedy requirement.[8] While the goodness of the common man is inherent to the genre, it is just as likely to be borne out in the down-home wisdom of a crackerbarrel people's representative like Will Rogers. That is, Rogers is the people. And as Roger Butterfield noted, the Rogers common man persona "was the image that many Americans like to make of themselves."[9]

Rogers was not, however, above returning the compliment to the people, as he does near the close of *So This Is London* (1930): "There isn't much difference in people. World over [they're] just about the same [good]." The film then nicely closes on the shared "harmony" of Rogers singing "My Country 'Tis of Thee" while his British counterpart in the film (Lumsden Hare) sings the English lyrics for "God Save the King." Thus, as this chapter will demonstrate, the Capra hero typically owes much to earlier crackerbarrel figures.

The crackerbarrel Yankee philosopher is characterized by five key elements: political involvement, rural or small-town residency, employment, capability, and fatherly leadership (all just the opposite of the comic antihero examined in the previous chapter).

Politics, the first crackerbarrel Yankee component, most obviously showcases its populist nature in Capra's *Mr. Smith Goes to Washington* (1939). The first name of hero Jefferson Smith (played by Jimmy Stewart) represents the populist belief in Jeffersonian democracy (the heart of populism), the faith in a rural small-town America in need of little interference by the federal government. His surname is literally a one-word definition of American's common man.

The Capra country philosopher constantly acts as a Jeffersonian brake on the dangers of Hamiltonian big government, or comparable powerful organizations bent upon dictating orders to the common man. Thus, while Jefferson Smith stops corruption in the Senate, John Doe (another Everyman, played by Gary Cooper) stops a fascist-like organization from assuming power in *Meet John Doe* (1941). And poet Longfellow (after the patriotic poet of the people) Deeds (also played by Cooper) offers a self-help small-farm solution to the Great Depression while foiling an influential, corrupt banker.

Capra's Jefferson Smith reminds one most of Seba Smith's crackerbarrel Yankee Jack Downing—America's first native comic figure (1830s).[10] Much of the Downing material is a chronicle of the character's trips to Washington to advise populist President Andrew Jackson on the state of the Union (the Downing figure can be seen as an early Uncle Sam figure). Thus, the idealistic, long-legged, backwoods Downing, who goes to Washington, anticipates in many ways the Capra figures—especially Smith (the idealistic, long-legged boys camp leader who also goes to Washington).

Capra's embracing of the political crackerbarrel Yankee approximately a hundred years after the pivotal 1830s is a natural for two reasons. First, while the antihero was clearly in ascendancy in American humor, the Depression had given the crackerbarrel figure some staying power as people searched for fundamental values in a difficult time. This is clearly demonstrated in the phenomenal early 1930s film success of Will Rogers—who is generally considered the last crackerbarrel figure of national significance. In fact, the year before his untimely 1935 death, Rogers was the number one box-office draw in American films.[11]

With Rogers's passing, American humor would never know another singular crackerbarrel Yankee writer of national significance. But the crackerbarrel Yankee film void was more than filled by Capra, starting with the 1936 *Mr. Deeds*. Although Capra's heroes were younger and more idealistic than the Rogers model (again, reminiscent of Jack Downing), they were clearly in the crackerbarrel Yankee tradition. In fact, Capra seems to even footnote his ties to Rogers with his pivotal casting and utilization of Harry Carey as the president of the Senate in *Mr. Smith Goes to Washington*. Besides bearing a striking resemblance to Rogers, Carey's folksy mannerisms are especially reminiscent of the humorist: the slouching posture, the bit of hair falling on the forehead, the half-suppressed smile. Though on paper Carey's is a seemingly small part, his largely visual support of the filibustering Smith is pivotal to this segment of the film, as well as being very entertaining.

Second, Capra also had a direct Rogers connection. Early in Capra's career (when he worked for Hal Roach), Rogers, on contract, had taken the young man under his wing. Capra speaks lovingly of the humorist, who made a very pleasant arrangement with the then-young gagwriter:

When he found out I had no office typewriter he said I could use his dressing room and typewriter and he'd charge me one gag a day—and oh, he'd throw in the coffee and doughnuts. We made a deal. For the next four months his dressing room was my office. I tried to give him one gag a day, but for my one he gave me twenty.[12]

It should always be kept in mind, however, that Capra idealizes the people more than does Rogers. The latter's people are not as perfect, though on balance they are more to the good. Indeed, at times they can be delightfully democratic in their actions, such as Eugene Pallette's ever so trusting Sheriff Rufe Jeffers (Jefferson?) in *Steamboat 'Round the Bend* (1935), who lets an accused murderer (later proved innocent) lock himself up. And then there is Francis Ford's comically democratic, tobacco-spitting juror in *Judge Priest* (1934)— forever undercutting the court remarks of the pompous Senator Maydew (Berton Churchill) with his unerring spittoon accuracy. This is not to deny the presence of the small-town busybody type, especially in Rogers's *Dr. Bull* (1933). But accordingly, one should then also mention a Rogers vehicle like *State Fair* (1933), a warm celebration of rural America without a villain in sight. In fact, its genuineness was so convincing that *Variety* was moved to observe: "Those who know their rural America will find it ringing true."[13] Regardless of the supporting players in a Rogers film, however, is the fact that this humorist represents the people.

Through the years there have been populist variations upon the Capra examples of this first crackerbarrel trait—positive political involvement or a people's "campaign" against an elitist minority. In the cynical post–World War II era trusting populism was sometimes revitalized by casting a woman in the focus role. Witness the Oscar-winning performances of Loretta Young in *The Farmer's Daughter* (1947) and Judy Holliday in *Born Yesterday* (1950). More recently, Goldie Hawn's *Protocol* (1984) might better have been titled *Judy Holliday Goes to Washington*. As with *Born Yesterday*, it is a populist *Pygmalion* with a *Mr. Smith* slant.

A classic collection of all that is Capra populism occurs in Sydney Pollack's underrated *The Electric Horseman* (1979). As Wes D. Gehring demonstrated in his article *"The Electric Horseman: A 'Capra' Film for the 1980s,"* contemporary cowboy Sonny Steele (Robert Redford) defeats an uncaring business conglomerate in a decidedly Capra-like world (see note 6). Besides the story's obvious fundamental populist confrontation, *The Electric Horseman* utilizes such Capra basics as the hero receiving help from a strong woman who initially had been an adversary (reporter Jane Fonda, reminiscent of Capra's use of Jean Arthur in *Deeds* and *Smith* and Barbara Stanwyck in *Doe*), and the people eventually rallying behind the hero.

The second crackerbarrell Yankee trait with direct ties to populism is rural and/or small-town residency. The Yankee is invariably from this setting, though he often enters cities and cures their problems, such as Jack Downing or Jefferson Smith in Washington, D.C. Moreover, he always longs to return to the country or the small town (just as a Washington or a Jefferson was anxious to lay down the mantle of national duty and return to his beloved land). Thus, Deeds is very anxious to return to Mandrake Falls. Doe is continually tempted by his friend and fellow traveler (Walter Brennan) to wander across the wilds of America, and Smith wants nothing more than to return to his woods and Boy Rangers.

An outgrowth of Europe's eighteenth-century Enlightenment, this glorification of nature is more specifically an outgrowth of eighteenth-century Deism—the belief that to know God was to know nature, and to prefer nature over what was man-made. As McKenna has insightfully observed, this is "the doctrinal underpinning for Jefferson's claim that the farmers are God's 'chosen people' and his preference for agriculture over industry."[14] No populist comedy better showcases this high regard for the rural "chosen people" than *The Farmer's Daughter* scene where title character Loretta Young and Joseph Cotton go to ask her father for permission to marry. This meeting, on a hilltop, is shot in such a manner as to suggest this immigrant farmer is nothing short of kingly in his importance.

Judy Holliday's *Born Yesterday* character comically verbalizes the same sentiment when she baldly but correctly interprets American humanist Robert Ingersoll's celebrated preference between Napoleon and a French peasant: "He himself would'a rather been a happy farmer." By the end of the film, so would Judy Holliday.

The dichotomy of nature versus the man-made is sometimes showcased in the populist crackerbarrel world as country versus city. More to the point, the city is a man-made evil. Visually, the evil urban setting is best portrayed in George Bailey's (Jimmy Stewart) nightmare run down the decadent streets of Potterville—the sin city which would have replaced Bedford Falls had it not been for Bailey's goodness. A more recent variation upon this is the scene in *The Electric Horseman* where Steele (Redford) rides the misused corporation symbol, the stallion Rising Star, down the ultimate anything-for-sale street—the Las Vegas strip. Appropriately, the saving of both hero and horse necessitates their return to nature and the beautiful wilds of the American West.

An interesting juxtapositioning of city and country occurs in Will Rogers's *David Harum* (1934), where the laid-back world of small-town banker and title character Will Rogers is contrasted with the complex environment facing him in a large urban setting like New York City. Though an 1890s period piece, roundabout Depression commentary is in this case provided, as the time is the economic panic of 1893. And the message is a familiar one, though with a special Rogers interpretation of Jeffersonain democracy. Moreover, the film is full of what now seem like Capra populist touches, such as Rogers's democratic interaction with a butler, the significance of Christmas, and the people coming together in comic song—"Ta-Ra-Ra-Boom-de-Ay"—to help Rogers win the story-closing trotter race.

Robert Redford's strong real-life commitment to environmentalist issues demonstrates one way in which the country issue has been revitalized in recent years. *The Electric Horseman* was shot near his rural Utah home, and his character's celebration of the land is consistent with the actor's own views. However, because the United States is predominantly urban, and has been for some time, the pro–small-town/rural accent is frequently softened or given special narrative assistance. For example, even in the 1930s Will Rogers's films were invariably set in an earlier time (generally turn-of-the-century America), where his crackerbarrel capableness and the inherent goodness of the common man were more palatable for a Depression audience grown cynical. More recently, the populist "Waltons" television series was also set back to that same Depression America of the 1930s, only now grown more attractive by the passage of time and the age-old myth of poor is better.

Of course, this does not mean a contemporary country/small-town populist comedy cannot be done. James Garner received a 1985 Academy Award nomination for just that sort of film in *Murphy's Romance*. Old is still superior, as best demonstrated by his antique automobile or the accentuated age difference between Murphy (Garner) and leading lady Sally Field. But Murphy is getting along just fine in the small town here and now.

More typical, however, of a contemporary populist slant upon the danger of city living is the film *Hero at Large* (1980). John Ritter is a struggling New York actor who finds part-time work as a costumed Batman-like figure at theaters where the films of a new caped crusader (Captain Avenger) are playing. But when Ritter starts performing actual good deeds (in costume) during off hours, a cynical city (and indeed an initially cynical heroine) is revitalized by this comic book crimebuster come to life. Thus, the evil of the city is also its deadening effect upon our basic humanity—a humanity which can be reawakened by a populist hero.

The third crackerbarrel component with populist underpinnings is gainful employment. With regard to populism, one might label it antielitism, or a variation of the celebration of the common man. Thus, if the Yankee is not of the ideal profession (farming), such as James Russell Lowell's Hosea Biglow, his is the next best thing—the everyday work world, from Thomas Chandler Haliburton's nineteenth-century clock peddler Sam Slick (who first appeared in 1835) to Will Rogers's twentieth-century cowboy and self-made adviser to Calvin Coolidge. Moreover, historian Richard Hofstadter goes so far as to claim that the most unique characteristic of populist thought is "its willingness to grant the moral legitimacy and political acceptability of anyone who did any kind of honest work." [15]

The crackerbarrel profession allows and often demands easy access to a large number of people. Indeed, the title "crackerbarrel philospher" is actually derived from a profession—the general store owner who serves up both basic goods and good advice. America's greatest nonfiction crackerbarrel figure was from just such a background: Abraham Lincoln ran a general store before entering law.

Genuinely interested in people and human rights, crackerbarrel service occupations give these figures both "blue-collar degrees" in psychology and sociology and a legitimate up-from-the-people background. This is, of course, central to their serving the people if, as is often the case in populist stories, the central figure enters public office. Thus, even before Loretta Young's farmer's daughter decides to run for Congress, she has a ready answer on what a representative should be: "Someone who would represent. . . . He should know what the people want and vote for what they want."

Keeping busy (working) also makes a more healthy life, both figuratively and literally. One stays in touch with the norm, and the normal. In fact, a people-related work ethic could be called a crackerbarrel motto. For example, at Will Rogers's Oklahoma ranch there was "a sign up on the bobwire gate at the section line: 'Nothing Allowed in That Will Interfere With the Work or Scare the Animals.' "[16] And near the close of *So This Is London,* Will Rogers observes that the "wrong people [are] doing the traveling. They're [the travelers] not the real [to be celebrated] people; they're at home working." However, it should be kept in mind that the populist figure is hardly a slave to work. He is never buried in some urban, workaholic grind aimed at success. The crackerbarrel type always has time for fun, whether it is Will Rogers's Judge Priest forever slipping away to fish (and democratically, too, since Stepin Fetchit is usually his partner), or Gary Cooper's propensity to chase after fire engines in *Mr. Deeds.*

The most fascinating application of work to a crackerbarrel Yankee story occurs in John G. Avildsen's *The Karate Kid* (1984). Avildsen (director of the original *Rocky*) has put together a populist feel-good film for the 1980s, with American immigrant Noriyuki (Pat Morita) spouting crackerbarrel wisdom, Japanese-style. Morita is an apartment building handyman who teaches a young man (Ralph Macchio) about individual human dignity—and karate. The unique work ethic slant occurs in the teaching of special karate hand movements which are identical to basic work hand movements—and up-down painting motion and a circular sanding motion.

Honest labor and antielitism are mainstream Capra. His views on these subjects are most amusingly presented in *Mr. Deeds Goes to Town.* The film fairly oozes this spirit, as Deeds brings democratic life to his inherited servants and gives a delightful shock to the opera company which comes expecting a handout and instead receives demands for self-sufficiency. Such an affectionately effective presentation is a natural for Capra, who came to America as a poor immigrant child from Sicily and worked his way to success. In fact, at one point in his autobiography Capra calls himself "another Horatio Alger."[17]

Possibly the most people-related profession of all crackerbarrel figures is

Irvin S. Cobb's Judge Priest, especially since much of this literature deals with the character's out-of-court "priestly" duties rather than with his work before the law. Appropriately, Cobb's friend and fellow crackerbarrel writer/actor Will Rogers played Judge Priest in the John Ford-directed 1934 film of the same name. Cobb also played a riverboat captain competing with Rogers in another Ford-directed crackerbarrel film—*Steamboat 'Round the Bend* (1935). Populist director Ford reused the *Judge Priest* characters and many other aspects of this film when he made *The Sun Shines Bright* (1953).

In the 1940s director Leo McCarey literally combined the priestly and the populist in his two phenomenally successful (critically and commercially) films of faith—*Going My Way* (1944) and *The Bells of St. Mary's* (1945). As film historian Jeffrey Richards noted when examining McCarey's populist ties, "Both films are based on the assumption that there is good in everyone and it only needs to be brought out, preferably by a crooning priest [Bing Crosby played central character Father O'Malley in each film] who here embodies the spirit of goodwill." [18]

Though one might not automatically associate populism and religion, both populism's inherent "love thy neighbor" policy and its celebration of the significance of the individual are at the heart of Christianity. Capra addressed this directly when he stated:

I think that the gospels are a comedy—good news. I think that the greatest comedy of all is the Divine Comedy—the Resurrection, victory over death. Every Sunday the Catholics celebrate the mass, celebrate a victory over death. That's what comedy means to me. . . . Sure, the good people—good hasn't taken over the earth. But neither has evil taken over the earth. And you shouldn't let it. [19]

The fourth crackerbarrel trait with direct populist ties is a capable nature. This implies an optimistic belief in a world where man can both implement and accept reasonable change. Remember, in England the Enlightenment was known as "The Age of Reason." To the populist, most people were both reasoning and reasonable. More precisely, as populist historian McKenna reminds us, this is what Jefferson meant when he referred to "self-evident" truths. [20]

The crackerbarrel figure lives in a rational world, and his common sense gets him through any situation. People who have difficulties are not organized and are not using their common sense, although a successful path is always available to them. A significant part of this is the ability to keep track of past experiences—simply what happened last time. In a rational universe events will repeat themselves and be quite predictable. This constitutes the basic formula for success. Thus, the Yankee figure is frequently an older man grown wise through a lifetime of experience, such as a Will Rogers. The most specific of examples is probably Hosea Biglow's comment on the Civil War: "I'm older'n you, an' I've seen things an' men, an' *my* experience, tell ye wut its ben."[21]

Capra more often, however, took a young man and gave him a wise older figure as a model, such as the martyred father of Mr. Smith, the father of George Bailey in *It's a Wonderful Life* (1946), and the writings of the late father of Ann Mitchell (played by Barbara Stanwyck) in *Meet John Doe*. While younger crackerbarrel Yankees were not unknown in literary circles (such as the very beginning figure of Jack Downing), Capra's inclusion of severe difficulties for the Yankee provided needed dramatic tension for the demands of a feature-length film and added character believability (the crackerbarrel Yankee can sometimes seem too perfect).

A younger hero also provides the perfect dramatic need for another populist key—a strong sense of nationalism, or more specifically, historical Yankee models of great patriotic significance, such as Jefferson, Jackson, and Lincoln. Thus, in *Mr. Smith,* besides the aforementioned use of the name Jefferson Smith, this character also visits most of what might be called the capital's crackerbarrel shrines (such as the Lincoln and Jefferson memorials), a plot line also followed in *Born Yesterday* and *Protocol*. Later, Smith returns to "worship" and gain strength at the Lincoln Memorial. (*Born Yesterday* and *Protocol* heroines return to the Jefferson Memorial.) Smith, who had earlier been described as having "Honest Abe's ideals," would soon go on to demonstrate the slain president's perseverance under duress. The ideals of such revered American heroes provide Jefferson Smith with a certain mythological aura all his own. As celebrated psychologist and cultural essayist Otto Rank observed in his famous, nearly book-length essay "The Myth of the Birth of the Hero," "the transference of mythical motifs from the life of the older hero to a younger one bearing the same name . . . [is] a universal process in myth formation."[22]

The most interesting populist comedy combination of crackerbarrel Yankee role models for a younger hero (after the hall of fame collection in *Mr. Smith*) occurs in *The Farmer's Daughter*. Besides its celebration of another real, martyred president, Woodrow Wilson, there are four prominent fictional characters. Two are the fathers of the story principals. The father farmer of the title (Harry Shannon) is an archetypal populist crackerbarrel model, from occupation to wise axioms ("If you don't want to fight for truth, then you shouldn't be in Congress"). The Joseph Cotton (Morley) father, though deceased, is a pivotal patriot memory—a U.S. senator and colleague of Wilson. Loretta Young's reading of his speech is an early indication of her political potential.

Additional worldly-wise parental populists are the Morley mother (Ethel Barrymore) and her husband-like, longtime butler Clancy (Charles Bickford). Together they create the most entertaining of crackerbarrel couples, with the matriarchal slant also nicely complementing the film's key variation upon the genre norm—casting a woman in the title role. Bickford, along with the brothers of the farmer's daughter, also provides the righteous muscle which occasionally overpowers the populist, at one point even dropkicking the Ku Klux Klan congressional opponent of Young from the Morley home (after Barrymore has metaphorically booted him from the party). One is reminded of similar Capra scenes, such as Deeds's punching of the elitist poets.

The final crackerbarrel Yankee trait (fatherly image) showcases many of the populist characteristics already discussed. Appropriately, they might be said to all coalesce around the populist celebration of the common man. To reiterate, this means a belief in the inherent goodness/righteousness of man and his ability to rise to heights of leadership during times of crisis (caused by an evil minority), only to return to his rural/small-town anonymity once the emergency is over.

This almost mysterious coming and going of the populist figure is also a basic convention of the mythological hero.[23] One is especially reminded of *The Electric Horseman* close, when Redford voluntarily disappears into the American West once his modern quest is done. An aerial camera quietly moves away from the scene. In the comic books it is the Lone Ranger slipping away to the refrain of "Who was that masked man?" In American history it is the Washingtons and Jeffersons and Franklins doing their patriotic duty but always preferring less celebrated lives as private citizens. In religion one only has to mention the cross, an analogy Capra often drew with his populist heroes. Thus, at its most fundamental level the populist is the stuff of an idealized father figure or parent, a wise but difficult-decision maker, forever wrought with personal sacrifice. The crackerbarrel populist's love of people merely reinforces this, bringing to mind Will Rogers's signature statement, "I never met a man I didn't like."

As already noted, Capra's young heroes frequently have older, crackerbarrel father types to guide them. But in the director's central trilogy of *Deeds, Smith,* and *Doe,* the most entertaining example of this figure still belongs to a younger character. It is found in the courtroom scene at the close of *Deeds,* where the title character defendant comically reduces his accusers to the childlike while increasing the childlike awe of his many admirers all the more. It is a comically insightful defense where the hero (perfectly cast with Gary Cooper) amusingly expands upon such things as the nature of being "pixilated," as well as introducing the term "doodling" into the American lexicon.

Capra's strongest trilogy father figure, moreover, is seemingly the youngest—the freshman senator of *Mr. Smith.* As the leader of the Boy Rangers (which Capra based on the Boy Scouts), Jimmy Stewart's Jefferson Smith is the surrogate father to thousands of boys everywhere. And Capra makes frequent and effective use of these children throughout the film, from the comically warm lobbying for Smith by the governor's children at the film's beginning, to the devastating attacks on the youngsters by the political machine near the film's close.

As is expected of the fatherly Yankee, Capra's models prove caretakers for the nation. Deeds provides a blueprint out of the Depression. Smith reveals corruption in the Senate. Doe stops an American fascist from taking power. Quite obviously, the crackerbarrel Yankee is an idealization of what America is all about—a variation on the real fact that the country's Uncle Sam figure evolved from this character.

Populist comedies outside of Capra abound with the same fatherly homage, be it Will Rogers forever assisting the young and the disadvantaged in film after film, or McCarey's Catholic "Father" O'Malley (Bing Crosby) and his *Good Sam* (short for Good Samaritan, 1948) doing the same. In fact, *Good Sam* finds Gary Cooper in a title role not unlike Jimmy Stewart's in *It's a Wonderful Life*.

The significance of the populist fatherly hosannas continues today. For example, in *The Karate Kid, Part II* (1986), Morita moves from being a surrogate father for Macchio (in the original film) to being his legal guardian. Goldie Hawn's father focus in *Protocol* (she was executive producer) even has a strong personal slant, because her real father, to whom the film is dedicated, provided the inspiration for the production with his stories of political corruption in Washington, D.C.[24]

These, then, have been the five key components of the crackerbarrel populist. However, three qualifiers need to be considered briefly before a full picture of the comedy genre is complete. The first and most obvious is that the dangers/evils of the modern world are becoming too complex for the crackerbarrel figure and the common man. It is simply no longer a rational world. As author Hamlin Hill observed in 1963, today's comedy figure is "incapable of inventing homespun maxims about hundred-megaton bombs, or feeling any native self-confidence in the face of uncontrollable fallout"[25]

Capra acknowledges this outdatedness in *It's a Wonderful Life*, where his populist hero is able to survive only through a deus ex machina plot device. Capra does tone down this heavenly intrusion by sending a second-class angel—Clarence Oddbody. But the Yankee is no longer able to cope, on a simple common-sense level, with the complex issues of the day. This moment has been foreshadowed by the near suicide of John Doe. But this time there are no friends who arrive at the eleventh hour (as they do in *Meet John Doe*); it takes an act of God. Note also how the title *It's a Wonderful Life* represents further capable hero displacement: it no longer showcases an individual's name.

Thus, since the 1940s the populist comedy has frequently required a healthy dose of the suspension of disbelief, if not outright fantasy. For example, the year after Capra was resorting to second-class angels (1947), writer-director George Seaton did a masterful job of recycling more than a little of *Mr. Deeds* into his delightful Christmas tale of Kris Kringle—*Miracle on 34th Street*. In both cases a caring populist hero attempts to dispense joy to the world, only to be branded insane. After these audience-identifying "ritualistic humiliations" (common to both Capra and many populist films in general), the faith of the people rekindles life in the heroes.[26] The difference, however, is that in 1936 it was largely played straight, whereas the post–World War II audience needed a Santa Claus fantasy to make it palatable. And Capra no doubt added further influence to *Miracle on 34th Street* when it is remembered that *It's a Wonderful Life* borrows generously from Dickens's *A Christmas Carol.*

It should be noted that additional populism lives on in such contemporary fantasies as the *Star Wars* sagas and *E.T.* (1982). And this is probably as it should be, since America's favorite fantasy, Frank Baum's *The Wonderful World of Oz,* was originally written as a populist allegory.

Populist fantasy of an indirect nature had been anticipated in McCarey's 1940s Catholic comedies of faith. And, of course, Richard Griffith originally applied the phrase "fantasy of good will," as previously noted, to Capra's populist films of the 1930s.

Another alternative for increased populist comedy acceptability, as opposed to the real-life miracle of a Deeds variety or the angelic intervention of *It's a Wonderful Life,* is to tone down the national accomplishments to more believable means. Thus, one has the neighborhood populism of *Hero at Large, The Karate Kid, Moscow on the Hudson,* and *Murphy's Romance.* One might also include Clint Eastwood's often-frustrated good Samaritan cowboy Bronco Billy (from the 1980 film of the same name). In a sense, Capra also anticipated this realist slant when he adapted the Howard Lindsay–Russel Crouse play *State of the Union* (1948). Though the central character is still a national populist (Spencer Tracy plays a presidential candidate), he drops out of politics because of the corruption. And while he promises to fight this problem, the film ironically closes with the backroom kingmakers calmly discussing who else they could manipulate into the presidency.

The resurgence of patriotism since Watergate, followed by the country's bicentennial celebration has, however, returned some credibility to even the more broad-based populist hero. Consequently, national populists have surfaced in productions like *The Electric Horseman* and *Protocol,* or on television's true fantasy of goodwill, "Highway to Heaven." No doubt because of the great critical and commercial success of *The Karate Kid,* the sequel also addressed much broader issues. Thus, Morita returns to his ancestral home, obtains major land reform, and in ultimate populist fashion, converts the villain. This is a most dramatic reversal from the populist film comedy's low ebb of the 1950s and 1960s, when rustics at their best were normally of the Ma and Pa Kettle variety.

The second crackerbarrel populist qualifier is that even the most idealistic can be corrupted by power. Sam Slick's observation is probably the most comically pointed on this subject: "Politics makes a man as crooked as a pack does a peddler. Not that they are so evil either, but it teaches a man to stoop in the long run."[27] This has been the fate of the once idealistic senior senator from Jefferson Smith's state, Joseph Paine (Claude Rains). A former friend and colleague of Smith's Yankee father (who, like Lincoln, was assassinated from behind, a martyr to his ideals), Paine had also been a "champion of lost causes." In fact, he tells Smith, "thirty years ago I had your ideals. I was you." But in becoming a senator he had to "compromise," as well as become a yes-man to political boss Jim Taylor (Edward Arnold).

There is also the danger that the crackerbarrel type could misuse the power himself—once he has used his populist traits to reach a position of power. Elia Kazan's *A Face in the Crowd* (1957, from a Budd Schulberg short story) later became the definitive film example of just that, with Andy Griffith (later television's definitive populist, crackerbarrel type) giving an excellent performance of this figure gone bad. It was also especially timely, with 1950s McCarthyism already being a strong populist defuser.

Moreover, regardless of how wise and wonderful the figure, his position of power sometimes sets dangerous precedents. For instance, even Peter C. Rollins's insightfully sympathetic biography of Rogers refers to the humorist's screen character as a "benevolent dictator."[28] And McCarey's 1952 populist melodrama *My Son John* (which examines a family which suspects their son may be a communist) is a reactionary workshop in the right-wing political dangers inherent in populism, whether one is "examining" communism, or Huey Long's "Share the Wealth" plan.

The third qualifier is that both the crackerbarrel type and the people can be fooled, with the former being turned into a puppet demagogue. Capra omnisciently showcases this vulnerability throughout *Meet John Doe*. In fact, film critic and theorist Andrew Sarris has labeled the naive, misused Doe a "barefoot fascist."[29] Ultimately, of course, the real fascist (Edward Arnold) is stopped, but he is hardly vanquished. And as historian C. Vann Woodward has observed, "Disenchantment of the intellectual with the masses was [already] well under way in the forties . . . [because of] mass support for evil caused in Germany and elsewhere."[30]

Even them, however, all was not black for populism. George Stevens's *The Talk of the Town* (1942) manages to out-Capra Capra. Though frequently compared to *Mr. Deeds, Talk of the Town* is most impressive because it so entertainingly works in *Mr. Smith* and *John Doe* country.[31] That is, while the people are again initially misled by the media control of a neofascist type, the close finds an American champion totally in charge—right down to another trip to Washington (Ronald Coleman's character becomes a Supreme Court Justice). And a dry intellectual (law school dean Coleman) has discovered both populist compassion and a dynamite punch, all thanks to Cary Grant's more practical *people*-oriented treatment of the law. Thus, while even a Lincoln could qualify his celebration of the people—"You can fool some of the people all the time, and all of the people some of the time, but you cannot fool all the people all the time"—the continued resiliency of populism underlines its integrality to the American experience.

## BIBLIOGRAPHICAL OVERVIEW

Source material here is overwhelmingly focused in nonfilm texts. Though references to populist film comedy are hardly obscure, extended analyses of the genre are something else. An excellent exception to this is "The Cinema of Populism" section in Jeffery Richards's *Vision of Yesterday* (1973). He devotes four chapters to the phenomenon—keying upon populist ideology and directors Capra, McCarey (focus on the 1940s), and Ford.

The richest area of related cinema study is best explored under the heading of Capra, populist comedy's archetypal director. Though there is seldom the direct coupling of director and populist genre which is present in the Jeffrey Richards material, it obviously demands attention. But this bibliographical overview will not attempt to open a Pandora's box of all possibly pertinent Capra material. Interested students of the director should, however, examine the chapter's notes section, where numerous Capra sources are cited.

The overview also continues to key upon *p*opulism as a general American phenomenon or ism and minimizes its attention to works devoted exclusively to the historically short-lived *P*opulist movement of the late nineteenth century.

The best book-length starting point for the study of populism as a basic American ideology is political scientist/professor George McKenna's *American Populism*. McKenna, after an insightful opening essay on the subject, has assembled an outstanding collection of populist writings chronicling the tendency through American history, from Jefferson to today. Most central is the category entitled "Vintage Populism," which includes such material as Jackson's 1832 congressional address, "Vetoing the Bank of 'The Rich and Powerful' " and excerpts from "Early Agrarian Protests" literature ("Shays' Rebellion" and "The Whiskey Rebellion"). This immediately establishes how innate populism is to the American experience.

An excellent companion piece to this anthology of original works is Ghita Ionescu and Ernest Gellner's *Populism: Its Meaning and National Characteristics,* an anthology of essays on the general phenomenon of populism. Most helpful for this chapter is Peter Wiles's essay "A Syndrome, Not a Doctrine: Some Elementary Theses on Populism," which examines twenty-four basic characteristics of populism.

Three additional works of interest which focus specifically upon the *P*opulist movement are John D. Hicks's *The Populist Revolt* (1931), Richard Hofstadter's *Age of Reform* (1955), and Norman Pollack's *The Populist Mind* (1967). They have been isolated for three reasons. First, Hicks's book is a pioneer study of the subject which treats the principals involved as heroes. It has had enormous influence and fittingly is of the same period (1930s) in which Capra came to populist prominence. Second, Hofstadter's volume is an influential revisionist look at Populism where the heroic common man is now seen to be much more easily misled. And just as Hicks's study matches the positive image of the 1930s populist, Hofstadter's doubts are consistent with the populist's fall from grace in the 1950s. Third, Pollack's *The Populist Mind* is both an anthology of pivotal 1980s Populist writing and a defense (in a lengthy introduction) against the 1950s stance which suggested links "between Populism and the proto-fascistic behavior that culminated with McCarthyism."[32] Beyond Pollack's convincing counterrevisionism is a fascinating collection of writing, ranging from Populist newspaper editorials to excerpts from Populist novels (focusing upon the work of Ignatius Donnelly, Populist activist and prolific author).

Probably the most significant of all novels is Donnelly's *Caesar's Column* (1890), an anti-utopian work which graphically predicts the sorry future facing man if the growing differences between the haves and the have-nots do not change. Though excerpted in Pollack's anthology, *Caesar's Column* merits a complete reading because of the richness with which it showcases so many general populist characteristics, anticipating the world of Frank Capra. Indeed, its Capra-like hero is another naive rural idealist who is nearly destroyed in the evil city but survives to fight for justice. Additionally, like Deeds, he also finds time to write romantic poetry to his future wife. Though the near-apocalypse ending of *Caesar's Column* might seem to distance itself from Capra, the haven found by the novel's central characters in a Shangri-la–like mountain retreat (which is also a depository of mankind's knowledge) is again pure Capra.

Besides the anthologized shorter works already noted, there are six additional essays which merit recognition. Film historian Richard Griffith's "The American Film" supplement to Paul Rotha's early history *The Film Till Now* deserves inclusion. Griffith's "fantasy of good will" concept (as applied to Capra) seems to have greatly influenced Jeff Richards's pivotal *Vision of Yesterday* essays. C. Vann Woodward's "The Populist Heritage and the Intellectual" nicely complements Norman Pollack's aforementioned introduction to *The Populist Mind*, both being historical surveys of the intellectual community on Populism. Ronald Lee's "The New Populist Campaign for Economic Democracy: A Rhetorical Exploration" best helps define the general ideology of populism, and its changing image through the years.

I also drew heavily upon related past writing of my own. Most pertinent were "McCarey vs. Capra: A Guide to American Film Comedy of the '30s" and *"The Electric Horseman:* A 'Capra' Film for the 1980s," both from the *Journal of Popular Film and Television;* "The Yankee Figure in American Comedy fiction," *Thalia: A Journal of Studies in Literary Humor;* and "Frank Capra: In the Tradition of Will Rogers and Other Yankees," *Indiana Social Studies Quarterly.*

## NOTES

1. George McKenna, ed., *American Populism* (New York: G. P. Putnam's, 1974), p. xii.

2. Lawrence Goodwyn, *Democratic Promise: The Populist Movement in America* (New York: Oxford University Press, 1976), p. xvi.

3. Harry Lazer, "British Populism: The Labor Party and the Common Market Parliamentary Debate," *Political Science Quarterly,* Summer 1976, p. 259.

4. Ronald Lee, "The New Populist Campaign for Economic Democracy: A Rhetorical Exploration," *Quarterly Journal of Speech,* August 1986, p. 288.

5. Ibid. See also Peter Wiles, "A Syndrome, Not a Doctrine: Some Elementary Theses on Populism," in *Populism: Its Meaning and National Characteristics,* ed. Ghita Ionescu and Ernest Gellner (London: Weidenfeld and Nicholson, 1969) p. 166; and Edward A. Shils, *The Torment of Secrecy* (London: William Heinemann, 1956), p. 98.

6. Wes D. Gehring has written extensively on the subject of crackerbarrel Yankee humor. The following pieces are especially pertinent with regard to this chapter: "McCarey vs. Capra: A Guide to American Film Comedy of the '30s," *Journal of Popular Film and Television* 7, no. 1, 1978, pp. 67–84; "The Yankee Figure in American Comedy Fiction," *Thalia: A Journal of Studies in Literary Humor,* Winter 1978–79, pp. 43–49; "Frank Capra: In the Tradition of Will Rogers and Other Yankees," *Indiana Social Studies Quarterly,* Fall 1981, pp. 49–56; and *"The Electric Horseman:* A 'Capra' Film for the 1980s," *Journal of Popular Film and Television,* Winter 1983, pp. 175–82.

7. See an overview of some positions taken by Capra scholars with regard to this subject, in Glen A. Phelps, "Frank Capra and the Political Hero: A New Reading of 'Meet John Doe,' " *Film Criticism,* Winter 1981, p. 49.

8. Richard Griffith, "The American film: 1929–48," (from "The Film Since Now" edition), in Paul Rotha's *The Film Till Now* (1949); repr. Norwich, England: Hamlyn Publishing Group, 1967), pp. 450–53.

9. Roger Butterfield, "The Legend of Will Rogers," *Life,* 18 July 1949, pp. 92, 94.

10. Walter Blair, *Native American Humor* (1937; repr. San Francisco: Chandler Publishing, 1960), p. 39.

11. Richard Gertner, ed., *International Motion Picture Almanac 1976* (New York: Quigley Publishing, 1976), p. 51.

12. Frank Capra, *The Name Above the Title* (New York: Macmillan, 1971), p. 40.

13. *State Fair* review, *Variety,* 31 January 1933, p. 12.

14. McKenna, *American Populism,* p.3.

15. Richard Hofstadter, "North America," in *Populism: Its Meanings and National Characteristics,* ed. Ionescu and Gellner, p. 17.

16. Will Rogers, *Letters of a Self-Made Diplomat to His President* (New York: Albert & Charles Boni, 1926), p. 234.

17. Capra, *The Name Above the Title,* p. 9.

18. Jeffrey Richards, "Leo McCarey: The Fantasy of Goodwill" (from "The Cinema of Populism" section), in *Visions of Yesterday* (London: Routledge & Kegan Paul, 1973), p. 262.

19. Richard Schickel, "Frank Capra," in *The Men That Made the Movies* (New York: Atheneum, 1975), pp. 87–88.

20. McKenna, *American Populism,* p. 4.

21. James Russell Lowell, "The Biglow Papers: Second Series," in *The Complete Poetical Works of James Russell Lowell,* ed. Horace E. Scuddler (1894; repr. Cambridge, Mass.: Riverside Press, 1924), p. 237.

22. Otto Rank. "The Myth of the Birth of the Hero" (1914), in *The Myth of the*

*Birth of the Hero and Other Writings by Otto Rank,* ed. Philip Freund (1959; repr. New York: Vintage Books, 1964), p. 63.

23. Ibid.

24. Richard David Story, "Hawn Exercises a Golden Touch," *USA Today,* 28 December 1984, p. 1D.

25. Hamlin Hill, "Modern American Humor: The Janus Laugh," *College English,* December 1963, p. 174.

26. Charles J. Maland, *American Visions: The Films of Chaplin, Ford, Capra, and Welles, 1936–1941* (New York: Arno Press, 1977), pp. 210–11.

27. Jennette Tandy, *Crackerbarrel Philosophers in American Humor and Satire* (New York: Columbia University Press, 1925), p. 41.

28. Peter C. Rollins, *Will Rogers: A Bio-Bibliography* (Westport, Conn.: Greenwood Press, 1984), p. 64.

29. Andrew Sarris, "Frank Capra," in *The American Cinema: Directors and Directions, 1929–1968* (New York: E. P. Dutton, 1968), p. 87.

30. C. Vann Woodward, "The Populist Heritage and the Intellectual," in *The Burden of Southern History* (New York: Vintage Books, 1960), p. 143.

31. See especially *The Talk of the Town* review, *New York Times,* 27 August 1942, p. 15; and *The Talk of the Town* review, *Variety,* 29 July 1942, p. 42.

32. Norman Pollack, ed., *The Populist Mind* (Indianapolis: Bobbs-Merrill, 1967), p. xxiii.

## BIBLIOGRAPHICAL CHECKLIST

Donnelly, Ignatius. *Caesar's Column* (novel). 1890; repr. Cambridge, Mass.: Harvard University Press, 1960.

Gehring, Wes. "*The Electric Horseman:* A 'Capra' Film for the 1980s," *Journal of Popular Film and Television,* Winter 1983, pp. 175–82.

———. "Frank Capra: In the Tradition of Will Rogers and Other Yankees," *Indiana Social Studies Quarterly,* Fall 1981, pp. 49–52.

———. "McCarey vs. Capra: A Guide to American Film Comedy of the '30s," *Journal of Popular Film and Television* 7, no. 1, 1978, pp. 67–84.

———. "The Yankee Figure in American Comedy Fiction," *Thalia: A Journal of Studies in Literary Humor,* Winter 1978–1979, pp. 43–49.

Griffith, Richard. "The American film: 1929–48" (from "The Film Since Now" edition). In Paul Rotha's *The Film Till Now.* 1949; repr. Norwich, England: Hamlyn Publishing Group Ltd., 1967, pp. 428–525.

Hicks, John D. *The Populist Revolt.* Minneapolis: University of Minnesota Press, 1931.

Hofstadter, Richard. *The Age of Reform.* New York: Alfred A. Knopf, 1955.

Ionescu, Ghita, and Ernest Gellner, eds. *Populism: Its Meanings and National Characteristics.* London: Weidenfeld and Nicholson, 1969.

Lee, Ronald. "The New Populist Campaign for Economic Democracy: A Rhetorical Exploration," *Quarterly Journal of Speech,* August 1986, pp. 274–89.

McKenna, George, ed. *American Populist.* New York: G. P. Putnam's, 1974.

Pollack, Norman, ed. *The Populist Mind.* Indianapolis: Bobbs-Merrill, 1967.

Richards, Jeffrey. Chapter 14, "The Ideology of Populism"; chapter 15, "Frank Capra: The Classic Populist"; chapter 16, "Leo McCarey: The Fantasy of Goodwill";

and chapter 17, "John Ford: The Folk Memory." In *Visions of Yesterday*. London: Routledge and Kegan Paul, 1973.

Woodward, C. Vann. "The Populist Heritage and the Intellectual." In *The Burden of Southern History*. New York: Vintage Books, 1960.


## SELECTED FILMOGRAPHY

1930   *So This Is London* (89 minutes).
A Fox Movietone Production. Director: John Blystone. Screenplay: Sonya Levien; Adaptation and Dialogue: Owen Davis, Sr.; Adapted by Arthur Goodrich from George M. Cohan's stageplay. Cast: Will Rogers (Hiram Draper), Irene Rich (Mrs. Hiram Draper), Frank Albertson (Junior Draper), Maureen O'Sullivan (Elinnor Draper), Lumsden Hare (Lord Percy Worthing).

1936   *Mr. Deeds Goes to Town* (115 minutes).
Columbia. Producer/Director: Frank Capra. Screenplay: Robert Riskin, from the Clarence Budington Kelland story "Opera Hat." Cast: Gary Cooper (Longfellow Deeds), Jean Arthur (Babe Bennett), Douglas Dumbrille (John Cedar).

1939   *Mr. Smith Goes to Washington* (125 minutes).
Columbia. Producer/Director: Frank Capra. Screenplay: Sidney Buchman, from the Lewis R. Foster story "The Gentleman from Montana." Cast: Jimmy Stewart (Jefferson Smith), Jean Arthur (Clarissa Saunders), Claude Rains (Senator Joseph Paine), Edward Arnold (Jim Taylor), Harry Carey (President of the Senate).

1941   *Meet John Doe* (135 minutes).
Warner Brothers. Producer/Director: Frank Capra. Screenplay: Robert Riskin, from a Richard Connell and Robert Presnell story. Cast: Gary Cooper (Long John Willoughby), Barbara Stanwyck (Ann Mitchell), Edward Arnold (D. F. Norton), Walter Brennan (The "Colonel"), James Gleason (Henry Connell).

1942   *The Talk of the Town* (118 minutes).
Columbia. Producer/Director: George Stevens. Screenplay: Irwin Shaw, Sidney Buchman; Dale Van Every adaptation of Sidney Harmon story. Cast: Gary Grant (Leopold Dilg), Jean Arthur (Nora Smelley), Ronald Coleman (Michael Lightcap), Edgar Buchanan (Sam Yates).

1946   *It's a Wonderful Life* (129 minutes).
Liberty Films. Producer/Director: Frank Capra. Screenplay: Frances Goodrich, Albert Hackett, Frank Capra, from the Philip Van Doren Stern story "The Greatest Gift," plus scenes by Jo Swerling. Cast: Jimmy Stewart (George Bailey), Donna Reed (Mary Hatch), Lionel Barrymore (Potter), Henry Travers (Clarence Oddbody, second-class angel).

1947   *The Farmer's Daughter* (97 minutes).
RKO release of a Dore Schary Production. Director: H. C. Potter. Screenplay: Allen Rivkin, Laura Kerr, from a Juhni Tervataa play. Cast: Loretta Young (Katrin Holstrom), Joseph Cotton (Glenn Morley), Ethel Barrymore (Mrs. Morley), Charles Bickford (Clancy), Harry Shannon (Mr. Holstrom).

1950   *Born Yesterday* (103 minutes).
Columbia release of a S. Sylvan Simon Production. Director: George Cukor.

Screenplay: Albert Mannheimer, from the Garson Kanin play. Cast: Judy Holliday (Billie Dawn), Broderick Crawford (Harry Brock), William Holden (Paul Verrall).

1979   *The Electric Horseman* (120 minutes).
Columbia release of a Ray Stark production. Director: Sydney Pollack. Screenplay: Robert Garland, from a Garland, Paul Gaer screen story, based upon a Shelly Burton story. Cast: Robert Redford (Sonny Steele), Jane Fonda (Hallie), Willie Nelson (Wendell), John Saxon (Hunt Sears).

1980   *Hero At Large* (98 minutes).
MGM. Producer: Stephen Friedman. Director: Martin Davidson. Screenplay: A. J. Carothers. Cast: John Ritter (Steve Nichols), Anne Archer (J. Marsh), Bert Convy (Walter Reeves).

1984   *Protocol* (96 minutes).
Warner Brothers. Producer: Anthea Sylbert. Director: Herbert Ross. Screenplay: Buck Henry. Cast: Goldie Hawn (Sunny), Chris Sarandon (Michael), Richard Romanus (Emir), Gail Strickland (Mrs. St. John).

# 9

# Parody

WES D. GEHRING

"You see, I wanted to be a detective, too. It only took brains, cour-
age, and a gun. And I had the gun."
Voice-over narrative by baby photographer Ronnie Jackson
(Bob Hope) in the film noir spoof *My Favorite Brunette* (1947).

Film parody is a comic, yet generally affectionate, and distorted imitation of a
given genre, auteur, or specific work. These parody variations are best demonstrated by the 1970s pied piper of the genre, Mel Brooks. His *Blazing Saddles* (1974) is a takeoff on the western genre. *High Anxiety* (1977) parodies the
mystery/thriller work of auteur Alfred Hitchcock. And Brooks's *Young Frankenstein* (1974) is largely a comic undercutting (or should one say distortion?)
of the classic horror film *Frankenstein* (1931) and some of its sequels, especially *Bride of Frankenstein* (1935).

Unlike other comedy genres discussed thus far, parody has been a mainstream part of American film comedy since the beginning. It was, in fact, a
pivotal ingredient in the works of America's film comedy father, Mack Sennett.
This comedy pioneer was at his best when parodying the melodramatic adventure films of his mentor, D. W. Griffith. For instance, Sennett's *Teddy at the
Throttle* (1916) is a delightful takeoff on Griffith's propensity for the last-min-
ute rescue, such as the close of his celebrated *The Birth of a Nation* (1915).

In the following examination of seven basic characteristics of parody, Sennett's significance to the genre is underscored by frequent references to his
work along with other pivotal directors, such as Brooks. First, while parody is
frequently humorous even without viewer expertise on the subject under comic
attack, it is most entertaining when one is familiar with the parody source.
Consequently, because Sennett was a former Griffith writer, his parody of the
master has an added comic edge for students of that director. For example, as

film comedy historian Gerald Mast reminds us, Sennett's *Help! Help!* (1912) is a "specific parody" of Griffith's *Lonely Villa* (1909), which the comedy filmmaker had written.[1]

Fittingly, the genre which easily seems to have inspired the greatest number of American film parodies is also considered the most inherently American (incomparably familiar)—the western. Thus, the vast majority of major American screen comedians have found time for a western spoof, such as Buster Keaton's *Go West* (1925), Laurel and Hardy's *Way Out West* (1936), W. C. Fields and Mae West's *My Little Chickadee* (1940), the Marx Brothers' *Go West* (1940), Abbott & Costello's *The Wistful Widow of Wagon Gap* (1947), and Martin and Lewis's *Pardners* (1956). Bob Hope even managed to do three western spoofs: *The Paleface* (1948), *Son of Paleface* (1952), and *Alias Jesse James* (1959), with Hope's version of the often adapted *Ruggles of Red Gap*— *Fancy Pants* (1950)—sometimes counted as a fourth. Naturally, the most celebrated of all parodies remains Brooks's *Blazing Saddles,* though western spoofs continue, be they the Saturday matinee variety of the Steve Martin–Chevy Chase–Martin Short *¡Three Amigos!* (1986), or the bawdy camp of *Lust in the Dust* (1985, with the gross-out leader of women impersonators, Divine, of John Waters fame).

Second, though the fundamental goal of parody is to be *funny,* this genre is also an educational tool, something which might best be defined as "creative criticism."[2] That is, to create effective parody one must be thoroughly versed in the subject under attack. (It is for this reason that parody is often comically affectionate in nature, because the artist is frequently a student of the target genre or auteur.) Thus, parody is the most palatable of *critical approaches,* offering insights through laughter. As applied to the classroom, I frequently teach a genre course where parody films are sometimes used to better define specific genres under discussion. Along the same lines, one better understands Griffith after viewing Sennett parodies of his work. Moreover, such parodies also provide a historical tenor of the times. In the case of Griffith, Sennett's period parodies demonstrate the initial popularity of this serious artist and also anticipate how Griffith could become passé during the 1920s when he seemed incapable of moving beyond the melodramatic structure that Sennett parodied.

The "creative criticism" significance of parody is important to keep in mind, because the genre often has been considered as something less than important, be it defined as a parasitic growth on true works of art or as a literary elitist form of Trivial Pursuits, where one needs to know an unnecessarily detailed collection of facts before even understanding the parody. Parody theorist Joe Lee Davis probably best demonstrated the genre's less than lofty image when he drew the following analogy: "As the pun [an abbreviated parody] has been called the lowest form of wit, so parody may often seem the lowest form of literary art."[3] Yet it takes just as much creative talent to both perceive a given structure and then effectively parody it as does to create a structure in the first place. Parody is simultaneously something old and something new. Kid a traditional structure, have fun with the content. That is, the parodist replicates the familiar pattern of a given genre or auteur while at the same time subjecting it to a fresh comic twist, such as the mysterious "elevator killer" of the Carl Reiner–Steve Martin *Man with Two Brains* turning out to be talk show host Merv Griffin. Besides being incongruously hilarious (Griffin's boringly nice image seemingly based in avoiding all controversy), it also offers comic insight about the contemporary horror film predator—it literally could be anyone.

Ironically, parody's focus on artistic structure would eliminate it from the traditional axiom that "art imitates life." As parody scholar David Kiremidjian observed, whereas "Hamlet argues that art should hold the mirror up to nature . . . parody . . . holds the mirror not up to nature but to another work of art." [4] Yet the modern era has never been limited by this axiom. Indeed, as early as Oscar Wilde's "The Decay of Lying" (1889), with its insightfully tongue-in-cheek observation, "Life imitates Art far more than Art imitates Life," defining the arts has been anything but traditional. [5] In today's world of self-conscious art, years after the "birth" of Andy Warhol's soup cans, there is no debating parody's artistic credentials.

Third, in a continued underlining of the significance of parody, the genre should not be confused with satire, of which it has sometimes been considered a lesser subcategory. As genre theorist Joseph A. Dane has observed: "The norms in parody and satire are different; parody deals with literary [or cinematic] norms (collective understanding of a text or genre), while satire deals with social norms." [6] Parody has affectionate fun at the expense of a given form or structure; satire more aggressively attacks the flaw and follies of mankind.

So why the confusion? Parody scholar Linda Hutcheon addressed this question in her seminal book, *A Theory of Parody:* "the obvious reason for the confusion of parody and satire, despite this major difference between them, is the fact that the two genres are often used together." [7] For example, Woody Allen uses his science fiction parody *Sleeper* (1973), where the comedian's screen persona awakens two hundred years in the future, as a perfect "historical setting" to also satirically refute the values of early 1970s America. And Brooks's most celebrated parody, *Blazing Saddles,* also makes pointed satirical comments on racism and violence in the generally glorified American West. Conversely, this book's chapter on black comedy (extreme satire) notes this genre frequently showcases parody, such as Stanley Kubrick's comic undercutting of the standard men-with-a-mission movie scene in *Dr. Strangelove* (1964), when Major "King" Kong (Slim Pickens) prepares his bomber crew for its ultimate test. Black comedy needs no more justification for including parody than its attacks on all "institutions," including celebrated genres and auteurs of its medium of expression. Parody is most likely to return the favor (include satire) if its target is especially vulnerable to the social statement, such as Brooks's sometimes dark commentary on the western in *Blazing Saddles.* A much milder example of social satire in a Brooks parody is his *Spaceballs* (1987) attack on the mega merchandising aspects of the *Star Wars* trilogy. While Brooks's work is primarily an affectionate spoof of George Lucas's films (indeed, Lucas's company did the sound effects for Brooks), *Spaceballs* does have a deliciously self-conscious segment where Brooks, as the Yoda-type character Yogurt, steps out of the storyline to hawk a seemingly limitless supply of *Spaceballs* items. And this is satirically compounded by reference to the punning sequel: *Spaceballs II: The Search for More Money.*

Still, the difference between parody and satire should be kept firmly in mind, with the understanding that the two need not go hand in hand. Indeed, the vast majority of American film parodies are much more concerned with undercutting the structure of a given genre and/or auteur, from the pioneer work of Sennett to the majority of the more recent Brooks examples. One receives the same form-over-social-comment message in the parody films of Bob Hope, who starred in a number of classic 1940s and 1950s examples of the genre. These included numerous solo spoofs, be they takeoffs of film noir or the western, as well as his *Road* pictures with Bing Crosby, where the parody was often of the adventure film, such as *The Road to Morocco* (1942). In fact, Hope even scooped Brooks's *High Anxiety* spoof of Hitchcock by decades, having starred in the excellent 1942 parody of Hitchcock's *The 39 Steps* (1935). The film, *My Favorite Blonde,* even co-starred Madeleine Carroll, who had a similar role in the original. This emphasis on dismantling structure over social statement continues in more recent parodies, be it *Airplane!*'s (1980) skewering of the *Airport* series (as well as *Zero Hour,* 1957), or the works of such comedy talents as Steve Martin (often in collaboration with Carl Reiner) and former Brooks disciple Gene Wilder. See especially the Martin-Reiner *Man with Two Brains* (1982) and Wilder's *The Adventures of Sherlock Holmes' Smarter Brother* (1975).

Fourth, there are essentially two kinds of film parodies—the broad and obvious puncturing of a genre or auteur, and a more subdued approach which manages to balance both comic deflation with an eventual reaffirmation of the subject under attack. Again, one might think of Sennett as a personification of the first and most mainstream of parody types. In fact, Sennett's parodies, and those of rival silent comedy producer Hal Roach, were sometimes so broad one need not go beyond their titles for a comedy payoff. For instance, both men produced short parodies later the same year of the 1923 epic silent western *The Covered Wagon.* Sennett's version was *The Uncovered Wagon;* Roach countered with *Two Wagons, Both Uncovered.* One should also make special note of the wonderfully overt Sennett parodies starring cross-eyed comic Ben Turpin. The pun-titled *The Shriek of Araby* (1923, which spoofs Valentino) and *A Harem Knight* (1926, a parody of Erich von Stroheim) are comic joys. Indeed, there is a special parody payoff just in seeing the diminutive, cross-eyed Turpin in the patented Stroheim white uniform and monocle or in the desert robes of Valentino's sheik. More recently, the spoofs of Brooks, Wilder, and Martin also leave little doubt that comedy is the message. One of Wilder's parodies, outside his work with Brooks, is also a Valentino takeoff—*The World's Great-*

*est Lover* (1977). Even the obvious parody tradition of Turpin's comedy de-
formity lives on in the comic bulging eyes of Brooks disciple Marty Feldman,
whose *Young Frankenstein* character of Igor is pronounced ''Eye-gore.'' Feldman also went on to direct, co-write, and star in an excellent spoof of his
own—*The Last Remake of Beau Geste* (1977, his best solo effort).

Parodies of reaffirmation are not so obvious. They are often confused with
the genre being undercut. A perfect example of this is John Landis's *An American Werewolf in London* (1981), where broad parody (such as the use of songs
like ''Bad Moon Rising'' and several versions of ''Blue Moon'') alternate with
shocking horror (graphic violence and painfully realistic werewolf transformations). This produces a fascinating tension between genre expectations (in this
case, horror—to be scared) and a parody which is comic without deflating the
characters involved. This is opposed to the more traditional horror parody of a
*Young Frankenstein*, where, for example, Feldman's Igor, with those eyes and
a roving hump, can never be taken seriously. Thus, the reaffirmation approach
adds a poignancy not normally associated with parody. One is truly saddened
by the death of the American werewolf (David Naughton). Even more deep-
felt emotions are elicited from the closing deaths of the central heroes in the
reaffirmation parody classics *Bonnie and Clyde* (1967) and *Butch Cassidy and
the Sundance Kid* (1969). Yet for many *Bonnie and Clyde* is merely a violently
offbeat gangster film, while *Butch Cassidy and the Sundance Kid* is no more
than another 1960s revisionist look at the western. But as with the later *American Werewolf in London,* both of these films maintain a mesmerizing tension
between genre expectations (the crime and violence of gangster and western
outlaw films) and an endearing sense of parody which encourages viewer identification. Consequently, Butch and Sundance are bumbling outlaws who make
their living by comically *avoiding* shoot-outs, just as Bonnie and Clyde are
outlaws who manage to exist quite nicely outside the gangster norm of the
predatory—asphalt jungle—city at night, frequently behaving like Sennett's
Keystone Cops in their slapstick, broad-daylight car chases with accompanying
upbeat banjo soundtrack music.

The reaffirmation parody of *Butch Cassidy and the Sundance Kid* is also
reminiscent of the tongue-in-cheek humor frequently found in the swashbuckling adventure film. Indeed, my correspondence with the film's screenwriter (William Goldman, who won an Oscar for best original screenplay) revealed that a key influence was the often comic banter between Cary Grant,
Victor McLaglen, and Douglas Fairbanks, Jr., in *Gunga Din* (1939).

It is not necessary, however, to limit oneself to modern cinema for examples
of the more complex reaffirmation parodies. Though neither as obvious nor as
prevalent as the traditional parody, they too have always been there. Buster
Keaton, silent film comedy's only rival to Charlie Chaplin, often essayed this
method. Appropriately, his greatest and most acclaimed film, *The General* (1927),
uses this approach, with Keaton having a Civil War backdrop of epically real
proportions. As if to underline the ambiguity between comedy and drama in

the reaffirmation parody, Disney later did the same story straight as *The Great Train Robbery* (1956).

Keaton, of course, was a master of both parody methods. His first feature, *The Three Ages* (1923), was a direct takeoff on Griffith's *Intolerance* (1916), as well as an interesting parody guide to Keaton's transition from short subjects to features. The epic *Intolerance*, with its examination of man's bigotry through the ages (ancient Babylon, the Judea of Christ, Renaissance France, and modern America), was a perfect parody invitation for Keaton to loosely join three short subjects into one feature. Parodying Griffith's historical structure, Keaton looks at love in three periods (the Stone Age, ancient Rome, and modern America).

Keaton's direct parody ease of transition here, from short subjects to features, is actually a phenomenon more frequently associated with the ambiguous reaffirmation method. For instance, film comedy historian Mast, while not addressing this basic parody dichotomy, has observed that since modern film parodies generally need to maintain their often slender premise for feature length (as opposed to an earlier period when short subject parodies were the norm), it is much easier to sustain viewer interest by actually blending in the real thrills and chills of the genre under comic attack.[8]

One final parody aside on Keaton: for him, as for Sennett and a number of other silent spoof artists, Griffith represented a favored target. Though Griffith was seldom so baldly parodied as in *The Three Ages*, Keaton (again like Sennett) was fond of skewering those Griffith cross-cutting conclusions, such as Keaton's athletically drawn out coming-to-the-rescue of the heroine in *College* (1927). Indeed, the fact that the *College* girl is actually being cornered in her own room by the film heavy is reminiscent of the cornered woman in *The Lonely Villa*.

Fifth, film parody, like other comedy approaches, is a genre of indeterminate time and space. It is not limited to one period and place, as is more apt to occur in a determinate time and place genre like the western. (See this volume's screwball comedy chapter for more on this distinction.) Thus, one might parody the science fiction genre by focusing on another galaxy in the twenty-second century. Or one could parody the western and go back to Dodge City in 1875. *But,* unlike the other comedy genres, once a specific parody choice has been made, time and place and all the icons which go with it (six-guns and ten-gallon hats, or space helmets and laser guns) are of the utmost importance.

Because parody is based on triggering a viewer's prior knowledge of a given genre or auteur, it is naturally important to showcase early on (through icons) which particular subject has been nominated for the comedy hotspot. Again, this accents the earlier point that parody keys upon having fun with a given structure or text.

The parodies of Brooks have been especially detailed in their attention to icons of a specific genre. In fact, he was even able to find and use the original laboratory set of the 1931 *Frankenstein* when he was making *Young Franken-*

*stein*. But Carl Reiner and Steve Martin actually go one step farther in their film noir parody *Dead Men Don't Wear Plaid* (1982). The movie is constructed around *real footage* from numerous 1940s noir classics, with Martin "interacting" with a who's who of the genre, including Humphrey Bogart. Though this one-gag parody eventually wears thin, the technical magic of matching new footage to old clips remains a fascinating achievement. It also reminds one that the technically authentic look of the film parody goes hand in hand with the icons. Again, *Young Frankenstein* is an excellent primer. Brooks apes the look of the 1930s film world by shooting his horror parody in black and white, using the old screen size, and resurrecting such archaic transitions as the iris-out and the wipe.

Another variation on parody recycling of a genre's icons involves casting cameo appearances by performers strongly associated with the type of film under attack. Thus, Bob Hope's film noir parody *My Favorite Brunette* opens with a pivotal cameo from celebrated noir performer Alan Ladd; his western parody *Alias Jesse James* closes with a corral full of western cameos, ranging from Jay Silverheels (Tonto) to Gary Cooper.

A further twist of actor as icon occurs in those film parodies where a performer imitates a classic screen persona. At its most ambitious, such films treat the actor as auteur, basing their parody on high points in the performer's career. For instance, Humphrey Bogart has been used so often along these lines he has nearly become a parody subgenre. The Neil Simon–authored *Cheap Detective* (1978) has a Peter Falk–Bogart parodying his way through most of the tough guy's classics, and those of a few others. *Variety* affectionately called it "Son of Casablanca" (June 7, 1978). The film was no doubt inspired by the earlier Simon parody *Murder By Death* (1976), where a Falk-Bogart joins a parody collection of celebrated detectives, though the names have all been changed (or at least slightly jiggled) to protect the innocent—producers. Thus, Falk's Sam Spade is called Sam Diamond, David Niven and Maggie Smith's *Thin Man* couple Nick and Nora Charles become Dick and Dora Charleston, and so on.

*The Black Bird* (1976), as more than suggested by the title, is a parody of *The Maltese Falcon* (1941), with George Segal starring as Sam Spade, Jr. *The Man with Bogart's Face* (1980) has Robert Sacchi essaying Bogart in a private eye case also suspiciously like *The Maltese Falcon*. And Woody Allen's *Play It Again, Sam* (1972) has Jerry Lacy's Bogart advising Allen on his love life, heavily filtered through *Casablanca* (1942, with a clip from the close acting as the start of the Allen film). Allen also periodically assumes Bogart's mannerisms and voice in the film, always with incongruously funny results, from trying to drink bourbon to trying to be a great lover. (*Play It Again, Sam*'s basic parody premise of getting romantic cues off the screen is also reminiscent of Keaton's wonderful *Sherlock Jr.*, 1924, where the great stone face plays a movie projectionist who learns about love via film.)

Bogart himself was directly involved in a send-up of *The Maltese Falcon*—

type films. He starred in John Huston's now celebrated cult film *Beat the Devil* (1954, scripted by Truman Capote and Huston), supposedly an adaptation of James Helvick's novel. Capote stated, "John and I decided to kid the story, to treat it as parody. Instead of another *Maltese Falcon* [which Huston had adapted and directed], we turned it into a . . . [spoof] on this type of film."[9] The Capote quote is included because the film is sometimes mistakenly described as a specific parody of *The Maltese Falcon*. Today, it would best be labeled a subtle parody of reaffirmation, which, while critically well-received, went over the heads of most 1954 viewers. Bogart himself was unhappy with the results, though it is hardly likely, as is sometimes suggested, that he also was unaware of its parody nature. After all, the man had lines like "Without money I become dull, listless and have trouble with my complexion."

It should be added that like a handful of other influential stars, such as John Wayne in the western, the Bogart persona actually goes beyond being just another film noir icon. As film critic Colin McArthur suggests, when certain performers have appeared numerous times in one particular genre, they have sometimes helped shape the evolution of that genre itself.[10] Thus, Bogart is such a film noir factor that the parody of this genre can result not only from imitating his persona but also from doing just the opposite. For instance, Robert Altman's spoofing adaptation of Raymond Chandler's *The Long Goodbye* (1973), with a delightfully laid-back Elliott Gould as Philip Marlowe, still has the viewer often laughingly thinking about how different Bogart's Marlowe was in *The Big Sleep* (1946). When spoofing film noir, Bogart is hard to deny.

Sixth, film parody repeatedly involves a compounding phenomenon. While parody usually has a focus genre or auteur under comic attack, it is frequently peppered with eclectic references to other structures or texts. For instance, although *Airplane!* makes parody mincemeat of the *Airport* movies, it still has irreverent time for other film targets, from a wonderful opening credit deflating of *Jaws* to later send-ups of John Travolta's white suit solo dance number in *Saturday Night Fever* (1977) and the beach scene in *From Here to Eternity* (1953).

The term *compounding* was selected because of the current interest in what is considered a "compound genre," in which one film displays strong characteristics of two or more genres. A comparable "compound parody" also occasionally occurs where two or more genres share the parody focus. Though it is not as common as the general parody phenomenon of stockpiling short comic references to other genres, examples have always existed. For instance, an excellent example from the early days would be Keaton's short, *The Frozen North* (1922). Though best celebrated as a comic assault on silent western star William S. Hart (said to have held a grudge for a year), the icy setting and related humor demonstrate more than a passing awareness of an earlier 1922 cinema sensation—Robert Flaherty's *Nanook of the North*, which is sometimes considered the beginning of the documentary movement. Consistently, the film includes a peppering of other parody elements, such as a comic broadside to the flamboyant 1920s actor/auteur Erich von Stroheim, whose *Foolish Wives* (1921) was his then most recent period sensation. (Stroheim remained a popular parody target into the 1930s, being most deliciously dissected in the Sennett two-reeler *The Pride of Pikeville,* 1927, where cross-eyed, anemic Ben Turpin emulates the virile star so successfully that he accidentally manages—thanks to those eyes—to flirt with two women simultaneously.) *The Frozen North* also anticipates the Klondike western parody elements of Chaplin's later classic, *The Gold Rush* (1925).

A more recent example of a "compound parody" is the superb *The Man with Two Brains,* which does a comedy blitz of both the mad scientist horror movie and film noir. The latter parody is largely through the inspired casting of Kathleen Turner, who does a comedy send-up of her classic noir woman from *Body Heat* (1981). Martin, as the gifted surgeon Michael Hfuhruhurr, inventor of the revolutionary screw-top brain operation, becomes involved with a brain in a jar, losing interest in his predatory wife (Turner). As "wild and crazy" as the premise seems, it then proceeds to showcase a laugh wave of "creative criticism" about the focus genres. For instance, when parodying a mad scientist scenario (doctors like Frankenstein, Jekyll, and Moreau—who risk the wrath of God and man for pure knowledge), what is more comically appropriate than having one fall in love with a brain in a jar? And what a refreshing twist this provides for the obligatory horror film search for available bodies, as Martin seeks a beautiful "home" for his steady brain. Martin even does a brief comic imitation of the perennial assistant in such horror film searches—Igor. The film also manages to close with a comic homage to the traditional message of mad scientist movies—man should not play God. That is, after Martin has successfully placed the brain (voice by Sissy Spacek) in Turner's body, it is revealed through a flashforward that his ideal noodle is a compulsive eater and the sensual Turner body has turned to blubber.

It should be noted that Woody Allen often pursues the compound parody approach in a less obvious manner, with one of his target genres not being typical mainstream cinema audience fare. For instance, in his directing debut, *Take the Money and Run* (1969), he mixes prison film parody with the conventions of the cinéma vérité documentary. In what he has sometimes called his favorite film, *Love and Death* (1975, which certainly keys upon his favorite themes), his parody takes on the romantic costume drama war film and art house cinema (particularly the works of Allen idol Ingmar Bergman and Sergei Eisenstein, besides every nineteenth-century Russian novel this side of a college literature class). Even his more general audience parody grab bag, *Everything You Always Wanted to Know About Sex (But Were Afraid to Ask)* (1972), includes a takeoff on the Italian films of director Michelangelo Antonioni.

Seventh, a final frequent trait of film parody is to self-consciously draw attention to the fact that it is a movie. This does not mean that movies about moviemaking, often now called "genre genre" films, are parodies. To honestly be incorporated into a parody format, this film self-consciousness must be used to complement an already ongoing attack on a target genre or auteur. For instance, Brooks's brilliant conclusion to *Blazing Saddles* has the parody becoming so broad that it quite literally breaks out of the film frame and spills over into a musical being shot on another set, followed by a comic invasion of the Warner Brothers lot and Hollywood proper. A smaller but just as exquisite Brooks example occurs in his Hitchcock parody, *High Anxiety,* when the famed director's fondness for the tracking shot is undercut. Whereas Hitchcock's camera obliquely travels through windows and walls, the Brooks camera attempts this only to break the window and draw the attention of all the actors before it embarrassedly backs out of the scene.

In either case, such movie self-consciousness represents the ultimate parody prick, since nothing deflates a celebrated genre or auteur faster than a comic reminder that this is, indeed, only a movie. Moreover, since parody is based on self-consciousness about a given subject, such filmmaking interjections represent a logical culmination of the parody experience—the comic deathblow to any remaining vestiges of the viewer's suspension of disbelief. In addition, as implied by theory historian Margaret A. Rose, the self-consciousness is one other way of "signaling" the audience that this is indeed a parody.[11]

These, then, are the seven pivotal characteristics of parody: a humor based on the distorted imitation of a familiar genre or auteur; "creative criticism"—offering educational insights; distinctive from satire (an attack on structure, not society); two basic types—overt parody and reaffirmation; a genre of indeterminate time and place *but* with a difference; the compounding of more than one target subject; and self-consciousness about the filmmaking experience. As demonstrated by the preceding overview, these traits have remained consistent from silents through sound. Still, parody does have a special turning point, and it would have to be the 1960s. Parody historians Nick Smurthwaite and Paul Gelder suggest that "not until the sixties was it generally accepted that the American cinema is made up of genres."[12] Certainly this is part of it, the decade when film study became a mainstream part of university study, catering to a student clientele weaned on the movie crash course made possible by 1950s television. After all, the 1960s has been called the "Fourth American Era" of movies (after the silents, the studio years, and the post–World War II period of transition), a time when a more educated and movie-conscious public began to constitute the bulk of the film audience.[13]

Five other factors, however, deserve at least brief attention in these 1960s parody developments. First was the late 1950s and 1960s influence of the French "New Wave" cinema movement. The innovative developments of directors like François Truffaut and Jean-Luc Godard has a major influence on American film. Ironically, it was the French homage to an earlier American cinema which helped this country both recognize the significance of its movie heritage and fuel the interest in its movie past, with the resultant mushrooming of parody films. One might note that Godard's celebrated first film, *Breathless* (1959, story by Truffaut), is a romanticized French gangster tale with Jean-Paul Belmondo sometimes aping his movie tough-guy idol, Bogart. Though not really a spoof, it often plays like a parody film of reaffirmation, with a range that extends from Belmondo comically trying to emulate a Bogart movie poster, to his death of betrayal in the streets, which certainly influenced the violent betrayal close of *Bonnie and Clyde*.

The French New Wave films frequently also had fun with the self-consciousness of the filmmaking process. For instance, in Godard's classic *Weekend* (1967), which moves from an epic traffic jam (reminiscent of Laurel & Hardy's *Two Tars,* 1928) to the do's and don'ts of joining a guerrilla band, there is a comic sequence where revolutionaries are moving through the jungle with a pulsating rock score seemingly in the soundtrack. *But* then the band members walk by the rock-producing group itself, incongruously playing in a jungle setting. Certainly this scene influenced the similar but more well-known Mel Brooks gag in *Blazing Saddles* where Gucci-attired black cowboy Cleavon Little is majestically riding through the time-honored vistage of the great American West, with the standard swelling musical accompaniment of the genre, *only* to come upon Count Basie and his orchestra as the source of that music.

Second, the 1960s also found the controversial American arrival of the auteur theory. While Andrew Sarris was the English language father/deliverer of this critical perspective, credit again goes to Truffaut and other New Wave directors who, before they entered film production, were influential young critics for the journal *Cahiers du Cinéma,* from whose 1950s pages auteurism was born. And obviously, like the general recognition of genre patterns in the 1960s, the appreciation of recurring auteur structures also encouraged increased interest in, and production of, parodies.

Third, the 1960s represented an early blossoming of several pivotal parody artists also connected to a common 1950s phenomenon—something called "Your Show of Shows" (1950–1954). This American television program was for the future parody what the 1970s edition of "Saturday Night Live" might someday represent for black comedy film. Like "Saturday Night Live," "Your Show of Shows" was a ninety-minute live comedy-variety program. Starring Sid Caesar and Imogene Coca and featuring Carl Reiner, "Your Show of Shows" included Mel Brooks, Neil Simon, and Woody Allen in its writing staff. Not surprisingly, one of the ongoing features of the show was film parody sketches. As with Sennett, the spirit of such parody was often captured in the titles— "From Here to Obscurity," "A Trolley Car Named Desire," and in comic honor of the drowning in *A Place in the Sun,* the spoof "A Place at the Bottom of the Lake." Because Caesar was a superb pantomimist, spoofs of silent movies were also common. Fittingly, the best thing about Brooks's later parody *Silent Movie* (1976) was the comedy of co-star Caesar.

While the feature film spoofs of Brooks, Allen, and Simon would be most fully realized in the 1970s, with Reiner as parodist coming into his own in the 1980s, the parody presence of the central duo (Brooks and Allen) was making itself known in the 1960s. Based upon the huge commercial success of the sexual satire *What's New, Pussycat* (1965, which Allen wrote and starred in), this stand-up comedian was able to make a parody transition to the big screen.

The following year, *What's Up, Tiger Lily?* (1966) appeared, Allen's comic redubbing of a 1964 Japanese secret agent film. It was an outrageous parody of the James Bond craze, which had taken off with the popularity of *Dr. No* (1963). *What's Up, Tiger Lily?*, which has to be *heard* to be believed, might best be summarized by simply stating that this left-field skewering of Bond was based in a plot line about recovering the missing recipe for the world's best egg salad. The next year Allen more directly addressed Bond parody in *Casino Royale* (1967), an overblown and uneven comic spoof of 007 in which the comedian appeared, and for which he did some uncredited writing. Suggested by a novel from Bond inventor Ian Fleming himself, Allen appears as little Jimmy Bond, the less than capable nephew of the secret agent. (The film's close, with Allen's delightfully surprising emergence as the mastermind of evil, provides the film's only sustained moments of quality comedy.) From this three-film foundation Allen launched his often parody-oriented film-directing career, with *Take the Money and Run* appearing in 1969.

Parody of Bond also figures prominently in the 1960s evolution of Brooks. He and Buck Henry developed and scripted the pilot for television's greatest comic undermining of the secret agent—''Get Smart'' (1965–1970). The show followed the exploits of Maxwell Smart, Agent 86 (Don Adams) and his beautiful assistant, Agent 99 (Barbara Feldon), with Smart comically bumbling his way through constant spy dangers, frequently using what became a nationwide catchphrase—''Would you believe?''—whenever he launched into one of his zany spy fabrications. Through the years ''Get Smart'' has remained very popular in syndication, eventually spawning a feature film version, *The Nude Bomb* (1980), where the world is threatened by a villain whose bombs will destroy all clothing. (On television it has been shown as ''The Return of Maxwell Smart.'')

Brooks's 1960s work in film is limited to two Oscar-winning properties, *The Critic* (1962, an animated short subject), and *The Producers* (1967). Both films favor satire over parody, but abundant examples of spoofing remain. *The Critic* is a collection of abstract Norman McLaren–like images from which Brooks, using a voice and attitude similar to that of his stand-up comedy persona, the 2,000-year-old man, attempts to make sense. The effect is reminiscent of the comic axiom of vagabond poet Sadakichi Hartmann—''If you think vaudeville is dead, look at modern art.''[14] Besides satirizing both abstract art and attempts made to analyze it, *The Critic* is a spoof of the art film genre, and more specifically, an affectionate parody of McLaren. *The Producers,* with a storyline focusing on the accidentally successful Broadway play *Springtime for Hitler* (a musical comedy about the Führer), is ultimately a satire on the absurd values, or lack of values, of a dark modern world. Because *The Producers* was also an unlikely success (this commercial hit was initially panned by most critics), Brooks's satirical point is doubly underlined. Satire aside, *Springtime for Hitler* is a rich parody of the musical, from specific scenes—a spoof of Busby Berkeley's patented overhead shot (in this case the pattern formed by the dancing girls is a giant swastika), for example—to the general comic irony of trying for a failure in a genre so strongly associated with the "Let's put on a show!" positive mindset of anything for a success.

Fourth, the 1960s represented a watershed of antiestablishment activity—fertile ground indeed for a genre (parody) based on the comic dismantling of what is often a long-standing entertainment structure. Moreover, the fact that the antiestablishment 1960s spawned the mainstream birth of black comedy (see this volume's chapter on this extreme form of satire) had even more direct impact on the spoof film. Because of the shared comic disregard each of these genres has for standard norms, there is a natural tendency for them to appear together (see this chapter's note 7). In addition, a number of more recent parodies, like *All That Jazz* (1979) and *An American Werewolf in London,* have been particularly attracted to this dark humor. Besides reflecting the increasingly macabre humor of the times, what more cuttingly direct way is there to parody a traditionally upbeat genre like the musical than the *All That Jazz* conclusion where the big show never gets put on and the director lies dead in a body bag? It should be remembered that another 1960s development helped make this possible—the end of official Hollywood censorship and the implementation of the rating system. Hitherto before unimagined scenes of graphic realism and/or shocking juxtapositionings were now possible.

Fifth, the ongoing success since 1963 of the Bond films also merits special attention. It has proven to be the most popular A-production series in the history of cinema, with the unique popularity of 007 generating a tidal wave of secret agent parodies, from the aforementioned Brooks and Allen examples to the delightful Pink Panther–Inspector Clouseau collaborations of writer-director Blake Edwards and Peter Sellers, starting in 1964. (Sellers, of course, was also one of the Bond impersonators in *Casino Royale,* where he could not be passed off as a "double agent," because he had a hard enough time being accepted as a single agent.) But as significant as the Bond film has been in encouraging parody, especially during the pivotal 1960s, when spoofs started to generate special attention, an additional factor frequently goes unnoticed.

The Bond films were very close to being parodies themselves, walking a thin line between action adventure and spy spoof (especially the many girls and gadgets), a line which became progressively thinner in later years when Roger Moore replaced Sean Connery as Bond. Thus, one might even make a case for defining the 007 films as parodies of reaffirmation. This tendency to want it both ways is more apparent in two short-lived film serials born of the Bond craze. James Coburn starred in the 007 spoof *Our Man Flint* (1966), which was followed by *In Like Flint* (1967). And Dean Martin was a campy poor man's Bond (with song) in the Matt Helm secret agent series also starting in 1966. The first film, *The Silencers,* was easily the best of the four Martin-as-Helm features made. Thus, a crucial 1960s parody legacy of Bond (beyond the obvious spoofs) was the incitement to play even the straight drama with tongue firmly in cheek.

Celebrated film critic Pauline Kael expressed concern with this tendency during the mid-1960s, though her irritation was precipitated not by Bond but by the western parody *Cat Ballou* (1965). Her complaint was that "Spoofing has become the safety net for those who are unsure of their [straight dramatic] footing. Unlike satire, spoofing has no serious objectives."[15] Yet Kael carries a safety net all her own when she closes her piece with the sudden, vague announcement that *Cat Ballou*'s spoofing is not really of a parody nature. (Normally parody and spoofing are used interchangeably.) Within the context of this chapter, Kael's attack on spoofing would seem to be directed at the ambiguous parody of reaffirmation. Yet *Cat Ballou*, while not without comic-dramatic duality, is hardly subtle with most of its western parody, be it the genre's symbol of civilization (schoolmarm Jane Fonda) becoming an outlaw, or a bad man (Lee Marvin) so coldly ruthless he has an artificial metal nose. Moreover, when noting an obvious 1960s parody of reaffirmation, such as *Bonnie and Clyde*, Kael is full of praise. More ironic still is the fact that her almost singular critical support of *Bonnie and Clyde*, at a time when most critics initially found the movie dangerously flippant about violence, helped establish her position as a pivotal American film critic.

It is important to dwell on this mid-1960s Pauline Kael–*Cat Ballou* controversy for four reasons. First, by its mere existence the more visible parody existence of the 1960s is underlined. This is especially true since Lee Marvin's double role as twin brothers (a drunken hired gun and the archvillain) was later rewarded with a film establishment Oscar for best actor, while the movie itself was a major commercial success. Second, Kael's acknowledgment and examination of a popular 1960s film tendency best labeled parody of reaffirmation is an indirect period example of the presence of a more sophisticated audience better able to recognize and enjoy subtle nuances in their parody—which is consistent with today's view of the audience metamorphosis then taking place. Kael and the subject of a more film-literate audience also brings to mind her early 1960s battle with Andrew Sarris over the merits of auteurism (which is dependent upon a viewer having seen several films by the same director). Kael found auteurism more redundant than artistic. And as in her later complaint with reaffirmation parodies, she essentially felt the film artist had not taken enough of a creative risk. Third, one might label Kael's critical flip-flop on this type of parody (from *Cat Ballou* to *Bonnie and Clyde*) as an additional example of her "convenient pluralism" (see criticism historian Edward Murray on this, though he does not address *Cat Ballou*).[16] However, another explanation is simply that the nature of reaffirmation parody was making the subject all the more complex to analyze, even for the influential critic. Certainly, Kael's semantic ambiguity over the terms *spoof* and *parody* represents more evidence of this. Fourth, besides encouraging further 1960s spoofs of the western, the fact that *Cat Ballou* both generated so much attention and is a milestone of sorts in the analysis of reaffirmation parody highlights again the importance of the western in the history of film spoofs.

Parody developments since the watershed 1960s, especially the video revolution, continue to encourage the ever greater film awareness of the general audience. And since the film spoof is based on such increased consciousness, the future for cinema parody has never seemed so great.

## BIBLIOGRAPHICAL OVERVIEW

While the preparation of this chapter was most dependent on essay-length writings, a pivotal book-length study was Linda Hutcheon's *A Theory of Parody*. Besides reflecting the more current stance of addressing parody as a genre (rather than as a subcategory in a satire superstructure), it showcases everything from parody's neglected importance as a serious form of art criticism to the most detailed of bibliographies. And as a basic foundation, its early chapter on "Defining Parody" is both insightful and challenging to the reader as few introductions are (see note 7).

An excellent companion volume of the Hutcheon book is David Kiremidjian's *A Study of Modern Parody*. Originally written as a 1964 doctoral dissertation at Yale, this revised version appeared in 1985. It had also appeared earlier, under the same title, in the *Journal of Aesthetics and Art Criticism* (Winter 1969). Unlike much scholarly writing, this is a very readable text, especially in its breakdown of parody fundamentals. I found most helpful chapter 2, "The Aesthetics of Parody," which in part addresses the basics of parody structure and behavior. Essentially, parody's comic upsetting of the balance between form and content in its target (genre or auteur) reveals the viewer's need to be aware of this union (form and content) in all art as well as demonstrating parody's importance as criticism (its second role after laughter).

Although not as crucial as the Hutcheon and Kiremidjian texts, Margaret A. Rose's *Parody // Meta-Fiction* is most helpful in mapping out the fundamentals of what it also considers a genre, including basic etymology and the attitude of parodist and audience alike. Fittingly, a variation of the first chapter is also the opening article, "Defining Parody," in a special parody issue of *Southern Review* (vol. 13, no. 1, 1980).

Of the shorter works one might best start with Gerald Mast's interestingly provocative "From Parody to Psychocomedy: Woody Allen and Others," from chapter 17 of his *The Comic Mind: Comedy and the Movies* (1979). Mast differentiates between 1920s spoofs and those of the 1970s (when his book first appeared) by noting that the recent examples tend to be both longer (feature films versus the earlier short subjects) and more immersed in the history of film rather than the 1920s tendency to spoof contemporary hits. Mast then rightfully suggests the special student-of-film demands this makes of the modern viewer.

Mast, however, overplays a parody point when he observes that the only 1970s spoof of a contemporary film was *The Big Bus* (1976, a takeoff on disaster movies).[17] Granted, the main 1970s parody thrust was in a historical and/or nostalgic overview nature, simply because there was more material from which to draw. But the spoof genre is never without some contemporary targeting. Thus, one can refute Mast's assertion by a simple utterance: "James Bond." Just as the 007 series has continued, so have the parodies. For instance, the Blake Edwards–Peter Sellers Pink Panther films skewered Bond an additional three times in the 1970s, starting with *The Return of the Pink Panther* (1975). The Inspector Clouseau sequels also are enriched by a parody-peppering (especially in the opening credits) of past *and present* film tastes. The most comic contemporary in-film spoofing occurs late in *The Revenge of the Pink Panther* (1978), when Sellers's Clouseau does a delightfully extended impersonation of Marlon Brando's title character from *The Godfather* (1972). Making it even more comically timely is the fact that Sellers's gangster costume makes him big enough to be a member of the celebrated 1970s Big Butt family of "Saturday Night Live"—reflecting the real-life aerial photograph–style weight gain of Brando.

Mast also posits four ways in which contemporary parodies extend their length beyond what used to be a short subject norm. His first and fourth suggestions are most valuable, with both demonstrating characteristics of reaffirmation parodies. The first method has the parodist nearly playing his material straight, maintaining viewer interest with serious carryovers of the genre or auteur under ambiguous attack. Number four is a variation along these lines, with the spoofer interjecting realistic traits into his work. For instance, Woody Allen's parody characters are typically more three-dimensional than the Brooks caricatures.

Mast's suggestions two and three are thought-provoking yet less unique because they recycle much of what one already expects of parody. For instance, number two plays on "multiplicity."[18] Thus, one Mast example is *The Cheap Detective*, where the multiplicity is equated with using as many Bogart films as possible for parody targets. There is no denying multiplicity here, but this sort of parody-peppering is so typical of the spoof film it hardly merits a special category. A stronger case exists for his other example—*Murder by Death*, with its parody of six celebrated detectives. Though *Murder by Death* is self-conscious about its mystery cast, most parodies are rich in character types from their target.

Mast's third point has spoof extension resulting from situations where something entirely alien to the specific parody narration is injected, such as the "sadomasochistic love scene between Dr. Montague (Harvey Korman) and Nurse Diesel (Cloris Leachman)."[19] Yet parody by definition is a genre where once the familiar structure of the target is replicated, the spoofing contents are supposed to surprise, including going outside the parody narrative. Examples might include Bob Hope finding one of Ray Milland's *Lost Weekend* (1945) bottles in *My Favorite Brunette*, or the literal genre breakout close of *Blazing Saddles*. That such a gifted comedy analyst as Mast should be so general in his assessment of parody (in a segment which still has much to recommend it) tells one that film parody merits much more attention.

The modern "Spoofing" section of Stuart Byron and Elisabeth Weis's *Movie Comedy* (1977) anthology also bears consulting. Seventeen short essays by a broad assortment of contemporary critics are showcased, including the previously noted Kael essay, which has been appropriately relabeled "Against Spoofing" (minus the *Cat Ballou* material). Moreover, as if in a further indirect rebuttal of Kael's position on *Cat Ballou,* the editors have included a very positive Judith Crist review of the film.

The majority of the "Spoofing" material, however, is devoted to pieces on Woody Allen and/or Mel Brooks (eleven of the seventeen). And the broadest lesson taught by the collection, besides the 1970s domination of the genre by these two, is that Allen was the darling of the critics, while praise for Brooks, when it occurred, was often apologetic. This was largely because of Brooks's Mack Sennett–like scattergun approach to parody.

A good measure of the more recent upturn in Brooks stock can be found in the Nick Smurthwaite and Paul Gelder book *Mel Brooks and the Spoof Movie* (1982), with four chapters devoted to Brooks, one to Allen, and one to other contemporary parodists. While numerous books have been done on both comedians, including the highly recommended volumes by Maurice Yacowar (*Loser Take All: The Comic Art of Woody Allen,* 1979, and *Method in Madness: The Comic Art of Mel Brooks,* 1981), the Smurthwaite-Gelder chapter breakdown probably best demonstrates the stronger association of Brooks with parody in the popular mind.

With regard to the overview nature of the survey work in hand, the most valuable Smurthwaite-Gelder chapter is "Spoofers in the Pack," which is a helpful reference guide to parodies of the recent past *outside* the work of Allen and Brooks. It starts with the parody films of Neil Simon and ranges from the affectionate spoofing of George Hamilton as Count Dracula in *Love at First Bite* (1979) to the black comedy parody of *An American Werewolf in London.*

Raymond Durgnat's excellent but eclectic look at film comedy, *The Crazy Mirror: Hollywood Comedy and the American Image* (1970), devotes a short chapter to parody—"Spoof and Satire." Though flawed by its vagueness with regard to the differences between parody and satire, it is valuable for its focus on the often neglected silent parodies, best represented by the attention Durgnat gives Raymond Griffith.

William K. Everson's chapter on private eye parody, "Comedy and Camp," in his book *The Detective in Film* (1972), is most valuable for an early aside he provides on the popularity of horror film spoofs. He reminds us of both the ease and appropriateness with which the traditionally cowardly comedian can be showcased in a horror film setting. This also anticipates the more recent, ongoing popularity of mixing black comedy and parody.

Along more theoretical lines are three additional essays which were influential in the writing of this chapter. Joe Lee Davis's "Criticism and Parody" *(Thought*, Summer 1951) and J. G. Riewald's "Parody As Criticism" *(Neo-philologus*, January 1966) were helpful in providing a further understanding of parody's significance as an important but neglected critical stance. And Joseph A. Dane's "Parody and Satire: A Theoretical Model" *(Genre*, Summer 1980) was convincingly thorough in demonstrating the separate genre nature of these two formats. This is especially important because many other examinations of the two have either ignored their relationship or been patently vague in differentiating between them, such as Durgnat's "Spoof and Satire."

It would be remiss to close this bibliographical guide without noting at least one preface to a parody anthology, as these collections appear in abundance and their openings are frequently insightful. My candidate would be Dwight Macdonald's Preface to his *Parodies: An Anthology from Chaucer to Beerbohm—and After* (1960). Besides touching on some parody basics already noted, such as its genre nature and its value as literary criticism, Macdonald also reminds us that "Parody ages faster" than any other format.[20]

While Macdonald's focus is on literary spoofing, the aging factor is equally true of film parody. For instance, Bob Hope spoofs are especially rich in references to period films and events, many of which are obscure to later audiences. Thus, in *My Favorite Brunette* the comedian tells supporting actor Lon Chaney, Jr. (in one of his patented feeble-witted roles), that he will bet him some rabbits. This is a direct comic reference to Chaney's earlier celebrated performance in the 1939 film adaptation *Of Mice and Men*, where the slow-witted Lennie (Chaney) has been promised that he and his friend George (Burgess Meredith) would eventually have a rabbit farm. Hope's rabbit reference remains funny, but is not nearly so obvious. However, one need not worry about the dating of the Hope parody films, as was once a concern directed at the parody-oriented *Road* pictures of Hope and Crosby.[21] These films are so densely peppered with still comic material that there is little chance they will become passé.

Since parody is the most tongue in cheek of genres it might be best to close with the famous observation of German parodist Robert Neumann, who comically but insightfully credited the genre's effectiveness to shooting "at a man with the weapon of his own form." Even in play, parody's focus on structure is not to be ignored.

## NOTES

1. Gerald Mast, Chapter 5, "Mack Sennett," in his *The Comic Mind: Comedy and the Movies*, 2d ed. (Chicago: University of Chicago Press, 1979), p. 47.
2. Joe Lee Davis, "Criticism and Parody," *Thought*, Summer 1951, p. 180.
3. Ibid., p. 185.
4. David Kiremidjian, *A Study of Modern Parody* (New York: Garland Publishing, 1985), p. 18.

5. Oscar Wilde, "The Decay of Lying," in *Criticism: The Major Texts*, ed. W. J. Bate (Chicago: Harcourt Brace Jovanovich, 1970), p. 642.

6. Joseph A. Dane, "Parody and Satire: A Theoretical Model," *Genre*, Summer 1980, p. 153.

7. Linda Hutcheon, *A Theory of Parody* (New York: Methuen, 1985), p. 43.

8. Mast, *The Comic Mind*, p. 308.

9. William F. Nolan, *John Huston: King Rebel* (Los Angeles: Sherbourne Press, 1965), p. 124.

10. Colin McArthur, *Underworld USA* (New York: Viking Press, 1972), p. 24.

11. Margaret A. Rose, *Parody // Meta-Fiction* (London: Croom Helm, 1979), pp. 25–26.

12. Nick Smurthwaite and Paul Gelder, *Mel Brooks and the Spoof Movie* (New York: Proteus Books, 1982), p. 7.

13. Gerald Mast, Chapter 15, "The Fourth American Era,' in his *A Short History of the Movies*, 2d ed. (Indianapolis: Bobbs-Merrill, 1976), pp. 475–503.

14. Gene Fowler, *Minutes of the Last Meeting* (New York: Viking Press, 1954), p. 95.

15. Pauline Kael, "Spoofing: *Cat Ballou*" (1965), in her *Kiss Kiss Bang Bang* (Boston: Little, Brown, 1968), p. 28.

16. Edward Murray, Chapter 6, "Pauline Kael and Pluralistic, Aesthetic Criticism," in his *Nine American Film Critics* (New York: Frederick Ungar, 1975), pp. 110–40.

17. Gerald Mast, "From Parody to Psychocomedy: Woody Allen and Others," in Chapter 17 of his *The Comic Mind: Comedy and the Movies*, p. 307.

18. Ibid., p. 309.

19. Ibid., p. 310.

20. Dwight Macdonald, Preface, in his *Parodies: An Anthology from Chaucer to Beerbohm—and After* (New York: Random House, 1960), pp. xi–xii.

21. For example, see Charles Higham and Joel Greenberg, *Hollywood in the Forties* (New York:: A. S. Barnes, 1968), p. 168; Raymond Durgnat, *The Crazy Mirror: Hollywood and the American Image* (1970; repr. New York: Delta, 1972), p. 170.

## BIBLIOGRAPHICAL CHECKLIST

### Books

Hutcheon, Linda. *A Theory of Parody*. New York: Methuen, 1985.
Kiremidjian, David. *A Study of Modern Parody*. New York: Garland, 1985.
Rose, Margaret A. *Parody // Meta-Fiction*. London: Croom Helm, 1979.

### Shorter Works

Byron, Stuart, and Elisabeth Weis, eds. Chapter 3, "Spoofing" (17 short essays). In *Movie Comedy*. New York: Penguin Books, 1977, pp. 102–37.
Dane, Joseph A. "Parody and Satire: A Theoretical Model," *Genre*, Summer 1980, pp. 145–59.
Davis, Joe Lee. "Criticism and Parody," *Thought*, Summer 1951, pp. 180–204.
Durgnat, Raymond. Chapter 17, "Spoof and Satire." In his *The Crazy Mirror: Hollywood and the American Image*. 1970; repr. New York: Delta, 1972, pp. 106–8.

Everson, William K. Chapter 12, "Comedy and Camp." In his *The Detective in Film*. Secaucus, N.J.: Citadel Press, 1972, pp. 210–20.

Kael, Pauline. "Spoofing: *Cat Ballou*" (1965). In her *Kiss Kiss Bang Bang*. Boston: Little, Brown, 1968, pp. 36–38.

Kiremidjian, G. David. "The Aesthetics of Parody," *Journal of Aesthetics and Art Criticism*, Winter 1969, pp. 230–42.

Macdonald, Dwight. Preface. In his *Parodies: An Anthology from Chaucer to Beerbohm—and After*. New York: Random House, 1960, pp. xi–xvi.

Mast, Gerald. "From Parody to Psychocomedy: Woody Allen and Others." In chapter 17 of his *The Comic Mind: Comedy and the Movies*, 2d ed. Indianapolis: Bobbs-Merrill, 1976, pp. 306–19.

Riewald, J. G. "Parody As Criticism," *Neophilologus*, January 1966, pp. 125–49.

Rose, Margaret. "Defining Parody," *Southern Review* 13, no. 1, 1980 (special parody issue), pp. 5–20.

Smurthwaite, Nick, and Paul Gelder. "Spoofers in the Pack." In their *Mel Brooks and the Spoof Movie*. New York: Proteus Books, 1982, pp. 67–92.

## SELECTED FILMOGRAPHY

Silent Era    Some Recommended Short Parodies:

Mack Sennett's *Teddy at the Throttle* (1916, with Gloria Swanson, Wallace Beery); Buster Keaton's *The Frozen North* (1922); Sennett's *Pride of Pikeville* (1927, with Ben Turpin). For additional short subject titles, see main text.

1937    *Way Out West* (65 minutes).
MGM release. Producer: Stan Laurel (for Hal Roach). Director: James W. Horne. Screenplay: Charles Rogers, Felix Adler, James Parrott, from a Jack Jevne, Charles Rogers story. Cast: Laurel and Hardy (themselves), James Finlayson (Mickey Finn), Sharon Lynne (Lola Marcel), Rosina Lawrence (Mary Roberts).

1940    *My Little Chickadee* (83 minutes).
Universal. Producer: Jack Gross (uncredited). Director: Edward Cline. Screenplay: Mae West, W. C. Fields. Cast: W. C. Fields (Cuthbert J. Twillie), Mae West (Flower Belle Lee), Joseph Calleia (Jeff Badger/masked bandit), Margaret Hamilton (Mrs. Gideon), Fuzzy Knight (Cousin Zeb).

1947    *My Favorite Brunette* (87 minutes).
Paramount release. Producer: Daniel Dare. Director: Elliott Nugent. Screenplay: Edmund Beloin, Jack Rose. Cast: Bob Hope (Ronnie Jackson), Dorothy Lamour (Carlotta Montay), Peter Lorre (Kismet), Lon Chaney, Jr. (Willie). Cameos by Alan Ladd and Bing Crosby.

1948    *The Paleface* (91 minutes).
Paramount release. Producer: Robert L. Welch. Director: Norman Z. McLeod. Screenplay: Edmund Hartman, Frank Tashlin, added dialogue Jack Rose. Cast: Bob Hope ("Painless" Peter Potter), Jane Russell (Calamity Jane), Robert Armstrong (Terris), Iris Adrian (Pepper).

1969    *Take the Money and Run* (85 minutes).
Palomar Pictures. Producer: Charles H. Joffe. Director: Woody Allen. Screenplay: Allen, Mickey Rose. Cast: Woody Allen (Virgil Stark), Janet Margolin (Louise), Jackson Beck (narrator).

1974   *Blazing Saddles* (93 minutes).
Crossbow for Warner Brothers. Producer: Michael Hertzberg. Director: Mel Brooks. Screenplay: Brooks, Norman Steinberg, Andrew Bergman, Richard Pryor, Alan Uger. Cast: Cleavon Little (Bart), Gene Wilder (Jim, The Waco Kid), Slim Pickens (Taggart), Harvey Korman (Hedley Lamarr), Madeline Kahn (Lili von Shtupp), Mel Brooks (Gov. William J. LePetomane/Sioux Indian Chief).

*Young Frankenstein* (108 minutes).
Crossbow Productions. Producer: Michael Gruskoff. Director: Mel Brooks. Screenplay: Gene Wilder, Brooks. Cast: Gene Wilder (Frederick Frankenstein), Peter Boyle (Monster), Marty Feldman (Igor), Madeline Kahn (Elizabeth), Cloris Leachman (Frau Blücher), Terri Garr (Inga).

1975   *Love and Death* (85 minutes).
Jack Rollins, Charles H. Joffe Productions. Producer: Joffe. Director/Screenplay: Woody Allen. Cast: Woody Allen (Boris), Diane Keaton (Sonia).

1976   *Murder By Death* (94 minutes).
Columbia release. Producer: Ray Stark. Director: Robert Moore. Screenplay: Neil Simon. Cast: Peter Falk (Sam Diamond), Peter Sellers (Sidney Wang), David Niven (Dick Charleston), Maggie Smith (Dora Charleston).

1980   *Airplane!* (88 minutes).
Paramount release. Producer: Jon Davison. Director/Screenplay: Jim Abrahams, David Zucker, Jerry Zucker. Cast: Robert Hays (Ted Striker), Julie Hagerty (Elaine), Lloyd Bridges (McCroskey), Peter Graves (Capt. Oveur).

1983   *The Man with Two Brains* (93 minutes).
Warner Brothers release. Producer: David V. Picker, William E. McEuen. Director: Carl Reiner. Screenplay: Carl Reiner, Steve Martin, George Gipe. Cast: Steve Martin (Dr. Michael Hfuhruhurr), Kathleen Turner (Dolores Benedict), David Warner (Dr. Alfred Necessiter), Paul Benedict (Butler).

# 10

## Black Humor

WES D. GEHRING

"If there's anyone out there who can look around this demented slaughterhouse of a world we live in and tell me that man is a noble creature, believe me, that man is full of bullshit."
—Newscaster Howard Beale (Peter Finch) to his television audience in the Paddy Chayefsky Oscar-winning script for *Network* (1976).

At its most fundamental, black humor is a genre of comic irreverence which flippantly attacks what are normally society's most sacredly serious subjects— especially that of death. In fact, death is both the ultimate black comedy joke and its most pervasive. Comedy, traditionally about optimistic new beginnings, frequently is symbolized by endings which celebrate a marriage or birth; thus, deathly black humor is sometimes even described as "anti-comedy." And like the avant-garde films of old, black humor is geared for shock effect, juxtaposing comedy and terrifying chaos (from individualized graphic violence to nuclear apocalypse). It dramatically personalizes in the viewer a jumble of conflicting emotions meant to reflect the on-the-edge absurdity of modern life. But there are no crackerbarrel solutions here, only black humor resignation, so nicely captured in Kurt Vonnegut, Jr.'s *Slaugherhouse-Five* repetition of "And so it goes" for every sorry event which afflicts his antihero Billy Pilgrim. Going beyond satire, the message is that there is no message, so audience members best steal a laugh before they are too dead to do even that.

Black humor is the midnight world of the comic antihero, the foundation for the screwball comedy genre (see chapter 7). But the absurdity of screwball comedy hardly registers on the chaos scale. It merely plays comically with its victims. It is a humor of frustration, not fatalities. In black humor, however, absurdity has become predator. Thus, even the modest daydream victories of

James Thurber's antiheroic Walter Mitty are no more, unless one translates them into the ultimate mind-game escape—black humor's "kind" offer of insanity, such as the final surprising Ambrose Bierce–like fate of Sam Lowry (Jonathan Pryce) in *Brazil* (1985).

There is nothing inherently new about dark or macabre humor. Jonathan Swift's baby-eating premise of "A Modest Proposal" was written in the eighteenth century, though one might look for such humor as early as Aristophanes. American literature boasts such pioneer dark humorists as Edgar Allan Poe, Ambrose Bierce, and the late work of Mark Twain. Though it has ties with the surrealism of the 1920s and 1930s and the existentialism of the 1940s and 1950s (see this chapter's Bibliographical Overview), black humor is more a post-1960s phenomenon. Indeed, the general acceptance of the term *black* humor/comedy (as opposed to references such as "gallows humor" or "sick humor") came into acceptance during that decade, where the phrase was frequently applied to the fiction of several authors just gaining critical recognition. Black humor theorist/historian Mathew Winston has noted two especially significant 1965 publications: a *Time* article entitled "The Black Humorists," chronicling the emergence of novelists like Joseph Heller, John Barth, Terry Southern, and Bruce Jay Friedman; and a Friedman-edited anthology of such works called *Black Humor*.[1] Winston might also have included black comedy author Conrad Knickerbocker's pioneer 1960s essay on the genre—"Humor with a Mortal Sting" (1964).[2] While it does not have "black" in the title, it immediately begins with a broad comparison of white (traditional) and black humor.

Despite the genre's ties to foreign isms and authors, America seems to have a corner on the market. As Japanese humor scholar Kōji Numasawa observed in his essay "Black Humor: An American Aspect," "American writers on the whole appear to be more articulate about it, and American audiences more susceptible to the form."[3] Central to this America–black humor connection was the social unrest of the 1960s, when the idealistic Great Society itself was failing—fragmented over issues like Vietnam and civil rights. The shocking violence so common to black humor was also a regular staple of the decade, from the political assassinations (especially Jack Ruby's live television assassination of an assassin) to television's evening news "body counts" from Vietnam, which eventually numbed themselves into being just another optionally noted box score. Black humor theorist/historian Douglas M. Davis has suggested this American affinity for the genre is an outgrowth, ironically, of the nation's unique ties with what might best be called populism (see chapter 8)— *but* "These beliefs do not stay the course. [The early promise for the 1960s goes unfulfilled.] They are rigid and break when they fall. Therein lies an invitation for black comedy.[4] Added inspiration for depictions of black humor absurdity was to be found in the American government's "unshakable insistence that black was white, that [Vietnam] escalation was really the search for peace, and that the war was being won."[5] Again, semantic word games were hardly 1960s innovations. One has only to think of the twisted humor of the Nazis, who used a Red Cross van to transport their deadly gas at Dachau and who placed the words "Arbeit Macht Frei" (work gives freedom) over an entrance to Auschwitz. The chilling latter precedent possibly inspired the Big Brother Party slogans of George Orwell's *1984:*

WAR IS PEACE
FREEDOM IS SLAVERY
IGNORANCE IS STRENGTH[6]

Regardless of the situation, such semantic manipulation makes truth and reality completely relative. In fact, Terry Gilliam's *1984*-inspired black humor film *Brazil* puts this even more graphically when it simply includes the "obscene" wall graffito "REALITY." In 1960s America such a "reality" seemed ominously close.

When the aforementioned *Time* article provides black humor examples outside of fiction, it fittingly starts with *Dr. Strangelove or: How I Learned to Stop Worrying and Love the Bomb* (1964), nicely describing the film as "treating the hydrogen bomb as a colossal banana peel on which the world slips to annihilation."[7] (The film was also co-scripted by acknowledged black comedy novelist Terry Southern.) Even today, *Dr. Strangelove* remains as both film's black humor archetype and a convenient starting point for the genre's emergence in American cinema, though the real onslaught started at decade's end.

Of course, earlier black humor film precedents exist. In fact, one could go back through cinema history and find numerous films with dark comic undercurrents, beginning with pioneer works from George Méliès and Mack Sennett. But that is usually what they are, simply undercurrents. Thus, for every legitimate pre-1960s black comedy antecedent, such as the comic attacks on Hitler and Nazism by both Charlie Chaplin and Ernst Lubitsch in *The Great Dictator* (1940) and *To Be or Not to Be* (1942), there are countless other movies which, while showcasing the characteristic occasionally, are best categorized in other, more traditional genres. For example, Chaplin's *The Gold Rush* (1925) features scenes of cannibalism comedy which were actually inspired by the tragic Donner Party's very real cannibalism. And the comic wall screen intrusions of the factory boss in Chaplin's *Modern Times* (1936) certainly inspired the Big Brother wall scenes of *1984*. But these early films are best defined as personality comedies. Other Chaplin contemporaries whose personality comedy personae sometimes embraced black comedy include cynics Buster Keaton, W. C. Fields, and the Marx Brothers (see the Bibliographical Overview). And this says nothing of the methodical "tit-for-tat" violence of Laurel & Hardy.

Howard Hawk's *His Girl Friday* (1940) quite literally incorporates "gallows humor," as the story revolves around an impending execution by hanging. But its interaction of characters, especially with an antihero focus upon Ralph Bellamy, more logically places it in the screwball genre. Another screwball comedy with black humor undercurrents would be *Arsenic and Old Lace* (1944), where two pleasantly batty little old ladies poison lonely elderly gentlemen.

Hawks's earlier gangster classic *Scarface* (1932), also has moments of black humor, especially those scenes which highlight the life and death of title character Paul Muni's private secretary Angelo (Vince Barnett)—the intense little man who does *not* know how to write, yet always takes calls during major gun battles. Other precursor directors whose works (like Chaplin's and Hawks's) often showcase black comedy elements include Billy Wilder and Alfred Hitchcock.

There is, however, one early black humor film which merits archetypal status on a level with that of *Dr. Strangelove*—Chaplin's *Monsieur Verdoux* (1947). The comedian's title character, his first complete break with his Charlie the tramp persona, makes a business of marrying and murdering little old ladies. Its key departure from the later *Dr. Strangelove* model is that while *Monsieur Verdoux* also focuses upon an absurd, predatory world, the film's black humor comes from a sympathetic individual who is given some justification for his deeds. He is merely paying back a harsh world in kind. Moreover, though the viewer only "meets" a single victim, her less than pleasant nature is presented as the norm, especially when coupled with the comically bitchy family of another victim (who assist in the eventual capture of Verdoux). That one should not be concerned about the demise of these women is further underlined by the case of Martha Raye's character, the only wife Verdoux fails to liquidate. Her nouveau riche loudmouth literally has the viewer rooting for her demise, though circumstances always intervene.

This Verdoux model, black comedy emanating from a sympathetic character, was the pre-1960s norm, and it continues to appear. The 1949 British black humor classic *Kind Hearts and Coronets* follows the same pattern, with Dennis Price superbly playing a wrongly disfranchised member of a titled family. Price methodically kills with comic coolness those less-than-sympathetic relatives (all played by Alex Guinness) who stand in his way of becoming a duke. More recently, the Blands (Paul Bartel and Mary Woronov) get back at a victimizingly sick world by killing sex "perverts" in *Eating Raoul* (1982).

An examination of a number of black comedies, with *Dr. Strangelove* and *Monsieur Verdoux* as the poles of the genre, disclosed three interrelated themes: man as beast, the absurdity of the world, and the omnipresence of death. Interestingly enough, these themes are generally just the opposite of the populist comedy. Thus, these contrasting values are briefly noted as the black comedy themes are examined.

First, unlike populist comedy's celebration of the inherent goodness of man, black humor takes a decidedly less idealistic view of the animal. Director Arthur Penn's 1970 adaptation of Thomas Berger's *Little Big Man* probably put it most baldly when the story's only collection of good people, the central character's (Dustin Hoffman) adopted Indian tribe, ironically call themselves the "Human Beings." This revisionist black comedy look at the white man's attempted genocide of the Indian, an indirect commentary upon genocide then occurring in Vietnam, was most focused in its celebrated toppling of the legend and heroic aura surrounding General George Armstrong Custer and his defeat at the Little Big Horn.

While other black comedies seldom have such a dramatic historic figure as Custer to showcase man as beast, it is the key upon which the genre is built. Visually, it is most dramatically presented in *Catch-22* (1970), when Alan Arkin is out after curfew. That night he witnesses a cross-section of human depravity in the streets: aberrated sexuality, children robbing a drunk, vicious beatings (man and animal), and the aftermath of a murder—a young, raped girl lying dead on the cobblestones. The black comedy send-up of all this is that no one is arrested—except Arkin, for breaking curfew.

A full chronicling of both the genre's depiction of man's inhumanity to man and the significance attached to human life would take a platoon of movie ushers decades to compile. But certainly one of the most definitive would be General "Buck" Turgidson's (George C. Scott) argument in *Dr. Strangelove* for a full-scale nuclear attack on the Russians: "I'm not saying we wouldn't get our hair messed. But I do say no more than ten to twenty million killed, tops—depending upon the breaks." Comically shocking, yet one is reminded of the real world revelations of *Atomic Cafe* (1982), a sort of black comedy documentary compilation film of America's often shocking approach to the nuclear age prior to *Dr. Strangelove,* such as the World War II decision to drop the atomic bomb on "virgin targets" (ones having suffered little previous war damage) like Hiroshima to better "see the total bomb damage." Moreover, as one critic later observed, *Atomic Cafe*'s "chilling" collection of 1950s misleading government educational films on the atom bomb, such as the "duck and cover" drills taught to adults and children alike (aimed at protecting them during a nuclear attack) nicely prepared the way for the subtitle of Kubrick's *Dr. Strangelove*—"How I Learned to Stop Worrying and Love the Bomb."[8]

Though the shock value of black comedy (such as the sudden mushroom culmination of *Dr. Strangelove* or the graphically portrayed U.S. cavalry massacre of Indian women and children in *Little Big Man)* is the genre's trademark manner of undercutting any concept of man's nobility, there is a more pervasive example—portraying his obsession with sex. This sexual negation of man has four variations. First, it is difficult to attach any significance to man's lofty ideals when serious subjects of concern are constantly displaced by sex. For example, the world ends at the close of *Dr. Strangelove* with the title character's (Peter Sellers) lecture on postwar survival having digressed to a scenario of ten women for every man. Thus, even with an approaching apocalypse, the mere thought of sex reduces man to the most base and selfish of animal needs. Such weakness also includes those black comedy characters initially shown as made of purer stuff—such as Robert Duvall's overly religious Frank Burns in *M\*A\*S\*H* (1970). Burns comically pays for his hypocrisy by having his sexual activities with another hypocrite (Sally Kellerman's Major Hot Lips) broadcast over the base intercom system. And in *Little Big Man* Faye Dunaway makes the startling switch from a parsonage wife to brothel prostitute.

Director Blake Edwards provides pointed commentary on this sexual vulnerability in *S.O.B.* (1981, with its fitting black comedy title), when his in-film director-producer makes a hit from a failed film with pornography and the bared breasts of its goody-goody star. The shock slant comes from Edwards casting wife Julie Andrews (with her equally goody-two-shoes, Mary Poppins image) as the star.

Sex also represents an absence of control, consistent with man's plight in black comedy. Loss of control is most comically presented in the bug-eyed panting of Yossarian (Alan Arkin) and his *Catch-22* company after they meet the sexy daughter of a visiting general (Orson Welles)—completely ignoring their bombing mission briefing. One is also reminded of Major King Kong (Slim Pickens) happily astride a falling phallic-shaped atomic bomb called Lolita, whooping his way to world oblivion. As Luis Buñuel, the most acclaimed foreign director of black comedy, observed, "in a rigidly hierarchical society, sex—which respects no barriers and obeys no laws—can at any moment become an agent of chaos."[9]

In addition, black comedy frequently makes direct links between sex and death—the ultimate lack of control. Most popular is the Bluebeard variety, of which *Monsieur Verdoux* is a prime example. But death can also appear as an ironic commentary on man's self-destructive lifestyle, such as Bob Fosse's *All That Jazz* (1979). The latter film, though best studied as a dark parody (see Chapter 9 in this volume), is the most direct about the subject—literally casting death as a sexy and flirtatious lady ironically dressed in white (Jessica Lange). Sex and death in black comedy can be a commentary upon man's sexual perversity, such as the *Eating Raoul* victims who were attracted by an advertisement promising kinky favors or Painless Pole (John Schuck) in *M\*A\*S\*H* who decides to commit suicide when an experience of impotency creates fears of latent homosexuality. One is also reminded of the pornography theatre conclusion of John Landis's *An American Werewolf in London* (1981). Though *Werewolf* is also best examined as dark parody, it is fascinating that the film's final transition of David (David Naughton) to beast should occur in a porno theatre (with the animalistic urges associated therein), and that the cries of pain which accompany David's change should be indistinguishable in the darkened theatre from the sexual moans emitted from the screen. Historically, death and sexual perversity often have found their ways into Buñuel's films. This even occurs as early as the still startling *Un Chien andalou* (1929), "when the man caresses the woman's bare breasts as his face slowly changes into a death mask."[10] In the sometimes black comedy of Kubrick's *A Clockwork Orange* (1971), one is also reminded of Alex's (Malcolm McDowell) murder of one female victim with a large, abstract sculpture of a penis. And the fulfillment of Sam Lowry's sexual fantasy in *Brazil* begins with a necrophilia joke.

The fact that sex frequently symbolizes the only solace even for the genre's nominal good guy is a further comment upon the pitiful condition of modern man. This is best showcased by sorry Billy Pilgrim's (Michael Sacks) love-making scenes with voluptuous movie star Montana Wildhack (Valerie Perrine) while the planet of Tralfamadore looks on in *Slaughterhouse-Five*.

Finally, even when sex is a positive story device, a sense of the comically shocking and unnatural remains. An example is the consummation of the relationship between title characters Bud Cort and Ruth Gordon in *Harold and Maude* (1972), where a nearly sixty-year age difference exists.

Consequently, sexual references abound in the genre, be it the large number befitting an archetype like *Dr. Strangelove* (which so moved one film critic to devote an entire article to the subject),[11] to the meandering philandering of Tom Conti's Scottish poet in the excellent but more modest black comedy *Reuben, Reuben* (1983). A sadly funny, final commentary upon sex and man in black comedy is provided in George Roy Hill's adaptation of John Irving's *The World According to Garp* (1982). Garp's mother (Glenn Close) has herself impregnated by a dying war veteran whose injuries have reduced him to a vegetable state. How appropriate that man can still perform the sex act without a mind, since the sexual organ always displaces the cerebral organ anyway, even when the brain is functioning.

Second, unlike the populist comedy's rational world fantasy, where justice prevails because of a man-of-the-people leader, black humor offers only an absurd environment, where the individual does not count. This absurdity is most obviously showcased by the fact that black humor's antiheroes often are not so much participants in the genre as they are unwilling spectators in a terrible, ongoing joke called life. This leaf in the wind characterization is best presented in the adaptations of *Little Big Man, Catch-22,* and *Slaughterhouse-Five,* but countless other examples exist, such as Steve Railsback's fugitive in Richard Rush's *The Stunt Man* (1980), where the tricks of filmmaking add to the antihero's vulnerability.

Black humor absurdity is usually presented in two ways—through the chaos of an unordered universe and through the flaws of mortal man. The first and most fundamental simply has man being victimized for merely trying to exist. For instance, in Martin Scorsese's *After Hours* (1985), Griffin Dunne's Mr. Normal character picks up a beautiful stranger (Rosanna Arquette). But the "after hours" date ends up a comic nightmare. It is never a good sign when your date commits suicide early, but things actually do get worse for Dunne. As he runs around late-night New York City (or should one say flees?) he has comically frightful encounters with a myriad of strange characters, from a vigilante-type ice cream lady to Teri Garr's equally lethal Monkees groupie. And one should not neglect the story's interweaving of petty criminals Cheech and Chong, who exist as a rather offbeat comic chorus reminder that yes, this is a comedy, a black comedy.

Seeing Dunne (who produced *After Hours*) as the ongoing victim of the world's absurdity also reminds one of his role in *An American Werewolf in*

*London.* Though a parody, *Werewolf* certainly has some black comedy credentials—beginning with a story that violently derails two hitchhiking tourists from a summer vacation to being werewolf victims. It is Dunne who dies early in this film but who continues to comically appear (in ever more graphic stages of physical deterioration), with the message that his friend must take his own life or else become a werewolf. Truly, this is not your run-of-the-mill comic chaos.

Jeff Daniel's naive, young tax consultant experiences an extended *After Hours–* type experience in Jonathan Demme's *Something Wild* (1986). Only this time, he is the one picked up—or, more comically correct, kidnapped—by a sexy but strange Melanie Griffith, who for a time sports both a Louise Brooks wig (bobbed black hair) and the nickname Lulu.

Of course, one need not leave the neighborhood in search of absurdity. It can always move in next door, as happened to John Belushi in the 1981 adaptation of Thomas Berger's *Neighbors* or it can pop up in the high school of *Teachers* (1984), where the best instructor is an escaped crazy and the worst one's in-class death goes unnoticed.

Other black comedy examples of the dangerous randomness of life range from Jack Lemmon and Tony Curtis accidentally dropping in on the "St. Valentine's Day Massacre" in Billy Wilder's *Some Like It Hot* (1959) to a hit man (Jack Nicholson) falling in love with a rival hit "man" (Kathleen Turner) in *Prizzi's Honor,* resulting in the genre's definitive "romantic" question—"Do I ice [kill] her, or marry her?" And *Reuben, Reuben* seems about to close on an upbeat note, with Tom Conti's poet deciding not to commit suicide (though he is still standing on a chair with neck in noose) and his years-long writing block ended. Ah, but then life's randomness hits, and the neighbor's big, friendly dog Reuben lumbers in, accidentally dislodges the chair, and a saved poet is lost.

For all the comic frightfulness of an unordered universe, man has been a strong contributor to the absurdity of the black comedy world. *Pogo* cartoonist Walt Kelly capsulized this nicely with his delightful pun of a famous axiom, "We have met the enemy and he is us." This man-made absurdity is the result of both general species incompetency and its perpetuation in human institutions.

*Dr. Strangelove* fairly shouts species incompetency, as do most Kubrick films, but it is often showcased in an institutionalized package. In fact, the film is a catchall for nearly every type of absurdity (including the chance occurrence of a person in power, like Sterling Hayden's General Jack D. Ripper, going crazy and playing God), but the overall point is that man is incapable of controlling what he has created. The irony is heightened by the fact that the scientific know-how needed to initially construct the bomb was immense; it is just that with humans in control, there can be no real fail-safe system. Leadership has never matched the technical strides made in science. And beyond the incompetence of major power leaders trying to indefinitely juggle the bomb, there is an army of other uniformed homo sapiens who could contribute to a nuclear apolcalypse, from the Third World intervention of *The Mouse That Roared* (1959) to a high school whiz kid accidentally tapping into the system in *War Games* (1983).

Species incompetency does not, of course, have to focus on state-of-the-art nuclear holocaust. Man has been unable to get along with man since the beginning of time. This endless involvement in war is his greatest tribute to incompetency, and a major ingredient of the absurd world he helped create. Vonnegut ironically paid tribute to this endless, insane legacy when he noted what one critic of antiwar books had advised as an equally productive subject—"Why don't you write an anti-*glacier* book instead?"[12]

Fittingly, black comedy often focuses on war, be it Wilder's *Stalag 17* (1953) or Altman's *M\*A\*S\*H,* because war is the perfect symbol for every man's ongoing battle for day-to-day survival. *M\*A\*S\*H* beautifully captures this dual nature absurdity (of shooting war and war as metaphor for life). First, what could be more fundamentally absurd about real war than the policy of medical miracles saving lives only to send them right back into battle? But *M\*A\*S\*H* does not show us the actual fighting—only the casualties—as the doctors mix humor and the graphic realism of the battlefield operating room. The plight of the civilian casualty of an absurd world follows a similar scenario. One does not witness the individual, internalized war most thinking human beings experience; it only comes to attention when someone is psychologically "wounded." And these casualties do not mend so easily, though like the recovered soldier, they too will find themselves back in the fray. (Of course, in a nuclear war, everyone would be on the "front lines.")

*M\*A\*S\*H* further accents the warlike nature of the civilian sector when it devotes considerable time to the football game between army units. As more and more commentators on the American scene have noted, football represents an excellent microcosm of this violent, competitive society. Director Robert Altman underlies the point by the comically aggressive, anything-for-a-victory attitude taken by both teams.

This interchangeable approach to war and life is also nicely borne out by the extended meaning to come out of Heller's phrase "Catch-22." As originally applied, it meant that combat flyer

Orr was crazy and could be grounded. All he had to do was ask; and as soon as he did, he would no longer be crazy [concern being a rational mental process] and would have to fly more missions. . . . If he flew them he was crazy and didn't have to, but if he didn't want to he was sane and had to.[13]

Quickly, this absurdity of war phrase was embraced by the general public— *before* Vietnam was an issue—and was applied to the homo sapiens–influenced absurdity of the world. It was even neatly classified in civilian dictionaries everywhere (an added tribute to man's absurdity—the need to organize his chaos), with dictionary crispness: "catch-22 n. (slang) a dilemma from which the victim has no escape." [14]

Of course, Paddy Chayefsky's script for *Network* is more direct and earthy about man-made absurdity. Newscaster Howard Beale (Peter Finch) explained why he had planned to commit suicide: "I just ran out of bullshit. . . . Bullshit is all the reasons we give for living." This brings one to the second chief source of man-made chaos—institutionalized absurdity. Finch, who won a posthumous Oscar for his role, goes from his indictment of the individual to that of religion: "If we can't think up any of our own [bullshit], we always have the God bullshit."

The often absurd actions/policies of establishment institutions (like the church or the military) are constantly under attack in black comedy. Their star target status is because they routinely propagate the lie, or "bullshit," that it is a rational world, and then their ongoing implementation of this lie results in mass dehumanization and/or death.

Institutionalized absurdity means man's chaos-making abilities attain irrevocable steamroller proportions. For instance, Monsieur Verdoux eventually goes to the guillotine for crimes eclipsed a million-fold by world governments—murder. As he drily observes, "Numbers sanctify." Institutionalized absurdity is further fueled by either additional goofs or greed—big business–style. The first, for which *Dr. Strangelove*'s less than fail-safe system might be the pivotal example, probably remains the most popular norm in the institutionalized absurdity category. Key black comedy examples continue to exist. For instance, in *Brazil* the state so flippantly executes its alleged enemies that a simple misspelling, caused by a squashed bug in a typewriter, can lead to an innocent victim's death—the event upon which the whole film turns. More importantly, however, institutionalized human incompetency is an easy comic caricature to create. For example, in *Harold and Maude,* the troubled and death-obsessed Bud Cort is sent to three institutional authority figures for help. And the film quickly has archetypes to undercut. Representatives of the church, the medical profession, and the armed forces meet with him—but are comically inneffective. This is especially true of the military figure, Uncle Victor (Charles Tyner), whose caricature is easily the most comically outrageous. Borrowing from Peter Sellers's zany interpretation of the Dr. Strangelove figure (with his comic malfunctioning—"heil Hitler"—artificial arm), one-armed Uncle Victor is equally demented, as well as being equipped with a malfunctioning mechanical device which is supposed to make his starched right sleeve salute. The gag is comically compounded when Uncle Victor is described as having once been "General MacArthur's right-hand man." Fittingly for this genre, the character recommends that going to war would be the best thing for his troubled nephew. Other black comedy examples of institutional incompetency range from the Woody Allen CIA of *Bananas* (1971), which sends military support to both sides in an insurrection to guarantee inclusion with the winners, to the core travesty of *Slaughterhouse-Five*—the firebombing of the non-military target city of Dresden (which actually occurred during World War II).

The big business approach to institutionalized absurdity finds craziness a by-product of the profit motive. *Catch-22*'s enterprising Milo (Jon Voight) is the perfect example of this phenomenon. His creation and direction of "M and M Enterprises" turns World War II into the most profitable of businesses, and the source of much of its planned and profitable absurdity. These enterprises range from his taking all the camp parachutes because he could obtain a good price on silk (Arkin's Yossarian only discovers this when he opens his pack to find his chute is replaced by two shares of M and M stock), to a Milo deal which has Americans bombing their *own* base in exchange for the German enemy *helping* Milo liquidate his unloadable stockpile of cotton! Fittingly, late in the film Voight's character paraphrases the famous, old General Motors big business axiom—"What's good for M and M Enterprises is good for the world."

This *Catch-22* model of organized and bankable absurdity is nicely complemented in the civilian world by *Network*—which chronicles the live television murder of a newscaster because he had "lousy ratings." (The murder also represented an excellent lead-in for a network show shot and produced by revolutionaries!) Early in the film network owner Arthur Jensen (Ned Beatty) puts this all in perspective when he observes, "There is no America, no democracy, there is only . . . [names corporation after corporation]. Those are the nations of the world." As if the metaphor needed further expansion, he goes on to say, "The world is a business; it has been since man crawled out of a slime." (See Chayefsky's skewering of another institution in 1971's *Hospital*, for which he also won an Oscar for script.)

Even the less global black comedies frequently play this analogy, be it Chaplin's killing of little old ladies to maintain his stock portfolio in *Monsieur Verdoux*, or the casual frying pan murders of *Eating Raoul* (truly a genre of *dead*-pan humor), where money is being raised for a restaurant while ridding the world of sex perverts. In fact, celebrated film critic Robert Warshow's "reading" of *Monsieur Verdoux* produced an axiom which could be applied to any number of these smaller black comedies—"Business is like murder and therefore murder is only a kind of business."[15]

Before I move to black comedy's third theme—the omnipresence of death—I should note that the genre's showcasing of absurdity is frequently reinforced by a fragmented narrative of less than linear proportions. At its extreme, such as in *Slaughterhouse-Five*, central character Billy Pilgrim is constantly time-tripping through events in his past, present, and future. Editing, which forever juxtaposes these worlds, makes the transitions as startling for the viewer as for the aptly named Pilgrim, thus reinforcing the genre's theme of absurdity. In *Catch-22* the flashbacks keep one scrambling for the narrative, especially the art film–like repetitions of Yossarian's discovery of the dying Snowden.

As with the formalistic editing, black comedy's self-conscious use of music is an additional commentary on the theme of absurdity. Thus, the mushroom cloud close of *Dr. Strangelove* is ironically accompanied by Vera Lynn's sentimental, romantic World War II song "We'll Meet Again." And *Brazil* takes its title from the upbeat, breezy 1930s Ary Baroso song of the same name, a song which frequently punctuates this dark comedy. Kubrick's *A Clockwork Orange* follows this same model by juxtaposing violence and "Singing in the Rain." Consequently, black humor is one comedy genre where formalistic techniques, such as self-consciously elaborate editing and music, reinforce theme.

This self-consciousness is also borne out in the genre's tendency to include scenes of film parody (see chapter 9). It is as if to say that black comedy attacks all "institutions," including celebrated auteurs and genres of its medium of expression, from the brief takeoff on Sergei Eisenstein's "Odessa Steps" sequence *(Battleship Potemkin,* 1925) near the close of *Brazil,* to the more lengthy Major "King" Kong's (Slim Pickens) preparation of his *Dr. Strangelove* bomber crew for its mission. In the latter case, much of what Kong says is ludicrous (such as his comments on their survival kit in case they bail out—but what would they be jumping into?), yet Kubrick so slickly apes the standard men-into-action scene of the war film (including "When Johnny Comes Marching Home Again" on the soundtrack) that the viewer ironically is tempted to root for success, despite what that would mean. Once again black comedy has put the viewer's emotions at comic cross-purposes. (In come cases, however, the parody is so pervasive that even a film with black comedy characteristics, such as *An American Werewolf in London* or *Bonnie and Clyde,* 1967, is best examined as parody.)

Third, unlike the populist comedy's romanticized celebration of family traditions and rituals (such as Capra's use of home and religion), which links mankind through the ages, black comedy focuses upon the awful finality of death. To borrow a Vonnegut metaphor (also echoed in the Chayefsky *Network* quote which opens the chapter), everyone is headed to the slaughterhouse. Death in populist films, especially those of John Ford, means a reaffirmation of past values and a promise for the future. In black comedy, death means THE END. To paraphrase a popular axion of the genre: "Life is awful, and then you die." Thus, death is the final joke of futile life. Black comedy merely obtains more mileage out of a terrible dilemma (death) by laughing at it. But there are no *final* happy endings, as Buñuel implies with the title of his autobiography—*My Last Sigh* (see note 9). The related taboos are those sacred things black comedy attacks which give meaning to death (religion) and reveal the less than dignified elements of pitiful life, from body functions to the sorry state of the body after death. (Laughter itself becomes a comforting "religion" in this genre.) The portrayal of black comedy death is also a compendium for all the genre's themes (man as beast and the absurdity of life) and subthemes (undercutting institutions).

There are four basic lessons to be learned or reaffirmed from the genre's obsession with death. First, death itself is a terrible absurdity. How can a once vital, passionate, thinking human suddenly be reduced to so much "garbage" in death? Yet that is black comedy's great revelation. It is borne out by the conclusion of Yossarian's pivotal repeated scene with wounded and dying Snowden in *Catch-22,* where his insides ooze to the floor. Poor Snowden's terrible secret is that "Man was matter. . . . Bury him and he'll rot like other kinds of garbage. The spirit gone, man is garbage." [16] Literary critic and black comedy theorist Sanford Pinsker calls this, rather than "Catch-22," the "heart of the novel" (something which applies equally to the film adaptation), while academic critics like Leslie M. Thompson and William R. Cozart term the scene the "ultimate description of technological atrocity." [17] By the time of *Eating Raoul,* Snowden's black comedy secret is a secret no more—Mrs. Bland's comment to her murderer husband as he experiences a modicum of guilt is a casual: "He [the victim] was a man, now he's just a bag of garbage." It is macabrely appropriate that in a genre where the individual is insignificant (the exact opposite of populism), he should also be physically destroyed.

Second, the casually random end-without-purpose unexpectedness with which death frequently appears underlies both the world's absurdity and the insignificance of man. For instance, the sudden execution in *Slaughterhouse-Five* of the caring former teacher Edgar Derby because of a misunderstanding about a glass figurine, the even quicker propeller slicing in half of Kid Sampson during a prank in *Catch-22,* and the death of Garp's child during another prank (the automobile accident) in *The World According to Garp* all document the transitory nature of man's stay on earth. That such events should also occur during moments of joy, be they comic pranks or Derby's initially happy surprise of finding a figurine like one from home in the rubble of Dresden, underline all the more the absurdity of life and death.

Third, the popularity of suicide in black comedies (Bud Cort in *Harold and Maude* or Chaplin's indirect one in *Monsieur Verdoux* by allowing himself to be caught) further accents man's earthly dilemma in six ways. First, it dramatically demonstrates that the genre's disregard for life actually begins with the individual, even by the indirect manner of working oneself to death, as in *All That Jazz.* Second, suicide is that rare activity where the black comedy individual can initiate the event instead of being the random recipient. How ironically fitting, however, that this act results in the total negation of the individual. Third, life is full of pain, and suicide provides a way around this, as the title to *M\*A\*S\*H*'s theme song dramatically shows: "Suicide Is Painless." That this escape has always been an alternative to life's suffering is practically underscored by Lubitsch entitling a pioneer black comedy with Shakespeare's celebrated wording for suicide—*To Be or Not To Be.* Fourth, on a metaphorical level, suicide is an apt phrase for the literal implementation of the death wish–like tendency of modern man to seemingly rush towards an apocalypse of his own making. Fifth, suicide is a modest example of something black comedy frequently showcases on a broader and more terrible scale—man playing God, from *Little Big Man*'s Custer and Chaplin's Hitler-inspired Great Dictator, to

Strangelove himself—whose ironic name is so fitting for these pain-producing "Creators." Sixth, black comedy suicides, or the attempts, often reveal that randomness is just as strong in suicide as in the frustrating lives it seeks to end. Thus, *Reuben, Reuben* documents an accidental suicide, after Tom Conti's character has decided to live; Sissy Spacek's Babe MaGrath comes closest to death in her various *Crimes of the Heart* (1986) suicide attempts after she decides against it, only to accidentally knock herself out trying to remove her head from the oven. *S.O.B.* works a variation on suicide and chance when the in-film director (Richard Mulligan) continually fails at suicide (while a nearby heart attack victim seeking help dies), only to later be shot and killed when he (Mulligan) has something to live for.

The fourth basic lesson to draw from the genre's obsession with death demonstrates man's callousness to shock. While viewers tend initially to be surprised, in-film black comedy characters often have the worn-down "And so it goes" attitude of *Slaughterhouse-Five*'s Billy Pilgrim, like the ho-hum complacency with which the Hitchcock characters treat the corpse in *The Trouble with Harry* (1955) or the even more subdued response Bud Cort's screen mother makes to his seemingly very real suicides in *Harold and Maude*. Of course, part of the audience's shock is this flippant response to the horrible. But any shock, if sustained, eventually produces a numbing effect. Faye Dunaway's character in *Network* addresses just this point when she describes the early 1970s American public as "clobbered on all sides by Vietnam, Watergate, the inflation, the depression, they've turned off, shot up, and fucked themselves limp and nothing else helps." Thus, black comedy's graphic portrayals of death are forever trying to produce new shocks for the viewing public, and occasionally even for the film characters themselves.

Related to these ever more shocking death scenes are other taboo-breaking examples, such as Altman's parodying the *Last Supper* in *M\*A\*S\*H* (borrowing from Buñel's *Viridiana,* 1961) or the *Catch-22* nurses who run human excrement back through the 100 percent bandaged body of a wounded flyer, simply by reversing his intake/outtake bottles. If one were to include the cult, underground, pre-*Polyester* (1981) films of John Waters in the genre, examples such as Divine's (Glen Milstead) downing of real dog excrement at the tacked-on close of *Pink Flamingo* (1972) would be further prime evidence of shock effect. Fittingly, Waters entitled his 1981 autobiography *Shock Value.*[18] Black comedy is a genre which respects nothing, including the values of its audience.

These, then, have been the three interrelated central themes of black comedy—man as beast, the absurdity of the world, and the omnipresence of death—all terrible realities which belie the veneer of rationality which "civilized" man too often accepts as the norm. Black comedy screams *Think about it!* as it scrambles one's complacency with juxtapositionings of humor and horror. Of course, "thinking about" the unanswerable is another application of Catch-22ism, but it does allow the individual to make his own separate peace.

As this chapter demonstrates, the genre embraces a wide cross-section of films, including some best examined as dark parodies. But this only begins to demonstrate the contemporary pervasiveness of black comedy: whether conscious or not, cruel humor helps get one through what are often cruel times. As Freud saw humor in terms of sexual taboos—laughter being an acceptable way of addressing a subject which many found difficult to discuss—black comedy applies that principle to the complete gamut of unmentionables which seem to now happen daily. Thus, the black comedy umbrella finds worthy topics in everything from nuclear apocalypse to the latest mass murder (or is that redundant?), with time out for jokes about the seven space shuttle astronauts who perished, or whatever is the tragedy of the day. Possibly perverse coping, but coping just the same. One is also reminded of the title for Tadeusz Borowski's now more widely celebrated 1940s concentration-camp stories, *This Way for the Gas, Ladies and Gentlemen*. Indeed, probably the greatest irony of black—sick—humor is that it is *the healthiest survivor outlook to take*.

## BIBLIOGRAPHICAL OVERVIEW

The most pivotal criticism applicable to American "black humor" film is drawn from the analysis of the 1960s movement of the same name in literature—often described as the most important development in American fiction since World War II. Black film comedy grew out of this literary beginning, with many of the works being adapted for the screen. As with most genres or movements, however, earlier precedents exist. For example, Bruce Jay Friedman's important 1965 anthology *Black Humor* was preceded by surrealist founder André Breton's 1939 *Anthologie de L'humour Noir*. Though the more central American thrust of the Friedman text is most pertinent to the subject at hand, surrealist Breton's pioneer overview provides a valuable, if eclectic, black humor foundation. Beginning with Swift's "A Modest Proposal," it includes a broad cross-section of artists as divergent as Lewis Carroll and Franz Kafka. If Breton's work was not quite ready to embrace black comedy as a genre (his introduction is more concerned with the generally antisentimental), neither was the period, which still predates the atrocities of World War II. In contrast, the 1960s embrace the genre as a timely reflection of a very chaotic contemporary world, though Friedman's firmly tongue-in-cheek Foreword (which claims he would just as soon define a corned-beef sandwich) comically presents the varied nature of even his 1960 selections.

As Breton's involvement suggests, black humor has ties with surrealism; I note in my 1987 Marx Brothers book the interest of surrealists in the team. Yet the brothers—more specifically, Groucho—could turn their Lewis Carroll absurdity into periodic black comedy, such as the costume party–like war scenes that close *Duck Soup*.[19] Also, Groucho's comic paranoia (as president of Freedonia) towards the intentions of a rival leader (Ambassador Trentino of Sylvania) nicely anticipates the equally comic paranoia of Sterling Hayden's General Jack D. Ripper towards the Russians in *Dr. Strangelove*.

More specific is black comedy's affinity for near-surrealistic scenes of fantasy, such as the winged flight of Sam Lowry (Jonathan Pryce) in *Brazil*. But the main difference between the genre and surrealism, as underlined by black comedy theorist/historian Max F. Schulz, is that surrealism keys upon "internal disorder" of the subconscious mind, while black comedy generally suggests that disorder is now the external, real state of things.[20]

Black humor also has ties with existentialism. Indeed, an early name for the former phenomenon was "Yankee Existentialism."[21] The two are most alike in their shared view of it being an absurd world. But an important difference to be recognized is that existentialism, at least the modern existentialism of Jean-Paul Sartre, presupposes meaning in life *if* the individual employs the power of choice. In contrast, black humor accents the absurdity, seldom offering any meaning in life, regardless of individual actions. This is emphasized by the sad bitterness of 121-year-old Jack Crabbe (Hoffman) at the close of his *Little Big Man* tale, as if further accented by a camera which purposely holds the final take long enough to make the viewer uncomfortable.

The most important book-length study of the genre is editor Douglas M. Davis's *The World of Black Humor: An Introductory Anthology of Selections and Criticisms* (1967). As the title suggests, Davis undertakes to present the best of both worlds, literary examples and critical definitions. Besides offering an excellent Introduction, Davis has assembled a valuable collection of criticism, including Conrad Knickerbocker's pioneer essay "Humor with a Mortal Sting" (1964) and another central piece from pivotal 1965—Richard Kostelanetz's "The Point Is That Life Doesn't Have Any Point," though it is anthologized as "The American Absurd Novel." Moreover, unlike Breton and Friedman, Davis attempts to be more insightful in his arrangement of black comedy authors, breaking his examples into three categories—twentieth-century beginnings, contemporary mainstream (1960s focus), and models of the genre's tendency for apocalyptic conclusions. The book's only major flaw is its neglect of Vonnegut, a frequent occurrence in 1960s black comedy assessments. Major critical recognition did not come to Vonnegut until the 1970s.

Appropriately, the best thing about Max F. Schulz's later book-length critical assessment of the genre, *Black Humor Fiction of the Sixties* (1973), after the excellent opening, "Towards a Definition of Black Humor," is a chapter entirely devoted to Vonnegut. The remaining three sections provide detailed analyses of additional black comedy authors. Obviously, other pertinent book-length assessments exist, but these are the most pointed. Interested readers are encouraged to seek out individual studies of specific film directors and novelists associated with the genre, some of which are noted in the main body of this text. A stimulating, more broadly based historical overview of dark humor can be found in Tony Hendra's massive 480-page *Going Too Far* (1987). But as its subtitle suggests *(The Rise and Demise of Sick, Gross, Black, Sophomoric, Weirdo, Pinko, Anarchist Underground, Anti-Establishment Humor)* this fascinating attention to related comedy variations often derails it from the more focused subject of this chapter.

Any number of shorter essays might be singled out, but two merit special attention—sociological theorist/historian Morris Dickstein's chapter "Black Humor and History: The Early Sixties," in his *Gates of Eden: American Culture in the Sixties* (1977), and Mathew Winston's *"Humour noir* and Black Humor," in comedy scholar Harry Levin's *Veins of Humor* (1972). Both these essays work on several levels. They provide a historically superb overview of the genre, as well as being rich in criticism citations. Just as significantly, they offer important critical assessments of their own. For instance, Winston suggests three ways the genre disorients one, besides the centerpiece juxtaposing of blackness and comedy: presenting the "patently impossible" as truth, constantly changing one's "distance from the characters," and "periodically shattering the illusion of a self-contained fictive world."[22] While Winston goes on to note direct address as an example of this break with suspension of disbelief, it also further explains the frequent presence of parody in the genre.

Few major works are without detractors. Thus, Terry Heller's "Notes on Technique in Black Humor" provocatively attacks Winston's essay as too narrow. Key evidence for Heller is Winston's decision (need?) to break black humor into two categories—one dominated by black (horror), the other by humor.[23] Ironically, Heller finds the division stimulating and proceeds to focus his essay upon a variation of the dichotomy, fine-tuning the possible mixtures of the continuums of humor and horror.

Other black comedy essays of note include *Time* magazine's "The Black Humorists," Kōji Numasawa's "Black Humor: An American Aspect," Burton Feldman's "Anatomy of Black Humor," Hamlin Hill's "Black Humor: Its Cause and Cure," Leonard Feinberg's "Black Humor: Aggression Against Everything," and Sanford Pinsker's "The Graying of Black Humor." As with the other pieces cited, the focus of these essays is fiction, but the black comedy principles presented are generally applicable regardless of the medium being examined. Hill's article underlines this through a black comedy subject matter which ranges from 1960s novelists to W. C. Fields and Lenny Bruce.

The recommended readings have been restricted to the most pointed of black humor focuses because, in truth, a floodgate of pertinent material exists as soon as one singles out a Kubrick or a Chaplin, though film study has been much less likely to broadly address black comedy. Still, I have my own personal floodgate of more focused material, from film historian Charles Maland's insightful *"Dr. Strangelove* (1964): Nightmare Comedy and the Ideology of Liberal Consensus" in the scholarly publication *American Quarterly,* to the provocative Terry Gilliam *(Brazil)* interview/article with the black comedy title "Kicking Ass," in the youth market *Spin* magazine.[24] Thus, for the student of black humor, this overview's keyed upon material represents just a beginning.

Of course, in today's increasingly darkly humorous world, we need not so much additional critical assessments as merely a daily newspaper. For instance, as this chapter was written (1986), two anniversaries occurred which brought home anew life's absurdity. In June the fortieth birthday of the bikini swimsuit reminded us that what is still the ultimate sexy costume was named after the Pacific atoll site of an American nuclear test. Moreover, the Bikini bomb had a picture of the sensually beautiful Rita Hayworth on it and was called Gilda— the 1946 title character of her then contemporary and most sexually provocative film. These facts also nicely complement the chapter's earlier correlation between sex and death/chaos. And how appropriate that the mistress of George C. Scott's sexually active character Buck Turgidson in *Dr. Strangelove* should first be seen in a bikini, as if this were her normal uniform. October 1986 saw the twenty-fifth birthday of Heller's *Catch-22,* and who should help the author celebrate but the United States Air Force Academy, where the book is part of the regular curriculum! To pun a *Catch-22* character promoted because of name, this seems a Maj. Major Major absurdity, "And so it goes."

## NOTES

1. Mathew Winston, *"Humour noir* and Black Humor," in *Veins of Humor,* ed. Harry Levin (Cambridge, Mass: Harvard University Press, 1972), p. 273; "The Black Humorists," *Time,* 12 February 1965, pp. 94–96; Bruce Jay Friedman, ed., *Black Humor* (New York: Bantam Books, 1965).

2. Conrad Knickerbocker, "Humor with a Mortal Sting," *New York Times Book Review,* 27 September 1964, pp. 3, 60–61.

3. Kōji Numasawa, "Black Humor: An American Aspect," *Studies in English Literature* (University of Tokyo), March 1968, p. 177.

4. Douglas M. Davis, Introduction, in *The World of Black Humor: An Introductory Anthology of Selections and Criticism,* ed. Davis (New York: E. P. Dutton, 1967), p. 20.

5. Morris Dickstein, Chapter 4, "Black Humor and History: The Early Sixties," in *Gates of Eden: American Culture in the Sixties* (New York: Basic Books, 1977), p. 117.

6. George Orwell, *1984* (1949; repr. New York: New American Library, 1961). The slogans occur frequently—for instance, pp. 7, 17, 87.

7. "The Black Humorists," *Time,* p. 94.

8. *"Atomic Cafe"* entry, in *TV Movies and Video Guide* (1987 edition), ed. Leonard Maltin (New York: New American Library, 1986, pp. 43–44.

9. Luis Buñuel, *My Last Sigh,* trans. Abigail Israel (1982; repr. New York: Random House, 1984), p. 14.

10. Ibid., p. 15.

11. Anthony F. Macklin, "Sex and Dr. Strangelove," *Film Comment,* Summer 1965, pp. 55–57.

12. Kurt Vonnegut, Jr., *Slaughterhouse-Five* (1969; repr. New York: Dell, 1974), p. 3.

13. Joseph Heller, *Catch-22* (1961; repr. New York: Dell, 1968), p. 47.

14. Eugene Ehrlich, Stuart Berg Flexner, Gorton Carruth, and Joyce M. Hawkins, eds., *Oxford American Dictionary* (1979; repr. New York: Avon Books, 1982), p. 131.

15. Robert Warshow, *"Monsieur Verdoux,"* in *The Immediate Experience* (1962; repr. New York: Atheneum, 1972), p. 213.

16. Heller, *Catch-22*, p. 450.

17. Sanford Pinsker, Chapter 2, "The Graying of Black Humor," in *Between Two Worlds: The American Novel in the 1960s* (Troy, N.Y.: Whitston Publishing, 1980), p. 23; Leslie M. Thompson and William R. Cozart, "The Technology of Atrocity," *Ball State University Forum*, Autumn 1984, p. 69.

18. John Waters, *Shock Value* (New York: Dell, 1981).

19. Wes Gehring, *Marx Brothers: A Bio-Bibliography* (Westport, Conn.: Greenwood Press, 1987).

20. Max F. Schulz, *Black Humor Fiction of the Sixties* (Athens, Ohio: Ohio University Press, 1973), p. 71.

21. Davis, Introduction, p. 15.

22. Winston, *"Humour noir* and Black Humor," pp. 275–77.

23. Ibid., pp. 277–78; Terry Heller, "Notes on Technique in Black Humor," *Thalia: Studies in Literary Humor*, Winter 1979–1980, p. 15.

24. Charles Maland, *"Dr. Strangelove* (1964): Nightmare Comedy and the Ideology of Liberal Consensus," *American Quarterly*, Winter 1979, pp. 697–717; Jack Mathews, "Kicking Ass," *Spin*, April 1986, pp. 97–98.

## BIBLIOGRAPHICAL CHECKLIST

### Books

Breton, André, ed. *Anthologie de L'Humour Noir*. 1939; repr. Paris: Editions du Sagittaire, 1950.

Davis, Douglas M., ed. *The World of Black Humor: An Introductory Anthology of Selections and Criticisms*. New York: E. P. Dutton, 1967.

Friedman, Bruce Jay, ed. *Black Humor*. New York: Bantam Books, 1965.

Hendra, Tony. *Going Too Far: The Rise and Demise of Sick, Gross, Black, Sophomoric Weirdo, Pinko, Anarchist, Underground, Anti-Establishment Humor*. New York: Doubleday, 1987.

Schulz, Max F. *Black Humor Fiction of the Sixties: A Pluralist Definition of Man and His World*. Athens, Ohio: Ohio University Press, 1973.

### Shorter Works

"The Black Humorists." *Time*, 12 February 1965, pp. 94–96.

Dickstein, Morris. Chapter 4, "Black Humor and History: The Early Sixties." In *Gates of Eden: American Culture in the Sixties*. New York: Basic Books, 1977, pp. 91–127.

Feinberg, Leonard. Chapter 8, "Black Humor: Aggression Against Everything." In *The Secret of Humor*. Amsterdam: Rodopi, 1978, pp. 153–68.

Feldman, Burton. "Anatomy of Black Humor," *Dissent*, March-April 1968, pp. 158–60.

Heller, Terry. "Notes on Technique in Black Humor," *Thalia: Studies in Literary Humor* (University of Ottowa), Winter 1979–1980, pp. 15–21.

Hill, Hamlin. "Black Humor: Its Cause and Cure," *Colorado Quarterly*, Summer 1968, pp. 57–64.

Knickerbocker, Conrad. "Humor with a Mortal Sting," *New York Times Book Review*, 27 September 1964, pp. 3, 60–61.

Kostelanetz, Richard. "The Point Is That Life Doesn't Have Any Point," *New York Times Book Review*, 6 June 1965, pp. 3, 28–30.

Numasawa, Kōji. "Black Humor: An American Aspect," *Studies in English Literature* (University of Tokyo), March 1968, pp. 177–93.

Pinsker, Sanford. Chapter 2, "The Graying of Black Humor." In *Between Two Worlds: The American Novel in the 1960s*. Troy, N.Y.: Whitston, 1980, pp. 11–28.

Winston, Mathew. *"Humour noir* and Black Humor." In *Veins of Humor*. Ed. Harry Levin. Cambridge, Mass.: Harvard University Press, 1972, pp. 269–84.

## SELECTED FILMOGRAPHY

1947    *Monsieur Verdoux* (122 minutes).
United Artists. Producer/Director: Charles Chaplin. Story/Screenplay: Charles Chaplin (from an idea by Orson Welles). Editing: Willard Nico. Cast: Charles Chaplin (Henri Verdoux), Martha Raye (Annabelle Bonheur), Isobel Elsom (Maria Grosnay), Marilyn Nash (girl).

1964    *Dr. Strangelove, Or: How I Learned to Stop Worrying and Love the Bomb* (93 minutes).
Columbia. Producer/Director: Stanley Kubrick. Screenplay: Kubrick, Terry Southern, and Peter George, based on Peter George's novel *Red Alert*. Editing: Anthony Harvey. Cast: Peter Sellers (Group Capt. Lionel Mandrake/President Muffley/Dr. Strangelove), George C. Scott (Gen. "Buck" Turgidson), Sterling Hayden (Gen. Jack D. Ripper), Keenan Wynn (Col. "Bat" Guano), Slim Pickens (Maj. T. J. "King" Kong), Peter Bull (Ambassador de Sadesky), Tracy Reed (Miss Scott).

1970    *M*A*S*H* (116 minutes).
20th Century-Fox. Producer: Ingo Preminger. Director: Robert Altman. Screenplay: Ring Lardner, Jr., based on Richard Hooker's novel. Editor: Danford B. Greene. Cast: Elliott Gould (Trapper John), Donald Sutherland (Hawkeye), Tom Skerritt (Duke), Sally Kellerman (Maj. Hot Lips), Jo Ann Pflug (Lt. Dish).

*Little Big Man* (150 minutes).
National General/Cinema Center. Producer: Stuart Millar. Director: Arthur Penn. Screenplay: Calder Willingham, based on Thomas Berger's novel. Editing: Dede Allen. Cast: Dustin Hoffman (Jack Crabbe/Little Big Man), Faye Dunaway (Mrs. Pendrake), Martin Balsam (Allardyce T. Merriwhether), Richard Mulligan (Gen. Custer), Chief Dan George (Old Lodge Skins).

*Catch-22* (121 minutes).
Paramount and Filmways. Producers: John Calley, Martin Ransohoff. Director: Mike Nichols. Screenplay: Buck Henry, based on Joseph Heller's novel. Editor: Sam O'Steen. Cast: Alan Arkin (Capt. Yossarian), Martin Balsam (Col. Cathcart), Arthur Garfunkel (Nately), Buck Henry (Col. Korn), Jon Voight (Milo Minderbinder), Orson Welles (Gen. Dreedle).

1971   *Harold and Maude* (90 minutes).
Paramount. Producers: Colin Higgins, Charles B. Mulvehill. Director: Hal Ashby. Screenplay: Higgins. Editors: William A. Sawyer, Edward Warschilka. Cast: Ruth Gordon (Maude), Bud Cort (Harold Chasen), Vivian Pickles (Mrs. Chasen), Charles Tyner (Uncle Victor).

1972   *Slaughterhouse-Five* (104 minutes).
Universal. Producer: Paul Monash. Director: George Roy Hill. Screenplay: Stephen Geller, based on Kurt Vonnegut, Jr.'s novel. Editor: Dede Allen. Cast: Michael Sacks (Billy Pilgrim), Ron Leibman (Paul Lazzaro), Valerie Perrine (Montana Wildhack), Eugene Roche (Edgar Derby).

1976   *Network* (121 minutes).
United Artists release of an MGM film. Producer: Howard Gottfried. Director: Sidney Lumet. Screenplay: Paddy Chayefsky. Editor: Alan Heim. Cast: Faye Dunaway (Diana Christensen), William Holden (Max Schumacher), Peter Finch (Howard Beale), Robert Duvall (Frank Hackett).

1982   *Eating Raoul* (83 minutes).
Independently made. Producer: Anne Kimmel. Director: Paul Bartel. Screenplay: Richard Blackburn, Bartel. Editor: Alan Toomayan. Cast: Paul Bartel (Paul), Mary Woronov (Mary), Robert Beltram (Raoul), Buck Henry (Mr. Leech), John Parragon (Sexshop Salesman).

1985   *Brazil* (131 minutes).
Universal. Producer: Arnon Milchan. Director: Terry Gilliam. Screenplay: Terry Gilliam, Tom Stoppard, Charles McKeown. Editor: Julian Doyle. Cast: Jonathan Pryce (Sam Lowry), Kim Greist (Jill Layton), Robert De Niro (Harry Tuttle), Katherine Helmond (Mrs. Ida Lowry), Michael Palin (Jack Lint).

# 11

## Clown Comedy

Wes D. Gehring

"Married! I can see you right now in the kitchen, bending over a
hot stove, but I can't see the stove."
——"Romantic" Groucho to Marx Brothers regular
Margaret Dumont in *Duck Soup* (1933).

The clown genre is both the most basic and the most obvious of comedy types.
Unlike other, more thematic-oriented, comedy approaches, the clown model is
dependent upon a front and center comic figure, or figures, around whom the
loosest of storylines is fashioned. One is reminded of the "Notice" with which
Mark Twain opens the adventures of his sometimes literary clown Huckleberry
Finn: "Persons attempting to find a motive in this narrative will be prosecuted;
persons attempting to find a moral in it will be banished; persons attempting to
find a plot in it will be shot." There are clown exceptions to this, such as the
generally tight narratives of Buster Keaton. However, *Variety's* August 11,
1948, rave review description of Red Skelton's greatest film, *A Southern Yankee,* could be applied to the majority of clown films—"an erratic jumble, pulled
together, only by a funny idea and Skelton's [or fill in the clown(s) of your
choice] knack for clowning."

This storyline of comedy convenience provides a humor hall tree on which
the film clown can "hang" his comic shtick—specific routines and/or variations of them which lend themselves to the establishing of the all-important
screen comedy persona. Thus, a Charlie Chaplin film invariably showcases the
underdog Tramp's ability to work a comic metamorphosis on inanimate objects, such as transforming a clock into a miniature patient in *The Pawnshop*
(1916) or dinner rolls into dancing feet in the delightful "Oceana Roll" of *The
Gold Rush* (1925). The more aggressive Eddie Murphy film is not complete
without one of his controlled comic tirades, where in a very tight spot Eddie

assumes an authority figure position and comically dresses down his potential antagonists, such as the redneck bar scene in *48 Hrs.* (1982), or the warehouse inventory confrontation in *Beverly Hills Cop* (1984).

Other classic material strongly associated with the comic persona of a film clown would include Groucho's baiting of Dumont or the surrealistic sight gags of Harpo, the comic word games of Danny Kaye (especially his "pellet with the poison's in the vessel with the pestle" from *The Court Jester*, 1956), the tit-for-tat exchanges of comic violence in Laurel & Hardy, W. C. Fields's fluctuations between huckster and antihero, Lou Costello's inability to understand bullying Bud Abbott's comments (such as their celebrated "Who's on first?" routine), Bing Crosby's propensity to "volunteer" his *Road* picture companion Bob Hope for comic danger, and the thrill comedy of Harold Lloyd, be it hanging from the clock in the silent classic *Safety Last* (1923) or the skyscraper ledge scenes in *The Sin of Harold Diddlebock* (1947, well into the sound era).

This is not to suggest that all clown films exist independent of other comedy genres. Indeed, there are few pure examples of any phenomenon. And as noted in earlier chapters, personality comedians sometimes have an affinity for the thematic comedy genres. Such ties are actually borne out of the clown personae themselves. Thus, the comic absurdity of the Marx Brothers sometimes lends itself to black comedy, the folksy crackerbarrel axioms of a Will Rogers celebrate populism, and Bob Hope's flip-flops between comic antihero and egotistical wise guy are nicely attuned to parody. Because of this, clown films sometimes work on more than one comedy level, with parody probably being the most frequent comedy sidekick genre. In fact, given that most clowns exhibit some incompetence, there is a degree of parody of the traditionally capable dramatic hero present in most clown films.

Be that as it may, clown films are certainly not dependent on such ties, and the majority exist outside all but the broadest of these comedy genre "marriages." And even where they do exist, the general public's focus remains on the clown. Consequently, as is sometimes noted, one frequently describes this viewing experience as having seen a Marx Brothers film, or a W. C. Fields film (fill in the clown of your choice), with little facts like storyline and even the film's title being superfluous to the conversation. Mere mention of the comedian's name so represents a given shtick that little further explanation is necessary.

The following discussion of the general characteristics of the clown genre—and most specifically the clowns themselves—draws examples from a history which breaks into three broad categories: the silents, the Depression, and the post–World War II era. First and still most celebrated is silent comedy, especially the traditional pantheon four—Charlie Chaplin, Buster Keaton, Harold Lloyd, and Harry Langdon, though strong cases can be made for countless others, from the well-known antiheroic exploits of Laurel & Hardy, to the more obscure, sophisticated comedy of Raymond Griffith.

Easily the most central is Chaplin, frequently considered cinema's most celebrated figure, comic or otherwise. It is hard to overestimate the significance of Chaplin to film comedy. Because of both the Everyman universality of his Tramp figure and the range of his mime, he remains *the* standard against which all cinema clowns are measured. Moreover, Chaplin's balancing of an equally celebrated pathos has become an ever elusive goal for other comedians. Because so many have failed (Langdon and Jerry Lewis are the most famous examples), Abbott & Costello biographer Bob Thomas has labeled the fixation the "Chaplin disease" (for a time, Lou Costello was similarly "afflicted").[1]

Directly related to the "Chaplin disease" was his ability to wear all the production hats; he wrote, directed, scored, starred in, and produced his own films. Many film comedians have since failed in the attempt to duplicate this accomplishment (again, Langdon and Lewis), but it remains the standard. For example, 1980s comedy star Eddie Murphy has frequently mentioned this as a goal.[2]

Chaplin's greatest artistic rival was Keaton, though he had never had the same contemporary critical and commercial success. Appropriately, three basic differences separate their work. Chaplin was about socially conscious underdogs winning. In *The Pilgrim* (1923) Charlie pantomimes the story of David and Goliath—it is a footnote to the source of all Charlie stories. The Keaton way was a comic battle not with man but rather with his machines, or with the elements themselves. And his victories were ones of unchanging endurance, as implied by his "Great Stone Face" nickname. If one scene encapsulates the Keaton milieu, it is his impossibly comic walk leaning into the tornado in *Steamboat Bill Jr.* (1928). Second, as is suggested by Chaplin's pathos and the unchanging Keaton visage, while the student of Chaplin is invariably first moved by the Tramp emotionally, the Keaton deadpan is more apt to move our minds, period. Third, to maximize the believability of his unique mime, Chaplin the filmmaker minimized technical special effects. Keaton, equally fascinated by machines in real life, was not averse to camera trickery for comedy, such as the elaborate masking of the lens for *The Playhouse* (1921), which allowed him to play all the parts.

In Lloyd, Chaplin had his greatest 1920s commercial rival. In contrast to Chaplin's Tramp, Lloyd was the proverbial boy next door, anxious to be a success. His greatest film, *Safety Last,* with its celebrated thrill comedy skyscraper-climbing scene, is the perfect metaphor for the Lloyd story—"climbing" to success. But the Lloyd films did not have the artistry of Chaplin's and Keaton's. Lloyd himself was without the physical grace and skills of Chaplin and Keaton, but he compensated for this with a nonstop manner consistent with his Puritan work ethic tendencies—a latter-day Horatio Alger on speed. Still, the Lloyd films are very funny because they merge ageless gags (the merely basted-together suit which begins to come undone in *The Freshman,* 1925) and a central character whose ambitious innocence is still winsome, though without the emotional complexities which make the Tramp so fascinating.

Chaplin's third silent rival, Langdon, came the closest in terms of pathos but he had nowhere near the comedy range of Charlie's Tramp. Appropriately, film critic James Agee described the Langdon persona as that of "an elderly baby" or "a baby dope fiend" (not unlike the face of Pee Wee Herman), who survived only through the grace of God.[3] But Langdon, whose stay at the top of silent comedy would be far shorter than that of any other pantheon member (a mere two years), had a comedy persona like the Blake Edwards/Peter Sellers Inspector Clouseau. For instance, though both have guardian angels, neither character is remotely aware such aid is being given. For example, Langdon's character mistakenly believes he has scared away the cyclone in *Tramp, Tramp, Tramp* (1926) and Inspector Clouseau becomes completely oblivious to the bumbling assassination attempts which become the comic centerpieces of the Pink Panther films. Unfortunately, Langdon was still the only pantheon member not fully cognizant of why his persona worked. Though some revisionist historians have recently attempted to disprove this position, his short but brilliant success still seems largely tied to the molding of writer-director Frank Capra, with whom he broke in 1927, seemingly afflicted by, and about to be the victim of, the "Chaplin disease." In fact, Langdon fan Bob Hope found himself on the same vaudeville bill in 1933, and was later advised by this comedy hero: "If you ever go out to Hollywood and become a star—and I think you could—don't make my mistake. Don't try to convince yourself that you're a genius."[4]

Second, the Depression era provided the impetus for the comedy success of older, more cynical comedy clowns, such as W. C. Fields, the Marx Brothers (especially Groucho), and Mae West. Moreover, two watershed developments added to this transition. First the ushering in of sound film provided the clown with a voice, except for Chaplin's Tramp and Harpo's trench coat–attired Pan. Second, American humor was undergoing a major change, as the childlike comic antihero (the totally frustrated modern man) took center stage away from the older, more capable crackerbarrel Yankee type—the early 1930s film success of Will Rogers's country philosopher notwithstanding. Earlier antiheroes had existed, of course, but they had not been the dominant norm in American humor before.[5] Thus, American film comedy had prior antiheroic precedents in the work of John Bunny (1910–1915, the country's earliest significant comedy star) and the often neglected silent features of W. C. Fields. But the best film breakthrough example of the antihero should be credited to the Leo McCarey–teamed and molded Laurel & Hardy, both because of their unique and timely full-blown articulation of the character, and because of the phenomenal popularity with which the public received it.[6]

While Laurel & Hardy successfully rode this development through the 1930s, W. C. Fields found great success during the sound era fluctuating between antihero and con man, from milquetoast husband in *It's a Gift* (1934) to carnival huckster in *Poppy* (1936, adapted from the 1923 Broadway play which so helped mold Fields the con man), which opens with Fields successfully selling a talking dog. Of course, both versions of Fields come liberally peppered with examples of the other. For example, in the picnic scene from *It's a Gift,* his wife forces the antiheroic Fields to share a sandwich with a son of whom he is none too fond. *But* even here a bit of larceny surfaces; Fields cheats when splitting the sandwich—he bends all the meat onto his side before dividing it.

Though not as apparent, there are even antiheroic elements in the Marx Brothers, or more precisely, in Groucho. While best remembered as a comic aggressor upon the world at large, he frequently plays the antiheroic brother within the team. In the standing gag of *Duck Soup* (1933), Harpo and his motorcycle sidecar always leave Groucho behind; in the tutti-frutti ice cream scene in *A Day at the Races* (1937), Chico sells Groucho a library of unnecessary betting books. Moreover, what Marx author Allen Eyles calls "Harpo's *tour de force* in outsmarting Groucho," the *Duck Soup* "mirror" scene imitation of the mustached one, is arguably the greatest of all Marx Brothers scenes.[7]

As a team, however, the Marxes were not so much victims as victimizers (though this aggression was toned down in their later MGM pictures). And that same aggression still brings one back to a comic antihero worldview. That is, physically and verbally, especially in their propensity for outrageous puns and malapropisms, the Marx Brothers declared that nothing, including the English language, was what it seemed. Thus, their *verbal* slapstick is not without some antiheroic ties to the tit-for-tat violence of Laurel & Hardy.

A more apparent influence of the Marxes was their early demonstration of the comic artistry potential of sound films, despite the often canned-theater nature of their first two movies. To the student of film comedy, their cross section of American humor team (con, dialect, mime) made the transition from silents to sound more palatable—especially with the mime of Harpo acting as a salve on the painful loss and/or decline of so many silent comedy stars. In fact, as early as 1937 perceptive popular culture critic Gilbert Seldes observed: "The arrival of the Marx Brothers and the reappearances of W. C. Fields saved screen comedy."[8] And the Marx Brothers' early film success was so great they paved the movie way for a whole series of other zany period comedy teams, such as the Ritz Brothers and Olsen & Johnson. Indeed, MGM's failed early 1930s attempt to team Buster Keaton and Jimmy Durante does not seem so unlikely if seen as a variation upon a Harpo-Groucho duo.

The third focus era (post–World War II) actually demonstrates some changes which had begun to take place during the war. Most obvious was the new breed of personality comedians who could fluctuate between the most incompetent of comic antiheroes and the cool, egotistical wise guy. Bob Hope was the unquestionable master, be it in a *Road* picture or as a Damon Runyan title character like *The Lemon Drop Kid* (1951).

Hope's comic duality complements modern humor's fascination with the schizophrenic. In fact, Woody Allen, today's greatest film comedian and most self-consciously shrink-oriented, follows the same antihero to wise-guy and back pattern. In *Play It Again, Sam* (1972), Allen bounces frantically between being a Bogart clone and the schlemiel of the week. Indeed, Allen, an admitted Hope disciple, at times even sounds like Hope. Comedy historian Maurice Yacowar notes that Allen's comment to a guard protecting all that remains of the evil leader in *Sleeper* (1973)—"We're here to see the nose. We hear it's running."—is pure Hope.[9]

In the 1940s and 1950s this antihero/wise–guy equation was sometimes given to two performers, or what was supposed to be two. For example, Danny Kaye frequently played dual roles in his films and was at his best in *Wonder Man* (1945), playing the most opposite of twins. The phenomenal 1940s commercial popularity of Abbott & Costello was also based in the antihero/wise-guy dichotomy. In addition, wise-guy Bud Abbott dished out more comic violence (especially slaps) to antiheroic Lou Costello than any comic this side of the Three Stooges' Moe Howard.

Martin & Lewis, *the* comedy team of the 1950s, often operated on the same antihero/wise-guy formula. Jerry Lewis's screen persona, which he calls the Idiot, is probably the ultimate antihero. Dean Martin has just as strongly been associated with the wise guy. Interestingly enough, Lewis's greatest solo work, *The Nutty Professor* (1963), finds him playing the same antihero/wise-guy quality that is often compared to the makeup of the Martin and Lewis team: Lewis plays both an absent-minded professor and a wise-mouthed crooner.[10]

While the duality has traditionally emphasized the antihero, sometimes to near neglect of the wise-guy persona, such as the excellent Red Skelton vehicles *The Fuller Brush Man* and *A Southern Yankee* (both 1948), some current film comedy personalities are reversing the emphasis. Both Bill Murray and Eddie Murphy are essentially cool comics who can weather antiheroic situations. While they do this in radically different ways (Murray is the original Mr. Laid Back; Murphy is the master of comic intensity), they comically deny the loss of control. Thus, unlike so many of their comedy predecessors, they are able to maintain their outrageousness in establishment positions. Murphy feigns angry outrage as he cheekily dresses down dangerous situations with an inimitable comic brassiness. In contrast, Murray's Mr. Cool character is based upon never seeming to be caught off-guard. Murphy creates the comic situation by confrontation; Murray's forte is responding to it.

While Murray and Murphy have been very influential (see especially the Murray-like nature of Michael Keaton and Tom Hanks), the emphasis on the antihero in the antihero/wise-guy quality still dominates. Examples would include the trials and tribulations of Chevy Chase as a father in search of "Wally World" in *National Lampoon's Vacation* (1983), Steve Martin's title-revealing tale *The Lonely Guy* (1984), Albert Brooks's attempt to be a Yuppy "Easy Rider" (substituting a Winabago for a motorcycle) in the so appropriately named *Lost in America* (1985), and Woody Allen's ongoing comic anxieties about life and death and other fun subjects in *Hannah and Her Sisters* (1986).

This, then, has been a brief historical overview of some major clowns during a three-part division of cinema history. But despite their numbers, the many years they represent, and their comic personality differences, five common characteristics link them in the clown genre—they are all generally identified with a specific comedy shtick which has lent itself to a winning screen comedy persona, physical/visual humor is a given, they are perennial underdogs who are often incompetent and/or amusingly unorthodox, they are frequently nomadic, and a "team" situation is commonly pivotal even with the most celebrated of "solo" comedians.

First is the significance of a specific comedy shtick (see this chapter's opening), variations of which are generally brought to each film. Interestingly enough, just such an example also represents the beginning of film in the United States. The earliest whole film on record is the comic *Fred Ott's Sneeze* (1891, from the American father of the movies, Thomas Edison).[11] Ott was an Edison engineer and resident funnyman whose material included a comic sneeze. And while this one-routine comedy "film" lasts mere seconds, it now holds the double distinction of first film and first film comedy. The more comically universal the shtick, the more likely the successful transition to film clown. For instance, Rodney Dangerfield has parlayed the most sweeping of stand-up shticks, "I don't get no respect"—which could be applied to 99.9 percent of the clown market—into an effective film comedy persona.

Second, American humor has always placed a high premium on physical/ visual comedy, whether in the movies or on the printed page. Thus, even the great literary comedians frequently showcase this phenomenon; witness the description of bouncing about in a stagecoach in *Roughing It* (1872) by the dean of American humor authors, Mark Twain:

Every time we avalanched from one end of the stage to the other, the unabridged dictionary would come too; and every time it came it damaged somebody. . . . The pistols and coin soon settled to the bottom, but the pipes, pipe stems, tobacco, and canteens clattered and floundered after the dictionary every time it made an assault on us. . . .[12]

But countless other examples also exist. America's celebrated antiheroic author (and "father" of Walter Mitty) James Thurber did a comic autobiography, *My Life and Hard Times* (1933), which was so full of physical/visual comedy (not to mention his delightful drawings) that even his episode titles create cartoon pictures: "The Night the Bed Fell," "The Day the Dam Broke," "The Dog That Bit People." Today comic antiheroic authors like Woody Allen continue to provide funny imagery, though it is often of a more surrealistically cerebral kind. For example, Allen's "The Kugelmass Episode," winner of the O. Henry Award for best short story of 1978, is about a machine which can project one into the storyline of any book. Unfortunately, yet apropos for an antihero, the Mitty-like Kugelmass falls victim to a total machine breakdown. Instead of finding himself in sexy *Portnoy's Complaint,* he is permanently thrust into an old *Remedial Spanish* textbook, where he is soon "running for his life over a barren, rocky terrain as the word *tener* ("to have")—a large and hairy irregular verb—races after him on its spindly legs."[13]

Naturally, with this kind of comic imagery on even the printed page, it is hardly surprising that the big screen should so strongly embrace it, at least in the clown genre. And for an American public so enamored with slapstick, it provides one more reason why the silent period has been on the film comedy pedestal since film critic James Agee's influential essay called it "Comedy's Greatest Era" in 1949.[14]

For the film genre clown the visual comedy often begins *before* the story—because clowns *look funny*. Through costume, makeup, body shape, and/or fluid contortions of face and body, they telegraph the obvious message—this will be a comedy. Thus, their funny appearance is a key icon in the clown genre, even when the comic personality might be more linked to verbal humor. For instance, while the machine-gun patter of Groucho is famous, it is more than a little dependent on the visual. Lillian Roth, the young heroine of *Animal Crackers,* best described the total Groucho *visual package* when she explained why she kept giggling into retakes a scene they had together:

The line itself wasn't so hilarious, but I knew Groucho was going to say it with the big cigar jutting from his clenched teeth, his eyebrows palpitating, and that he would be off afterwards in that runaway crouch of his; and the thought of what was coming was too much for me.[15]

Groucho himself, once accused of underselling some comedy material on a 1930s MGM road-testing tour for a future film, observed that he could attain a laugh with any line as long as he wiggled his eyegrows. Thus, he was purposely eliminating such actions in order to discover what was intrinsically most amusing. Even then, he had a head start. As the great 1930s film critic Otis Ferguson observed in his *A Night at the Opera* review, Groucho "would be funny in still photographs."[16]

Groucho contemporary Mae West is also famous for her dialogue, invariably of a sexual innuendo nature. But this ongoing joke is largely made possible by both West's exaggerated hourglass figure, which seems to have been poured into a Gay Nineties dress, and such suggestive physical actions as her provocative strut. Thus, West is already a visual satire on sex before she pursues that same theme verbally.

Regardless, countless comedians have showcased comic costumes and/or contortions through the years, such as Charlie Chaplin's Little Tramp "uniform" and funny shuffle from the "east-and-west feet";[17] Harpo's magic-pocketed trenchcoat and the "Gookie" grimace of a "Neanderthal idiot";[18] and the simpler costume of Woody Allen—wrinkled clothing, disheveled hair, and the all-important antiheroic glasses (visually reminiscent of Lloyd's bespectacled character, especially in Allen's *Sleeper,* 1973).

After the clown has established a comedy tone through appearance, time is frequently reserved for physical/visual humor. And though the silent 1920s were the golden age of the phenomenon, clown films of the early sound era continued to highlight visual shtick. Indeed, Chaplin kept Charlie the Tramp silent until 1936, and Harpo forever maintained the tradition. Close scrutiny of even such distinctly voiced comedy clowns as Laurel & Hardy and W. C. Fields finds much of their work based in the visual gag. This is especially true of Laurel & Hardy; witness their Oscar-winning attempt to deliver a piano up a huge flight of stairs in *The Music Box* (1932), or those little habitual gestures which so endear them to an audience, such as Hardy's exasperated look at the camera (the viewer) when Laurel has pulled a major boner or Laurel's absent-minded scratching at the top of his head when perplexed. Moreover, their body shapes are the classic comedy contrast for clowns: stout and skinny.

Fields, the former vaudeville juggler, invariably included a great deal of physical humor in his work, such as his field goal–like booting of Baby LeRoy in *The Old-Fashioned Way* (1934) or the domestic skirmishes as he tries to shave in the "family" bathroom of his greatest film, *It's a Gift* (1934). And like Laurel & Hardy, the Fields persona has numerous patented gestures, such as his ever-present comic difficulty with his hat and cane, or the comic surprise derived from his collection of bent, limp, and otherwise temperamental pool sticks and golf clubs. Field's copyrighted sketches at the Library of Congress document his interest in the visual.[19]

In the 1940s the sight gag of the clown genre was more thoroughly usurped by the verbal, though its decline was greatly exaggerated. For instance, as strong as Agee's aforementioned essay is on the silent clowns, he underestimates the physical abilities of Bob Hope and also neglects the unique visual gifts of clowns like Red Skelton, especially in such special outings as *The Southern Yankee*. The film includes Skelton's inspired hike between military lines during battle wearing the ultimate "two-piece" suit—a Northern uniform on the Yankee side of his body, a Southern outfit on the Confederate side. Fittingly, he also carries a two-sided flag. Thus, for a time he is a hero to be applauded by both armies, *but then the wind changes* (also a nice metaphor for the plight of most comedians). Each army suddenly sees the wrong flag and the battle commences again, but this time Skelton is now designated hit*ee*.

One might best measure the ongoing significance of physical comedy in the 1940s by the fact that even in the very verbal films of Abbott & Costello, slapstick sequences are still very effective. Examples might include Costello's comic difficulties in learning how to march in *Buck Privates* (1941) or the many bits of visual mischief he can cause as a ghost in *The Time of Their Lives* (1946). Moreover, even the verbal routines of this duo feature slapstick punctuation, be it the fat man/thin man dichotomy again, or Costello's exasperated expressions and Abbott's perennial manhandling of his partner.

In the years since, physical comedy has remained an important part of the clown genre, being best showcased in the 1950s and 1960s work of Jerry Lewis, especially his gag-focused directing debut in *The Bellboy* (1960). And even

America's most cerebral of clowns, Woody Allen, is very generous with his visual comedy. Indeed, his funniest film, *Sleeper*, is dominated by it, including the giant chicken and vegetable scene, his attempts to fly with a malfunctioning whirlybird backpack, the *Modern Times*–like conveyor belt scene, and fighting off the huge blob of chocolate pudding while comically dressed as a twenty-second century domestic robot. In fact, through the 1970s much of Allen's most memorable material remained sight gags: trying to play a cello in a marching band *(Take the Money and Run,* 1968), the take-out order for an army *(Bananas,* 1971), the delightfully nervous meeting of a blind date *(Play It Again, Sam,* 1972), basic training problems and flirting at the opera *(Love and Death,* 1975; not to mention being shot from a cannon, which figured prominently in the film's advertising), and trying to catch runaway lobsters and kill spiders *(Annie Hall,* 1977). With all this in mind, it is not so startling to discover that prior to scheduling conflicts, Jerry Lewis had originally been slated to direct *Take the Money and Run.*

One might add such 1970s and 1980s visual footnotes as the arched eyebrows of John Belushi and his fat man grace so reminiscent of Fatty Arbuckle; Marty Feldman's bulgingly misdirected peepers, in a class with Ben Turpin's crossed eyes; the otherworld appearance and movements of Pee Wee Herman, so like the now forgotten silent star Larry Semon; the silly pothead antics of Cheech & Chong, who brought a whole new meaning to the term *dopey* comedy team; and the return of Inspector Clouseau, courtesy of the ongoing slapstick tradition of Blake Edwards.

The third characteristic of clowns finds them underdogs who frequently exhibit comically incompetent behavior. Fittingly, this characteristic is often directly related to the physical humor of point two. That is, the incompetent clown's inadequacies are often showcased in some basic physical task, such as Laurel & Hardy trying to put a radio antenna on the roof, with predictable results, in *Hog Wild* (1930); Jerry Lewis's lab-exploding tendencies in *The Nutty Professor* (1963), and Woody Allen's bumper car–like attempt to drive an automobile in *Annie Hall.*

Teams, even of the merely occasional variety, such as Hope & Crosby, often use the capable/incompetent dichotomy for their humor focus. This is the case with Abbott & Costello, Martin & Lewis, and Hope & Crosby. Much of the teams' comedy comes from the capable type taking advantage of "the stooge," fittingly also a title of a 1953 Martin & Lewis film. In the *Road* pictures, Bob Hope is frequently the stooge. For instance, Crosby generally wins Dorothy Lamour by the end of each film. Even at the close of *The Road to Utopia* (1946), where it seems Hope's luck has finally changed since one sees him and Lamour as a now elderly married couple, the ski-nosed comic is a loser. When their now grown only child appears, he is the mirror image of (and played by) Bing Crosby. Conversely, there are teams where the same capable/incompetent framework is established despite there being no able character in sight. Humor then arises from one team member *thinking* he is the more enlightened and taking chaotic charge. This is true of both Laurel & Hardy and The Three Stooges, with the latter team title nicely demonstrating their *stooge equality*.

While it is tempting to focus entirely on incompetent behavior for this third point, it would be misleading. For instance, much of the motivation behind my 1983 biography of Chaplin was to address the clown's oversubscribed image as a loser. To examine his Tramp films closely is to more often find a very capable clown, be it his amazing brick-stacking skills in *Pay Day* (1922) or his ballet-like grace on roller skates in *The Rink* (1916) and *Modern Times* (1936).

The Tramp's interaction with mechanical objects is more problematic, but his dexterity almost always wins out. Frustrating moments can occur, such as the debilitating conveyor belt of *Modern Times*. But for every such stumbling block there are numerous mechanical victories: the Chaplin cop of *Easy Street* (1917), who so adeptly manages to etherize the giant bully (Eric Campbell) with a gas street lamp, or the Chaplin soldier of *Shoulder Arms* (1918), who converts a Victrola horn to a breathing device so he can sleep underwater in his partly submerged bunker.

Consequently, clowns are as likely to be unorthodox as incompetent. Besides Chaplin's magic, or the magic pockets of Harpo, one might note such diverse examples as the inherently wise and warm crackerbarrel humor of Will Rogers, Eddie Murphy's aggressively comic way of bluffing himself through any problem, and Buster Keaton's ability to work eccentric, mechanical miracles with large machines. For instance, Keaton manages to transform an ocean liner galley—originally constructed to feed thousands—into a personalized kitchen for one in *The Navigator* (1924). Unorthodox or incompetent, most clowns qualify as underdogs and outsiders—going against the establishment norm. While few assume the up-front comic attack posture of the Marx Brothers, most would at least qualify as comedy fifth columnists, going against the regimented seriousness of society. This is probably best demonstrated by W. C. Fields's mumbled asides in times of comic frustration.

The fourth characteristic, appropriate for comedy outsiders, is that film clowns are frequently nomadic, with direct literary ties to such picaresque heroes as Don Quixote and Huck Finn.[20] Fittingly, cinema's greatest clown, Chaplin's Charlie, is closely linked to the picaresque, be it his identity as a wandering tramp or the celebrated imagery of him quite literally shuffling down life's highways. Not coincidentally, the inspired teaming of Hope and Crosby is based on a series of *Road* pictures, as the duo comically meander about the globe. In fact, some episodes even devote time charting their helter-skelter movements on a map.

There are four comedy reasons for going on the road. The first is that it gives the clown an endless supply of new settings for his comedy, from Harry Langdon's nomadic ways in the cross-country walkathon *Tramp, Tramp, Tramp* and the touring assistant to *The Strong Man* (both 1926), to Pee Wee Herman's trip to the Alamo in search of his bike in *Pee Wee Herman's Big Adventure* (1986) and the inspired road humor of the fittingly entitled Steve Martin-John

Candy film: *Planes, Trains and Automobiles* (1987). The picaresque carnival huckster of *Poppy* (1936) is what established W. C. Fields both on Broadway (1923) and in the movies—Fields starred in D. W. Griffith's original silent adaptation, *Sally of the Sawdust* (1925). And Fields's cinema con man continued to focus on the nomadic, in his steamboat comedies *Tillie and Gus* (1933) and *Mississippi* (1934), or on another carnival huckster type in *You Can't Cheat an Honest Man* (1939, where he is circus owner Larson E. Whipsnade). Moreover, even his more domestic, antiheroic roles sometimes find time for the picaresque, such as his celebrated cross-country automobile trip to California in *It's a Gift*. And Will Rogers quickly established a critical and commercial success in sound films by playing the "American innocent abroad" in films such as *They Had to See Paris* (1929) and *So This Is London* (1930).

The mode of transportation can also become an end in itself; Will Rogers took a *Steamboat 'Round the Bend* (1935), and the Marx Brothers made use of an ocean liner in *Monkey Business* (1931) and *A Night at the Opera* (1935), and of a train in *At the Circus* (1939) and *Go West* (1941). The machine-oriented Keaton had, of course, led the way with his own ocean liner in *The Navigator* and the ultimate nonstop train picture—*The General* (1927). W. C. Fields's *Never Give a Sucker an Even Break* (1941) manages to use a commercial plane to both recycle part of an earlier Fields train compartment sketch, as well as justify a bit of comic travel surrealism—he survives jumping out of a plane (without benefit of a parachute) in pursuit of a wayward liquor bottle and lands in the bizarre mountaintop fortress of a Mrs. Hemoglobin (Margaret Dumont).

A second comic reason for travel is that placing a clown in some unlikely settings *can be* an ongoing joke itself, and is often the starting point for parody. (For more on the genre, see this volume's parody chapter.) Thus, seeing Chaplin's Klondike-bound Charlie (in full Tramp costume) shuffling around a glacier in *The Gold Rush* (1925) is delightfully incongruous, just as the traditional garb of Laurel & Hardy is comically out of place on their trek into the cowboy country of *Way Out West* (1936). Conversely, seeing the traveling clown of your choice in the appropriate garb for some nomadic situation can also make for great comic incongruity. The countless comedy changes Hope & Crosby go through in their wandering *Road* pictures exemplify this best, but there are innumerable other illustrations. Richard Pryor and Gene Wilder must don chicken costumes at one point in *Stir Crazy* (1980), and Bette Midler and Shelley Long wear "masculine" outfits to visit a brothel in *Outrageous Fortune* (1987). In *Spies Like Us* (1985), Chevy Chase and Dan Aykroyd even provide the viewer with an updated, unofficial "Road picture," nicely continuing the earlier serie's comic style show tradition, especially in their hilarious Nanook of the North parkas, or the equally comic glowing floor lamp–like UFO alien costumes.

A third travel reason for comedy is that it justifies introducing a broad cross-section of supporting comedy characters (not to mention Dorothy Lamour) such as the zany Wiere Brothers of *The Road to Rio* (1947); the laid-back George Carlin of *Outrageous Fortune;* the truckload of on-the-road types in both *National Lampoon's Vacation* and *Pee Wee Herman's Big Adventure* (especially the phantom trucker Large Marge); and Bronson Pinchot's scene-stealing bit (from Eddie Murphy, no less) in *Beverly Hills Cop* (1984), playing a gay California gallery worker to Murphy's New York cop. And these are but a fragment of the examples showcased. Indeed, to better understand the multitude of comic types encountered, one might quote the original theater poster's description of Midler and Long's plight in *Outrageous Fortune:*

The CIA is trailing them
The KGB is tracking them
The phone company is tracing them
The police are chasing them
The cowboys are herding them
And the Indians are hunting them

Are they going to fall for all of that? [with "fall" punning the poster's visual—Midler and Long hanging from a cliff—more visual humor]

   This ad copy leads into a fourth fundamental reason for comedy travel—the appropriately billed fourth item: "The police are chasing them." From the Keystone Cops to *Smokey and the Bandit* (1977) and beyond, "picaresque comedian" is often an artsy way of saying "funny person on the run." Besides the obvious reminder that the humorous chase is just what the comedy doctor ordered for *moving* pictures, one can also use the chase as a composite of the three previously mentioned main characteristics of the film comedian—shtick, physical humor, and being the underdog, as well as the nomadic given. To illustrate, comedian shtick often involves movement—Charlie Chaplin's beguiling slide on one foot as he takes a corner too fast; the hurried, mincing walk of Bette Midler; Harpo chasing girls, both on foot and with his trusty bike; the ever speedy, loping walk of Groucho; and fast cars, whether the surrealistic paddy wagon of the Keystone Cops or a Burt Reynolds speeding car. In addition to the obvious visual humor such examples represent, they encourage countless other bits of slapstick, such as wrecked cars (from Laurel & Hardy Model-Ts to the *used* car lot total of *The Blues Brothers,* 1980), or simply the broad humor associated with most hide-and-seek chase scenes— Charlie Chaplin successfully pretending to be a floor lamp in *The Adventurer* (1917), the stowaway exploits of the Marxes in *Monkey Business* or Hope & Crosby in *The Road to Rio,* the encyclopedic survey provided by an army of comics in *It's a Mad, Mad, Mad, Mad World* (1963), Gene Wilder's attempt to pass as Richard Pryor's "brother" in *Silver Streak* (1976), and Bette Midler and Shelley Long's ride down an airport baggage conveyor belt in *Outrageous*

*Fortune*. Finally, what better way is there to comically peddle an underdog-outsider persona than to be a funny fugitive from the law—film comedy has used the device since the beginning. And even when a clown comedy is not particularly picaresque in nature, there seems to be an unwritten law that a chase, especially as a rousing conclusion, be added.

A fifth and final common characteristic of these clowns is the often unnoted importance of a "team" interaction. Even "solo" clowns frequently need someone off whom to bounce their humor. Indeed, their comic interactions with others are what begin to differentiate pure shtick (the concert film) from a clown film. Obviously, little needs to be said about the acknowledged comedy teams, but the unofficial ones merit attention. Many important clowns have been at their comedy best when periodically teamed: Wallace Beery and Marie Dressler, Hope and Crosby, Pryor and Wilder, even Walter Matthau and Jack Lemmon. Also, the young Jerry Lewis teamed with Dean Martin is generally to be preferred over the former's solo efforts. Fittingly, Lewis's best individual effort, *The Nutty Professor,* occurs when he seems to play both main parts of an old Martin & Lewis movie. Besides his patented zany, he plays sexy, egotistical crooner Buddy Love, a character rather like the early Martin persona. Even some acknowledged teams are better understood when studied as comedy duos. For example, the Marx Brothers are much more likely to appear in two-somes of Groucho and Chico or Harpo and Chico, with the less celebrated Chico actually being most necessary in order to maintain comedy lines of communication. When all three are together on screen, translator Chico is all the more indispensable. The main exception to this is still another popular Marx Brothers film duo—Groucho and Margaret Dumont. (Zeppo Marx's appearances in the team's Paramount films were most often in modest support of Groucho.)

Unofficial teamings are often less apparent because the supporting member is neither a star nor a regular repeater—though the comedy type is. For instance, W. C. Fields's antiheroic humor was frequently in need of a nagging wife and/or the standard comic female busybody. Through the years a number of women nicely essayed the part, though occasional repeater Kathleen Howard was the best. Moreover, Fields constantly peopled his films with comic physical types who were both visual jokes and fitting targets for Fields one-liners and/or double-takes. The skinny-as-a-rail American Gothic–type Bill Wolf seemingly was given a number of cameo parts in Fields films just because of his physique, and on more than one occasion an unusually small person was cast so that the comedian could utilize the line, "Is he standing in a hole?" As is so often true of Fields, his cinema inclinations were true in real life, where his entourage invariably included at least one undersized and/or oddly shaped member.[21]

Other comedy types used more ambitiously by Fields would include Franklin Pangborn's patently prissy persona (shades of another busybody wife) bank examiner J. Pinkerton Snoopington in *The Bank Dick* (1940), or Fields's loyal

Indian companion Clarence (George Moran) in *My Little Chickadee*. The latter film, of course, is best known for Fields's most famous teaming—with Mae West.

Fields's teaming with Clarence was probably inspired by a previous, popular teaming of Fields in the newspaper comic strips of the day. In 1936 he was the inspiration for the Great Gusto, a prominent character in the strip *Big Chief Wahoo*, of which Fields was very fond. Wahoo played the stooge to Gusto, who had a medicine show—the classic con-man setting for Fields since his Broadway success as a medicine show huckster in *Poppy* (1923).

An additional period teaming of Fields in another medium would also eventually surface in the movies. In 1937 Fields started doing comic verbal battle with Edgar Bergen's lippy "child" Charlie McCarthy on radio's very popular "Chase & Sanborn Hour." Though they teamed only once in the movies *(You Can't Cheat An Honest Man,* 1939), the key to their successful, comic rivalry was based in Fields's long-established film premise that he hated children. And Charlie McCarthy was just a Baby LeRoy (an earlier Fields nemesis) grown into a smart-aleck kid.

The coming of sound films greatly encouraged the team concept, because sound defused the comic centralness of the silent clowns. Dialogue, after all, necessitates the interaction of two or more people. But even in the silents, unofficial teams were forever lurking. The W. C. Fields–like comedy pioneer John Bunny was often tied to another shrewish wife (Flora Finch), whose skinniness also comically contrasted with Bunny's roundness. Harry Langdon was frequently paired opposite big men like Vernon Dent, who would later often surface in the early Three Stooges films. Even Chaplin found numerous ways to create teams. As examined in my Chaplin biography, Charlie was teamed frequently through a dual-focus comic narrative. In certain films, especially the short subjects, this dual focus meant that his actions repeated or paralleled actions of another central character. This is best exemplified by his work with giant Eric Campbell (his comic rival in the Mutual films, 1916–1917), especially in *Easy Street* (1917). But similar big man/little man pairings occurred both earlier, such as Fatty Arbuckle and Campbell-like Mack Swain for Mack Sennett, and later with Swain in *The Gold Rush* and Jack Oakie in *The Great Dictator* (1940).

The dual focus also surfaced both when Chaplin played two parts himself *(A Night in the Show,* 1916; *The Idle Class,* 1921; *The Great Dictator)*, and when Charlie became the model for another character's copying, instead of the copier himself, as was usually the case in his teaming with big men. The best example of the former occurs in *The Kid* (1921), where Jackie Coogan's title performance "is clearly another presentation of Charlie, so that we have in this film a dual personality, the adult and the child Charlie."[22]

Consistent with this Charlie "team" concept is the fact that, as with W. C. Fields's 1930s cartoon strip pairing in *Big Chief Wahoo,* during the 1910s Charlie sometimes emerged as part of a duo in the strip *Charlie Chaplin's Comic Ca-*

*pers.*[23] His occasional partner was an undersized character named Luke, physically not unlike Jiggs of the then very popular cartoon strip *Bringing Up Father*. However, the inspiration for this more normal-sized duo possibly came from Chaplin's occasional teaming with the normal-sized Ben Turpin while both were at Essanay, before Turpin's crossed eyes became the focus of his comedy.

These, then, have been the five major characteristics which link film clowns. Of course, it should go without saying that clowns share one more trait from which all others emanate—they make us laugh—a commonalty about which there is nothing common.

## BIBLIOGRAPHIC OVERVIEW

Everybody loves clowns, and everybody writes about them, including this author, who has books on Charlie Chaplin, W. C. Fields, and the Marx Brothers. Thus, on an individual basis, there is no shortage of clown books and articles available. The situation is not nearly so rich when survey overviews are requested. However, some excellent sources do exist, and in the interest of time and space I will note a top-ten book pantheon plus the proverbial "one extra."

The book with which to begin in Gerald Mast's *The Comic Mind: Comedy and the Movies* (1973). Both an ambitious history and an analytical guide to American film comedy, it is an insightful work in an area where little recommendable competition exists. The Mast text is flawed only by not devoting enough time to sound comedy's clowns, who are herded together into one chapter. (His work assumes a more theme-oriented focus in the sound era.) Surprisingly, the 1930s work of Will Rogers is not even cited.

*Movie Comedy* (1977), edited by Stuart Byron and Elisabeth Weis, is also a valuable source. Essays on American film comedy are arranged under five headings: "The Silent Era," "The Sound Era," "Spoofing" (see this volume's parody chapter), "Sex and Marriage," and "Social Satire." It is a quick and convenient collection of influential but concise essays by many of America's leading film critics, including Pauline Kael, Richard Schickel, and Andrew Sarris.

British film historian Raymond Durgnat's *The Crazy Mirror: Hollywood Comedy and the American Image* (1972) is another important, and always critically provocative, volume. However, the material is often rather eclectic, as the author attempts to touch bases with a seemingly limitless number of comic references, resulting in an almost stream-of-consciousness style, as if Virginia Woolf were its co-author. Consequently, gems of astuteness often share the page with rather peripheral material.

A more structured examination is prolific critic and author Leonard Maltin's *The Great Movie Comedians: From Charlie Chaplin to Woody Allen.* (1978) Each of twenty-two chapters is devoted to a single comedian or team. Besides the universally celebrated, Maltin also has sprinkled in chapters on important but neglected figures, such as Raymond Griffith and Marie Dressler. More recently slighted figures, such as Danny Kaye and Red Skelton, also receive chapters. Two additional recommended companion volumes to Maltin's work are James Robert Parish and William T. Leonard's detailed clown guide *The Funsters* (1979), and James L. Neibaur's *Movie Comedians: The Complete Guide* (1986). One should also note Maltin's *Movie Comedy Teams* (1974). Though not quite on a par with his *The Great Movie Comedians,* it remains *the* book on teams.

Among the other studies which have a more specialized subject, *New York Times* critic Walter Kerr's *The Silent Clowns* (1975) is easily the best. Besides his insightful, in-depth look at seemingly every silent comedian of note, including the often neglected silent films of W. C. Fields, the book showcases a wealth of beautiful stills. Two additional silent comedy volumes of note are Kalton C. Lahue's *World of Laughter: The Motion Picture Comedy Short, 1910–1930* (1966), and Lahue and Samuel Gill's *Clown Princes and Court Jesters* (1970). The last volume consists of fifty short chapters, each devoted to a silent comedian or team. However, it avoids being a silent comedy version of Maltin's *The Great Movie Comedians* (which it predates) by often focusing on the lesser known comedians. It purposely omits Chaplin, Keaton, and Lloyd.

Donald W. McCaffrey's *The Golden Age of Sound Comedy: Comic Films and Comedians of the Thirties* does for this decade what Kerr's work does for the silents. While not quite on a par with *The Silent Clowns,* it is an excellent look at both the period's clowns and other comedy genres (though not labeled as such). Gerald Weales's impressively researched *Canned Goods as Caviar: American Film Comedy of the 1930s* (1985) should be a close bookshelf neighbor to the McCaffrey text. It is a fascinating trip through the decade by way of focusing on twelve pivotal comedies, nearly half of which are clown vehicles: *City Lights* (1931, Chaplin), *She Done Him Wrong* (1933, Mae West), *Duck Soup* (1933, Marxes), *It's a Gift* (1934, Fields), and *Steamboat 'Round the Bend* (1935, Rogers). It is especially rich in his discussion of pivotal 1930s critics and his notation of a wealth of source material. Unlike so many film comedy texts, which are often simply overgrown picture books, Weales puts the intellectual excitement of several good books in each chapter.

## NOTES

1. Bob Thomas, *Bud & Lou* (Philadelphia: J. B. Lippincott, 1977), p. 130. See also Wes D. Gehring's *Charlie Chaplin: A Bio-Bibliography* (Westport, Conn.: Greenwood Press, 1983).

2. See especially Gene Lyons (with Peter McAlevey), "Crazy Eddie," cover article, *Newsweek,* 7 January, 1985, pp. 53, 55; *"Ebony* Interview with Eddie Murphy," cover article, *Ebony,* July 1985, p. 46.

3. James Agee, "Comedy's Greatest Era," in *Agee on Film,* vol. 1 (New York: Grosset and Dunlap, 1969), p. 8. (Originally appeared in *Life,* 3 September, 1949.)

4. Bob Hope and Bob Thomas, *The Road to Hollywood: My 40-year Love Affair with the Movies* (Garden City, N.Y.: Doubleday, 1977), p. 12.

5. See Chapter 7, on screwball comedy in this volume, as well as Wes D. Gehring's *Leo McCarey and the Comic Anti-Hero in American Film* (1980) and *Screwball Comedy: A Genre of Madcap Romance* (1986).

6. See both Gehring's aforementioned Leo McCarey text and his *W. C. Fields: A Bio-Bibliography* (1984).

7. Allen Eyles, *The Marx Brothers: Their World of Comedy* (1966; repr. New York: Paperback Library, 1971), p. 106.

8. Gilbert Seldes, Chapter 5, in *The Movies Come from America* (New York: Charles Scribner's Sons, 1937), p. 41.

9. Maurice Yacowar, *Loser Take All: The Comic Art of Woody Allen* (New York: Frederick Ungar, 1979), p. 156.

10. For example, see Andrew Sarris, "Jerry Lewis," in *The American Cinema: Directors and Directions, 1929–1968* (New York: Dutton, 1968), pp. 242–43.

11. Gerald Mast, *A Short History of the Movies*, 3d ed. (Indianapolis: Bobbs-Merrill, 1981), p. 15.

12. Mark Twain, *Roughing It* (1872; repr. New York: New American Library, 1962), p. 42.

13. Woody Allen, "The Kugelmass Episode," in *Side Effects* (New York: Random House, 1980), p. 55.

14. James Agee, "Comedy's Greatest Era," in *Agee on Film*, vol. 1 (New York: Grosset and Dunlap, 1969), p. 8. (Originally appeared in *Life*, 3 September, 1949).

15. Lillian Roth (with Mike Connolly and Gerald Frank), *I'll Cry Tomorrow* (New York: Frederick Fell, 1954), p. 85.

16. Otis Ferguson, *A Night at the Opera* review, *New Republic*, 11 December, 1935, p. 130.

17. Carl Sandburg, "Carl Sandburg Says Chaplin Could Play Serious Drama," in *Authors on Film*, ed. Harry M. Geduld (Bloomington: Indiana University Press, 1972), p. 264. (Originally in *Chicago Daily News*, 16 April, 1921.)

18. Alexander Woollcott, "A Strong Silent Man," *Cosmopolitan*, January 1934, p. 108.

19. Besides Gehring's Fields book, see his "W. C. Fields: The Copyrighted Sketches," *Journal of Popular Film and Television*, Winter 1986, pp. 65–75.

20. Gerald Mast, "Comic Climate," in Chapter 1 of his *The Comic Mind: Comedy and the Movies*, 2d ed. (Chicago: University of Chicago Press, 1979), p. 7.

21. Robert Lewis Taylor, *W. C. Fields: His Follies and Fortunes* (Garden City, N.Y.: Doubleday, 1949), p. 174. When Fields worked for Ziegfeld he had even employed a dwarf known as "Shorty" to be his valet and general man Friday. Originally hired to spook a superstitious Ziegfeld, Shorty eventually crossed the line of reality versus illusion when Fields also included him in his famous golf routine. And Fields's professional and personal interest in the diminutive stooge continued during his Hollywood days.

22. Peter Cotes and Thelma Niklaus, *The Little Fellow: The Life and Works of Charles Spencer Chaplin* (1951; repr. New York: Citadel, 1965), p. 109.

23. See the collection *Charlie Chaplin Up in the Air* (Chicago: M. A. Donohue, 1917).

# BIBLIOGRAPHICAL CHECKLIST

Byron, Stuart, and Elisabeth Weis, eds. *Movie Comedy*. New York: Penguin Books, 1977.

Durgnat, Raymond. *The Crazy Mirror: Hollywood Comedy and the American Image*. 1969; repr. New York: Dell, 1972.

Kerr, Walter. *The Silent Clowns*. New York: Alfred A. Knopf, 1975.

Lahue, Kalton C. *World of Laughter: The Motion Picture Comedy Short, 1910–1930*. 1966; repr. Norman: University of Oklahoma Press, 1972.

Lahue, Kalton C., and Samuel Gill. *Clown Princes and Court Jesters*. South Brunswick, N.J. A. S. Barnes, 1970.

McCaffrey, Donald W. *The Golden Age of Sound Comedy: Comic Films and Comedians of the Thirties,* New York: A. S. Barnes and Company, 1973.

Mast, Gerald. *The Comic Mind: Comedy and the Movies,* 2d ed. 1973; repr. Chicago: University of Chicago Press, 1979.

Maltin, Leonard. *Movie Comedy Teams*. 1970; repr. New York: Signet, 1974.

————. *The Great Movie Comedians: From Charlie Chaplin to Woody Allen*. New York: Crown, 1978.

Neibaur, James L. *Movie Comedians: The Complete Guide*. Jefferson, N.C.: McFarland, 1986.

Parish, James Robert, and William T. Leonard (with Gregory W. Mank and Charles Hoyt). *The Funsters*. New Rochelle, N.Y.: Arlington House, 1979.

Weales, Gerald. *Canned Goods as Caviar: American Film Comedy of the 1930s*. Chicago: University of Chicago Press, 1985.

# SELECTED FILMOGRAPHY

1923  *Safety Last* (81 minutes).
  Hal Roach Studios. Director: Fred Newmeyer, Sam Taylor. Story/Screenplay: Hal Roach, Sam Taylor, Tim Whelan. Cast: Harold Lloyd (The Boy), Mildred Davis (The Girl), Bill Strothers (The Pal).

1925  *The Gold Rush* (82 minutes).
  Chaplin–United Artists. Producer/Director: Charlie Chaplin. Story/Screenplay: Charlie Chaplin. Cast: Charlie Chaplin (lone prospector), Georgia Hale (Georgia), Mack Swain (Big Jim McKay).

1926  *The Strong Man* (75 minutes).
  First National Picture. Director: Frank Capra. Screenplay: Arthur Ripley, Frank Capra, Hal Conklin, Robert Eddy. Cast: Harry Langdon (Paul Bergot), Mary Brown (Priscilla Bonner), Gertrude Astor (''Gold Tooth''), Arthur Thalasso (Zandow the Great).

1927  *The General* (74 minutes).
  United Artists. Director: Buster Keaton, Clyde Brickman. Screenplay: Al Boasberg, Charles Smith, from a Keaton/Brickman story. Cast: Buster Keaton (Johnnie Gray), Marian Mack (Annabelle Lee).

1933  *Duck Soup* (70 minutes).
  Paramount. Producer: Herman Mankiewicz. Director: Leo McCarey. Screenplay: Bert Kalmar, Harry Ruby. Additional Dialogue: Arthur Sheekman, Nat Perrin.

Cast: Groucho (Rufus T. Firefly), Chico (Chicolini), Harpo (Pinkie), Zeppo (Bob Rolland), Margaret Dumont (Mrs. Teasdale).

*Sons of the Desert* (68 minutes).
MGM. Producer: Hal Roach. Director: William A. Seiter. Story: Frank Craven. Cast: Stan Laurel (himself), Oliver Hardy (himself).

1934    *It's a Gift* (73 minutes).
Paramount. Producer: William LeBaron. Director: Norman McLeod. Based upon an original story by Charles Bogle (W. C. Fields; see especially his copyrighted stage routine "The Sleeping Porch" and the multi-copyrighted "The Family Ford") and adopted from J. P. McEvoy's musical comedy revue *The Comic Supplement*. Cast: W. C. Fields (Harold Bissonette), Kathleen Howard (Amelia Bissonette), Baby LeRoy (Baby Dunk).

1945    *Road to Utopia* (90 minutes).
Paramount. Producer: Paul Jones. Director: Hal Walker. Story/Adaptation: Norman Panama, Melvin Frank. Cast: Bing Crosby (Duke Johnson), Bob Hope (Chester Hooton), Dorothy Lamour (Sal), Robert Benchley (Narrator).

1948    *A Southern Yankee* (90 minutes).
MGM. Producer: Paul Jones. Director: Edward Sedgwick. Screenplay: Harry Tugend, original by Melvin Frank and Norman Panama. Cast: Red Skelton (Aubrey Filmore), Arlene Dahl (Sallyann Weatharby).

1951    *Sailor Beware* (104 minutes).
Paramount. Producer: Hal Wallis. Director: Hal Walker. Screenplay: James Allardice, Martin Rackin; added dialogue, John Grant; adaptation, Elwood Ullman, from Kenyon Nicholson, Charles Robinson play. Cast: Dean Martin (Al Crowthers), Jerry Lewis (Melvin Jones).

1973    *Sleeper* (88 minutes).
United Artists. Producer: Jack Grossberg. Director: Woody Allen. Screenplay: Allen, Marshall Brickman. Cast: Woody Allen (Miles Monroe), Diane Keaton (Luna Schlosser), John Beck (Erno Windt).

# THE FANTASTIC

# 12

# Horror Film

## GERALD C. WOOD

"It is practically the only question of the age, this question of primitivism and how it can be sustained in the face of sophistication."
—Jean Renoir[1]

"I aim to provide the public with beneficial shocks. Civilization has become so protective that we're no longer able to get our goose bumps instinctively. The only way to remove the numbness and revive our moral equilibrium is to use artificial means to bring about the shock. The best way to achieve that, it seems to me, is through a movie."
—Alfred Hitchcock[2]

Genre films are created on the intense, nervous playground where America's most sacred beliefs and fantasies confront what is most unthinkable, most unspeakable in the dominant culture. The major genres traditionally give the audience a peek at discomforting images but then quickly draw a curtain over the troubling sights. Westerns, for example, show man alone on a friendless landscape, then reassure us that solitude fosters an integrity and moral purity not available in groups. As long as the cowboy's alienation is pictured as leading to a higher self-sacrifice, the gap between private wants and public needs in westerns doesn't surface as an unresolvable tension. Similarly, in the classical musical seeming social injustice and immobility become trivial matters when in the final scenes love conquers all, everyone has a partner, and there is singing and dancing in the streets of every American town. Even screwball behavior, so potentially disruptive to society, becomes normative as long as appropriate mates are found and the screwballs discover room to be themselves in a surprisingly open and expansive landscape. Before they become more interested in variations than traditions, revisions than affirmations, most genres are expert at imagining a calming truce, sometimes a perfect fusion, among all the combatants on the field of anxiety.

But if the most popular genres work hard to reinforce traditional values, the very existence of other genres, the darker ones, is an embarrassment to the average American. The gangster film, for example, never enjoyed the luxury of a fully developed classical phase in the early 1930s (as did the musical, for example) because of intense pressure to apologize for its seductive imagery and to recast its stories as solvable, isolated social problems. The denial of the American Dream and the easy violence of lower-class, alienated heroes in films like *Little Caesar, Scarface,* and *Public Enemy* were quickly understood as subversive of the myths and fantasies of their audiences. Explanatory titles were added, and the pure gangster was transformed into the delinquent or law-man long before the end of the decade.[3] The illegitimate younger brother of the gangster, film noir, was more successful, but noir developed after World War II, when all genres were entertaining revisions. Because Americans didn't want to become too conscious of the dark themes in this popular style, the French were the first to explain the nature of film noir—and to give the style a name. Most obviously, the sexually explicit film, whether erotic or porno-graphic, has from the early days of this century been a topic for moral discussion and social control. Crime, despair, and sexual license have lived an underground, though vital and sometimes very profitable, existence in the popular American imagination.

From the early days of film, the horror genre has been attractive and successful because, more than either the legitimate or subversive films, it has been able to keep a hairy paw in both worlds. In its first thirty years—from the first years of the twentieth century until the mid-1930s—the horror film was acceptable because it drew from three "ennobling" sources: its stories came from respectable literature, its look was artily European (German and Scandinavian), and its monsters were sentimentalized as misunderstood, good-hearted sacrificial lambs.[4] There was no pressing need for apology and control of this genre, for it showed the bitter fruits that grew when men tampered with God's natural world. Reason, love, and control of the dark side were integral to these stories. Nevertheless, the imagery and tension of the horror film were drawn from the world of less acceptable things. Insanity, alienation, sexual deviance, obsession, and violence were as ingrained in the horror film as in the gangster or pornographic film. The popularity of the genre was assured as long as it maintained a delicate balance between the goodness it showed as powerful and eventually victorious and the fascinating evil it made visible but then returned to the closet.

The appearance of horror in the early silent period was based primarily on the literary tradition, which offered familiar stories and a sense of higher culture much coveted by the new medium. *Dr. Jekyll and Mr. Hyde,* for example, was an especially popular topic in the silent period. After initially being filmed in 1908, the story was photographed in at least three other versions by 1915.

In 1920 two more remakes appeared, bringing the total to more than a half dozen. The werewolf story was filmed as early as 1913 and 1914. And Mary Shelley's *Frankenstein,* which was to become a film classic in the 1930s, was first filmed in 1910, then redone in 1915 as *Life Without Soul.*[5] Other film works in the horror genre were similarly adapted from literature by Edgar Allan Poe, H. G. Wells, and Jules Verne.[6] As Les Daniels has noted, it wasn't until 1932, with the release of *The Mummy,* that an important American horror film was made from other than a literary source.[7]

The classical period of horror actually developed a little later, however. It was in the first half of the 1930s when this relatively minor tradition of literary horror and sentimental monsters was transformed into a major genre by forces within and outside the film industry. The 1920s had set the stage by creating an unprecedented growth in national consensus and awareness, which in turn led to a new emphasis on popular entertainment and diversion. Movies and the star system were part of a general public interest in things American, including radio personalities, sports (for example, baseball, boxing, and football), jazz, and national heroes like Charles Lindbergh. Within Hollywood itself, the studio system sought to create and repeat familiar stories and images, to shape as well as reflect this national consciousness. And, of course, the Depression became an ever-present horror from which the new industry and audience desperately tried to escape. Artistically, the major influence came from Germany as first the styles of *Caligari* and *Nosferatu* were imitated, then the artists themselves immigrated to the Los Angeles area. Especially at Universal Pictures, where the most influential films were produced, German camerawork translated the literary work of the British novel and short story onto celluloid, while continuity was established by the stars and the American horror tradition of the 1910s and 1920s.[8]

True to its century-old literary sources and its own brief tradition as a film genre, the horror film of 1930–1935 was supportive of the values of the dominant culture. In the face of the Depression, the *Frankenstein* cycle, for example, warned of the dangers of tampering with the natural order. According to these stories, science and other distractions from romantic love and the traditional family would eventually lead to disaster and loneliness, maybe even eternal damnation. Similarly, sexual temptations in the form of European outsiders like Dracula must be overcome in the interest of the family and church. Heterosexual love and sexuality sanctified by marriage (and thus the authority of institutional religion) were the norms that had to be upheld in times of disorder. The classical horror film was also politically reactionary. In *King Kong* the transition from the terrible but majestic world of nature to the cynical and materialistic landscape of the urban and industrial modern world was viewed as a tragic loss of creative and sexual power.[9] Or if (as in *Dracula*) the city was unavoidable, urban evil had little relation to the political and social structure of American society. Darkness in the classic horror film came from the foreign aristocracy which could only be defeated by "some intelligent bourgeois from some metropolitan and educational centre. . . . [who] comes to the aid of the people against the aristocracy."[10]

While the closure at the end of these films reassured the audiences of the importance of old-fashioned values—those before the Roaring Twenties and the Depression—the horror film nevertheless left a legacy of unresolved tensions and troubling images to which later filmmakers would return. The sympathy for the monsters and the fascinating imagery associated with the forces of darkness were richly problematic even in the classical period.[11] In *Dracula* the innocence and naivete of the Sewards and Jonathan Harker seem crippling and paralyzing. It takes a rare knowledge of esoteric lore and nearly superhuman courage to confront the darker forces and rescue these powerless normals. Van Helsing is too special and Lucy too attracted to Dracula for the conclusion to be totally convincing. Similarly, the death of Kong and the Frankenstein monster are at best mixed blessings for their societies. The loss of primitive forces, whether natural or artificial, creates a sense of melancholy from which even the classical horror film is never immune. Despite its obvious preference for order and tradition, the genre demonstrates the price that must be paid to establish and maintain civilization. Tod Browning's *Freaks* makes this theme explicit by imagining a world where normals impose a life-denying control over the freaks. The injustice is so oppressive, in fact, that the victims band together in violent revolt against their oppressors.

The next major figure in the development of motion picture horror was Val Lewton, a producer, who held an unprecedented interest in and respect for the dark forces which had been treated so ambivalently in the classical period. Between 1942 and 1946 Lewton was responsible for the creation of seven horror fims variously directed by Robert Wise, Mark Robson, and Jacques Tourneur. Beginning with *Cat People* and concluding with *Bedlam*, these films, by Lewton's own definition, were films of "psychological horror."[12] They relied heavily on suggestive imagery and suspense rather than explicit horror, and their characters were typically in emotional or religious crisis. The healthiest characters created by Lewton and his collaborators accept the reality of the dark forces at work in the world—whether sexual, irrational, or aggressive. In a modern world which tries to make everything clear, orderly, and rational, the path to sanity leads through a dark and mysterious exploration of the irrational, these films contend. At the heart of Lewton's work is the humanism which informs both the literature from which classical film horror was borrowed and the film tradition which had flourished ten years before. All seven films in the Lewton canon fear the alienation of the individual from his or her whole humanity, especially in the obsessive need for order that characterizes the modern temper.

But Lewton's films were more than just the culmination of classical humanism and gothic expressionism.[13] While they looked backward in their desire to reattach man with the ancient world of community myth and depth of feeling, they also anticipated the preoccupation with repression—sexual and political—

that was to follow in the next three decades. *Cat People,* for example, deals with sexuality, especially female sexuality, its troubling power and the dangers of its repression. *Curse of the Cat People* examines the restraints on imagination imposed by middle-class needs for order and control, particularly on the female imagination. *Bedlam* places these conflicts in a more explicitly social frame; the sanitarium becomes a metaphor for political and social oppression of the disadvantaged, an oppression which is opposed by a young woman who first removes her self-delusive fantasies, then becomes an active force for social change. By working with the small budgets of the B film, Lewton was able to make more personal films which continued the humanist tradition in horror films and also expanded the genre's potential interest in women's issues and political themes.

While Lewton's use of expressionistic stories and settings was exceptional, his films were still tied to the studio sets and their obvious artifice. The dreamlike appearance of his work was one of the major achievements of the studio tradition, but that style of filmmaking was soon to pass. By the late 1940s, more certainly by the 1950s, the movies started using more contemporary places and images. Not coincidentally, the horror film began to leave the world of fable and literary story for more current social and political issues.

Included in this contemporaneous spirit was a search for new styles and tones, especially those that would reflect a younger audience. As the Hammer films from England showed, those people who were enticed away from their new televisions were willing to watch more colorful splashes of violence and explicit sexuality than ever before. The subtexts of aggressive and unusual erotic acts in the Dracula series, for example, could literally become the focus of the horror films of the 1950s. Or, as Hollywood soon found out, teenagers themselves could become the innocent victims of adult machinations in such youth classics as *I Was a Teenager Frankenstein* and *I Was a Teenage Werewolf,* both released in 1957, or *The Blob* (1958). Better yet, by the end of the 1950s Roger Corman was to imagine a new blend of the comic and horrific, this time with a cynical, darker tone that prefigured the later Hitchcock (like *Frenzy*) and the black comedy of *Dr. Strangelove* and beyond. Corman's *A Bucket of Blood* and *The Little Shop of Horrors* (1959 and 1960) reduced the sympathy between audience and protagonists by creating mechanical, ridiculous characters and plots which appealed to a more alienated and jaded audience.

Mainline horror of the 1950s, on the other hand, often drew heavily from the revived interest in science fiction and, like the western, began to focus on the psychological and political themes which until the 1950s had been found only in the subtext of horror films. Popular fare during this decade dealt with zombies, aliens, and various visitors from outer space, figures found in the ice of the Cold War, the jet stream of the space race, and mushroom clouds of the atomic bomb (*Godzilla* was released in the United States in 1956).[14] Most interesting are *The Day the Earth Stood Still* (1951), which anticipates *Close Encounters of the Third Kind* in its declaration that fear of the unknown is a greater threat than forces from the outside, and *Them!* (1954), which shows the modern landscape under siege by gigantic mutant ants formed on the site of atomic tests.

Early in this period *The Thing* (1951) became the most coherent and thoroughgoing study of sexual desire up to that time. The Wolfman and Jekyll and Hyde films, as well as Frankenstein and Dracula, had indirectly made statements about the necessity of controlling human sexuality for the good of society and the family. But in previous films this subject had been one of many. In Howard Hawks's film the discovery and thawing of the monster at an arctic research station is correlated with the arrival of Nikki, an old girlfriend of Captain Hendry, a leader on the expedition. As in *King Kong,* the victory over the monster parallels Hendry's acceptance of his responsibilities toward the woman and commitment to her. But Hawks varied the classical text so that Nikki understands Hendry's desire and accepts his sexuality (which is light-years beyond Ann Darrow's hysteria).[15] Also Hendry and Nikki's predicament is not portrayed as common or normative; their socialization takes place within a group which is largely alienated from an impersonal society. These typical Hawksian themes are significant additions to an otherwise traditional horror film.

A more substantial variation from the tradition was made by Don Siegel's *Invasion of the Body Snatchers* (1956). This story of the invasion of American life by seedpods which replace ordinary people and carry on a feelingless and passive existence brought an unusual satiric tone to the horror film. The loss of fellow feeling and community is especially effective in this film because, like much of 1950s horror, it is placed in a simple, realistic setting, a small town where the rituals of family life and community action are carried out religiously. Even the budding love affair between Miles Bennell and Becky Driscoll dies when Becky falls asleep (thus becoming a replicant) and sides with the zombies against Miles.

Though he is often remembered as one of the major directors of horror, Alfred Hitchcock was sixty years old before he made a horror film, and only two of his works can be considered major works of the genre. In fact, with the possible exception of *Frenzy* (1972), his last five films did little to advance the art of horror; they are not up to his other creative efforts. But Hitchcock's vision, even in other genres like the suspense film and the romantic melodrama, was preoccupied with the horrific. And the two films of 1960 and 1963 *(Psycho and The Birds)* are seminal works of horror film, the first for its formal characteristics, the second for its imagery and themes.

*Psycho* is a cartoonish story of oedipal conflict and multiple personalities, whose explanation of motivation is not particularly believable. But its use of audience manipulation to tell this thin story was a tour de force. Hitchcock used a leering, voyeuristic camera to peep into the lives of the film's adulterers, thieves, and psychopaths to the point where the audience feels uncomfortable with looking, guilty for watching. To this discomfort he adds disorientation when first the heroine and then the private investigator are murdered. Used to identifying with one character or another, the audience is even led to see the action through the eyes of Norman Bates, the psychopath. By breaking the rules of the traditional horror film, Hitchcock raised the anxiety level of the viewer, expanded the use of subjective camera for manipulation, and created new, more self-reflexive ground for the horror films that would follow.[16]

If *Psycho* gives the audience little time to rest comfortably on the conventions of horror, *The Birds* is almost too leisurely in its development. In the second film Hitchcock makes the audience wait, wait, wait for the bird attacks, and along the way the director is quite content to interject long interludes where a storekeeper gives directions or the protagonists, safely posed on a hilltop, discuss their childhood. As much as *Psycho* asks the audience to feel anxiety and shame about watching, *The Birds* asks for microscopic inspection of desperate people searching for connections in a suicidal world. As the natural world of the birds turns against the human beings, the traditional order of the family is fractured (represented by the death of the father). The characters either isolate themselves by a profound narcissism (Mitch, Melanie, and Mrs. Brenner), or they stay on the fringe, maintaining empty rituals of sham attachment (Annie and her gardening, Cathy and her surrogate mothers). The birds attack whenever these evasions and defenses start to break down. If the final scenes of *The Birds* suggest that intimacy may be returning to the Brenner household, the blackbirds of death are nevertheless foregrounded. Cathy's lovebirds, which are rescued from the house, may be a sign of hope, or they might be deadly.[17]

The apocalypse glimpsed in the endings to *Invasion of the Body Snatchers* and *The Birds* became an accepted part of the form of horror by the end of the 1960s. The watershed year was 1968, when Roman Polanski's *Rosemary's Baby* gained international popularity by picturing the birth of the anti-Christ. But the film which has become more influential has been 1968's *Night of the Living Dead*, directed by George Romero. This film combined the zombie theme of *Body Snatchers* with the decay of family and community life of *The Birds* to produce an apocalyptic horror more disturbing than even Polanski's. From the opening scenes where the American flag flies over a graveyard, *Night of the Living Dead* imagines a world where family members devour each other, power is in the hands of vigilantes more actively evil than the zombies, and the black man (a representative of good liberal causes and individual courage) is shot down in cold blood. Romero's film portrays a society on the verge of disintegration from the lack of family, religious, or social cohesiveness. The survivors are a band of cold fascistic killers.

Since the beginning of the 1970s the horror film has achieved an unprecedented popularity and critical respectability. *The Exorcist* (William Friedkin, 1973) and *Jaws* (Steven Spielberg, 1975) are usually credited with beginning this revival, which has supported the work of talented young directors and established ones alike. The horror films of John Carpenter (*Halloween*, 1978) and Brian DePalma (*Carrie*, 1976, and *Dressed to Kill*, 1980) have been especially popular. Even Stanley Kubrick has joined the action with *Clockwork Orange* (1971) and later *The Shining* (1980). But the most creative and enduring contributions have come from less well-known artists, for whom the attraction of young people to the genre has offered an unusual opportunity to enter the industry. Roger Corman has been a significant contributor to this revival by fostering the work of many talented young directors. But the best work has actually been done by supposedly second-rank directors who are part of no clear front or organization. David Cronenberg's influence from Canada (especially *The Brood*, 1979) should be included in this list, as should that of Tobe Hooper (*Texas Chain Saw Massacre*, 1974), Larry Cohen (*It's Alive*, 1973, and *The Stuff*, 1985), Wes Craven (*The Hills Have Eyes*, 1977, and *Swamp Thing*, 1982), and more recently Abel Ferrara (*Ms. 45*, 1981).

With the popularization of the horror film has come a diversity of intent and styles rarely achieved in the history of the genre. The most pervasive influence has probably come from the teenage audience, which dominates the moviegoing population. More horror films than ever before have babysitters, teen drunks on the beach, or young horror film addicts as their protagonists. The stories show young people attacked in their houses or in sorority houses, dormitories, summer camps, or hospitals. Whether the films are well made or shoddy, adolescents seem willing to pay to see images of themselves and their lifestyles— under attack. Particularly important to this audience, if the movies are good indicators, is anxiety over sexual experimentation.[18]

If sex has become more explicit in the horror film, violence also has become more graphic and, with the development of special effects, an end in itself. Part of the reason for this escalation in the amount of violence has been the need for the adolescent audience to test themselves, to ride the roller coaster of fear and survive. But it is just as true that the horror films reflect a preoccupation with the brutality of the times as advertised by the media. Although there is no definitive conclusion about the effect of all this violence, it is probably true that there is a pattern of (1) initial revulsion, (2) desensitization that helps the viewer cope with violence in the real world, and (3) saturation, which leads to apathy toward violent acts in both film and life outside the theater.[19]

The horror film has never been a pure genre; it has easily borrowed from the sentimental monster film and science fiction, for example. But in the last decade or so the genre has been especially open to modification, from parody *(Young Frankenstein* and *Love at First Bite)* to a radical blend of comedy and horror *(An American Werewolf in London* and *Survivors)* or fantasy and horror *(Gremlins)*. The run on remakes *(The Thing, Invasion of the Body Snatchers)* suggests the self-reflexive nature of much recent horror. And lest we forget, the conservative religious tradition of *Rosemary's Baby*, *The Omen*, and *The Exorcist* continues to be profitable, though the best experimental work is still being done in the dehumanization films led by George Romero and Larry Cohen. While many of the young directors have been seduced by big budgets and the special effects explosion, Romero's popular *Living Dead* trilogy and Cohen's less visible examinations of corporate irresponsibility have become major works of horror film. The most striking experiment in form in the last few years has been *Ms. 45*, which takes the revenge motif and turns the genre on its ear by putting the violence in the hands of a woman who has been raped. In a genre which has tended to cast women as victims or mere objects of veneration, this well photographed and acted film is a refreshing inversion of things.[20] Not as inventive but especially successful at the box office have been horror films dealing explicitly with taboo relationships (incest in the remake of *Cat People*) or the old union of horror and science fiction *(Alien, Blade Runner)*.

The development of the horror film is not really as neat and linear as this brief survey might suggest.[21] Variations and recapitulations exist side by side throughout the history of this genre. Nevertheless, there has been a general shift from the early conservative horror tradition in which nearly all the films considered monstrous anything which opposed the traditional order of society expressed as patriarchal authority, the church, romantic love, and the family. In the best films of the middle phase—the 1940s and 1950s—the forces of darkness needed to be regulated in the interest of society, but what was repressed was never to be denied or excessively inhibited. Since the end of the 1950s, there has been increasing fear that society itself can be monstrous, that there are forces at work which will alienate man from his better nature. And yet in its most anarchic moments, the horror film has respected knowledge, tradition, and meaning. Very lately, there has even been a new conservatism of form and content, a reaction against the apocalyptic tendencies of the past twenty years.

In any case, if the horror film is well made, it will take the viewer beyond simple fear into profound anxiety about the forces that threaten his or her well-being and sense of meaning and justice. As long as the spectator shares the vision of the film, permits the fear to rise, and keeps a sense of aesthetic distance, the horror film will transport the viewer into a dark world rarely imagined in most other genres.[22] In the horror experience the best viewers bathe themselves in a creative regression that can vitalize their lives:

The arts . . . help us master the world by making explicit fears that have been merely implied for too long . . . the arts sensitize us to what we can feel, if we give ourselves permission, and provide us with the means of expression. . . . It is . . . one of the missions of the novelist, the playwright, the filmmaker, and the artist . . . to stir people up and upset the apple carts of hardened assumptions, notions, and life-styles which have gone undisturbed so long that consciousness is dulled.[23]

Since at least 1908 many filmmakers have been upsetting the emotional apple carts of their audiences with what Hitchcock called "beneficial shocks." When the aesthetic of horror is done well, these artists use the shocks to reintroduce us to the living "primitivism" Jean Renoir feared would be lost in our sophisticated modern age. The horror film is one of the most effective allies in this mission of sensitization.

## BIBLIOGRAPHICAL OVERVIEW

Because horror films historically have been considered not quite legitimate, there has been relatively little work of interpretation until the last fifteen years or so. Most works until then were picture books or vehicles for stars. There has been an excessive amount of attention to specific actors and classic films but little consideration of themes and forms. For the most part, horror-as-genre has been considered only in the wake of the new focus on genre in general.

And even then horror has tended to lag behind. Of the book-length studies of genre, Stuart Kaminsky's discussion in *American Film Genres* (1974) is a quite useful introduction to the themes of horror. While Stanley Solomon's *Beyond Formula* (1976) gives more space to horror and more attention to specific films, it is less coherent and useful as an introduction than Kaminsky. Stephen Neale's work, *Genre* (1980), gives little attention to horror, but his few comments on the genre are stimulating, especially if the reader has some basic understanding of the history of the horror film. Thomas Schatz's book on genre study is exemplary in most respects; it has both careful analysis of specific films and a clear sense of the tradition and the pressure for variation. The one major weakness of *Hollywood Genres* (1981) is its omission of a chapter on horror.

The first wave of significant work on the horror film came in the late 1960s and early 1970s. It began with the publication in 1967 of two histories of the genre: Ivan Butler's *The Horror Film* (later revised in 1970 as *Horror in the Cinema*) and Carlos Clarens's *An Illustrated History of the Horror Film*. These books brought the genre together as a historical form with a coherent and dignified tradition. But three other works, all articles, actually defined the areas in which the horror film would be most fruitfully examined; (1) its relation to social contexts, (2) its religious implications, and (3) its implicit psychological themes.

Although it has now become commonplace to state that horror films reflect the fears of their audiences, it was John D. Denne's essay "Society and the Monster," in *December* magazine (1967), which developed the historical categories (the atmosphere, bipartite, and social monster films) that described a development in the form. Denne found an evolution from the pre-1940s where the monster lived in his own fantastic world, through the contested space of the 1950s, up to the realistic world where the monster is out of place. In this vein an especially provocative essay was written in the *Kenyon Review* (1970) by Frank McConnell ("Rough Beast Slouching"), who, among other things, discovered the relationship between Dracula and the "old consciousness" of Europe and Frankenstein and the new world's obsession with materialism. McConnell also defined in this article the important shift from liberal humanism to the art of dehumanization. Among more recent attempts to show the relationship between horror film and social contexts, Harlan Kennedy's "Things

That Go Howl in the Id,'' in *Film Comment* (March/April 1982), has outlined the role of Vietnam and Watergate in the popularization of the modern horror film. Stephen King, in chapters 6 and 7 of *Danse Macabre* (1981), has shown how a number of popular horror films reflect substantial, but usually transitory, conflicts and anxieties in American culture.

The key work on the religious dimensions of the horror film has been written by R.H.W. Dillard. This contribution, like Denne's, appeared in 1967 when Dillard published "Even a Man Who Is Pure at Heart," in *Man and the Movies,* edited by William R. Robinson. In this essay the classical film texts are considered as expressions of a Christian mythos; Dillard found that the films of 1931–1945 centered on the need for salvation in the face of death, a theme borrowed from the Christian morality plays. His later essay ("Drawing the Circle," in *Film Journal,* January–March 1973) and the book *Horror Films* (1976) showed less interest in questions of genre than in close examination of the film texts. Dillard's emphasis moved toward how auteurs have used the tradition and participated in a "devolution" of the classical vision.

In December of 1970 and January of 1971 *Films and Filming* published Margaret Tarratt's seminal work on the psychology of the horror film—"Monsters From the Id." For her, the science fiction horror films of the 1950s and beyond dramatize "the individual's anxiety about his own repressed sexual desires, which are incompatible with the morals of civilised life."[24] A year later Dennis L. White, in "The Poetics of Horror," *Cinema Journal* (Spring 1971), shifted the emphasis from the texts themselves to the viewers and their fears of the "id," "rejection and perfection," and "chaos." According to White, horror films help people face and deal with such everyday fears. Walter Evans followed in the fall of 1973 and the spring of 1975 with two essays in the *Journal of Popular Film* which focused on the problems of adolescents. The first argued that the horror film deals with fears and adjustments to adult sexuality, a point of view later developed by James Twitchell into the book *Dreadful Pleasures: An Anatomy of Modern Horror* (1985), which traced these themes into the literary and folk sources for the films.[25] Evans's second essay linked horror movies and rites of initiation in other cultures. A discussion of a number of horror films from a more rigorously clinical viewpoint was offered by Harvey R. Greenberg in chapters 9–11 of his book *The Movies on Your Mind* (1975). He related the stories to, for example, masochistic fantasies, good/bad mother interpretations, birth fantasies, and masturbatory imagery. Most satisfying are his discussion of adolescent sex/love issues in *King Kong* and fusion anxiety in the science fiction film. Much later, Noel Carroll, in "Nightmare and the Horror Film" (*Film Quarterly,* Spring 1981), found that oedipal issues in contemporary horror reflect feelings of powerlessness and rage; for Carroll, simple sexual interpretations of horror films fail to take into account the influence on the genre of more complex social issues.

The most ambitious attempt at uniting the psychological approach with a "social/political" view has been that undertaken by the writers of *The Ameri-*

*can Nightmare* (1979). The general position of this work is best outlined in the essay by Robin Wood (reprinted from *Film Comment*) which defines the "basic formula for the horror film" as "normality is threatened by the Monster" and goes on to describe as "progressive" films which deviate from this formula.[26] Although it at times oversimplifies complex creations and social forces, the work of Wood and Tony Williams has raised a number of important issues about the intimate politics of the horror film. Of particular interest is their discussion of the decline of the family. A number of essays built on the positions in *American Nightmare* also appear in *Planks of Reason,* edited by Barry K. Grant (1984).

With the appearance of four other books, there is finally a body of work on horror film *as a genre.* The first of these was the relatively brief overview by Andrew Tudor in *Image and Influence* (1974). This sociological approach traced the history of the form, but also suggested the social and cultural contexts which had shaped the works. The most recent full-length work has been Gregory A. Waller's *The Living and the Undead* (1986), which places the films in their literary and dramatic traditions. Waller's emphasis is on close textual analysis, and he demonstrates how the literary and film productions express the artistic visions and ethos of their times. S. S. Prawer's *Caligari's Children* (1980), like Waller, puts a strong emphasis on textual study and intertextual influence, again between literature and film. But Prawer adds a more complete survey of the history and sociology of the genre, as well as related issues like violence in film and the aesthetics of fear. Focusing on the "modern" horror film, Charles Derry defined the three major strains as the horrors of "personality," "armageddon," and "the demonic" (*Dark Dreams,* 1977).

And any survey of the horror film is incomplete without substantial reading about individual artists, including the major directors of horror film. The classical directors who achieved a distinctive style—F. W. Murnau, James Whale, Tod Browning, and the directors who worked with Val Lewton—need to be included. Also Howard Hawks and Donald Siegel are major directors who have worked in a number of genres, including horror. Of course, study of Alfred Hitchcock and Roman Polanski should be part of an examination of the transition to contemporary horror. And with the recent emphasis on horror, longer works are available on many of the latest generation of directors—Brian DePalma and David Cronenberg, for example.

## NOTES

1. Quoted in Joseph McBride and Michael Wilmington, *John Ford* (New York: Da Capo Press, 1975), p. 175.

2. François Truffaut, *Hitchcock,* rev. ed. (New York: Simon & Schuster, 1983), p. 201n.

3. Thomas Schatz, *Hollywood Genres* (New York: Random House, 1981), pp. 82, 95–102.

4. See, for example, Andrew Tudor, *Image and Influence* (New York: St. Martin's, 1974), p. 204; and James B. Twitchell, *Dreadful Pleasures* (New York: Oxford, 1985), p. 57.

5. "Filmography," in *Focus on the Horror Film*, ed. Roy Huss and T. J. Ross (Englewood Cliffs, N.J.: Prentice-Hall, 1972), pp. 170–71; Twitchell, *Dreadful Pleasures*, pp. 216, 244–45; and Walter Evans, "Monster Movies and Rites of Initiation," *Journal of Popular Film*, Spring 1975, p. 138n.

6. James Brosnan, *Future Tense: The Cinema of Science Fiction* (New York: St. Martin's, 1978), pp. 16–25.

7. Les Daniels, *Living in Fear: A History of Horror in the Mass Media* (New York: Charles Scribner's Sons, 1975), p. 133.

8. Stephen Pendo, "Universal's Golden Age of Horror," *Films in Review*, March 1975, pp. 155–56.

9. X. J. Kennedy, "Who Killed King Kong?" in *Focus on the Horror Film*, p. 109.

10. Tudor, *Image and Influence*, pp. 209–10.

11. Ibid., p. 218.

12. Quoted in J. P. Telotte, *Dreams of Darkness: Fantasy and the Films of Val Lewton* (Urbana: University of Illinois Press, 1985), p. 100. See also Michel Perez, "The Puritan Despair," in *Focus on the Horror Film*, p. 132; and Twitchell, *Dreadful Pleasures*, p. 58.

13. T. J. Ross, Introduction, in *Focus on the Horror Film*, p. 2.

14. See, in addition to the general histories, Robert Brustein, "Film Chronicle: Reflections on Horror Movies," *Partisan Review*, Spring 1958, pp. 288–96; and Brian Murphy, "Monster Movies: They Came from Beneath the Fifties," *Journal of Popular Film*, Winter 1972, pp. 31–44.

15. Margaret Tarratt, "Monsters from the Id," *Films and Filming*, December 1970, p. 41.

16. Robin Wood, *Hitchcock's Films* (New York: A. S. Barnes, 1965), pp. 118–19.

17. Donald Spoto, *The Dark Side of Genius: The Life of Alfred Hitchcock* (New York: Ballantine, 1983), p. 487.

18. Walter Evans, "Monster Movies: A Sexual Theory," *Journal of Popular Film*, Fall 1973, pp. 353–65; and Twitchell, *Dreadful Pleasures*.

19. S. S. Prawer, *Caligari's Children: The Film as Tale of Terror* (New York: Oxford University Press, 1980), pp. 272–73.

20. See Stephen Neale, *Genre* (London: British Film Institute, 1980), p. 61:

Most monsters tend, in fact, to be defined as "male," especially in so far as the objects of their desire are almost exclusively women. Simultaneously, it is women who become their primary victims. In this respect, it could well be maintained that it is women's sexuality, that which renders them desirable—but also threatening—to men, which constitutes the real problem that the horror cinema exists to explore, and which constitutes also and ultimately that which is really monstrous.

21. For a thorough and extremely useful discussion of the complex interaction of the social, economic, political, and artistic factors in the shaping of film history, including genres, see Robert C. Allen and Douglas Gomery, *Film History: Theory and Practice* (New York: Knopf, 1985), especially Chapter 4, "Aesthetic Film History."

22. See Martin Gratjahn, "Horror—Yes, It Can Do You Good," *Films and Filming*, November 1958, p. 9; and Morris Dickstein, "The Aesthetics of Fright," *American Film*, September 1980, pp. 32–37, 56–59.

23. Edrita Fried, *The Courage to Change* (New York: Grove Press, 1981), pp. 60, 86.

24. Tarratt, "Monsters from the Id," p. 38.

25. Twitchell calls the films "fables of sexual identity" (p. 7).

26. Robin Wood, "An Introduction to the American Horror Film," in *The American Nightmare* (Toronto: Festival of Festivals, 1979), pp. 14, 23.

## BIBLIOGRAPHICAL CHECKLIST

### Books

Britton, Andrew, et al. *American Nightmare: Essays on the Horror Film.* Toronto: Festival of Festivals, 1979.

Butler, Ivan. *Horror in the Cinema.* New York: Warner Paperback Library, 1970. (Originally published as *The Horror Film.*)

Clarens, Carlos. *An Illustrated History of the Horror Film.* New York: Putnam, 1967.

Daniels, Les. *Living in Fear: A History of Horror in the Mass Media.* New York: Charles Scribner's Sons, 1975.

Derry, Charles. *Dark Dreams: A Psychological History of the Modern Horror Film.* New York: A. S. Barnes, 1977.

Dillard, R.H.W. *Horror Films.* New York: Monarch, 1976.

Grant, Barry K. *Planks of Reason: Essays on the Horror Film.* Metuchen, N.J.: Scarecrow Press, 1984.

Huss, Roy, and T. J. Ross, eds. *Focus on the Horror Film.* Englewood Cliffs, N.J.: Prentice-Hall, 1972.

Prawer, S. S. *Caligari's Children: The Film as Tale of Terror.* New York: Oxford University Press, 1980.

Twitchell, James. *Dreadful Pleasures: An Anatomy of Modern Horror.* New York: Oxford University Press, 1985.

Waller, Gregory A. *The Living and the Undead.* Urbana: University of Illinois Press, 1986.

### Shorter Works

Alloway, Lawrence. "Monster Films," *Encounter,* January 1960, pp. 70–72. Repr. in Huss and Ross, *Focus on Horror Film,* pp. 121–24.

Brustein, Robert. "Film Chronicle: Reflections on Horror Movies," *Partisan Review,* Spring 1958, pp. 288–96.

Carroll, Noel. "Nightmare and the Horror Film: The Symbolic Biology of Fantastic Beings," *Film Quarterly,* Spring 1981, pp. 16–25.

Denne, John D. "Society and the Monster," *December,* nos. 2 and 3, 1967, pp. 180–83. Repr. in Huss and Ross, *Focus on Horror Film,* pp. 125–31.

Dickstein, Morris. "The Aesthetics of Fright," *American Film,* September 1980, pp. 32–37, 56–59.

Dillard, R.H.W. "Drawing the Circle: A Devolution of Values in Three Horror Films," *Film Journal,* January–March 1973, pp. 6–35.

———. "Even a Man Who Is Pure at Heart: Poetry and Danger in the Horror Film." In *Man and the Movies.* Ed. William R. Robinson. Baltimore: Penguin, 1967.

Durgnat, Raymond. "Scream Louder, Live Longer: An Introduction to Screen Violence," *Listener,* 3 December 1964, pp. 880–82.

Evans, Walter. "Monster Movies: A Sexual Theory," *Journal of Popular Film,* Fall 1973, pp. 353–65.

———. "Monster Movies and Rites of Initiation," *Journal of Popular Film,* Spring 1975, pp. 124–42.

Gratjahn, Martin. "Horror—Yes, It Can Do You Good," *Films and Filming,* November 1958, p. 9.

Greenberg, Harvey R. Chapter 9, "Horror and Science Fiction—The Sleep of Reason" (pp. 195–212); chapter 10, "The Sleep of Reason—II" (pp. 213–31); chapter 11, "The Sleep of Reason—III" (pp. 232–63). In his *The Movies on Your Mind.* New York: Saturday Review Press, 1975.

Kaminsky, Stuart. Chapter 7, "Psychological Considerations: Horror and Science Fiction." In his *American Film Genres.* Dayton, Ohio: Pflaum, 1974.

Kennedy, Harlan. "Things That Go Howl in the Id," *Film Comment,* March–April 1982, pp. 37–39.

Kennedy, X. J. "Who Killed King Kong?" *Dissent,* Spring 1960, n.p. Repr. in Huss and Ross, *Focus on the Horror Film,* pp. 106–9.

King, Stephen. Chapter 6, "The Modern American Horror Movie—Text and Subtext," and chapter 7, "The Horror Movie as Junk Food." In his *Danse Macabre.* New York: Everest House, 1981.

McConnell, Frank. "Rough Beast Slouching: A Note on Horror Movies," *Kenyon Review,* 1970, pp. 109–20. Repr. in Huss and Ross, *Focus on the Horror Film,* pp. 24–35.

Murphy, Brian. "Monster Movies: They Came from Beneath the Fifties," *Journal of Popular Film,* Winter 1972, pp. 31–44.

Pendo, Stephen. "Universal's Golden Age of Horror: 1931–41," *Films in Review,* March 1975, pp. 155–61.

Rockett, W. H. "The Door Ajar: Structure and Convention in Horror Films That Would Terrify," *Journal of Popular Film and Television,* Fall 1982, pp. 130–36.

Solomon, Stanley, Chapter 3, "The Nightmare World." In his *Beyond Formula: American Film Genres.* New York: Harcourt Brace Jovanovich, 1976.

Tarratt, Margaret. "Monsters from the Id," *Films and Filming,* December 1970 and January 1971, pp. 38–42 and 40–42. Repr. in *Film Genre: Theory and Criticism.* Ed. Barry K. Grant. Metuchen, N.J.: Scarecrow Press, 1977, pp. 161–81.

Telotte, J. P. "Faith and Idolatry in the Horror Film," *Literature/Film Quarterly,* Summer 1980, pp. 143–55.

———. "The Horror Mythos and Val Lewton's Isle of the Dead," *Journal of Popular Film and Television,* Fall 1982, pp. 119–29.

———. "Through a Pumpkin's Eye: The Reflexive Nature of Horror," *Literature/Film Quarterly,* Summer 1982, pp. 139–49.

Tudor, Andrew, "Horror Movies." In his *Image and Influence: Studies in the Sociology of Film.* New York: St. Martin's Press, 1974, pp. 203–12, 223–25.

White, Dennis L. "The Poetics of Horror," *Cinema Journal,* Spring 1971, pp. 1–18. Repr. in *Film Genre: Theory and Criticism.* Ed. Barry K. Grant. Metuchen, N.J.: Scarecrow Press, 1977, pp. 124–44.

Williams, Tony. "Horror in the Family," *Focus on Film,* October 1980, pp. 14–20.

Wood, Robin. "Gods and Monsters," *Film Comment*, September–October 1978, pp. 19–25. Repr. in Britton, *American Nightmare*, pp. 75–86.
———. "Neglected Nightmares," *Film Comment*, March–April 1980, pp. 24–32.
———. "Return of the Repressed," *Film Comment*, July–August 1978, pp. 24–32. Repr. in Britton, *American Nightmare*, pp. 7–28.

## SELECTED FILMOGRAPHY

1931    *Dracula* (75 minutes).
Universal. Producer: Carl Laemmle, Jr. Director: Tod Browning. Screenplay: Garrett Fort, from play by Hamilton Deane and John L. Balderston and novel by Bram Stoker. Photography: Karl Freund. Art Direction: Charles D. Hall. Makeup: Jack Pierce. Editing: Milton Carruth. Cast: Bela Lugosi (Count Dracula), Helen Chandler (Mina Seward), David Manners (Jonathan Harker), Edward Van Sloan (Dr. Van Helsing), Dwight Frye (Renfield), Herbert Bunston (Dr. Seward), Frances Dade (Lucy Weston), Charles Gerrard (Martin).

*Frankenstein* (71 minutes).
Universal. Producer: Carl Laemmle, Jr. Director: James Whale. Screenplay: Richard Schayer, Francis Edwards Faragoh, Garrett Fort, Robert Florey, and John L. Balderston, from play by Peggy Webling and novel by Mary Shelley. Photography: Arthur Edeson. Art Direction: Charles D. Hall. Makeup: Jack Pierce. Cast: Boris Karloff (the Monster), Colin Clive (Dr. Henry Frankenstein), Mae Clarke (Elizabeth), Frederick Kerr (Baron Frankenstein), Edward Van Sloan (Dr. Waldman), John Boles (Victor Morris), Dwight Frye (Fritz).

1932    *Freaks* (61 minutes).
MGM. Producer/Director: Tod Browning. Screenplay: Leon Gordon and Willis Goldbeck, from a story by Tod Robbins. Photography: Merritt B. Gerstad. Art Direction: Cedric Gibbons. Musical Direction: Gavin Barns. Cast: Olga Baclanova (Cleopatra), Harry Earles (Hans), Henry Victor (Hercules), Leila Hyams (Venus), Roscoe Ates (Roscoe), Daisy Earles (Freida), Wallace Ford (Phroso, the clown), Daisy and Violet Hilton (Siamese twins), Edward Brophy and Matt McHugh (Rollo brothers), Prince Randian (the Living Torso).

1933    *King Kong* (100 minutes).
RKO. Producer: David O. Selznick. Directors: Merian C. Cooper and Ernest B. Schoedsack. Screenplay: Ruth Rose and James Creelman, from story by Edgar Wallace and Merian C. Cooper. Photography: Edward Lindon, Vernon L. Walker, and J. O. Taylor. Art Direction: Carroll Clark and Al Herman. Special Effects: Willis O'Brien. Music: Max Steiner. Cast: Fay Wray (Ann Darrow), Robert Armstrong (Carl Denham), Bruce Cabot (Jack Driscoll), Frank Reicher (Captain Englehorn), Sam Hardy (Weston), Noble Johnson (Native Chief), James Flavin (Briggs).

1935    *Bride of Frankenstein* (80 minutes).
Universal. Producer: Carl Laemmle, Jr. Director: James Whale. Screenplay: William Hurlbut and John Balderston. Photography: John Mescall. Art Direction: Charles D. Hall. Special Effects: John P. Fulton. Makeup: Jack Pierce. Editing: Ted Kent and Maurice Pivar. Music: Franz Waxman. Cast: Colin Clive

(Dr. Henry Frankenstein), Boris Karloff (the Monster), Elsa Lanchester (Mary Shelley and the Bride), Ernest Thesiger (Dr. Septimus Pretorius), O. P. Heggie (Blind Hermit), Dwight Frye (Karl), Valerie Hobson (Elizabeth Frankenstein), Una O'Connor (Minnie), E. E. Clive (Burgomeister), Gavin Gordon (Lord Byron), Douglas Walton (Percy Shelley).

1942    *Cat People* (75 minutes).
RKO. Producer: Val Lewton. Director: Jacques Tourneur. Screenplay: DeWitt Bodeen. Photography: Nicholas Musuraca. Art Direction: Albert D'Agostino and Walter E. Keller. Music: Roy Webb. Cast: Simone Simon (Irene Dubrovna), Kent Smith (Oliver Reed), Jane Randolph (Alice Moore), Tom Conway (Dr. Judd), Alan Napier (Carver), Jack Holt (Commodore), Elizabeth Russell (Barbara Farren), Alec Craig (zookeeper).

1951    *The Thing* (87 minutes).
RKO/Winchester. Producer: Howard Hawks. Directors: Howard Hawks and Christian Nyby. Screenplay: Charles Lederer, from story by John W. Campbell, Jr. Photography: Russell Harlan. Art Direction: Albert D'Agostino and John J. Hughes. Special Effects: Donald Stewart and Linwood Dunk. Music: Dmitri Tiomkin. Cast: Kenneth Tobey (Captain Hendry), Margaret Sheridan (Nikki Nicholson), James Young (Lt. Dykes), Dewey Martin (Sgt. Bob), Paul Frees (Dr. Voorhees), Robert Cornthwaite (Dr. Carrington), Douglas Spencer (Ned Scott), Robert Nichols (Lt. MacPherson), Eduard Franz (Dr. Stern), John Dierkes (Dr. Chapman), James Arness (The Thing), William Self (Corporal Barnes).

1956    *Invasion of the Body Snatchers* (80 minutes).
Allied Artists. Producer: Walter Wanger. Director: Don Siegel. Screenplay: Daniel Mainwaring, from "The Body Snatchers" by Jack Finney. Photography: Ellsworth Fredricks. Art Direction: Edward Haworth. Music: Carmen Dragon. Cast: Kevin McCarthy (Dr. Miles Bennell), Dana Wynter (Becky Driscoll), King Donovan (Jack Belicec), Carolyn Jones (Theodora Belicec), Larry Gates (Dr. Kaufman), Ralph Dumke (Sheriff Grivett), Jean Willes (Sally Withers), Sam Peckinpah (Charlie Buckholtz), Virginia Christine (Wilma Lentz), Bobby Clarke (Jimmy Grimaldi), Beatrice Maude (Grandma Grimaldi), Everett Glass (Dr. Pursey), Richard Deacon (Dr. Bassett), Whit Bissell (Dr. Hill), Dabbs Greer (Mac).

1960    *Psycho* (109 minutes).
Paramount/Shamley. Producer/Director: Alfred Hitchcock. Screenplay: Joseph Stefano, from book by Robert Bloch. Photography: John L. Russell. Art Direction: Joseph Hurley, Robert Clatworthy, and George Milo. Special Effects: Clarence Champagne. Editing: George Tomasini. Music: Bernard Herrmann. Cast: Anthony Perkins (Norman Bates), Janet Leigh (Marion Crane), Vera Miles (Lila Crane), John Gavin (Sam Loomis), Martin Balsam (Milton Arbogast), John McIntire (Sheriff Chambers), Frank Albertson (Tom Cassidy), Simon Oakland (Dr. Richmond), Vaughn Taylor (George Lowery), John Anderson (car salesman), Patricia Hitchcock (Caroline).

1963    *The Birds* (120 minutes).
Universal. Producer/Director: Alfred Hitchcock. Screenplay: Evan Hunter, from story by Daphne du Maurier. Photography: Robert Burks. Art Direction: Robert Boyle. Special Effects: Lawrence A. Hampton. Editing: George Tomasini. Sound

Consultant: Bernard Herrmann. Cast: Rod Taylor (Mitch Brenner), Tippi Hedren (Melanie Daniels), Jessica Tandy (Mrs. Brenner), Suzanne Pleshette (Annie Hayworth), Veronica Cartwright (Cathy Brenner), Ethel Griffies (Mrs. Bundy), Charles McGraw (Sebastian Sholes), Ruth McDevitt (Mrs. MacGruder).

1968    *Night of the Living Dead* (90 minutes).
Continental/Image 10. Producers: Russell Streiner and Karl Hardman. Director/ Photography: George Romero. Screenplay: John A. Russo and George Romero. Special Effects: Regis Survinski and Tony Pantanello. Cast: Judith O'Dea (Barbara), Russell Streiner (Johnny), Karl Hardman (Harry), Duane Jones (Ben), Keth Wayne (Tom), Judith Ridley (Judy), Kyra Schon (Karen), Marilyn Eastman (Helen).

1973    *It's Alive* (91 minutes).
Warner Brothers/Larco. Producer/Director/Screenplay: Larry Cohen. Photography: Fenton Hamilton. Special Makeup Effects: Rick Baker. Editing: Peter Honess. Music: Bernard Herrmann. Cast: John Ryan (Frank Davies), Sharon Farrell (Lenore Davies), James Dixon (Detective Perkins), Michael Ansara (the Captain), Andrew Duggan (Dr. Perry), Guy Stockwell (Clayton), William Wellman, Jr. (Charlie), Robert Emhardt (the Executive).

1974    *The Texas Chain Saw Massacre* (81 minutes).
New Line/Bryanston/Vortex. Producer/Director: Tobe Hooper. Screenplay: Tobe Hooper and Kim Henkel. Photography: Daniel Pearl. Art Direction: Robert A. Burns. Special Makeup: W. E. Barnes. Editing: Sallye Richardson and Larry Carroll. Music: Tobe Hooper and Wayne Bell. Cast: Marilyn Burns (Sally Hardesty), Paul A. Partain (Franklin Hardesty), Gunnar Hansen (Leatherface), Allen Danziger (Jerry), Teri McMinn (Pam), William Vail (Kirk), Edwin Neal (hitchhiker), Jim Siedow (old man), John Dugan (grandfather).

1981    *Ms. 45* (84 minutes).
Rochelle/Navaron. Producer: Rochelle Weisberg. Director: Abel Ferrara. Screenplay: Nicholas St. John. Photography: James Momel. Art Direction: Ruben Masters. Editing: Christopher Andrews. Music: Joe Delia. Cast: Zoe Tamerlis (Thana), Albert Sinkys (Albert), Darlene Stuto (Laurie), Helen McGara (Carol), Nike Zachmandglou (Pamela), Jimmy Laine (first rapist), Peter Yellen (burglar), Editta Sherman (Mrs. Nasone), S. Edward Singer (photographer), Jack Thibeau (man in bar).

# 13

## Science Fiction

VIVIAN SOBCHACK

"The essence of technology is nothing technological."
—Martin Heidegger, "The Question of Technology,"
in *Martin Heidegger: Basic Writings.*

The American science fiction (SF) film has always taken as its distinctive generic task the poetic mapping of social relations as they are created and changed by new technological modes of "being-in-the-world." Thus, SF is a genre which tends to be less concerned with individual psychology and personal crises than it is with public situation and social crises. Its basic plot conflicts arise from the unexpected and broad cultural consequences of technological accomplishment, and its dramatic action tests the ability of society and its institutions to withstand or embrace the challenge of radical (and usually global) transformation.

As a result of this focus, the narrative scope of the SF film is temporally and spatially macrocosmic and fluid rather than microcosmic and stable. The genre's extrapolative and speculative time travels occur across a range of imagined presents, pasts, and futures—from the vast temporal (as well as spatial) journey of *2001: A Space Odyssey* (1968) to the "long, long ago . . . in a galaxy far, far away" of *Star Wars* (1977). As fluidly, the genre locates itself in places as exotic and extraterrestrial as the war-torn imaginary planet Metaluna in *This Island Earth* (1955), or as familiar and mundane as the suburbs of Muncie, Indiana, in *Close Encounters of the Third Kind* (1977).

Not circumscribed by determinate temporal and spatial boundaries like those which mark off the western or the gangster film, the iconography of the SF film is also fluid and plastic. While we tend to characterize SF in terms of its spaceships, robots, extraterrestrials, and special effects, these are not necessary to the genre, and even when they do appear, their visualization and narrative meaning are transformed from film to film. Rather than constituting a determinate and specific iconography, such figures evoke not their own generic consistency, but the general "feel" of the genre—its broad focus on the transformational powers of advanced science and applied technology and its narrative and visual attempts to make these sensible. Indeed, if there is any visual constancy to the SF film, it corresponds to the genre's consistent thematic emphases on the wonderfully functional and functionally wonderful aspects of advanced science and technology. The genre's primary visual project is to produce wondrous and unfamiliar imagery—and it tends to do so according to two quite distinct (and often budget-dependent) formal strategies.

The big-budget SF films usually foreground not only "brave new worlds" and spectacular machinery, but also the latest technological developments in the cinema's own means of expression. Their privileged displays of flamboyant and novel "special effects" function to challenge and transform not only the film's narrative world but also the very stability and complacency of the medium itself. The fact that both the narrative and the cinema are figuratively and literally able to *contain* such awesome technological power informs the big-budget SF film with a certain optimism—even when its narratives are sometimes cautionary about what the technologized future holds in store for us. Certainly, this optimism about the transformational wonders and opportunities offered by advanced technology is apparent in such celebratory works as the early *Destination Moon* (1950) or the more recent *Close Encounters of the Third Kind*. However, a degree of technological optimism also informs those films whose narratives figure advanced technology as alien or alienating. That is, even though *War of the Worlds* (1953) visualizes the powerful machinery of the invading Martians as annihilatingly alien, even though *Forbidden Planet* (1956) suggests that advanced technology will ultimately give concrete form and expression to our most primal and destructive impulses, and even though *Alien* (1979) or *Blade Runner* (1982) criticizes a cold, corporate, and technologized future in which human life has minimal value, each of these films also tends to celebrate the transformative power and beauty of this technology and to offer us a vision of it which resonates with thrilling and positive poetic force.

In contrast, lower-budget SF seems informed by pessimism or irony. Less likely to use elaborate special effects to emphasize the technologically transformed nature of modern existence, the visual strategy of films like *It Came from Outer Space* (1953), *Them!* (1954), or more recent works like *Repo Man* (1984) and *The Brother from Another Planet* (1984) is a negative one. In an attempt to create imagery at which we will wonder, these films work to disrupt our comfortable relations with the terrestrial world, to alienate us from what first seem completely familiar landscapes, objects, animals, and people. *It Came from Outer Space* and *Them!* are exemplary of the negative poetics of the generally low-budget SF films of the 1950s. Their images create a wonderfully anxious pessimism about the future as they estrange both the narratives' protagonists and the films' spectators from the very terrestrial ground beneath their feet and transform the Earth itself into an alien and unknown planet which harbors invasive extraterrestrials or radiation-induced insect mutations. The visual strategy of these films is to reenergize the commonplace, to constitute a specular paranoia toward the familiar. Much more recent low-budget films like *Liquid Sky* (1983) and *Repo Man* borrow upon the strategy of their low-budget 1950s counterparts, but amend 1950s pessimism and paranoia to an attitude more representative of the "postmodern" culture of the 1980s.[1] These films evidence reflexive irony toward big-budget SF's privileging of "special" effects and technological "novelty" in a society so totally technologized and commodified that alien-ation and cultural estrangement are as unspecial and familiar as they still are "awesome." Pessimism and paranoia become re-signed as unflappable curiosity about the constant transformations which mark contemporary American culture as lived "science fiction." The extraterrestrials in both these films have nothing on the terrestrials—who look and act as alien and alienated as might any visitors from outer space. Indeed, elaborating upon the initial defamiliarization and transformation of "mother" Earth by their 1950s predecessors, these films begin with the planetary transformation long accomplished: Earth *is* outer space, and a Los Angeles all-night convenience store and New York's Harlem are estranged landscapes worthy of the most alien planet.

In sum, the SF film gives concrete narrative shape and visible form to our changing historical imagination of social progress and disaster, and to the ambiguities of being human in a world where advanced technology has altered both the contours and meaning of personal and social existence. Its very spatial and temporal fluidity, its visual plasticity and focus on technological transformation, mark SF not merely as a genre of the fantastic but also as the film genre most readily able to symbolically respond to and poetically figure the anxieties and hopes that inform its contemporaneous historical context.

It is hardly surprising, then, that the American SF film was first produced in quantity and first critically acknowledged as a cinematic grouping in the early 1950s.[2] The genre initially emerges and flourishes as a symbolic response to the period's most visible and culturally significant technological markers: the inconceivably powerful atomic and hydrogen bombs; the incomprehensibly rational and then still "impersonal" (and frighteningly emotionless) computer; and the magical and instantaneous electronic representations of television. The "essence" of these technological innovations were "more than technological." Their existence radically altered not only the everyday life-world of Americans in the 1950s, but also constituted a new recognition of the vast power and consequences of science and technology, a new consciousness of time and space, a new sense of global community, of physical and geographical vulnerability, and of political enmity—the latter culturally articulated in the novel term *Cold War*. Within this newly technologized, sociopolitical context, the SF films of the 1950s poetically figure its wonderful and fearsome *novelty* and symbolically dramatize both its new pleasures and its new forms of cultural "alien-ation."

The vision of these films, whether celebratory or paranoid, is markedly cool—
"either bearing documentary 'witness' to the new world space and technology,
or manifesting visual response in a removed and estranged state of 'undecida-
bility' as to what sort of affective behavior might be appropriate in such suddenly original situations."[3] Indeed, the two key films which together initiated
the genre represent the period's strong ambivalence toward a radically transformed existence which, on the one hand, seemed to offer the expansive promise of progress, discovery, and a new colonialism and, on the other, opened up
the threatening possibilities of massive social change, foreign invasion, and
even total human extinction.

*Destination Moon* celebrated American science, technology, and capitalist
expansion in a narrative which led to the moon, but suggested future conquest
of the stars. Its images emphasizing the literally shiny novelty of futuristic
technology and the beauty of new cosmic frontiers, the film was meticulously
concerned with conveying both its own prophetic authenticity and the realistic
wonders of scientific achievement. Indeed, its set design and special effects
drew upon the expertise of a real astronomical artist and an actual rocket designer. Shot in Technicolor on a relatively large budget and using a range of
special effects which foregrounded the liberation of human being and vision
from terrestrial gravity and an earthbound perspective, *Destination Moon*'s was
a positive vision of the technologically transformed future.

In contrast, *The Thing* (1951) emphasized the period's pessimism and fear
about the consequences of new scientific discoveries and the application of
advanced technology. It dramatized terrestrial sky and space as negatively open
and vulnerable to penetration, invasion, and colonization by an alien Other. Set
in the empty and hostile Arctic where a spaceship is discovered beneath the ice
and its extraterrestrial passenger accidentally "thawed out," xenophobic in its
figuration of the alien as a murderous "creature," and cautionary about the
dangers of scientific curiosity, *The Thing* is paranoid in both narrative and
style. While its plot centers around how a team of "regular guys" in the U.S.
Air Force battle this "intelligent vegetable" against the wishes of an "obsessed" scientist, its tone is dark and its mise-en-scène and editorial style construct a deep mistrust of off-screen space. Shot in black and white on a relatively low budget, using few special effects, earthbound and claustrophobic,
*The Thing*'s negative vision of the future ended with the warning message:
"Keep watching the skies."

These two films set the boundaries and tonal range for most of the films
which followed to constitute what now (through hindsight) might be called the
first Golden Age of the American SF film. But for some few exceptions like
*War of the Worlds* (1953) and *Invaders from Mars* (1953) which were earthbound nightmares of alien invasion, the legacy of the big-budget, Technicolor,
special effects–laden *Destination Moon* were films that visually went "where
no man has gone before"—into outer space and alternate times. And even
when the narratives of these films expressed ambivalence about the ultimate

consequences of advanced (and alien) technology, their mise-en-scène simultaneously celebrated that technology and elaborated it in awesome and poetic images of graceful, glitteringly new machinery and startlingly beautiful extraterrestrial landscapes and spacescapes. There were far fewer of these films produced, however, than those cautionary films which echoed the thematics and visual style initiated by *The Thing*.

Dramatizing what Susan Sontag has called "the imagination of disaster," the poetry of one group of these films derived from "the aesthetics of destruction," from "the peculiar beauties to be found in wreaking havoc, making a mess."[4] Black and white visions of massive urban destruction featured atomically awakened or mutated creatures which mindlessly stomped cities and transformed social order into mass chaos. Embodying the threat of nuclear annihilation in generally regressive and primal forms, these creatures most often took the shape of insects or prehistoric beasts, and the films bore titles like *The Beast from 20,000 Fathoms* (1953), *Tarantula* (1955), *It Came from Beneath the Sea* (1955), *The Deadly Mantis* (1957), and *The Black Scorpion* (1957). Breeding in the drains under Los Angeles, destroying well-known urban landmarks like Coney Island, wreaking mass havoc and causing mass hysteria, these creatures condensed in their gigantic size, primitive biology, and acts of mindless destruction not only the affective charge of a massive and annihilating energy out of control and run amok, but also physically evoked a sense of a primal, pre- (and post-) human-inhabited Earth. Although generated by the bomb, then, the very primal nature of the creatures displaced attention from their technologically generated return from civilization's repressed prehistory. This displacement of attention (and responsibility) allowed, on the one hand, for the symbolic representation of technological catastrophe and, on the other, for a technological salvation. As Brian Murphy points out: "Those beasts and things . . . , we could deal with them only by going back to the very people who spawned them: the scientists working 'in full cooperation' (such an important word, that 'cooperation') with the military."[5] It was the scientists and the military who used advanced technology against the destructive creature (just as they had against the Japanese): to bomb it, incinerate it, or poison it with "radioactive isotopes." Ritual in structure and mythic in function, these creature films dramatized and narratively (if not culturally) resolved the period's intense and contradictory feelings about science, advanced technology, and their historically destructive (and military) applications.[6]

A second group of low-budget 1950s films gave symbolic shape and drama to another kind of historically located anxiety—the fear of "alien" invasion, of being "taken over" by a powerful and inhuman Other who would radically alter human (and American) consciousness. Again, the imagery of the films condensed and displaced the real historical sources of such cultural anxiety: the Cold War with the Soviets—which might, at any moment, turn radioactively "hot" and obliterate humanity; Communism—(mis)understood as a dehumanizing program to flatten and homogenize human individuality, will, and emotion, and intent on infiltrating and invisibly "taking over" the free world; "brainwashing"—a fascinating and yet terrifying new and war-related articulation of mind control. These anxieties were given concrete form in two types of "invasion" dramas.

The first, like the creature films, drew upon the "aesthetics of destruction" to feature urban America under attack from alien invaders whose weaponry blasted the likes of Hoover Dam, razed New York City, or demolished sacred national monuments in Washington, D.C. In rare cases like *Invasion U.S.A.* (1952), the "aliens" were not extraterrestrials, but unspecified "foreigners" (visually coded, if not narratively identified, as Russians). More often, however, invasion was dramatized as global, and the enemy was figured as extraterrestrial and a threat to all nations on the planet. Again and again, films like *Earth vs. the Flying Saucers* (1956) condense the culture's xenophobia, its fear of the scope of atomic warfare and its consequent "yearning for peace," and its contradictory "hunger for a 'good war,' which poses no moral problems" and leads to a "UN fantasy . . . of united warfare" as resolution.[7] Indeed, only one SF film of the 1950s—*The Day the Earth Stood Still* (1951)—dared to focus on the period's intense and often hysterical xenophobia, and to challenge its fantasy of united warfare as the ground for international peace. One of the first SF films of the decade, featuring an alien protagonist and terrestrial villains, speaking out against irrational fear and pointing to the vast scope of nuclear destruction, *The Day the Earth Stood Still* is an SF classic, but had little thematic influence on the xenophobic films which immediately followed it.[8]

The second type of "invasion" film was more visually paranoid and negative in both its style and narratives. *Invaders from Mars* (exceptional for its color), *It Came from Outer Space* (1953), *Invasion of the Body Snatchers* (1956), *It Conquered the World* (1956), and *The Day Mars Invaded the Earth* (1963) focus on an insidious and invisible alien invasion and locate themselves in the ordinary and familiar world of small-town and suburban America. Poetically condensing and displacing the fear of communist infiltration and brainwashing, and the fear of the dehumanizing aspects of that superrationality represented by scientists and their technology, the aliens in these films "take on" human form and "take over" human minds. They are figured as fathers and mothers and Uncle Ira, as telephone linemen and the cop on the beat, as psychiatrists and as lovers.

Those "taken over" are marked as alien not by flamboyant and powerful displays of their difference, but rather by their small failures of appropriately human response to ordinary human situations. Pretending to be human, they fail in the most visibly subtle and negative of ways (not blinking at the sun, not responding passionately enough to a kiss), and consequently cause a kind of visual paranoia in the spectator as well as in the films' protagonists (who, usually not believed when they first discover the spreading menace, spend most of the narrative's time trying to convince others they are not paranoid and that the threat is real). The invasion in these films is quietly pervasive, and the goal of the aliens seems not only to be the takeover of the planet, but also the transformation of human beings into more "rational" and less "emotional" creatures. Expressing extremely ambivalent feelings about the new implications of both human reason and emotion in a nuclear age, the aliens in these films croon chilling (but also appealing) promises which speak to the cultural anxieties and desires of the 1950s: "Love, desire, ambition, faith. Without them, life is so simple" (this from *Invasion of the Body Snatchers,* arguably the best of these paranoid fantasies).

By the end of the 1950s, the relative popularity of SF had severely declined. There were many reasons; the most overt was that an increasing number of SF films were made on increasingly low budgets, were increasingly repetitious, and were increasingly produced as B movies slanted toward an adolescent audience. Less obvious was the economic pressure television exercised on a film industry which could no longer count on an entertainment monopoly or a homogenous family audience. The traditional studio system was breaking down, and although the industry had tried to regain its former primacy by introducing new technology unavailable to television (wide-screen and 3-D), it was not in a financial position to support those genres whose special needs cost extra money. (Along with SF, the musical also suffered a decline in the 1960s.)

We might also speculate that the SF film lost much of its symbolic and poetic force because while it tended to repeat and replicate itself on lower and lower budgets and with less and less imagination, its historical context was rapidly changing. Cold War tensions eased in the 1960s, but domestic problems were on the increase. The "aliens" that worried Americans now were closer to home: blacks who demanded their civil rights, and flower children who "spaced out" and rejected their parents' values. As well, we had grown used to living with the bomb and in a technological world no longer quite so new and shiny and unfamiliar. America's real space program in the 1960s far outpaced changes in its cinematic space program, culminating in the documentary (and televised) representation of the first manned moon-landing in 1968 (a momentous year for many other cultural reasons as well). These events challenged the now-dated futurism of SF with an intensely present reality, but one which was also in many ways socially and politically peripheral. Thrilling as transmissions from space were to all who watched, our present and future were more terrestrially bound—to an ambiguous and unpopular war in Southeast Asia that clearly contradicted old, optimistic SF fantasies about American might, colonial expansion, and economic opportunism, and to massive civil unrest marked by assassinations, bloody riots and demonstrations, and general disenchantment with cultural institutions from the government to the family.

Although there were a number of SF films released from the 1960s to the mid-1970s, some of which attempted (perhaps too successfully) the expression of contemporaneous and domestic social concerns, the genre itself seemed to slip from view—except for the epic *2001: A Space Odyssey* which, while not extraordinarily popular at the box office, did stand in the public consciousness and seemed to set a new cinematic standard for SF. Not only were its special effects elaborately and meticulously done, but the film's intellectual demands suggested that SF could be made for adults. Nonetheless, *2001* was a singular phenomenon and the SF films that followed shared neither its scope nor its open and transformational vision of the future. Indeed, SF's general lack of success at the box office may have been due to its narrative and visual inability to sufficiently transform and displace current and terrestrial concerns. Audiences of the period were hardly keen on cinematic visions which badly represented the end of frontiers and the negative aftermath of technological progress. Speaking about the films released between 1968's *2001* and 1977's blockbuster *Star Wars,* Joan F. Dean points to the genre's major themes between 1970 and 1977 as overpopulation, food shortages, ecology, and old age. "Consequently," she tells us, "space travel appeared only infrequently" and "extraterrestrial visitors to this planet diminished in number."[9]

Yet in 1977 it was precisely space travel and extraterrestrial visitors that reenergized the genre in the two works which mark the renaissance of the SF film and begin its second Golden Age: *Star Wars* and *Close Encounters of the Third Kind.* These films were suddenly and radically different in narrative focus and style from either their 1950s counterparts or their more recent and baleful predecessors. Both films seemed unprecedentedly hopeful about human existence and cultural transformation, and both joyfully embraced what used to be the threateningly different and repulsive Other. Mechanical or biological, alien beings were visualized as cuddly if also powerful innocents. Both films were also playful in ways that SF had never been playful before—purposefully humorous in part, and often reflexive about their own generic existence. As well, both films were hardly cool and detached in their vision, or cautionary and pessimistic about advanced technology. All the new hardware seemed as comfortable as it was novel, and was figured more for its aesthetic and emotional appeal than for its scientific plausibility. In this regard, both *Star Wars* and *Close Encounters* also evidenced a generically original "emotionalism"— transforming what used to be an "objective" vision of high technology and display of special effects into a "subjective" expression of new technological "highs" and their sublimely pleasurable special "affect." And while one might have expected this kind of euphoric optimism in a big-budget SF film, it became apparent as the genre flourished that low-budget SF also had a new, playful, and self-conscious tone, also shared delight at what amounted to sublimely visible forms of literally alien-ated affect. (An independent film released in 1986 aptly bears the playful title *UFOria.*)

After the huge successes of *Star Wars* and *Close Encounters,* SF again became mainstream family entertainment—and big business. Indeed, it is interesting to speculate on the many possible cultural reasons for the genre's changes and its renaissance in popularity, but clearly one major factor was economic. The new sentimental SF film had box-office appeal across a range of previously fragmented audiences. The *Star Wars* trilogy, the *Star Trek* movies, films like *E.T.: The Extraterrestrial* (1982), *Starman* (1984), *Back to the Future* and *Cocoon* (both 1985) were popular not only with children and adolescents, but also with adults who longed to regain an innocence and hope lost to years of enforced historical sophistication and despair. These films combined regressive nostalgia with reflexivity—promoting both identification with childhood innocence, and awareness that such innocence was less a fact of life than a figment of past textual imagination.

If there was any challenge to the *Boy's Life* vision initiated by *Star Wars* and *Close Encounters,* it came not from those few SF films which resonated with 1950s paranoia (several of them remakes of 1950s films), but from films which evidenced another and less squeaky clean form of nostalgia. In their visual conservation and celebration of urban waste and material clutter, these SF films have been called postindustrial, but might be more properly characterized as postmodern. Their nostalgia is, on the one hand, often intertextual; although often set in the future, the films tend to refer backward to a stylistic past—particularly to the urban darkness of 1940s film noir. On the other hand, their nostalgia also takes a most material form. Although they may contain certain cautionary and critical narrative elements (as do *Blade Runner,* 1982, and *The Terminator,* 1984), they nostalgically collect, save, and recycle bits and pieces of an advanced technology and material culture which are always already figured as so familiar that they're old. Unlike those films of the 1970s which figured overpopulation and pollution as both a narrative and visible problem, films like *Blade Runner* take them narratively for granted, but visibly *eroticize* their negative material effects. Garbage, junk, exhaust, acid rain, and urban squalor are visualized as beautiful, and the "alienation of daily life in the city" is presented to the spectator in a vision filled with "a strange new hallucinatory exhilaration."[10]

This visual pleasure in collection, in gathering together bits and pieces of material culture in surprising and often unmotivated relation, is even more evident in those SF films made on the margins of the industry and the genre. Delighting in the totalized alien-ation of a fully industrialized, commodified, and media-conscious culture, films like *Liquid Sky, Strange Invaders* (both 1983), *The Adventures of Buckaroo Banzai, Night of the Comet, Repo Man* (all 1984), and *UFOria,* radically articulate the very "science-fictionalization" of American culture. In these films, everyday life is extraterrestrially strange (witness "Hawaiian Days" in the local supermarket) and everyone is marvelously freaky and alien (from punkers to repo men, to religious fanatics, to readers of the *National Enquirer*).

In sum, the reemergence of SF as a popular genre in the mid-1970s and its continued success in the 1980s offers us new symbolic maps of our social relationship to others in what has become the familiarity (rather than the novelty) of a totally technologized world. One map posits and sentimentalizes a simpler and more innocent world, one in which technology is benign and even emotionalized, in which cultural Others are just like us. The other map posits and celebrates a world so complex, so heterogeneous, so totally "affected" by technology, that novelty and constant transformation are familiar—and nothing is especially alien, even if everything is sublimely strange. Indeed, now the aliens are us.

## BIBLIOGRAPHICAL OVERVIEW

Substantive critical literature about the American SF film is relatively sparse. Most of the serious work done on the genre has appeared only in the last decade or so—generally corresponding to the genre's renaissance in 1977, and to the growing influence of structuralist, psychoanalytic, and Marxist methods of textual analysis on cinema studies. With some few exceptions, most of the books available on SF film to this time were picture books pitched to fans rather than to scholars. Indeed, until recently, film scholars have tended to take a fairly contemptuous attitude toward the SF film—possibly because of the genre's own poetic decline during the 1960s (the decade in which cinema studies and scholarly publication on film began to flourish), and possibly because there were not yet critical methods sufficient to the genre's structural and ideological complexity.

There are, therefore, very few sustained book-length explorations of the SF film written in English. John Baxter's *Science Fiction in the Cinema* (1970) was the first major work to provide a thoughtful overview of the genre's major themes and films, but its broad and international scope also limited the depth of its analysis as it surveyed films from Georges Méliès's *A Trip to the Moon* (1902) to Kubrick's *2001: A Space Odyssey* (1968). Nonetheless, Baxter's work remains useful—not only for its intelligent identification of generic themes and motifs, but also for some of its insights and its initial—if contentious—discussion of the differences between SF film and literature. As well, Baxter is one of the first critics to point to a major source of the genre's power. He tells us that "whatever its sociological importance, SF cinema is basically a sensuous medium. It is the poetry of the atomic age, a shorthand evocation of the pressures that are making us what we are and will be." [11] The book is organized in general accordance with the genre's chronological development in chapters also usefully stressing major themes; thus, headings range from "First Contact" and "Utopischefilme" through "The End of the World, Plus Big Supporting Programme" to "Renaissance in *2001*." There is a brief bibliography, even briefer filmography, and unfortunately no index.

Following Baxter's work and echoing its broad international scope and general thematic emphases, John Brosnan's *Future Tense: The Cinema of Science Fiction* appeared in 1978. His chapters also are arranged chronologically, beginning with "Yesterday's Tomorrow (1900–30)" and ending with "A Close Encounter with Star Wars (1977–78)." Brosnan's unique elaborations on Baxter are found in his informative, if anecdotal, discussions of production details and in his accessible technical descriptions of special effects, a subject about which he had previously published a book.[12] Also useful is a special appendix: a "videography" of SF on television and an index. Despite all its virtues and its obvious fascination with the films, *Future Tense* nonetheless continues *Science Fiction in the Cinema*'s negative comparisons of SF film with SF literature, and its relatively superficial analyses of the genre's plots and themes.

It is to these sorts of prejudiced comparisons and surface descriptions that Vivian Sobchack's *The Limits of Infinity: The American Science Fiction Film, 1950–75* (1980) attempts to respond. Narrowing the broad focus of previous books, the work deals only with the American SF film and only with its (then) major period of production. It attempts a structural analysis not only of the films' themes but also of their generically particular social functions and formal aesthetics. Thus, the first chapter, "The Limits of the Genre: Definitions and Themes," discusses the films' thematic specificity and social function in relation not only to SF literature but also to the cinematic genres of fantasy and horror. The second, "Images of Wonder: The Look of Science Fiction," analyzes the implications of the plasticity of the genre's iconography and the specific visual functions of the genre's imagery, with an emphasis on how wondrous imagery is created through speculation and extrapolation, through the cinematic subversion of the mundane and familiar, and through an "aesthetics of collision" constituted by a mise-en-scène in which both the familiar and the fantastic are visibly brought together. The third chapter, "The Leaden Echo and the Golden Echo: The Sounds of Science Fiction," discusses the strange banality or pretensiousness of SF dialogue as a peculiar strategy by which the genre authenticates or grounds its fantastic imagery, and also describes the way in which spoken language is transformed—not only by its context but also in its very substance. Music and sound effects are also analyzed in terms of their generic functions. An expanded edition of the book, newly titled *Screening Space: The American Science Fiction Film* (1987), not only surveys those SF films released after 1975 in an added chapter, "Postfuturism," but also focuses on the ideological implications of the genre's new aesthetics, particularly as they relate to a "postmodern" world whose cultural logic has been transformed by both advanced technology and late capitalism.

One subsequent book-length study of the genre also deserves mention: Bill Warren's *Keep Watching the Skies! American Science Fiction Movies of the Fifties, Volume I, 1950–1957* (1982). It is a chatty but focused survey of films released in these peak years of early SF production, and although it is more evaluative than analytic in approach, it also often transcends its aficionado perspective to provide a wealth of valuable description and production information. That it has no bibliography is an indication of its casual attention to previous scholarship on the genre, but it makes up for this oversight with several extremely useful appendices: one a filmography; one on the films' order of release, one of announced (but not produced) films, and one on SF serials released in the 1950s. The work is also indexed.

Shorter discussions of the SF film are, of course, more numerous than book-length explorations. The most substantial have tended to appear as chapters in works focusing on topics in some way related to SF, in anthologies, and in specialized journals. As early as 1967, Carlos Clarens devoted two chapters of *An Illustrated History of the Horror Film* to SF. Chapter 7 ("Keep Watching the Sky!") and chapter 9 ("No End Title") respectively treat the American films of the 1950s and later foreign SF like Jean-Luc Godard's *Alphaville* and François Truffaut's adaptation of Ray Bradbury's *Fahrenheit 451*.[13] More specifically focused, however, are chapters on SF in two more recent works exploring 1950s American culture and ideology through cinema. Nora Sayre's *Running Time: Films of the Cold War* (1982) discusses the political paranoia of 1950s SF in chapter 7 (again titled "Watch the Skies"). Peter Biskind's *Seeing Is Believing: How Hollywood Taught Us to Stop Worrying and Love the Fifties* (1983) in chapter 3 ("Pods and Blobs") and a section called "Us and Them" explores the sources and implications of the decade's xenophobia as it is represented on the screen: the fear that the "Russians Are Coming" is illustrated through analyses of *Them!* and *The Thing*, the fear of "Mind Managers" through *Invasion of the Body Snatchers*, and the yearning for "Friends in High Places" through *The Day the Earth Stood Still* and *It Came from Outer Space*. These books are particularly valuable for placing the SF film of the 1950s in both cinematic and social context.

There are also several significant anthologies of the genre—the first major one still among the best. William Johnson's *Focus on the Science Fiction Film* (1972) is a broad collection of short pieces which address not only the SF film's "Beginnings: 1895–1940's" and its "Popular Years: The 1950's," but also, in "Taking Stock: Some Issues and Answers" and "Moving On: The 1960's and After," the genre's aesthetics and production. What is most valuable about the Johnson collection (besides the editor's astute introduction) is that it includes a number of translations of fascinating ideological and aesthetic readings of the genre originally written in French and Italian, and that it reprints one of the earliest pieces on the SF film published in a specialized film journal. First appearing in *Film Quarterly* in 1959, Richard Hodgens's "A Brief, Tragical History of the Science Fiction Film" takes SF seriously and bemoans its corruption in the likes of the creature films of the 1950s. However contentious, Hodgens's piece is a "must" for the serious student of the genre. Johnson's anthology also includes a most useful bibliography, filmography, and index.

A more eccentric anthology is Thomas R. Atkins's *Science Fiction Films* (1976). Besides the editor's introduction ("Notes on Science Fiction on the Screen"), it contains only six essays which—because they range across the breadth and chronology of the genre—seem somewhat randomly collected. The pieces themselves, however, offer developed explorations of particular themes and films; Gene D. Phillips's "Fritz Lang on *Metropolis*"; Fred Chappell's "The Science Fiction Film Image: *A Trip to the Moon* to *2001: A Space Odyssey*"; Vivian Sobchack's "The Alien Landscapes of the Planet Earth: Science Fiction in the Fifties''; Stuart M. Kaminsky's *"Invasion of the Body Snatchers:* A Classic of Subtle Horror'' and ''Don Siegel on the Pod Society''; and Lee Atwell's *"Solaris:* A Contemporary Masterpiece.''

Finally, there have been two extremely useful anthologies published recently. *Omni's Screen Flights/Screen Fantasies: The Future According to Science Fiction Cinema* (1984), edited by Danny Peary, is pitched to a general readership yet contains a number of extremely sophisticated essays. Part 1 has the volume's most theoretical pieces and explores the significance, aesthetics, and structure of the genre through considerations of SF's depiction of the future, the city as SF ''character,'' sex in the SF film, and the relation between scientists and their creations. Part 2 contains briefer critical articles and interviews which focus on specific films (many of them firsthand accounts by filmmakers and performers), and part 3 continues this strategy but also opens out to include thoughtful discussion of SF production design and special effects. Again, international in scope and chronologically exhaustive, the anthology's biggest virtues are its intelligence, size, variety (310 pages yield forty-one articles and interviews, a ''Checklist of Futuristic Films,'' and an index), and its wealth of material on relatively recent films.

*Shadows of the Magic Lamp: Fantasy and Science Fiction in Film* (1985), edited and introduced by George Slusser and Eric S. Rabkin, is a more probing collection. It brings together fourteen essays originally presented at an academic conference on SF and fantasy film. Nine of these concern the SF film and were written by well-known film scholars who have specialized in genre theory and criticism. Thus, Leo Braudy gives us ''Genre and the Resurrection of the Past''; Bruce Kawin, ''Children of the Light''; Vivian Sobchack, ''The Virginity of Astronauts: Sex and the Science Fiction Film''; Peter Biskind, ''Pods, Blobs, and Ideology in American Films of the Fifties''; H. Bruce Franklin, ''Don't Look Where We're Going: Visions of the Future in Science Fiction Films, 1970–1982''; Albert J. LaValley, ''Traditions of Trickery: The Role of Special Effects in the Science Fiction Film''; Garrett Stewart, ''The 'Videology' of Science Fiction''; George Slusser, ''Fantasy, Science Fiction, Mystery, Horror''; and Frank McConnell, ''Born in Fire: The Ontology of the Monster.''

Anthologies are obviously most useful in collecting and presenting articles often scattered across time and a diversity of periodicals. Thus, it is most unfortunate that one of the best early essays written on the American SF film has not been included in an SF anthology: Susan Sontag's ''The Imagination of Disaster.''[14] In 1965, Sontag attempted her own structural analysis of the genre by proposing model SF scenarios and looking to the genre's unconscious poetics and politics. While she sees the films as providing a remarkable and often beautiful ''sensuous elaboration'' of catastrophe, she primarily takes them to task—not only for their often patent silliness and banality, but also as culturally symptomatic of ''the inadequacy of most people's response to the unassimilable terrors that infect their consciousness'' in the new nuclear age.[15] As fantasy, she suggests, SF films ''inculcate a strange apathy concerning the processes of radiation, contamination, and destruction,'' and finally function to allay anxiety and "normalize what is psychologically unbearable."[16]

Other essays are more easily found than Sontag's, for they appear in specialized journals focusing on either film or science fiction—and, indeed, these often publish "special issues" (for film journals, on genres, and for SF journals, on film). For example, issue #13 (1986) of *camera obscura* (a journal emphasizing feminist film theory) is devoted to the SF film—while issue #22, volume 7, part 3 (November 1980) of *Science-Fiction Studies* (a journal generally, emphasizing SF literature) is devoted to a consideration of "Science Fiction and the Non-Print Media" and includes not only a fascinating "Symposium on *Alien*," but also such fine essays as Michael Stern's "Making Culture into Nature: or, Who Put the 'Special' into 'Special Effects'?" and Andrew Gordon's *"The Empire Strikes Back:* Monsters from the Id."[17]

Given its general interest in popular film genres, the *Journal of Popular Film and Television* has been regularly publishing articles on SF film since its first issue in 1972, while other journals like *Film Quarterly, Literature/Film Quarterly, Film Criticism,* and *Jump Cut* do so less frequently. The less academic *American Film* has also addressed generic issues ranging from SF's forms of futurism to the wizardry and business of its special effects, and *Cinefantastique* still stands as the one periodical which, however fanzine its tone, consistently provides a wealth of technical information on SF film production. Currently, the SF film is at the height of its new popularity. It is quite likely, therefore, that theoretical and critical writing on the genre will be on the increase for years to come.

## NOTES

1. A full definition and description of the postmodern and its cultural and aesthetic characteristics can be found in Fredric Jameson, "Postmodernism, or The Cultural Logic of Late Capitalism," *New Left Review,* no. 146 (July–August 1984), pp. 53–92.

2. Films which might be considered SF date back to the very beginnings of American cinema, but their production was sporadic and they were regarded as unrelated by those who reviewed them.

3. Vivian Sobchack, *Screening Space: The American Science Fiction Film* (New York: Ungar Press, 1986).

4. Susan Sontag, "The Imagination of Disaster," *Commentary,* October 1965, p. 44. Reprinted in *Against Interpretation* (see Bibliography).

5. Brian Murphy, "Monster Movies: They Came From Beneath the Fifties," *Journal of Popular Film,* Winter 1972, p. 32.

6. I am using the term *myth* here to refer to the work of structural anthropologist Claude Lévi-Strauss, who writes that the basic cultural function of myth "is to provide a logical model capable of overcoming a contradiction (an impossible achievement if, as it happens, the contradiction is real)." See his "The Structural Study of Myth," in *The Structuralists from Marx to Lévi-Strauss,* ed. Richard DeGeorge and Fernande DeGeorge (Garden City, N.Y.: Doubleday, 1972), p. 193. For further discussion of the mythic and ritual dimensions of film genres, see Vivian Sobchack's "Genre Film: Myth,

Ritual, and Sociodrama,'' in *Film/Culture: Explorations of Cinema in Its Social Context,* ed. Sari Thomas (Metuchen, N.J.: Scarecrow Press, 1982), pp. 147–65.

7. Sontag, "The Imagination of Disaster," p. 46.

8. Interestingly, it is the SF that borrows upon the thematics of *The Day the Earth Stood Still:* the humane alien, human villains who through fear or self-interest threaten the alien's person and peaceful mission, positive relationships between humans and aliens figured as emotional and even sexual. These elements are present in *E.T.* and *Cocoon,* but *Starman* stands as the most obvious reworking of the 1950s classic.

9. Joan F. Dean, "Between *2001* and *Star Wars,*" *Journal of Popular Film and Television,* vol. 7, No. 1, 1978, pp. 36–37.

10. Jameson, "Postmodernism," p. 76.

11. John Baxter, *Science Fiction in the Cinema* (New York: A. S. Barnes, 1970), p. 13.

12. John Brosnan, *Movie Magic: The Story of Special Effects in the Cinema* (New York: St. Martin's Press, 1974).

13. Carlos Clarens, *An Illustrated History of the Horror Film* (New York: Capricorn Books, 1967).

14. This may have to do with copyright issues, since the essay is included in *Against Interpretation,* an anthology of the author's own wide-ranging essays. See Bibliography.

15. Sontag, "The Imagination of Disaster," p. 48.

16. Ibid., p. 42.

17. Although a number of film scholars have written on SF, Andrew Gordon's work has been among the most prolific and sustained. See his *"Star Wars:* A Myth for Our Time"* (*Literature/Film Quarterly,* Fall 1978, pp. 314–26), which precedes the cited article, and *"Return of the Jedi:* The End of the Myth" (*Film Criticism,* Winter 1984, pp. 45–54), which follows it, as well as "The Power of the Force: Sex in the *Star Wars* Trilogy," in *Erotic Universe: Sexuality and Fantastic Literature,* ed. Donald Palumbo (Westport, Conn.: Greenwood Press, 1986). In addition, he has also written *"Close Encounters:* The Gospel According to Steven Spielberg" (*Literature/Film Quarterly,* 8, no. 3 [1980], pp. 156–164), and *"E.T.* as Fairy Tale," (*Science-Fiction Studies,* vol. 10, 1983, pp. 298–305). J. P. Telotte's work is also worth mention. See his "The Doubles of Fantasy and the Space of Desire" (*Film Criticism,* Fall 1982, pp. 56–68); "Human Artifice and the Science Fiction Film" (*Film Quarterly,* Spring 1983, pp. 44–51); and " 'The Dark Side of the Force': *Star Wars* and The Science Fiction Tradition" *(Extrapolation,* Fall 1983, pp. 216–26).

## BIBLIOGRAPHIC CHECKLIST

### Books

Atkins, Thomas R., ed. *Science Fiction Films.* New York: Monarch Press/Simon & Schuster, 1976.

Baxter, John. *Science Fiction in the Cinema.* New York: A. S. Barnes, 1970.

Brosnan, John. *Future Tense: The Cinema of Science Fiction.* New York: St. Martin's Press, 1978.

Johnson, William, ed. *Focus on the Science Fiction Film.* Englewood Cliffs, N.J.: Prentice-Hall, 1972.

Peary, Danny, ed. *Omni's Screen Flights/Screen Fantasies: The Future According to Science Fiction Cinema*. Garden City, N.Y.: Doubleday, 1984.

Pohl, Fredrik, and Fredrik Pohl IV. *Science Fiction Studies in Film*. New York: Ace Books, 1981.

Slusser, George, and Eric S. Rabkin, eds. *Shadows of the Magic Lamp: Fantasy and Science Fiction in Film*. Carbondale: Southern Illinois University Press, 1985.

Sobchack, Vivian. *Screening Space: The American Science Fiction Film*. New York: Ungar Press, 1987. (Originally published in 1980 as *The Limits of Infinity: The American Science Fiction Film, 1950–75*.)

Strickland, A. W., and Forrest J. Ackerman. *A Reference Guide to American Science Fiction Films*. Bloomington, Ind.: T.I.S. Publications, 1981.

Warren, Bill. *Keep Watching the Skies! American Science Fiction Movies of the Fifties, Volume I, 1950–1957*. Jefferson, N.C.: McFarland, 1982.

## Shorter Works

Biskind, Peter. Chapter 3, "Pods and Blobs" (pp. 101–59) and the "Us and Them" section. In his *Seeing Is Believing: How Hollywood Taught Us to Stop Worrying and Love the Fifties*. New York: Pantheon Books, 1983.

Clarens, Carlos. Chapter 7, "Keep Watching the Sky!" (pp. 118–37), and chapter 9, "No End Title" (pp. 161–71). In his *An Illustrated History of the Horror Film*. New York: Capricorn Books, 1967.

Hodgens, Richard. "A Brief, Tragical History of the Science Fiction Film," *Film Quarterly*, Winter 1959, pp. 30–39.

Sayre, Nora. Chapter 7, "Watch the Skies." In her *Running Time: Films of the Cold War*. New York: Dial Press, 1982, pp. 191–214.

Sontag, Susan. "The Imagination of Disaster," *Commentary*, October 1965, pp. 42–48.

## General Periodicals of SF Interest

*American Film*. (Prints articles of general SF interest.)

*camera obscura*. (#15, 1987, was devoted to the SF film.)

*Cinefantastique*. (Articles containing SF technical, film production information.)

*Journal of Popular Film and Television*. (Prints articles of general SF interest.)

*Science-Fiction Studies*. (#22, Vol. 7, November 1980, was devoted to "Science Fiction and the Non-Print Media.")

## SELECTED FILMOGRAPHY

1950    *Destination Moon* (91 minutes).
Eagle-Lion. Producer: George Pal. Director: Irving Pichel. Screenplay: Rip Van Ronkel, Robert A. Heinlein, and James O'Hanlon, loosely based on the novel *Rocketship Galileo* by Robert A. Heinlein. Production Design: Ernst Fegte. Special Effects Supervisor: Lee Zavitz. Cast: John Archer (Barnes), Warner Anderson (Cargreaves), Tom Powers (General Thayer), Dick Wesson (Sweeney), Erin O'Brien Moore (Mrs. Cargreaves).

1951    *The Thing (From Another World)* (87 minutes).
Winchester/RKO. Producer: Howard Hawks. Director: Christian Nyby, with Howard Hawks (uncredited). Screenplay: Charles Lederer from the novella *Who Goes There?* by John W. Campbell, Jr. Art Direction: John J. Hughes and Albert S. D'Agostino. Special Effects: Linwood Dunn and Donald Stewart. Cast: Kenneth Tobey (Capt. Patrick Hendry), Margaret Sheridan (Nikki), Robert Cornthwaite (Dr. Carrington), Douglas Spencer (Skeely), Dewey Martin (Crew Chief), James Arness (The Thing). Remade in 1982 (Director: John Carpenter).

*The Day the Earth Stood Still* (92 minutes).
Fox. Producer: Julian Blaustein. Director: Robert Wise. Screenplay: Edmund H. North from the story "Farewell to the Master" by Harry Bates. Art Direction: Lyle R. Wheeler and Addison Hehr. Special Effects Director: Fred Sersen. Cast: Michael Rennie (Klaatu), Patricia Neal (Helen Benson), Sam Jaffe (Dr. Barnhardt), Hugh Marlow (Tom Stevens), Billy Gray (Bobbie Benson), Frances Bavier (Mrs. Barley), Lock Martin (Gort).

1954    *Them!* (93 minutes).
Warner Bros. Producer: David Weisbart. Director: Gordon Douglas. Screenplay: Ted Sherdeman from a story by George Worthington Yates, adapted by Russell Hughes. Art Direction: Stanley Fleisher. Ant Effects: Dick Smith. Cast: Edmund Gwenn (Dr. Harold Medford), James Whitmore (Sgt. Peterson), James Arness (Robert Graham), Joan Weldon (Dr. Patricia Medford).

1956    *Forbidden Planet* (98 minutes).
MGM. Producer: Nicholas Nayfack. Director: Fred McLeod Wilcox. Screenplay: Cyril Hume from a story by Irving Block and Allen Adler and suggested by Shakespeare's *The Tempest*. Art Direction: Arthur Lonergan, Mentor Huebner, A. Arnold Gillespie, and Irving Block. Cast: Walter Pidgeon (Dr. Morbius), Anne Francis (Altaira), Leslie Nielsen (Commander Adams), Warren Stevens (Lt. Ostrow), Jack Kelly (Lt. Farman), Earl Holliman (Cookie).

*Invasion of the Body Snatchers* (80 minutes).
Allied Artists. Producer: Walter Wanger. Director: Don Siegel. Screenplay: Daniel Mainwaring with rewrites by Sam Peckinpah, based on Jack Finney's *The Bodysnatchers*. Production Design: Edward Haworth. Special Effects: Milt Rice. Cast: Kevin McCarthy (Dr. Miles Bennell), Dana Wynter (Becky Driscoll), King Donovan (Jack Belicec), Carolyn Jones ("Teddy" Belicec), Larry Gates (Dr. Daniel Kaufman), Virginia Christine (Wilma Lentz). Remade in 1978 (Director: Philip Kaufman).

1968    *2001: A Space Odyssey* (138 minutes).
MGM. Producer/Director: Stanley Kubrick. Screenplay: Stanley Kubrick and Arthur C. Clarke. Production Design: Tony Masters, Henry Lange, and Ernest Archer. Art Direction: John Helsi. Special Effects: Stanley Kubrick and Douglas Trumbull. Cast: Keir Dullea (Bowman), Gary Lockwood (Poole), Douglas Rain (voice of HAL), William Sylvester (Dr. Heywood Floyd), Leonard Rossiter (Smyslov), Margaret Tyzack (Elena).

1977    *Star Wars* (121 minutes).
Fox. Producer: Gary Kurtz. Director and Screenplay: George Lucas. Art Direction: Norman Reynolds and Leslie Dilley. Special Effects: John Dykstra. Cast:

Mark Hamill (Luke Skywalker), Harrison Ford (Han Solo), Carrie Fisher (Princess Leia), Peter Cushing (Grand Moff Tarkin), Alec Guiness (Ben Kenobi), Anthony Daniels (C3PO), Kenny Baker (R2D2), Peter Mayhew (Chewbacca), David Prowse and the voice of James Earl Jones (Darth Vader). Followed in 1980 by Lucas-produced *The Empire Strikes Back* (Director: Irvin Kershner), and in 1983 by *Return of the Jedi* (Director: Richard Marquand).

*Close Encounters of the Third Kind* (135 minutes).
Columbia. Producers: Julia and Michael Phillips. Director and Screenplay: Steven Spielberg. Production Design: Joe Alvez. Art Direction: Dan Lomino. Special Effects: Steven Spielberg and Douglas Trumbull. Cast: Richard Dreyfuss (Roy Neary), François Truffaut (Claude Lacombe), Terri Garr (Ronnie Neary), Melinda Dillon (Gillian Guiler), Cary Guffey (Barry Guiler), Bob Balaban (Interpreter Laughlin). "Special Edition" released in 1980.

1979  *Alien* (124 minutes).
Fox. Producers: Walter Hill, Gordon Carol, and David Giler. Director: Ridley Scott. Screenplay: Dan O'Bannion. Production Design: Michael Seymour. Art Direction: Leslie Dilley and Roger Christian. Special Effects: Brian Johnson and Nick Alider. Cast: Sigourney Weaver (Ripley), Tom Skerritt (Dallas), Ian Holm (Ash), John Hurt (Kane), Harry Dean Stanton (Brett), Yaphet Kotto (Parker), Veronica Cartwright (Lambert). Sequel in 1986, *Aliens* (Director: James Cameron).

*Star Trek—The Motion Picture* (132 minutes).
Paramount. Producer: Gene Roddenberry. Director: Robert Wise. Screenplay: Harold Livingston. Production Design: Harold Michelson. Special Effects: Industrial Light and Magic. Cast: William Shatner (James Kirk), Leonard Nimoy (Mr. Spock), DeForest Kelly (Dr. McCoy), James Doohan (Scott), Nichelle Nichols (Uhura), Walter Koenig (Chekov), George Takei (Sulu), Stephen Collins (Decker), Persis Khambatta (Ilia). Sequels in 1982, *Star Trek II: The Wrath of Khan* (Director: Nicholas Meyer), in 1984, *Star Trek III: The Search for Spock* (Director: Leonard Nimoy), and in 1986, *Star Trek IV: The Voyage Home* (Director: Leonard Nimoy).

1982  *Blade Runner* (124 minutes).
Ladd/Warner Bros. Producer: Michael Deeley. Director: Ridley Scott. Screenplay: Hampton Fancher and David Peoples from Philip Dick's novel, *Do Androids Dream of Electric Sheep?* Production Design: Lawrence G. Paull. Visual Futurist: Syd Mead. Art Direction: David Snyder. Special Effects: David Dreyer, Richard Yuricich, and Douglas Trumbull. Cast: Harrison Ford (Rick Deckard), Rutger Hauer (Roy Batty), Sean Young (Rachel), Edward James Olmos (Lt. Gaff), William Sanderson (J. F. Sebastian), Daryl Hannah (Pris), Joe Turkel (Tyrell), Joanna Cassidy (Zhora), Brion James (Leon).

*E.T.: The Extra-Terrestrial* (115 minutes).
Universal. Producers: Steven Spielberg and Kathleen Kennedy. Director: Steven Spielberg. Screenplay: Melissa Mathison. Production Design: James D. Bissel. Special Effects: Dennis Muren. "E.T.": Carlos Rimbaldi. Cast: Dee Wallace (Mary), Henry Thomas (Elliot), Peter Coyote ("Keys"), Robert McNaughton (Michael), Drew Barrymore (Gertie).

1984  *Starman* (115 minutes).
Columbia. Producer: Larry J. Franco. Director: John Carpenter. Screenplay: Bruce A. Evans and Raynold Gideon. Production Design: Daniel Lomino and William J. Durrell, Jr. Special Effects: Roy Arbogast, Bruce Nicholson, and Michael McAlister. Cast: Jeff Bridges (Starman), Karen Allen (Jenny Hayden), Charles Martin Smith (Mark Sherman), Richard Jaekel (George Fox).

*Repro Man* (92 minutes).
Universal. Producers: Jonathon Wacks, Peter McCarthy, and Michael Nesmith. Director and Screenplay: Alex Cox. Art Design: J. Rae Fox and Linda Burbank. Cast: Emilio Estevez (Otto), Harry Dean Stanton (Bud), Olivia Barash (Leila), Tracy Walter (Miller).

*The Terminator* (108 minutes).
Orion. Producer: Gale Ann Hurd. Director: James Cameron. Screenplay: James Cameron and Gale Ann Hurd. Art Direction: George Costello. "Terminator" Effects: Stan Winston. Cast: Linda Hamilton (Sarah Connor), Michael Biehn (Kyle Reese), Arnold Schwarzenegger (The Terminator).

1985  *Back to the Future* (116 minutes).
Amblin/Universal. Producers: Bob Gale and Neil Canton. Director: Robert Zemeckis. Screenplay: Robert Zemeckis and Bob Gale. Production Design: Lawrence J. Paull. Art Direction: Todd Hallowell. Special Effects: Industrial Light and Magic. Cast: Michael J. Fox (Marty McFly), Christopher Lloyd (Dr. Emmett Brown), Lea Thompson (Lorraine Baines McFly), Crispin Glover (George McFly).

# 14

## Fantasy

WADE JENNINGS

"Toto, I have a feeling we're not in Kansas anymore."
—*The Wizard of Oz* (1939).

Fantasy is one of the most enduring of film genres and yet one of the most difficult to define or even to describe. The largest problem in discussing fantasy is that the term is exceptionally broad and has been used indiscriminately throughout the history of film criticism. As Stuart A. Kaminsky says in his book-length study of film genres, "Genre in film, if it is to have meaning, must have a limited scope, a limited definition."[1] It is unlikely that we can ever restrict fantasy to such a limited scope or definition, but it is nonetheless too important a type of film to ignore. The following discussion of fantasy will attempt to synthesize critical views of fantasy and to provide description where definition is impossible.

The elements that fantasy films typically share are largely narrative ones—similarities in plots, characters, and themes. Perhaps the only indispensable element in a fantasy is a central situation that defies rational or even pseudo-scientific explanation. In fact, the chief distinction between fantasy and science fiction is that in science fiction the drive is toward explanation, toward resolution of the mystery and its attendant problems, whereas in fantasy the situation cannot be explained; it must simply be accepted. How is it that in Oz witches can fly on broomsticks? No one within a fantasy film asks such questions, nor should the audience. The comforts of rational explanation must be left behind when one enters the world of fantasy.[2]

Often the inexplicable world is contrasted to a conventional "reality" from which the characters have come and to which they may return. This framing technique makes it easier for the audience to accept the new world since they are discovering it along with the characters in the film. The fantasy world may be nothing more than the ordinary world transformed by some fantastic event or character, but more often it is a place like Oz, Shangri-La, or Tarzan's jungle.

The problems of definition are compounded by the fact that although such inexplicable central situations must exist in all fantasy films, not all films with such situations are best understood as fantasies. By custom as well as theory, many types of films with fantastic elements are treated as separate genres. As we have already discussed, science fiction films differ from fantasy films in their emphasis on scientific explanation, no matter how strained. Horror films use fantasy for only one main purpose, to terrify the audience, though of course the distinction here is sometimes a difficult one to make. Films that are essentially symbolic or allegorical in nature (*The Seventh Seal,* for example) have little in common with fantasy films, nor do experimental or surreal films with little narrative coherence resemble the traditional fantasy film in important ways. Because of the highly specialized techniques involved, animated films and films that depend greatly on puppetry are treated separately from fantasy, as are films in which supernatural elements are explained in conventionally religious terms, films in which fantasy is used largely to produce comic effects, erotic effects, or to introduce the musical numbers that are the real interest in the film. In spite of these necessary distinctions, fantasy films may in fact borrow heavily from these other types of films in creating their central situations.

When we examine the plots in those films that we do term fantasies, we find a bewildering variety of stories—those about supermen who fight to save civilization, lovers who escape time, old people who discover a source of eternal youth, boys who turn into dogs. In spite of the diversity, however, plots in fantasy films do share certain elements that are clearly distinguishable in film after film. For example, most fantasy films involve a quest, literal or metaphorical, a journey that leads to necessary self-discovery, to a rejection of conventional values or previous understanding, and to a climax in which the protagonist makes a choice between two worlds in which he may live.

The journey motif resembles in many ways the quest in traditional romances in which a young squire must meet many tests before he can claim his knighthood. In some films based on myth, such a heroic quest is of course a natural element, films such as *Die Niebelungen* (1924) or *Dragonslayer* (1981), but the quest is just as important in films with quite different subjects. In *The Wizard of Oz,* for example, Dorothy must first find the Wizard and then the witch's castle before she is ready to understand the truth about herself and the power that she has possessed all along. Similarly, Luke Skywalker in the *Star Wars* trilogy (beginning in 1977) must travel through the galaxy to find the secret of the force that has been with him through the whole adventure.

Other journeys are more metaphorical than physical in fantasy films that emphasize elements other than action. In *Berkeley Square* (1933), for instance, a young man travels to the past and back to discover his ability to love, while in *Cocoon* (1984), the old people have to discover within themselves the courage and joy to live before they are ready to complete the journey into the unknown.

One of the most important discoveries on these journeys is that conventional knowledge and conventional values are not adequate in the new world that is discovered. Characters are either shocked into a recognition that what they have always believed is not true, or they are taught that lesson by those in the new reality. In *The Miracle on 34th Street,* for instance, the character played by Maureen O'Hara is firmly locked into a practical view of existence that has no room for imagination, fun, or love—that most impractical of emotions. When fantasy intrudes into her world in the person of Kris Kringle, she stubbornly resists, but her journey to enlightenment begins when she is forced to recognize that the qualities that he represents are stronger and more real than those to which she has clung. In short, she has to surrender knowledge and reason and become childlike enough to believe before she can be redeemed. The young heroine of *Death Takes a Holiday* faces an even more difficult test when she is forced to reconsider her whole notion of death, to leave conventional understanding behind, and to accept the paradox of love coexisting with death. Only in leaving behind other human beings who cling to the traditional understanding can she free herself for the grand adventure.

The journey to self-knowledge and the surrender of conventional understanding in fantasy films leads to a climax in which the character is forced to choose between two worlds. The choice is unpredictable: Dorothy chooses to leave Oz with all of its beauty and adventure to return to Kansas, a place she now values. In *Lost Horizon* (1937), on the other hand, the protagonist returns to reality only long enough to tell his story and make the preparation to return to the world of fantasy that he recognizes as his natural home. Whatever the choice of worlds at the end of the films, the protagonists typically embrace it with joy that springs from a sense of having found that which they sought.

Given the similarity in central plots, it is not surprising that fantasy films also share several important themes that arise naturally from such situations. The most intriguing of these is a questioning of what constitutes "home." How can the characters make the choices which confront them at the ends of the films except by examining their values and deciding under what circumstances they can live freely and happily given those values? The answer in some cases is that home is that place where one finds love, no matter what the other circumstances; we understand why the protagonist in *Splash* (1983) gives up his humanity for the sake of the creature he loves, just as we understand why another man chooses to return to the world of conventional reality and leave the fantasy behind as in *Heaven Can Wait* (1979). Each is choosing the world in which he can be the self he has discovered, the world in which he can love, the world in which he is at home. When one considers the significance of the theme of home in fantasy films, Dorothy's concluding statement at the end of her film is transformed from platitude to a resonant declaration: "Auntie Em . . . there's no place like home."

The most characteristic theme in fantasy, however, one related closely to the other themes and to the plots, is the discovery of joy. Characters whose lives have had no meaning, who have lived what Thoreau calls "not life," find that life is rich, full, and wondrous. We often find this theme celebrated in the conclusions of fantasy films. At the end of the sound version of *The Thief of Bagdad,* for example, the young thief proclaims to the happy lovers: "You've found what you wanted, now I'm going to find what *I* want—some fun and adventure at last!" The sheer exuberance of the moment is captured at the ends of other fantasies as well—the kite-flying scene in *Mary Poppins,* the Christmas celebration in *It's a Wonderful Life* (1946), and the reunion in *The Wizard of Oz,* all show the natural reward of the completed quest, the return to home.

The most significant theme in fantasy films, however, is freedom; this theme transcends and unifies the others. Characters have to find that they are free and can therefore choose, that their choices are necessarily personal—not bound by duty or unhappy commitments, and that this freedom brings with it the possibility for fulfillment and happiness. The very fact that fantasies deny natural laws opens the door to such freedom, as does the fact that the characters learn to overcome social and intellectual limitations that block the freedom of characters in realistic genres. Self-knowledge, home, and joy—the realization of all these possibilities comes from the insistence in fantasy films that one is finally not bound by any forces that he cannot overcome, that he is free. The freedom, of course, is the freedom from mortality, from death and the fear of death. It is not surprising that so many fantasy films illustrate such liberation: *Death Takes a Holiday, On Borrowed Time* (1939), *Cocoon,* and dozens of other fantasies show that death is either a release or an illusion. In either case, recognition of that fact frees us from that ultimate limitation.

The characters in fantasy film are often not as distinctive in type as those in other genres; in fact, fantasy often borrows characters from melodrama, comedy, and adventure films. At least three character types, however, belong essentially to fantasy films and in one form or another show up in most of them.

The most obvious fantasy character is the superman—the hero or villain who has "powers beyond those of mortal men." Tarzan, a man capable of talking with animals and traveling through the treetops at great speed, is an obvious example of such a character. Powerful wizards, witches, and near-human monsters often demand a human hero's most courageous and cunning opposition, and good superhuman creatures often protect the hero from evil. Such supernatural creatures in fantasy films range from angels to devils, from Greek gods to legendary heroes, but they share the possibility of violating natural law when they choose, thus setting the stage for the fantasy which follows.

A more interesting type in fantasy film is the child hero. These characters often have to struggle alone in a world of adults without completely understanding what they have been called upon to accomplish. The discovery that most of these children make is simply that their natural innocence and goodness is more powerful than the supernatural evil which they face or the mysteries which terrify them. Dorothy's accidental triumph over the Witch of the West, the children's discovery of eternal truth in *The Bluebird* (especially the 1940 version), and Elliott's triumph over the adult world in *E.T.* (1982) illustrate the character convention at work in such cases. The child is superior to the well-meaning adults in his world and, often unknowingly, stronger than the dangerous ones. Perhaps the best incarnation of the type is Sabu's young thief in *The Thief of Bagdad* (1940).

Finally, many fantasy films include a character who is a supernaturally wise mentor to the human hero. Glinda, the good witch in *The Wizard of Oz*, for example, advises Dorothy and sets her upon the road to the necessary self-discovery that she must earn. Likewise, Ben Kenobi and Yoda guide young Skywalker in his pursuit of the powers of the force just as Kris Kringle leads mortals to understand Christmas and faith. Benevolent or wise advisers also instruct heroes such as Arthur *(Excalibur,* 1982), George Bailey *(It's a Wonderful Life)* and Robert Conway *(Lost Horizon).* Sam Jaffe's High Lama in the last film is in fact an apotheosis of the type: patient, loving, all-knowing, he is able to watch the hero's slow growth to knowledge in the certain knowledge of his eventual success. He sees the eternal questions while the others struggle with the momentary problems.

While these considerations of plot, theme, and character elements in the genre are necessarily broad, they do indicate that the genre has a unity of content and vision that may not be obvious on first glance. Certainly the subject deserves a more extended consideration than it has yet been given.

The history of fantasy films is much easier to discuss. It falls into four distinct periods, each with its own emphases and prevalent subgenres.

Not surprisingly, the first important period, beginning with the first attempts at narrative filmmaking and lasting until the advent of sound, was dominated by the interest in special effects, effects possible for the first time in this new medium. Georges Méliès, a French magician turned pioneer filmmaker before the turn of the century, discovered to his delight that fantastic illusions were possible in moving pictures with very little effort. Simply by stopping a shot, removing or inserting new elements, and resuming it, miraculous appearances and disappearances could be suggested. Equally simple techniques allowed the filmmaker to make small things seem gigantic and vice versa.

An experienced showman, Méliès used his newly acquired tricks to make one of the first great fantasy films, *A Trip to the Moon* (1902). Although the film begins in the tradition of Jules Verne and H. G. Wells as science fiction, showing scientists planning a trip by rocket to the moon, Méliès quickly abandons scientific pretense in favor of fun: chorus girls help to launch the rocket that—in the most famous shot in the film—lands in the eye of a most literal and agitated man in the moon. Méliès thus makes the point that in the world of this film rationality is not compelling—anything can happen and will. The celebration of freedom that will continue in the genre as a dominant theme is thus established.

Although other early filmmakers also recognized and sometimes made use of film's capacity for creating fantastic illusions, both producers and audiences preferred films more firmly rooted in reality. Only occasionally in the silent period did fantasy achieve what it might. In Hollywood, the best example of fantasy filmmaking at its best in this period was the Douglas Fairbanks's version of *The Thief of Bagdad*. Although the film made use of the larger-than-life Fairbanks persona and the audience's acceptance of him as a hero, it also exploited imaginatively the special effects that the plot allowed. Fairbanks fought dragons and sea spiders, overcame wicked wizards with supernatural powers, and took his princess at the end off to the land of love on his flying carpet. As both producer and star, Fairbanks had the power and money to make the fantasy work. The audiences, however, preferred him in slightly less fantastic settings as Zorro or Robin Hood, so the investment in the special effects did not seem worthwhile after all.

In the same year in Germany Fritz Lang made even more spectacular use of special effects in his re-creation of the heroic myth of *Die Niebelungen*. Lang realized that film could capture both the epic sweep of Siegfried's adventure and the poetic lyricism of the source. With the help of the German government, Lang constructed hugely expensive effects such as a dragon that had to be operated by seventeen men, a gigantic set that dwarfed the human figures, and great wind and fog machines. The result is a fantasy film that amazed audiences but appealed to them less than the much more inexpensive *Dr. Mabuse* that Lang also created. Audiences on both sides of the Atlantic agreed: fantasy films were not worth the exorbitant efforts and expenses involved. Industry tycoons understood that message, and the great special-effects fantasy films became unusual endeavors. Producers could more safely follow the example of Cecil B. de Mille and provide the special effects in more palatable religious spectacles or adventure films.

With the advent of sound, however, a new kind of fantasy imported from the stage became more common in film. Romantic fantasy emphasized imaginative situations that did not need elaborate special effects, only the audience's willingness to suspend disbelief. The basic subject in such films was the power of love, a power greater than even time or death. For over two decades in films like *Death Takes a Holiday, Berkeley Square, The Enchanted Cottage* (1945), and *Portrait of Jennie* (1948), the plot sees lovers separated by supernatural circumstances and yet faithful to their love beyond reason. Their reward is, of course, a miraculous reunion with the beloved in life or in death.

Other romantic fantasies emphasized comic rather than melodramatic aspects of the supernatural love affair. In films like *The Ghost and Mrs. Muir* (1947) or *Here Comes Mr. Jordan* (1941), love between living and nonliving people proves inconvenient and often amusing, but not insurmountable. Again, love proves stronger than the obvious problems, again transcending even death.

Although many of the romantic fantasies were modest box-office successes, others were not. Obviously, fantasies in whatever form were a riskier gamble for studios than almost surefire genres like westerns and gangster films.

Fantasy comedies—those films in which comic elements are subordinate to interest in the central fantasy—also had a somewhat feeble interest for the public in the first two decades of sound pictures. As a subgenre, it has somewhat more distinctive characteristics than romantic fantasy. Usually in fantasy comedies a supernatural character or group of characters play dominant roles, making life difficult for the ordinary mortals who become involved with them. Ghosts, like the ones in *The Ghost Goes West* (1936) and *The Canterville Ghost* (1943), are usually harmless creatures in the comedies, more sinned against than sinning, but witches (*I Married a Witch,* 1942), leprechauns (*The Luck of the Irish,* 1948), and even angels are more troublesome to mortals. Angels are particularly common in fantasy comedies, ranging from the unfortunate victim in *The Horn Blows at Midnight* (1945) to the suave charmer in *The Bishop's Wife* (1947).

In the other usual fantasy-comedy formula, ordinary people find themselves involved in supernatural situations that turn their lives upside down. This type of fantasy obviously has strong connections to other comedy genres, including screwball comedy. *Topper* (1937), for example, overlaps any reasonable boundaries between the types. Clearer examples of the fantasy comedy per se are *It Happened Tomorrow* (1944), a film in which a young man is able to read the next day's paper, and *It Grows on Trees* (1952), a comedy in which a middle-class housewife discovers a tree that produces money instead of leaves. Like most other fantasies, these were never very popular and also waned in the film industry's hard times after 1950.

The heroic fantasy aimed primarily at the children's audience was much more dependable at the box office than the others. These films were often constructed around the adventures of a superhero like Tarzan or Superman, but they also included surprisingly entertaining fantasies based on literary works or simple myth, films such as *She* (1934), *The Wizard of Oz* (1939), *The Thief of Bagdad,* and *Jason and the Argonauts* (1963). The market for such films waned, particularly after cheaply made imports flooded the market after 1960. The taste for fantasy was met by the much more popular science fiction and horror films of the next two decades, some of which were almost as much fantasy as they were the other. *Forbidden Planet* (1956) is a particularly clear instance of fantasy and science fiction blending so thoroughly that it may be impossible to decide which is in fact the dominant genre.

The greatest films in any genre and any period defy easy generalizations, of course. In the 1930s and 1940s, a few fantasy films drew widely and imaginatively on all the possibilities in all the subgenres to produce a result greater than the sum of its parts. Perhaps the best example in this period of such a film is Jean Cocteau's *Beauty and the Beast* (1946). The film is obviously based on a fairy tale, unapologetically so. Cocteau writes about the film, "to bring good luck to us all, let me say to you four magic words, the true 'Open Sesame' of childhood: 'Once upon a Time. . . .' "[3] However, the film is also a romantic fantasy for the adult audience. The beast at the end speaks lines that could serve as a thematic statement for many such films: "Love can make a man a beast—love can also beautify ugliness." In short, love transcends all obstacles. Finally, the film is an almost allegorical reaffirmation of the possibility of innocence, beauty, and love in a world that had recently seemed impossibly separated from such things. The special effects and fairy-tale simplicity may have appealed to children, but the insistence on faith and courage was an ideal for adults in a war-ravaged world.

Despite such moments of greatness, fantasy films had not found the audiences that make it possible for a genre to continue to thrive. As the film industry throughout the world experienced the slump of the early 1950s, such financially risky genres tended to disappear. The period from about 1952 to about 1977 was a particularly devastating one in the history of fantasy films. Only the Disney studios turned out many profitable films with traditional fantasy elements, and even these films usually subordinated the fantasy to slapstick comedy. One glowing exception to the trend was Disney's fantasy with music, *Mary Poppins* (1964). The film was aimed at the traditional Disney market, children and their parents, but its zest, unforced exuberance, and delight in pretense made it a popular success on a much wider scale. The attempts to capitalize on the film's success proved to be disasters, however, and films like *Dr. Dolittle* (1967) simply confirmed the view that fantasy, with or without music, was box-office poison.

Although science fiction also lost some of its appeal in the turbulence of the 1960s and early 1970s, horror films continued to please audiences who sought release in the fantastic. Many other genres had also died in this same period, with only occasional films reminding us of what we had once enjoyed. Fantasy seemed the most hopelessly unrevivable of them all since its natural emphasis on wonder and optimism ran so counter to the spirit of the time.

In 1977, however, a film appeared that was to change the course of filmmaking over the next decade. George Lucas had great trouble financing his *Star Wars* project; it is no wonder. Although it had elements of science fiction, of the western, and of the heroic adventure films of the past, it was at the core a fantasy, a story of a young man's quest to discover who he is and what is the nature of the reality he meets. With its themes strongly flavored by Eastern mysticism and its plot dependent on a central concept called the Force, a mysterious supernatural power, the film did not seem likely to appeal to any particular audience.

The film did not appeal to a particular group—it appealed to everyone. Perhaps Lucas was lucky and the time was right for a return to fantasy and its basic optimism. Gerald Mast points out that "the best American films since 1976 reflect a movement away from social rebellion and toward something else . . . something to believe in . . . myths to unify our culture."[4] One may debate whether Lucas benefited from such a trend or whether he created it. Certainly the *Star Wars* trilogy reintroduced to American film a subgenre that had long been dormant, the philosophical fantasy.

The point of philosophical fantasy is to examine basic values, the very meaning of life, from the distance offered by the fantasy. Such films may take us "far, far away" from ordinary reality, but it is nonetheless that reality that they comment upon.

Two films by Frank Capra from the 1930s and 1940s illustrate the quite different philosophical conclusions that such films may reach. In *Lost Horizon,* a diplomat from a world on the brink of a great war is transported to a world of timeless peace, order, and beauty. When circumstances and a sense of duty take him back to that other world, he stays only long enough to tell his story. He belongs in Shangri-la, not in a world that he cannot be of use to. He has the right and the need to seek his personal salvation in the fantasy.

In *It's a Wonderful Life,* made just after that war, another young man also despairs of the world that he finds himself in. At the beginning of the film rather than the conclusion he decides to leave that world, to commit suicide. It takes angelic intervention and a miraculous journey to the world that would have been had he not lived to convince the protagonist that he is necessary to that world, that he has been a force for good and will continue to be, and that in that world he already has the love and the possibility for happiness that he had overlooked in his despair. The fact that both fantasies end affirmatively is of course more important than that they reach different conclusions about how happiness is to be achieved.

George Lucas shows his characters torn by the same conflicts. They, too, long to escape a world where the odds are hopeless, but both Luke Skywalker and Han Solo, alter egos of the hero, discover that they must continue the struggle and that they can win. The plots and themes in the trilogy take the viewers back again and again to the basic philosophical considerations in the film: which is stronger, good or evil? What is the nature of power? How can love conquer hate? The questions are simple but not simple-minded.

In the immensely popular films that followed *Star Wars*, other aspects of fantasy were reexplored. In Steven Spielberg's *E.T.*, for example, the minor interest in scientific explanation is subordinate to the basic theme of home. Both the little boy and the alien in the film need to find that place, and by the end of the film as they soar over a rainbow that deliberately reminds us of another such search in another fantasy film, they succeed in their quest.

Continuing both the box-office success and the thematic explorations of *Star Wars* and *E.T.*, recent films such as *Splash, Cocoon,* and *Back to the Future* engage their characters in fantastic journeys that lead inevitably to the single question of how one lives in a world of confusion, mortality, and failure. As in Capra's films, the answer is either to leave the world or to transform it. In fantasy, one has the power to do either.

To the surprise of most film historians, fantasy has not only been reborn, it has revitalized the film industry. Uniting elements from many other genres and boldly insisting on the central fantasy that does not have to be "explained," these films have also brought together audiences of all ages, cultural and social background, and even nationalities. Film thus once again becomes one of the most important shared experiences in a fragmented world.

The artistic and cultural significance of such films is all the more remarkable when we realize that all fantasy begins with a very simple question: "What if . . . ?" The history of fantasy film continues to make clear in how many directions one may travel down the Yellow Brick Road and with what joy one may make that journey.

## BIBLIOGRAPHIC OVERVIEW

In this book-length study of film genres, Stuart Kaminsky concludes the chapter on horror and science fiction with a short paragraph beginning with this curious sentence: "Although we will not explore in this book a third genre related to science fiction and horror, it is worthwhile to acknowledge the existence of the fantasy genre."[5] Even this grudging recognition is more than most film historians and theorists have given fantasy. It is simply not part of the material that critics have found interesting. Even reviewers for the most part have treated the genre with condescension, if not contempt.

The early reviews of fantasy films, like the films themselves, focused on special effects and the illusions that the films managed to create. Such reviews also made clear that such films were escapes, presumably in contrast to the more realistic films that offered social criticism or artistic depth. These reviews indicated repeatedly that such films are for children or those adults who are willing to be children for the course of the film. The only notable exception to this consistent view was offered by William Rose Benét and Amy Loveman in an essay called "Prospero and the Pictures." As the title suggests, these writers argued that fantasy in film has potential power and that it is more natural to the form than the realism that had become more popular.[6] Although this essay was not a major theoretical discourse on the form, it at least acknowledged the comparative worth of the genre.

Through the 1930s and 1940s, that period dominated by romantic fantasy, the critics were no more interested or respectful. James Agee's review of *The Enchanted Cottage,* for example, is vitriolic and includes a line that might have been used by most reviewers of such films in the period: "Everything about it embarrasses me too much for clear thought."[7]

The reviewers for less serious magazines and newspapers often gushed about "sweet" and "charming" fantasy films, but even they favored diminutives when discussing them. A favorable review of *Miracle on 34th Street,* for instance, called it a "witty, tender little fantasy."[8] Such films obviously did not merit anyone's respect, a fact that no doubt irritated critics like Agee who attempted to lead his public to believe that film at its best deserved their attention. He concluded at one point that "when studios try to make it [fantasy], duck and stay hid until the mood has passed."[9]

Of the American film critics, Parker Tyler was the only one who examined fantasy as a legitimate and sometimes successful form of serious filmmaking. His eclectic interests in myth theory, in Freudianism, and in sexual politics colored his view of fantasy as they did everything else, however, and he is more successful in raising questions about possibilities in these films than in thoroughly answering such questions. In both *The Hollywood Hallucination* and *Magic and Myth of the Movies,* Tyler breaks ground in genre criticism. In a chapter entitled "Supernaturalism at Home" in the latter book, he points out that art does not have to adhere to "modern rational convention" and that "many modern movies illustrate the latter-day vestiges of very remote but serious beliefs of mankind that now have the appearance of mere symbolic fantasy."[10] He even traces such assumptions through brief discussions of filmmakers such as Méliès and René Clair. Tyler's mythic view of film fantasy did not create much interest in the critical community, but it did open a discussion that has become more heated in the last ten years.

Another of Tyler's consistent observations is that film by its very nature provides a way of understanding the workings of the unconscious mind; he particularly noted, long before most psychologists had discovered the fact, that film and dreams were similar in many ways, especially those films in which fantasy was allowed to dominate explanation. Tyler writes of the fact that by the mid-1940s "the dream has been found so photogenic and the emotional atmosphere of psychoanalysis, with its obvious kinship to the sinister sex of monster movies, has been so flexible as screen idiom" that Hollywood might make up its "many sins of omission in respect to psychology." Tyler's tongue-in-cheek approach to the subject does not penetrate far into the subject of fantasy film and psychology, but again it both treats films of this sort as legitimate and equal works of art and opens the door for later critics who will explore the dream connection fully.[11]

In the 1950s and 1960s, there was little significant discussion of fantasy film, but one peculiar development was that a few reviewers began to mourn the loss of the "great" fantasy pictures of the past, pictures that had hardly been so valued in their own time. Raymond Fielding, for example, describes "The Dearth of Fantasy" in a 1959 essay in *Films in Review.* Although the title suggests the argument of the essay, this elegy does offer a theoretical explanation of the superiority of traditional fantasy films that is more provocative than one might expect in such an essay. He argues that in earlier films that had depended more on the audience's willingness to "believe" than on its interest in special effects, we experience "a state of mind, a fever of the imagination that frees us, momentarily, from the hegemony of reason and habit. In the psychological sense, escapism involves a conceptual disengagement from perceptual reality. . . . True fantasy always has a rich, schizoid flavor to it, forcing the viewer's mind to turn back upon itself, surrealistically, to augment and embellish the dramatist's fantasy-line with the imagery of half-forgotten dreams."[12] Fielding thus picks up, in somewhat rhapsodic terms, several of Tyler's basic observations about the nature of such films.

The publishing industry's interest in the glossy, picture-filled film books of the 1970s led quickly to several books that lumped science fiction, horror, and fantasy. None of these books offered much new insight into the nature of fantasy, but again they treated the subject as seriously as the format permitted and thus helped further to legitimatize a genre that had still not evoked much sympathy or interest among critics. In *Cinema of the Fantastic,* Chris Steinbrunner and Burt Goldblatt provide good synopses and glowing praise for two fantasy films, *A Trip to the Moon* and *Beauty and the Beast.*[13] In David Annan's *Movie Fantastic: Beyond the Dream Machine,* the text among the pictures does make cryptic but occasionally interesting points about the connection between fantasy film and folk myth and other arts. Again, however, the editor is far more interested in horror and science fiction than in the fantasy film per se.[14] This and other books of the kind would perhaps not be worthy of comment were it not for the fact that there was little else being written about fantasy film at a time when other genres were beginning to be examined in some depth.

The new schools of critical theory that emerged in the 1960s and 1970s have had little to say about fantasy as a genre or about the films that belong in that group. Like Kaminsky, some critics occasionally give a brief nod to such films, but their interest continues to lie elsewhere. This indifference is especially surprising in the case of feminist critics; fantasy films would seem to offer a particularly interesting view of gender identification, the nature of women, and the social roles appropriate to women, but no extended study of such subjects has yet been published.

With the transforming success of fantasy in recent film history, some critics and historians have begun to look at the topic at last. In the most recent edition of Gerald Mast's *A Short History of the Movies,* he provides a brief but satisfying discussion of fantasy in German films of the silent era and a few pages on George Lucas's and Steven Spielberg's fantasies; he calls them "the master mythmakers of the era," though he undercuts the significance of that designation by wondering if they are best considered filmmakers or showmen. Clearly they are no auteurs of the old school, he concludes.[15]

Most of the introduction to film books aimed at the student market do not discuss fantasy as one of the major film genres. Even when such books do consider the genre, they often offer a slanted view of fantasy that may not be entirely consistent with the entire genre. Thomas and Vivian C. Sobchack in their *An Introduction to Film* spend about a page in the chapter on genre discussing fantasy, asserting among other things that children are the chief audience for the genre and that "little emphasis is placed on the social effect of the hero's triumph."[16] Both points are debatable, of course, especially the first. But the Sobchacks provide a brief working description of the genre and compare it to other significant genres, again giving it a validity that most other film books do not grant it.

Recent journal articles concerning fantasy films have focused on theme for the most part, and while they are successful in their relatively modest undertakings, they do not help to deepen our basic awareness of fantasy as a genre.[17] Contemporary reviews may thoughtfully acknowledge the importance of the genre's success without giving fantasy itself much dignity in their discussions. In a recent review in *Nation,* for example, Andrew Kopkind calls the new fantasy films "epic cartoons" but goes on to concede that they are "surely the most entertaining, sociologically interesting, and commercially successful cultural products of this period" and that they have given us our language and our heroes of the moment.[18] Obviously, critics and reviewers like Kopkind are still basically as suspicious and contemptuous of the genre as was James Agee forty years ago.

Perhaps the most provocative critical reaction to fantasy films recently has been Robin Wood's chapter "Papering the Cracks: Fantasy and Ideology in the Reagan Era" in his history and analysis of Hollywood from the Vietnam War to the present. In his usual polemical fashion, Wood asserts that the undeniable appeals of such "pure fantasies" as the *Star Wars* trilogy and *E. T.* are neither pure nor sociologically insignificant. He sees such fantasies as symptoms of an age of "reassurance" that sees audiences reduced to children in their response to the films and middle-class, male values celebrated at the expense of all social and cultural movements toward reform in the 1960s and 1970s.[19] Whether one finds Wood's arguments compelling or not, they certainly treat the fantasy genre with as much serious attention as any type of film has ever received. The staggering audience reaction has made such attention mandatory.

After decades of critical neglect, fantasy seems on the verge of being discovered as a significant genre worthy of the most intensive consideration by the whole spectrum of film critics and social historians.

## NOTES

1. Stuart A. Kaminsky, *American Film Genres* (Chicago: Nelson-Hall, 1984), p. 7.

2. This basic distinction is made in Thomas Sobchack and Vivian C. Sobchack's *An Introduction to Film* (Boston: Little, Brown, 1980), p. 225.

3. Quoted by Chris Steinbrunner and Burt Goldblatt in *Cinema of the Fantastic* (New York: Saturday Review Press, 1972), p. 201

4. Gerald Mast, *A Short History of the Movies,* 4th ed. (New York: Macmillan, 1986), p. 496.

5. Kaminsky, *American Film Genres,* p. 131.

6. William Rose Benét and Amy Loveman, "Prospero and the Pictures," *Saturday Papers* (New York: Macmillan, 1921), pp. 43–48.

7. James Agee, *Agee on Film* (Boston: Beacon Press, 1958), p. 156.

8. Quoted by Agee, p. 274.

9. Agee, p. 105.

10. Parker Tyler, *Magic and Myth of the Movies* (New York: Henry Holt, 1947), p. 81.

11. Ibid., p. 113. For a more thorough treatment of the subject, a useful book is Robert T. Eberwein's *Film and the Dream Screen: A Sleep and a Forgetting* (Princeton: Princeton University Press, 1984).

12. Raymond Fielding, "The Dearth of Fantasy," *Films in Review,* November 1959, p. 534.

13. Steinbrunner and Goldblatt, *Cinema of the Fantastic.*

14. David Annan, *Movie Fantastic: Beyond the Dream Machine* (New York: Bounty Books, 1974).

15. Mast, *Short History of the Movies,* pp. 496–500.

16. Sobchack and Sobchack, *Introduction to Film,* pp. 225–26.

17. See the articles by Andrew Gordon and Anne Lancashire in *Film Criticism,* Vol. 8, No. 2, 1984, concerning the mythic elements in the *Star Wars* trilogy.

18. Andrew Kopkind, "The Cartoon Epic," *Nation,* 26 January 1985, pp. 86–87.

19. Robin Wood, *Hollywood from Vietnam to Reagan* (New York: Columbia University Press, 1986), pp. 162–88.

## BIBLIOGRAPHICAL CHECKLIST

### Books

Annan, David. *Movie Fantastic: Beyond the Dream Machine.* New York: Bounty Books, 1974.

Cocteau, Jean. *Diary of a Film: La Belle et la Bête.* New York: Ray Publishers, 1950.

Frazer, John. *Artificially Arranged Scenes: the Films of Georges Méliès.* Boston: G. K. Hall, 1979.

Lee, Walt. *Reference Guide to Fantastic Film.* 3 vols. Los Angeles: Chelsea-Lee Books, 1972.

Mast, Gerald. *A Short History of the Movies,* 4th ed. New York: Macmillan, 1986.

Meyers, Richard. *The World of Fantasy Films.* South Brunswick, N.J.: A. S. Barnes, 1980.

Nichols, Peter. *The World of Fantastic Films.* New York: Dodd, Mead, 1984.

Pollock, Dale. *Skywalking: The Life and Films of George Lucas.* New York: Harmony Books, 1983.

Rovin, Jeff. *The Fabulous Fantasy Films.* South Brunswick, N.J.: A. S. Barnes, 1977.

Slusser, George, and Eric S. Rabkin, eds. *Shadows of the Magic Lamp: Fantasy and Science Fiction in Film.* Carbondale: Southern Illinois University Press, 1985.

Steinbrunner, Chris, and Burt Goldblatt. *Cinema of the Fantastic.* New York: Saturday Review Press, 1972.

Tyler, Parker. *Hollywood Hallucination.* 1944; repr. New York: Simon and Schuster, 1970.

———. *Magic and Myth of the Movies.* 1947; repr. New York: Grove, 1970.

### Shorter Works

Benét, William Rose, and Amy Loveman. "Prospero and the Pictures." In *Saturday Papers.* New York: Macmillan 1921, pp. 43–48.

Clifton, N. Ray. "Fantasy-Allegory-Abstraction." In *The Figure in Film*. Newark: University of Delaware Press, 1983, pp. 332–47.

Dyer, Peter John. "All Manner of Fantasies," *Film and Filming*, June 1958, pp. 13–15.

Fielding, Raymond, "The Dearth of Fantasy," *Films in Review*, November 1959, pp. 534–36.

Gordon, Andrew. *"Return of the Jedi:* The End of the Myth," *Film Criticism* 8, no. 2, 1984, pp. 45–54.

Kaminsky, Stuart A. "Psychological Perspective: Horror and Science Fiction." In *American Film Genres*, 2d ed. Chicago: Nelson-Hall, 1985, pp. 119–33.

Kopkind, Andrew, "The Cartoon Epic," *Nation*, 26 January 1985, pp. 85–88.

Lancashire, Anne. *"Return of the Jedi:* Once More with Feeling," *Film Criticism* 8, no. 2, 1984, pp. 55–66.

Markety, Constance. "Birth and Rebirth in Current Fantasy Films," *Film Criticism* 7, no. 1, 1982, pp. 14–25.

Sobchack, Thomas, and Vivian C. Sobchack. "Genre Films." In *An Introduction to Film*. Boston: Little, Brown, 1980, pp. 189–248.

Telotte, J. P. "The Doubles of Fantasy and the Space of Desire," *Film Criticism*, vol. 7, no. 1, 1982, pp. 56–68.

Wood, Robin. "Papering the Cracks: Fantasy and Ideology in the Reagan Era." In *Hollywood from Vietnam to Reagan*. New York: Columbia University Press, 1986, pp. 162–88.

## SELECTED FILMOGRAPHY

1902   *A Trip to the Moon* (one reel).
Star Films. Produced, directed, and written by Georges Méliès. Cast: uncredited.

1924   *Die Niebelungen* Part 1: *Siegfrieds Tod;* Part 2: *Kriemhilds Rache* (22,283 feet).
Decla-Bioscop-Ufa. Producer: Erich Pommer. Director: Fritz Lang. Screenplay: Thea von Harbou, from *Die Nibelungenlied* and Norse sagas. Cast: Paul Richter (Siegfried), Margarete Schon (Kriemhild), Theodor Lops (Gunter), Hanna Ralph (Brunhild).

*The Thief of Bagdad* (11,230 feet).
United Artists. Producer: Douglas Fairbanks. Director: Raoul Walsh. Screenplay: Lotta Woods, from a story by Elton Thomas. Cast: Douglas Fairbanks (The Thief of Bagdad), Snitz Edwards (His Evil Associate), Charles Belcher (The Holy Man), Julanne Johnston (The Princess), Anna May Wong (The Mongol Slave).

1933   *Berkeley Square* (87 minutes).
20th Century-Fox. Producer: Jesse L. Lasky. Director: Frank Lloyd. Screenplay by Sonya Levien, from a play by John L. Balderston. Cast: Leslie Howard (Peter Standish), Heather Angel (Helen Pettigrew), Valerie Taylor (Kate Pettigrew), Irene Browne (Lady Ann Pettigrew).

1934   *Death Takes a Holiday* (78 minutes).
Paramount. Producer: E. Lloyd Sheldon. Director: Mitchell Leisen. Screenplay: Maxwell Anderson, Gladys Lehman, and Walter Ferris, from a play by Alberto

Casella of the same name. Cast: Fredric March (Prince Sirki-Death), Evelyn Venable (Grazia), Sir Guy Standing (Duke Lambert), Katherine Alexander (Alda), Gail Patrick (Rhoda).

1937    *Lost Horizon* (118 minutes).
Columbia. Producer: Frank Capra. Director: Frank Capra. Screenplay: Robert Riskin, from the novel by James Hilton of the same name. Cast: Ronald Colman (Robert Conway), Jane Wyatt (Sondra), Edward Everett Horton (Alexander P. Lovett), John Howard (George Conway), Thomas Mitchell (Henry Barnard), Margo (Maria).

1939    *The Wizard of Oz* (101 minutes.)
MGM. Producer: Mervyn LeRoy. Director: Victor Fleming. Screenplay: Noel Langley, Florence Ryerson, Edgar Allan Wolfe, from the novel by L. Frank Baum of the same name. Cast: Judy Garland (Dorothy), Frank Morgan (Professor Marvel/The Wizard), Ray Bolger (Hunk/The Scarecrow), Bert Lahr (Zeke/The Cowardly Lion), Jack Haley (Hickory/The Tin Woodman), Billie Burke (Glinda), Margaret Hamilton (Miss Gulch/The Wicked Witch of the West).

1941    *Here Comes Mr. Jordan* (93 minutes).
Columbia. Producer: Everett Riskin. Director: Alexander Hall. Screenplay: Seton I. Miller, Sidney Buchman, from a play by Harry Segall of the same name. Cast: Robert Montgomery (Joe Pendleton), Evelyn Keyes (Bette Logan), Claude Rains (Mr. Jordan), Rita Johnson (Julia Farnsworth), Edward Everett Horton (Messenger 7013), James Gleason (Tony Abbott).

1943    *A Guy Named Joe* (118 minutes).
MGM. Producer: Everett Riskin. Director: Victor Fleming. Screenplay: Dalton Trumbo, based on an original story by Charles Sprague, David Boehm, and Frederick H. Brennan. Cast: Spencer Tracy (Pete Sandridge), Irene Dunne (Dorinda Durston), Van Johnson (Ted Randall), Ward Bond (Al Yackey), James Gleason (''Nails'' Kilpatrick), Lionel Barrymore (The General).

1946    *It's a Wonderful Life* (129 minutes).
RKO. Producer and Director: Frank Capra. Screenplay: Frances Goodrich, Albert Hackett, and Frank Capra, based on the short story ''The Greatest Gift'' by Philip Van Doren Stern. Cast: James Stewart (George Bailey), Donna Reed (Mary Hatch), Lionel Barrymore (Mr. Potter), Thomas Mitchell (Uncle Billy), Horace Travers (Clarence), Beulah Bondi (Mrs. Bailey).

1947    *The Miracle on 34th Street* (96 minutes).
20th Century-Fox. Producer: William Perlberg. Director: George Seaton. Screenplay: George Seaton. Cast: Maureen O'Hara (Doris Walker), John Payne (Fred Gailey), Edmund Gween (Kris Kringle), Gene Lockhart (Judge Henry X. Harper), Natalie Wood (Susan Walker).

1948    *Beauty and the Beast* (93 minutes).
Discina Release in the United States (French version released in 1946). Producer: André Paulve. Director: Jean Cocteau. Screenplay: Jean Cocteau, based on a story by Madame Leprince de Beaumont. Cast: Jean Marais (The Beast/Avenant), Josette Day (Beauty), Marcel André (The Merchant), Nane Germon (Felicity), Mila Parely (Adelaide).

1948    *Portrait of Jennie* (101 minutes).
Selznick International. Producer: David O. Selznick. Director: William Dieterle. Screenplay: Paul Osborn and Peter Berneis, based on the novel of the same name by Robert Nathan. Cast: Jennifer Jones (Jennie Appleton), Joseph Cotten (Eben Adams), Ethel Barrymore (Miss Spinney), Lillian Gish (Mother Mary of Mercy).

1964    *Mary Poppins* (140 minutes).
Walt Disney Studio. Producer: Walt Disney. Director: Robert Stevenson. Screenplay: Bill Walsh, from a book of the same name by P. L. Travers. Cast: Julie Andrews (Mary Poppins), Dick Van Dyke (Bert/Old Dawes), David Tomlinson (Mr. Banks), Glynis Johns (Mrs. Banks), Hermione Baddeley (Ellen), Karen Dotrice (Jane Banks), Matthew Garber (Michael Banks), Elsa Lanchester (Katie Nanna), Ed Wynn (Uncle Albert).

1977    *Star Wars* (119 minutes).
20th Century-Fox. Producer: Gary Kurtz. Director: George Lucas. Screenplay: George Lucas. Cast: Mark Hamill (Luke Skywalker), Harrison Ford (Han Solo), Carrie Fisher (Princess Leia Organa), Alec Guinness (Ben–Obi-Wan–Kenobi), Peter Cushing (Grand Moff Tarkin), David Prowse, with the voice of James Earl Jones (Lord Darth Vader).

1978    *Superman* (142 minutes).
Warner Brothers. Producer: Pierre Spengler. Director: Richard Donner. Screenplay: Mario Puzo, David Newman, Leslie Newman, and Robert Benton, from a story by Mario Puzo. Cast: Marlon Brando (Jor-el), Gene Hackman (Lex Luther), Christopher Reeve (Clark Kent/Superman), Ned Beatty (Otis), Jackie Cooper (Perry White), Glenn Ford (Pa Kent), Margot Kidder (Lois Lane).

1981    *Excalibur* (140 minutes).
Orion. Producer and Director: John Boorman. Screenplay: John Boorman and Rospo Pallenberg, based on *Le Morte d'Arthur* by Sir Thomas Malory. Cast: Nigel Terry (King Arthur), Helen Mirren (Morgana), Nicholas Clay (Lancelot), Cherie Lunghi (Guinevere), Paul Geoffrey (Percival), Nicol Williamson (Merlin), Robert Addie (Mordred).

1982    *E. T., the Extra-Terrestrial* (120 minutes).
Universal. Producers: Steven Spielberg and Kathleen Kennedy. Director: Steven Spielberg. Screenplay: Melissa Mathison. Cast: Henry Thomas (Elliott), Dee Wallace (Mary), Robert McNaughton (Michael), Drew Barrymore (Gertie), Peter Coyote (Keys).

1983    *Splash* (111 minutes).
Buena Vista. Producer: Brian Grazer. Director: Ron Howard. Screenplay: Lowell Ganz, Babaloo Mandel, and Bruce Jay Friedman from a story of the same name by Brian Grazer. Cast: Tom Hanks (Allen Bauer), Daryl Hannah (Madison), Eugene Levy (Walter Kornbluth), John Candy (Freddie Bauer), Dody Goodman (Mrs. Stimler), Shecky Greene (Mr. Buyrite).

# SONGS AND SOAPS

# 15

## The Musical

JAMES M. COLLINS

The musical is simultaneously the most accessible and complex film genre—
accessible because the plots are transparent, the numbers based on the familiar
popular music of the day, and the visual style is seldom if ever confusing or
elliptical. In many ways the clichéd reactions to ''new style'' filmmaking in
the 1960s reflected a nostalgia for exactly this sort of film, as the nostalgia
vehicle *That's Entertainment* (1974) rather definitively proves. At the same
time these films devoted shamelessly to pure entertainment are based on a complicated visual-narrative style that integrates the use of space and of spectator
in unparalleled fashion, as well as integrating an acute awareness of the contemporary culture surrounding them and the historical traditions preceding them.
They may indeed be ''just entertainment,'' but as recent popular culture studies
have shown quite convincingly, defining ''entertainment'' involves confronting
a whole range of interconnected issues. To enjoy musicals is effortless; to appreciate their cultural significance is among the most challenging tasks in film
study.

   The standard place to begin a history of the musical is quite obviously with
the advent of sound, since the first semitalkie was *The Jazz Singer* (1927) and
the first 100 percent all-talking, all-singing movie was *Broadway Melody* (1929).
Musicals were among the most popular films of the early sound era since they
could show off the new technology to its best advantage. But to begin here
distorts the relationship between film and musical material that has been vital
to the medium since its inception. Edison's original motivation in developing
the Kinetoscope was to provide a visual accompaniment for the phonograph,
which he considered the more important of the two devices.[1] Edison's dream
of creating a prototype of the ''home-entertainment center'' was never fully
realized, but its very conception inaugurates the desire to connect music and
images. Throughout the silent era, musical accompaniment for the images simply was a given, and the size and sophistication of the ensemble were con-

sidered a decisive factor in establishing the quality of a theater. Even more important, film in the silent period was seldom silent since more often than not film was only one spectacle or "act" on a diversified bill. The earliest nickelodeons featured song slides (of the follow-the-bouncing-ball variety) that encouraged group sing-alongs.[2] Later, when films moved out of remodeled cigar stores and pawn shops into legitimate vaudeville houses throughout the country, they remained for several years one facet of an evening's entertainment that featured a wide range of live musical acts.[3] The presence of these live musical acts led, oddly enough, to the development of the first experiments with sound films. In 1926, the first Vitaphone preludes premiered in Warner's Theatre in New York. These preludes featured various musical acts (the most prominent being stars from the Metropolitan Opera) and were clearly intended to serve the same function as the "live" musical preludes in the film theater. The success of these Vitaphone preludes was an essential step in the development of the sound feature since they were instrumental (no pun intended) in creating a new market for sound film in the film-going public.

The significance of the ongoing tension between live musical acts and film presentation goes beyond simple financial concerns. Vaudeville, the music hall, and Broadway were established musical institutions before the advent of film, but they are relevant to the film musical beyond mere precedent or sources for adaptation. Musical films, while seeming to provide a great advance over live acts, also meant the end of the spontaneous, intimate relationship between show and audience. From the earliest film musicals to the present one encounters this tension between the increasing technological sophistication of the medium (allowing it easily to outdo mere theater) and the sense of nostalgia for a direct relationship with the audience. In her seminal study on the musical, Jane Feuer describes this tension in the following manner. "The Hollywood musical as a genre perceives the gap between producer and consumer, the breakdown of community designated by the very distinction between performer and audience, as a form of cinematic original sin."[4] This brief overview of the history of the genre will focus on the ways musicals have attempted to resolve that tension by concentrating on the ever-shifting relationship between performance, spectacle, and audience.

## The 1930s: Diversification, Contradiction, and Refinement

The thirties were perhaps the golden age of the musical since at no other time were they as diversified artistically or as successful with the general public. While certain common denominators can be located, the differences among the musicals produced by competing studios reveal the most about the evolution of the genre. The popular images of Fred Astaire, Maurice Chevalier, and lines of dancing Golddiggers are all fixtures in American popular imagery, but each was associated with decidedly different types of entertainment. Any history of Hollywood at this time therefore must be studio sensitive since at least three distinct styles emerged: the operetta tradition at Paramount, the "backstage" show at Warner Brothers, and the elegant-romantic approach at RKO.

Some of the first great musical successes in the 1930s were among the most conservative in their nostalgic reliance on earlier forms of musical entertainment. The films featuring Maurice Chevalier (*Love Parade,* 1929 and *Love Me Tonight,* 1932) and later Nelson Eddy and Jeanette MacDonald (*Naughty Marietta,* 1935; *Rose Marie,* 1936; *Maytime,* 1937; *Sweethearts,* 1939) were basically nineteenth-century operettas in their use of fairy-tale plots and settings and in their reliance on quasi-"high art" singing, especially the romantic duet. The use of space (with a few important exceptions like *Love Me Tonight*) was primarily static and extremely theatrical. Produced by Paramount (the most European in orientation of all Hollywood studios) and directed by the likes of Ernst Lubitsch and Rouben Mamoulian, these films have a refined, witty, but basically stagy quality since their model of what constituted fine musical entertainment was decidedly antiquated by the 1930s.

The musicals produced by Warner Brothers were diametrically opposed to the nineteenth-century operetta tradition. Three films in particular produced in 1933—*Footlight Parade, Forty-Second Street,* and *Gold Diggers of 1933*— represented a radically different aesthetic that was American, contemporary, and popular. These films were filled with obsessive theater directors, hustling hoofers, art deco sets, tough-talking dames, and any form of semicontrolled energy. These films took as their model the contemporary Broadway show and recent popular music. They bear a greater resemblance to the Warner gangster films of the same decade than to Paramount musicals, since like the gangster films, these musicals presented a gritty, street-smart set of individuals driven to succeed at any cost. More specifically, as musicals they were instrumental in developing a new, thoroughly twentieth-century definition of musical entertainment.

*Footlight Parade* epitomizes the contemporary spirit of this new form of film musical and reveals quite clearly the tensions, even contradictions, that made them so distinctive. The narrative premise is a perfect example of the recuperation of live entertainment that Feuer describes. James Cagney plays a musical director down on his luck who decides there's a fortune to be made in producing "live" musical preludes for film theaters throughout the country. His "shows" travel from theater to theater in chain-store fashion, while he creates new numbers in New York. But the emphasis on "live" entertainment is more thoroughly worked out in the "backstage" conceit pervading the film. Cagney constantly makes and remakes numbers so that each one appears to be in the process of creation. In the last section we see the finished product, but at this point a fascinating series of contradictions arise. While the rehearsals leading up to this grand finale are all clearly situated on a theatrical stage, the finished numbers are contructed around a cinematic use of space. The best example is Busby Berkeley's (who directed only these last three numbers—Lloyd Bacon was responsible for the rest) extravaganza "By a Waterfall." The number begins "onstage" in a theater complete with proscenium arch and audience. As the number progresses, theatrical space gives way to completely cinematic space in which the camera changes perspective constantly, moving from underwater shots between the legs of the dancers to high overhead shots of the entire ensemble. The Berkeley-signature overhead shots are perhaps the greatest violation of theatrical space since they represent an impossible perspective, created specifically for the camera, in which the positioning of characters and sets is subservient to the overall visual pattern within the frame.

*Forty-Second Street* manifests many of the same structural features (the maniacal director in the process of putting on a "live" show, the "blue-collar" dancers, the buffoonish financial backers, several of the same actors and actresses) and many of the same tensions between theatrical and cinematic space. We see, once again, countless rehearsal scenes, and here the finished product includes numbers like "Shuffle Off to Buffalo," presented "onstage" in a limited, two-dimensional space. But the title number obeys a different spatial logic. It begins simply and statically—Ruby Keeler sings the title song (and dances to it after a fashion) onstage, but when the chorus takes over, cinematic space takes over as well. The camera begins a long tracking crane shot that moves through "the city" that clearly could not exist onstage. Especially interesting here is the motivation for this transition. When the entertainer performs for the people the space remains theatrical, but when "the people" begin to sing and take the song with them into the street and their homes, suddenly the whole world becomes "musicalized" and only the fluidity of the cinematic medium captures its all-pervasive spontaneity. In the process, performance gives way to spectacle, theater gives way to film, "act" gives way to "life itself."

One finds in this depiction of "life in the streets" the central ideological tensions of these early Warner musicals, perhaps best illustrated by the opening and closing numbers of *Gold Diggers of 1933*. In the opening, assembled chorus girls are clad in giant coins as they sing "We're in the Money," a scene which is surely one of the most preposterously optimistic reflections on the Depression in film history. Here the Hollywood musical offers the viewer a saccharine alternative to economic hard times outside the confines of the movie theater, entertainment as escapism pure and simple. But the last number in *Gold Diggers* is "My Forgotten Man," which couldn't be more opposed to the opening number in visualization and tone. Where the first number is a glittering ensemble number presented as pure spectacle, "Forgotten Man" begins with a solitary singer (Joan Blondell), who is clearly supposed to be a streetwalker. As she finishes singing about the "forgotten men" (who once fought the wars and tilled the earth but now stand in bread lines) the camera begins a track throughout the city (à la *Forty-Second Street)* introducing shots of forgotten men everywhere. The number remains a production number, but the sense of static presentation for the audience, as in "We're in the Money," dissolves into a kind of Berkeleyesque fanfare for the common man.

The tension between entertainment as escapism and entertainment as musicalized social commentary makes application of simple political labels a rather Procrustean activity. In his perceptive essay on the Warner Brothers musicals, Mark Roth has argued for their direct connections with the New Deal—that they embody a spirit of optimism, of the collective effort succeeding where individuals fail, that they even include FDR models in the figures of the director, etc.[5] Roth's analyses are often quite convincing, but they suffer from all the shortcomings of standard "reflection" theory that seeks to explain in one-to-one equivalences how film "x" reflects social situation "y" in direct, uncomplicated fashion. While many of the structural features Roth seizes on may be "New Deal-ish," Jeffrey Richards's work on Frank Capra's comedies[6] and the *Cahiers du cinéma* collective text on *Young Mr. Lincoln*[7] both see many of the same features as avowedly populist and anti-Roosevelt by explicit design. Part of the problem obviously arises in defining the points of contact (and departure) between collective action and the New Deal as a whole, but the more far-reaching issue concerns the complete lack of any notion of "mediation" in most of these readings of 1930s films. In his essay on Columbia Pictures, Edward Buscombe argues for a more rigorous and extreme investigation into Hollywood's representation of social experience going beyond simple reflection theory.[8] Although he says little about musicals specifically, Buscombe's insistence that we see Hollywood as a force which mediated reality, even produced reality (as opposed to simply reflecting it), serves as a starting point for ideological analysis of 1930s musicals.

The best way to understand this mediation, and at the same time evaluate the musical in its most sophisticated form during the decade, is to examine the Astaire-Rogers films from RKO (*The Gay Divorcee*, 1934; *Top Hat*, 1935; *Follow the Fleet*, 1936; *Swing Time*, 1936; *Shall We Dance?*, 1937; *Carefree*, 1938; *The Story of Vernon and Irene Castle*, 1939). Within the traditions that emerged in the early sound musical, these films may be seen as a hybrid of the operetta and contemporary backstage musicals. In many ways the Astaire-Rogers dances may be seen as part of the duet-dominated operetta tradition, and the stylized sets and fairy-tale plots resemble *Love Parade* far more than *Footlight Parade*. At the same time, these films were avowedly "backstage," Astaire and Rogers always playing show people who come together romantically as they join professionally. They were explicitly "contemporary" in their incorporation of currently popular jazz and ballroom music and dance movements (especially in their use of scores by George Gershwin, Jerome Kern, and Irving Berlin).

Two significant ramifications of this hybrid form were a greater integration of numbers with narrative and a far greater diversification of the musical numbers. In the Warner's films of the early 1930s the numbers were more often than not fully detachable from the narrative, musical breaks that postponed the development of relationships between the characters until the number had ended, at which point the "plot" continued. As a result, performance space and time, and narrative space and time, appeared only tangentially and intermittently related, a throwback no doubt to an earlier period when the number was part of an elaborate musical review where spectacle followed spectacle without any suturing narrative continuity. The Astaire-Rogers films introduced an entirely different relationship in which songs and dances became thoroughly narrativized—the most significant developments in the characters' relationships coming not only when they were dancing and singing together, but *because* they were doing it together.

A significant amount of critical attention has been devoted to the dances of Astaire-Rogers, but the most significant feature of those dances remains their diversity.[9] In another essay I have tried to differentiate the various dances according to their function within the text as a whole—those thoroughly "private" dances which suggest the sexual power of the dance ("Cheek to Cheek"), those which glorify the power of dancing itself ("The Continental"), and those emphasizing the relationship between entertainment and spectators ("Shall We Dance").[10]

The third category of dances remains the ideological center of these films since they simultaneously suggest the dance as the only viable alternative to despair (financial or otherwise). These numbers, unlike the escapism of "We're in the Money" or the semiserious social commentary of "The Forgotten Man," are part of an elaborate transformation of values in which an entertainment economy replaces a financial economy, and success becomes redefined in the terms of the musical. This shift in economies is accompanied by an explicitly "discursive" visual and verbal relationship with the spectator. Many theorists of spectatorship insist upon the voyeuristic nature of the film viewing state,[11] but the numbers in these movies address themselves directly to the audience, thereby establishing a different text-to-spectator relationship than other Hollywood genres. A subtle explanation of this phenomenon is beyond the scope of this survey, but at least two aspects of this discursive relationship need to be commented upon here. The first concerns the actor's direct gaze at the camera, and by extension at the spectator. In other genre films looking directly into the camera is admissible only within the context of a point-of-view shot or for a comic effect, for example, Bob Hope winking at the camera in any number of films. The title number in *Top Hat* exemplifies the difference. The song opens onstage, sung to a diegetic audience, but as the number progresses that audience disappears in reframing, and Astaire sings directly to the actual spectators in the movie theater. This direct gaze, or *regard,* is accompanied by an explicit verbal discursiveness that constantly emphasizes the *you,* as in *Let Yourself Go.*

The ideological ramifications of this discursiveness are far-reaching since they provide the foundation of the spectator's involvement in the text. If an ideology is at work in the musicals of the 1930s, it cannot be defined in traditional "political" terms. The "politics" of entertainment need to be explored if we are to understand how these texts position themselves vis-à-vis American culture and as they attempt to position their spectators in the process.

### The Freed Unit: The Folk and the Self-Reflexive Musicals

The early 1940s mark a relative low point in the history of the musical compared to the diversified invention of the 1930s. During the war years many war effort musicals were produced (*Cover Girl*, 1944; *The Gang's All Here*, 1943), but no new pattern emerged comparable to the 1930s musical. A series of Dan Dailey–Betty Grable–Carmen Miranda vehicles appeared (*Springtime in the Rockies*, 1941; *Mother Wore Tights*, 1947, etc.), but they have been largely ignored by film historians, not so much because they are egregiously bad (certainly the case), but because they represent no significant development over the films of the 1930s.

The Freed Unit musicals produced at MGM continue to generate greater critical interest because of their refinement of so many of the central features of the genre. Arthur Freed had worked in a variety of capacities making musicals throughout the 1930s, but not until he became a producer in the 1940s was his impact felt. The term *Freed Unit* refers to the distinct style that emerged in the films he produced, even though different directors, actors, and choreographers were involved in them. Since most of the acknowledged "masterpieces" of the genre from *Meet Me in St. Louis* (1944) to *The Bells Are Ringing* (1960) are Freed products, anything like a careful examination of each film is impossible. Instead, I will briefly differentiate between two basic styles that emerged and discuss how other non-Freed films followed suit throughout the fifties.

Vincente Minnelli's *Meet Me in St. Louis* is a quintessential example of a Freed Unit "folk" musical. The term *folk musical* is used by Rick Altman[12] to describe those musicals that depart from the backstage tradition by using music and dances indigenous to a particular temporal and geographic setting. Musicals such as *Oklahoma!* (1955), *Brigadoon* (1954), *Seven Brides for Seven Brothers* (1954), *Annie Get Your Gun* (1950), *Gigi* (1958), and *West Side Story* (1961) all develop a set of songs and dances which grow directly out of the rhythms and costumes of their settings. One finds few official performances or shows in such films. Instead, numbers seem to be a spontaneous but still "anthropologically" correct outpouring of a given culture. *Meet Me in St. Louis* serves as a perfect example because all of the numbers have an organic relationship with their environment. Songs are either generated by times of year (Christmas—"Have Yourself a Merry Little Christmas"), daily activity (riding the trolley—"The Trolley Song"), or special sing-along parties ("Under the Bamboo Tree") or events particular to that setting (the World's Fair—"Meet Me in St. Louis"). In each case the shift from day-to-day life to musical life appears completely natural, the distinctions purposely blurred—life is not *like* a song, it *is* a song. Explicit "stage" settings are avoided, and when any kind of proscenium is used, it is thoroughly "natural"—window archways, front porches, etc.

Running parallel with these folk musicals was a series of films that develop in sophisticated ways the backstage format. *Summer Stock* (1950), *Singin' in the Rain* (1952), *The Band Wagon* (1953), and *Silk Stockings* (1957) all contain strong self-reflexive elements that not only expose the mechanisms of production but seemingly investigate the nature of entertainment itself. Numbers like "That's Entertainment" *(The Band Wagon)* and "Gotta Dance" *(Singin' in the Rain)* are emblematic of this desire to make entertainment *about* entertainment. In "That's Entertainment," the history of Western culture is "musicalized"—all major cultural achievements, whether *Oedipus Rex, Hamlet,* or Broadway shows, share a common purpose, to entertain the spectator. Not coincidentally, this number is sung directly to the camera/real audience without any diegetic audience to serve as a justification. The song becomes its own justification, its own legitimation of its privileged status as entertainment. "Gotta Dance/Broadway Melody" similarly attempts to musicalize existence by providing a past history that justifies/ensures the success of entertainment in the present.

This structure becomes especially baroque in the "Born in a Trunk" number in *A Star Is Born* (1954)—not a Freed Unit musical, but MGM-produced and clearly inspired by the Freed Unit. The scene opens on Vicki Lester (Judy Garland) and Norman Maine (James Mason) in a theater watching Lester's film debut. The "show" within the movie concludes, and as an encore the character Lester plays approaches the edge of the stage and sings about how she got to this point, inaugurating an elaborate series of flashbacks, some situated on other earlier "stages" in her career, others in imaginary agents' offices, etc. In the process, two significant conflations occur. The stages and real-life locales become interchangeable, thereby producing a musicalized autobiography in which the distinctions between the two appear negligible. The other, more elaborate conflation concerns the various audiences involved. When we see the character that Lester portrays singing for the first time on her own in a flashback, four different but thoroughly interrelated audiences are engaged at once—the diegetic music hall audience in the flashback, the diegetic theater audience that Vicki Lester's character sings to in her film, the diegetic film theater audience within *A Star Is Born* (of which Lester is a part), and the actual audience of *A Star Is Born,* seated in actual film theaters. This "Chinese box" structure erects spatial and temporal distinctions only to dissolve them entirely through the power of the entertainment that makes all audiences and all shows collapse into one grand megatext that is the Garland persona.

The self-reflexivity in the MGM musicals operates at varying levels of sophistication and employs a wide range of textual mechanisms—"persona" references, hymns to the greater glory of entertainment itself, films about films in the process of creation, intertextual references, etc. Direct commentary on the actual apparatus of production is the basis of several numbers: "Technicolor, Cinemascope and Stereophonic Sound" *(Silk Stockings,* 1957); "You Were Meant for Me" *(Singin' in the Rain),* in which Don constructs the set for his song to Kathy; the disastrous effects in *The Band Wagon* rehearsals; and the nonproduction production number Garland does in her living room in *A Star Is Born*.

While the all-pervasiveness of the self-reflexive elements clearly differentiates the MGM musicals from other Hollywood genre films, one cannot confuse this type of hyper–self-consciousness with that associated with the films of Jean-Marie Straub, Jean-Luc Godard, etc. Jane Feuer locates the crucial difference between musical and modernist self-reflexivity in the textual function; the latter seeks to "deconstruct" the classical text by violating its conventions, but the former "demystifies" those conventions only to "remystify" them, thereby securing the status of traditional entertainment.[13] The three songs mentioned above that refer directly to the actual aspects of production do so only in order to establish a "second-order" discursiveness in which the text's exposure of its mechanisms is itself a textual mechanism at another level. The musical is thus able to have its self-reflexive cake and dance on it too. The mechanisms of entertainment are exposed only so long as they remain entertaining. At this point the film musical is no longer an ersatz imitation of the music hall or a watered-down imitation of the European operetta, but a superior mode of entertainment unto itself. The MGM musical represents not just the zenith of self-reflexivity within the genre, but Hollywood's very vision of itself as entertainment capital of the world.

## The Decline and Return of the Classical Musical

The musicals that appeared after the golden age of the genre in the 1950s gravitated toward different, often contradictory, extremes: the "blockbuster" that attempts to continue and even outdo the "quality" of the Freed Unit (*West Side Story*, 1961; *The Sound of Music*, 1965; *Camelot*, 1967; *On a Clear Day You Can See Forever*, 1970; the nostalgic compilation film (*That's Entertainment*, parts 1 and 2) which simply edits together the "greatest hits" of MGM, thereby acknowledging that the Golden Age is indeed over; the "deconstructive" musical that explodes codes and conventions in an attempt to parody or critique the genre (*The Boyfriend*, 1971; *All That Jazz*, 1979; and *Pennies from Heaven*, 1981).

The last category has received the most serious critical interest since in their "deconstruction" these films further elaborate the possibilities of the genre, continuing the self-reflexivity found in the Freed Unit musicals but in a more explicitly metafictional manner. They have replaced the affirmation of "That's Entertainment" with the interrogative "What's Entertainment?" In each case the status of entertainment is actively investigated—from the perspective of the director (*All That Jazz*), the spectators (*Pennies from Heaven*), or the spectacle itself (*The Boy Friend*). While Bob Fosse's film at times bears closer resemblance to $8\frac{1}{2}$ than *Singin' in the Rain*, its attempt to demystify the genre and entertainment as a whole still reveals an element of the same "re-mystification'' found in the MGM musical, although here entirely *personalized* in the figure of the director, who may be driven to amphetamines and sexual promiscuity, but lives and quite literally dies for ''Showtime.''

The metafictional and nostalgic compilation films of the 1970s appear to mark the end of the classical Hollywood musical. Several films have appeared within the last decade, though, that suggest that formulas, codes, and conventions are still viable ways of constructing musical entertainment. The advent of the rock musical, which by its rhythms, characters, and intended audience appears to mark definitively the end of the classical musical, has ironically signaled the return of many of its central features. *Footloose* (1984) is especially representative. The chief source of conflict in the film is between the town preacher, Reverend Moore, who detests rock music and dancing, and the young outsider, Ren, who lives for it. The struggle over the dance at the prom is set in traditional terms of spontaneity vs. stolidity, personal expression vs. public repression. Ren manages, like Astaire or Kelly before him, to transform a wide variety of natural spaces (barns, football fields, etc.) into dance spaces, thereby ''musicalizing'' as much of the world as possible. Ren's victory over the preacher signals the greater victory of the dance over traditional social order.

Perhaps the most surprising evidence of a return to many of the conventions of the traditional musical has come in the form of rock videos. The emergence of rock music, and most specifically the rock festival films of the 1960s like *Woodstock* and *Monterey Pop,* has been considered proof positive that musical narrative had been replaced by musical performance as the dominant mode of disseminating popular music. Yet rock videos of the past ten years represent a significant reversal of that process. The performance mode of the 1960s has been completely transformed into a narrative mode of the 1980s. The vast majority of rock videos have either done away with outright performance, or placed it entirely within a narrative context, so that very few videos maintain anything like a ''concert'' aesthetic. Most surprising about this transition is that very often the narrativization appears entirely unjustified by the song lyrics, yet the band members ''act out'' those lyrics, sometimes in period costumes and settings, thereby attempting to narrativize spatially and temporally songs about atemporal ''states of consciousness,'' for lack of a better term. With the return of narrative to musical entertainment the history of the genre has hardly reached an end point.

## BIBLIOGRAPHICAL OVERVIEW

The state of scholarship devoted to the musical has drastically improved in the eighties. While other Hollywood genres were rediscovered by serious film historians in the 1960s, the musical was virtually ignored by academic criticism until the late 1970s. A number of book-length studies appeared before this, but these were generally coffee-table volumes lavishly illustrated with production stills, but little else. These have varied only in the sophistication and quality of their formats. Arlene Croce's *The Fred Astaire and Ginger Rogers Book* (1972) attempts to capture their most important dances, but other more recent attempts like Ethan Mordden's *The Hollywood Musical* emphasize only the nostalgia element, substituting personal taste lists (Best Performances, Worst Performances, Dullest Person, Ruby Keeler Award for Least Overacted Role, etc.) for production stills.

Two books, *Genre: The Musical* (1981), edited by Rick Altman, and Jane Feuer's *The Hollywood Musical* (1982), establish the critical parameters for serious study of the musical. Both texts purposely avoid the production still/ nostalgia style in an effort to examine the basis of musical entertainment through close stylistic, ideological, and psychoanalytic analysis. Applying theoretical concepts from Christian Metz, Louis Althusser, and Jacques Lacan to films by Vincente Minnelli and Busby Berkeley struck many nonacademic or quasi-academic critics as nonsensical. In conflict here are the presuppositions involved; to those who were dismissive of using contemporary critical theory in regard to the musical, these films were simple entertainment, not open to serious analysis. To the contributors to the Altman anthology, using such theoretical approaches was essential to an understanding of the nature of entertainment within its cultural context.

Altman provides short introductions describing the main thrust of each essay in *Genre: The Musical,* making an article-by-article overview superfluous here. I will instead concentrate on those essays not discussed in the preceding historical outline that develop significant approaches to the genre. A more thorough critique of Altman's anthology may be found in Charles Wolfe's review article "What's Entertainment? Recent Writing on the Film Musical" in *Quarterly Review of Film Studies,* Spring 1986.

Richard Dyer's "Entertainment and Utopia" has proven a seminal essay since it is one of the few essays devoted to *any* genre that investigates the diverse functions entertainment may perform within a specific cultural context. He takes clichés like "escapism" and "wish fulfillment" and carefully examines how these values are constructed by certain forms of entertainment. Dyer stresses that musicals appear to be utopian solutions to real social contradictions, but their success in resolving those contradictions is due to their ability to redefine them within the terms of the genre. Musicals create false contradictions that they already have the answer to, thereby resolving problems through an elaborate substitution process. Dyer invokes the work of Suzanne K. Langer, developing his own categories to subtly characterize both the representational and nonrepresentational aspects of entertainment. In the process he addresses central issues like the relationship between the musical numbers and the narrative.

In her essay "The Image of Woman as Image: The Optical Politics of *Dames,*" Lucy Fischer applies a feminist approach to the genre that develops a series of issues and questions ignored by most studies on the musical. The cornerstone of Fischer's essay is the production and consumption of women as images catering to the pleasure of the male eye. She argues convincingly that those optical politics involve a sexual coding of the gaze as in other genres, but that within the musical the fluidity of the mise-en-scène and the emphasis on the plastic nature of cinematic composition are linked directly to the body of women. Women became thoroughly objectified in Berkeley's mise-en-scène, and his camera fetishizes, fragments, and "penetrates" the bodies of women, thereby positioning a thoroughly male-identified spectator. While her remarks on Berkeley are most convincing, their applicability to other musicals is debatable. Nonetheless, her essay remains a significant attempt to bring a feminist mode of analysis to a genre that depends on female audiences as much as, if not more than, any other genre.

Alan Williams's essay, "The Musical Film and Recorded Popular Music," is also concerned with spectator positioning (as are the essays by Fischer, Feuer, and Collins in the Altman anthology), approaching it from an often overlooked, but vitally important perspective. Williams focuses on the relationship between the musical and the recording process itself, concentrating on the technological and stylistic aspects of the *auditory* "apparatus" (normally characterized in exclusively *visual* terms in the work of Jean-Louis Comolli, Jean-Louis Baudry, Stephen Heath, etc.). By shifting emphasis onto the spectator as *auditor,* and situating these films within the history of popular music, Williams is able directly to confront the explicitly *musical* nature of the genre in an unprecedented manner.

Jane Feuer's *The Hollywood Musical* is the single most ambitious book devoted to the genre, exploring a series of interrelated issues that constitutes the self-reflexivity distinctive of the genre. Her assertion "The musical is Hollywood writ large" sums up quite neatly the book's central presupposition: to understand the musical is to understand Hollywood as an entertainment industry since it is in these films that Hollywood articulates its vision of itself, thereby creating its own mythology and asserting its privileged status within American culture and the history of entertainment.

Feuer's first chapter, "Mass Art as Folk Art," establishes both a historical and a theoretical context for the genre. For the former, she discusses the musical film's direct antecedents, the music hall and vaudeville, setting the terms of the transition from live to recorded entertainment. For the latter, she stresses the film musical's ability to present itself as "folk art" (spontaneous, of the community, etc.), even though it is by its very nature "mass art" (fixed, produced by an industry, etc.). A variety of textual mechanisms make this possible: "nonchoreographed" choreography, group dances as community rituals, use of natural settings as dance floors, inclusion of diegetic spectators who participate directly or indirectly in the show, and an overall emphasis on entertainment as bricolage.

The second chapter, "Spectators and Spectacle," develops many of Feuer's central points concerning spectator positioning and the ideological ramifications of the genre's self-reflexivity discussed above. The next two chapters, "The Celebration of Popular Song" and "Dream Worlds and Dream Stages," examine the relationships between the musical and more "elite" art (opera, ballet, symphony), and the development of a heterogeneous diegesis in the musical that establishes differences between the world, the stage, and dream states, only to erase them in ever-shifting hybrid combinations of all three. In the final chapter, "The History of the Hollywood Musical: Innovation as Conservation," Feuer historicizes self-reflexivity through an analysis of intertextual history, tracing the complicated, ubiquitous process of citation found in these films.

Two recent articles that are ostensibly extended reviews of the Altman anthology have expanded much of that work in significant ways. Robert Burgoyne's "Enunciation and Generic Address" discusses the various approaches to enunciation and spectator positioning in the Altman anthology (particularly the Feuer, Collins, and Fischer essays), but places them in a broader context of enunciation theory by also focusing on Stephen Neale's *Genre* (1980) and Annette Kuhn's *Woman's Pictures* (1982). Burgoyne's essay lucidly locates the key problematics in this work and provides a thorough overview of their ongoing development. Charles Wolfe's aforementioned "What's Entertainment? Recent Writing on the Film Musical" also provides a thoroughly developed context for understanding the Altman and Feuer books, as well as an insightful elaboration of what still needs to be developed in the study of the genre. Wolfe is especially sensitive to a weakness of both books—that while certain issues concerning textuality have been thoroughly developed, they have not been sufficiently historicized. Moreover, a comprehensive history of the musical remains to be done since these two books have rescued the genre from coffee tables in regard to theoretical issues, but not in regard to subtle historical analysis.

This significant omission should be rectified by Rick Altman's *The American Film Musical* (University of Indiana Press, 1987), which promises to be the definitive history of the genre for some time to come. Altman's book should represent a quantum leap over previous histories of the genre since it combines exhaustive factual material with a theoretical sophistication lacking in Clive Hirschhorn's *The Hollywood Musical* (Crown, 1981) and Ted Sennett's *Hollywood Musical* (Abrams, 1981), both of which are encyclopedic in scope but ultimately superficial and aggressively evaluative in the worst "film-buff" tradition.

## NOTES

1. David Cook, *A History of Narrative Film* (New York: Norton, 1981), p. 5.
2. Russell Merritt, "Nickelodeon Theaters, 1905–1914: Building an Audience for the Movies," in *The American Film Industry,* ed. Tino Balio (Madison: University of Wisconsin Press, 1985), pp. 83–102.
3. Robert C. Allen, "The Movies in Vaudeville: Historical Context of the Movies as Popular Entertainment," in *American Film Industry,* pp. 57–82.
4. Jane Feuer, *The Hollywood Musical* (Bloomington: Indiana University Press, 1982), p. 3.

5. Mark Roth, "Some Warners Musicals and the Spirit of the New Deal," in *Genre: The Musical*, ed. Rick Altman (Boston: Routledge and Kegan Paul, 1981), pp. 41–58.

6. Jeffrey Richards, "Frank Capra and the Cinema of Populism," in *Movies and Methods*, vol. 1, ed. Bill Nichols (Berkeley: University of California Press, 1976), pp. 65–77.

7. The Editors of *Cahiers du cinéma*, "John Ford's *Young Mr. Lincoln*," in *Movies and Methods*, pp. 493–528.

8. Edward Buscombe, "Notes on Columbia Pictures Corporation 1926–1941," *Screen*, Autumn 1975, pp. 65–82.

9. Arlene Croce, *The Fred Astaire and Ginger Rogers Book* (New York: Galahad Books, 1972).

10. Jim Collins, "Toward Defining a Matrix of the Musical Comedy: The Place of the Spectator Within the Textual Mechanisms," in *Genre: The Musical*, pp. 134–46.

11. See especially Christian Metz, "Story/Discourse: Notes on Two Kinds of Voyeurism," and Laura Mulvey, "Visual Pleasure and Narrative Cinema," in *Movies and Methods*, vol. 2, ed. Bill Nichols (Berkeley: University of California Press, 1986), pp. 543–48 and 303–14.

12. Rick Altman, *The American Film Musical* (Bloomington: Indiana University Press, 1977).

13. Feuer, p. 3.

## BIBLIOGRAPHICAL CHECKLIST

### Books

Altman, Rick, *The American Film Musical*. Bloomington; Indiana University Press, 1987.

Altman, Rick, ed. *Genre: The Musical*. Boston: Routledge and Kegan Paul, 1981. (An exhaustive, annotated bibliography by Jane Feuer is included.)

Babington, Bruce, and Peter William Evan. *Blue Skies and Silver Linings: Aspects of the Hollywood Musical*. Manchester, England: University of Manchester Press, 1985.

Croce, Arlene. *The Fred Astaire and Ginger Rogers Book*. New York: Galahad Books, 1972.

Feuer, Jane. *The Hollywood Musical*. Bloomington; Indiana University Press, 1982.

Fordin, Hugh. *The World of Entertainment: Hollywood's Greatest Musicals*. New York: Doubleday, 1975.

Kobal, John. *Gotta Sing, Gotta Dance: A Pictorial History of Film Musicals*. London: Hamlyn, 1971.

Mordden, Ethan. *The Hollywood Musical*. New York: St. Martin's Press, 1981.

Sennett, Ted. *Hollywood Musicals*. New York: Henry H. Abrams, 1981.

Taylor, John Russel, and Arthur Jackson. *The Hollywood Musical*. New York: McGraw-Hill, 1971.

### Shorter Works

Altman, Rick. "A Semantic/Syntactic Approach to Film Genre," *Cinema Journal*, Spring 1984, pp. 6–18.

Belton, John, "The Backstage Musical," *Movie*, Spring 1977, pp. 36–44.

Braudy, Leo. "Musicals and the Energy from Within." In his *The World in a Frame: What We See in Films.* New York: Anchor/Doubleday, 1976, pp. 139–163.

Burgoyne, Robert. "Enunciation and Generic Address," *Quarterly Review of Film Studies,* Spring 1985, pp. 135–42.

Cook, Jim. "On a Clear Day You Can See Forever," *Movie,* Spring 1977, pp. 61–62.

Delamater, Jerome. "Busby Berkeley: An American Surrealist," *Wide Angle,* Spring 1976, pp. 30–37.

Hasbany, Richard. "The Musical Goes Ironic: The Evolution of Genres," *Journal of American Culture,* Spring 1978, pp. 120–37.

Hogue, Peter, "The Band Wagon," *Velvet Light Trap,* Winter 1974, pp. 33–34.

Johnson, Albert, "The Films of Vincente Minnelli," *Film Quarterly,* Winter 1958, pp. 21–35.

Lloyd, Peter. "Stanley Donen," *Brighton Film Review,* March 1970, pp. 17–19.

Mellencamp, Patricia. "Spectacle and Spectator: Looking Through the American Musical Comedy," *Cine-Tracts,* Summer 1977, pp. 28–35.

Patrick, R., and W. Haislip. "Thank Heaven for Little Girls," *Cineaste,* vol. 6, 1973, pp. 22–25.

Scheurer, Timothy, "The Aesthetics of Form and Convention in the Movie Musical." *Journal of Popular Film,* Fall 1974, pp. 307–24.

Spiegel, Ellen. "Fred and Ginger Meet Van Nest Polglase," *Velvet Light Trap,* Fall 1973, pp. 17–22.

Turim, Maureen. "Gentlemen Consume Blondes," *Wide Angle,* Spring 1976, pp. 68–76.

Wolfe, Charles. "What's Entertainment? Recent Writings on the Film Musical," *Quarterly Review of Film Studies,* Spring 1985, pp. 143–52.

## SELECTED FILMOGRAPHY

1929    *Love Parade* (110 minutes).
Paramount. Director: Ernst Lubitsch. Screenplay: Ernest Vajda, Guy Bolton, based on the play *The Prince Consort* by Leon Xanrof, Jules Chancel. Music: Victor Schertzinger. Cast: Maurice Chevalier, Jeannette MacDonald.

1933    *Forty-Second Street* (98 minutes).
Warner Brothers. Director: Lloyd Bacon. Screenplay: Rian James, James Seymour, based on the novel by Bradford Ropes. Music: Al Dubin, Harry Warren. Choreography: Busby Berkeley. Cast: Warner Baxter, Bebe Daniels, Ginger Rogers, Dick Powell, Ruby Keeler.

*Gold Diggers of 1933* (96 minutes).
Warner Brothers. Director: Mervyn LeRoy. Screenplay: Avery Hopwood, Ben Markson, David Boehm, Erwin Gelsey, James Seymour, based on the play *The Gold Diggers* by Avery Hopwood. Music: Al Dubin, Harry Warren. Choreography: Busby Berkeley. Cast: Warren William, Joan Blondell, Ruby Keeler, Dick Powell.

1935    *Top Hat* (101 minutes).
RKO Radio. Director: Mark Sandrich. Screenplay: Dwight Taylor, Allan Scott, derived from the musical *The Gay Divorcee* by Dwight Taylor and a play by Alexander Farago, Aladar Laszlo. Art Direction: Van Nest Polglase, Carroll Clark.

Music: Irving Berlin. Choreography: Fred Astaire, Hermis Pan. Cast: Fred Astaire, Ginger Rogers, Edward Everett Horton, Helen Broderick.

1937   *Maytime* (133 minutes).
MGM. Director: Robert Z. Leonard. Screenplay: Noel Langley based on a play by Rida Johnson Young. Music: Sigmund Romberg. Cast: Jeannette MacDonald, Nelson Eddy, John Barrymore.

1944   *Meet Me in St. Louis* (113 minutes).
MGM. Director: Vincente Minnelli. Screenplay: Irving Brecher, Fred F. Fomklehoffe, based on stories by Sally Benson. Music: Hugh Martin, Ralph Brant. Cast: Judy Garland, Margaret O'Brien, Mary Astor, Lucille Bremer, Leon Ames.

1952   *Singin' in the Rain* (102 minutes).
MGM. Director: Gene Kelly, Stanley Donen. Screenplay: Adolph Green, Betty Comden. Music: Nacio Herb Brown, lyrics by Arthur Freed. Cast: Gene Kelly, Debbie Reynolds, Jean Hagen, Donald O'Connor.

1953   *The Band Wagon* (112 minutes).
MGM. Director: Vincente Minnelli. Screenplay: Adolph Green, Betty Comden. Music: Howard Dietz and Arthur Schwatz. Cast: Fred Astaire, Cyd Charisse, Oscar Levant, Nanette Fabray, Jack Buchanan.

1954   *A Star Is Born* (154 minutes).
Warner Brothers. Director: George Cukor. Screenplay: Moss Hart. Music: Harold Arlen, Ira Gershwin. Cast: Judy Garland, James Mason, Charles Bickford, Jack Carson.

1957   *Silk Stockings* (117 minutes).
MGM. Director: Rouben Mamoulian. Screenplay: Leonard Gershe, Leonard Spigelgass, based on the musical play suggested by *Ninotchka* (Lubitsch, 1939). Music: Cole Porter. Cast: Fred Astaire, Cyd Charisse, Jules Munshin, Peter Lorre.

1958   *Gigi* (116 minutes).
MGM. Director: Vincente Minnelli. Screenplay: Alan Jay Lerner, based on the novel by Collette. Music: Alan Jay Lerner, Frederick Loewe. Cast: Leslie Caron, Maurice Chevalier, Louis Jordan, Hermione Gingold.

1979   *All That Jazz* (123 minutes).
Columbia. Director: Bob Fosse. Screenplay: Bob Fosse, Robert Alan Arthur. Music supervision: Stanley Lebowsky. Cast: Roy Scheider, Jessica Lange, Anne Reinking, Ben Vereen.

1981   *Pennies from Heaven* (107 minutes).
MGM. Director: Herbert Ross. Screenplay: Dennis Potter. Music: Johnny Burke, Arthur Johnson. Cast: Steve Martin, Bernadette Peters, Christopher Walken.

# 16

# Melodrama

STEVEN N. LIPKIN

Of all film genres, melodrama may be one of the easiest to identify and yet one of the most difficult to define. It is too many things. There is no predominant formal element that distinguishes melodrama. We may know a western because of its setting, a musical because of the importance of singing and dancing in the film, or a horror film because of the presence of the uncanny. Perhaps the most consistently agreed-upon feature of film melodrama is that it emphasizes the "domestic" or "maternal" elements of family life.

The problem of definition is common to most who have written about melodrama. George Bernard Shaw defined melodrama as "a simple and sincere drama of action and feeling, kept well within that vast tract of passion and motive which is common to the philosopher and the laborer, relieved by plenty of fun, and depending for variety of human character . . . on broad contrasts between types of youth and age, sympathy and selfishness, the masculine and the feminine, the serious and the ridiculous."[1] Eric Bentley felt simply that melodrama "represented the theatrical impulse."[2] While both statements are extremely broad, Bentley's points out the near-universality of melodrama as a mode of expression, and Shaw's suggests two of the central components of the genre, the emphasis on the signification of emotion, and dependence on structures of typicality within which the narrative develops particular characters. Frank Rahill offers a more comprehensive assessment of the genre that acknowledges the cross-modality of melodrama while delineating its defining characteristics:

Melodrama is a form of dramatic composition . . . partaking of the nature of tragedy, comedy, pantomime, and spectacle, and intended for a popular audience. Primarily concerned with situation and plot, it calls upon mimed action extensively and employs a more or less fixed complement of stock characters, the most important of which are a suffering heroine or hero, a persecuting villain, and a benevolent comic. It is conventionally moral and humanitarian in point of view and sentimental and optimistic in temper, concluding its fable happily with virtue rewarded after many trials and vice punished. Characteristically it . . . introduces music freely, typically to underscore dramatic effect.[3]

In his landmark historical overview of film melodrama, Thomas Elsaesser emphasizes the importance of music in melodrama as punctuation of emotional effects. The interrelation of music and the filmic presence of emotion create a textual complement to the film's storyline.[4] While virtually all conventional film narratives portray and generate emotion, melodrama not only emphasizes emotionality, but it must situate affect within a clearly delineated moral system. Robert B. Heilman notes that one of the essential functions of melodrama is to portray "the world's evil in characters of singlemindedness rather than tragic dividedness."[5] Melodrama must then tell an essentially emotional story within a universe with a clear moral structure. The musical punctuation of emotional/ moral contrasts in film melodrama will create a pattern of visual excess that ultimately reinforces the film's ideological structure.

The troubling difference between "melodrama" and what is "melodramatic" underlies efforts to characterize the genre. Melodrama is as much a mode of expression as it is a kind of film. In part, the problem of "the melodramatic" results from the excessiveness of the mode.[6] The clear opposition of good and evil in melodrama easily becomes "conflict" in virtually any kind of narrative film, so that a story becomes "melodramatic" to the extent that its presentation of conflict is excessive.[7] "Action" films and melodrama ("passion" films) conceivably constitute opposite sides of the same coin. "Conflict" in action films will be more broadly externalized; characters' actions will establish their identities. "The family melodrama, by contrast, though dealing largely with the same oedipal themes of emotional and moral identity, more often records the failure of the protagonist to act in a way that could shape the events and influence the emotional environment, let alone change the stifling social milieu."[8] In his discussion of the "wholeness" of melodrama, Heilman shows how the very clear-cut nature of good and evil gives even war stories an inherently melodramatic structure.[9] The essential characteristics of melodrama—strong presentation of affect, strong moral contrasts—also become a general means of presentation, a stylistic, economic mode of expression adaptable for many kinds of film narratives. While the potential ubiquity of the "melodramatic" mode of expression has profound implications for us as film viewers within a specific cultural milieu,[10] it remains that there is still a kind of film called "melodrama" with distinct parameters and a clear history of development from French, British, and American theatre and literature.

Both Thomas Elsaesser and Peter Brooks suggest that the roots of melodrama begin in the period following the French Revolution. Brooks notes the "desocialization" of art after the revolution and the subsequent rise of the novel, with its "exploitation of the drama latent in the quotidian and the domestic."[11]

Elsaesser traces the roots of film melodrama to the consistently portrayed opposition between external, social constraints, and the internal experience of
characters that links the novels of Victor Hugo, Honoré de Balzac, and Charles
Dickens, suggesting that "perhaps the current that leads more directly to the
sophisticated family melodrama of the '40s and '50s . . . is derived from the
romantic drama which had its heyday after the French Revolution and subsequently furnished many of the plots for operas, but which is itself unthinkable
without the c18th [18th century] sentimental novel and the emphasis put on
private feelings and interiorised (puritan, pietist) codes of morality and conscience."[12] Martha Vicinus similarly sees the Victorian novel and theater providing a form of cultural therapy. Melodrama allowed a means to cope with
the wedge a burgeoning capitalist economy had driven between home and work,
the workplace becoming the site of "action," the home "the setting for passion, sacrifice, suffering, and sympathy":

Faced with cataclysmic religious, economic, and social changes, most Victorians could
feel powerless on occasion, believing that all traditional values were in danger of being
turned upside down. The family became the refuge from change and the sustainer of
familiar values. But . . . it also became the arena for the most profound struggles
between good and evil. Melodrama's focus on the passive and powerless within the
family made it particularly appealing to the working class and women, two groups
facing great dangers without economic power or social recognition.[13]

According to Frank Rahill, not only were successful nineteenth-century British dramatic works imported wholesale to the United States, but also many
nineteenth-century American dramas blatantly imitated the themes and structures of their British precedents. Examples of two important contributions of
the nineteenth-century American theater to the film melodramas subsequently
made from many of them included the thematic conflict between city and country developed in the "frontier" play, and the development of character types
conceived visually for largely immigrant audiences.[14] A variety of subtypes of
theatre melodrama provided a wealth of material for film, including courtroom
dramas, murder mysteries, gothic dramas, "cloak and sword" dramas, "sensation" dramas and the "problem play"; literally scores of stage melodramas
had become films in the first two decades of the American film industry, most
notably titles such as *Judith of Bethulia, Monte Cristo* (Rahill states that this
was made as a film eleven times before 1937), *Enoch Arden, Under Two Flags,
Under Gaslight, Way Down East, Two Orphans,* and *The Clansman.*[15]
    The last three titles in this list merely underline the importance of the career
of D. W. Griffith in linking works of nineteenth-century European literature
and theatre to American film. Griffith's work overall clearly manifests the basic
melodramatic function of balancing the emotions and desires of the films' central characters against impersonal, if not evil, exploitative social forces. *Way
Down East* (1920) translates the contrast between rural and urban values into

the conflict between individual moral strength and social hypocrisy, set, in the film's penultimate scene, against the near-catastrophic ravages of nature. One of Griffith's ultimate melodramatic accomplishments remains *Orphans of the Storm* (1922), which manages to maintain its focus simultaneously on the physical and social vulnerability of the Gish sisters, their main source of strength in their love for each other, the omnipresent, exploitative cruelty of the pre-Revolutionary French society within which they have become displaced, the honor, immorality, and ruthlessness of the main representatives of the forces which will eventually clash in the Revolution, and the Revolution itself. One example suffices to suggest the melodramatic essence of the work, as the desires of worthy individuals are constrained by unfeeling, corrupt social powers: the blind Louise (Dorothy Gish), enslaved as a street beggar by the evil Mme. Frochard, sings as she slowly works her way down a Parisian street; she is heard by her sister Henriette (Lillian Gish), standing on a balcony above, who has been looking for Louise in vain throughout the film. At that instant, an aristocratic father who would block Henriette's impending marriage to his son has her arrested, preventing Henriette from touching Louise. Louise knows Henriette is near because she has heard her sister call her name. The long shot view of the crisis moment of the scene shows Louise standing on the sidewalk reaching for Henriette, and Henriette on a balcony, in the same space but just across the way, being restrained and carried off. The critical formal element in the scene is the implied sound of the dialogue, which we must appreciate largely from the point of view of Louise, the blind sister. Ironic as this may be in a silent film, it is quintessential melodramatic use of sound as emotional punctuation. Griffith's melodramas render the sociopolitical as personal and cinematic. One can see silent film melodramas of the late 1920s configuring sight, sound, and emotion with comparable complexity in films such as F. W. Murnau's *Sunrise* (1927) and Frank Borzage's *Seventh Heaven* (1927).

Before considering how subsequent films place the family in a position of central importance, it is worth exploring further the problem of morality in film melodrama. The historical development of melodrama through classic Hollywood cinema clarifies the moral functions of the genre. In Martha Vicinus's view of Victorian culture, melodrama "served as a cultural touchstone for large sections of society that felt both in awe of and unclear about the benefits of the new society being built around them."[16] Melodrama lent a necessary perspective when basic values and norms began to change. Peter Brooks develops this thesis to its logical conclusion. Melodrama "comes into being in a world where the traditional imperatives of truth and ethics have been violently thrown into question, yet where the promulgation of truth and ethics, their instauration as a way of life, is of immediate, daily concern."[17] The desacralized world, lacking eternal truths, seizes upon melodrama as a means to signify right and wrong. The imaging of good and evil in melodrama provides a "cultural touchstone" by lending a clear moral perspective. Melodrama makes real and accessible the signification of good and evil:

While its social implications may be variously revolutionary or conservative, it is in all cases radically democratic, striving to make its representations clear and legible to everyone. We may legitimately claim that melodrama becomes the principal mode for uncovering, demonstrating, and making operative the essential moral universe in a post-sacred era.[18]

The simplicity, the utter clarity that melodrama often may be faulted for, becomes, in this view, one of its most essential functions. Melodramatic representations must be highly legible. Virtue triumphs visibly, marking "a democratization of morality and its signs":

On the stage they are used virtually as pure signifiers, in that it is their spectacular, their visual interaction that counts. . . . The familial structure of melodrama's persons and problems persistently suggests this, and the use of a rhetoric that names pure states of being and relationships can legitimately be read as a breaking-through of repression, reaching toward a drama of pure psychic signs. . . . Desire achieves full satisfaction in enunciation of the integral psychic condition. Morality is ultimately in the nature of affect, and strong emotion is in the realms of morality: for good and evil are moral feelings.[19]

Melodrama tends to manifest its moral clarity as visual excess. "Excess" in this sense is overstatement. Brooks argues that excess in melodrama pushes the work past the visual surface of reality to a sense of inner truth.[20] Stage melodrama emphasizes gesture and tableaux so as to offer clear signs of emotional and moral states. Film melodrama translates the music at the root of *melo* drama into the counterpoint between decor, framing, color and wide screen (in many 1950s works), and the emotional and moral dilemmas of its characters. For Thomas Elsaesser, cinematic overstatement structures the emotional fluctuation that marks the domestic melodrama, which

is iconographically fixed by the claustrophobic atmosphere of the bourgeois home and/ or the small-town setting, its emotional pattern is that of panic and latent hysteria, reinforced stylistically by a complex handling of space in interiors . . . and a 'thematisation' of objects which develop the existential antithesis of the individual in a closed society into the more directly philosophical point about a world totally predetermined and pervaded by 'meaning' and interpretable signs.[21]

The broad, therapeutic function of presenting an excessively visible moral system is clearly evident within 1930s domestic melodramas. Films such as Frank Borzage's *A Man's Castle* (1933), John Stahl's *Imitation of Life* (1934), Leo McCarey's *Make Way for Tomorrow* (1937), and King Vidor's *Stella Dallas* (1937) center on the family as a potential refuge from external constraints. Here the family becomes the moral center of the films' respective universes; we will see in film melodramas of the 1940s and 1950s the family itself becoming more clearly a source of repression. In these films character morality is measured through his/her willingness to make sacrifices in deference to the family. The family, with all of its conflicts, is situated within the larger, ambivalent socioeconomic context necessitated by the films' Depression-decade settings and audience.

The visual qualities of a family's environment conveys the most immediate, tangible sense of "family"—houses and apartments signify changing economic status. In Stahl's *Imitation* the Pullman clan moves from the secure house to the uncertainty of the "rooms" at the back of the store, and then to their plush town house. The home connects inextricably with the Pullman business interests. Mrs. Pullman at first works out of the house, selling door to door on the boardwalk; then the entire group lives at the back of the store, virtually a total commitment to "family" business; finally, the view from the terrace of their plush town house offers the hugely lit neon sign announcing the size and success of their pancake business. (Douglas Sirk's 1959 remake of *Imitation of Life* shares a similar progressive iconographic strategy.) The progression in Borzage's *A Man's Castle* from shanty dwelling to a home (with checkered curtains and a stove) forwards the developing domestication of the Spencer Tracy–Loretta Young relationship and the Tracy character in particular. Here the home as home becomes the basis for the relationship. On the other hand, the loss of their house is the most prominent cause of the disruption of the marriage of the elderly couple in McCarey's *Make Way for Tomorrow*. Once they can't pay for their house anymore, they lose it, losing the possibility of finding any comfortable niche anywhere, together or separately. The mother's squeaky rocking chair, and the sick father, hastily and reluctantly shifted from the couch to a bed when the doctor calls, punctuate their homelessness.

In each instance what might comprise a "home" depends on the nature of the sacrifice the individual character is willing to make to the family as a whole. Sacrifice becomes a measure of larger moral qualities. In *Make Way* it is the unwillingness of the children to make any sacrifices for their parents that most effectively points up the failure of the family's home life. Bill, the Tracy character in *A Man's Castle,* realizes that he should sacrifice his own independence for the sake of forming a family. He returns from the freight he's hopped to "marry" his pregnant mistress. In both cases the key to moral strength remains with the most vulnerable characters, who must be strong in the situation of the film and impart that strength to others. It is the elderly and homeless parents who must "show" their children how callous they've been as children, by standing them up for the "last dinner" they'll have together as a family. Similarly, it takes the frail, slender Loretta Young character to stand up to Bill's coarseness like a bulldog, hanging on until she can confront him with the news that he can leave if he wants to, but "no matter what" she has "a part of him." The vulnerable characters stimulate any new awareness of what "family" is, and that awareness creates a sense of right and wrong.

Two of the most important counterbalances to the 1930s films' ostensible moral positioning of the nuclear family are the desires of women, particularly women as mothers, and the related presence and significance of children. These counterbalances are essentially pressure points, showing the potentially repressive nature of the family. The extensive critical examination given Vidor's *Stella Dallas* recently by feminist film critics centers precisely on the issue of the instructive value of Stella's sacrifice for the sake of her daughter at the end of the film. The thrust of this inquiry is to explore how the film's presentation of Stella positions the spectator of the film ideologically.[22] In this view the family is not simply a source of moral reference, but more importantly is the site of patriarchal hegemony. Before the specific steps of this argument are examined, it is worth seeing how some representative films of the 1940s offer divergent views of the moral function of the nuclear family.

Major subtypes of 1940s melodramas include nostalgic tributes to family and "Mother," including such films as Elia Kazan's *A Tree Grows in Brooklyn* (1945), Frank Capra's *It's a Wonderful Life* (1946), and George Stevens's *I Remember Mama* (1948); gothic melodramas and films noir with strong melodramatic components, such as Alfred Hitchcock's *Rebecca* (1940) and Michael Curtiz's *Mildred Pierce* (1945); "social problem" films exemplified by William Wyler's *Best Years of Our Lives* (1946); and films such as David Lean's *Brief Encounter* (1946) that exhibit the growing self-consciousness in melodrama that would flower in the work in the 1950s of Douglas Sirk and Nicholas Ray. Marriage and family provide primary reference points against which central characters (and we) measure feelings, desires, and the appropriateness of behavior. For example, Francie in *A Tree Grows in Brooklyn* must consider sacrificing her desire for education in order to help support her fatherless family; George Bailey's commitment to Bedford Falls continually disrupts his plans for education and travel in *It's a Wonderful Life;* and Laura mulls over her "brief encounter" with another man while in her sitting room with her husband, who's "glad she's back" from her brief foray away from marriage. *Best Years of Our Lives* examines the tension between socioeconomic constraints and the needs and desires of individuals, as it contrasts the homecoming of three newly returned veterans. Al would like to do something meaningful in his profession as a banker; Fred wants a secure home life for his wartime marriage; Homer wants people to treat him like anyone else despite the loss of his hands in the war. In their most affirmative view of marriage, the family, and/or society at large as the yardsticks of moral values, these films show a confluence of family dynamics and individual desires. These moments tend to be emotionally powerful due to affective instructions the films provide us as viewers. Family configurations—such as the conferences around the kitchen table to determine whether or not going to school will have to be financed by "going to the bank" in *I Remember Mama,* the overwhelming demonstration of family and town support for George Bailey in the Christmas-time conclusion of *It's a Wonderful Life,* or Fred and Peggy moving into the kiss that cements their future together while Homer and Wilma complete their marriage ceremony in Wilma's living room at the conclusion of *Best Years*—give the clearest demonstrations of how individual desires ultimately contribute to the greater social whole.

*A Tree Grows in Brooklyn* generates affect in support of ideology with explicit instructiveness, and exemplifies the generally affirmative tenor with which we see families in 1940s melodramas. Strategies of excess mesh smoothly with thematic and ideological structure as crucial emotional moments place the film's viewer in the position of watching or listening to characters in the film reading written words. The film's ideology links family, education, and the quality of future life. Francie's graduation provides a notable example. The flowers she finds on her desk are densely loaded signs, not only of love, growth, and even death, but also for Francie of her potential for beauty, her adolescence becoming adulthood, and completion. Her father's note with the flowers validates education as an ideal now realized. We see Francie noticing the note in the flowers; when she opens it we see what it says through her eyes. Although the message is simple ("To Francie on her graduation day—Love from, Papa") her aunt's explanation that Johnny wrote the note before Christmas (he dies on Christmas Eve, trying to find work) reinforces the preliminary, uncanny effect of seeing the writing of one who is dead. The affective power of the note is devastating. Thanks to Sissy's mediation Johnny comes to life because of his ability to keep his word. Because we read his message as Francie reads it, our direct, unmediated access to his writing directly implicates us within this moment of growth, a moment rich with the continuity of the Nolan family. Francie's response to Johnny's writing instructs our own: her display of released emotion allows the affective climax of the film.

While no less patriarchal, the sense of moral order in films such as *Rebecca* or *Mildred Pierce* becomes more explicitly repressive, explaining the fundamentally different (but perhaps equally potent) affect separating gothics and films noir from domestic melodramas. For feminist film critics these darker "women's films" provide a means for understanding how women (as characters in films and as viewers) have been positioned by film and culture. Gothics show vulnerable heroines consistently the potential victims of clearly evil forces (usually their husbands), thus reinforcing simultaneously a clear moral code and women's relationship to it. In an analysis of *Mildred Pierce* Pam Cook notes:

Mildred's take-over of the place of the father has brought about the collapse of all social and moral order in her world: Monty and Veda are on the point of breaking the ultimate taboo: that against father incest. In the face of impending chaos and confusion the patriarchal order is called upon to reassert itself and take the Law back into its own hands, divesting women completely of any power they may have gained while the patriarchal order was temporarily impaired. This involves establishing the truth without a doubt, restoring "normal" sexual relationships and reconstituting the family unit, in spite of the pain and suffering such repressive action must cause.[23]

The tendency to generate increasingly repressive socioeconomic atmospherics characterizes film melodramas through the 1950s, and is best seen in light of feminist film theory's view of the psychological and ideological positioning of women by these works.

E. Ann Kaplan explains that "woman" in conventional cinema "is presented as what she represents for man, not in terms of what she actually signifies. Her *discourse* (her meanings as she might produce them) is suppressed in favor of a discourse structured by patriarchy in which her real signification has been replaced by connotations that serve patriarchy's needs."[24] Kaplan and others draw on Lacan's view of our entry into language to theorize how the interrelationship of language and vision psychically inscribes women within a patriarchal ideological system.[25] Their analyses of melodramas then center on the "instructiveness" of these films on the most profound levels: the kind of self-sacrifice urged by domestic melodrama becomes ongoing reinforcement of a masochistic displacement and repression of desire in order to preserve the dominance of the socioeconomic structure the family embodies.[26]

One effect of the increasing self-consciousness of 1950s melodramas is to make more transparent the sense of coerced obedience. Geoffrey Nowell-Smith has observed that "the question of law or legitimacy, so central to tragedy, is turned inward from 'Has this man a right to rule (over us)?' to 'Has this man a right to rule a family (like ours)?' This inward-turning motivates a more directly psychological reading of situations, particularly in the Hollywood melodrama of the '50s."[27]

George Stevens's *A Place in the Sun* (1951) exemplifies the shift characteristic of 1950s melodramas from portraying the family as a shelter, a bulwark against the pressure of socioeconomic constraints on individuality, to the family itself as a medium of repression. Explicitly parental authority figures or explicitly coded social/familial spaces serve in *A Place in the Sun* to enforce moral strictures. The first moments in the film when George Eastman (Montgomery Clift) sees and desires Alice (Shelley Winters) and then Angela (Elizabeth Taylor) serve to demonstrate the film's processes of displaying simultaneously desire and its repression through familial influences. George sees Alice his first day at his new job in his uncle's bathing suit factory; she is his co-worker, placed just across and up from his station at the end of a conveyor belt. Just before this, George has been told by his cousin Earl, the son of Charles Eastman, owner of Eastman Mills, that "company policy forbids dating among employees. My father asked me *specifically* to tell you that." The continuation of the sequence further underlines George and Alice's joined separation in repressive company space: a dissolve through images of a time clock and a calendar finds George and Alice (now in a two-shot) at the end of their shift. The low angle shows them dwarfed by huge "It's an Eastman" advertisements (a reclining woman wearing a bathing suit) on the walls above their heads.

Alice and George notice each other within a work code that proscribes the implications of their glances. They repress and so increase their desire, eventually having a furtive relationship. Angela appears, on the other hand, precisely for the purpose of being seen, framed by her gown, her shawl, and the foyer arch of the Eastman mansion. The same socioeconomic code that proscribes George's gaze at Alice validates the full display of Angela before George and the eyes of the other members of his family. Social codes reinforced by space, decor, costume, and blocking define their differences as characters. Eventually, social places become repressive, increasing the desire of both couples to be inaccessible to social scrutiny. Loon Lake, wholly from society and wholly natural, logically becomes the last place George can "be" freely with either woman physically. They ultimately strive to reach an amoral place, free from social, moral, and legal constraints. Angela takes George and speeds away from a group of their friends at her house (only to be ticketed by a motorcycle cop who apparently has stopped her many times before); George murders Alice. Both extralegal acts reflect their desires to be with each other unburdened by social baggage, friends, or laws. The fundamentalist seed planted in him by his mother can only make George's desire to evade responsibility increase his guilt; to speed away with Angela or to plunge alone into the woods represents his last desperate effort to embrace the intolerable, amoral place, free and beyond social grasp.

   *A Place in the Sun* creates a sense of desire not only by images that suggest its presence but also by the coding of influences that act to repress it. These are elements of character, decor, and space that convey familial and/or social codes. These strategies have received scrutiny in particular in other 1950s melodramas, notably of Douglas Sirk, Nicholas Ray, and Vincente Minnelli, and, as Thomas Elsaesser suggests, invite critical attention to the social systems external to the films but which exert detectable determining influences:

The critique—the questions of "evil," of responsibility—is firmly placed on a social and existential level, away from the arbitrary and finally obtuse logic of private motives and individualised psychology. . . . This is why the melodrama, at its most accomplished, seems capable of reproducing more directly than other genres the patterns of domination and exploitation existing in a given society, especially the relation between psychology, morality and class-consciousness, by emphasizing so clearly an emotional dynamic whose social correlative is a network of external forces directed oppressingly inward, and with which the characters themselves unwittingly collude to become their agents.[28]

Film critics as diverse in method and purpose as Thomas Schatz, Charles Affron, and Noël Carroll have examined the relationship between irony in the films of Douglas Sirk and the repressive atmosphere of his imaging of families.[29] *Magnificent Obsession* (1954), *All That Heaven Allows* (1955), *Written on the Wind* (1956), and *Imitation of Life* (1959) have provided particularly rich examples of the tensions Sirk generates in his treatment of family situation, decor, and casting. Charles Affron suggests that, ultimately, Sirkian irony functions sympathetically in its instruction of its viewer:

[*Imitation of Life*'s] profusion of ironies leads us not to some stable value, but rather to the value of the ironic processes and their multiple, unresolved readings. The nonvalues of bad/good, black/white, mother/actress/woman are ironic muddles that catch the muddles of an industry and a society, muddles intolerant of even a patently false resolution. The elements that constitute the muddles remain distinct as they submit to the cruelties of irony. Lora is "five years too late" in starting her career. Lana's career started more than twenty years before, and she too is too late. Civil rights are centuries too late. And another mordant irony is reserved for Hollywood itself, feeding on itself in remakes like *Imitation of Life,* trying to hang on to its illusory beauty with the cosmetics of wide screen and Eastmancolor, but as over-the-hill as the film's star. Sirk's irony draws us to this kind of knowledge, to sympathy for blacks in a white society and for stars in Hollywood.[30]

Any effort to understand melodrama demands attention to the moral universe these works construct as much as to the importance of emotion in conveying moral value. While film melodrama from the 1920s through the 1950s (and, arguably, into the 1980s with works such as *Terms of Endearment* or *On Golden Pond*) finds the family as a segment of larger society as the most consistent source of its visually excessive moral and affective instruction, it is the ideological and psychological implications of this larger instructive process that occupies the attention of those studying the genre. It is worth noting a major irony of melodrama spectatorship: while melodrama provides "instructive" image patterns which are repressive in their own right, melodramatic form as a whole conceivably parallels the process of psychoanalysis in establishing conflict, imaging the dynamics of repression, and providing a means of articulation of these tensions, allowing a liberation, a "victory over repression."[31] The ideological action of melodrama is matched in affective power by generic conventions which allow it to say and show fully that which cannot otherwise be said or shown any other way.

## BIBLIOGRAPHICAL OVERVIEW

Writing on melodrama generally and film melodrama in particular divides into several major categories: works that provide historical/conceptual overviews of the genre; works that describe the maternal/domestic melodrama, centering on "the woman's film"; works relating melodramatic form and theories of readership in film; and analyses of individual films often from a specific theoretical perspective.

Probably the most important overview of melodrama in any medium is Peter Brooks's *The Melodramatic Imagination* (1974). Brooks focuses on Balzac and Henry James in examining the origins and evolution of melodrama on stage and in literature. Brooks argues that the essence of melodrama is to provide moral instruction: melodrama resituates morality in a "desacralized" world, a world lacking a source of eternal truth. Brooks locates more traditional concerns within the visible surface of melodrama, such as displays of extreme emotion within the moral/semantic systems of the melodramatic stage. By relating melodrama's meanings to a larger project of moral clarification Brooks ultimately explains the resilience of the genre, and provides a belletristic perspective from which one can view recent discussions of melodrama by feminist, semiotic, and psychoanalytic film theorists.

Martha Vicinus manages to match the breadth of Brooks's book in an article on the "Helpless and Unfriended: Nineteenth Century Domestic Melodrama" (1981). Vicinus offers a clear historical view of the cultural functions of melodrama, focusing on the importance of the family as a shelter from changing socioeconomic constraints during the eighteenth and nineteenth centuries. While drawn from literary and stage melodrama, the thesis Vicinus develops applies directly to family imagery in maternal/domestic film melodrama. Christian Viviani's "Who Is Without Sin?" (*Wide Angle* 4), for example, shows how the ritual of maternal suffering in a large number of film melodramas also sheds light on hypocritical, repressive social values. In a chapter on Hollywood melodramas primarily of the 1950s (and focusing in particular on the major films of Douglas Sirk), Thomas Schatz in *Hollywood Genres* (1981) suggests that the family itself is the primary source of repression of main (usually female) characters. Schatz shows through several "variations" in family iconography how these films throw domestic repression into sharp relief.

Perhaps the most comprehensive summary in film literature of the literary, theatrical, and musical sources of film melodrama remains Thomas Elsaesser's "Tales of Sound and Fury" (1972). Elsaesser suggests how the musical form at the root of "melodrama" may be translated into filmic equivalents. This overview also suggests the richness of film melodramas as texts for analysis: Elsaesser traces film melodrama as the place "where Freud left his Marx on the American home" through a multitude of examples from 1930s, 1940s, and 1950s American film. Geoffrey Nowell-Smith's more specifically focused "Minnelli and Melodrama" (1977) extends the approach of Elsaesser's article, viewing melodrama within an analytic framework that sees that "the 'subject positions' implied by the melodrama are those of bourgeois art, in a bourgeois epoch, while the 'represented object' is that of Oedipal drama" (p. 114).

Three other more general, conceptual overviews of the genre are worth mentioning. Robert B. Heilman's *Tragedy and Melodrama: Versions of Experience* (1968) compares the two modes on the basis of character dividedness. Tragic characters are essentially divided in what Brooks would explain as their moral perspective; undivided characters in melodrama can conceivably become limited when realized in film. Frank Rahill's *The World of Melodrama* (1967) offers a helpful history of melodrama in theater, examining not only historical precedents of the theatrical form but also delineating major theatrical subtypes of the genre. An interesting description of melodramatic structure as defined in non–Anglo-American theory appears in Daniel Gerould's "Russian Formalist Theories of Melodrama" (1978). Gerould finds that in the 1920s there was serious interest on the part of Russian formalists in the viability of melodramatic form, not just in literature but also in film.

The thrust of recent writing about film melodrama has been toward defining maternal/domestic melodrama and describing its ideological and psychological implications. Perhaps the first major, relatively recent work to provide historical perspective on "the women's film" has been Molly Haskell's *From Reverence to Rape: The Treatment of Women in the Movies* (1973). Haskell situates the functions of melodrama within the overall context of film's imaging of women: noting the traditional, destructive stereotyping of male and female roles in narrative films, Haskell traces the tendency for central women characters to be self-sacrificing. The self-sacrifice thematic becomes a platform from which the films ostensibly reinforce traditional role models.

Recent feminist writing on film melodrama places the overall process of filmic reinforcement Haskell describes within the larger functions of the patriarchal ideological system that characterizes conventional culture. Important among the feminists writing about film melodrama are Tania Modleski, who in *Loving with a Vengeance: Mass Produced Fantasies for Women* (1982) situates the melodramatic theme of maternal self-sacrifice within narrative, ideological, and psychological structures. Modleski considers not only films but also gothic literature and television soap operas in demonstrating the repressive actions of "women's" cultural forms on their primary readers. E. Ann Kaplan overviews the critical treatment of melodrama in literary theory and provides a clear, comprehensive summary of feminist film theory's analysis of spectatorship and gender in *Women and Film: Both Sides of the Camera* (1983) and her shorter "Theories of Melodrama: A Feminist Perspective." Kaplan's concern with the development of theoretical positions makes her work an excellent introduction to the writings of Laura Mulvey, Annette Kuhn, and Mary Ann Doane. Laura Mulvey's "Visual Pleasure and Narrative Cinema" appeared in *Screen* 16 (1975) and cleared the ground for subsequent psychoanalytically oriented feminist film theory. Drawing on Lacan's reading of Freud, Mulvey describes the positioning of the female spectator in relation to narrative pleasure: by terming the "look" of the viewer (of either sex) at characters on the screen as an objectifying, controlling gaze, Mulvey shows how "psychoanalytic theory . . . as a political weapon, demonstrat[es] the way the unconscious of patriarchal society has structured film form" (p. 6). Annette Kuhn in *Women's Pictures: Feminism and Cinema* (1982) and Mary Ann Doane, Patricia Mellencamp, and Linda Williams (in *Re-Vision: Essays in Feminist Film Criticism,* 1983) have furthered the line of thought initiated by Mulvey theoretically and in the analyses of specific film texts. Kuhn's work, like Kaplan's, sets out very clearly the ideological implications of the "dominant mode of representation," poses the need for an alternative, challenging feminist cinema, and examines works that begin to fulfill that function. Doane explores in depth the basic notion of female spectatorship. In *Re-Vision* she, Mellencamp, and Williams define "vision" as "both seeing differently and wrenching the 'look' (and the 'voice') from their previous structures" (p. 14). In "Film and the Masquerade: Theorizing the Female Spectator" (1982) Doane argues that female spectatorship conventionally structured forces objectification and fetishization of the image, and seizes the notion of the "masquerade" as a point of resistance to patriarchal positioning of the female spectator which simultaneously asserts its femininity (pp. 81–82).

The energy of feminist film theory has logically extended to a number of analyses of individual film melodramas, most notably King Vidor's 1937 version of *Stella Dallas* and Joan Crawford's rendition of *Mildred Pierce* (1945). Linda Williams in "Something Else Besides a Mother: *Stella Dallas* and the Maternal Melodrama" (1984) debates with E. Ann Kaplan the positioning of Stella (and consequently the film's spectator) at the film's conclusion. The flashback structure of *Mildred Pierce* has resulted in critical concern with the film's structuring of viewer response through both formal and ideological elements in Joyce Nelson's *"Mildred Pierce Reconsidered"* (1977). Janet Walker (in "Feminist Critical Practice: Female Discourse in *Mildred Pierce,*" *Film Reader* 5) sees the film's depiction of relationships between women as "powerful enough to threaten a system in which men dominate" (p. 171). Pam Cook similarly sees the film shedding light on the "enforced repression of female sexuality" in its "problematic need to reconstruct a failing patriarchal order" ("Duplicity in *Mildred Pierce,*" in *Women in Film Noir,* ed. E. Ann Kaplan, 1978). Sandy Flitterman showcases the applications of feminist film theory's concerns with the ideological and psychoanalytic implications of melodrama's imaging of female characters in her analysis of the little-known *Guest in the House* ("*Guest in the House:* Rupture and Reconstitution of the Bourgeois Nuclear Family," *Wide Angle* 4).

The problem of readership appears throughout discussions of film melodrama discussed so far. The whole theoretical area of spectatorship/readership/reception, although applied primarily in feminist approaches to film melodrama, has received other treatment worth mentioning separately. Notably, Robert C. Allen's *Speaking of Soap Opera* (1985) draws cogently on theorizing about literary readership in developing a view of serial readership. A worthy preliminary to Allen's work is Modleski's chapter on soap operas noted above (in *Loving with a Vengeance*) where Modleski shows how soap opera's serial structure demands a retraining of conventional readership skills. Perhaps the most insightful, systematic description of how the reader and the process of reading is inscribed within the form of film texts is Charles Affron's *Cinema and Sentiment* (1982). Affron draws comprehensively on a wide range of theoretical positions and critical methods, including traditional, psychoanalytic, and semiotic film theories, in explaining the film viewer's affective response.

## NOTES

1. From *Our Theatres in the Nineties*, London, 1932, I, p. 93, quoted in Earl F. Bargainnier, "Melodrama as Formula," *Journal of Popular Culture*, vol. 9, 1975, p. 22.

2. Cited in Peter Brooks, *The Melodramatic Imagination* (New Haven: Yale University Press, 1976), p. xi.

3. Frank Rahill, *The World of Melodrama* (University Park: Pennsylvania State University Press, 1967), p. xiv.

4. Thomas Elsaesser, "Tales of Sound and Fury," *Monogram*, vol. 4, 1972, p. 5.

5. Robert B. Heilman, *Tragedy and Melodrama: Versions of Experience* (Seattle: University of Washington Press, 1968), p. 287.

6. "The 'melodramatic' occurs in examples of 'excess' where signification exceeds expectations of the 'real' in behavior or representation." Frank Krutnik, *"The Shanghai Gesture:* The Exotic and the Melodrama," *Wide Angle*, vol. 4, no. 2, 1980, p. 36.

7. Heilman, for example, notes that "in general usage the term *melodrama* certainly implies the combat of 'good guys' and 'bad guys' . . . in this structure, man is pitted against a force outside of himself—a specific enemy, a hostile group, a social force, a natural event, an accident or coincidence." *Tragedy and Melodrama*, p. 79.

8. Elsaesser, "Tales," p. 9.

9. "Openly we shrink from the hardships of war, its shocks, its terrors, and its griefs; but quietly, inwardly, and perhaps unconsciously we find in it the joy of wholeness, the exhilarating freedom from doubt and self-awareness, the gratifying order in which evil is without and we can ride unified and inspirited on a wave of blame and indignation." Heilman, *Tragedy and Melodrama*, p. 106.

10. Peter Brooks argues that melodramatic form offers a moral clarity for a "desacralized" world, an argument that I will take up below in some detail; however, here he suggests moreover that melodrama creates a mind-set: "Melodrama substitutes for the rite of sacrifice an urging toward combat in life, an active, lucid confrontation of evil. It works to steel man for resistance, it keeps him going in the face of threat." *Melodramatic Imagination*, p. 205.

11. Ibid., p. 82.

12. Elsaesser, "Tales," p. 3.

13. Martha Vicinus, "Helpless and Unfriended: Nineteenth Century Domestic Melodrama," *New Literary History*, Autumn 1981, pp. 128, 131.

14. Rahill, *The World of Melodrama*, pp. 258, 278.

15. Bargainnier, "Melodrama as Formula," p. 731.

16. Vicinus, "Helpless and Unfriended," p. 128.

17. Brooks, *Melodramatic Imagination*, p. 15.

18. Ibid.

19. Ibid., pp. 44, 28, and 54.

20. Ibid., pp. 2, 115.

21. Elsaesser, "Tales," p. 13.

22. See, for example, E. Ann Kaplan's discussion of the film in *Women and Film: Both Sides of the Camera* (New York: Methuen, 1983) and Linda Williams's response in "Something Else Besides a Mother: *Stella Dallas* and the Maternal Melodrama," *Cinema Journal*, Fall 1986, pp. 2–27.

23. Pam Cook, "Duplicity in *Mildred Pierce*," in *Women in Film Noir*, ed. E. Ann Kaplan (London: BFI, 1978), p. 75.

24. Kaplan, *Women and Film*, p. 18.

25. See, for example, Mary Ann Doane, Patricia Mellencamp, and Linda Williams, eds., *Re-Vision: Essays in Feminist Film Criticism* (Los Angeles: AFI Monograph Series, 1983); Doane's "Film and the Masquerade: Theorizing the Female Spectator," *Screen*, September–October 1982, pp. 74–87; Laura Mulvey, "Visual Pleasure and Narrative Cinema," *Screen*, Autumn 1975, pp. 6–18; and Annette Kuhn, *Women's Pictures: Feminism and Cinema* (London: Routledge and Kegan Paul, 1982). Here the female is positioned as a passive observer from the mirror stage on, and has been forced to locate herself as an object, rather than a subject. "Assigned the place of object (lack), she is the recipient of male desire passively appearing rather than acting. Her sexual pleasure in this position can thus be constructed only around her own objectification." Kaplan, *Women and Film*, p. 26. Positioned submissively, the female has no means to enact her own desires except as a substitute male. The irony of "women's films" stems from women spectators watching images of women, offered no other psychological options than to objectify and fetishize these images.

26. Molly Haskell has traced this tendency in the form of a self-sacrifice thematic which ostensibly ennobles the image of the housewife but ultimately deflates feminine assertiveness and identity. *From Reverence to Rape* (New York: Holt, Rinehart and Winston, 1973); see pp. 159–63.

27. Geoffrey Nowell-Smith, "Minnelli and Melodrama," *Screen*, Summer 1977, p. 115.

28. Elsaesser, "Tales," p. 14.

29. Thomas Schatz, *Hollywood Genres* (New York: Random House, 1981); Charles Affron, *Cinema and Sentiment* (Chicago: University of Chicago Press, 1982); Noell Carroll, "The Moral Ecology of Melodrama: The Family Plot and *Magnificent Obsession*," in *Melodrama*, ed. Daniel Gerould (New York: New York Literary Forum, 1980).

30. Affron, *Cinema and Sentiment*, p. 156.

31. Brooks, *Melodramatic Imagination*, pp. 201, 41.

## BIBLIOGRAPHICAL CHECKLIST

### Books

Affron, Charles. *Cinema and Sentiment*. Chicago: University of Chicago Press, 1982.

Brooks, Peter. *The Melodramatic Imagination*. New Haven: Yale University Press, 1974.

Gerould, Daniel, ed. *Melodrama*. New York: New York Literary Forum, 1980.

Haskell, Molly. *From Reverence to Rape: The Treatment of Women in the Movies*. New York: Holt, Rinehart and Winston, 1973.

Heilman, Robert B. *Tragedy and Melodrama: Versions of Experience*. Seattle: University of Washington Press, 1968.

Kaplan, E. Ann. *Women and Film: Both Sides of the Camera*. New York: Methuen, 1983.

Modleski, Tania. *Loving with a Vengeance: Mass Produced Fantasies for Women*. Hamden, Conn.: Archon Books, 1982.

Rahill, Frank. *The World of Melodrama*. University Park: Pennsylvania State University Press, 1967.

### Shorter Works

Bargainnier, Earl F. "Melodrama as Formula," *Journal of Popular Culture* 9, 1975, pp. 726–33.

Elsaesser, Thomas. "Tales of Sound and Fury," *Monogram,* vol. 4, 1972, pp. 2–15.

Gerould, Daniel. "Russian Formalist Theories of Melodrama," *Journal of American Culture,* Spring 1978, pp. 152–68.

Kaplan, E. Ann. "Theories of Melodrama: A Feminist Perspective," *Women and Performance: A Journal of Feminist Theory,* Spring-Summer 1983, pp. 40–48.

Mulvey, Laura. "Notes on Sirk and Melodrama," *Movie,* Winter 1977–1978, pp. 53–57.

Nowell-Smith, Geoffrey. "Minnelli and Melodrama," *Screen,* Summer 1977, pp. 113–18.

Schatz, Thomas. Chapter 8, "The Family Melodrama." In his *Hollywood Genres.* New York: Random House, 1981, pp. 221–60.

Vicinus, Martha. "Helpless and Unfriended: Nineteenth Century Domestic Melodrama," *New Literary History,* Autumn 1981, pp. 127–43.

Viviani, Christian. "Who Is Without Sin?" *Wide Angle,* Spring 1980, pp. 4–17.

Williams, Linda. "Something Else Besides a Mother: *Stella Dallas* and the Maternal Melodrama," *Cinema Journal,* Fall 1984, pp. 2–27.

## SELECTED FILMOGRAPHY

1921  *Orphans of the Storm* (125 minutes).
United Artists. Producer/Director: D. W. Griffith. Screenplay: Griffith, based on Palmer/Jackson version of the play *The Two Orphans* by Adolphe Philippe d'Ennery and Eugene Cormon. Cast: Lillian Gish (Henriette Girard), Dorothy Gish (Louise Girard), Joseph Shildkraut (The Chevalier), Lucille LaVerne (Mme. Frochard).

1933  *A Man's Castle* (75 minutes).
Columbia. Producer/Director: Frank Borzage. Screenplay: Jo Swerling. Cast: Spencer Tracy (Bill), Loretta Young (Tina), Walter Connelly (Ira).

1934  *Imitation of Life* (106 minutes).
Universal. Director: John Stahl. Producer: Carl Laemmle, Jr. Screenplay: William Hurlbut (from novel by Fannie Hurst). Cast: Claudette Colbert (Bea Pullman), Warren Williams (Steven Archer), Ned Sparks (Elmer), Louise Beavers (Delilah).

1937  *Make Way for Tomorrow* (92 minutes).
Columbia. Producer/Director: Leo McCarey. Screenplay: Vina Delmar (from the novel *The Years Are So Long,* by J. Lawrence). Cast: Victor Moore (Barkley Cooper), Beulah Bondi (Lucy Cooper), Fay Bainter (Anita Cooper), Thomas Mitchell (George Cooper).

1945  *A Tree Grows in Brooklyn* (128 minutes).
20th Century-Fox. Producer: Louise D. Lighton. Director: Elia Kazan. Screenplay: Tess Slesinger and Frank Davis. Cast: Dorothy McGuire (Katie Nolan), Peggy Ann Garner (Francie Nolan), Joan Blondell (Aunt Sissy), Lloyd Nolan (Officer McShane), James Dunn (Johnny Nolan).

1946  *The Best Years of Our Lives* (172 minutes).
Goldwyn. Producer: Samuel Goldwyn. Director: William Wyler. Screenplay: Robert E. Sherwood (from verse novel by M. Kantor). Cast: Fredric March (Al), Dana Andrews (Fred), Harold Russell (Homer), Myrna Loy (Millie), Teresa Wright (Peggy), Cathy O'Donnell (Wilma).

1946    *Brief Encounter* (103 minutes).
Cineguild. Producers: Noel Coward, Anthony Havelock-Allan, and Ronald Neame.
Director: David Lean. Screenplay: Coward, Lean, and Havelock-Allan. Cast:
Celia Johnson (Laura), Trevor Howard (Alec), Stanley Holloway (Fred).

1948    *I Remember Mama* (134 minutes).
Paramount. Producer: Harriett Parsons. Director: George Stevens. Screenplay:
DeWitt Bodeen (based on a play by John Van Druten, based on *Mama's Bank
Account,* a novel by Kathryn Forbes). Cast: Irene Dunne (Mama), Barbara Bel
Geddes (Katrin), Oscar Homolka (Uncle Chris), Philip Dorn (Papa).

1951    *A Place in the Sun* (122 minutes)
Paramount. Producer/Director: George Stevens. Screenplay: Michael Wilson, Harry
Brown, from the novel *An American Tragedy* by T. Dreiser. Cast: Montgomery
Clift (George Eastman), Shelley Winters (Alice Tripp), Elizabeth Taylor (Angela
Vickers).

1959    *Imitation of Life* (124 minutes).
Universal. Producer: Ross Hunter. Director: Douglas Sirk. Screenplay: Eleanor
Griffin and Allen Smith (from novel by Fannie Hurst). Cast: Lana Turner (Lora),
John Gavin (Steve Archer), Juanita Moore (Annie), Sandra Dee (Susie), Susan
Kohner (Sara Jane).

# NONTRADITIONAL GENRES

# 17

# The Social Problem Film

CHARLES J. MALAND

What's wrong with pictures about people who have problems?
—Stanley Kramer

The entertainment picture is no place for social, political and economic argument.
—Martin Quigley

A film play can provide diversion and at the same time have something to say.
Darryl F. Zanuck

If you want to send a message, use Western Union.
—Attributed to several Hollywood producers

The public will buy "message" pix but they gotta be good.
—*Variety*[1]

As the preceding comments suggest, the social problem film is something of an anomalous form in Hollywood, a subject of considerable debate. In an industry traditionally devoted to providing "pure entertainment," its advocates propose that films should treat serious issues. To those who argue that movies should let viewers "escape" their worlds for two hours in a darkened theater, they counter that audiences can be more genuinely and deeply engaged by watching "hard-hitting" and "relevant" stories about contemporary life. To flights of fantasy, they claim to offer the grit of reality. To the requirement of pleasing the audience, they add the aim of informing or instructing them. Discussing the social problem film engages the critic in a long-standing debate about the proper character and social function of movies in American culture.

It is impossible to give an exhaustive treatment of the social problem film in the space of a chapter. Rather, in this opening historical/analytical section I have focused on defining what constitutes a social problem film and then on examining ten representative American social problem films from the 1930s to the 1980s by discussing them in light of several narrative conventions of the Classical Hollywood Cinema.

## DEFINING THE SOCIAL PROBLEM FILM

Before I try to define what constitutes a social problem film, it is worthwhile to consider the term *social problem* in isolation.[2] While it would be perverse to claim that what is widely perceived as a social problem in a society has no genuine basis in social phenomena, it would be just as misleading to claim that every relatively widespread phenomenon in society which leads to human deprivation, conflict, or suffering is automatically considered a social problem.

Sociologist Lee Rainwater, after surveying the field, found that nearly every attempt by a sociologist to define the term *social problem* included at least two references: the first to an objective social condition, the second to a subjective evaluation that defines the condition as undesirable.[3] One can elaborate to make several points about such a notion of "social problem." First, a social problem refers to an undesirable social condition affecting a significant number of people. Second, it must be perceived by a considerable segment of society to be a problem. Third, the definition of what constitutes a social problem presupposes power: an individual or a group must have enough power in society to get the matter into public debate, or the condition may never be considered a social problem. Finally, implicit in the very notion of the term *social problem* is the belief that something can be done about it—that the problem has a solution. If people generally believe that an undesirable social condition results from something ineradicable in human nature—for example, that physical assault is simply a manifestation of an ineluctable aggressiveness in human beings—it most probably would not be considered a social problem because nothing could be done to eliminate it.

Given these presuppositions, we can propose the following definition: a social problem is a harmful condition which affects many people and which may, through social action or reform, be ameliorated.

So what constitutes a "social problem film"? Since defining sometimes proceeds by negation, we might begin by stating what the social problem film is not. Strictly speaking, it is not a film *genre,* at least as the term has come to be used. In *Hollywood Genres,* Thomas Schatz writes that a genre film "involves familiar, essentially one-dimensional characters acting out a predictable story pattern within a familiar setting."[4] Schatz goes on to distinguish between genres of order, like westerns and gangster films, and genres of integration, like musicals and screwball comedies. He also delineates the characteristic settings, iconography, character types, plot structures and conflicts, and thematic concerns central to the various genres. If we use Schatz's definition of genre and his general approach to genre study as a guide, the social problem film is not a genre. Social problem films simply are too various in their narrative and thematic characteristics to warrant the label "genre."

Nevertheless, a working definition of the social problem film is possible: it is a narrative feature film whose central narrative concern or conflict relates to or includes the presentation of a social problem. The social problem film also has a contemporary setting, though it may include scenes from the past that lead up to that contemporary setting and help to explain the roots of the problem. In *The Grapes of Wrath,* for example, flashbacks showing Dust Bowl storms and the driving of Muley's family from the land provide background historical information that allows the narrative to proceed. Finally, the social problem film is generally animated by a humane concern for the victim(s) of or crusader(s) against the social problem and, often, by an implicit assumption that the problem can be treated or even eliminated through well-intentioned liberal social reform. In American film history, at least from the Depression on, the social problem film has generally been associated with a cautiously reformist liberalism.

This definition excludes several kinds of films that resemble or exhibit some characteristics of social problem films. It excludes films like *Big Jim McClain* or *Dirty Harry* which also foreground what they take to a social problem—the dangers of communist subversion, the "pampering" of criminals by the judicial system—but which propose the simple use of repressive violence as the solution to the problem. Pauline Kael has pointed out the similarity between right- and left-wing "morality plays" in the American cinema, principally in their use of the Manichean moral assumptions of melodrama, and it is true that some social problem films resemble a film like *Dirty Harry* in their moral simplicity (or oversimplicity) and clarity. But *Dirty Harry* elicits a scorn for, rather than confidence in, liberal social reform.[5]

The definition also excludes films set in the past and distinctively genre films which, through the use of metaphor, present a contemporary social problem through the filter of history or the conventional framework of a film genre. For example, some biographical films about historical figures—*Juarez* is a good instance—treat a social problem as a central part of the narrative. The massacre of the Indians in a western like *Little Big Man,* which was released during the Vietnam War, almost inevitably brought to viewers' minds the killing of Vietnamese by Americans. In the 1950s, both *High Noon,* a western, and *Invasion of the Body Snatchers,* a science fiction film, were widely taken by some viewers as metaphorical considerations of the conflicts of the McCarthy era; unfortunately for the makers who hoped to express a liberal perspective to their viewers, sometimes these metaphors were so vague or loose that they could be misunderstood or even completely missed. None of these is a social problem film, for the first two lack a contemporary setting, and the last two fail to present their problems overtly, as an important dimension of the narrative. They are instead oblique and metaphorical.

This is not to deny that established film genres in American cinema draw from the characteristics of social problem films. Some of the most interesting critical examinations of American cinema in the past decade have established beyond doubt that American films, often the most challengingly provocative ones, blend genres. I need only mention Robin Wood's essay on *Shadow of a Doubt* and *It's a Wonderful Life,* in which he convincingly argues that both films derive some of their disturbing power from their blending of small-town domestic comedy and film noir.[6] Social problem conventions often appear in films that are distinct examples of a film genre, such as the social problem/ screwball comedies of Frank Capra (see *Mr. Deeds Goes to Town, Mr. Smith Goes to Washington,* and *Meet John Doe*). But the working definition here places such films at the periphery of the form.

Finally, social problem films, according to the working definition, can focus on problems relating both to domestic issues *(Grapes of Wrath)* and international issues *(Fail Safe, Missing).* The historical treatment below emphasizes those films which focus on domestic issues. Numerically, they were more common than those focusing on issues of an international scope. This is partly because the censorship restrictions of the Hays Code and considerations of foreign distribution (which made producers wary of film subjects that could offend nations in which their films were distributed) made it doubly hard to make such "foreign policy" problem films. Nevertheless, enough were made so that one could have surveyed ten or twelve key social problem films focusing on foreign problems.

To reiterate, a social problem film is a film with a contemporary setting whose central narrative concern focuses on a negative condition in society that is perceived as a problem and whose portrayal of the victims of or crusaders against the social problem is empathetic.

## REPRESENTATIVE AMERICAN SOCIAL PROBLEM FILMS, 1930s–1980s

Social problem films have existed nearly from the time that American movies began telling stories. D. W. Griffith's *A Corner in Wheat* (1909), with its criticism of how money-hungry speculators enrich themselves at the expense of both the urban and rural poor, is an early example. Similarly, Kay Sloan has shown how social problem films in the 1910s functioned to serve the purposes of Progressive reform; sometimes they were even financed by reform groups like the National Child Labor Committee, the National American Woman Suffrage Association, and the National Committee of Prison Labor.[7] This tendency sets something of a pattern for the social problem film: *in general* the film industry and viewers have been more likely to tolerate or even embrace social problem films during eras of reform (the Progressive Era, the Depression, the late 1960s and into the 1970s) and to reject them during periods of a more conservative cultural climate (the 1920s, the 1950s, and 1980s).

The epigrams at the beginning of this essay suggest the opposing views held toward the social problem film within the movie industry. The dominant and more conservative view holds that "message" movies violate the canons of "entertainment" so central to Hollywood. Therefore, they will not make adequate profits and hence ought not be made.

On the other hand, a minority group of generally more liberal filmmakers views social problem films as a way for the industry to show concern for the quality of life in the United States (and incidentally to gain prestige for themselves, too). Defenses of the social problem film by those inside the industry sound very similar from era to era. In 1949, for example, liberal screenwriter Philip Dunne defended social problem films in an article about his screenplay for *Pinky*. "Entertainment," he wrote, is not only the domain of westerns and musicals; it "can also be fashioned from the raw materials of contemporary life." For Dunne, such materials ought to be presented "not as preachments, but as living dramatic stories." Like his producer Darryl F. Zanuck, Dunne felt that problem films needed to emphasize the dramatic dilemmas of individual people. Nearly forty years later, Jack Lemmon—an actor associated with a number of social problem films—discussed social problem films in much the same way: "When you can combine art and politics successfully, then I think you can move people . . . and you can enlighten them by making them think more." Yet Lemmon, like Dunne, believed that drama had to be kept in mind: "I don't think it is necessary for a film to have a political, social or economic point of view. Primarily a film should entertain. . . . The wonderful thing is that sometimes you can combine the two, as in the case of *Missing* or *The China Syndrome*, and that brings a level of craft up to a level of art."[8] Both Dunne and Lemmon, like most successful Hollywood figures involved with social problem films, look over their shoulders as they defend their involvements, constantly aware of the shadows which the giant "Entertainment" casts over them. The American social problem film never long ignores that presence.

If conservatives and liberals argue about whether social problem films should even be made, observers further left on the political spectrum comment on the timidity of social problem films once they *are* made. To Russell Campbell, for example, they "depict social problems as aberrations within a fundamentally sound system." To John Hill, social problem films ultimately advocate "social control, the maintenance of social order by either assimilation or containment." Robin Wood states this perspective most broadly: "Hollywood's intermittent concern with social problems has, in fact, almost never produced radically subversive movies (and if so, then incidentally and inadvertently)."[9] All three believe that social problem films end up as apologies for the system.

If social problem films constitute not a genre but rather a persistent and anomalous form in Hollywood, how can we usefully discuss them? Perhaps the most fruitful avenue of inquiry can be begun first by citing an observation by David Bordwell, Janet Staiger, and Kristin Thompson in *The Classical Hollywood Cinema*. "Any complete account of Hollywood filmmaking," they write, "must recognize deviations from the norm. Hollywood itself has stressed differentiation as a correlative to standardization."[10] From this perspective, Hollywood films must be similar enough (roughly two hours long, subordinating style to story) to provide its audience with something familiar, yet different enough to provide that audience with something new, fresh, or interesting. Following this insight, the social problem film can be usefully explored as one example of deviation or difference—in this case, treating an involving social problem as part of the central narrative conflict of the film—within the standard patterns of Classical Hollywood Cinema (hereafter, CHC).

We shall do this by examining ten representative social problem films from the early 1930s to the present. The films were selected for several reasons. All of them present a social problem as part of the central narrative conflict. In addition, they represent every decade from the 1930s to the 1980s, yet they varied in the degree to which they were successful by industry and box-office standards. Sometimes it can be as useful to explore a less successful film when attempting to define the contours and appeal of a particular film form. In chronological order, followed in parentheses by the year of release and the foregrounded social problem, the films are *I Am a Fugitive from a Chain Gang* (1932—the southern chain gang and judicial systems), *Grapes of Wrath* (1940—the plight of the Okies displaced by the Dust Bowl), *Lost Weekend* (1945—alcoholism), *Gentleman's Agreement* (1948—anti-Semitism), *On the Waterfront* (1954—corruption in waterfront unions), *Storm Center* (1956—McCarthyite curbing of First Amendment freedom of expression), *Guess Who's Coming to Dinner?* (1967—interracial marriage), *Coming Home* (1978—treatment of the handicapped, women's rights, and Vietnam veteran readjustment), *The China Syndrome* (1979—dangers of nuclear power plants and profit-seeking corporations), and *Alamo Bay* (1985—tensions between Vietnamese refugees and Anglos on the Texas Gulf Coast). For the sake of brevity, the longer film titles will be presented in abbreviated form for the rest of the essay.

While all ten are social problem films, they varied in the degree to which they were successful by the industry's artistic standards (as measured by the Academy Award nominations) and at the box office (as measured by *Variety*'s annual list of twenty top-grossing films). If we examine first the number of major Oscars (for best film, director, actress, actor, and screenplay) for which each film was nominated and then the number which they won, the list looks like this: *Fugitive* (2, 0), *Grapes of Wrath* (4, 1), *Lost Weekend* (4, 4), *Gentleman's Agreement* (5, 2), *On the Waterfront* (4, 4—plus Oscars for best supporting actress and cinematography, and three nominations for best supporting actor), *Storm Center* (0, 0) *Guess* (5, 2) *Coming Home* (5, 3), *The China Syndrome* (3, 0), and *Alamo Bay* (0, 0). In addition, six of the films were on *Variety*'s list of the twenty-top grossing films of that year: *Grapes of Wrath, Lost Weekend, Gentleman's Agreement* (8th), *On the Waterfront* (15th), *Guess* (2nd), and *China Syndrome* (12th).[11] (The last film, which dealt in part with the potential dangers of nuclear power plants, was helped at the box office by the publicity surrounding the accident at Three Mile Island, which was first reported less than two weeks after the film was released.)

Thus, we can see that at times the industry respects social problem films as prestigious products and that social problem films can do very well, though rarely spectacularly, at the box office. One should note that the very strong box-office performance of *Guess* was related partly to factors of stardom: it was the final Tracy-Hepburn film, Tracy having died shortly after shooting. In addition, it touched on a subject—interracial marriage—that had been taboo because of the code, yet presented it through the nonthreatening narrative conventions and tone of a drawing room comedy. All these elements contributed to its unusually strong box-office performance.

Potential makers of social problem films have had to fight for the right to make them within the institutional structures of Hollywood. During the studio era (1930–1950) social problem films seem to have been approved for one of three reasons. First, the studio and/or a particular producer within the studio would encourage them as a way of differentiating the product from those of other studios or producers. Second, the film could be an adaptation of a popular and widely discussed novel, hence creating a ready-made market for the film. Finally, a social problem film could be made to capitalize on a cycle of social problem films begun by the financial success of one of them.

The first method seems to have fostered *Fugitive*. In the early years of the Depression Warner Bros., encouraged by studio head Jack Warner and production chief Darryl F. Zanuck, developed a policy that stimulated the production of social problem films. As a way to make efficient and inexpensive films, yet differentiated enough from others to draw in audiences, Warner and Zanuck pursued the policy of making "topicals": films based on newspaper headlines. As Warner said in 1933, "Newspapers will be watched this year as they were last for ideas and plots."[12] Such topicals included gangster films like *Little Caesar* and newspaper films like *Five Star Final,* later films about unions like *Black Legion* and oppressed women like *Marked Women.* The topicals also included *Fugitive*.

Of the other pre-1950 films discussed here two others also were pushed by a producer, in both cases Zanuck again. After moving from Warners to 20th Century-Fox in 1933, Zanuck moved away from social problem films until the late 1930s. Then, in the 1940s he produced a number of social problem films, including *Grapes of Wrath* and *Gentleman's Agreement.*[13]

In addition, *Grapes of Wrath, Gentleman's Agreement,* and *Lost Weekend* were all based on popular novels of the same title. John Steinbeck had focused on the plight of the dispossessed Oklahoma farmers in *Grapes of Wrath,* Charles Jackson delineated the psychology of the alcoholic in *Lost Weekend,* and Laura Z. Hobson had traced modes of anti-Semitism in America in *Gentleman's Agreement.* All had become best-sellers, particularly *Grapes of Wrath* and *Gentleman's Agreement.* All went on to be successful films at the box office.

*Gentleman's Agreement* also was part of a larger cycle of social problem films about the fate of minorities in American society between 1947 and 1950. That cycle offers one of the only examples in American film history of a cycle of social problem films being made in an era not particularly noted for reform. That period was a transitional one in American history, as the New Deal reform spirit had waned and the political climate of the Cold War began to dominate public debate. The social problem cycle during the period may have been stimulated in part, however, by the growing American sensitivity to the fate of minorities in the United States following World War II (the war was fought, after all, against a country which systematically persecuted its Jewish minority) and by the publication of Gunnar Myrdal's study of blacks in American society, *An American Dilemma* (1944). Whatever the case, *Gentleman's Agreement* helped to initiate the cycle, which included another film touching on anti-Semitism, *Crossfire,* and five films dealing with blacks in American society: *Lost Boundaries, Home of the Brave, Pinky, Intruder in the Dust,* and *No Way out,* but it became a victim of the Cold War by the end of 1950. That *Gentleman's Agreement* did so well at the box office is no surprise when one considers that it was produced by a prominent producer known for his social problem films, Darryl F. Zanuck, that it was based on a popular novel, that it received some publicity as being part of this social problem cycle, and finally that it starred Gregory Peck.

As the studio system began to break up in the late 1940s and early 1950s due to antitrust action against the industry, competition from television, and various other factors, independent production—what Bordwell, Staiger, and Thompson (ch. 26) call the "package-unit" system of production—became much more prominent. In the package-unit system a producer organizes a film project by securing the financing, hiring workers for that particular project, and arranging the equipment and the locations for the film. Under this system, a prominent producer, director, actor, or writer (or some combination of the four) could provide the impetus for making a social problem film. And for the films discussed here made after 1950, each had an individual or small group that pushed for the independent production of the film. *On the Waterfront* originated as a script by Arthur Miller about waterfront crime, based on a series of newspaper articles by Malcolm Johnson. Budd Schulberg and Elia Kazan—both liberals with leftist political roots in the Depression years—pushed the project and got Sam Spiegel to produce it.[14] *Storm Center* came about thanks to the efforts of Daniel Taradash. Though he had hoped to make the film as early as 1951, Taradash had to wait until after winning an Oscar for his *From Here to Eternity* screenplay; that, and his screenplay for the acclaimed *Picnic,* gave him enough clout to get his picture financed under his own direction for a 1956 release.[15] *Guess* came about thanks to the efforts of producer/director Stanley Kramer, one of Hollywood's most persistent advocates of social problem films (he also was involved with such films as *Home of the Brave, The Defiant Ones, On the Beach,* and *Judgement at Nuremburg*). After commissioning William

Rose to do a screenplay about interracial marriage, Kramer secured the services of Sydney Poitier, Katharine Hepburn, and Spencer Tracy, and the production was set.[16]

The three final films on the list also were independent productions. Both *Coming Home* and *The China Syndrome* came about partly through the efforts of Jane Fonda, along with her associate producer Bruce Gilbert. After Fonda became associated with leftist politics in the late 1960s, she co-founded the IPC (Indochina Peace Campaign), which became dedicated to making popular, "progressive" films. Both *Coming Home* and *China Syndrome* were IPC connected. *China Syndrome* itself actually originated in a script by documentary filmmaker *(The Murder of Fred Hampton)* Mike Gray, who interested producer Michael Douglas in the project about the time Douglas was riding high as producer of *One Flew Over the Cuckoo's Nest*.[17] Finally, *Alamo Bay* was initiated by French director Louis Malle, who read an article in 1980 on the experiences of Vietnamese immigrants living on the Gulf Coast of Texas. After hiring Alice Arlen (co-screenwriter of *Silkwood*) to do the script for the film, Malle obtained modest financing from Tri-Star Pictures and made the film.[18]

Thus the ten films were made through the efforts of a variety of people committed to the notion of social problem films, often working against the grain of conventional Hollywood wisdom. Yet as the comments above by Philip Dunne and Jack Lemmon indicate, the social problem embedded in the film had to be presented within accepted conventions of "entertainment." With that in mind, the question of the extent to which these ten films follow the central narrative conventions of the CHC can be pursued.

According to the recent work of such scholars as Noel Burch, Robert Ray, and Bordwell, Staiger, and Thompson, the system of filmmaking that evolved in the American film industry from the 1910s on became quite systematized by the sound era.[19] This CHC is characterized by a variety of stylistic and narrative conventions. The primary aim of the CHC is to tell a story as smoothly, clearly, and absorbingly as possible. Cinematic style in the classical Hollywood system is thus subordinated to the purposes of the narrative and rarely calls attention to itself. Thus, although the CHC consists of both stylistic and narrative conventions, for our purposes, four narrative conventions are especially relevant:

1. a clearly defined, usually male, *protagonist* who is animated by a desire introduced early in the film

2. a *romantic companion* for the protagonist

3. an *antagonist,* usually an individual, whose traits or goals oppose those of the protagonist

4. a *linear plot* that is clearly *resolved* in the ending

A look at the extent to which these ten films follow the conventions indicates how fully they are wedded in most ways to the classical Hollywood model of filmmaking.

CHC films most often center on the problems of a central male protagonist, and five of the ten films exhibit this convention most clearly: *Fugitive* (James Allen, played by Paul Muni), *Lost Weekend* (Don Birnam, played by Ray Milland), *Gentleman's Agreement* (Phil Green, played by Gregory Peck), *On the Waterfront* (Terry Malloy, played by Marlon Brando), and, arguably, *Guess* (Matt Drayton, played by Spencer Tracy). Allen desires only a chance to succeed as a builder in America, Birnam to be an acclaimed writer, Green to write about anti-Semitism in a meaningful way, Malloy to make a relatively decent living (and later to avenge the death of his brother), and Drayton, to decide what is best for his daughter.

Of the remaining five films, four contain central male protagonists who share their role with at least one more character, while only *Storm Center,* starring Bette Davis as Alicia Hull, focuses on a single female protagonist. *Grapes of Wrath* focuses especially on Tom Joad (Henry Fonda) and Ma Joad (Jane Darwell), with the growing awareness of the social problem embodied in Tom's character. *Coming Home* is one of the most complex and skillfully intertwined of the films: it focuses on three characters: Luke Martin (Jon Voight), a paraplegic Vietnam veteran trying to readjust to civilian life; Capt. Bob Hyde (Bruce Dern), a gung-ho Marine who goes to Vietnam in search of heroism; and Sally Hyde (Jane Fonda), who stays home when Bob leaves, seeking meaningful activities as a woman separated from her husband. *China Syndrome* has two protagonists, both caught uncomfortably within profit-making institutional structures: Kimberly Wells (Jane Fonda) in a television news unit, Jack Godell (Jack Lemmon) in a nuclear power plant. Kimberly's desire to do hard news stories intertwines with Jack's desire to alert the public about the unsafe conditions in the power plant. One might argue that *Alamo Bay* has a major and minor protagonist. The major protagonist is Glory (Amy Madigan), who returns to the coastal town to help her ailing father operate his shrimp distribution business, then gradually begins to fight for social justice for the local Vietnamese immigrants. The minor protagonist is Dinh (Ho Nguyan), a Vietnamese immigrant who hopes to realize the American Dream by buying his own fishing boat. It is interesting to note that the final three films, each of which has an important female protagonist, were all made after the women's movement. Social problem films from the mid-1970s on—*Country, The River,* and *Norma Rae* are other examples—very frequently feature strong women characters who function as something more than what Hollywood during its classical period called "the romantic interest."

Two other elements relate to the protagonist in many social problem films. First, the protagonist often goes through an experience of education about the social problem as the film develops, beginning the narrative naive about or ignorant of the problem. As the narrative develops, he or she becomes aware of the problem and sometimes committed to fighting against it. James Allen in *Fugitive,* Tom Joad in *Grapes of Wrath,* Phil in *Gentleman's Agreement,* Terry (to some extent) in *On the Waterfront,* Alicia Hull in *Storm Center,* both Kimberly and Jack in *China Syndrome,* and Glory in *Alamo Bay* all follow this pattern. These protagonists all become victims of or crusaders against the problem (or sometimes both victims and crusaders).

Second, as the protagonists become educated about or victims of the social problem, they are often assisted by another character, often a minor character, who helps educate the protagonist about the problem or suggests some way of confronting it. James Allen's clergyman brother in *Fugitive,* Casey in *Grapes of Wrath,* Dave in *Gentleman's Agreement,* Father Barry in *On the Waterfront,* the cafe owner in *Storm Center,* and Father Ryan in *Guess Who's Coming to Dinner* all fit this function. Note that in four of the six cases, the character is a religious spokesman and that in every case but one, the perspective of these characters is vindicated; the heroes act on their advice or follow their moral suggestions to their own benefit. The sole exception is *Fugitive.* There Allen's brother counsels patience and acceptance, for which Allen is victimized by another term on the chain gang. Significantly, *Fugitive* is also the film of those listed above with the most pessimistic conclusion: at the end James Allen has no clear defenders as he tries to avoid being sent back to the chain gang.

The romantic companion is the second key narrative convention of the CHC. Most often in the CHC the protagonist had a romantic partner of the other sex. Only three of our ten films—*Grapes of Wrath, Storm Center,* and *China Syndrome*—lack that romantic double. Neither Tom Joad nor Alicia Hull is romantically involved, even though a minor romantic subplot (Rosasharn and Connie, Alisha's library aide and Paul Duncan) exists in both films. *China Syndrome* resists getting Kimberly Wells romantically involved, though the bachelor Jack Godell does subtly approach her in one bar scene. Of the remaining seven, three function very traditionally, with the woman acting as a moral influence on the protagonist: *Lost Weekend*'s Helen, the long-suffering lover hoping to cure Don of his alcoholism; *On the Waterfront*'s Edie Doyle, who with Father Barry pressures Terry to inform the authorities about the murder of her brother; and Christina Drayton in *Guess,* who accepts her daughter's marriage to a black man (the key romantic relationship in the film) soon after she learns of the plans, then seeks—again with the help of a clergyman (Monsignor Ryan)—to get Matt to go along with their daughter's wishes.

Romantic relationships in the other four films function in a variety of ways. In *Fugitive* James Allen is pressured by Marie into a marriage, when she threatens to expose him. Allen also has a "good" romantic double, Helen, whom he returns to briefly in the film's final scene. In *Gentleman's Agreement* Phil Green is portrayed as such a somber, admirable character that his romantic double, Kathy, does not need to "reform" him; in fact, she must learn to live up to *his* exacting standards. The final two films function very similarly: in both *Coming Home* and *Alamo Bay,* women function as protagonists and have difficult, even crumbling, relationships with characters who could be considered antagonists: Bob Hyde in the first and Shang in the latter. In addition, in both films married characters (Sally, Shang) carry on relationships outside of marriage (with Luke and Glory). Finally, in both films the central female character is not defined in the narrative solely by her relationship with a protagonist, as was often the case during the studio era.

The antagonist in CHC films is usually a single character who obstructs the central character from fulfilling his or her desire. In social problem films, partly because the problem itself shapes the central conflicts, the antagonist is not always embodied in a character. For example, in *Fugitive* the antagonist seems much more systemic: the chain gang system and the corrupt courts—represented by a whole array of guards, wardens, and legal officials—cause the problems. Antagonists in *Grapes of Wrath* include natural causes (the "dusters") and distant economic forces (the bankers "back East"), though the thugs of orchard owners are also in evidence. In *Lost Weekend,* the problem is *within* the protagonist—the compulsion to drink. In both *Gentleman's Agreement* and *Guess,* the antagonist is discrimination against minorities, manifested in a variety of forms in both movies. In neither film does a single predominant individual embody the problem; rather, different forms of anti-Semitism and different attitudes toward interracial marriage are expressed by different characters. In general, social problem films tend to "broaden" the antagonist, defining the social problem through a number of characters and various forms that obstruct the desire of the protagonist.

In several of the other films, however, an "evil" individual *is* stressed: *On the Waterfront*'s Johnny Friendly, the corrupt labor leader; *Storm Center*'s Paul Duncan, the opportunistic anticommunist politico; *China Syndrome*'s Evan McCormack, the corporate head of the nuclear power company; and Mac, the leader of the Ku Klux Klan in *Alamo Bay.* In each case the antagonist is physically large, and except for *Storm Center,* the antagonists are physically unattractive and surrounded by henchmen or followers of some sort who help them carry out their plans (the latter element is another way to "broaden" the antagonist). Each of these villains functions to "locate" or embody the problem: corrupt labor practices, denial of civil liberties, corporate greed and irresponsibility, intolerance toward immigrants. In these instances, it could be argued that by identifying the problems so closely with evil individuals, the film narratives displace the social problem onto a single person, implicitly suggesting that the problems will disappear if the evil person is eliminated. As Bordwell, Staiger, and Thompson have observed, the CHC exhibits "a persistent habit of reconciling social antagonisms by shifting the emphasis from history and institutions to individual causes and effects" (82). This often—but not always—happens in social problem films.

The final narrative convention of the CHC is a linear plot in which the central conflict or conflicts are clearly resolved in the ending. If CHC films use flashbacks, they are clearly integrated and motivated, included to provide information central to the development of the narrative. Only two of these ten films have flashbacks: Muley's stories about the "dusters" and the invasion of the "cats" (Caterpillar tractors) in *Grapes of Wrath* and Don's reminiscences about the development of his relationship with Helen in *Lost Weekend*. In both cases, the flashbacks begin with the character in the present telling the story and end by returning to the character again, providing no disruption in the narrative.

Social problem films have been attacked by some critics for following the convention of the closed, happy ending, which—according to those critics—tends to defuse the social criticism and to suggest to the audience that the problem is easily solved. Though nearly all ten of our films are linear, their endings—even when closed—often try *not* to suggest that solutions to the problem presented are easy. *Fugitive* has the most open ending: in a famous scene, the fugitive James Allen, asked by his girlfriend how he survives, backs into the darkness while uttering tersely, "I steal." In the final scene of *Grapes of Wrath,* which comes immediately after Tom Joad leaves the family to fight for his people, Ma Joad delivers a speech about the ability of the common people to endure. The speech mutes Tom's actions and the more overt social criticism of the novel.[20] *Lost Weekend* and *Gentleman's Agreement* both have pat endings: Don, under Helen's influence, apparently stops drinking and goes back to his novel; Kathy, after *acting* against anti-Semitism by offering to let Phil's Jewish friend Dave live in her summer house—thus reforming her "nice" anti-Semitism and satisfying Phil—ends in Phil's embrace. In *On the Waterfront*'s much discussed conclusion, the savagely beaten Terry Malloy struggles successfully to walk to the waterfront warehouse, leading the rank-and-file union members to work while Johnny Friendly ominously cries, "I'll be back."[21]

*Storm Center* and *Guess* probably conform (or at least attempt to conform) most closely to the CHC narrative conventions. In the former, Alicia Hull—fired from her job for refusing to remove a book about communism from the public library shelves—watches the burning of the library with her fellow townspeople, castigates herself for not fighting more rigorously for her rights earlier, and vows to remain in the town and help rebuild the library. The ending is singularly unconvincing: the boy who set fire to the library was once an avid reader under Alicia's influence but became psychologically unstable after the town ostracized her. The ending asks us to believe that the town will welcome Alicia back into the fold; in the context of the narrative, however, it seems more likely that the town will *blame* Alicia for her evil influence on the boy and reject her even more fully (this implausible ending is one reason for the film's lack of success, however interesting it is as a social problem film). In comparison, the ending of *Guess* is completely sunny: the problem of interracial marriage is displaced by the problem of the generation gap in the second half of the film (both fathers object to the marriage), then romantic love conquers all. Matt Drayton, the white father blesses the marriage. The black father apparently (we must surmise through reaction shots) agrees. And the whole group goes jovially into the dining room.

Although the three most recent films do resolve their narrative conflicts to some extent, they also leave some disturbing implications. *Coming Home* intercuts between Bob Hyde swimming to his suicide in the ocean and Luke Martin speaking to a high school assembly against his and his country's involvement in Vietnam. Sally's reaction to Bob's death and her relationship with Luke are left unresolved: in the final shot, just after the final extreme long shot of Bob swimming out in the distant ocean, Sally opens a grocery store door that has the word "Lucky" appearing just above the word "OUT," implying visually that Bob's suicide is less painful than the physical and psychological suffering survivors like Luke will have to bear. In *China Syndrome* Jack Godell is killed by a SWAT team at McCormack's orders after Godell briefly but ineffectively speaks to Kimberly and her crew about the dangers at the plant. After another nuclear tremor, Kimberly interviews Godell's friend Ted Spindler, who defends the legitimacy of Jack's criticisms. The last shots are of a microwave oven commercial on a video monitor and then the video color test bars that opened the film. We're left to reflect on what has transpired, wondering about the extent to which the nuclear corporation's power will obstruct or manipulate the investigation. *Alamo Bay* concludes with a shootout reminiscent of a western. After Shang shoots one of Dinh's Vietnamese friends and is beating Dinh, Glory kills Shang with a handgun after warning him to stop. As the local sheriff arrives to lead Glory away, the final shot is a freeze-frame close-up of Glory, accompanied by the inscription, "Today, more than 15,000 Vietnamese live and work on the Gulf Coast of Texas." All three films end with deaths, with lingering problems, and with inconclusive romances, failed romances, or no romances at all. These endings qualify the general rule which Bordwell, Staiger, and Thompson articulate: "Narrative resolution can work to transcend the social conflict represented in the film, often by displacing it onto the individual . . . , the couple . . . , the family, or the communal good" (82).

In general, then, the ten social problem films examined here follow—though not slavishly—the narrative conventions of the CHC, particularly the films made before the 1970s. The most variation occurs in the ending of *Fugitive* and in the three most recent films. This can be attributed both to the broader influences of American cultural history and to the economic evolution of the film industry. The open, despairing ending of *Fugitive* can easily be linked to the more general American cultural uncertainty in 1931 and 1932, the most severe years of the Depression. The refusal to bow fully to the conventions of male protagonists, romance, and rigidly closed happy endings in the films of the 1970s and 1980s stems from at least three factors. First, the audience for films has shrunk and become more specialized since the 1950s, and a sizable segment of the remaining audience was made up of viewers influenced by the critical spirit of the late 1960s and early 1970s. That segment was willing to accept critical assessments of contemporary American life. Second, the women's movement made it much more difficult for filmmakers after the early 1970s to make a social problem film with a central female character who served only as a "romantic interest."[22] Finally, just as filmmakers radicalized during the 1930s influenced the social problem films of the 1940s, filmmakers made politically conscious in the late 1960s (stars like Jane Fonda, producers like Bruce Gilbert, writers like Mike Gray, directors like Hal Ashby) influenced the social problem films of the 1970s and 1980s.[23]

Excluding *Fugitive* and to some extent *Grapes of Wrath,* however, none of the pre-1970 films questions the fundamental soundness of the American system. *Lost Weekend,* treating a social problem involving substance dependency, does not raise the issue. Phil Green in *Gentleman's Agreement* often inveighs against anti-Semitism because it violates American political ideals. In *On the Waterfront* appeals of good citizenship by Edie and Father Barry pressure Terry to testify against the corruption of Friendly, and a conspicuous line points out that the waterfront and its corruption are like no other place in America. Alicia Hull alludes to Jefferson when she refuses to remove *The Communist Dream* from the bookshelves, even though she stresses that she believes the ideas in the book are ''preposterous,'' making *Storm Center* a model liberal film. And *Guess* never questions the liberalism and generous spirit of the wealthy Draytons (he's a newspaper owner; she operates an art gallery), and given the tremendous accomplishments of the black man their daughter has chosen to marry, their spirit is not severely tested, anyway. Especially in the 1950s, when an American consensus and the legacy of McCarthyism cast a shadow over the film industry, social problem films were extremely tentative about questioning the soundness of American ideals or institutions.

In fact, given the economic imperative that a movie must appeal to a large audience and the necessary lag time between the initial idea for a movie and its completion, social problem films in American culture often appear well after the issues they consider are most controversial. Appearing in 1940, *Grapes of Wrath* presented a problem that was much less acute than it was in the mid-1930s, in part because the outbreak of World War II in Europe was beginning to stimulate the American economy. *Storm Center*'s focus on McCarthyite denial of civil liberties would have been a courageous film in 1951, when Taradash first hoped to make it; McCarthy had been out of the public eye for two years by the time the film was released. Similarly, the integrationist optimism of *Guess* appeared at a point when black nationalism and black pride were encouraging a militancy and separatism not even hinted at in the film. Even with Louis Malle's reputation and his enthusiasm for the *Alamo Bay* project, five years elapsed between the time he became interested in the Vietnamese situation on the Texas Gulf Coast and the time the film was released. Perhaps *China Syndrome* and *Coming Home* were the most timely films. Yet the latter appeared three years after the American presence in Vietnam ended. And though Three Mile Island turned *China Syndrome* into the most topical of the ten films, controversy about the safety of nuclear power plants was alive through most of the 1970s. In American film, social problem films may be generated from headlines, but the headlines are often stale news before the films reach an audience.

Nevertheless, though the social problem film has been much maligned from both the left and the right, it does, at its best, stem from honorable impulses. The attempt of narrative art to depict and criticize the manners and morals of society is perhaps as old as narrative itself. And the social problem film at its best carries on that tradition. The final words here belong to Andrzej Wajda, the Polish filmmaker whose films like *Ashes and Diamonds, Without Anesthesia,* and *Man of Marble* are rooted in the same impulse as many American social problem films. "The artist *does* help shape opinions, and can function as a kind of conscience of the nation," Wajda once told an interviewer. Such a filmmaker must function on the slender line "between the permissible and impermissible," but function there he must, for "the most important thing is to tell the audience something, to make people think, to initiate a dialogue."[24] These comments reside centrally within the impulse that generates social problem films.

## BIBLIOGRAPHICAL OVERVIEW

The social problem film, as a separate and distinguishable film type, has not been written about nearly so much as more clearly identifiable forms like the western, gangster, horror, and musical films. This is partly because, as suggested above, it is not really a film *genre,* if by that term we mean a class of films similar in character type, setting, narrative patterns, and iconography. This absence of easily distinguishable and definable generic conventions in the social problem film has also contributed to a problem of terminology. The class of films I am calling the "social problem film" in this essay has been known, inside and outside the film industry, by a number of different terms: topicals, message films, social exposé films, problem films, and social consciousness films. Nevertheless, whatever the difficulties of definition and terminology, the social problem film has generated some critical and scholarly interest, and this section will discuss some of the most interesting and useful considerations of the social problem film.

Since only one book, Peter Roffman and Jim Purdy's *The Hollywood Social Problem Film* (1981), is devoted entirely to an examination of the form, it is a good place to begin.[25] Subtitled "Madness, Despair, and Politics from the Depression to the Fifties," the book contains an introduction in which the authors attempt to define the form in the context of the Hollywood system. The bulk of the text then discusses a broad spectrum of films in four parts: "The System Breaks Down: The Individual as Victim, 1930–33"; "The System Upheld: The Individual Redeemed, 1933–1941"; "Fascism and War"; and "The Postwar World."

Two important characteristics distinguish Roffman and Purdy's approach to the social problem film. First, their definition is very broad. "The problem film," they write, "combines social analysis and dramatic conflict within a coherent narrative structure. Social content is transformed into dramatic events and movie narrative adapted to accommodate social issues as story material through a particular set of movie conventions."[26] This broad definition permits Roffman and Purdy to discuss films from a wide variety of genres as social problem films.

A second important characteristic of *The Hollywood Social Problem Film* stems from its historical boundaries. Roffman and Purdy root the social problem film in the Depression, when, as they put it, "a strong sensibility of social concern was given play in America." That sensibility provided the impetus for the social problem film, but "between the death of Roosevelt [1945] and the censure of McCarthy [1954], this sensibility faded, partly due to McCarthyism itself and largely due to the changed social perspectives of the prosperous fifties." While Roffman and Purdy note that "the late sixties saw a revival of Hollywood social concern," they argue that the "most important aspect of this revival was not the renewal of the social problem film but the infusion of an explicitly antisocial subtext that the Formula had previously prohibited."[27]

The book is well documented and includes a useful selected bibliography, as well as filmographies of over 200 films discussed in the text. In my view this otherwise useful book contains two main weaknesses. First, the definition of the social problem film is somewhat imprecise (particularly in the use of terminology like "social issues" and "social content," and in the lack of specificity of what "conventions" are part of the genre) and too broad, for it allows them to include such different movies as *The Front Page, Footlight Parade, You Can't Take It With You,* and *Citizen Kane* in the category of social problem films. Second, I believe that—relative to the entire output of Hollywood in the 1930s and 1940s—they overestimate the importance of the social problem film in Hollywood during the period (strong though it was) and underestimate the extent to which the social problem film has been a persistent, if minority, type in Hollywood since the decade of the teens.

A number of articles have discussed the social problem film. Two particularly useful essays specifically concerned with defining and analyzing social problem films are John Hill's "The British 'Social Problem' Film: *Violent Playground* and *Sapphire*" and Russell Campbell's "The Ideology of the Social Consciousness Movie: Three Films of Darryl F. Zanuck."[28] Hill's understanding of the social problem film is similar to the one described in the historical/analytical section of this essay. As he puts it, "What is distinct in the 'social problem' film is not any set of exclusive characteristics (such as specific iconography) but its specific mobilization of more general conventions, especially those of narrative and realism." To Hill, a central element of the social problem is "its adoption of the conventions of narrative as a means of sugaring the didactic pill." Because the traditional conventions of narrative develop and then resolve conflict, such narratives always in one sense "solve" problems. Working within these narrative conventions, the social problem film most often exposes a social problem in the central conflict of the narrative, then stresses "the reformist solution, the capacity for social accommodation," in its conclusion. Despite this tendency toward neat resolution in social problem films, Hill does not dismiss them as unimportant. Quoting John Ellis, he argues that by presenting a problem through narrative conflicts, social problem films do "work through" and even "refresh" ideological problems central to the culture in which the films are made.[29]

Campbell's article is an analysis of three social problem films produced by Darryl F. Zanuck which focus on the oppression of a minority or under-privileged group: *Grapes of Wrath, Gentleman's Agreement,* and *Pinky.* After discussing the controversies that such films generated, Campbell attempts to define the core of the "social consciousness movies." Such films, writes Campbell, form "part of the liberal branch of bourgeois ideology. . . . The liberal purpose of focusing attention on a social problem in order to provoke corrective action remains uppermost." Much like Hill, Campbell believes that the social problem film, "while portraying negative aspects of American soci-ety, celebrates the system for being flexible and susceptible to amelioration." Functioning in the movie industry much as the left wing of the Democratic party functions in the American political process, social problem movies absorb protest and "depict social problems as aberrations within a fundamentally sound system rather than pointers to the inherently exploitative nature of a capitalist economy." Ultimately, concludes Campbell, social problem films serve as "warnings and exhortations" to middle-class viewers, suggesting that "those who have must be willing to give a little, to sacrifice, . . . to bend," if the system is to survive.[30]

Another exploration of social problem films appeared when sociologist Her-bert Gans defined and defended them from a liberal pluralist perspective in the 1960s. His essay, "The Rise of the Problem-Film: An Analysis of Changes in Hollywood Films and the American Audience," defines the problem film as one which

deals explicitly with social, sexual, and political problems and their solution. The typi-cal problem-film shows how an individual or group is beset by the problem, weaves a plot around the causes and consequences of the problem, describes the moral or ethical issues—and dilemmas—raised both by the problem and possible solutions, and finally ends with the hero taking appropriate action, usually including a morally difficult choice, which solves the problem, at least for him and loved ones.

Unlike Purdy and Roffman, who see the social problem film as characteristic of the 1930s and 1940s, Gans sees it primarily as a phenomenon of the late 1950s and early 1960s, following the brief vogue for problem films about race in the late 1940s and early 1950s. He also sees three causes for the growth of problem films: the emergence of television and "its takeover of the old fantasy themes"; the change and increased education among moviemakers; and the breakdown of the movie audience into "subcultures of taste," at least one subculture of which is attracted to problem films. In discussing the future of problem films, Gans takes the classical liberal stance. Because problem films "provide information for the citizenship role even as they entertain," they may enable American movies, despite the decline in movie attendance from the late 1940s on, to "assume a more significant role in American society."[31]

Finally, Richard Dyer, in "*Victim:* Hermeneutic Project," offers a Marxist analysis of Basil Dearden's *Victim* (Rank, 1961)—a British social problem film about homosexuality starring Dirk Bogarde—within the broader context of the British social problem film. The essay offers three particular contributions to those interested in the social problem film. First, it treats the cycle of British social problem films between 1956 and 1963, which—unlike most American social problem films before the mid-1960s, at least partly because of the Hays Code—focused especially on issues of sex and the family. Second, Dyer suggests that although British social problem films do present an aura of reality— a "true-to-life gloss," in his words—they tend to conceive the problems "as being outside of class and history" and thus "avoid the struggle inherent in class society." This reminds one of Campbell's suggestion that American social consciousness movies tend to depict social problems vividly without suggesting that any fundamental restructuring of society is needed to ameliorate them. Finally, in one of the most interesting sections of the essay, Dyer outlines a scheme for understanding the various ways a viewer might have responded to (in his words, "decoded") *Victim*. Drawing on work by Stuart Hall, he suggests six different categories: a dominant, negotiated, or radical reading for those who disliked the film, and the same three possibilities for those who liked it. Dyer's schematic rendering of various audience responses is of particular interest to those seeking to understand the important question of the various ways American social problem films have been received and understood by audiences.[32] Anyone who has taught social problem films to large groups or argued about the value of a particular social problem film with others of different ideological predispositions knows how different the responses to social problem films can be.

The above are probably the most useful works for those interested in the theory and analysis of social problem films. However, a number of other works also relevant to the subject ought to be mentioned briefly. Kay Sloan, in "A Cinema in Search of Itself: Ideology of the Social Problem Film during the Silent Era," examines a number of feature films in the 1910s "made by filmmakers who actively sought social reforms during the Progressive Era."[33] In his *Rise of the American Film,* particularly chapters 9 and 25, Lewis Jacobs touches on the "significant content" of some American movies before World War I and during the 1930s.[34] While these works treat the beginnings of the social problem film, two recent works suggest how the social problem film has also moved to prime-time television in the past decade and what ideological operations are at work in them: Elayne Rapping's "Made for TV Movies: The Domestication of Social Issues" and Laurie J. Schulze's "*Getting Physical:* Text/Context/Reading and the Made-for-Television Movie."[35]

Since social problem films often get made because of the intervention of particular studios, producers, directors, or stars drawn to and identified with the form, other kinds of documents are also relevant to the student of the social problem film. Studies of the particular studios, autobiographies by or biographies of appropriate figures, and interviews with people involved in the projects often yield interesting results. Nick Roddick's *A New Deal in Entertainment: Warner Brothers in the 1930s,* while providing a vivid picture of the studio which was often identified with social problem films in the 1930s, also reminds us that such films constituted but a small portion of the entire studio output in that decade.[36] Useful autobiographies and biographies include Jack Warner (with Dean Jennings), *My First Hundred Years in Hollywood* (New York: Random House, 1965); Mel Gussow, *Don't Say Yes Until I Finish Talking: A Biography of Darryl F. Zanuck* (New York: Doubleday, 1971); Michel Ciment, *Kazan on Kazan* (New York: Viking, 1974), and Thomas H. Pauley, *An American Odyssey: Elia Kazan and American Culture* (Philadelphia: Temple University Press, 1983); Donald Spoto, *Stanley Kramer: Film Maker* (New York: Putnam's, 1978); and Fred Guiles, *Jane Fonda: an Actress in Her Time* (New York: Doubleday, 1982). Articles by or interviews with people making social problem films can also be illuminating. They include—among many, many more—Adrian Scott (producer of *Crossfire*), "You Can't Do That!" *Screenwriter,* August 1947, pp. 4–7; Philip Dunne (co-screenwriter of *Pinky*), "Approach to Racism," *New York Times,* 1 May 1949, sec. 2, p. 5; Stanley Kramer, "The Great Stone Face," *Journal of the Producer's Guild of America,* June 1960, pp. 11–12; Gary Crowdus and Dan Georgakas, "Spread a Little Sunshine: An Interview with Jack Lemmon in Havana," *Cineaste,* 14, no. 3 (1986), pp. 4–10. *Cineaste* magazine has been particularly good over the past decade at providing interviews with filmmakers interested in making films of political or social relevance; Georgakas and Lenny Rubenstein have collected a number of them in *The Cineaste Interviews* (1983). Finally, Jim Cook and Alan Lovell, editors of *Coming to Terms with Hollywood* (1981), examine the aesthetic and political views of a number of leftists—including Kazan, Lillian Hellman, Joseph Losey, Abraham Polonsky, and Robert Rossen—who became associated in various degrees with the social problem film in the 1940s and 1950s.

In conclusion, I believe it is important that social problem films be understood in the larger context of American film history. As such, the following books which treat the broader context of American film history ought to be mentioned: Garth Jowett, *Film: The Democratic Art* (Boston: Little, Brown, 1976); Robert Sklar, *Movie-Made America* (New York: Random House, 1975); Robert Ray, *A Certain Tendency in Hollywood Cinema, 1930–1980* (Princeton: Princeton University Press, 1985); and David Bordwell, Janet Staiger, and Kristin Thompson, *The Classical Hollywood Cinema: Film Style and Mode of Production to 1960* (New York: Columbia University Press, 1985).

## NOTES

1. Stanley Kramer, "The Great Stone Face," *Journal of the Producer's Guild of America,* June 1960, p. 11; Martin Quigley, *Motion Picture Herald,* 27 January 1940; Darryl F. Zanuck, quoted in *Variety,* 7 January 1949, p. 6; *Variety,* 9 October 1949, p. 1.

2. The following two paragraphs are influenced by several sources: Howard Becker, ed., *Social Problems: A Modern Approach* (New York: Wiley, 1966); Paul B. Horton and Gerald R. Leslie, eds., *The Sociology of Social Problems* (New York: Appleton-Century-Crofts, 1970); Lee Rainwater, ed., *Social Problems and Public Policy* (Chicago: Aldine, 1974); and John Hill, "The British 'Social Problem' Film: *Violent Playground* and *Sapphire,*" *Screen,* February 1985, pp. 34–48.

3. Rainwater, *Social Problems and Public Policy,* p. 1.

4. Thomas Schatz, *Hollywood Genres* (New York: Random House, 1981), p. 6. The most interesting recent attempt to define a genre, based on an exhaustive survey and close viewings of films, is Jeanine Basinger's *The World War II Combat Film* (New York: Columbia University Press, 1986). I doubt that a similar attempt to define the social problem film as a genre would yield the same fruitful results that Basinger found in her study.

5. Pauline Kael, "Morality Plays Left and Right," in *I Lost It At the Movies* (Boston: Little, Brown, 1965), pp. 319–46.

6. Robin Wood, "Ideology, Genre, Auteur," *Film Comment,* January–February 1977, pp. 46–51.

7. Kay Sloan, "A Cinema in Search of Itself: Ideology of the Social Problem Film During the Silent Era," *Cineaste* 14, no. 2, 1985, pp. 34–37, 56.

8. Philip Dunne, "Approach to Racism," *New York Times,* 1 May 1949, sec. 2, p. 5: Interview with Jack Lemmon, *Cineaste,* vol. 14, no. 3, 1986, p. 7.

9. Russell Campbell, "Three Films of Darryl F. Zanuck," *Quarterly Review of Film Studies,* Winter 1978, p. 60; Hill, "The British 'Social Problem' Film," p. 36; Robin Wood, *Hollywood from Vietnam to Reagan* (New York: Columbia University Press, 1986), p. 202.

10. David Bordwell, Janet Staiger, and Kristin Thompson, *The Classical Hollywood Cinema* (New York: Columbia University Press, 1986), p. 70. For a fuller discussion of the interplay of standardization and differentiation within the film industry, see chapters 7 and 9.

11. The Oscar nominations and awards are listed in Richard Shale, *Academy Awards,* 2d ed. (New York: Ungar, 1982); box-office figures are compiled in Cobbett Steinberg, *Reel Facts* (New York: Random House, 1978), pp. 339–54. Since *Variety* did not begin ranking the top twenty films until 1947, *Grapes of Wrath* and *Lost Weekend* are not ranked.

12. Quoted in Harry Alan Potamkin's "The Year of the Eclipse," *The Compound Cinema,* ed. Lewis Jacobs (New York: Columbia University Press, 1977), p. 203 (the article originally appeared in *Closeup,* March 1933). On Warner Brothers during the 1930s, see also Nick Roddick, *A New Deal in Entertainment* (London: British Film Institute, 1983).

13. Zanuck's involvements with social problem films at Fox in the middle and late 1940s is treated in chapter 9 of Mel Gussow, *Don't Say Yes Until I Finish Talking: A Biography of Darryl F. Zanuck* (New York: Doubleday, 1971).

14. See Ken Hey, "Ambivalence as a Theme in *On the Waterfront* (1954): An Interdisciplinary Approach to Film Study," in *Hollywood as Historian,* ed. Peter Rollins (Lexington: University of Kentucky Press, 1983), especially pp. 153–61.

15. Daniel Taradash, "Check This," *New York times,* 14 October 1956, sec. 2, p. 5.

16. Donald Spoto, *Stanley Kramer: Film Maker* (New York: Putnam's, 1978), pp. 283–91.

17. Fonda discusses her attitudes toward Hollywood as of 1974 in "Jane Fonda: 'I Prefer Films That Strengthen People,' " collected in *The Cineaste Interviews,* ed. Dan Georgakas and Lenny Rubenstein (Chicago: Lake View Press, 1983), pp. 105–18. See also the interview with her colleague, the associate producer of *Coming Home* and *The China Syndrome,* Bruce Gilbert (pp. 248–64). Fonda and Mike Gray are both discussed in Barbara Zheutlin and David Talbot, *Creative Differences: Profiles of Hollywood Dissidents* (Boston: South End Press, 1978), pp. 131–43, 309–21.

18. John Culhane, "Louis Malle: An Outsider's Odyssey," *New York Times Magazine,* 7 April 1985, pp. 28–31, 68.

19. The following paragraphs are indebted to those scholars, particularly to Ray's *A Certain Tendency in Hollywood Cinema, 1930–1980* (Princeton: Princeton University Press, 1985), chapter 1; Bordwell, Staiger and Thompson, *Classical Hollywood Cinema,* especially chapter 15; and Bordwell and Thompson, *Film Art,* 2d ed. (New York: Knopf, 1986), pp. 98–99.

20. See George Bluestone's chapter on *Grapes* in *Novels into Film* (1957; repr. Berkeley: University of California Press, 1973).

21. See Lindsay Anderson, "The Last Sequence of *On the Waterfront,*" *Sight and Sound,* January–March 1955, pp. 127–30.

22. This is not to say that Hollywood has become a bastion of feminism, but rather that more strong women characters have appeared in American films during the past ten years when compared, say, to the 1950s. Two searching explorations are found in Wood, *Hollywood from Vietnam,* chapter 10, and Elayne Rapping, "Hollywood's New 'Feminist' Heroines," *Cineaste* 14, no. 4, 1986, pp. 4–9.

23. The influence of this 1930s generation on American film is discussed in *Coming to Terms with Hollywood,* ed. Jim Cook and Allen Lovell (London: British Film Institute, 1983), while more recent figures are discussed in Zheutlin and Talbot.

24. Interview with Andrzej Wajda, in *The Cineaste Interviews,* pp. 317, 321, 324.

25. Peter Roffman and Jim Purdy, *The Hollywood Social Problem Film* (Bloomington: Indiana University Press, 1981).

26. Ibid., p. viii.

27. Ibid., pp. ix, 297–98.

28. Hill, "The British 'Social Problem' Film," pp. 34–38; Russell Campbell, "The Ideology of the Social Consciousness Movie: Three Films of Darryl F. Zanuck," *Quarterly Review of Film Studies,* Winter 1978, pp. 49–71.

29. Hill, "The British 'Social Problem' Film," pp. 36–37, 48.

30. Campbell, "Ideology of the Social Consciousness Movie," pp. 60, 69–70.

31. Herbert Gans, "The Rise of the Problem-Film: An Analysis of Changes in Hollywood Films and the American Audience," *Social Problems,* Summer 1963, pp. 327, 336.

32. Richard Dyer, "*Victim:* Hermeneutic Project," *Film Forum,* Autumn 1977, pp. 12, 19–22.

33. Kay Sloan, "A Cinema in Search of Itself: Ideology of the Social Problem Film during the Silent Era," *Cineaste* 14, no. 2, 1985, pp. 34–37, 56.

34. Lewis Jacobs, *Rise of the American Film* (1939; repr. New York: Columbia University Press, 1967).

35. Elayne Rapping, "Made for TV Movies: The Domestication of Social Issues," *Cineaste* 14, no. 2, 1985, pp. 30–33; Laurie J. Schulze, "*Getting Physical:* Text/Context/Reading and the Made-for-Television Movie," *Cinema Journal,* Winter 1986, pp. 35–50.

36. Roddick, *A New Deal in Entertainment.*

## BIBLIOGRAPHICAL CHECKLIST

### Books

Cooks, Jim, and Alan Lovell, eds. *Coming to Terms with Hollywood.* Dossier 11. London: British Film Institute, 1981.

Georgakas, Dan, and Lenny Rubenstein, eds. *The Cineaste Interviews.* Chicago: Lake View Press, 1983.

Roffman, Peter, and Jim Purdy. *The Hollywood Social Problem Film.* Bloomington: Indiana University Press, 1981.

Zheutlin, Barbara, and David Talbot. *Creative Differences: Profiles of Hollywood Dissidents.* Boston: South End, 1978.

### Shorter Works

Campbell, Russell. "The Ideology of the Social Consciousness Movie: Three Films of Darryl F. Zanuck," *Quarterly Review of Film Studies,* Winter 1978, pp. 49–71.

Dyer, Richard. "*Victim:* Hermeneutic Project," *Film Forum,* Autumn 1977, pp. 12–22.

Gans, Herbert. "The Rise of the Problem-Film: An Analysis of Changes in Hollywood Films and the American Audience," *Social Problems,* Summer 1963, pp. 327–36.

Hill, John. "The British 'Social Problem' Film: *Violent Playground* and *Sapphire,*" *Screen,* February 1985, pp. 34–48.

Jacobs, Lewis. Chapter 9, "Pre-war Films: Significant Trends," and Chapter 25, "Significant Contemporary Film Content," in his *The Rise of the American Film.* 1939; repr. New York: Columbia University Press, 1967.

Maltby, Richard. Chapter 8, "A Little Understanding: Liberal Realism and the Politics of Displacement," and Chapter 9, "Rhetoric Without a Cause: The Liberal Cinema," in his *Harmless Entertainment: Hollywood and the Ideology of Consensus.* London: Scarecrow, 1983.

Rapping, Elayne. "Made for TV Movies: The Domestication of Social Issues," *Cineaste* 14, no. 2, 1985, pp. 30–33.

Schulze, Laurie J. "*Getting Physical:* Text/Context/Reading and the Made-for-Television Movie," *Cinema Journal,* Winter 1986, pp. 35–50.

Sloan, Kay. "A Cinema in Search of Itself: Ideology of the Social Problem Film during the Silent Era," *Cineaste* 14, no. 2, 1985, pp. 34–37, 56.

Wood, Robin. "Images and Women," in his *Hollywood from Vietnam to Reagan.* New York: Columbia University Press, 1986.

## SELECTED FILMOGRAPHY

1932   *I Am a Fugitive from a Chain Gang* (93 minutes).
Warner Brothers. Director: Mervyn LeRoy. Screenplay: Howard J. Green and Brown Holmes, from the story by Robert E. Burns, "I Am a Fugitive from a Georgia Chain Gang." Cinematography: Sol Polito. Cast: Paul Muni (James Allen), Glenda Farrell (Marie Woods), Helen Vinson (Helen), Preston Foster (Pete), Allen Jenkins (Barney Sykes), Berton Churchill (Judge).

1940   *Grapes of Wrath* (128 minutes).
20th Century-Fox. Producer: Darryl F. Zanuck. Director: John Ford. Screenplay: Nunnally Johnson, from the novel by John Steinbeck. Cinematography: Gregg Toland. Cast: Henry Fonda (Tom Joad), Jane Darwell (Ma Joad), John Carradine (Casey), Charley Grapewin (Grampa), Russell Simpson (Pa Joad), Doris Bowdon (Rosasharn), John Qualen (Muley).

1945   *Lost Weekend* (101 minutes).
Paramount. Producer: Charles Brackett. Director: Billy Wilder. Screenplay: Brackett and Wilder, from novel by Charles R. Jackson. Cinematography: John F. Seitz. Cast: Ray Milland (Don Birnam), Jane Wyman (Helen St. James), Phillip Terry (Wick Burnam), Howard da Silva (Nat), Doris Dowling (Gloria), Frank Faylen (Bim).

1947   *Gentleman's Agreement* (118 minutes).
20th Century-Fox. Producer: Darryl F. Zanuck. Director: Elia Kazan. Screenplay: Moss Hart, from the novel by Laura Z. Hobson. Cinematography: Arthur Miller. Cast: Gregory Peck (Phil Green), Dorothy McGuire (Kathy), John Garfield (Dave), Celeste Holm (Anne), Anne Revere (Mrs. Green), Jane Wyatt (Jane), Dean Stockwell (Tommy), Sam Jaffe (Professor Lieberman).

1954   *On the Waterfront* (108 minutes).
Columbia. Producer: Sam Spiegel. Director: Elia Kazan. Screenplay: Budd Schulberg, based on newspaper series by Malcolm Johnson. Cinematography: Boris Kaufman. Cast: Marlon Brando (Terry Malloy), Rod Steiger (Charlie), Eva Marie Saint (Edie Doyle), Lee J. Cobb (Johnny Friendly), Karl Malden (Father Barry), Pat Henning ("Kayo" Dugan).

1956   *Storm Center* (85 minutes).
Phoenix (distributed by Columbia). Producer: Julian Blaustein. Director: Daniel Taradash. Screenplay and story by Taradash and Elick Moll. Cast: Bette Davis (Alicia Hull), Brian Keith (Paul Duncan), Kim Hunter (Martha Lockridge), Paul Kelly (Judge Robert Ellerbe), Kevin Coughlin (Freddie Slater), Joe Mantell (George Slater), Sally Brophy (Laura Slater).

1967   *Guess Who's Coming to Dinner* (112 minutes).
Columbia. Producer/Director: Stanley Kramer. Original Screenplay by William Rose. Cinematography: Sam Leavitt. Cast: Spencer Tracy (Matt Drayton), Katharine Hepburn (Christina Drayton), Sidney Poitier (John Prentice), Katharine Houghton (Joey Drayton), Cecil Kellaway (Monsignor Ryan), Isabell Sanford (Tillie).

1978   *Coming Home* (120 minutes).
United Artists. Producer: Jerome Hellman. Director: Hal Ashby. Screenplay by Waldo Salt and Robert C. Jones, based on a story by Nancy Dowd. Cinematographer: Haskell Wexler. Cast: Jane Fonda (Sally Hyde), Jon Voight (Luke Martin), Bruce Dern (Capt. Bob Hyde), Penelope Milford (Vi Munson), Robert Carradine (Bill Munson), Robert Ginty (Sgt. Dink Mobley).

1979   *The China Syndrome* (122 minutes).
Columbia. Producer: Michael Douglas. Director: James Bridges. Original screenplay by Bridges, Mike Gray, and T. S. Cook. Cinematography: James Crabe. Cast: Jane Fonda (Kimberly Wells), Jack Lemmon (Jack Godell), Michael Douglas (Richard Adams), Scott Brady (Herman DeYoung), Wilford Brimley (Ted Spindler), Daniel Valdez (Hector Salas), Richard Herd (Evan McCormack).

1985   *Alamo Bay* (105 minutes).
Tri-Star Pictures. Producers: Louis and Vincent Malle. Director: Louis Malle. Screenplay by Alice Arlen, based on Ross Milloy's article, "Vietnam Fallout in a Texas Town." Cinematographer: Curtis Clark. Music: Ry Cooder. Cast: Amy Madigan (Glory), Ed Harris (Shang), Ho Nguyen (Dinh), Donald Moffat (Wally), Truyan V. Tran (Ben), Rudy Young (Skinner), William Frankfather (Mac).

# 18

## Biographical Film

CAROLYN ANDERSON

An amalgam of literature, history, psychology, and sociology, contemporary biography offers new variations on the ancient art of telling life stories. In the 1980s it may be the preferred form of reading in America.[1] Its filmic equivalent, the bio-pic, reaches back to the earliest days of moviemaking, and although never the most prolific nor the most popular of genres, the biographical film has a rich tradition, but one that has rarely been recognized in film scholarship. This chapter examines the bio-pic as a distinctive film type by creating a generic profile based on a sample of over 200 biographical features with special attention to the ways in which key films demonstrate characteristic generic patterns. Although there were biographical films in the silent era, this sample includes only sound films, ranging chronologically from *Disraeli* (1929) to *Sid and Nancy* (1986). Only U.S. productions made for theatrical distribution are included in the creation of the generic profile, but some American deviations from the commercial mainstream are discussed.

To consider films in generic terms one must entertain notions of boundaries. The next natural, but by no means easy, step is the creation of taxonomies or generic subsets. The noted biographer Paul Murray Kendall has divided biographies into categories by their relation to facticity: (1) novel as biography, (2) fictionalized biography, (3) interpretive biography, (4) super biography, (5) scholarly biography, (6) life and times biography, (7) research biography, and (8) compilation of source materials.[2] As with most category systems, the interior divisions blur, but the edges stand out. If Kendall's system were adapted to the cinema, *Seraphita's Diary* (1982), a fiction film that posed as autobiography, would be at one end of the continuum and newsreel compilations of historic figures, such as *King: A Filmed Record, Montgomery to Memphis* (1970), would stand at the other end. The majority of bio-pics would probably fall into the fictionalized or interpretive biography categories.

Hayden White's reminder to fellow historians holds true for biography as well: "The same set of events can serve as components of a story that is tragic *or* comic, as the case may be, depending upon the historian's choice of plot structure that he considers most appropriate for ordering events . . . into a comprehensible story."[3] Thus, the genre could be divided by tone, with the hagiographic bio-pic offering a model of achievement, like *Edison, the Man* (1940), at one extreme, and a satire, such as *Buffalo Bill and the Indians, or Sitting Bull's History Lesson* (1976), with its attitude of aggressive debunking, at the other.

The genre both parts and merges by the central content of the life story told and, therefore, biographies of entertainers (*Funny Girl* [1968]) can be grouped together and also considered a subgenre of the musical, the lives of racketeers (*Al Capone* [1959]) share characteristics with the gangster movie, accounts of outlaws (*The Left-Handed Gun* [1958]) follow norms of the western, and so forth.

Rather than using one of these categorization systems, I will present the key biographical films in chronological order as a reminder that biographical films do have their own historical progression as a genre. I agree with Colin McArthur that "no matter what period history-writing or historical drama is ostensibly dealing with, in reality it is providing for the ideological needs of the present."[4]

Influenced by the German *Kostümfilm* of the late teens and early 1920s and encouraged by the great success of the British biographies of the early 1930s, American studios produced more than fifty bio-pics in the 1930s and 1940s. Despite the variety of the genre, one combination of talents shaped its image: the Warners production directed by William Dieterle, starring Paul Muni. Thomas Elsaesser cogently describes the "collage of motives" operating at Warners and locates the founding of the genre "in the dialectic between the external threat of censorship and a potential disturbance from inside: too great a desire for autonomy by the individual parts (the star and the director) creating an excess of 'personality' in the system and thus requiring a countervailing force of integration: the bio-pics were in some sense this counterforce."[5] Warners wanted to improve its image and, according to Elsaesser, constructed a self-consciously civic mode of address in a series of bio-pics about idealists.

In *The Story of Louis Pasteur* (1936) Muni plays the scientist as a genius at odds with society, a tension reconciled by Pasteur's acceptance into the Académie Française. Characteristic of this era, the protagonist is non-American and noncontemporary. Besides content distance, the style of spatial construction and the sense of continuity in these films differed from other Warner productions. Scenes were often staged frontally, reducing the illusion of spatial depth; point of view structure was rarely used, resulting in lives "that appeared as if already set in the picture frame of history."[6] Warners marketed *Pasteur* emphasizing its cultural merit and its commitment to historical accuracy. The film was enormously successful in the United States and abroad.

Although Warners is the studio most remembered for bio-pics, 20th Century-

Fox actually produced more biographies in our sample than Warners. (Fox produced 20 percent, Warners 18 percent, MGM 15 percent, and Paramount 11 percent of 204 films.) Kenneth Macgowan was the producer responsible for many Fox bio-pics, including *Young Mr. Lincoln* (1939), directed by John Ford and starring a promising contract player, Henry Fonda. As its title suggests, *Young Mr. Lincoln* limited itself to the re-creation of an early segment of a well-known life. In contrast to the problem of providing an audience with information sufficient to create a context for an unfamiliar figure,[7] here the challenge was to create suspense. The dramatic core of the film is a tumultuous trial in which Lincoln successfully defends two brothers falsely accused of murder.

No biographical film has been the subject of a more influential analysis than the one given *Young Mr. Lincoln* by the *Cahier du Cinéma* editors.[8] In a complex ideological reading, they claim that the film disparages politics, presenting a morality superior to politics. Lincoln "can only be inscribed as a Fordian character at the expense of a number of distortions and reciprocal assaults."[9] They argue that biography locates history unproblematically in the human, which falsely implies that history resides in the subjectivity of its participants and their individual perceptions of events.

Two biographies produced as the United States entered World War II demonstrate the optimism and sentimentality of the bio-pics of the early 1940s and the eagerness of stars to extend their acting range through the demands of biographic impersonation. In *Pride of the Yankees* (1942) Gary Cooper played the baseball star Lou Gehrig. Released only a year after Gehrig's death from a form of sclerosis that would later bear his name, *Pride of the Yankees* featured Gehrig's teammates (most notably Babe Ruth) playing themselves, a practice which lends a special credibility to the bio-pic, yet often simultaneously introduces the awkwardness of clashing styles of presentation and highlights the artifice of the biographic project.

By the end of the 1930s, Cooper was Hollywood's top earner. He had established a persona of courage based on his classic, lean, wholesome good looks and the earnestness of his roles. *Pride of the Yankees* deepened the image of Cooper as the "idealized common man."[10] Gehrig is presented as a fine and humble man, rather than a great athlete: the shy young Gehrig loves his mother, works hard, and enjoys a clumsy romance. *Pride of the Yankees* lacks the conflict that moves drama forward until Gehrig's fatal illness. This modest film highlights the biographer's dilemma: most people, even famous ones, don't live their lives dramatically.

In *Yankee Doodle Dandy* (1942) James Cagney demonstrated not only his versatility but his patriotism. As a response to his stereotyped gangster screen image and to charges of communist associations in his off-screen life, Cagney persuaded Warners to let him portray George M. Cohan, a patriotic song and dance man, who died shortly after the film's release. The resulting bio-pic was a tremendous financial and critical success. Receipts for its New York premiere were converted into war bonds and donated by Warners.[11] Cagney won an Oscar for his masterful impersonation of Cohan from youth through old age. So forceful was the performance that "the Cagney voice" that impersonators mimic is the hoarse, breathy voice the actor used for the elder Cohan, not Cagney's natural voice.[12] But, of course, audiences know actors through their roles; the performance is often more memorable than the life. Just as print biographies display a penchant for recalling the lives of literary figures, the film biography privileges the performer as central figure. Entertainers are featured in 31 percent of the films in our sample, composers 16 percent, and sports figures 10 percent. Combined, these three kinds of performers account for more than half of the total. Because of its emphasis on the individual, the biography genre easily operates as a star vehicle. Often playing against type, leads in bio-pics frequently win acting awards. Cagney's protrayal of George M. Cohan is an unforgettable tour de force. The penultimate Hollywood musical, *Yankee Doodle Dandy* celebrates American entertainment and displays its integral connection with American politics.

Since the primary material of biography, the actual lives of people, exists prior to its use in stories of those lives, the biographical construction process follows norms of history and journalism as well as fiction. Certainly great differences exist among biographers in their access to public figures, living or dead, but at one level the material resides in the public domain: the life stories are there for the telling. Fame attracts biographers; biographies contribute to fame. What lives Hollywood chooses to commemorate when and how depends on a complicated web of motives and exigencies. Because of its empahsis on the past, the bio-pic tends to be a conservative genre. Not surprisingly, the most active period for the genre from our sample was 1946–1955.

One of the most convoluted bio-pic projects of that era was *Viva Zapata!* (1952), which created for screenwriter John Steinbeck, producer Darryl F. Zanuck, and director Elia Kazan the dilemma of making a movie about a revolutionary figure in a repressive political atmosphere. In his careful case study of the film, Paul Vanderwood describes the ideological confusion among the various participants: "No documents better reveal the problems of political focus which beset the intellectual left in postwar America than the succession of Steinbeck-Kazan screenplays which preceded the filming of *Viva Zapata!* What began as an endorsement of revolution with determined leadership as the means to social change ended up as a rejection of power, strong leadership, and rebellion in favor of a grass-roots democracy which promises little, if any, change at all."[13] Vanderwood offers substantial evidence to confirm that Zanuck was more concerned with Stalinism than Zapatismo, that this historical film of a Mexican agrarian rebel was shaped by the contemporary shadow of the House Un-American Activities Committee.

Zapata's corruption by power is part of the dark side of the bio-pic. A continuing motif runs through much of the genre: success has its price. The genre accommodates itself as easily to the twist of the cautionary tale as to the sweep of the inspirational fable. The brilliant artist who remains personally inadequate is a type featured in numerous bio-pics: "Filmmakers gravitate toward the odd, flamboyant, often tragic figures." [14] In *Lust for Life* (1956), Kirk Douglas channeled his ever-present intensity into a moving portrayal of the tormented artist, Vincent Van Gogh. Director Vincente Minnelli, who had been a celebrated theater designer early in his career, created a rich visual story that matched the narrative for its emotional power.

Douglas prepared for his role by reading the painter's voluminous correspondence with his brother, Theo. Based on those letters, Douglas formed an interpretation of Van Gogh as a latent homosexual, a characterization that remained implicit due to the Production Code. [15] *Lust for Life* was adapted from a best-selling "historical novel" by Irving Stone that takes great liberties with Van Gogh's life. In our sample, 34 percent of films were credited adaptations: 17 percent biographies or historical novels, 10 percent autobiographies, and 7 percent plays. Print biographies have always enjoyed more freedom than films in examing the sexual lives of their subjects, but Leon Edel has noted great changes in the literary biography during his career as a biographer. While he thinks biography has "profited enormously" from the new sexual directness, Edel nevertheless cautions biographers to "learn all over again the lessons of relevance." [16]

The most popular and influential biographical film of the 1960s, *Bonnie and Clyde* (1967), presented the sexual frustrations of its subjects as an integral part of their personalities. Director Arthur Penn's interest in Bonnie Parker and Clyde Barrow was more thematic than historic: "I don't think the original Bonnie and Clyde are very important except insofar as they motivated the writing of the script and our making of the movie. Whether they are violent or not violent, whether we are sympathetic to them or not sympathetic, doesn't matter. They were part of an event, they were there when it was happening. So we hung our movie on them, but we don't confine it to them." [17] The film tapped pools of discontent in audiences throughout the country and was seen and enjoyed as a challenge to the status quo.

Part of the appeal of *Bonnie and Clyde* to media-savvy audiences is the film's reflexivity about mythmaking. The film investigates how historical figures become captives of their own legends. The opening credits present still photographs of Bonnie and Clyde with brief biographies. On the sound track we hear a camera clicking and then a phonograph playing "Deep in the Arms of Love." The documentary photographs dissolve into the faces of Warren Beatty and Faye Dunaway, as the names of the actors are listed and the credits turn from white to red. The fit among historical personage, legend, and star is emphasized. That fit is intentionally loose in *Bonnie and Clyde;* a modernist reading accepts the slack. [18]

Very much a product of the camera-as-star era, the film's lulling Technicolor functions both romantically and ironically. One of the best examples of the film's glossy romanticism and ironic counterpoint is Bonnie's reunion with her family. The special photographic textures of soft focus, filters, and slow motion create a dusty pastoral of considerable beauty as the sequence works both as nostalgia and as a self-conscious comment on manufactured nostalgia. Bonnie's writing of "The Ballad of Bonnie and Clyde" and its publication link character and audience in the inevitability and fatalism that accompany tragic causality, yet the result is something far more ambivalent than straightforward tragedy.

The 1966–1975 period was a time when notions of the heroic were problematic for many Americans. Not surprisingly, fewer biographical films were made in this decade than in any other from our sample. Many of the bio-pics that were produced reflected a core ambivalence toward their subjects, who were often social outcasts. *Patton* (1970) polarized audiences by its presentation of the controversial World War II general. Frank McConnell describes and challenges common reactions to the film:

Released at the height of the American involvement in Vietnam, *Patton* managed, remarkably enough, to please both hawks and doves, to be taken both as an essay on the glories of armed conflict—a mechanized *Iliad*—and as a satire on the megalomania of the professional soldier—another *Catch-22*. In fact it is neither of these things. But it is one of the subtlest and most moving examinations we have, in either film or literature, of the terrible seduction of the heroic ideal and the terrible price that ideal requires of those who, at their peril, attempt to live as if it were attainable in an age which will not allow it to be attained.[19]

George C. Scott plays Patton as an anachronism who understands the art of combat, but not his part in a modern, corporate war. So memorable was Scott's impersonation of Patton that he was convinced to revive it in a 1986 made-for-television movie *The Last Days of Patton*.

*Lady Sings the Blues* (1972) is somewhat unusual in its attention to a female protagonist (28 percent of the subjects in our sample were women), far more unusual in that the biographical subject is black (only 2 percent of our sample), but conventional in its focus on an entertainer's life. Billie Holiday is introduced not as a brilliant jazz artist but as a junkie. Under the opening credits, she's hauled into jail and bound in a straight-jacket. The melodrama begins with the sad last chapter of Holiday's life. Like many bio-pics of female entertainers, the film emphasizes early hardships and the star's inability to maintain a satisfying marriage.

The musical bio-pic invites audiences to remember *and* forget their memories of celebrated performances. The genre asks the same contradiction of its leading players, since the original recordings are normally not used and bio-pic actors are usually accomplished performers in their own right. Pauline Kael's reaction to *Lady Sings the Blues* is typical: She complains that Diana Ross isn't able to reproduce the pain in Holiday's voice *and* that Ross's singing is *too* close to Holiday's. Her final appraisal of the film reveals low expectations for the genre:

The keys to Holiday's life are in her art, and that's not in the movie. (It almost never is in movies, because how do you re-create the processes of artistic creation?) *Lady Sings the Blues* is as good as one can expect from the genre—better, at times—and I enjoyed it hugely, yet I don't want Billie Holiday's hard, melancholic sound buried under this avalanche of pop. When you get home, you have to retrieve her at the phonograph; you have to do restoration work on your own past.[20]

Biographical purists contend that an adequate life story can never be told until after a person's death, but 27 percent of the subjects in our sample were alive when films based on their lives were released. Levels of collaboration between subject and production vary; three men still in their thirties—athletes Bob Mathias and Muhammad Ali and war hero Audie Murphy—"played themselves" in bio-pics. *Raging Bull* (1980) contrasts with the essential optimism in most biopics about living subjects. Loosely based on boxer Jake La Motta's autobiography, *Raging Bull* emphasizes the sense of guilt and inadequacy that permeates La Motta's own account. The dominant feature of La Motta's personality and his boxing style is "his tendency, his need, to overcome simply by absorbing as much punishment as his opponent can dish out. La Motta flings himself against the wall of fate."[21]

Director Martin Scorsese builds the film on La Motta's violent animalism; almost all scenes are in the home or the fight ring, both the locus of violence. The fight scenes, with titles giving names of opponents and dates, have a documentary flatness, yet also an expressionistic, almost mystical quality. Shot with a single camera, the fights are pictured in slow motion with lushly romantic music. As Pauline Kael notes, *Raging Bull* is "a biography of the genre of prize fight films."[22] Film school graduate Scorsese uses those conventions in new ways. The black-and-white film begins and ends with a flash-forward of an aging La Motta, played by a startlingly bloated Robert De Niro, rehearsing his act in a seedy nightclub. The routine includes an imitation of Marlon Brando in *On The Waterfront,* one of many exmaples of a life shaped by the movies.

*Reds* (1981) continues the modern fascination with the construction process in the biographical enterprise. Producer/co-writer/director/star Warren Beatty challenges the omniscient tone of the illusionary cinema by injecting documentary footage and then voice-overs of thirty-two elderly "witnesses." The recollections of these contemporaries of John Reed and Louise Bryant function as a narrative device and a contradiction of the notion of a single or fixed biographical truth.[23] Even more radical is the film's celebration of the life of an American Communist. Yet, despite the Brechtian device of the witnesses' testimony and the controversial subject matter, overall *Reds* remains a technically conservative romance about the personal life of an admirable man who died young.

The first section of the 190-minute epic earns the film's plural title as it creates a group profile of the intellectuals, artists, and workers who shaped the American Socialist party between 1915 and 1920.[24] Reed's friends and comrades in Greenwich Village, Provincetown, and Croton-on-Hudson naturally fall out of the narrative as the journalist goes to Russia to report on and participate in the Bolshevik Revolution. There, ironically, the story becomes increasingly individual. Reed's final romantic reunion with Bryant (Diane Keaton) and his subsequent death are shaped into a conclusion dominated by the conventions of the melodramatic love story. The off-screen voice of the last witness tries to retrieve a sense of political cause: "Grand things are worth living and dying for. He himself said that." Hollywood rewarded this tribute to personal idealism by nominating it for more Academy Awards than any other film for the previous fifteen years.

As *Reds* reminds us, point of view is both an aesthetic and a political choice. Problematic in every genre, point of view becomes especially complicated in the bio-pic. *Frances* (1983) serves as an example of authorial complexity. The film opens with the announcement "This film is based on the true life story of Frances Farmer." After the credits, we hear the voice of the adolescent Frances (Jessica Lange), reading from her diary. Since Farmer wrote an autobiography *(Will There Ever Be a Morning?)*, the film could have illustrated and enacted that text with Frances as narrator. The autobiography goes uncredited, but incidents and even lines of dialogue from it are presented in the film.[25] Frances soon drops out as narrator, replaced by Harry York (Sam Shepard). York does not appear in Farmer's autobiography, but in the film he appears within the story as the actress's advocate, friend, and lover and also functions as narrator, commenting on Frances's troubled life and linking separate chronological periods. Technically a continuous voice-over would make dialogue impossible, and supposedly York would not have access to all the horrors that beset Frances, so most of the film is presented from the omniscient camera's "point of view." But, of course, there are not three points of view—Frances's, Harry's, no one's—technically and conceptually the film is a construction with its own, however befuddled, narrative voice. The film could pose as autobiography even if Frances had not written one. Conversely, no matter how religiously an adaptation might follow the Farmer autobiography, it could never duplicate it. Certainly *Frances* was influenced by Farmer's and others' views about her rebellious life, but finally, its "point of view" remains that of its makers. Biography may be a humble art, but it is an art nonetheless.

*Frances* and *Silkwood* (1983) are two of a group of bio-pics produced in the last decade about strong-willed, outspoken women who are punished for their independence. *Frances* traces almost thirty years of the actress's life—from 1931 when she won a national contest with an essay explaining her agnosticism to her postlobotomy television appearance in 1958. *Silkwood* tells the story of the last year in the life of a factory worker who didn't live to be thirty. The film shows how Karen Silkwood, contaminated by plutonium herself, tries to organize her co-workers into protesting the hazardous conditions at the Kerr-McGee Cimarron Plant in Oklahoma. Her activism strains her relationship with her lover and jeopardizes her employment. On her way to a meeting with a reporter, she is killed in a mysterious single-automobile accident.

No climax compares to sudden death in dramatic intensity. Bio-pics about subjects who died in accidents (6 percent), as suicides (3 percent) or victims of murder (6 percent) or execution (3 percent), are far more likely to picture the death than those that tell the stories of people who died of illness (35 percent) or old age (8 percent). The pull toward visual spectacle also results in a frequent concentration on moments of physical suffering: we see Billie Holiday jailed and straightjacketed, Karen Silkwood forced into a high-pressure shower and scrubbed with an abrasive brush, Frances Farmer given shock treatments and lobotomized. The iconography of these scenes of terror resembles that in many melodramas, but the visual power of the pain is intensified by our knowledge that these lives have been lived rather than simply imagined.

In addition to the biographies inspired by current headlines like *Silkwood,* the genre continues its never-abandoned, but diminished, practice of featuring the greats of former eras. Often these old lives are told from new perspectives, such as *Amadeus* (1984), which explores the effects of envy as much as it profiles Wolfgang Amadeus Mozart. Adapted by Peter Schaffer from his hugely successful play, *Amadeus* is a lavish period picture with costumes and sets to rival its music for audience attention. The tale unfolds as a memory of Mozart by his far less talented rival, Salieri (F. Murray Abraham). Biographical inaccuracies can be defended by a clever dramatic conceit: the story is the delusion of an unreliable narrator. Yet, for many moviegoers, Tom Hulce's madcap is the only Mozart they will ever know.

Many bio-pics have looked to the distant past: 15 percent of the subjects were born prior to 1800, 57 percent from 1800 to 1900. People who led long lives have often been featured (32 percent lived past sixty-six years), yet 13 percent of the subjects died before age thirty-five. Mozart's death at thirty-five is pictured in *Amadeus* as a result of his dedication and Salieri's treachery. The final act of this extravagant film plays a variation on the popular bio-pic theme that artistic production is equated with suffering. *Amadeus* pleased audiences and won a number of Oscars, including Best Picture. As a genre, the bio-pic has been well rewarded: 44 percent of our sample films have received Academy Award nominations and 19 percent have earned Oscars.

The creators of bio-pics about writers often confront the difficult task of turning people whose fame is based on their written words into people whose actions make compelling drama. Sometimes authors do lead dramatic lives. Yukio Mishima certainly did, but co–scenarist-director Paul Schrader was restricted from exploring many aspects of the controversial author's life by conditions laid down by Mishima's widow. In *Mishima: A Life in Four Chapters* (1985) Schrader creates an experimental design that imitates Mishima's elaborate sense of style, his fascination with structure, and his tendency to divide his life into distinct units. Separated into chapters labeled ''Beauty, Art, Ac-

tion, and The Harmony of Pen and Sword," the film interweaves three types
of content, each with its own visual style: the last day of Mishima's life with
his elaborate preparation for the performance of *seppuku* (ritual suicide) is photographed in muted color, docudrama style; flashbacks of his childhood and
youth are shot in black and white; excerpts from three of his novels are staged
theatrically in extravagantly stylized sets, filmed in garish color. Schrader acknowledges that *Mishima* is "not coy. It states up front that this is going to be
an intellectual and individualistic enterprise. It's quite the opposite of art pretending to be just entertainment."[26] The film was attacked by many critics as
pretentious and ignored by most Americans. Nevertheless, Schrader has no
interest in making a "straight bio-pic." He insists "the bio-pic is now in the
provinces of television. You have to have an original approach if you try to do
a cinematic biography."[27]

Since the late 1960s, the telefilm or made-for-television movie has been the
most popular form of bio-pic production in the United States. As cinematic
biographies became more experimental or ironic in tone and as movie audiences grew younger, television producers revived the style of sentimental storytelling that characterized bio-pics of the 1930s and 1940s. Just a few examples:
*Brian's Song* (1971) told the sad story of a talented athlete who died young;
the first docudrama miniseries was a joint biography, *Eleanor and Franklin*
(1976); *Elvis* (1979) beat two Hollywood blockbusters, *Gone With the Wind*
and *One Flew Over the Cuckoo's Nest,* in the audience ratings; HBO's first
made-for-pay-TV movie was a biography, *The Terry Fox Story* (1983). Several
characteristics of television programming are well served by biographical content: its tendency toward intimacy and personal revelation; its attention to the
topical; its malleability to serialized form. Biography provides an excellent vehicle for presenting a social issue or a historical era in personal terms. Biographical docudramas follow the pattern of strong star identification common
in continuing series, yet the productions are promoted as "specials" of particular seriousness and worth. Values and attitudes that would seem anachronistic
in a contemporary setting become tolerable, even laudable. Three examples
from the 1980s illustrate these characteristics.[28] The seven-part *Oppenheimer*
(1982), jointly produced by BBC and PBS, chronicles the life of America's
most famous and most controversial scientist. Played by Sam Waterson, J.
Robert Oppenheimer is presented as a flawed hero, overwhelmed by inferior
enemies. Ambiguous in its attitude toward the bomb, the production explores
the complex intersection of physics with politics and war through the scientific
triumphs and human disappointments of the leader of the Manhattan Project.
Far less subtle is the HBO production of *Murrow* (1986). The portrayal of CBS
radio and television journalist Edward R. Murrow (by Daniel J. Travanti) strongly
contrasts a man of unswerving integrity with the venality of the corporate world
that broadcasting became during his career. Like many docudramas, *Second*

*Serve* (CBS, 1986) is unabashedly a message movie. Like many of the bio-pics broadcast on commercial television, it builds its message from recent headlines. In the demanding role of the transsexual Renée Richards, Vanessa Redgrave brings a sense of dignity and felt suffering to a banal script.

Often broadcast on television and, less often, exhibited in commercial theaters, another variant of the film biography must be acknowledged—the biographical documentary. It, too, has a long tradition, one that reaches back to turn-of-the-century actuality filming. Five contemporary biographies—*Showman; Nana, Mom, and Me; Georgia O'Keeffe; N!ai;* and *The Times of Harvey Milk*—demonstrate the range of the subgenre. In *Showman* (1962), Albert and David Maysles follow film producer and distributor Joseph E. Levine making deals, attending a Boston homecoming, presenting Sophia Loren with her Oscar, and so forth. A very early example of direct cinema, *Showman* offers the rhythm of Levine's life as it is lived, a slice of the present, so to speak, in strong contrast to the retrospective nature of most documentary biographies.[29] In *Nana, Mom, and Me* (1974), Amalie R. Rothschild employs some of the patterns of direct cinema, but also stages interviews of her grandmother and mother in an autobiographical exploration of family life. Interviews form the core of *Georgia O'Keeffe* (1977) and *N!ai: The Story of a !Kung Woman* (1980). In both films extraordinary women reflect on their own lives. They speak to an off-camera interviewer and, thus, seem to be telling their stories to us in the audience. Director Perry Miller Adato utilizes archival photographs and early home movies of the artist's early years, plus the visual excitement of O'Keeffe's remarkable work. In *N!ai* John Marshall and Adrienne Miesmer contrast footage Marshall shot of N!ai and her people throughout the 1950s with 1978 images to demonstrate the changes in !Kung life in southern Africa over three decades. N!ai's poignant account serves the goals of both biography and anthropology.*The Times of Harvey Milk* (1984) won an Oscar for Robert Epstein as the best feature-length documentary. Made after Milk's assassination, the film presents the charismatic gay activist's career as both political biography and social history. Narrated by Harvey Fierstein, constructed through news footage and interviews, *The Times of Harvey Milk* continues the hagiographic tone that has always been central to the biographic enterprise.

What lies ahead for the biographical film? I assume the genre will continue to accommodate itself to both change and stasis. Aggressively avant-garde, revisionist works like *Sigmund Freud's Dora: A Case of Mistaken Identity* (1979) find expression in the genre as easily as formulaic celebrations of the heroic, such as the CBS series *Heroes: Made in the U.S.A.* (1986). Docudramas will continue to mine the headlines for sensational accounts of wives who burn their husbands and boys who must live in plastic bubbles. The nature of the heroic bends with time and the artist's sensibility; forms will vary, but filmmakers will never tire of telling life stories.

## BIBLIOGRAPHICAL OVERVIEW

This analysis of biographical film as a genre has been informed by work that can be divided into three lines of inquiry: (1) a general study of biography as an amalgam of literature and history; (2) a general examination of film genres; and (3) a specific exploration of biographical film. Scholarly attention to the three areas is, as one would expect, far from evenly divided. A long and developed tradition of criticism surrounds the (literary) biography; a rapidly growing and increasingly sophisticated body of research has focused on film genre; hardly any serious work has been devoted exclusively to an analysis of the biographical film.

### Biography

At the close of World War I, Lytton Strachey and others opened a new ear of biographical writing in English letters, abandoning the hagiographic tone of most Victorian biographies and replacing it with an irreverent attitude toward the past. The influence of Strachey's debunking style has diminished with time, but his interest in the personalities and motives of his subjects and his devotion to the novelist's craft of vivid actualization and imagination have helped shape contemporary biographical writing. So, too, have these interests and practices engendered an ongoing debate on the goals and procedures of biographical writing. Since the 1920s there has been a steady growth in the literature of biographical criticism. In 1928 Harold Nicolson published a fine historical survey of the form, *The Development of English Biography,* soon followed by Dana Kinsman Merrill's *The Development of American Biography* (1932). Also in 1928 French biographer André Maurois presented six lectures on "aspects of biography" at Trinity College, Cambridge. Delivered in English, revised in written French, then translated back into English for publication, these lectures followed by a year E. M. Forster's Cambridge lectures on "aspects of the novel." Maurois's seminal book presented a view of a new and renewed biographical form; its influence remains strong. Other practicing biographers who have contributed to the tradition of writing general reflections on the biographical enterprise include Catherine Drinker Bowen, Leon Edel, Paul Murray Kendall, and James L. Clifford. Bowen, in *Biography: The Craft and the Calling* (1969), writes directly for the biographer-to-be while Edel's *Literary Biography* (1957) is essentially an account of the psychological and narrative methods he used in writing his acclaimed multivolume life of Henry James. In *The Art of Biography* (1965), Kendall presents a historical survey of biographical writing, with an emphasis on contemporary work, and also a study of biographical problems. Clifford's *From Puzzles to Portraits: Problems of a Literary Biographer* (1970) concentrates on examples of the author's own research followed by an analysis of the special conundrums of a highly developed subgenre, the literary biography.

A number of edited collections contain similar combinations of practical advice, theoretical analysis, and personal anecdote from working biographers. Marc Pachter's *Telling Lives: The Biographer's Art* (1981), Stephen B. Oates's *Biography as High Adventure: Life Writers Speak on Their Art* (1986), and *Introspection in Biography: The Biographer's Quest for Self-Awareness* (1985), edited by Samuel H. Baron and Carl Pletsch, are but three recent examples of such collections.

For those interested in historical surveys of the form, Clifford's anthology *Biography as an Art: Selected Criticism 1560–1960* (1962) provides both a diverse collection of essays and an extensive bibliography on biographical criticism. Edward H. O'Neill also offers a developed bibliography in *A History of American Biography, 1800–1935* (1961) in addition to his historical overview. Richard Altick continues the survey approach in *Lives and Letters: A History of Literary Biographies in England and America* (1965). Roy Pascal presents a historical survey and a study of the central problems, opportunities, and varieties of autobiography in *Design and Truth in Autobiography* (1960).

## Film Genres

Recent scholarly attention to film genre builds on a long literary tradition of genre studies. Paul Hernadi's *Beyond Genre: New Directions in Literary Classification* (1972) responds to that tradition. No single work of contemporary literary criticism has been more broadly influential than Northrop Frye's *Anatomy of Criticism* (1957), a book of four essays, the fourth of which is "Rhetorical Criticism: Theory of Genres." Frye set the agenda for much subsequent scholarship on genre: "The purpose of criticism by genres is not so much to classify as to clarify such traditions and affinities, thereby bringing out a large number of literary relationships that would not be noticed as long as there was no context established for them."[30] In that 1957 work Frye challenged the description of autobiography as "nonfiction," a challenge that has been only recently developed by film scholars who are exploring the boundaries of narrative form.

Literary critic John G. Cawelti's work on popular culture has directly influenced the study of film genres, especially the work of Stuart M. Kaminsky and Stanley J. Solomon. In 1974 Kaminsky wrote the first book in English devoted specifically to the general topic of genre and film, *American Film Genres: Approaches to a Critical Theory of Popular Film*. Solomon's study *Beyond Formula: American Film Genres,* which takes a genre masterpieces approach, appeared two years later, soon followed by the first critical anthology exclusively concerned with the subject of genre in film, *Film Genre: Theory and Criticism* (1977), edited by Barry Keith Grant. During the 1970s many outstanding studies of individual genres appeared (discussed elsewhere in this volume) and many film critics included analyses of the function of genre within larger explorations, for example, Leo Braudy's cogent section on "Genre: The

Convention of Connection'' in *The World in a Frame* (1976). Articles on film genres have regularly appeared in the *Journal of Popular Film and Television,* which devoted three issues to genre and made available a comprehensive bibliography on the topic, written by Larry N. Landrum (Fall 1985). Also during the 1980s, Thomas Schatz published the thoughtful survey *Hollywood Genres: Formulas, Filmmaking and the Studio System* (1981) and Kaminsky (1985) and Grant (1986) both issued considerably revised editions of their important work in genre studies.

During the 1970s, interest in understanding American film through genre theory also occupied the attention of a group of British writers. Often influenced by semiotic theory and self-consciously political, these film critics explored notions of genre, especially in British Film Institute publications such as *Screen* and *Film Reader 3* (1978).

One of the most sophisticated and provocative discussions of genre is Stephen Neale's *Genre* (1980). Paul Willemen has written a lucid preface to *Genre* in which he historically situates how and why genre theory occupied a special and specific place in film theory in the late 1960s and early 1970s. First, he sees genre theory as a challenge to and displacement of the ''dominant notions of cinema installed and defended on the basis of the assumed excellence of the 'taste' of a few journalists and reviewers.''[31] Second, he notes that genre theory developed in the wake of the recognition that all artistic productions are rule-bound activities firmly embedded in social history and, thus, any theory of cinema must discover the structures which underpin groups of films and give them their social grounding.

Neale argues that Hollywood film must be understood on two levels of abstraction: first, as constituting a machine for the production of certain forms of narrative structure, subject position, and psychological lures; second, as organized around certain genres that offer more specific constructions within the overarching system. He sees genre study as a productive way to provide knowledge about cinema and the way it functions as a social institution.

### Biographical Film

Although it is not uncommon for film rental catalogs to have sections on biographies and for film glossaries to include definitions of the bio-pic (for example, the University Film Association's *Glossary of Film Forms* (1978) contains the entry ''Biographical film, biography, biog, biopic: A biographical feature film'')[32] and, far more important, for producers and audiences to share a conception of what constitutes the genre, the biographical film has gone largely ignored in critical writing, even in a period of heightened attention to genre as a central way of organizing meaning in film.

Often the filmic biography is included in discussions of historical drama and, to use a more current label, docudrama. Grant's revised and expanded anthology, *Film Genre Reader* (1986), contains a chapter on docudrama by Seth

Feldman. More often—for example, in the writing of Michael Arlen ("Adrift in Docudrama")—docudrama is discussed as a television form. In several articles, Tom W. Hoffer and Richard Alan Nelson (1978 and 1980) have created a taxonomy of docudrama and charted the evolution of this genre on American television.

In a perceptive article, "The Invasion of the Real People" (1977–1978), David Thomson posits that "more than any other movie genre, the biopic has been transformed to suit new attitudes to history and unstable schemes of reality."[33] Thomson notes the increasing amount of material on screens of all sizes in which the boundaries of feature and documentary are discarded, yet most people consent to these uneasy portrayals of themselves. In contrast to the tidy bio-pic of the past, these contemporary hybrids that fluctuate between illusion and authenticity produce an effect "on our stability and our sense of a reliable external reality that has to be shuddered at."[34] Thomson's concern is not shared by Ronald Bergan in his compact survey "Whatever Happened to the Biopic?" (1983). Bergan claims, "We should not go to a biopic, as we do a literary biography, to learn the facts of the lives under scrutiny. Therefore, much criticism of the genre has been misdirected."[35] Bergan remains comfortable with the bio-pic's expectation that audiences suspend their knowledge of a subject while fact is transmuted into fiction.

The most thorough examination of the biographical film is Caroline Merz's dissertation (1981), which, unfortunately, remains unpublished. In considering the generic boundaries and goals of biographies, Merz draws heavily on theories about the nature and meaning of nineteenth century biography. In England and the United States, biography embodied the ideology of bourgeois thought, centering on self-determination and individual improvement. Another romantic variant was the biography which stressed the inspirational nobility of sacrifice without expectations of reward. Merz recognizes a similar ideology with an emphasis on individualism in the bio-pic. She considers the contract of biography the promise to deliver up a life; a biography's success or failure is judged on whether it creates a coherent personality.

Merz's work was discussed as part of a weekend school on the bio-pic sponsored by the British Film Institute in 1983 and reported on in *Screen* by Mary Joannou and Steve McIntyre (1983). Topics included the nature and structure of the bio-pic and its filmic specificity and the relation of the viewer to the biographical film text. Participants considered "how a closed discourse centering on an individual is constructed out of the open facts of a real life" and found that the typical Hollywood solution was to "follow a more or less unproblematic historical trajectory of the individual towards the achievement by which he or she is best known to the public."[36] Alan Madsen's thoughtful response (*Screen*, February 1984) to Joannou and McIntyre's report challenges the conference's dichotomy of "closed discourse" and "open facts" and argues that the bio-pic is not a contrasting of a construct and the unconstructed. Madsen recognizes the enigma at the heart of biographical film: "Whereas the cinema is most certainly a representation, it is not that which represents the once present, but that which represents the already represented."[37]

## NOTES

1. Stephen B. Oates, *Biography as High Adventure* (Amherst: University of Massachusetts Press, 1986), p. ix.

2. Paul Murray Kendall, *The Art of Biography* (New York: Norton, 1965), pp. 126–27.

3. Hayden White, *Tropics of Discourse* (Baltimore: Johns Hopkins University Press, 1978), p. 84.

4. Colin McArthur, *Television and History* (London: British Film Institute, 1980), p. 40.

5. Thomas Elsaesser, "Film History as Social History: The Dicterle/Warner Brothers Bio-pic," *Wide Angle,* Spring 1986, p. 21.

6. Ibid., p. 28. The perceptive stylistic notations are Elsaesser's.

7. See William Dieterle, "Thoughts about Directing," in *Hollywood Directors, 1914–1940,* ed. Richard Koszarski (New York: Oxford University Press, 1976), p. 344, for his description of the opening of *Pasteur.*

8. "John Ford's *Young Mr. Lincoln*" (1970), translated and reprinted in *Movies and Methods,* vol. 1, ed. Bill Nichols (Berkeley: University of California Press, 1976), pp. 493–529. See Nichols's challenge to the *Cahiers* critics in the same volume, pp. 618–21.

9. *Cahiers du Cinema* collective text, p. 501.

10. See Donald Spoto, *Camerado: Hollywood and the American Man* (New York: New American Library, 1978), p. 32. Spoto links Cooper and Fonda as having similar screen images in this period.

11. Patrick Gilligan, *Cagney: The Actor as Auteur* (New York: DaCapo, 1979), p. 94.

12. See Gilligan, p. 211.

13. Paul Vanderwood, "American Cold Warrior: *Viva Zapata!*" in *American History/American Film: Interpreting the Hollywood Image,* ed. John E. O'Connor and Martin A. Jackson (New York: Frederick Ungar, 1979), p. 189.

14. Garson Kanin, as quoted in Beth Curtin, "Reel Artists," *Films in Review,* January 1981, p. 20.

15. Kirk Douglas, in Curtin, pp. 20–21.

16. Leon Edel, "Biography and the Sexual Revolution—Why Curiosity Is No Longer Vulgar," *New York Times Book Review,* 24 November 1985, p. 14.

17. Arthur Penn, "*Bonnie and Clyde:* Private Morality and Public Violence," reprinted in *Hollywood Directors 1941–1975,* ed. Richard Koszarski (New York: Oxford University Press, 1977), p. 360. Also see Lawrence L. Murray, "Hollywood, Nihilism, and the Youth Culture of the Sixties: *Bonnie and Clyde,*" in *American History/American Film,* pp. 237–56.

18. Comments on the film are adapted from Carolyn Anderson and Gary Edgerton, "Genre as Constraint and Catalyst: Modernizing the Popular in *Breathless, Bonnie and Clyde* and *The American Friend,*" Paper presented at the University Film Association Convention, Ithaca, N.Y., 1979.

19. Frank McConnell, *Storytelling and Mythmaking: Images from Film and Literature* (New York: Oxford University Press, 1979), p. 128.

20. Pauline Kael, "Pop versus Jazz," reprinted in *Reeling* (New York: Warner Books, 1976), p. 69. *Sweet Dreams* (1985) is an exception to the performance rule: the original Patsy Cline recordings are lip-synced by non-singer Jessica Lange.

21. Richard Combs, "Hell Up in the Bronx," *Sight and Sound,* Spring 1982, p. 131.

22. Pauline Kael, "Religious Pulp, or the Incredible Hulk," in *Taking It All In* (New York: Holt, Rinehart and Winston, 1984), p. 107.

23. See "Reds on *Reds,*" *Jump Cut,* April 1983, pp. 6–10. John Hess and Chuck Kleinhans collect opinions in the spirit of the film's witnesses.

24. See Margot Peters, "Group Biography: Challenges and Methods," in *New Directions in Biography,* ed. Anthony M. Friedson (Honolulu: University of Hawaii Press, 1981), pp. 41–51.

25. Anne Fischel, "Hollywood as Historian: A Critical Reading of *Frances,*" Unpublished Paper, 1986, p. 1.

26. Paul Schrader in Karen Jaehne, "Schrader's *Mishima:* An Interview," *Film Quarterly,* Spring 1986, p. 13.

27. Ibid.

28. In "Footnote to Fact: The Docudrama" in *Film Genre Reader* (Austin: University of Texas Press, 1986), Seth Feldman offers a thoughtful comparison of docudrama on U.S., British, and Canadian television. John Caughie's "Progressive Television and Documentary Drama," reprinted in *Popular Television and Film* (London: British Film Institute, 1982), is a perceptive analysis applied to British programming.

29. See Charles Reynolds, "Focus on Al Maysles," in *The Documentary Tradition,* 2d ed., ed. Lewis Jacobs (New York: W. W. Norton, 1979).

30. Northrop Frye, *Anatomy of Criticism* (Princeton: Princeton University Press, 1957), pp. 247–48.

31. Paul Willemen, Preface to *Genre* by Stephen Neale (London: British Film Institute, 1980), p. 1.

32. John Mercer, comp. *Glossary of Film Forms* (Philadelphia: Temple University, University Film Association, 1978), p. 11.

33. David Thomson, "The Invasion of the Real People," *Sight and Sound,* Winter 1977–1978, p. 18.

34. Ibid., p. 21.

35. Ronald Bergan, "Whatever Happened to the Biopic?" *Films and Filming,* July 1983, p. 22.

36. Mary Joannou and Steve McIntyre, "Lust for Lives: Report from a Conference on the Biopic," *Screen,* April–May 1983, p. 147.

37. Alan Madsen, untitled letter, *Screen,* January–February 1984, p. 86.

## BIBLIOGRAPHICAL CHECKLIST

### Books

Altick, Richard. *Lives and Letters: A History of Literary Biographies in England and America.* New York: Knopf, 1965.

Baron, Samuel H., and Carl Pletsch, eds. *Introspection in Biography: The Biographer's Quest for Self-Awareness.* Hillsdale, N.J.: Analytic Press, 1985.

Bowen, Catherine Drinker. *Biography: The Craft and the Calling*. Boston: Little, Brown, 1969.

Braudy, Leo. *The World in a Frame*. Garden City, N.Y.: Anchor Press/Doubleday, 1976.

Cawelti, John G. *Adventure, Mystery, and Romance: Formula Stories as Art and Popular Culture*. Chicago: University of Chicago Press, 1976.

———. *From Puzzler to Portraits: Problems of a Literary Biographer*. Chapel Hill: University of North Carolina Press, 1970.

Clifford, James L., ed. *Biography as an Art: Selected Criticism 1560–1960*. New York: Oxford University Press, 1962.

Davenport, William H., and Ben Siegel, eds. *Biography Past and Present*. New York: Charles Scribner's Sons, 1965.

Edel, Leon. *Literary Biography*. London: R. Hart-Davis, 1957.

———. *Writing Lives: Principia Biographica*. New York: W. W. Norton, 1984.

Friedson, Anthony M., ed. *New Directions in Biography*. Honolulu: University of Hawaii Press, 1981.

Frye, Northrop. *Anatomy of Criticism*. Princeton: Princeton University Press, 1957.

Garraty, John A. *The Nature of Biography*. London: Jonathan Cape, 1958.

Grant, Barry Keith, ed. *Film Genre: Theory and Criticism*. Metuchen, N.J.: Scarecrow Press, 1977; revised as *Film Genre Reader*. Austin: University of Texas Press, 1986.

Hernadi, Paul. *Beyond Genre: New Directions in Literary Classification*. Ithaca, N.Y.: Cornell University Press, 1972.

Kaminsky, Stuart M. *American Film Genres: Approaches to a Critical Theory of Popular Film*. Dayton, Ohio: Pflaun, 1974; 2d ed., Chicago: Nelson-Hall, 1985.

Kendall, Paul Murray. *The Art of Biography*. New York: Norton, 1965.

Maurois, André. *Aspects of Biography*. Trans. by Sydney Castle Roberts. New York: Frederick Ungar, 1966 (originally published in 1929).

Merrill, Dana Kinsman. *The Development of American Biography*. Portland, Maine: Southworth Press, 1932.

Meyers, Jeffrey, ed. *The Craft of Literary Biography*. New York: Schocken Books, 1985.

Nadel, Ira Bruce. *Biography: Fiction, Fact and Form*. New York: St. Martin's Press, 1984.

Neale, Stephen. *Genre*. London: British Film Institute, 1980.

Nicolson, Harold. *The Development of English Biography*. London: Hogarth Press, 1928.

Oates, Stephen B., ed. *Biography as High Adventure: Life-Writers Speak on Their Art*. Amherst: University of Massachusetts Press, 1986.

O'Neill, Edward H. *A History of American Biography, 1800–1935*. New York: A. S. Barnes, 1961.

Pachter, Marc, ed. *Telling Lives: The Biographer's Art*. Philadelphia: University of Pennsylvania Press, 1981.

Pascal, Roy. *Design and Truth in Autobiography*. Cambridge, Mass.: Harvard University Press, 1960.

Schatz, Thomas. *Hollywood Genres: Formulas, Filmmaking and the Studio System*. New York: Random House, 1981.

Solomon, Stanley, J. *Beyond Formula: American Film Genres*. New York: Harcourt Brace Jovanovich, 1976.

Winslow, Donald J. *Life-Writing: A Glossary of Terms in Biography, Autobiography, and Related Forms*. Honolulu: University of Hawaii Press, 1980.

## Shorter Works

Arlen, Michael J. "Adrift in Docudrama." In *The Camera Age*. New York: Farrar, Straus, and Giroux, 1981.

Bergan, Ronald. "Whatever Happened to the Biopic?" *Films and Filming*, July 1983, pp. 21–22.

Buscombe, Edward. "The Idea of Genre in the American Cinema," *Screen*, March–April 1970, pp. 33–45.

Collins, Richard. "Genre: A Reply to Ed Buscombe," *Screen*, August–September, pp. 66–75.

Curtin, Beth. "Reel Artists," *Films in Review*, January 1981, pp. 17–22, 44–45.

Elsaesser, Thomas. "Film History as Social History: The Dieterle/Warner Brothers Biopic," *Wide Angle*, Spring 1986, pp. 15–31.

Feldman, Seth. "Footnote to Fact: The Docudrama." In *Film Genre Reader*. Ed. Barry Keith Grant. Austin: University of Texas Press, 1986.

———. "The Electronic Fable: Aspects of the Docudrama in Canada," *Canadian Drama*, Spring 1983, pp. 39–48.

Hoffer, Tom W., and Richard Alan Nelson. "Docudrama on American Television," *Journal of the University Film Association*, Spring 1978, pp. 21–27.

———. "Evolution of Docudrama on American Television Networks: Content Analysis, 1966–1978," *Southern Speech Communication Journal*, Winter 1980, pp. 149–63.

Hoffer, Thomas W., Robert B. Musburger, and Richard Alan Nelson. "Docudrama." In *TV Genres: A Handbook and Reference Guide*. Ed. Brian G. Rose and Robert S. Alley. Westport, Conn.: Greenwood Press, 1985.

Joannou, Mary, and Steve McIntyre. "Lust for Lives: Report from a Conference on the Biopic," *Screen*, April–May 1983, pp. 145–49.

Landrum, Larry N. "Recent Work in Genre," *Journal of Popular Film and Television*, Fall 1985, pp. 151–58.

Merz, Caroline. "An Examination of Biography in Film and Television." Ph.D. diss., University of East Anglia, 1981.

Musburger, Robert B. "Setting the Stage for the Television Docudrama," *Journal of Popular Film and Television*, Summer 1985, pp. 92–101.

Ryall, Tom. "The Notion of Genre," *Screen*, March–April 1970, pp. 22–32.

Small, Edward S. "Literary and Film Genres: Toward a Taxonomy of Film," *Literature/Film Quarterly*, Fall 1979, pp. 209–19.

Thomson, David. "The Invasion of the Real People," *Sight and Sound*, Winter 1977–1978, pp. 18–22.

## SELECTED FILMOGRAPHY

1936  *The Story of Louis Pasteur* (85 minutes).
Warner Bros. Producer: Henry Blake. Director: William Dieterle. Screenplay: Sheridan Gibney and Pierre Collings. Cast: Paul Muni (Louis Pasteur), Anita

Louise (Annette Pasteur), Josephine Hutchinson (Marie Pasteur), Donald Woods (Jean Martel).

1939   *Young Mr. Lincoln* (101 minutes).
20th Century-Fox. Producer: Kenneth Macgowan. Director: John Ford. Screenplay: Lamar Trotti. Cast: Henry Fonda (Abraham Lincoln), Pauline Moore (Ann Rutledge), Marjorie Weaver (Mary Todd), Donald Meek (John Felder), Ward Bond (J. Palmer Cross).

1942   *Pride of the Yankees* (128 minutes).
RKO. Producer: Samuel Goldwyn. Director: Sam Wood. Screenplay: Jo Swerling and Herman J. Mankiewicz. Cast: Gary Cooper (Lou Gehrig), Teresa Wright (Eleanor Gehrig), Babe Ruth (Babe Ruth), Walter Brennan (Sam Blake).

*Yankee Doodle Dandy* (126 minutes).
Warner Bros. Producers: Jack L. Warner and Hal B. Wallis. Director: Michael Curtiz. Screenplay: Robert Buckner and Edmund Joseph. Cast: James Cagney (George M. Cohan), Joan Leslie (Mary Cohan), Walter Huston (Jerry Cohan), Rosemary DeCamp (Nellie Cohan).

1952   *Viva Zapata!* (113 minutes).
20th Century-Fox. Producer: Darryl F. Zanuck. Director: Elia Kazan. Screenplay: John Steinbeck. Cast: Marlon Brando (Emiliano Zapata), Anthony Quinn (Eufemio Zapata), Harold Gordon (Franciso Madero), Jean Peters (Josefa Zapata).

1956   *Lust for Life* (122 minutes).
MGM. Producer: John Houseman. Director: Vincente Minnelli. Screenplay: Norman Corwin. Cast: Kirk Douglas (Vincent Van Gogh), Anthony Quinn (Paul Gaugin), James Donald (Theo Van Gogh).

1967   *Bonnie and Clyde* (111 minutes).
Warner Bros. Producer: Warren Beatty. Director: Arthur Penn. Screenplay: David Newman and Robert Benton. Cast: Warren Beatty (Clyde Barrow), Faye Dunaway (Bonnie Parker), Michael J. Pollard (C. W. Moss), Gene Hackman (Buck Barrow).

1970   *Patton* (170 minutes).
20th Century-Fox. Producer: Frank McCarthy. Director: Franklin J. Schaffner. Screenplay: Francis Ford Coppola and Edmund H. North. Cast: George C. Scott (George S. Patton, Jr.), Karl Malden (Omar N. Bradley), Michael Strong (Hobart Carver), Karl Michael Vogler (Erwin Rommel).

1972   *Lady Sings the Blues* (144 minutes).
Paramount. Produced by Motown. Director: Sidney J. Furie. Screenplay: Terence McCloy, Chris Clark, and Suzanne de Passe. Cast: Diana Ross (Billie Holiday), Richard Pryor (Piano Man), Billy Dee Williams (Louis McKay).

1980   *Raging Bull* (128 minutes).
United Artists. Producers: Irwin Winkler and Robert Chartoff. Director: Martin Scorsese. Screenplay: Paul Schrader and Mardik Martin. Cast: Robert De Niro (Jake La Motta), Joe Pesci (Joey La Motta), Cathy Moriarty (Vickie La Motta).

1981   *Reds* (190 minutes).
Paramount. Producer/Director: Warren Beatty. Screenplay: Warren Beatty and

Trevor Griffiths. Cast: Warren Beatty (John Reed), Diane Keaton (Louise Bryant), Maureen Stapleton (Emma Goldman), Jack Nicholson (Eugene O'Neill), Edward Hermann (Max Eastman), Jerzy Kosinski (Gregory Zinoviev).

1983    *Frances* (131 minutes).
A Brooks Film Production. Released by Universal. Producer: Jonathan Sanger. Director: Graeme Clifford. Screenplay: Eric Bergen, Christopher Devere, and Nicholas Kazan. Cast: Jessica Lange (Frances Farmer), Kim Stanley (Frances's mother), Sam Shepard (Harry York).

*Silkwood* (128 minutes).
An ABC Motion Picture. Released by 20th Century-Fox. Producers: Mike Nichols and Michael Houseman. Director: Mike Nichols. Screenplay: Nora Ephron and Alice Arlen. Cast: Meryl Streep (Karen Silkwood), Kurt Russell (Drew Stephens), Cher (Dolly Pelliker), Diana Scarwid (Angela).

1984    *Amadeus* (158 minutes).
Orion. Producer: Saul Zaente. Director: Milos Forman. Screenplay: Peter Schaffer. Cast: Tom Hulce (Wolfgang Amadeus Mozart), F. Murray Abraham (Antonio Salieri), Elizabeth Berridge (Constanze Mozart), Jeffrey Jones (Emperor Joseph II).

1985    *Mishima: A Life in Four Chapters* (122 minutes).
A Zoetrope Studios/Film Link International/Lucasfilm Ltd. Production. Released by Warner Bros. Producers: Mata Yamamoto and Tom Luddy. Director: Paul Schrader. Screenplay: Paul Schrader and Leonard Schrader. Cast: Ken Ogata (Yukio Mishima), Mashayuki Shionoya (Morita), Junkichi Orimoto (Mashita).

# 19

# The Art Film

WILLIAM C. SISKA

A viable conception of film genre as a means to understanding the film experience must necessarily include as a genre the art film, though its most prominent representatives come from Europe. This genre, which a nonrigorous approach might dismiss as simply "foreign films," has been commercially popular in the United States since the late 1950s. It has had a marked influence on the Hollywood cinema, and a number of American film directors, among them Arthur Penn and Robert Altman, can be placed in company with key European art film directors like Ingmar Bergman and Michelangelo Antonioni without any sense of cultural dislocation. This chapter will treat the art film as an international genre, while looking distinctly for its effect on American audiences and American films.

The notion that there are two film cultures, an entertainment cinema directed towards a mass audience and a serious art cinema aimed at an intellectual audience, is not a recent one. In the 1920s in England, Alfred Hitchcock and Ivor Montagu were active in an organization called the Film Society whose purpose was to import from the Continent those films deemed the pathfinding artistic achievements of the time, namely the Soviet films of dialectical montage, and the expressionist films of the Universum Film A. G. (UFA) studios in Germany. At about the same time artists in the dadaist and surrealist movements in Paris began producing short films as extensions of their work in other plastic media, attracting three men who planned only a career in the cinema, Luis Buñuel, René Clair, and Jean Renoir. In the Hollywood of the 1930s and 1940s John Ford distinguished between the artistic aspirations of literary adaptations like Sean O'Casey's *The Informer* (1935) and Eugene O'Neill's *The Long Voyage Home* (1940), and the popular genre films that he also directed to pay for the adaptations. And soon after the end of World War II came the release of *Open City* (1945), *Paisa* (1946), and *Bicycle Thieves* (1948), the masterpieces of Italian neorealism, another conscious art film movement.

But the term *art cinema* or *art film* applied to a specific group of movies that had enough common characteristics to comprise a film genre did not come into general use until the late 1950s. Five films released during this period became standard-bearers for the movement and helped set the conventions of the genre. Ingmar Bergman's *The Seventh Seal* (1956) and *Wild Strawberries* (1957), Alain Resnais's *Hiroshima, Mon Amour* (1959), Michelangelo Antonioni's *L'Avventura* (1960), and Federico Fellini's *La Dolce Vita* (1960), aided by the response of audiences at international film festivals (particularly at Cannes in 1959 and Venice in 1960) that ranged from impassioned enthusiasm to outrage, gained a notoriety that made them marketable in major European and American cities.

These films jolted their audiences with their open confrontation of the spiritual malaise of contemporary bourgeois culture, their frank treatment of sexuality, and stylistic innovations borrowed from modern painting, drama, and literature. Unlike the best popular genre films, which on the surface are first to please, and in the guise of pleasure tell us something about our lives, these art films were more interested in the development of ideas than in entertainment values, a fact recognized both by hostile critics who castigated the films as boring as well as by those viewers refreshed by the films' adult treatment of serious issues. Angst, alienation, the secular sweep of urban values, the fear of nothingness—the common concerns of high art and intellectual culture were on the screen, it seemed to most viewers, for the first time.[1] Like the earlier path-breaking film movements—Soviet and German films of the 1920s, Italian neo-realism in the 1940s—the art film opened moviegoers' eyes to a new understanding of what the cinema was capable of doing.

Alongside the unusual complexity with which these art films treated intellectual issues, they also departed from the popular genres in their use of film form. They eschewed the precise, generally upbeat and optimistic endings of the entertainment cinema in favor of open-ended, ambiguous, or negative conclusions. Whereas the popular genres focused on the literal depiction of action, the art film foregrounded visual symbols, and often employed metaphor and allegorical action to communicate its themes. The art film tended to break with plot-oriented storytelling, choosing more often an episodic, if no less tightly structured narrative designed to explore a central theme rather than follow a character to his goal. And the more daring of the art films stylistically, like *Hiroshima, Mon Amour,* jumped freely back and forth in time, and between reality and fantasy, without cueing the viewer with the traditional dissolves and fades.

The art film as a genre is defined as those narrative films in which abstract issues are dealt with overtly in dialogue and by direction of the viewer to symbolic or metaphorical images. At the center of each art film is a "raised" problem rather than the "lived" problems which form the core of traditional narratives. A raised problem is an abstract question that invites discussion and exploration. A lived problem, on the other hand, demands a singular solution. Consider a person coming to a busy street corner he needs to cross. He can wait for the light to change, stopping traffic, or, if impatient, he might gauge a break in traffic and dart partway across the street, dodge a bus and truck, and zigzag to the other side. This man has solved a lived problem. Now, if instead of planning and executing the crossing, he were to watch the drivers isolated in their steel shells whooshing this way and that, and ask himself "What does it mean to cross the street?" we have a quintessential art film protagonist. Crossing is turned from a simple activity into a problem for contemplation.

The popular genre film is built on the solving of lived problems: "How do I protect the pioneer cabins from the Indians?" "How do I entrap the murderer?" "How do I convince the person of my dreams to marry me?" As these are presented in the traditional movie, they are concrete, particular problems solved by action. The art film, on the other hand, poses such questions as "How does the ethical person behave?" "What does it mean to act?" "What is the meaning of life?" These are metaphysical problems not solved through simple, straightforward action.

Ingmar Bergman's *The Seventh Seal* provides an accessible, startling paradigm for the art film genre. *The Seventh Seal,* in its storyline, might be a historical adventure film. A disillusioned knight, played by Max von Sydow, returns north from the Holy Land after years on a futile crusade, to find the bubonic plague laying waste the land. While the framework of the medieval adventure story provides a palpable appeal for the film, Bergman soon makes clear that his theme is more modern and events are to be understood as metaphor.

The knight is a twentieth-century man engaged on a quest for the meaning of life, in the face of the modern experience of the silence of God. The knight asks of God some sign of his existence, and wonders aloud that if God does not exist, "Then life is an outrageous horror." Thus, the exterior ravages of the plague—swept landscape reflect the interior trauma of the knight who demands meaning but must live in uncertainty. The setting also suggests Bergman's view of life in the mid-1950s, at the height of the Cold War, with the threat of arbitrary annihilation in a nuclear holocaust weighing heavily on the powerless, the European observers of the East-West chess match between the United States and the Soviet Union.

The raised problem of *The Seventh Seal,* addressed so clearly in words, is also reinforced by a panoply of striking images carrying metaphorical and symbolic meaning. For example, after confessing to Death his fear of nothingness, the knight holds his arm up high and clenches his fist, watching as blood pulses through a throbbing vein. Caught in that image is his resolve to continue his quest for meaning as long as he is alive. Later, the reverential treatment given the bowl of strawberries and cream by camera and actors raises its presence to the symbolic level of the best this life has to offer: the peace and fellowship of sharing a meal.

The predicament of modern man as an isolated individual in an indifferent universe depicted in *The Seventh Seal* is shared by the other early art films as well. In Bergman's *Wild Strawberries,* the protagonist is a public success but a private failure, a man esteemed by the scientific community of which he is a part, but loathed and pitied because of his coldness by those who live with him. Again the journey metaphor is used, this time as the aged professor travels by auto through the district where he grew up, traveling through his inner life as he does so. Touched by the devotion of his loving daughter-in-law, he confronts his failure and achieves a belated redemption through love. In the Italian art films *La Dolce Vita* and *L'Avventura,* the decadent consumption of material goods and the replacement of genuine feelings with mechanistic maneuverings cloud the terror of the unknown from the characters in the films, except for the protagonists (played by Monica Vitti in *L'Avventura* and Marcello Mastroianni in *La Dolce Vita*) who are repelled by the fruits of secular technological society. Again, as in Bergman's films, mere animal existence is posed against the necessity of transcendent meaning. But the protagonists' recognition leads to inner pain rather than action, because no transcendent meaning is evident.

All these films, and Alain Resnais's *Hiroshima, Mon Amour,* share with the modern art that began in the 1890s a romantic belief in the value of love and a romantic pessimism concerning its possibility in the modern world. While all the films are modernist in form, breaking with the Aristotelian rule of the primacy of plot in favor of abstraction, it is *Hiroshima, Mon Amour* which makes the most violent departure from traditional aesthetics. Scripted by *nouveau roman* novelist Marguerite Duras, Resnais's film broke all rules of temporal and spatial unity, and even of storytelling: past and present are freely intermixed, but past is presented as memory and fantasy. The objective historical reality of World War II—the Nazi occupation of France, the nuclear holocaust in Japan—is seen through and reshaped by the subjectivity of the French and Japanese protagonists, two lovers who seek communion across time and culture. In its playing with form, this film most clearly identifies itself with the modern art of Picasso, Schoenberg, Faulkner, and Joyce. All these art films, and those that followed, can best be understood in relation to the key concepts that define modernism: the self, self-consciousness, reflexivity, relativity, subjectivity, and open texture.

The critical notoriety and box-office success of these seminal art films—produced on low budgets, they didn't need a mass audience to ensure profitability—made possible continued work by these directors and the infusion of many new directors and their art films as well. François Truffaut followed his autobiographical *The Four Hundred Blows* (1959), which premiered at Cannes the same year as *Hiroshima, Mon Amour,* with two pictures which displayed a modernist self-consciousness towards form. After the gangster-film inspired *Shoot the Piano Player* (1960), Truffaut adapted Henri-Pierre Roché's novel celebrating Bohemian life in early twentieth-century France, *Jules and Jim* (1961). This film intercuts documentary World War I footage, grotesquely stretched from its standard ratio to fill Truffaut's wide screen, to serve as a comment on the hideousness of war. Truffaut uses freeze frames of the heroine, Catherine, to draw attention to the fact that we are watching a film, as well as to reflect the desire of the male characters to freeze Catherine in their own image, and to turn a vital, complex individual into a coherent, simplified work of art.

Jean-Luc Godard began his career as a feature filmmaker with a modernist gangster film, *Breathless* (1959), replete with jumpcuts and a narrative as seemingly arbitrary and aimless as its protagonist, Poiccard, played by Jean-Paul Belmondo. Godard justly has the reputation as the most radical of feature film directors in the self-consciousness of his form, but other established art film directors moved towards greater reflexivity as well.

Reflexive, or self-referential films, are movies that either draw attention to the process of moviemaking or to the problems of the moviemaker. Movies about moviemaking (as distinct from movies about show business, like *A Star Is Born* or *All About Eve*) have a checkered history, with many of the most successful being comedies: Buster Keaton's *The Cameraman* (1928), W. C. Fields's *The Bank Dick* (1941), and Preston Sturges's *Sullivan's Travels* (1941). All three have fun with the process of moviemaking, and the personal element in the Sturges film makes that work a poignant masterpiece. The reflexivity in these films is not modernist, however, as filmmaking in them is seen as a "lived" problem rather than a conceptual issue. This is true as well of some more recent reflexive films, like François Truffaut's Oscar-winning *Day For Night* (1973), which presents the joys and trials of a director coping with the vast assemblage of equipment and manpower involved in making a movie.

But it's in Frederico Fellini's magnificent *8½* (1962) that modernist reflexivity comes to the fore. Here the problem is not the process of moviemaking, not "How do I make a movie?" as it is in *Day For Night*, but rather the raised problem: "What do I make a movie for?" Fellini's alter ego, Guido, played again by Mastroianni, does not seem at all stymied by the men and material necessary for this production, but is paralyzed by the problem of deciding what he wants his movie to mean. He tries to meld the spiritual confusion of his own life with the same malaise of bourgeois society that marked *La Dolce Vita* and find a solution to them through art. Guido faces the dilemma, as does Italian society, of living in a world where the Catholicism of his upbringing, with its moral certainties, has proven irrelevant to the complexities of modern life, and yet there has emerged no other answer. We are drawn to images of entrapment—Guido locked in the glass cage of his automobile in a massive traffic jam in an underpass—and escape—Guido sailing in the clouds in free flight. Guido's film is about social salvation brought about by mass flight to another planet, but at the end of the film, in a cathartic sequence, all the persons from his past and present life march down the launching scaffold symbolizing their return to Earth. There, they parade behind Guido in a circus ring, a ritual dance of harmony and peace. Guido's final narration verbalizes the raised problem of the film, when he says that the confusion in his relationships has resulted from the confusion inside him, and that the answer, for the time being, lies in acceptance of that turmoil and doubt.

If Fellini's *8½* is the model for a film that is reflexive towards the filmmaker, it is in Godard's films that we find the epitome of reflexivity towards form. Godard's films from the very beginning evinced a dissatisfaction with traditional narrative and generic conventions even while taking pleasure in them. Thus, Belmondo in *Breathless* plays a gangster, but an aimless one: a gangster without a job to do, a passive man who lets his associates call the shots, the very opposite of the Bogart hero whom he admires on a movie poster. In *Les Carabiniers* (1963) Godard makes a war film but refuses to show us any battles, and even the skirmishes we do see have no defined foe to the nonheroic protagonists he gives us. Thus Godard's characters are hard to identify with, the emotional power of his films comes from the way he imposes himself, energetically, even frantically, on his material. Interrupting the storyline with graphics, chapter headings, postcards, in-jokes, and direct address, he constructs what can better be described as film essays than as film narratives. This intertextuality, or open texture, is brought to its height in *Weekend* (1967). *Weekend,* along with two films that preceded it, *Masculine-Feminine* (1965) and *Two or Three Things That I Know About Her* (1966), marks a break with the standard themes and form of the first art films, and a movement into a new phase, in which politics and the political analysis of aesthetic form come into play.

The classic art films focus on the problem of the self in a universe where God is silent and technology has irremediably altered the individual's relationship to time, space, and other people. The themes of alienation, sexual frustration, failure of communication and the individual's anguish at his personal situation that had run through serious novels and dramas since the beginning of the twentieth century had finally found their way into the theatrical cinema. Antonioni followed his *L'Avventura* with three more pictures that developed these themes, *La Notte* (1960), *L'Eclisse* (1962), and *The Red Desert* (1964); Bergman brought forth his Silence Trilogy of *Through a Glass Darkly* (1959), *Winter Light* (1961), and *The Silence* (1962); Fellini followed *8½* with *Juliet of the Spirits* (1964); and Luis Buñuel returned to prominence with *Viridiana* (1963).

These films and those discussed earlier established the art cinema as a viable genre and led to certain expectations that both audience and critics brought to the films. The first of these expectations was that art movies were more difficult to understand than popular genre films. The art film viewer had to be initiated into the conventions of modern art and philosophy before the goals and stylistics of the art cinema could be appreciated, the same way one might have needed to have Picasso explained to him whereas Norman Rockwell was easy to understand without any introduction. The second assumption was that all art films were auteur films, personal statements of their directors in the way that a novel or a poem was the statement of its author.

Art films were often marketed in the United States by way of the name recognition of their directors, like Truffaut, Buñuel, and Bergman, rather than by the names of the featured actors, who were not as well known. American films of the period, with the exception of Alfred Hitchcock's (whose name recognition after all owed itself to his television series) were almost invariably marketed by the names of the stars. The names of John Wayne and William Holden played a much more prominent role in the selling of *The Horse Soldiers* (1959) than did its director John Ford's.

The third assumption was that art films were more "real" than popular genre films; that is, that they dealt in serious ways with contemporary issues. Persons attending an art film expected an experience that was confrontational rather than escapist, that was more intellectually demanding than simply entertaining, and showed us "real" people facing situations that might actually be encountered by members of the audience. It was not unusual for regular art film viewers to look forward to the next Bergman, Antonioni, or Fellini film with the expectations usually reserved for some serious novelists and prominent social philosophers: that their work would offer fresh insights into the human experience.

The claim to greater realism was made in reaction to the propensity in popular genre films for the moral equilibrium of the world to be restored, for good to triumph over evil and life to go on happily for the protagonists. If the art film has a greater claim to reality over its Hollywood counterparts, it lies in its focus on ordinary people in ordinary situations. The escapist genre film, after all, offers us extraordinary people (heroes and stars, rather than people like us), in extraordinary situations and settings. Finally, for the intellectual audience, the "happy ending" too often went against the reality of "the world out there" where the knowledge of death as the end of all human life demanded attention.

That these early art films had a chance to become financially profitable in the United States at all is the product of four factors. First, the enforcement of the Paramount Decrees, sent down by the Supreme Court in 1952 requiring the studios to divest themselves of their theater chains, broke the major Hollywood production companies' stranglehold on exhibition. No longer could substantial competition to Hollywood's product be effectively choked off by refusing an opportunity for theater play.

When the studios were forced to sell their theaters, they were no longer assured of exclusive exhibition of their product. Divestiture had the effect intended by the framers of the Sherman Antitrust Act that had led to this decision: it opened up the market place to free trade. Independent producers and small distributors began to peddle their product with impunity. In 1963 no fewer than 800 foreign films were released in the United States by a grand total of eighty different distributors.

The Supreme Court's "Miracle Decision," also handed down in 1952, suggested that motion pictures were a significant art form and were therefore protected by First Amendment rights. This new freedom of expression for the movies made possible the importation of European films which were generally more explicit and frank in their treatment of sensitive topics than their Hollywood competitors.

Further opening the market for European art films was Hollywood's refusal in the early days of television to recognize that it was no longer the mass entertainment medium it was in the 1930s, when it made films with simultaneous appeal to all spectra of the audience. Television had taken over that highly lucrative position; the audience for movies was now fragmented, and for a significant fragment the art film exercised a strong appeal. This audience fragment was well-educated, upwardly mobile, frequently suspicious of movies as a mindless diversion, yet looking for a valid reason to indulge their attraction to films. Hollywood was slow to make movies for this group.

In addition to the two Supreme Court decisions and the rise of the fragmented audience, the fourth factor conducive to the viability of the art cinema was the increasing importance of the international film festivals to domestic distributors. Films by directors unknown to American distributors would be tested by the festival audiences—if they met with an enthusiastic reception, they would likely be picked up for distribution in the United States. The careers of Alain Resnais and François Truffaut were initially boosted by the success of their first films at the Cannes festival in 1959. Beginning about the same time, the festivals brought to the public the dynamic, politically daring cinema of East Europe, highlighting such directors as Andrzej Wajda, Miklós Jancsó, and István Szabó.

The art film became a "European" genre *par excellence,* suited perfectly to the exigencies of the smaller European production companies with their limited financial resources vis-à-vis the major Hollywood studios. Low budgets and a modest-sized but highly loyal audience virtually assured the profitability of art films made by prominent directors. This made possible the increasingly innovative explorations into film form by those directors. One reason Jean-Luc Godard was able to make so many avant-garde feature films was that his movies generally earned their money back in Paris alone, so that any foreign distribution provided pure profit.

The subject matter of the early art films by Bergman, Antonioni, and Fellini was well-suited to the temper of their times. At the end of the 1950s the Western world was in the midpoint of the longest unbridled economic growth in its history. The postwar rebirth of Europe led to an entrenched bourgeoisie that was beginning to question the spiritual and emotional consequences of this prosperity. Politics, where it enters at all, as in Fellini's protagonists' encounters with Marxists in both *La Dolce Vita* and *8½,* is simply another obstacle for the individual to learn to cope with, like the influence of religion or an overbearing lover.

But this first phase of the art film ends around 1965, as art film directors respond to their environment and politics seeps into their films in a more meaningful way. In Antonioni's *Blow Up* (1966) antinuclear demonstrators in the

Bertrand Russell tradition march down a busy street waving placards; in Bergman's *Persona* (1965) the mute actress shies away from a television screen replaying the immolation of a Buddhist monk in Saigon. But in Godard's films from *Pierrot le Fou* (1965) onwards politics plays the role of a moral imperative reshaping the form of the films themselves. The open texture of Godard's *Weekend* (1967) juxtaposes a tawdry B-movie story of a married couple hoping to rid themselves of the wife's mother with sequences of grisly highway carnage, political diatribes from Third World garbage men, readings from Friedrich Engels's sociological tracts, playful riddles reminiscent of Lewis Carroll, and finally a confrontation with a hippie band of guerrillas who kill and eat the unfortunate members of the bourgeoisie who happen to cross into their territory.

The narrative of the debased couple as they travel to the mother's country home is carried through from beginning to end, where the wife, now a member of the hippie band, munches on one of her slaughtered husband's ribs. But the disgressions are as important as the story—even the intertitles reading "A Film Found on the Scrapheap" and "A Film Lost in the Cosmos"—and combine in an organic black comic vision of a society in chaos, a civilization that "autodestructs." This brilliant film is more essay than narrative, a poetic cry of rhetorical thunder that ranks with Rabelais, Swift, and Voltaire.

In *Weekend* politics is not merely a part of life, but the raison d'être of the filmmaker's life, forcing Godard to constantly interrupt his story to inject his personal feelings about social issues into the film. Other directors, notably the Japanese Nagisa Oshima, working independently of the Godardian influence which touched so many of the films of the period, produced his own disjunctive, passionate essays on student life in Tokyo in *Diary of a Shinjuku Thief* (1967) and an attack on capital punishment in *Death by Hanging* (1968). Godard's great contribution to cinema seems to have been made because of the political imperatives which drove him to experiment with new forms and his own inability to keep himself out of his works. In Godard's films more regularly than others the form of the art loses its transparency, ceases to be an invisible window on a fictive world, and asserts its own reality to us. Like the Buster Keaton of *Sherlock Jr.* (1924), the prototype of the modernist metacinema, Godard is conceptualizing, giving us an illustrated example of what the filmmaking apparatus can do. It's Godard's playfulness that makes his films contradictory revelations, giving us what Susan Sontag calls films at once "achieved and chaotic, 'works in progress.' "[2]

Though the art films of the 1970s coming out of Western nations abandoned political didacticism as their central theme, the events of the late 1960s left an indelible mark on many of these films.

A film that specifically dealt with the events of the late 1960s from the distance of time and brought those events into the present was Alain Tanner's *Jonah Who Will Be 25 in the Year 2000* (1976). Tanner, working with the Marxist art critic and novelist John Berger as his scenarist, brings together a group of late 1960s activists in Geneva who find they must come to terms with their failed dreams as life goes on in the mid-1970s. Tanner mixes voice-over quotation from the writings of Jean-Jacques Rousseau (a native of Geneva) with the lives of myriad characters, each reflecting a different commitment to principles that generated the events of 1968.

Another film of open texture, *Jonah* presents its characters as exemplars of certain countercultural positions; among them, Max the leftist ideologue, who has gone into a seven-year funk and has visions of suicide; Marco, the innovative history professor who wraps his Marxist viewpoint in entertaining, hands-on lectures involving the slicing of blood sausage and beating of rhythms to illustrate the concept of history as fragments of time; and Marie, who fights a bloodless revolution by undercharging pensioners for their groceries.

The triumph of the film lies in a structure which allows each character to expostulate her position with rhetoric—the abstract issues are all discussed as such—and then shows us how they act on them. Max is seen as a selfish depressive, who nevertheless starts the ball rolling by telling a farming family not to sell to a real-estate front man who's trying to buy up the countryside and turn it into high-priced apartment blocks. But it's Mathieu, a laid-off factory worker, and his wife Mathilde who are Berger and Tanner's real heroes. Mathieu does not shy from new work to support his family, and is hired on by the farm at low wages and the most demeaning job: king of the manure pile. Mathilde dreams of the new baby she desires, symbolic of an act of faith in a better future, a faith necessary if there's to be progress in history. *Jonah* is that rarity among art films, an intellectual film that doesn't shy away from hard truths, yet ends with a credible optimism.

If art films like those discussed have given emotionally powerful portrayals of the world we live in, and have occasionally been inspirational to the educated audience for whom they have been most accessible, Andrzej Wajda's *Man of Marble* (1977) shows us a kind of film whose power is not only aesthetic but political as well. This has more to do with the situation of the film, coming out of an Eastern bloc nation, than with its modernist style. Wajda uses modernist film techniques pragmatically, insofar as they enhance the themes he wants to develop. Wajda made the highly Western, apolitical *Everything for Sale* (1967), a film as personal and self-reflexive as Fellini's *8½*. But in *Man of Marble* he succeeds in using reflexivity to communicate a political message of great power.

*Man of Marble* uses art film techniques: open-texture in the cross-cutting, from reconstructed documentaries of the past to the present, and to re-creations of the past as seen by the characters in the present; and reflexivity: the film as an adventure in filmmaking, and a meditation on the power of film to mold mass opinion. Foremost, however, is the use of filmmaking as a metaphor for the discovery of the truth. As we journey with Agnieszka from bureaucrat to bureaucrat, live through her battles with timid and compromised producers, and finally discover how Birkut met his end in the workers uprising of 1970, we share the excitement of bringing to light both the glories and debacles of the Polish past.

Woody Allen's *Annie Hall* (1977) is the crossover film between the art cinema and the popular film. Its Oscar for Best Picture of 1977 marked the belated acceptance of modernist techniques by the Hollywood establishment, and its box-office success, although not of blockbuster proportions, showed that the art was accessible, under certain circumstances, to the mass audience. Conditioned by the comic persona of Woody Allen, known from his television appearances and earlier films like *Take the Money and Run, Bananas,* and *Sleeper,* the audience was ready for the horseplay and parody that marked the earlier films, and for the philosophical musings in comic framework that characterized his stage monologues. But the surprising thematic coherence of *Annie Hall*, its autobiographical frankness, and its playfulness with the conventions of romantic comedy account for its critical acclaim. Just as Fellini makes only half-hearted attempts to distance himself from his alter ego, Guido Anselmi, in $8\frac{1}{2}$, Allen and his character Alvy Singer are inextricably linked.

In the film, Allen jumps out of character to address the audience, not an unknown convention of screen comedy (Groucho Marx turns to the audience and suggests they go out into the lobby during a sequence in *Horsefeathers* [1932]), but Allen's direct address is part of a pattern of breaking down the straightforward narrative to transpose the form into confession. He meditates aloud on his problem, the raised problem of the film: What does it mean to have a relationship? The fragmentation of the narrative does not follow the logic of the detective story, flashing back to past events, in order to provide clues to the completion of a puzzle that will lead us to a coherent piece of knowledge, but in order to follow the emotional progress of Allen's/Singer's resolution of his failed love.

While adhering to the formula of romantic comedy—man wins woman, woman expresses dissatisfaction with being dominated and leaves man, man undergoes series of trials to win woman back—Allen ends his film with a modernist twist: in the end he doesn't get Annie back. The problem with this age-of-feminism, realistic conclusion, Allen is saying, is that while that's the way life really is, it doesn't make him happy. In this way *Annie Hall* critiques the escapist formula of romantic comedy while at the same time telling a realistic tale that conforms to the lives of sophisticated urbanites in the 1970s.

While *Annie Hall* acknowledges the realm of politics—Alvy meets his first wife at a political fund-raiser, and later becomes obsessed with the political ramifications of the Kennedy assassination—the film harks back more strongly to the early Bergman, Fellini, and Antonioni art films than it does to the overtly political films of Tanner and Wajda. Allen is concerned with the problem of love in an age of angst, freedom, and equality.

*Annie Hall* is exceptional in that it's an American art film that was also an unqualified commercial success. While the art cinema was never explicitly banned in Hollywood, its problems made it unpopular with producers. Yet the art movie impulse in Hollywood is almost as old as the feature film industry itself. D. W. Griffith made the standard-bearer for the screen spectacle and also for the melodrama in *A Birth of a Nation* (1915); but when he followed it up with an "art" film, *Intolerance* (1916), his more daring and experimental epic, it was too demanding for the mass audience that had flocked to his earlier picture and failed to recoup its costs. *Citizen Kane,* whose mixing of documentary and narrative modes and Jamesian view of truth as a collection of subjective interpretations makes it a prototype for the art cinema of the 1960s and 1970s, was also a financial failure, a film that lost money despite its Oscar for screenplay and four additional nominations.

Only the success of the European art films playing on American screens in the 1960s opened Hollywood to the possibilities of indigenous production. Even so, few Americans seemed inclined to embrace the modernist narrative. John Cassavetes's *Shadows* (1959) was produced independently of Hollywood, as was Arthur Penn's *Mickey One* (1964). Dennis Hopper directed his hyperreflexive *The Last Movie* (1971) for Universal on the heels of the unexpected box-office bonanza from *Easy Rider* (1969), but *The Last Movie* offered none of the simple countercultural pleasures of the earlier film; and with the narrative complexity of a Godard picture together with the roughness of an American experimental film, it was doomed with both popular and art house audiences, who were either unable or unwilling to deal with its vision of chaos.

The most important American director of the 1970s is also the one most infatuated with art film techniques, and most successful in their application. And while Robert Altman's modernism made him a cultural oasis for likeminded American filmmakers and their audience, it also "did him in" in Hollywood terms. Altman's 1970s output splits between popular genre films transformed by modernist techniques, among them *Brewster McCloud* (1971), *McCabe and Mrs. Miller* (1972), and *The Long Goodbye* (1973); and the European-style art films *Images* (1973), *Three Women* (1977), and *Quintet* (1979).

The former group, capped by the magnificent *Nashville* (1975), is the more trenchant of Altman's work, the innovations contained in them exerting considerable influence on other filmmakers. *Nashville* employs a multifaceted narrative following the lives of several protagonists who are brought together during a political campaign not unlike Tanner's later use of the same technique in *Jonah.* Refreshingly original was Altman's use of natural sound levels in *McCabe and Mrs. Miller,* which produced an aura of authenticity that forever changed the western. After *McCabe,* the myths of the western look empty compared to the raw emotive power of the rugged, uncivilized environment. *The Long Goodbye* also undercuts a myth by the injection of naturalism. The romanticized detective of the 1940s is paraded as a hapless anachronism in the figure of Elliott Gould's "Rip Van Marlowe" (as Altman referred to the character).

*Quintet* (1979), with its mixed cast of popular movie star Paul Newman and European art film mainstays Fernando Rey and Bibi Andersson, was the last in a string of financial failures that drove Altman from Hollywood. *Quintet,* with its handsome metaphorical construct of civilized persons trapped in an ice-bound city and forced to play a game which ends in their deaths one by one, had a somberness that disappointed Newman fans, and a stark simplicity that failed to involve art film enthusiasts. Altman has shown a remarkable resilience, though, and has lately been filming plays on low budgets with considerable success, including David Rabe's *Streamers* (1983) and Sam Shepard's *Fool For Love* (1986). With his version of Christopher Durang's *Beyond Therapy* (1987) he has shown welcome signs of returning to the stylistics and themes of his work of the early 1970s.

One of the most fruitful cross-fertilizations of modernist concerns and popular narrative forms is in the modernist thriller. In this form, the adventures of the protagonist-investigator in the nightworld of the thriller becomes a metaphor for the modernist journey to self-discovery. Arthur Penn's *Night Moves* (1975) provides a model of its kind. Penn, working with what was originally a straight detective story about a private investigator hired to return a runaway daughter to her mother, replaced the hard-sell payoff of the conventional thriller, in which questions are turned to certainties through the detective's discoveries, with a web of confusion and ambiguity in which each of detective Harry Moseby's (Gene Hackman's) forays into the underworld does not complete the picture but opens up into further uncertainties. This thriller as journey to self-discovery motif can also be found in Antonioni's *The Passenger,* and in Nicholas Roeg's *Bad Timing* (1980), and Volker Schlondorff's *Circle of Deceit* (1982).

For a time in the late 1970s it looked as if the art film market would prosper, with major studios opening what they called "Classics" divisions to handle the more specialized art film product, and with the success of *Annie Hall* signaling the possibility of an increasing modernist presence in the popular cinema. But ballooning production and exploitations costs—the expense of making prints, advertising, and promoting a feature film—have discouraged experimentation in the popular cinema. The Classics divisions, and even the daring small distribution companies that have established themselves, like Cinecom International, seem to favor traditional narrative films over modernist work.

Even so, substantial numbers of interesting and vital modernist films are still being made. Third World film movements, like that of Brazil, make powerful, innovative films that seem to adapt modernist techniques for the same reason as do the East Europeans—because they work so well to fulfill the social function of film art: to explore national consciousness and serve as a tool in the search for the truth. But it is becoming increasingly difficult to see these films, as the flooding of screens with teenage products and with the films of proven mass audience movie stars like Clint Eastwood and Sylvester Stallone (which open on as many as thirteen hundred screens simultaneously) squeezes out "the little guy."

On a more positive note, the art cinema in the late 1980s has seen its role strengthened both in terms of box-office receipts and critical acclaim, as strongly demonstrated by the 1986 and 1987 Academy Awards, in which *Kiss of the*

*Spider Woman* (1985) and *A Room with a View* (1986) won major awards. But what has also been clear is that the move in these contemporary art films is away from the self-conscious modernism and stylistic innovation that marked the art film successes of the 1960s and 1970s to a more traditional narrative structure.

Also notable in the 1960s is the emergence of a commercially viable English language art cinema. This art cinema has found its home both in the American independent film movement, which was responsible in part for both *Kiss of the Spider Woman* and *A Room with a View,* and the renaissance of the British cinema, in particular the films produced by David Puttman's Enigma Films, including *Cal* (1984) and *The Killing Fields* (1985); and Channel Four, which produced Peter Greenaway's *The Draughtsman's Contract* (1982). If there has been a dearth of foreign language art films on American screens, there has in its place been the excitement of watching a native-language art film movement unfold.

But no matter what the language or nation of origin, as long as persons have the deep-felt need to express themselves, the art cinema will crop up in some form. In 1984 Andrei Tarkovsky left the Soviet Union, where he had produced esoteric, obscure, demanding masterpieces like *Stalker* (1980) and *The Mirror* (1981), as well as the enigmatic epic *Andrei Rublov* (1966). Tarkovsky stated his position at the Telluride Film Festival in 1984: that unless one explores the preoccupations of the self and the spiritual dilemmas of the age, art has no value. One would guess that such an artist would have difficulty finding backing for a project in this day and age. But Tarkovsky has managed to make one film in Italy, *Nostalghia* (1985), which won three major Cannes Film Festival awards, and *The Sacrifice* (1986), which shared the top prize at the 1986 Cannes Festival. Regrettably, Andrei Tarkovsky died in 1986. His career, however, shines as an example to the film makers who will pursue his ideals.

## BIBLIOGRAPHICAL OVERVIEW

While there has been relatively little published work dealing with the art film as a genre, there is a correspondingly abundant amount of published work on art film directors. The following bibliography contains, therefore, several articles and books which, while not addressing the art film directly, nevertheless are very useful in understanding either the concept of modernism or the work of particular directors.

Of the works dealing with the art film directly, Roy Armes *The Ambiguous Image* (1976) offers insightful essays on a large number of directors. Armes perceptively identifies the art film as a modernist genre; his book's weakness lies in that he does not offer a definition of modernism. William C. Siska's *Modernism in the Narrative Cinema: The Art Film as a Genre* (1976) connects the art film to modernist perception as exercised by other prominent modernists including Henry James, James Joyce, Pablo Picasso, and Paul Klee. David

Bordwell's article "The Art Cinema as a Mode of Film Practice" (1979) links the art film that emerged in the late 1950s with earlier art filmmakers such as Sergei Eisenstein and Carl Dreyer. Steve Neale's "Art Cinema as Institution" (1981) takes a Marxist position on the possibilities of the art film as a counter-strategy to the dominant Hollywood narrative. Siska's "Metacinema: A Modern Necessity" (1979) defines and analyzes the difference between traditional and modernist narratives that are reflexive either towards the psyche of the filmmaker or toward the process of film production.

Among the other books and articles, the content of those whose titles announce them as being about the works of particular directors is self-evident. Of the others, Ian Cameron's *Second Wave* (1970) contains insightful essays on important art film directors Nagisa Oshima, Dusan Makavejev, and Jerzy Skolimowski. Paul Coates's *Story of the Lost Reflection* (1985) relates art films from Central and East Europe to the Romantic aesthetic of the late nineteenth and early twentieth century, and is particularly interesting in its treatment of the Romantic notion of the double, which relates to the modernist thriller. James Roy MacBean's *Film and Revolution* (1975) gives strong analyses of middle-period Godard films like *Two or Three Things That I Know About Her* and *Weekend,* as well as essays on Makavejev, Rossellini, and Third World cinema. James Monaco's *The New Wave* (1976) is good on Godard and Truffaut, and also has a section on an intriguing modernist, Jacques Rivette.

Thomas Schatz's "Modernist Strategies in the New Hollywood" (1983) offers a delightful analysis of Woody Allen's *Annie Hall* in the context of modernism and popular entertainment. Andrew Tudor's chapter "Critical Method: Auteur and Genre," in his *Theories of Film* (1973), lays out some of the problems with analyzing any genre, including the art film, while Peter Wollen's fine essay "Counter Cinema: *Vent D'Est*" (1985) poses traditional against modernist narrative strategies using Godard's *Vent D'Est* as an example of the latter. Finally, Carl E. Schorske's *Fin-De-Siècle Vienna: Politics and Culture* (1981) may seem out of place in a chapter about recent cinema, but Schorske's book relates well the obsessions and perceptions of many key early modernists, and in its linking of aesthetics to politics and other cultural movements provides a stimulating example for others to follow.

## NOTES

1. Of course, these art films had their forebears in the experimental films of the French avant-garde, notably Luis Buñuel's and Salvador Dali's *L'Age d'Or* (1930) and Jean Cocteau's *The Blood of a Poet* (1930). In the theatrical cinema, precursors of the art film genre include D. W. Griffith's *Intolerance* (1916), the films of Sergei Eisenstein, and Orson Welles's *Citizen Kane* (1941). Closer in feeling and texture to the art films under discussion are Robert Bresson's *The Diary of a Country Priest* (1950), Roberto Rossellini's *Strangers, Voyage to Italy* (1953), Fellini's *La Strada* (1954), and Carl Dreyer's *Ordet* (1955).

2. Susan Sontag, "Godard," in *Styles of Radical Will* (New York: Dell, 1969), p. 149.

## BIBLIOGRAPHICAL CHECKLIST

### Books

Armes, Roy. *The Ambiguous Image*. Bloomington: Indiana University Press, 1976.
Bondanella, Peter. *Federico Fellini: Essays in Criticism*. New York: Oxford University Press, 1978.
Cameron, Ian, ed. *Second Wave*. New York: Frederick A. Praeger, 1970.
Chatman, Seymour. *Antonioni, Or, The Surface of the World*. Berkeley: University of California Press, 1985.
Coates, Paul. *The Story of the Lost Reflection*. New York: Schocken Books, 1985.
Kaminsky, Stuart, ed. *Ingmar Bergman: Essays in Criticism*. New York: Oxford University Press, 1975.
MacBean, James Roy. *Film and Revolution*. Bloomington: Indiana University Press, 1975.
Monaco, James. *The New Wave*. New York: Oxford University Press, 1976.
Mussman, Toby, ed. *Jean-Luc Godard*. New York: E. P. Dutton, 1968.
Schorske, Carl E. *Fin-De-Siècle Vienna: Politics and Culture*. New York: Alfred A. Knopf, 1981.
Simon, John. *Ingmar Bergman Directs*. New York: Harcourt Brace Jovanovich, 1972.
Siska, William C. *Modernism in the Narrative Cinema: The Art Film as a Genre*, 1976; repr. New York: Arno Press, 1980.
Tarkovsky, Andrei. *Sculpting in Time: Reflections on the Cinema*. London, 1986. (Available through A. Zwemmer, Ltd., London.)
Wood, Robin. *Arthur Penn*. New York: Frederick A. Praeger, 1969.

### Shorter Works

Bordwell, David. "The Art Cinema as a Mode of Film Practice," *Film Criticism,* Fall 1979, pp. 56–64.
Neale, Steve. "Art Cinema as Institution," *Screen,* Spring 1981, pp. 11–39.
Schatz, Thomas. "Modernist Strategies in the New Hollywood." In *Old Hollywood/ New Hollywood: Ritual, Art, and Industry*. Ann Arbor: University of Michigan Research Press, 1983.
Siska, William C. "Metacinema: A Modern Necessity," *Literature/Film Quarterly,* Autumn 1979, pp. 285–289.
Sontag, Susan. "Bergman's *Persona*" and "Godard." In *Styles of Radical Will*. New York: Dell, 1969.
Tudor, Andrew. "Critical Method: Auteur and Genre." In his *Theories of Film*. New York: Viking Press, 1973.
Wollen, Peter. "Counter Cinema: *Vent D'Est*." In *Movies and Methods,* vol. 2, ed. Bill Nichols. Berkeley: University of California Press, 1985.

## SELECTED FILMOGRAPHY

1956    *The Seventh Seal* (95 minutes).
Production Company: Svensk Filmindustri. U.S. Distributor: Janus Films. Director: Ingmar Bergman. Screenplay: Ingmar Bergman. Photography: Gunnar Fischer. Cast: Max von Sydow (Knight, Antonius Block), Gunnar Bjornstrand (Squire, Jons), Bengt Ekerot (Death), Nils Poppe (Jof), Bibi Andersson (Mia), Ake Fridell (Plog, the blacksmith), Inga Gill (Lisa, Plog's wife), Maud Hansson (Witch), Gunnel Lindblom (servant girl), Erik Strandmark (Skat).

1959    *Hiroshima, Mon Amour* (91 minutes).
Production Company: Argos Films/Como Films (Paris)/Daiei (Tokyo)/Pathé Overseas. U.S. Distributor (current): New Yorker Films. Executive Producer: Samy Halfon. Director: Alain Resnais. Script: Marguerite Duras. Photography: Sacha Vierny and Mikio Takahashi. Cast: Emmanuele Riva (She), Eiji Okada (He), Bernard Fresson (The German), Stella Dassas (The Mother), Pierre Barbaud (The Father).

*Breathless* (90 minutes).
Production Company: Georges de Beauregard/Société de Nouvelle de Cinéma (Paris). U.S. Distributor (current): New Yorker Films. Producer: Georges de Beauregard. Director: Jean-Luc Godard. Script: Jean-Luc Godard. Based on an idea by François Truffaut. Photography: Raoul Coutard. Cast: Jean-Paul Belmondo (Michel Poiccard alias Laszlo Kovacs), Jean Seberg (Patricia Franchini), Daniel Boulanger (Police Inspector).

1961    *Jules and Jim* (105 minutes).
Production Company: Les Films Carosse/SEDIF. U.S. Distributor: Janus Films. Director: François Truffaut. Script: François Truffaut and Jean Gruault, from the novel by Henri-Pierre Roché. Photography: Raoul Coutard. Cast: Jeanne Moreau (Catherine), Oscar Werner (Jules), Henri Serre (Jim), Marie Dubois (Therese).

1962    *8½* (138 minutes).
U.S. Distributor (current): Corinth Films. Producer: Angelo Rizzoli. Director: Federico Fellini. Script: Federico Fellini, Ennio Flaiano, Tullio Pinelli, Brunello Rondi. Photography: Gianni di Venanzo. Cast: Marcello Mastroianni (Guido Anselmi), Anouk Aimee (Luisa), Sandra Milo (Carla), Claudia Cardinale (Claudia).

1967    *Weekend* (95 minutes).
Production Company: Comacico/Les Films Copernic/Lira Films (Paris)/Ascot Cineraid (Rome). U.S. Distributor (current): New Yorker Films. Director: Jean-Luc Godard. Script: Jean-Luc Godard. Photography: Raoul Coutard. Cast: Mireille Darc (Corinne), Jean Yanne (Roland), Jean-Pierre Calfon (Leader of the F.L.S.O.), Juliet Berto (Girl in the Car Crash/Member of F.L.S.O.), Jean-Pierre Leaud (Saint-Just/Man in Phone Booth).

1975    *Night Moves* (110 minutes).
Warner Brothers. Producer: Robert M. Sherman. Director: Arthur Penn. Script: Alan Sharp. Photography: Bruce Surtees. Cast: Gene Hackman (Harry Moseby), Jennifer Warren (Paula), Melanie Griffith (Delly), Susan Clark (Ellen Moseby).

1976   *Jonah Who Will be 25 in the Year 2000* (110 minutes).
Production Company: Citel Films Geneva and Action Films Paris. U.S. Distributor: New Yorker Films. Executive Producer: Yves Peyrot. Director: Alain Tanner. Screenplay: John Berger and Alain Tanner. Photography: Renato Berta. Cast: Jean-Luc Bideau (Max), Jacques Denis (Marco), Dominique Labourier (Marguerite), Miou-Miou (Marie), Rufus (Mathieu).

1977   *Man of Marble* (160 minutes).
Production Company: Polish Corporation for Film Production. U.S. Distributor: New Yorker Films. Director: Andrzej Wajda. Script: Aleksander Scibor-Rylski. Photography: Edward Klosinski. Cast: Krystyna Janda (Agnieszka), Jerzy Radziwitowicz (Mateusz Birkut), Taduesz Lomnicki and Jacek Lomnicki (Burski), Krystyna Zachwatowicz (Hanka Tomczyk).

*Annie Hall* (93 minutes).
United Artists. Producer: Charles Joffe. Director: Woody Allen. Script: Woody Allen and Marshall Brickman. Photography: Gordon Willis. Cast: Woody Allen (Alvy Singer), Diane Keaton (Annie Hall), Tony Roberts (Rob), Carol Kane (Allison), Paul Simon (Tony Lacy).

# Index

# About the Editor and Contributors

CAROLYN ANDERSON received her Ph.D. from the University of Massachusetts–Amherst where she is currently assistant professor in the Department of Communication, teaching courses in film and telelvision history and criticism. Her recent publications include chapters in *Current Research in Film: Audiences, Economics, and the Law* (Vol. 3), *Film and the Arts in Symbiosis: A Resource Guide* (Greenwood Press, 1988), and *Image Ethics: The Moral Rights of Subjects in Photography, Film and Television*. With Thomas W. Benson she is co-author of *Reality Fiction: The Films of Frederick Wiseman*.

JAMES M. COLLINS teaches film, television, and cultural study in the Department of Communication and Theatre at the University of Notre Dame. He has recently finished the book *Starting Over: Cultural Analysis in a Post Modern Context*.

WES D. GEHRING is Professor of Film at Ball State University. He received a Ph.D. in film studies from the University of Iowa. He is the author of *Leo McCarey and the Comic Anti-Hero in American Film* (1980), *Charlie Chaplin: A Bio-Bibliography* (Greenwood Press, 1983), *W.C. Fields: A Bio-Bibliography* (Greenwood Press, 1984), *Screwball Comedy: A Genre of Madcap Romance* (Greenwood Press, 1986), and *The Marx Brothers: A Bio-Bibliography* (Greenwood Press, 1987). His articles have appeared in numerous journals.

WADE JENNINGS is Professor of English at Ball State University. He is editor of the anthology of short fiction, *FICTIONS*, and the author of a number of papers, articles, and reviews dealing with literature and film in such journals as *Quarterly Review of Film Studies* and *Post Script*. He is currently writing a book about the career of Judy Garland for the Greenwood Presss bio-bibliography series on figures in American popular culture and is a member of the editorial board of *Post Script: Essays in Film and the Humanities*.

KATHRYN KANE is the author of *Visions of War: The Hollywood Combat Films of World War II* (1982). She received her doctorate in film criticism from the University of Iowa and has received numerous awards for writing and publications. She is currently director of communications and marketing for one of the largest association management firms in the country.

STEVEN N. LIPKIN, Associate Professor of Communication, teaches film and video at Western Michigan University. His current research examines melodramatic structures in Vietnam war films.

CHARLES J. MALAND is an Associate Professor and Chairperson of the Cinema Studies Program at the University of Tennessee, where he teaches film, American Studies, and American literature. Besides publishing articles on film and American culture in a variety of journals, he is the author of *American Visions: The Films of Chaplin, Ford, Capra, and Welles, 1936–1941* (1977), and *Frank Capra* (1980). His third book, *Chaplin and American Culture: the Evolution of a Star Image*, will be published in 1988.

JACK NACHBAR is a professor of popular culture and director of the Film Studies Program at Bowling Green State University in Ohio. He is co-editor of the *Journal of Popular Film and Television* and has written or edited several books on film and on popular culture, including *Focus on the Western, Movies as Artifact,* and *The Popular Culture Reader.* Current projects include a book on *Casablanca* and an article on film noir and the western.

JOHN RAEBURN is professor and chair of English and professor of American Studies at the University of Iowa. He is co-editor of *Frank Capra: The Man and His Films* and the author of *Fame Became of Him: Hemingway as Public Writer.*

THOMAS SCHATZ teaches in the Department of Radio, Television, and Motion Pictures at the University of Texas at Austin. He is the author of *Hollywood Genres: Formulas, Filmmaking, and the Studio System* (1981). He is currently finishing a book on the studio as auteur.

WILLIAM C. SISKA is Director of the Film Studies Program at the University of Utah. He is author of *Modernism in the Narrative Cinema* and writer/ director of award-winning independent films *Make Your Own Steps* and *Hannah.*

THOMAS SOBCHACK, Associate Professor of Film Studies at the University of Utah, is co-author of *An Introduction to Film,* 2d ed. (1987). His articles on genre subjects have appeared in *The Journal of Popular Film and Television* and *Literature/Film Quarterly.* He is currently finishing a book on *Critical*

*Approaches to Film* for Longman's and researching the connections between "the Brighton School" of British silent film and American films of the period.

VIVIAN SOBCHACK teaches film studies at the University of California, Santa Cruz, and in addition to her publications on the American Science Fiction film, she is also the co-author of *An Introduction to Film* and the author of the forthcoming *The Address of the Eye: A Phenomenology of Film Experience*.

GERALD C. WOOD is Professor of English and Coordinator of the Department of English at Carson-Newman College, Jefferson, Tennessee. He is presently both editing the short plays of Horton Foote and writing a book on Foote's career as a playwright and screenwriter. His articles, which range in subject from Lord Byron to teaching film in the liberal arts college, have appeared in several journals.